Politics and Ideas in Early Stuart England

Politics and Ideas in Early Stuart England

Essays and Studies

Kevin Sharpe

Pinter Publishers
London and New York

© Kevin Sharpe, 1989

First published in Great Britain in 1989 by
Pinter Publishers Limited
25 Floral Street, London WC2E 9DS

Front cover illustration: reproduced by permission of The British Library
(ref. 11623aaa29 TP 8873734)

ISBN 0-86187-708 x

British Library Cataloguing in Publication Data
A CIP catalogue record for this book is available from the British Library

Library of Congress Cataloging-in-Publication Data

Sharpe, Kevin.
    Politics and ideas in early Stuart England: essays and studies/
  Kevin Sharpe.
        p.   cm.
    Bibliography: p.
    Includes index.
    ISBN 0-86187-708-X
    1. Great Britain — Politics and government — 1603-1649. 2. Politics
and culture — Great Britain — History — 17th century. I. Title.
DA390.S53   1989
306.2′0941 — dc20   89-4016
                                                                        CIP

DA
390
.S53
1989

Filmset by Mayhew Typesetting, Bristol, England
Printed and bound in Great Britain by Biddles Ltd of Guildford

Contents

Acknowledgements

Compiling this collection has renewed my sense of how much I have owed to the generosity of many scholars and friends over nearly twenty years. To describe these intellectual debts would itself require another substantial essay — and even that would be inadequate acknowledgement. I would, however, like particularly to thank George Bernard, John Morrill, David Riggs, Keith Thomas, Greg Walker and Steve Zwicker for their careful criticisms of and comments on earlier drafts of the introductory essay. And more generally, as well as them, I thank warmly those scholars who through encouragement, criticism, and generosity with their time and knowledge have made these pieces possible: Gerald Aylmer, Keith Baker, Christopher Brooks, Bliss Carnochan, John Elliott, Conrad Russell, Lawrence Stone, Hugh Trevor-Roper and Anne Whiteman.

I should like here to again express my thanks to those institutions and societies which provided the time and resources that made the research for these essays possible: the British Academy, The Wolfson Foundation, Oriel College Oxford, the Fulbright Commission, the National Endowment for the Humanities, the Institute for Advanced Study, Princeton, Stanford Humanities Center, the Henry E. Huntington Library and the Committee for Advanced Studies, University of Southampton.

For permission to reprint articles and essays, I am grateful to the following: Longman Publishers and the editors of the *English Historical Review* (2); Gerald Duckworth & Co. (4); Longman and David Starkey (5); the Past and Present Society and Christopher Brooks (6); the late Charles Schmitt (8); Professor Steven Zwicker and the University of California Press (9); The Historical Association (10); the editor, *The Huntington Library Quarterly* (11).

Preface

During the years over which these essays were penned, the study of early modern English history has been completely transformed. The old whig story of escalating constitutional crisis over the decades before the Civil War can no longer convincingly be told, despite the efforts of some to preserve it, with minor adjustments, for the historical canon. On the other hand, the revisionists' new tales of factional intrigue, personal interest and local politics have left critics feeling, rightly I think (and have always thought), that something is missing from the story. The passions and principles, ideas and values which creatively fermented in the cultural and political life of early Stuart decades find little or no place in some revisionist narratives of parliaments and high politics.

But we must beware that we do not from a sound criticism leap to an unsound conclusion, or from a proper dissatisfaction with some new explanations drift desperately and uncritically back to the old. For the traditional whig history of seventeenth-century England was premised on an inevitably mounting ideological as well as political polarization. The ideas and values of early Stuart England were anachronistically read from the later perspective of the war between 'Cavalier' and 'puritan'. In some recent work there is again a worrying tendency to write simplistically of 'court' and 'country' or 'absolutist' and 'constitutionalist' as contending ideologies. Political historians, however, have demonstrated beyond doubt that the court was not a monolith but a world of individuals with different preferences and policies. And it is important to recognize that there was no one court culture or set of values or styles uniting men at Whitehall. In an essay on Thomas Howard, Earl of Arundel, I endeavoured to show how cultural pursuits and values could both bind a circle and yet divide courtiers, as they did Arundel and Buckingham. In a more recent study of Thomas Carew I argue that the very categories of 'court', 'country' and 'Cavalier' obstruct rather than facilitate a reading of a famous court poet. If ideas and values must recover their proper place in the history of early Stuart England, they should be those of the seventeenth century, not those of the nineteenth and twentieth centuries.

Indeed it is the ideas, values and terms that recur again and again in early Stuart England that were passed over by those whig historians who looked only for intellectual changes which seemed to explain the war or inculcate a new age. The divine, natural and patriarchal foundations of royal authority and the power of the king's person provide an obvious example. In early Stuart England the king was expected to stand as a model for public and private life; the monarchical styles of James I and Charles I shaped the different cultural and political texts of their reigns. The concern with *honour*, to take another case, is important for understanding Charles I's frustrations, the hostility to favourites, the Earl of Pembroke's attitude to foreign alliances and affairs, and Ben Jonson's view of society. Most of all, if we are to comprehend early Stuart politics — Charles I's aims and ideals, or Laud's view of the role of the universities — we need to appreciate the obsession with *order* in early modern England, an order that was perhaps always more of an ideological construct than a political reality.

Because ideas like those of kingship, honour and order are traditional they may seem hard to historicize, and so appear to offer us little insight into their force at particular periods. Particular events, often political events, however, at times enable us clearly to see the specific application and force of traditions and so to recognize their historical importance at particular moments. The hegemony of George Villiers, Duke of Buckingham, for example, sharpened and focused discussions of aristocratic virtue, social hierarchy and royal counsel in the 1620s. The political circumstances of James I's reign, as is argued below, led Sir Edward Coke to a new emphasis upon the role of precedent in legal decision and to a novel concern that the common law be deemed certain and immutable. Particular circumstances in other words gave even seemingly timeless tropes a specificity. William Camden told his history lecturer, Degory Wheare, that he was the man for his age; as Wheare himself introduced the classical histories as the appropriate texts for an 'unsettled age'. Ideas, events and circumstances shaped each other and no history of one should exclude the other.

Nor should ideas be separated from the instruments of government. In a government of personal monarchy based on a network of personal relationships, the art of government was the art of winning compliance, and one of its principal instruments was patronage. As the circles of Prince Henry and the Earl of Arundel demonstrate, however, ties of patronage could be formed by values as well as by connections of family and locality. Moreover, as the criticisms of Buckingham's dispensation of favour remind us, there were ideas of patronage as well as patronage of ideas. At all points of the chain of command the effectiveness of the agents and instruments of government was bound up with ideals, traditions, customs, expectations and hopes. Power and its exercise, as we have begun to appreciate, rested on such perceptions.

Such perceptions, I suggest in my first essay, are articulated not only in the self-consciously political tracts, sermons and speeches of the period. They are embedded in metaphors — and analogues such as that of the body; they are encoded in genres like politic histories and Petrarchan love poems. Changes and manipulations of genre — the decline of the romance and the rise of the picaresque, for instance — announce important social and political as well as intellectual changes.

The essays that follow are studies in the interactions of ideas and events, of ideas and the instruments of government in early Stuart England. They consider the interrelationships of values and politics at court, and in universities, in parliaments and the localities, among lawyers and antiquarians, ministers, magistrates and poets. The appraisals attempt an assessment of recent work, much of it informed by other disciplines, which has done most to reorient the study of cultural, intellectual and political history. The first essay looks at the history of ideas and politics in the wake of its 'linguistic turn' and ventures into other territories of meaning which await exploration. They were all written, like my books on historical thought and Caroline literature, from a strong conviction that political history and intellectual history should not be divorced. It can only be hoped that they demonstrate that revisionist history of early Stuart England need not be a history with the ideas left out, indeed that a better understanding of the seventeenth century requires a fuller study of the relationship of ideas, values and styles to politics and the exercise of power.

I Approaches

1. A commonwealth of meanings: languages, analogues, ideas and politics

I Approaches

The relationship of ideas in the broadest sense, what in less sophisticated days we might have called climates of opinion, to events, to actions at specific historical moments, has been, perhaps, the most central of all historical problems. Certainly the question of that relationship — even if it has never satisfactorily been resolved — has stimulated since classical times the greatest works of historical interpretation. It would not have occurred to historians from Thucydides to Ranke to study intellectual and political history, the history of thought and action, apart. In particular no historian of the English Civil War before this century could have conceived of writing about that upheaval without addressing ideas as well as actions, principles as well as interests.[1]

In recent years this has not been the case and for this there are two broad reasons. Since the war, the narrower specialization that accompanied the professionalization of the historical academy has made it difficult (if not dangerous) for the historical artist to paint with broad strokes on a large canvas. Historians separated into their own studios (intellectual, political, economic and social) to refine their own techniques and compose exquisite miniatures. Accordingly intellectual historians studied the development of ideas as the independent products of an autonomous intellect, as phenomena which had their own distinct history. And historians influenced by the methods of Sir Lewis Namier turned to the history of politics as the study of patronage and connections founded on interests and personal relationships.

Where the seventeenth century is concerned, there is a more particular reason for the lack of interest in the relationship between ideas and events: the recent revisionist scholarship has widened the gulf between intellectual and political history.

Professor Pocock warned that narrow concentration on the practice of high politics reduces discourse to insignificance.[2] Professor Stone, as usual, is more polemical and more graphic: the revisionists, he writes, 'write detailed political narratives which implicitly deny that there is any deep-seated meaning to history except the accidental whim of fortune and personality . . . they are now busy trying to remove any sense of ideology or idealism from the two English revolutions of the seventeenth century'.[3] There is much substance in the criticism, but the passage quoted gives rise to a concern that was (and is) central to revisionists' historiography. For Stone equates ideology with a 'deep-seated meaning to history', with, I take that to mean, a belief that the past has been leading somewhere, indeed leading to the establishment of certain principles and values. This of course, though Stone might not like the term, is another manifestation of the whig interpretation of history which the revisionist historians, especially those of the seventeenth century, set out to challenge.[4] From Macaulay to Gardiner those historians who studied the Stuart century as a crucial stage in the evolution of parliamentary government were as whig in their history of ideas as in their history of politics; to question their political narrative as anachronistic is also to invalidate the history of seventeenth-century beliefs as they approached it — searching for those who heralded the future glories of the English constitution.[5] The revisionists rejected the teleological approach to the history of beliefs, as to the history of politics, but they were not intrinsically or necessarily hostile to the place of principle or ideology.[6] As yet, they have not written a revisionist history of ideas, but we have to consider how it might be written.

Over the last two decades, while the political history of the seventeenth century has been rewritten, a far more important revolution has taken place in the discipline of intellectual history. It is a revolution that can confidently be said to have been led by two scholars: John Pocock and Quentin Skinner.[7] Greatly influenced by linguistic philosophers and semioticians, Pocock and Skinner have reoriented the methodology and practice of intellectual history to a study of languages in which, they argue, the beliefs and attitudes of an age are encoded. Such an approach has emancipated intellectual history from the limitations of the 'great texts' to study the vocabularies of the past revealed in all discourse — letters, sermons and plays, as well as pamphlets and political treatises. Quentin Skinner has argued that the great texts are in some respects the least representative of the thought of an age, rather the response to new problems — a response which in turn led to the reshaping of languages and ideas. For Pocock the great texts of political theory exemplify the most powerful minds of an era 'exploring the tension between established linguistic usages and the need to understand words in new ways'.[8] In order to comprehend those very texts, and more generally to understand the prevalent attitudes of the age, Pocock has proclaimed in methodological essays the need for the broadest study of vocabularies and languages, especially those languages that in any era become accredited to take part in public speech, or that were institutionalized.[9] The history of the changes in linguistic paradigms and accredited vocabularies, he has shown in practice, may then document the fundamental shifts in values — from a concern with grace to concern with custom and law, from a perception of virtue founded on civic humanism to one associated with the new world of rights, property and commerce.[10]

The history-of-languages approach to the history of thought has contributed far greater sophistication to the study of intellectual history and rightly problematized some simplistic (or even unpondered) notions. The old idea of 'influence' has fallen to the new approach; problems of authorial 'intention' and the reception of texts have been complicated and clarified (if not resolved) by a developed understanding of the linguistic contexts of any discursive performance.[11] Perhaps most important of all, Professor Pocock's discussion and demonstration of a 'shared yet diverse linguistic context'[12] has furthered our understanding of the common beliefs and assumptions that still underlie the articulated tensions of an age, as in 1628 when crown lawyers no less than MPs argued in the language of custom and law.[13]

Yet for all these benefits, there are problems within Pocock's and Skinner's study of languages, and, more generally, limitations to and weaknesses within the linguistic methodology itself. Critics have drawn attention to fundamental philosophical problems of interpretation that have not been entirely satisfactorily resolved: the problems of the precise nature and definition of text and the related problems of the hermeneutic circle — that is the need to interpret texts from our broader knowledge of vocabularies which knowledge itself we derive from texts.[14] Despite his methodological injunctions, Skinner's own study of early modern political thought has still focused on the 'great' texts. And his exploration of the languages which provide the discursive context of those texts has been selective and even anachronistic: concentrating for example on natural law, but not theology or canon law. More generally, neither Skinner nor Pocock have pursued the relationships of languages to meanings or the perceptions of that relationship in the early modern period. Was language in the seventeenth century, as we might at times be led to deduce from a reading of the philological scholars or Ben Jonson's *Discoveries*, synonymous

with the object ('Nomen et esse go together')?[15] Or did contemporaries perceive words, as did Bishop Arthur Lake's biographer,
as a mode of representing meaning 'fitly compared by the ancients
to a picture'?[16] What did contemporaries understand by
metaphor? How did they distinguish, as does Pocock, between
rhetorical and institutional languages? How conscious were they of
the linguistic turn as an ideological act?

Another unresolved difficulty is the old one — the precise relationship within the linguistic methodology of ideas to events.
Pocock attempts to resolve the problem by (rightly) closing the
difference between speech and action — by seeing discourse as
performances at moments in time. But this approach does not itself
explain *why* at any given moment languages undergo a shift, nor
how changed events bring about linguistic and ideological sea-
changes.[17] Quentin Skinner, as Professor Tully pointed out,
acknowledges that ideologies are poor guides to action[18] and ends
up (curiously given his methodological injunctions) in the *Foundations of Modern Political Thought* with a blend of whig history of
ideas and a resort to war as the motive force of political change —
which leaves the relationship of languages and events (the starting
point of Skinner's theorizing about intellectual history) far
behind.[19] What both these unresolved problems may suggest is
that the relationship of ideas to events, of intellectual and political
history, cannot satisfactorily be explored *only* through the history
of verbal languages. Events not only lead men to recast inherited
terms, vocabularies and syntaxes. They sometimes lead them to *act*
and *experience* — I shall argue that the Civil war is one such case
— in ways that their language does not, cannot, represent or
accommodate, at least until some time after.[20]

This leads to an unfortunate (but not necessary) consequence of
the linguistic approach to the history of ideas: the neglect of other
aesthetic and cultural practices in which values and assumptions
are encoded. The tendency of all recent discussion has been to see
verbal discourse as the locus where all meaning is constituted.[21]
Skinner defines an ideology entirely in discursive terms as 'a
language of politics defined by its conventions and employed by its
writers'.[22] This, however, is to ignore the picture and the
building, the public procession and religious ritual, the games and
pastimes in all of which the meaning a society identifies for itself
is embodied and represented. In his discussion of 'the state of the
art' of intellectual history, Pocock says nothing of the art of the
state. In a period where a relationship of aesthetics to ideology is
assumed, he therefore fails to explore important material for
elucidating ideology and cultural values.[23] In their fruitful borrowings from semioticians, Pocock and Skinner have hitherto paid too

little attention to the equally rich offerings of symbolic anthropology, for elucidating the ideologies of cultural practices.[24] At the
beginning of the decade, reviewing the state of intellectual history
William Bouwsma called for 'an expanded concern with the meanings expressed by every kind of human activity in the past'.[25] He
saw the study of the history of music and dance as providing
perhaps the most valuable future areas of study. His agenda has not
yet been followed, but in the extension of Pocock's and Skinner's
approach into these territories may lie the most profitable future
research.

Here the early modern period of English history offers especially
rich possibilities, which may not have been fully appreciated. In the
early modern period, as we have long known, men idealized a
divinely ordained system which, never descriptive of the world,
nevertheless presented a powerful normative depiction of it. In that
representation, from the highest sphere of the planets, through the
arrangements of societies, the composition of the individual and the
hierarchy of beasts, a naturally appointed order was replicated.[26]
Accordingly, the king of the commonweal corresponded to God in
the heavens and the sun in the cosmos or to the father in the family
and the lion, ruler of beasts, in the animal kingdom. Within man
himself in his divine state the reason or soul was perceived to be the
monarch; and by corollary the state was conceived as a human
body, consisting of head and members, sinews and humours. These
correspondences or analogues ran in both or several directions; that
they were mutually adaptable was one of the ingrained habits of
mind of early modern culture.

These analogues cannot be reduced to mere metaphor. Contemporaries were quite able to distinguish metaphor, which was a
rhetorical device, from analogical thinking which 'discovered new
truth by arguing from known to unknown'.[27] Pym, in reply to
Strafford's long speech at his trial in which the Earl had referred to
the state by architectural, corporal and musical analogies,
mentioned his 'metaphor of the intoxicating cup'; the analogues he
took without comment as truths.[28] (Evidently Bacon did likewise
when he described Aesop's fables as 'parabolic wisdom'.)[29] To be a
father, in early modern England, *was* to be a king, and the reverse
was also true. To observe the world of nature with its own hierar-
chies and laws was also a political experience; to master one's own
unruly appetites and passions, to ride a horse and tame the
unruliness of its nature, was to practise government and reconfirm
the natural order of divine government.[30] It may take a
considerable imaginative leap for us to comprehend that bee-
keeping might be or become an ideological act. But when we turn
from such practices to the discourse that in turn they generated,

the need to make that imaginative leap is made both more compelling and easier. For we soon come to appreciate as we read
seventeenth-century books and speeches how familiar and natural
the transferences were: animal fables were popular moral texts not
least because the animal kingdom corresponded to the human
commonweal;[31] the *Game at Chess* was a powerful political
polemic not least because the game was readily seen to replicate
political action. The language of treatises on the body, on the
family, on riding, on music, on the Government of Cattle, was
highly political because each of these analogues (and others)
corresponded in some way to the commonweal, as it related to
them. Once we perceive this, we may see not only the cultural
practices but the texts they generated become invaluable
documents of political ideas. Moreover, as we observe and read
them from this perspective, we may discern that authors were not
only aware of the political force of the seemingly apolitical matter,
but capable of a sophisticated manipulation of the correspondence
— bringing it into now closer, now more distant, focus.[32] So
familiar were these correspondences that they often run quite
casually across the various planes of the macrocosm, appearing to
us liked mixed metaphor. So, in *God Save the King*, Henry Valentine could speak of the king as the sun and 'The Sun is the beauty
and bridegroom of nature'.[33] Similarly the preface to the
Commons Journal on 19 March 1604 depicted the commonweal in
a few lines in architectural, corporal and familial terms.[34] The
analogies and correspondences came naturally to mind and were as
naturally interrelated.

As well then as texts and languages, we shall need to study
aesthetic documents, cultural practices, analogues, correspondences and the discourse that they in turn generated and which we
have not been used to studying as political texts. An appreciation,
however, of these ingrained habits of mind as political ideas
requires the political historian as much as the historian of ideas,
and it is here that the separation of the sub-disciplines has
impoverished each. For in a general sense many actions in early
Stuart England were political and political moments must be understood in the context of ingrained habits and cultural assumptions.[35] That is why Pocock sees political theory as emerging from
ordinary political discourse in times of crisis, and why Professor
Salmon found himself 'often unable to distinguish between
political theory and political history'.[36] But more particularly, it is
the political historian who may see the highly topical, immediate
and (perhaps) radical comment in the articulation at a specific
moment of the timeless trope or convention.[37] To discuss, in
highly political terms, the reciprocal relations of love and duty

between husband and wife, to urge that neither press it to a 'question of law' but for them to strive who should be most careful of each other's good, is one thing; in the year after Bate's case and the quarrel over the rights of kings and subjects it is sharply to specify a general analogy.[38] To rearticulate a conventional discourse of love between monarch and subjects at a time when that discourse was being redefined by the king was, as I recently argued in the case of Thomas Carew, to turn a gesture of praise into criticism.[39] Again contemporaries often exhibited a sophisticated capacity to manipulate the dialectic between the conventional trope and the moment — a sophistication which Jonson announced for example in declaring that his masques (which drew on Neo-Platonic philosophy) were also to 'sound to present occasions'.[40] At times the 'occasion' that gives a conventional language or action its specificity may be beneath the surface of the broad familiar story: Davenant's poem *Madagascar*, I suggested, addresses the debate in Council in the winter of 1636–7 over aid to the Elector Palatine as well as a project to conquer the island.[41] Far then from revisionist historiography being intrinsically hostile to the history of ideas, a closer, detailed narration of political moments and manoeuvrings may enable us to historicize and particularize the timeless general troupe and so to study the discursive performance or cultural act both as a political event and ideological gesture.

II The world picture

Traditionally studies of political ideas in the seventeenth century have moved quickly (and with an audible sigh of relief) to Hobbes, bemoaning the poverty of theory during the earlier decades of the century. Such studies equate political thought with political philosophy, with self-conscious theorizing of fundamental problems about the nature of the state. Others, the works of Christopher Hill chief among them, have attempted to explain the early deficiency of theory in comparison to a later ferment in political thought by reference to the operation of censorship before the 1640s.[42] Government censorship, however, not least because there were no adequate institutions or mechanisms through which to exercise it, was largely ineffective even when attempted and the evidence suggests it was attempted only in extreme cases. This myth of widespread censorship needs to be, and is currently being, dispelled.[43] More recently, however, scholars have questioned the absence of theory: an eminent medievalist has drawn attention to the fourteenth-century foundations of ideas voiced in the 1640s;[44] a literary scholar has demonstrated the familiarity of early Stuart England with the political treatises of George Buchanan;[45] most generally, a survey of political ideology has forcefully argued that the early Stuart English could draw from rich wells of indigenous intellectual traditions and continental theorists to justify their resistance to the monarch in 1642.[46]

While such scholars have greatly enriched our knowledge, their arguments, I believe, fail to convince. For though ideas of resistance, contract and popular sovereignty were available from the past and from the continent, they were not questions theorized or addressed by early Stuart Englishmen. To acknowledge that men did not articulate these ideas, that they did not see the relevance or the force of ideas that had emerged from political crises until they confronted their own crisis, may come close to saying (since all thinking is an act of selecting) that they did not think them. What is certain is that such theories were not in the foreground of their thinking about politics. And I would suggest that in general concentration on and search for such theorizing of political problems in early seventeenth-century England is anachronistic.[47] It is anachronistic because political theory approaches politics as both a sphere of its own and as a set of problems: it addresses the questions of political obligation, of why citizens should be subject or subject themselves to the authority of the state. It takes, that is, the state as an artifice which needs to be justified. This is a premise and approach essentially alien to early Stuart thinking. It is one of the many marks of Hobbes's revolutionizing of political thought that he conceived his state as an artificial creation: 'for by art is created that great Leviathan called a Commonwealth . . . which is but an artificial man'.[48]

For before the events of civil war shattered the assumptions, the state was seldom conceived abstractly or as an 'other'. The commonweal, the term usually employed, was represented as a natural organism, like the family from which it grew. Man fulfilled himself as a man in so far as he was part of the commonweal, and had no social existence (Aristotle would have said no fulfilment of his humanity) outside it. Everything good in the created world, a preacher at the assizes in 1629 told his auditories, was ordered and under government: celestial bodies, beasts, men.[49] In a clock, he noted (revealing that even the observations of mechanisms could then complement rather than confront this world view), the great wheels guided the small. And so the government of the commonweal reflected the divine plan and government of all nature.

We cannot but discern a justificatory tone to the preacher's assertions; he claimed authority for the government of the day —

implicitly against its critics — by equating it with *an ideal*: of the divine government of nature. But that idealization itself manifests that in early modern England the question of order in the state was part of that of natural order — and of moral order in all human affairs, secular and spiritual. Political theory did not really exist as an independent study because politics was not a distinct and separate arena of thought or action.[50] That is not to say that there was no political thought, no debates or differences, no attitudes to politics. Rather the reverse: to reflect on the universe, the relationship of man to God or the hierarchy in the animal kingdom was also to reflect on the nature of the commonweal and of the order and degrees within it. As J. Robinson put it succinctly in his *Observations Divine and Moral*, 'It is a kind of impeachment of Authoritie to examine the Reasons of Things'.[51]

We tend in modern political discussion to think about various relationships: of individuals to each other, to institutions, of each to principles or ideals. In early modern England, commentators tended rather to represent the commonweal as an organism in which there was only one relationship: that of all to all, and of everything to one divine truth. Because there was held to be one truth, there could no more be a contention over fundamental values in secular matters than in spiritual; the two, the state and the church, promulgated and preached God's truth; out of the bosom of the church, it was officially decreed, 'there is no ordinary salvation'.[52] Again the organic conception was an ideal, but the religious divisions and social dislocations that increasingly disrupted it led not to the abandonment but the more forceful articulation of organic unity. Hooker reasserted that those who questioned the church of England upset all order, as indeed their questioning reflected the disruption of their human order. Bishop Henry King denounced those 'giddy' men who 'prefer their own fantasies' to public doctrines;[53] Gyles Fleming wrote of the need to prefer 'the unity of God's church before our own private phantasies and particular humours'.[54] Anglican apologists and antiquaries were so anxious to establish the historical origins of the Church of England in the time of the apostles because it was essential to exonerate their church from the charge of schism.[55] For there could be only one true religion; neither God nor his magistrates on earth could really tolerate another faith. In a real sense recusants and nonconformists who rejected the church were also outside the commonweal; their only hope was to come to see the light of truth.[56] This assertion of the unity and oneness of truth was by no means just an official doctrine of the church hierarchy. It was a normative ideology for long just powerful enough to contain the tensions that might have fractured it.

Despite the logic of the Calvinist doctrine of election — that is
mass separation — and the tensions to which (as we shall see) it
gave rise,[57] surprisingly few puritans were willing to separate
from the church. Robert Bolton, a Northamptonshire preacher, in
the *Saints Sure and Perpetual Guide* revealed his unease with the
Laudian church, but counselled the godly not to separate.[58] The
religious sceptics and rationalists too, for all they appear at times
to herald a future more liberal position, held to the idea of one
indivisible truth and religious community. Sir William Davenant,
who appears to have desired a more rationalist theology, upbraided the puritans for separating themselves, like the Jews, as a
sect.[59] The philosopher Lord Herbert, though impatient with
dogma, in the words of his biographer, 'in spite of the appearance
of some hard-hitting pragmatism responds to the idea of truth as
to a mysteriosum fascinosum whose ultimate characteristic is the
unification of all diversity'.[60] Herbert indeed responded to the
sceptical Montaigne's contention that all was diversity by asserting
(not arguing, for it was an axiom not to him in need of demonstration) that all was integrated by correspondences into one ordered
universal structure.[61]

As idealized, then, the commonwealth was bound by one truth.
It was also held, ideally, to express one good. The state, Aristotle
had maintained, existed to make the virtuous life possible. It was
a moral community and because it was both a moral and an
integrated community there could theoretically (the practical
tensions we will explore at length)[62] be no confrontation between
the good of the individual and the good of the whole. The good
of each person derived from and depended on the good of the
community. What over a century later Rousseau went to elaborate
lengths to argue (and failed), could be asserted in seventeenth-
century England as a commonplace: 'That which tends to the
common peace and safety must be practised by all'.[63] The
imperative itself suggests a recognition that not all adhered to that
commonplace. Indeed the most acute of the Tudor common-
wealthsmen revealed a realistic awareness of the tensions that
could exist between the individual and the community. But, for all
that realization, they adhered to the traditional concept of society
as an organism, 'depending for its health on the proper functioning
of all its parts for the good of the whole body'.[64] After the
religious disputes, economic crises and political tensions of the late
sixteenth and early seventeenth centuries, John Pym could declaim
in 1628 that:

> The form of government is that which doth actuate and dispose every
> part and member of a state to the common good; and as these parts give

strength and ornament to the whole, so they receive from it again strength and protection in their several stations and degrees. If this mutual relation and intercourse be broken, the whole frame will quickly be dissolved.[65]

It may from hindsight seem ironic that Pym's speech was delivered at the impeachment of Mainwaring. Certainly that context powerfully reminds us that ideals are often asserted at the very moments when they are being undermined in practice; that a shared language about how things ought to be may mask damaging political conflicts about how to restore them to perfection. But it is equally important to note that when contemporaries recognized threats to common good and order posed by interests, personal acquisitiveness, selfish behaviour or circumstance, they responded — the Jacobean dramatists provide an excellent example — by a reassertion of community and integrity.[66]

Those who preferred a private course were, like the fanatics who followed the dictates of their own consciences, dismissed as irrational men. 'The order of reason', Nicholas Faret observed in *The Honest Man*, 'requires that the interests of private men should yield to the public'.[67] What we would delineate as 'private interest', distinct from and in confrontation with public roles and duties, was not accepted in early modern England.[68] Economic and social theorists such as Clement Armstrong, a philosopher like Thomas More, could discern it but never really accommodate or accept it.[69] Any society organized around service relationships may find it difficult to distinguish private and public realms and in early modern England there were few who did not either give or receive service; most did both. The politicization of the body expressed this world and these integrations.[70] Indeed what later ages would understand as private, the early seventeenth century viewed as 'privatus', deprived of the order and good of the commonweal, of, as the Solemn League and Covenant could still put it, 'the true public liberty, safety and peace of the kingdom, wherein everyone's private condition is included'.[71] What we would separate as private and public interest, the individual and the state, were harmonized in the concept of the commonweal.

Indeed the commonweal was represented generally as a condition of harmony. In this quality of course it corresponded in microcosm to the harmony of the celestial bodies and took as its model the harmony of God's creation. It also macrocosmically corresponded to the harmony of humours in the well-ordered man. These are familiar statements but their implications have not perhaps sufficiently been pondered. For as God authored and maintained the harmony of the world so it was the role of the king to sustain the harmony of the commonweal.[72] Harmony is synonymous with balance and the balance is the symbol of justice. The business of kingship, then, is less the exercise of power than the distribution of justice to maintain, as an assize sermon of 1629 put it, 'proportion'.[73] In the natural body of man, health depended on a harmony of the various humours, on a balanced constitution; and so, again, as the physician of the state, it was the duty of the king to preserve a balanced *constitution* (the word takes on its political sense in our period)[74] in the body politic.

These ideas of harmony are essential contexts for any under-standing of attitudes to power in early modern England, and in particular help to make sense of what to us seem irreconcilable contradictions — such as Sir Thomas Smith's references to parlia-ment as the highest power in the realm *and* to the king as absolute.[75] They also importantly suggest how disagreements and even disruptions could for long be accommodated to ideas of unity and wholeness: by treating political upheavals not (as we naturally do) as rival contests for power, but rather as temporary imbalances in the body politic.[76] The subject and the sovereign were not only analogues to the body and the soul, wrote Forset in his *Comparative Discourse*; they existed in the same balance.[77] What secured that balance, or harmony, was moderation — the avoidance of any extremes. In Aristotle's *Ethics*, moderation, the pursuit of the mean, was equated generally with virtue and specifically with justice.[78] Echoing Aristotle, Ralph Knevet writing in 1628 defined the most virtuous men, the aristocracy, as those who most harmonized or moderated their own parts.[79] In *The English Gentleman*, Richard Braithwaite wrote: 'Moderation is a subduer of our desires to the obedience of reason'.[80] The ruler then was a moderator who, controlling his own appetite and balancing humours, sought to avoid all excess or extremes in the commonweal.[81] James I, who did not always succeed in the moderation of his personal pleasures, specifically proclaimed this as his axiom: 'I am for the medium in everything . . .'[82] Charles I's courtiers, I recently argued, reasserted the doctrine to a monarch who, they believed, had upset the balance both in his practice and theory of government.[83] The idea of cosmic harmony — of balance and moderation — far from a validation of un-restrained authority, was a normative ideology of self-restraint for rulers.

Power we most obviously think of as residing in individuals (or institutions), as the sway wielded by a superior over an inferior and as related to the exercise of the will. None of these associa-tions gets to the heart of early seventeenth-century attitudes.[84] Early modern perceptions of power, it must be admitted, are beset by ambivalences and hard to pin down; but these, like the infrequent use of the term, may be revealing as well as frustrating for the historian. The power of the king, we know, was described as analogous to that of God. Yet, as James Daly pointed out, the position of God himself in the cosmic theory (like much of that theory) was itself ambiguous, since He was both the author of the chain of correspondences and also part of that chain.[85] Not surprisingly then, in itself the analogy of royal with divine power could support both relatively unrestrained action and action circumscribed by the need to act according to the principles — or laws — that maintained the cosmos in harmony. Most contemporaries, however, saw God as acting usually through the divine laws according to expectations discernible by reason, deploying only exceptionally His power of miracle which operated outside of natural law. That power was explicitly compared to the king's prerogative; in the words of John Donne: 'Nature is his Prerogative'.[86] Royal prerogative, the Earl of Strafford added in 1641, 'must be used as God doth his omnipotency', that is only on 'extraordinary occasions'.[87] The analogy of the king with God then limited as well as validated royal power. Moreover the king's inferiority to God and his derivation of power from God made the due exercise of that power an *obligation*.

Early modern Englishmen were more used to thinking in terms of duties than of rights: Fulke Greville referred to the 'mutual duties to which man is born';[88] Francis Bacon wished to digest the duties of men to a science.[89] Notions of duty and obligation came more easily than the concept of power to a society organized around patron–client relationships. The more frequent assertions of the obligations and duties than power of the king (even their equation) therefore should not surprise us. The most obvious obligation was the need to account to God, in respect of whom, Owen Feltham put it in his *Resolves*, 'the greatest Monarch is more base than the basest vassal'.[90] P. Scot in his *Table Book for Princes* was more graphic: kings were never to forget their imminent need to account before the strictest of all judges — 'who knoweth but tomorrow they may be (where all kings before them are) the food of serpents and worms'.[91] Accountability to God, however, was not the only obligation. The king was obliged to subject his own will, not only to the regulation of his own reason, but to the common good, the custody of which defined his function.[92] In *A Looking Glasse for Princes and People*, a thanksgiving sermon for the birth of Prince Charles, the preacher William Struther reminded his congregation that the power of princes was 'not of themselves but lent of God and not for themselves but for him and his people'.[93] Charles I needed no reminding of this — even though he felt others did. 'Let me remember you', he told his

Commons in 1628, 'that my duty most of all and everyone of yours according to his degree, is to seek the maintenance of this church and commonwealth'.[94] Charles I and his audience in 1628 evidently had a different sense of the good of the church and commonwealth. But what is important is that he, as they, believed that royal power was in no way synonymous with the king's will.[95] In the *Emperour of the East*, Massinger has a character go so far as to proclaim that 'absolute Princes/Have, *or should have* in policie less free will then such as are their vassals'.[96] His caveat strikes to the root of the political problems left unresolved by theory: what was to be done if the monarch did not behave as he ought? To this problem the normative ideology had no answer other than a reassertion of the ideal. The exercise of royal power was, or ought to be, the exercise of self-restraint.[97] Sovereigns, Forset put it, governed by laws.[98] Power thus perceived and law were not at odds — which is why Knolles, in translating the *Six Livres de la République*, could combine praise of a Bodinian theory of sovereignty with celebration of the English common law.[99] Governing — exercising power — in early modern England was seen not as an individual act of will but as the expression of a cosmic and communal order by a monarch whose public body and will were inseparable from that order and community. Thomas Hobbes in his *Leviathan* came to see power in very different terms. But significantly before the Civil War he defined power in communal terms — as having its foundation in the 'belief of the people'.[100]

The community participated in the exercise of power through the giving of counsel and presentation of petitions against things amiss. Juan de Santa Maria put the place of counsel boldly: 'Kings which do not hear by consequence do not understand. And not understanding they cannot govern'.[101] Here again the analogy with God reinforced the king's obligation to heed the voice of his subjects. Kings, John Bastwick argued (for once uncontroversially), are like gods 'in respect of invocation, only to be sought to and called upon of their subjects', as God was invoked by prayer.[102] We are familiar with the pervasiveness in early Stuart political discourse of the necessity for, and the king's obligation to heed, good counsel.[103] Indeed once again mounting anxieties about the course of government lay behind the persistent reiteration of the ideal. In good counsel, it was frequently argued, lay the very health of the body politic.[104] But we may be less familiar with how far the obligation could be pressed. In the English translation of Juan de Santa Maria's *Christian Policie*, for example, the monarch who resolves business alone 'therein breaks the bounds of a Monarchie and enters into those of a tyrannie'.[105] Moreover, he is equally guilty if he acts 'against the opinion of his counsellors' — a point also made by George More in his *Principles for Young Princes*, a treatise which in general not only emphasized the obligations of princes but catalogued the horrible ends met by tyrants.[106] The obligation on the king to subordinate his own will to the concurrence of his councillors underlines how far the early seventeenth century was from seeing power as a distinct act of the individual will. And it is a further reminder why, despite the tensions in practice, it was not easy for them to theorize about the (potential) conflicts of prerogative and law.

On the continent, circumstances had forced England's neighbours to reflect on these and other fundamental political questions and problems. Such reflections had produced important and radical texts of political theory — especially in those countries where religious wars had led to violent antagonism between conscience and obedience, religious and secular obligations. Works such as the famous *Vindiciae Contra Tyrannos*, Buchanan's *De Iure Regni Apud Scotus* and several Dutch justifications of their revolt, were disseminated and well known in England.[107] Sympathy for the Dutch cause among the Sidney circle meant that even apologia for resistance could be received favourably, for all the Queen's disapproval. The Sidney circle also had connections with French polemicists and with Buchanan, and questions concerning resistance and tyranny permeate Sidney's *Arcadia*.[108] After the 1550s, however, English Calvinists were not faced with the threat of suppression. Even in the ideological decades of the 1560s to 1580s, when the cause of international Protestantism perforce involved England in the European debates about the limitations to authority and obedience, there was in England no reinvestigation of the foundations of political theory.[109] Sir Thomas Smith's *De Republica Anglorum* was premised on the symbiosis, not conflict, of authority and law.[110] After the threat to England receded in the 1590s, and after the peace with Spain of 1604, though travel to the continent was opened, England may have been in some respects more insulated from radical Protestant thought than before.[111] The Gunpowder Plot reinforced James I's desire for a polemical retort to the Jesuits and ultramontanes, but his reply was an ideological reinforcement of the commonweal (and church of England).[112] James's Calvinism seemed to ease remaining tensions in radical Protestant political thought as in theology, and the king himself ruled Buchanan out of season.[113] As for the Catholics, despite their political proscription and marginalization, they proved, by the end of Elizabeth's reign, more anxious to demonstrate their loyalty than to flirt with resistance theories.[114]

The Continental treatises of political thought that were translated into English in the early seventeenth century either emphasized the unitary nature of the commonweal and the need for monarchical authority, as did Bodin's *Six Books of a Commonweal*, or reiterated existing English conventions about monarchy and the state. Philip Bethune's *The Counsellor of Estate*, translated from the French in 1634, though it resonates with echoes of Commines, Machiavelli and Botero, defined the state as 'no other thing but an order' and stressed the necessity for religious unity, for good laws, mild government, counsel and sovereign monarchy.[115] Juan de Santa Maria's *Christian Policie*, published two years earlier, discussed the king analogically and conventionally as the reason, the father, the shepherd and the physician of the state, along with the traditional injunctions that the ruler must be just and virtuous. In places the language of such translations makes it clear that continental texts were being anglicized — not to censor their content but to make it comprehensible to English experience and convention.[116]

On occasions, however, even in the early seventeenth century, the very different nature of continental experience and ideas was made manifest. J.F. Le Petit's treatise *The Low Country Commonwealth* (translated in 1609) boldly concluded that the King of Spain had acted wrongly and the Dutch had 'been forced to oppose themselves and shake off his yoke'.[117] But there is almost no evidence that such knowledge or claims posed new questions about the commonweal in England. As Professor Salmon concluded: 'It was difficult for Englishmen to appreciate the relevance of . . . ideas remote from their own legal traditions until an open breach between King and Parliament, an overt contest for the sovereign law-making power forced them to do so'.[118] In the 1630s and 1640s, circumstances led the Scots to draw anew on Buchanan;[119] in 1647 the declaration of the Army referred to the rebellious Netherlanders and Portuguese 'proceeding from the same principles of right and freedom' as the soldiers claimed.[120] But before the divide, the fact and literature of resistance — on the continent or in the past — seem to have been of little relevance to early Stuart Englishmen. The exception to that generalization is the Cambridge lectures on Tacitus by Isaac Dorislaus in which, as well as defending the Dutch, the lecturer was believed to have hinted too at the application of his text to England. The episode caused a furore and the lecturer was silenced.[121] It is an episode that may demonstrate as much the paranoia of the king and government as any radical intents of the lecturer or his patron. In either case it suggests that the applicability of continental to English experience never required a long leap. Yet the fact remains that for most of the years before the civil war it was a step which was not taken.

To apply the experiences and values of another country or culture to one's own world, to re-examine one's own organization and premises in the light of them, seems to us an obvious, indeed unavoidable gesture. It is, however, a gesture that depends upon a relativism largely absent from the world-view of early modern England.[122] Just as there could be no toleration of other faiths because God's truth was one, so other societies, or modes of government, were seen as imperfect or diseased organisms. French foppishness and tyranny, Dutch avarice and selfishness, Spanish unreliability and pride, Italian chicanery and amorality, were stereotypes not eroded by travel. It has been persuasively argued that in sixteenth-century Spain, the impact of the discovery of the Amerindian prompted a fundamental reappraisal of ideas about society, man and the state of nature.[123] There is little evidence that such rethinking percolated to England. Rather the travel literature of the early Stuart years displays either a curiosity with the bizarre (like that which led to the building of cabinets of curios) or a cultural imperialism discomforting to some modern readers. Sir Thomas Herbert's *A Relation of some Yeares Travaile . . . Into Afrique and the Greater Asia* offers some fascinating insights into the ceremonies and habits of the peoples but displays prurience and superiority more than a real desire to understand without judging.[124] Henry Lord's *Display of Two Foreign Sects in the East Indies* showed him only 'how Satan leadeth those that are out of the pale of the church around in the maze of error and gentilism'.[125] Travel in fact appears to have taught him, as it has so many Englishmen through the ages, the wisdom of staying at home. With regard to the experience of the other, 'I know not wherein it may be more profitable than to settle us in the the solidness of our own faith'.[126] Heylyn's aptly titled *Microcosmus* did just what many English scholars since have: surveyed the globe from his study at Oxford and found it by English standards wanting.[127] Even those whose temperaments or circumstances made them sympathetic to other cultures appear incapable of evaluating them for themselves — as other, different. A *Revelation of the Successfull Beginnings of the Lord Baltemore's Plantation in Maryland* went to great lengths to paint the Indians in good colours, as chaste, grave and friendly; but their greatest quality was their proximity to Christianity (only language hindered a complete conversion) and English civilization, their residence with a central fire being compared to the old baronial halls of England![128] The understanding of Indian culture was not likely to develop from comparisons of their idols with children's dolls in England, but the comparison does typify how other cultures, when experienced, were seen.[129] Societies were judged by one set of standards as churches by (theoretically) one gospel.

The greatest challenge to such a world-view was presented by the essays of Michel de Montaigne, translated into English by John Florio in 1603.[130] Montaigne found in nature no common uniform law discernible by man's reason: 'we see an infinite difference and variety in this world'.[131] As a consequence, systems of morality, law, order were also relative. The radical implications of Montaigne's assault on the metaphysical universe of the Renaissance did not pass unnoticed in England. Samuel Daniel, in a preface to the English translation, acknowledged the alternatives posed if Montaigne were right. Either men were unlearned, 'or els that truth hath other shapes then one'.[132] Lord Herbert of Cherbury engaged with Montaigne and reasserted man's capacity to discern the 'common notions' of one natural order.[133] Montaigne's relativism won no converts in England. Though he deserves, perhaps, an important place in Professor Shapiro's story of 'the gradual erosion of the distinction between knowledge and probability', it is a story with no really important chapters before the middle of the century.[134]

III Tensions

A commonweal united as one, all its parts in harmony, all its citizens combined in the common interest, its ruler restraining his own will and governing for the public good, a realm untouched by the conflicts on the continent and the fundamental reappraisals of government which they had forced: it will already have been more than apparent that what I have sketched is an idealized picture, not an accurate representation of Tudor and Stuart society.[135] This idealization, however, is not that of the historian; it is a contemporary idealization, a representation that encodes the meaning that early modern Englishmen (especially those in authority) discerned in their universe and which they in turn represented to themselves and to each other. They were not of course ignorant that there were threats to their world, contradictions within it, indeed tensions which could become conflicts. Separatists challenged the very foundations of society, state and church, and, most seriously, rejected their integration. Theorists and pamphleteers wrote of economic self-interest and the quest for power; dramatists staged naked ambition; magistrates and MPs daily encountered political differences; the populace at times rose in revolt. If then we are to maintain that before the civil war such realizations and experiences did not shatter their world-view, did not rewrite the vocabulary of political thought, we must examine these tensions, and how they were perceived and accommodated.

In the early seventeenth century, the tensions pervade the entire chain of being from the celestial plane to the little kingdom of man. The great speech on order from *Troilus*, cited by Tillyard as the summation of a world-view, is itself undermined by the character's position in the play. We have become all too familiar with Donne's lines from the first Anniversary about the impact of the new cosmology.[136] But it is worth quoting from the less well known Thomas Scot's *Philomythie* (1616) to see how closely the disharmony of the planets is associated with the subversion of all moral order:

> This earth we live on and do steadfast call
> Copernicus proves giddy brainde and all
> Those other bodies whose swift motions we
> So wonder at, he settled finds to be
> Till sanctified Ignatius and his brood
> Found out the lawfull way of shedding blood,
> And proved it plainly that a subject might
> Murther his Prince, we fondly usde t'indite
> Such persons of high treason: Now before them
> We kneele, we pray, we worship and adore them.[137]

At the other end of the chain, Thomas Browne was no less convinced of the macrocosmic significance of his own personal turmoil. In himself, rather than all being order, a mass of contrarieties contended for the mastery: 'the battle of Lepanto, passion against reason, reason against faith, faith against the Devil, and my conscience against all'.[138] In general the ordering of human sexual appetites was (and is) regarded as an important social problem: understandably so if the author of *The Lawes Resolutions of Women's Rights* was correct in arguing that without the protection of law no woman 'being above twelve years of age and under an hundred . . . should be able to escape ravishing'.[139] That sexual passion was often an analogue for man in the state of nature made this a problem of universal import. Social and political tensions were not comprehended only analogically (important though this is) from corresponding disorder in the macrocosm or microcosm; they were explicitly acknowledged in the commonweal. Jacobean city comedies and rogue literature speak to an obvious recognition of disharmony;[140] sermons and injunctions to hospitality, Herrick's poetry and Jonson's later drama address 'the breakdown of a system of communal obligations'.[141] James I acknowledged that though 'we are of all nations the people most loving and most reverently obedient to our Prince, yet we are . . . too easy to be seduced to make rebellion'.[142] George Wither's *Britaine's Remembrancer* is permeated with a fear of imminent 'distraction', 'desparation' and specifically deplores those who have put their persons before the public weal.[143] The popularity of satire and criticism of the prince was freely recognized, [144] even though it sat uneasily with assertions concerning the love that existed between the king and his people.[145] Sir Thomas Wentworth even acknowledged that there were some who sought to divide the ruler from his people and sovereignty from subjection 'as if their ends were distinct, not the same, nay in opposition'.[146] A recurrent theme of tragedy was the tension between ideal and natural rulers. Juan de Santa Maria, for all his conservatism, almost took it for granted that no kings could be found without faults.[147] And so the catalogue could go on. But it is more important to ponder these acknowledgements of tension than it is to list more of them. What is immediately striking is how often they surface in works which may also be read as conventional treatises of cosmic harmony: Shakespeare's plays offer a vivid example, but Scot's treatise and Wentworth's speech of 1628 offer more prosaic instances.

In fact in most of the texts we examine, some recognition of division and dislocation is juxtaposed with the theory of unity and order.[148] There may be general reasons for that as well as particular ones: Clifford Geertz once observed (significantly while discussing Elizabethan England) that 'Heresy is as much of a child of orthodoxy in politics as it is in religion'.[149] But their acknowledgement of disorder does not make our texts self-consuming artefacts. Rather in themselves subsuming those tensions within a theory of order, our writers may have textualized that exquisite poise that was normative for (though never simply descriptive of) social behaviour. Richard Hooker's *Laws of Ecclesiastical Polity*, often and rightly cited as a classic statement of harmony, is itself a document of tensions *and* of an attempted resolution of them — the reconciliation for example of consent and order.[150] In this context it is noteworthy that some of our best evidence of contemporary debate comes from early Stuart drama. Not only, one suspects, because the dramatic medium is one of debate, but because the state offers a laboratory for the examination of a difficulty, displaced — but not too far — from reality. On the stage in Jacobean England therefore we find plays that lack closure, as dramatists dared to imagine their world without meaning. Ben Jonson, the author of one of the best of them, *Bartholomew Fair*, took the broken compass as his own mark.[151] The imaginary permits this licence because it enables reflection without practical consequences.[152] On the political stage such experiment was not possible: the tensions, though acknowledged, had to be resolved; the circle had to be complete; there had to be closure. The royal texts therefore, the *Basilikon Doron* of James I and the *Eikon Basilike* of his son, had to find that balance which secured the harmony of the commonweal. Interestingly, a concern with exquisite poise, the resolution of tension, has recently been discerned in the paintings and architecture, as well as the literature, of Caroline England.[153] In each case the documents of kingship replicated and reinforced the picture of order not by ignoring its opposites but by controlling them. And this was the function of the king in practice: the act of recognizing threats, neutralizing them, reconciling contradictions — his own and others — preserving balance through the destabilizing passage of time. Governing, Juan de Santa Maria acknowledged, was difficult;[154] had all been naturally harmonious, of course, it should not have been. The king's very position was ambivalent: he drew his authority from a world-view which at times only the due exercise of his authority could sustain.

Far then from a simple idealization removed from reality, the idea of correspondences, the metaphysical idea, was itself a way of resolving tensions, a way of holding the world together through coincidentia oppositorum.[155] The world was held together by an act of consciousness — though we would add a consciousness that was also translated into action. It is no accident that it was Francis Bacon who could clearly articulate what others only dimly suspected and even feared: human understanding, he wrote, 'easily supposes a greater degree of order and equality in things than it really finds; and although many things in nature be sui generis and most irregular, will yet invent parallels, conjugates and relatives where no such thing is'.[156] Along with the certainties and truths of the Elizabethan world picture went the realization that all was not as it was represented, that authority could easily become overrigorous, that kings could fail to take counsel, that the balance of humours was precarious, that order was on the edge of confusion. When these tensions were themselves systematized, encoded into a different representation of meaning or order, they posed the profoundest challenges to the prevailing ideology, perhaps challenges from which it never completely recovered. We must turn to examine three of these: the challenges of scepticism, Machiavellianism and of Calvinism.

Scepticism and rationalism, we might think, posed the greatest threat to the Elizabethan world picture and commonweal. To question the power or nature of God might analogically be thought to challenge his magistrate on earth. Certainly some of the activities of the sceptics caused scandal. In tearing leaves out of a Bible in order to dry his tobacco the philosopher Thomas Allen quite literally deconstructed one of the prime texts of authority.[157] The sordid death of Christopher Marlowe pleasantly confirmed to many the swift arm of divine retribution against one who had danced

with the devil. Yet the sceptics of the early Stuart age, I would
suggest, were men of different, less radical stripes than their Elizabethan predecessors. It was not, perhaps, a small or insignificant
group that took in Raleigh, Lord Herbert, Inigo Jones, the Earl of
Arundel, the poet Sir John Suckling, the playwright Sir William
Davenant, as well as the distinguished circle at Great Tew —
especially Lord Falkland.[158] But listing them we see that these
were very much men of the court and establishment. Their scepticism consisted in a rationalist, undogmatic approach to religion,
in an emphasis on man's reason and capacity to discern the good,
in a concern with ethical rather than narrowly doctrinal priorities.
Accordingly in *Philomythie*, Thomas Scot allegorizes the sceptic as
a chameleon; 'His Reason is his God'.[159] 'They make', William
Pemble observed, 'the understanding the seat of all speculative
habits'.[160] The ethics of the sceptics were derived as often from
classical as Christian sources: they knew 'some Philosophy no
Divinity', Scot charged.[161] In his popular treatise on *The English
Gentleman* (1630) Richard Braithwaite asked: 'have we not read
how divers naturally addicted to all licentious motions by reading
moral precepts and conversing with Philosophers became absolute
commanders of their own affections?'[162] In another widely
disseminated *Guide of Honour* (1634), Anthony Stafford counselled his noble readers to love goodness in whatsoever religion
they found it.[163] Both tenets confirm a sense that a more secular
approach to ethics was a fashion among the upper classes and
perhaps most of all the court milieu in the late 1620s and
1630s:[164] Sir Thomas Wentworth (to whom *The English
Gentleman* was dedicated) and the Earl of Arundel were both
Stoics;[165] Inigo Jones, like his patron Arundel, paid more attention
to the didactic qualities of classical art and architecture than to
devout piety.

Some historians have gone further and posited a close connection between the sceptics and rationalists and the dominance of the
Arminians at the court of Charles I.[166] There are some general
reasons and particular passages to support this view.[167] Lord
Herbert, for one, concluded that 'this principle of Evil cannot be
derived from Adam, for all our sins and transgressions are our own
meer voluntary acts'.[168] Meric Casaubon, dedicating to Laud the
meditations of Marcus Aurelius Antoninus, announced it as, though
the work of a heathen, one of the best guides to living virtuously.[169] Robert Harris, pastor of Hanwell, in *A treatise of the
New Covenant* seems to suggest theological connection: 'for who-
soever is capable of Reason, the same is also capable of Grace (for
what is Grace but reason perfected and elevated . . .)[170] Laud himself, however, would have none of it; he showed little sympathy

for other courtiers' ease with the integration of the sacred and the profane. When his friend Wentworth sent him a treatise on the vanity of the world replete with references to poetry, art and the classics, Laud replied with unusual frostiness: 'If you will read the short book of Ecclesiastes you will see a better disposition of those things than in any anagrams of Dr Donnes or any designs of Van Dyck'.[171] The Laudian God, as Malcolm Smuts has put it, was a more 'tranquil deity'[172] than the interventionist God of the puritans; the Laudian Christopher Dow described as accidents events that Burton had catalogued as God's punishments of sabbath-breakers.[173] But neither Laud nor the Arminians walked with the rationalists and sceptics and significantly none of their enemies (who hurled every other accusation) charged them with doing so.

Yet though there was no obvious connection between Laudianism and the rationalists, the court of Charles I was especially conducive to a classical, pagan, as well as Christian world view. Those like Alexander Grosse who counselled preachers to cite the Scriptures rather than secular authorities, or Richard James who urged that 'from Christ better than from the Stoic porch' morality may be learned, express the fear that a clear line between pagan and Christian culture was being eroded.[174] This may well have upset many — and not only the puritans. But it demonstrates that the rationalists and sceptics did not present a threat to the ideological foundations of the commonweal as perceived by the king and court. Rather, for all his piety, Charles I's own political values appear to synthesize classical and Christian influences.[175] The radical scepticism of Montaigne, we have seen, enjoyed little influence in England, and even the potential radicalism of the Elizabethan 'School of Night' faded into nought with the death of a generation. In the scepticism of Caroline figures such as Lord Herbert there was an intrinsic conservatism: the principle that since certainty was elusive, one should place one's trust in the laws and conventions of the realm.[176]

If Montaigne cast only a shadow across the moral horizon of the Elizabethan world, Machiavelli darkened its skies to near blackness. The impact of Machiavelli is all the more powerful when we recall that no English edition of *The Prince* was published until 1640, and no edition of the *Discourses* before 1638.[177] And yet Machiavelli was sufficiently popularly known to be represented on the stage as the devil himself,[178] the phrase 'old Nick' being his legacy to folklore. The man himself, or his reputation, became a text — debated, refuted, yet possessing power. Given that he was not widely read, except by the learned who could read him in Latin or Italian, [179] the fear that he aroused, the vehemence with which he was denounced, require explanation. At the simplest level, an explanation must be that Machiavelli not only challenged but subverted all the premises of the early modern English common-weal. He disrupted the notions of unity and wholeness by acknow-ledging and advocating the pursuit of interests; he substituted for ideas of divine harmony the capricious goddess Fortuna; he separated the exercise of power from virtuous action and detached authority from obligation; he broke the correspondence between divine and regal behaviour by a defence of dissimulation. He opted for fear over love as the basis of government.[180] More traumatic-ally, he effected this bouleversement of conventions through a discourse that employed the very vocabulary that had sustained them and so drew attention to the tensions which that language had concealed.[181] He divested *reason* and *nature* of their divine, metaphysical, ethical, their normative value.[182] A more sophisti-cated explanation for the fear that Machiavelli excited must be related to the ambivalence of this conservative vocabulary and radicalism of meaning. Machiavelli, to put it another way, was feared because he powerfully articulated existing tensions that the normative conventions and discourse had kept in delicate control. And this ambivalence, I would suggest, revealingly surfaces in the treatises that denounce him as well as those that adapt, adopt and attempt to neuter him. We need say little about the latter: the 'Machiavellianism' of men like Raleigh and Bacon has been exten-sively argued;[183] politic historians such as John Speed anglicized and moralized but nevertheless appropriated his goddess Fortuna (in English garb she was reconciled, if not always synonymous, with Providence) as a driving force of history.[184]

The denunciations are more interesting. Even diatribes such as *Machiavells Dogge* (1617) take their agenda from him, setting back upright each of the premises he was believed to have over-turned.[185] One wonders too whether in his conventional counsel to princes, George More did not, in spite of scorning him, also see Machiavelli's relevance to recent English experience: 'where Matchevils [sic] principle taketh effect, there the subjects must be made poor by continual subsidies, exactions and impositions that the people may be always kept under as slaves'.[186] In other works, the connection between Machiavelli and the tensions within and the fragility of the conventions seems consciously to be explored. In Scot's *Philomythie*, in which animals in turn deliver moral tales, Aesop has to face the argument of Tortus (Cardinal Bellarmine's chaplain, who may stand for Machiavelli) that his morality may easily be inverted. Tortus charges that:

In Kings he would no other vertue see
Then what in lyons and in Eagles bee
To prey on all, to make their will a law,
To tyrannize, to rule by force and awe[187]

Aesop's moral fables are subverted by Tortus just as Machiavelli overturns the normative paradigms of the age. The frontispiece depicts Aesop and Tortus, representing virtue and vice, contesting for the globe — we might say for the interpretative authority to determine values.[188] In *The Uncasing of Machiavelli's Instruction to His Son* the very structure of the treatise addresses ambivalence. The first half *is* a Machiavellian treatise in which (?ironically) all are counselled to follow their own interest, wealth and power, to flatter and deceive, to use, not love their fellow men, to think of the present not the afterlife:

Get all contentment that the world can give
For after death, who knoweth how we live.[189]

The second half of the tract, however, offers 'The Answer to Machiavelli's Uncasing'. Here the coin is flipped and the reader is urged to ignore all that has preceded except 'by ill to know the good';[190] the anonymous author proceeds to conventional invocation to honesty, charity, honour, virtue, piety. Not only does this work acknowledge the force of Machiavelli's impact, it acknowledges too that the relationship of the ill and the good is as close (as well as opposite) as the two faces of a coin. The author shows Machiavelli's vain courses *and* how to avoid them. He counsels virtue but (unwittingly?) concedes that the interpretation of his janus text (the moral decision) rests with the reader: 'Machiavel's rules deny, yet use them as thy pleasure'.[191] Is the ambivalence of the last line unconscious? For we may deny Machiavelli's rules and yet live by them and thereby (rather than rejecting them) pursue *pleasure* (rather than virtue). The coin may be turned over again and again. It may be such a recognition that prompted the remarks of Edward Dacres in his preface to the translation of *The Prince*. Machiavelli's maxims were condemned as pernicious by all, he confessed, but 'if thou consider well the actions of the world, thou shall find him much practised by those that condemn him'.[192] Dacres could not himself mask his grudging respect for the Italian even whilst penning a critical commentary on his amoral tenets. Once again too he sees that Machiavelli had demonstrated how this was the coin-edge that divided the two heads. The ethical politics which Dacres's own day 'presuppose[d]', 'will never allow this rule, as that a man may make *this small difference* between virtue and vice'.[193] But Machiavelli had made only a small difference between them and it was only a *presupposition* (not quite the same as a truth) that stood in his way. Old Nick raised demons that could never be completely exorcized.

Machiavellianism and scepticism are ideologies which it is hard to define rigidly. Puritanism, the last of our cases, appears from recent historiography to be in danger of losing all meaning,[194] and the question of its importance in relation to politics and the crisis of 1642 has dissolved into disagreement and confusion. Gardiner had no doubt that in an important sense the English Civil War was a puritan revolution; in our own century, from a different perspective, Christopher Hill concurred and Michael Walzer in a stimulating study probed the revolutionary ideology and language of the saints.[195] More recent historiography has questioned the radicalism of the puritans, has claimed that few theological differences distanced them from the established church, and even depicted them as the vanguard defence of the status quo against the innovating Arminians, on whose shoulders the blame for the crisis now rests.[196] Such revisions have not (at least to this reader) proved convincing. For the moment let us leave that controversy to make a different observation.

For that two quite contrary interpretations can be powerfully argued might lead us to suspect that both within puritanism and the church of England there were ideological tensions to which circumstances could give a conservative or revolutionary face. Since much has been written of late about the former, it is probably appropriate here to re-emphasize the second, for strict Calvinist theology on several points squared uneasily with the theological and philosophical bases of the Elizabethan world picture. First the logic of double predestination threatened the separation of grace (the gift only of God) from nature seen as irredeemably corrupt and fallen. This was potentially to question the divine, natural and normative condition of society which could now only be itself a product of the fall. Richard Hooker, seeing the danger of their challenge, forcefully argued for God as the author of nature and man's reason as capable of acting according to the good.[197] The controversy about nature and grace was not resolved: Sidney's *Apology for Poetry* is a splendid document of the ambivalent perceptions of nature;[198] and the word continued throughout our period to be used in not only different but quite contrary senses — as the fallen and as the perfect state of man. It may be the rationalist classicism of the 1620s and 1630s, as well as the Arminians, that rearticulated and reintensified the differences. Both Burton and Prynne, of course, blamed the Arminians and went to great lengths to deny the ascription of grace to nature.[199] Classical humanism, however, was as difficult to reconcile with strict predestination as was Arminianism and the resulting tension, as Milton and the radical sects of the 1650s testify, was not just between theological enemies.[200]

With predestination came another emphasis that jarred with the conventional ideology: the emphasis on the power and will of a God who acted purely according to his volition and by no means necessarily in accordance with any rules or laws discernible to man.[201] In the Elizabethan world picture the universe, as we have seen, was idealized as operating according to divine laws; God's exercise of his prerogative — miracle — was only an occasional intervention in a rational system: his will and his law were complementary not at odds. The Calvinist emphasis implied their separation and hence substituted a voluntarist for a legal perception of power in general; this by correspondence questioned the harmony between prerogative and law in the commonweal as well as created world. James I, in a little-quoted passage of his famous speech on monarchy, recognized the importance of the parallel and reasserted the symbiosis of prerogative and law as well as of the divine and secular realms. Kings like God had power to create or destroy:

> But now in these our times we are to distinguish between the state of
> kings in their first original, and between the state of settled kings . . .
> for ever as God, during the time of the Old Testament, spake by oracle
> and wrought by miracles, yet how soon it pleased him to settle a church
> . . . then there was a cessation of both, he ever after governing his
> people and Church within the limits of his revealed will; so in the first
> original of kings . . . their wills at that time served for law, yet how
> soon kingdoms began to be settled in civility and policy then did kings
> set down their minds by laws . . .[202]

We perhaps need to look again at the perception of law in the sermons and speeches of puritans.[203] For though the logic of the voluntarist emphasis of Calvinism was not always pursued, there is a sense in which Hobbes's determinism drew on the puritans he hated.[204]

As well as emphasizing a wilful God operating outside a perceived system of law, Calvinism placed the personal conviction and personal relationship with God above the codes or community of the commonweal. The Calvinist community of the elect could not logically be synonymous with the community of the visible church. Whilst some ministers did not choose to press this to its conclusion, the puritans did distinguish themselves by their behaviour — by the zeal of their devotion to sermons, by the sobriety of their lives and by their distancing themselves from the pastimes of their neighbours whom they regarded as profane.[205] James I and others scorned the puritans as a 'sect rather than Religion', a term that expresses the challenge they presented to the

ideology of communalism.[206] There can be little doubt that the
Books of Sports which licensed traditional pastimes were intended
as responses to the puritan challenge to society as well as the
church, and it may be that we need to study the pastoral idealizations of rural harmony that are a recurring motif of the literary and
visual arts in Caroline England not as an innovation, but as a
reassertion of conventional ideas of unity.[207] In their insistence on
uniformity of ceremonies, Charles I and Laud appear, whatever the
fear of their critics, to have been more concerned with the unity
of the church and realm than with the theological and sacerdotal
aspects of the liturgy.[208] The puritans, however, put conscience
before uniformity, parish community, and indeed before family.
This could not but have consequences for a society built on those
very pillars, as contemporaries — not all fellow travellers with the
high church party — were quick to recognize. In *The Looking-
Glasse of Schisme*, Peter Studley, a minister at Shrewsbury, related
the gory story of one of his parishioners, Enoch ap Evan, who had
axed his brother and mother to death for kneeling in church.[209]
To Studley the moral was clear: schism and zeal threatened the
church and realm; it was natural to conclude in early Stuart
England that fratricide was but one step from regicide. Owen
Feltham found political language came naturally in describing those
who 'in things but ceremonial' spurned at 'the grave authority of
the church': 'I suppose we may call him a church *rebel*, or one that
would exclude order that his brain might rule'.[210] Even the
moderate Robert Saunderson who denounced the Arminians and
went to some lengths to deny the 'effectual holiness' of ceremonies still condemned those who would fashion their own liturgy
according to their taste: 'whereof what other could be the issue
but infinite distraction and unorderly confusion'?[211] The stress on
the individual conscience and the distinctness of the godly were,
and were seen to be, political as well as religious and social
gestures.

   What then of the political conservatism of the puritans recently
argued by historians?[212] This must I think be open to major
qualification if not rejection. For in England as in Europe the
loyalty of the puritans to princes was always conditional: in the
case of Thomas Cartwright, as Scott Pearson put it, 'of such a conditional nature as to render it suspect'.[213] The author of *Christ's
Confession* illustrates the point: whilst he maintained that Christ's
kingdom was not prejudicial to Caesar's, he warned princes that if
they were not obeyed by subjects it was because they did not seek
Christ's kingdom.[214] And those who were not with Christ were
against him. A godly man could serve his king when the monarch
walked the path of God: 'But if the prince they serve be an

idolator, an heretic or wicked, they can hardly hold their places
. . .'[215] *Christ's Confession* closes with a prayer that the king may
see the light and leaves the possible consequence of his not doing
so undiscussed. The implications, however, are those expressed
more obviously in *The Fall of Babylon*, a diatribe against the
bishops published in Amsterdam in 1634: kings are lords over men
only in so far as they are subjects not as they are Christ's
disciples.[216] The unconventional division points to the radical
core of Calvinist political thought: the unnaturalness (in the normative sense) of the state and its subordination to the rule of the
saints.[217] For much of our period the radical, political implications
of Calvinism were quiescent. But they were not, as Johan Sommerville would have it, of no importance.[218] For the Calvinists alone
perhaps in 1642 had a set of beliefs that could turn the world
upside down. 'At the beginning of the English Civil war, the work
of ideological opposition to the king was still done (largely) by the
radical Calvinism of the sixteenth century and its derivatives.'[219]

Our excursus into scepticism, Machiavellianism and puritanism
may seem to have led us far away from the commonweal of truth,
harmony and virtue which we earlier described. It is important
therefore to recall that we have not travelled to other realms, that
sceptics, Machiavels and puritans inhabited the commonweal even
when others found it hard ideologically to incorporate them. Not
only were they part of the commonweal, they articulated clearly
ambivalencies and tensions at its philosophical and theological
centre. The perception of a rationally ordered universe intelligible
to human reason always contained the possibility of a more secular
world view; in Protestant theology lay always the potential for a
more individual relationship to a wilful God; and many in practice
acted (and were seen to act) according to Machiavelli's principles.
The Elizabethan world picture was not a flat, two-dimensional
canvas. The frame only just contained a swirl of action and
contradiction, an interplay of dark and light. Viewed from a
different perspective all could take on a different appearance. Or,
to change the metaphor to a language that contemporaries frequently used, it was a drama which at first sight appears a simple
morality play but on closer reading resonates with tensions and
subversions only just held in artistic control. Until 1642, the early
modern world was just that: held together by art, by the texts
which mediated its ideological premises. As we turn to those
authorizing texts, vocabularies, cultural practices and analogues,
we must remain alert to the ambiguities and contradictions they
reveal and endeavour to control.

IV Texts and languages

It is a mark of how approaches to the history of ideas have been revolutionized that where once we founded that history on key texts, the very existence or nature of a text is now called into question and doubt. It was called into question by literary critics who observed that what we call a text is no more than a speech act of agent (a) (whom we describe as an author) which is reinterpreted and hence rewritten by a set of subsequent agents (b to n) (whom we call readers, commentators, critics, etc.). These agents from their own linguistic and cultural paradigms reconstitute the meaning of the original verbal performance, themselves therefore become authors, and so by appropriating de-authorize, in both senses (displacing both the author and the authority of), the original performance. Many historians have ignored the radical challenge posed by Stanley Fish's question: *Is There a Text in This Class?*[220] John Pocock, however, has addressed it and reasserted 'the persistence of a literary artefact of a certain authority and *duree*'.[221] The historian, Pocock argues, can, indeed does, accommodate the acts of reinterpretation and appropriation without abandoning the idea of text, viewed as 'a certain set of formulas or paradigms, which are to be applied each time the authority of the text is invoked'.[222] This goes a long way to answering the textual Pyrrhonists. One might here adduce to support Pocock's argument seventeenth-century instances in which a destruction of a text acknowledged an authority which could not easily be deconstructed. We have mentioned Thomas Allen's tearing up of his Bible; James I's ripping of the Protestation from the Commons Journal in 1621, and other concerns about entries in that Journal imply a recognition of its textual authority.[223] More generally the growing anxiety exhibited by the Privy Council over records and libraries — Sir Robert Cotton's was closed in 1629, Sir Edward Coke's papers were sequestered on his death — may reveal, if not the autonomous power of legal and historical documents, at least the greater authority of some readings than of others.[224] Indeed the need to reinterpret and appropriate certain texts itself bears witness to their authority.[225] It was essential to claim Biblical endorsement for almost any action in early modern England, and the same was almost as true for Aristotle. Hugo Grotius, as Richard Tuck has pointed out, had to comb Aristotle in search of passages to support a very un-Aristotelian thesis.[226]

Yet this example reminds us too that textual authority and its subversion may be in a more complex relationship than Pocock allows. Texts, even as a set of linguistic formulas, may remain. But the authority of a *name* may become the veil for a subversion of the *meanings* originally connected to (we will not worry the problem of intended by) that name, leaving the survival of the text as original meaning act in doubt. A good case of this is offered by Charles Schmitt's rich study of Renaissance Aristotelianism.[227] Aristotle, Schmitt reminds us, was read from many different types of text — most of them printed with some form of commentary: 'like . . . Biblical knowledge, Aristotelian doctrine was available in many different forms, from the most learned annotated editions of the Greek text to the sketchiest of compendia in Latin or a number of different vernaculars'.[228] Centuries-old disputes over the editions and translations of the Bible, the difference between the Scriptures in the Vulgate and Geneva Bible forms, are enough to indicate how editions complicate speaking of the authority of the text. Not least because he was read in so many forms, and in so many different circumstances, in courts, in literary academies, in schools and universities, 'Aristotle could serve as a starting point for many investigations and result in varied approaches to understanding the world'.[229] At times the only unifier of such variety was Aristotle's name. Similarly the Platonism of the Renaissance has been recently defined as 'a kernel of Plato's doctrines along with Aristotle's reinterpretations admixed with Pythagorean mathematics, Stoic ethics, Plotinian and Christian mysticism, Hermeticism, Patristic theology, and cosmology, Florentine humanism and Neo-Platonism, a number of occult symbolisms, several types of logical theory and method, and a turbulent current of religious reformation . . .'[230] To what extent was there a Platonic text in this class? Clearly there was in the sense that Renaissance Platonists were so described and derived authority for their meaning from him. But as editions also lead us to recall, texts as well as conveying power are authorized by and dependent upon it. Their publication required licence; their teaching and discussion in schools and universities involved the support of teachers or a place in the curriculum. The authority of a text in other words always interacted with the institutions of power, political, social and intellectual. As Schmitt put it, 'The longevity of Aristotelian philosophy . . . certainly was tied . . . to the whims of those in political control, as well as to the structural continuity and acceptance of traditional practices'.[231]

Those texts which continued to have authority, then, may be those whose original meanings had least stability or rigidity; their formulas or paradigms, to dissent from Pocock, may not be so much reapplied as recast. They may have been authoritative because they have to a wide extent permitted and yet contained their own reinterpretations. Eclecticism, however, cannot ultimately be contained; as John Selden put it, 'Scrutamini Scripturas:

These two words have undone the world'.[232] Nor are there *no*
bounds to eclecticism. When the world in 1642 was undone, its
authorizing texts were dethroned along with the king. The authority and subversion of the Bible, Aristotle and other 'texts' is
inseparable from the history of authority and subversion themselves.

The close interplay of 'texts' and 'authority' is in particular
demonstrable from a study of interpretations. Certain interpretations made by those in power became thereby authoritative in the
broader sense of influencing other readings. Elizabeth I's identification of herself with Richard II[233] or James I's reading of the
Faerie Queen as a commentary on his mother's (Mary Queen of
Scots) trial shaped contemporary readings and responses.[234] But,
as recent work has begun to demonstrate, the relationship between
textual authority and organs of power may, especially in Renaissance England, be broader and closer still. Once we see a text as
a set of paradigms that have acquired authority but which are also
reinterpreted in time and circumstance, we may come to include
as 'texts' other such performances, both discursive and enacted —
especially by those in authority. Indeed James I's desire to have the
story of his mother's reign rewritten[235] may become more
explicable when we understand that royal authority itself in early
modern England rested more on a set of presumptions and perceptions than on the instrument of power.[236] The power of a text,
we might say, could then be crucial for the performance of power.
And the monarchy itself we might study as a text — not least
because the comparison came easily to contemporaries. Ben Jonson
always regarded the king and poet as brothers in authority and
shaped his own artistic performance in close parallel to royal
speech and action: his *works* appeared the same year as those of
James I.[237] Shakespeare, David Bergeron has argued, fashioned his
plays about families and politics from the model of the royal
family, which became a text for him as much as the 'authorities'
— North's *Plutarch*, Greene's *Pandosto* and others — on which he
drew.[238] More importantly, the identification of monarch and
artist came as naturally to the former as the latter: their roles as
actors, icons and texts were acknowledged by Elizabeth, James and
Charles and by their subjects.[239] The *Table Book for Princes* put it
directly: kings are 'the subjects of all discourse; the objects of all
men's eyes'.[240] The lives of princes, another wrote in 1634,
'should be set forth unto their people as specula, a supereminent
watch tower whom their subjects everywhere might behold . . .
and as speculum, a mirror wherein they might gaze on and strive
to imitate their sovereign . . .'[241] In a mirror, however, one sees
oneself. And these last lines from the preface to a life of Alfred

indicate that the actions and lives of monarchs, like other texts, were also reinterpreted; their original formulas or paradigms were rewritten.[242] By the 1610s and 1620s Elizabeth I's reign was employed as the hold-all of a set of values some of which she would have deplored.[243] *England's Elizabeth* was appropriated, albeit unconsciously, to authorize later attitudes.[244]

Texts then can be regarded as clusters of values which derive authority often from the name which holds them together; their histories may see the name and certain associations invoked, while the values are rewritten. In an important sense the text as object remains, as does the mirror, but historical subjects find in it representations of themselves. Though few historians would dissent from this formulation, many have not exploited the possibilities it presents. The phrases 'conventional' (often 'merely conventional') or 'familiar trope' are often employed by historians of ideas to denigrate the importance of a view or thinker:[245] the 'timeless' trope, by its label, has no history. But no conventions or tropes are without a history; and the changing selection, articulation and deployment of them requires, perhaps, closer attention than it has received. Consider the classicism of Ben Jonson and the Caroline poets and playwrights: literary scholars have for years been content to elucidate the 'imitations' of 'borrowings' from and 'influence' of Horace, Martial, Ovid and so on; and historians have fallen into the trap of dehistoricizing those who appeared to want to live outside of their own age. The classicism of English Renaissance poets, however, does not make them unoriginal.[246] We may say of them, as Professor Oestreich said of Justus Lipsius: though superficially he seems to be lost in the classical authorities he cites, 'yet it is his own pregnant formulations that stick in the mind'.[247] Indeed, the chronology of imitation and appropriation raises important questions. Why, we need to ask generally, was a pagan culture celebrated in decades of religious passion and division?[248] Why, we must ponder more specifically, does an interest in the classical motif of the happy country life come into vogue in the second quarter of the seventeenth century?[249] Poets like Jonson, it has been suggested, treated their classical sources in the way that antiquaries drew on precedents:[250] they selected from a past what might convey qualities for living properly in the present; their texts and circumstances were in a dialogue.

Historians who can learn from eavesdropping on such conversations might pay more attention to the editions of and prefaces to classical texts, and still more perhaps to the genre of *observations* on authors who were popular in the early modern period. In these the re-readings and reconstitutions in the light of contemporary experience are obvious: in *The Honest Man or The Art to Please in Court*, (translated into English in 1632), Nicholas Faret admitted that he had so mingled his own views with those of the ancients that he did not know how to unravel them.[251] Joshua Sylvester, in his prefatory remarks to C. Edmondes's *Observations Upon Caesar's Commentaries*, wondered whether Caesar or Edmondes deserved the greater praise;[252] Samuel Daniel thought the observations 'Makes Caesar more than Caesar to contain'. Ben Jonson revealingly described Edmondes as recreating Caesar.[253] A perusal of the work shows these comments to be more than mere praise. Edmondes draws for his commentary on other authors ancient and modern, on Livy and Guicciardini;[254] more importantly he invests Caesar's age with the cosmology of seventeenth-century England. Edmondes commends Caesar's address to his soldiers who had taken fright at the Germans, and his endeavour 'by the authority of his speech to restore reason to her former dignity, and by discourse . . . to put down a usurping passion, which had so troubled the government of the soul'.[255] In Edmondes's pages, recent historical figures such as the Admiral Coligny inhabit a world alongside Caesar and Tacitus. Similarly in *Augustus* (1632) Peter Heylyn drew on Guicciardini, moved easily to the reign of Richard III and never left behind his experience of the reign of Charles I.[256] These Commentaries and Observations are only one way in which classical conventions were rewritten and re-specified. Jonson's *Epigrams* and country house poems both imitate the ancients and address themselves specifically to the present; what is selected *and not selected* from each, the use of a trope to arouse an expectation which is then not pursued, such devices and strategies give specificity to each act of classical imitation rather than dissolve them into timeless conventions.[257] In early modern England, the familiarity of anyone educated with the classical texts so adapted meant the specificity of such manoeuvres did not pass unnoticed.

This is true not only of the classics. Simon Birkbeck in *The Protestant's Evidence* recruited Geoffrey Chaucer as a Protestant in his effort to prove the historicity of his faith;[258] the 1606 edition of *The Ploughman's Tale* announced that it showed 'by the doctrine and lives of the Romish clergie that the Pope is anti-Christ'.[259] Histories, ancient and modern, were frequently rewritten in the light of circumstances or as polemical gestures. By 1630, Elizabeth I's reign was being rewritten to demonstrate the queen's desire for further religious reform and her allegedly ever-harmonious relations with her parliaments.[260] More generally, as Annabel Patterson has cogently demonstrated, the fable tradition from its beginnings denies the distance between convention and specificity: the question of its author is itself one of historical interpretation; the fables are universal and political; they are both authoritative and open to endless different readings.[261] 'The story of the fable in England in the seventeenth century', Patterson concludes, 'is one that can teach us more than moral commonplaces. It helps to explain how ideology finds expression and how cultural formations appear and disappear in response to historical circumstances'.[262] We may take an illustration of our own from Scot's *Philomythie*, where he relates the tale of the sea horse and the crocodile contending to be kings of the Nile. The crocodile is lulled into a false sense of security by 'antique shews and masking merriments' and is warned:

> Beware of him that does extol you so
> And like a God adores ye as ye go[263]

The story is explicated as a moral about honour and baseness. As well as this moral commonplace, however, the author (Scot) recognizes historical circumstances: 'If any man enquire further after the tale, let him call to mind the late death of that renowned King of France . . .'[264] The invitation to historical readings is opened, seemingly to be closed by one. But 'if any man enquire [yet] further after the tale' . . . one lulled by 'masking merriments' and flatterers in 1616 might well evoke more domestic and topical applications. Political and social circumstances, in other words, gave timeless fables constantly renewed specificity — as indeed they did other conventions and traditions.

This specificity itself has a longer and shorter historicity. In general the intellectual life of early modern London must be seen in relation to recent social developments: the residence in the fashionable West End of nobles and gentry for much of the year; the popularity of a gentry education at universities and the Inns; the emergence of the court as a cultural centre.[265] Professor Malcolm Smuts has made the interesting suggestion that the vogue for love poetry in the 1620s and 1630s reflected the return of powerful ladies to court, with the succession of Henrietta Maria.[266] The interdependency of ideas and circumstances can, also, have a much more detailed history. The publication and editions of texts emerge from present concerns: Professor Salmon observed that the *Vindiciae Contra Tyrannos* was translated into English at a time when England planned to intervene in the Low Countries.[267] Other historians have drawn attention to the vogue for Machiavellian works in 1650–1.[268] We might note the republication of Elizabethan and Jacobean writers about the same time, and the spate of Elizabethan material published around 1617–18, as further instances of circumstance as the motor for publication — a subject greatly in need of further study.[269]

Altered conditions and experiences in our period led to some famous and some less well-known rewritings and reinterpretations, across relatively short periods of time. Sir Edward Coke's view of the common law, we know, was coloured by his career and especially by his dismissal from office as Lord Chief Justice. Hobbes after 1642 abandoned his earlier equivocation to argue for the impossibility of renouncing man's right to self-defence and revised his account of the state of nature accordingly.[270] In the 1625 edition of his *Essays*, Francis Bacon recast his 'of Ambition' to accommodate ambitious natures as he had not before, and in general exhibited less enthusiasm for a civil science that might explain human behaviour by precepts and laws.[271] When, in 1535, Marsilio of Padua's *Defensor Pacis* was translated into English, his translator, William Marshal, omitted the chapter on the correction of secular magistrates as 'nothing appertaining to this realm of England'.[272] More careful analysis of these editions, translations and rewritings could provide valuable insights into important intellectual shifts.

Still more illuminating than such rewritings, however, is reflection about how seemingly unaltered conventions were *re-read* in different circumstances. At times such a study of reception and reader-response may be elusive. There can be little doubt about the suggestion that the ancient tales of murder and intrigue took on renewed vividness in the context of seventeenth-century phobias about Catholic plots, but it is difficult to pin down and document.[273] However, the publication of works around celebrated historical occasions clearly does suggest the likelihood of re-reading and specifying conventions. George More's reiteration of timeless counsel to justice, mercy and liberality in his *Principles for Young Princes* gained at least a renewed immediacy in the year after the creation of the first Prince of Wales since Henry VIII.[274] P. Pelletier's *Lamentable Discourse upon the parricide . . . of Henry the Fourth* gave particular poignancy to the argument for sovereign authority in the year of the French monarch's assassination and that nation's drift into anarchy.[275] Two works (at least) published in 1628 clearly addressed the assassination of the Duke of Buckingham and the issues he had aroused as much as the lives of Aelius Sejanus and Edward II which were their avowed subject.[276] Sejanus (with whom Buckingham had been identified in parliament) was depicted as ensuring Tiberius trusted no one else; Tiberius (with whom Charles I had identified himself) as regarding the attacks on his favourite as directed against him.[277] In *The Deplorable Life of Edward II*,[278] Gaveston is portrayed as corrupting the king by masques, by cutting him off from counsel, and by advising him that his will was above the law.[279] Sometimes an

action other than publication gives the general a specific and
political turn. It would be hard to deny this, for example, in
Henrietta Maria's escorting the visiting Elector Palatine to the
Blackfriars to see a revived Elizabethan play about the sufferings of
Germany under a medieval Spanish tyrant.[280] More generally we
can only imagine *how* a gesture, tone or aside made specific and
topical a history play, a sermon or a lecture.[281]

Fortunately we are in no doubt that audiences and readers were
quick to make such applications, and that writers responded to
their enthusiasm to do so. In Massinger's *Roman Actor*, Paris
protests, with less than conviction, his innocence if some found
themselves specifically touched by what was only generally represented.[282] Thomas Scot's *Philomythie*, an Aesopian collection of
fables (the moral ambivalence of which we have discussed), dis-
claims any particular application beyond the conventional moral:

> If ought beside the moral you invent,
> Call it your owne, by me 'twas never ment.[283]

The disclaimer, however, turns out to be an invitation. As we
begin to read in the fables, the story of the bird of paradise's
divorce from the Phoenix to marry 'An unknowne foule, by
th'ayre begot and bred' appears to have in 1616, the year of the
Overbury scandal, a more particular force than the injunction to
chastity.[284] And as we progress further we discern that the very
structure of the work subverts the disclaimer in order to assist
closer parallels with Jacobean England. After the first part of
Philomythie, we meet a section entitled *Certain Pieces of This Age
Parabolized*; as the generalities of the first part had specific
resonance so here the particulars of Jacobean experience are raised
(if that is the right word) to moral texts. In the *Second Part* the
two come together as ideals, moral tales and Jacobean experience
are synthesized — in order to praise, counsel and criticize the king
and court in the light of the moral qualities they mirror or neglect.
'O Princes', ends the debate between the hart, the horse and the
bull, 'banish faction from the Court'.[285]

Circumstances could lead to the rewritings and rereadings of
conventions to the point where they overturn rather than adjust
the paradigms. One cannot but wonder how conscious John Pym
was in 1640 when he refashioned the traditional identification of
the king as the soul of the commonwealth and physician of the
state to support his claims:

> A parliament is that to the Commonwealth which the soul is to the
> body, which is only able to apprehend and understand the symptoms
> of all such diseases which threaten the body politic. It behoves us
> therefore to keep the faculty of that soul from distempers.[286]

The conceit was entirely traditional; its application radically novel. Some historians of ideas who prefer to find more autonomously intellectual influences behind changes in ideas might reflect that Thomas Hobbes who had evidently become a Cartesian mechanist by 1630, did not develop his mechanist theory of the state until he experienced disruption and Civil War.[287] A political crisis prompted a radical reappraisal, just as earlier, less traumatic, events had led to reinterpretations of existing texts and paradigms.

We have observed that the world-view of early modern Englishmen contained ambivalences and tensions. We have seen that social and political circumstances reinterpreted, some would have said subverted, the authoritative texts of that world picture. As we turn from specific texts to the languages, cultural practices and analogues, through which early modern Englishmen mediated the meaning they identified in their society, we must keep in mind the dialectic of the ideal and actual, the stable and unstable which characterized the intellectual and political realms. Languages themselves operate simultaneously in many different and contrary ways. Speech acts are individual and yet, since the function of language is to communicate, are premised on what is shared; they not only convey ideas; they too evoke other responses — emotions, prejudices, past experiences, fantasies, in all of which, as well as in thought, meanings are constituted.[288] A common language runs throughout the commonweal of discourse, but performs quite differently in its various territories. It is not clear that Pocock's method allows sufficiently for this, especially where his accredited and institutionalized languages are concerned. Legal language, his first study, was undoubtedly an important idiom of political discussion in early modern England, but that shared language had different meanings and evoked different responses in law courts, in the Commons, and in common speech — as today economic terminology functions differently in business and everyday parlance.[289]

The shared language may be in general evidence of common values and ideals, but it is not synonymous with shared experience or meanings. All — James I, Charles I, Pym, those outside the political arena — saw the king's prerogative and the common law as complementary, but experience showed them that they did not mean the same by that. In Hampden's case, for example, Fortescue was invoked by both sides.[290] Revealingly and importantly, however, the realization that a common, shared language could articulate different, even contrary positions did not lead to an abandonment of the legal idiom as a vocabulary for the discussion of political questions, but to a wish to codify the law as a means to resolving political problems.[291] (MPs as late as 1628 believed that once the law was *clear* their apprehensions would be settled;[292] and Charles I acted as though he believed the same thing in taking knighthood fines and ship money to the decision of the courts in the 1630s.)[293] James I, as so often, expressed the belief best. In the context of recent questions about the relationship of royal prerogative, civil and common law, James expressed his wish that the laws were in English, that contrary precedents and statutes be resolved and clarified, ('all contrarieties should be scraped out of our books'), most of all that the law might have 'a settled text'.[294] A settled text might effectively end arbitrariness and dispute. Such a belief was echoed throughout the first four decades of the century — and even beyond in the interregnum interest in law reform.[295] The quest for that text demonstrates that, for all the tensions and disputes of the early Stuart decades, politics was still not conceived as a contested pursuit of power, but as a matrix of duties and rights held harmoniously in balance by law. It also suggests a belief that words might themselves possess an authority which permitted no different interpretation — a belief that may open up an important aspect of the relationship between ideas and politics in early modern England.

The language of the ancient constitution is, of course, an historical as well as legal language. Among the gentry and educated of early modern England it was a common language, although the study of history had, until the 1620s, no formal place in the university curriculum. History was valued among the governing classes because, like the law, it was seen to offer rules for the conduct of affairs and especially statecraft. Historical thought and the languages and values bequeathed by the study of the past in the seventeenth century still await a comprehensive study.[296] What seems worthy of note, however, is that the philological studies of the Elizabethan period were not developed into a sophisticated sense of anachronism; rather in the early Stuart years the favoured histories were essentially didactic treatises peppered with axioms and often populated by figures who seem as shaped by present concerns as by evidence from the past.[297] History was not the study of the past as we would understand it but a glass in which man might observe universal truths: 'there', Bethune put it in *The Counsellor of Estate*, 'is seen the life of the world . . . the divers establishments of estates, the beginning, progress, middest and end, and the causes of the increase and ruin of empires'.[298] Hobbes in his preface to Thucydides' Peloponnesian Wars praised 'the actions of honour and dishonour' which were guides to the 'government of . . . life'.[299] The first history lecturer at Oxford, Degory Wheare, instructed his students to seek out from the particulars of their texts '*universals* . . . by which we may be instructed to live

well and happily'.[300] Gentlemen's commonplace books make it
clear that the reading of historical works led often to collections
of maxims and axioms evidently compiled as guides for the
present.[301] The past and the present were not perceived as
different; as there was theoretically one universal truth that united
the divine system, so there had been one truth through all time. As
the idea of one ordered universe prevented relativism, so it stayed
the development of anachronism — even when the technical skills
for its comprehension, philology and archaeology for example,
were emerging. The past like the present was studied not by the
historical criteria of successful or unsuccessful but according to the
moral absolutes of good and bad. Like the Scriptures, history
offered the way to the good life.

It did not escape contemporaries that from the past men justified
their wrongdoings and rebellions, as evil men claimed the Bible for
their authority. Such only demonstrated, however, that one
needed to learn to read the past and perhaps that, like the laws,
histories needed codification to distil the moral precepts which
they yielded. Though in histories men read of tyrants, as well as
virtuous rulers, coups and rebellions as well as the calm of
Augustan empire, none dissented from the view that history was an
ethical text, moral philosophy taught by examples, nor from the
position that good actions had the warrant of the past. It was the
Civil War that severed the cord between past and present, between
history and morality.[302] The Levellers came to claim rights intrinsic to man whether or not they had existed in the past; Hobbes
claimed that the Civil War had been caused by the reading of
histories.[303] Once again it was a political crisis rather than the
philological method itself that changed thinking about the past. In
the later seventeenth and early eighteenth century, scholars began
to develop the antiquarian scholarship of the Elizabethan age into
what looks more recognizable as a modern historicism. And simultaneously, but gradually, history began to lose its status as the
accredited language of politics. In early Stuart England, history, for
all the different meanings it might permit and conceal, was a
language both normative and shared.

History, in seventeenth-century England, was a branch of literae
humaniores, and the language it bequeathed was part of the discourse of humanism and classicism. To the scholar, it is scarcely an
exaggeration to say that history was classical history; in England in
the early seventeenth century, the antiquarian interest in the
medieval past fell subject to ancient history and histories penned
according to classical models.[304] An absorption in classical antiquity led to an absorption in classical vocabularies and values, the
significance of which we still have not pursued.[305] Thomas

Godwin's *Romanae Historiae Anthologia . . . An English Exposition of the Roman Antiquities* drew very exact parallel between England and Rome, and the ease with which seventeenth-century Englishmen employed classical terms, such as senate, points to a widespread identification.[306] In the ancients, some came to believe, was 'all that was requisit to be known'; classical values therefore might form the source of the good life.[307] In Ben Jonson we discern a clear belief that classical culture might be the powerful instrument of moral reform. Not least because Horace and Virgil located virtue in the rural estate, he revived and adapted their vision in the country house poem *To Penshurst*, as he restaged their world in Roman plays.[308] It was a vision widely shared. In *The School of Policie* published in 1605, H. Crosse discussed virtue in predominantly classical terms.[309] Anthony Stafford's *Guide to Honour* counselled a moderation of the passions and liberality which he called 'humanitas'.[310]

This secular classicism, as we observed, existed in tension with more spiritual priorities and texts; as Professor Kearney put it, there were 'two contrasting ideals of what a humanist education should be, the one drawing its inspiration from the values of the Italian courts, the other from the city states of Strasburg, Geneva, Basle and Zurich'.[311] One was lay, the other clerical. In discussing the common languages of early modern England, however, it is necessary to observe that even these tensions did not de-authorize classical idiom. The strict Calvinists shared an education with their less spiritual peers and the classics were as familiar to them.[312] Sir Simonds D'Ewes recalled immediately on learning of Henri IV's assassination Tacitus's account of the poisoning of Germanicus; Leighton and Prynne, puritans, addressed the House of Commons as 'senators'.[313] Professor Rostvig pointed long ago to similar praise of the classical value of the via contemplativa in the poetry of Catholics such as William Habington, of Anglicans like Drummond and Herrick, and of Milton.[314] Evidently Meric Casaubon and Thomas Wentworth found Marcus Aurelius's Meditations complementary to their Christian beliefs.[315] The classical idiom, in other words, was another shared language of values among the governing classes of England. It was an idiom that reinforced a vision of a moral universe and a harmony secured through moderated passions. Classical culture was a culture of discipline and self-regulation for governors and for subjects. In the 1650s, however, as Zera Fink has shown, the republican apologists found in the classics (especially in Cicero) authority for their radical cause.[316] In doing so they broke the link between the Elizabethan world picture and the ancient world and put an end to the classical idiom as one of shared values. When the Augustans after the years of upheaval

rearticulated classical values they did so, it has been argued, more
consciously and strategically, not naturally — in both its early
modern senses. 'The superb formal imitations of Pope, Swift and
Doctor Johnson', take us far from the classical world of Ben Jonson;
they 'adjust the idiom of familiars who have lost their numinous
ghostliness'.[317]

V Aesthetics and cultural practices

A belief that imitation of the classics might revivify the civilizing,
moral force of the ancient world in early modern England was an
ideology not confined to the literary arts. The adoption (and adaption) of Roman styles in buildings, portraits, dress and manners
expressed similar values and ideals. As Malcolm Smuts recently
brilliantly explicated it, Inigo Jones's philosophy drew on Vitru-
vius's parallel between architecture and the human body.[318] The
right proportion and harmony in stone might by correspondence
promote a more rational ordering of the senses and the appetites in
man; and in the body politic, by correspondence, the architect was
partner to the statesman in moulding the raw materials of nature
into a harmonic order. Inigo Jones thought that Stonehenge had
been erected by the Romans in order to civilize the ancient Britons
and his projected palace at Whitehall was to have served the same
purpose. In default of its being completed the proscenium arches he
designed for the masquing stage at Whitehall, most often in the
Banqueting House which had been built as the first stage of the
larger plan, announce the claim of architecture as a moral force and
agency of government.[319] Jones's claims appear to have baffled or
disturbed Ben Jonson.[320] But they were not, I would suggest,
unusual, except in the complexity of Jones's philosophical explica-
tions. The architectonic analogue came naturally to early modern
England. Wentworth's famous speech about the arch of order seems
to transcend a mere metaphor or simile for government: the authority of the king '*is* the keystone of the arch of order and government', he claimed.[321] In 1641 at his trial, he was to rearticulate the
point. The 'pillars of this monarchy' had been fixed 'that each of
them keeps due measure and proportion with other'.[322] Sir Edward
Coke depicted the common law in the same terms, as 'the main
pillars and supporters of the fabric of the commonwealth'.[323] The
analogue came naturally because the architect (like the poet) is a
maker; like God (and his magistrate, the king) he creates that harmony which distils the order of perfect nature, and which holds the
cosmos and commonweal together. The architect was a statesman
in presenting models of harmony and proportion that might lead

men to balance their own humours and so regulate the realm of
their body, enabling subject and ruler in turn to love each other,
as the father taught and loved his children.

In considering the relationship of aesthetics to politics, it is
important to emphasize that the Elizabethan world picture was just
that: a picture, a representation of the ideology of the cosmos and
commonweal. The word cosmos means both order and beauty.[324]
The beautiful therefore was an ordering, a governing in itself.
Beauty was, one writer put it in *An Apology for Women*, 'a kingdom without a general'.[325] It was 'called of Plato a prerogative of
nature',[326] that is the effective power of a perfect nature holding
all in harmony, or, in Owen Feltham's words, 'Beauty is the wit
of Nature put into the frontispiece'.[327] Physical beauty was
expected in Renaissance thought to express an inner perfection, a
perfect harmony of humours in the microcosm of man or woman,
or indeed beast. A horse was regarded as the noblest of creatures
'for the verdict of reason must pass according to the evidence of
proportion'.[328] Men's characters and qualities were read from
their faces; outward beauty was praised only in so far as it
reflected inner virtue.[329] If external beauty did not correspond to
inner perfection the disjuncture had social and cosmic implications. For as beauty led men to the perfection of nature, artifice
corrupted nature and the commonweal. False representation struck
at an important foundation of the Elizabethan world picture, the
Neo-Platonic philosophy of the relationship of perfect form to
matter. It is such import that lies behind Ben Jonson's denunciation
of fashion (and flattery) as the corruption of men and society.[330]
Owen Feltham addressed the consequences in directly political
language: 'Wickedness in beauty is a traitor of the bedchamber'.[331]
When Laud spoke of the 'beauty of holiness' he voiced the same
belief: that there must be a corresponding harmony, unity and
order in the outward face of religion as there was in God, in his
created world and in the soul wherein the beauty of created man,
his natural power to order himself, resided. The liturgy, like Inigo
Jones's buildings, indeed like St. Paul's Cathedral to the refur-
bishing of which Laud devoted so much energy, might assist in
bringing about an inner spiritual order. Church towers, Gyles
Fleming reminded his congregation, expressed the triumph of the
Christian over the pagan; and the act of ordered worship expressed
a harmony between the worshipper and God.[332]

The corollary to the belief that the beautiful might bring about
order and harmony is the belief that models of order should be
visually represented. In histories and poems, characters of virtue
and vice were verbally presented so that men might hence derive
a moral sense. The visual representation of order had the same

(some argued more) force.[333] 'Julius Caesar', one author claimed, 'but looking upon the image of Alexander the Great was thereby excited to the undertaking and performance of things truly great'.[334] The source of order in the commonweal was the monarch, who was, the phrase is often used, made in God's image. The true king, as the Oxford play *The Royal Slave* reminds us, displayed his virtue, his regality, in his looks.[335] The King's image might therefore lead others to emulate his goodness. God stamped princes with majesty in their countenance, the preacher William Struther observed in *A Looking Glasse for Princes and People*. (The recurrent employment of the metaphor, in mirrors for magistrates, almost certainly relates to the belief that outward appearances revealed inner qualities.)[336] The countenance of the good monarch then could itself order and harmonize the raw materials of nature and society.[337] 'In the light of the King's countenance', Bishop Hall wrote, 'is life';[338] 'Every King . . .' Bishop Henry King concurred, 'is a rich medal cast in Christ's mould'.[339] It is no coincidence that the period of the English Renaissance in which the ordered picture of the cosmos was the predominant ideology was also the age in which monarchs took an interest in their own visual representation: in statues and pictures, on coins, medals and seals. This was neither vanity nor simple propaganda.[340] In an age when the King's touch cured scrofula and his word could be life and death, his image (which authorized coins as currency) conveyed power. Elizabeth I, we know, was converted by portraits into an iconic symbol, at times like the statue of a saint.[341] The queen loses her personality in a larger story of divine import, which both glorifies the queen *and* reminds us of that greater majesty to which she owes obeisance. Few if any portraits of English monarchs in the late sixteenth and seventeenth centuries appear to me as straightforward announcements of a king's power. Scholars have observed that in Van Dyck's portraits of Charles I, the king with the most sophisticated appreciation of the representation of kingship, one discerns rather a 'psychic balance', than swagger.[342] The calm of the king's demeanour, his subduing of a powerful horse, symbolize the passions ordered and thereby represent the king as the best ruler.[343] The monarch is depicted as an image of self-regulation. Interestingly in Massinger's *Emperor of the East*, Pulcheria, Beauty, makes the point explicitly: absolute princes have less free will than vassals.[344] Beauty, balance and order were seen as one in the cosmos, in society, and in the individual. The ideology of the visual and plastic arts still awaits careful explication. But in the canvases of Van Dyck we may see the contained tension between the majestic individual who through his own power might impose order on his environment and the monarch subsumed in a larger picture of order, subject to natural laws.

The history of these ideas cannot be limited to the study of texts, languages and visual artefacts. There is a politics of performances as well as a politics of discourse, and it may be that historians have not only largely ignored the former but erected over-rigid boundaries between the two. Ideology, in any culture, is encoded in symbolic systems, of which language is only one.[345] Like established texts and languages, certain cultural practices become accredited because they mediate shared values from which in turn they derive authority.[346] Such practices reveal the tensions within shared values and customs. As a consequence they offer the historian rich documents of perceptions of power and of the submerged differences beneath common practices. The artificiality of the distinction between discourse and other performances is most obvious in the case of the monarchy itself. Kings addressed their subjects in words — in speeches, proclamations — and through their actions — ceremonies, progresses, processions to chapel — and also through their manners, style, choice of advisers, organization of court and household, eating habits and so on.[347]

James I and Charles I had very different senses of their own performances. James chose to represent himself mostly through his words: few other monarchs published not only their political testament but their *Works* as he did,[348] and contrarily showed so little concern for the consequences of his actions, his conduct. When he spoke of royal action, he soon came back to discourse: 'King's actions . . . are as the actions of those that are set upon the stage . . . and I hope never to speak that in private which I shall not avow in public'; 'One of the maynes for which God hath advanced me upon the lofty stage of the supreme throne is that my words . . . might with greater facility be conceived.'[349] In Jacobean England, the royal actor was an orator. Charles I, by contrast, seldom chose to represent himself through words. His affection, he wrote to Louis XIII, was to be found more in actions than words, 'me montant toute ma vie par mes actionnes'[350] Unlike his father Charles regarded his daily conduct as a representation of his rule, and encouraged others in authority to do so. He was chaste, reserved, grave, moderate in his diet and dress, and ordered his court as a model of decorum, believing that 'every man should be a rule of order and abstinence in his own house'.[351] When — rarely — he spoke at any length, the words were still subordinate to other forms of representation. When he set down his declaration after the dissolution of parliament in 1629, the King explained that he had written 'that we may appear to the world in the truth and sincerity of our *actions*, and not in those colours in which we

know some . . . would represent them to the public view'.[352]
Discourse will not take us far into the nature of Charles I or his
values, and it can never be more than one source for the study of
monarchical ideology.

Historians have of course begun to study rituals of state. The
coronation ceremony, we learn, 'acted out the reciprocal obligations owed the prince by the people, owed the people by the
prince, and owed to God by the prince and people, within the
frame of order and degree'.[353] Changes in the ceremony or in
behaviour at the ceremony could subtly tilt its message. Yet we
need to extend our study to more familiar practices and to the
subtle but revealing shifts in such familiar customs and practices.
The removal of the Garter ceremony from Windsor to London (by
Elizabeth) or back again (by Charles) reflected very different
emphases within the theory of order — perhaps from a civic to a
more theological conception of monarchical ritual and authority.[354] The ending of jousts, the monarch's dancing (or not dancing), dining publicly (or not) all need explicating, as they have not
been, as ideological performances. Performance, action, not mere
'external representation', Juan de Santa Maria wrote in *Christian
Policie*, is the essence of kingship.[355] Every act was then also a
real presentation of the monarchy and the system of order that it
partook of.

Ceremonies, culturally accredited performances, especially by
those in some position of authority, we are used to studying as
symbols and enactments of values. This is not least, perhaps,
because contemporaries often wrote about them and announced
their political import. The allegorical pageants of Elizabeth's reign
were recounted often in early Stuart England;[356] masques were
published as texts (at times with high print-runs), as were some
civic rituals. In 1629, the order of the mayor, aldermen and
sheriffs of London 'for their meetings and wearing of their appar-
rell throughout the whole year' was set down — presumably for
a public wider than their eminences themselves.[357] Ceremonies
were attended by a public which was evidently well schooled in
reading their symbolic codes.[358] Recent work on the politics of
popular ritual and festival has begun to open our understanding of
the broader place of ceremonies throughout the symbolic commonweal.[359] Like royal coronations and progresses, village
customs and rituals — may day festivities, beating the bounds,
rituals of inversion — were both expressions of and reinforcements
of the ideology of wholeness, harmony and order. They represented its ideal form; they acknowledged and contained its
tensions. Popular festival served, Leah Marcus recently put it, 'to
meld individuals into their *natural* surroundings and into a larger

collective entity'.[360] That festivals were ideological and political performances is obvious from the political disputes to which they gave rise: magisterial complaints of disorder and subversion, arguments about the cohesion of the community and the importance of exercises to defence, the sharp divisions over the question of Sunday sports. Professor Underdown has recently, suggestively albeit not persuasively, argued that differing rural pastimes and festivals helped to *explain* political divisions in 1642.[361]

Historians of political ideas need to pay closer attention to the accredited rituals and ceremonies of social communities. And, in this context, religious practices would repay further study too. For again ecclesiastical historians have paid more attention to discourses — to sermons, theological works, polemical tracts and diatribes — than to religious performances, the art of preaching, pastoral care and acts of charity, the act of administering and receiving the sacraments and, importantly, the diversities in all such practices. The Northamptonshire preacher Robert Bolton was strong in his belief that the word read had not the force of the word preached; he prescribed elaborate preparation for the delivery of and listening to sermons, attaching, as did most puritans, importance to the *practice* of a sermon as well as the word.[362] *An Alarm to wake Church Sleepers* literally offers such counsel, urging the congregation actively to participate by uttering short ejaculations during the sermon.[363] Others less precise in their religious inclinations also saw the importance of the performance of preaching. Owen Feltham thought that the stage had lured men away from the pulpit through the power of its performances: 'We complain of drowsiness at a sermon, when a play of doubled length leads us on still with alacrity. But the fault is not all in ourselves. If we saw divinity *acted* the gesture and variety would as much invigilate . . . The stage feeds both the ear and the eye and through this latter sense the soul drinks deeper draughts. Things *acted possess us more* . . .'[364] The word itself had to be performed to have most power. Yet the power of religion did not lie only in the word but in the sign, in the sacraments, in the gestures (kneeling, standing), in the place — cathedral, parish church, private chapel, or house. The sacraments, Christopher Dow defended in 1637 as 'moral instruments to convey those graces unto the receivers which the outward signs visibly represent . . .'[365] To some churchmen they were in other words efficacious in instilling grace. The relative importance of the word and the sacraments was, of course, the subject of theological and indeed political controversy. But this was not a controversy between word and action, discourse and performance. Performance was at the heart of religious beliefs, puritan, Anglican and Catholic, and

at the very centre of the ideology of order. When we consider
religion as performance, it may lead us to see that many, some
seemingly trivial, cultural practices also symbolically revealed and
reaffirmed that ideology.

The symbolic significance of cultural practices in earlier ages has
left its stamp on some familiar idioms. Perhaps no political
metaphor has been more enduring and familiar than that of the
ship of state. In the seventeenth century it came to speakers and
writers naturally as a depiction of order and government. In *A Free
Will Offering*, Samuel Hinde spoke of the church in these terms:
'In the ship of our English church sits the sovereign majesty of our
Lord and King. His nobles, lords, judges, Councillors as representative pieces of his own Majesty sit in the steerage of estate and to
them is committed the helm of government'.[366] The clergy, he
added, were the pilots of that ship. The metaphor was open, of
course, to various interpretations and left room for a radical
deployment.[367] But what, I think, we need to consider here is the
practice that produces the metaphor: the act of sailing, navigating,
provisioning a large ship, of commanding its crew, of steering
through rocks and storm-tossed seas. Did not such an experience
actually replicate the art of ordering the self, the family, the
commonweal in a world beset by tempests internal and external?
In the case of the puritan emigrés, as David Cressy has recently
shown, the experience of crossing the ocean was a spiritual as well
as physical journey.[368] I would suggest that we need to reflect
more generally and imaginatively on the meaning of such experiences, on, in other words, correspondences between such an
action and an ideology in early modern England. Not least, because
contemporaries give us warrant to do so. For example, the
ubiquity of the theatrical metaphor, the frequent depiction of
social and political life as a play, may lead us to understand that
experiencing a play in early Stuart England was itself an extension
of political as well as social life.[369] The popularity of the satirical
Game at Chess might indicate too that it was not only plays and
politics that shared a discourse and meaning; the chess-board
seemed naturally to replicate the political world. Arthur Searle's
manual *The Famous Game of Chess Play* announced the game as
'an exercise . . . fit for princes' and its language is politicized at
every turn.[370] Searle observed the limitations to the king's
freedom of movement for all his importance; the power of a
queen; the capacity of a mere pawn to threaten the king; the
relative strength of dukes (rooks) and knights in comparison to
bishops; most of all the need for co-operation among all the orders
for security and success.[371] Other players clearly left the board
with political reflections to the fore: 'there is much difference

between the king and the pawn', Owen Feltham noted in his popular *Resolves*; 'that once ended they are both stuffed into the bag together . . . and who can say whether was most happy, save only the king had many checks, while the little pawn was free and secure . . .'[372] The force of Middleton's play seems more compelling in this context. No less, a full appreciation of the country house poem requires a similar imaginative grasp of the Stuart perception that gardening, ordering the raw material of nature, was an ideological and political pursuit.[373] We find these connections across a broad range of cultural practices. In *The Art of Archerie*, for instance, Gervase Markham linked the sport to the inculcation of virtue, reminding his readers that Aristotle had defined virtue as the mean and that the archer practised so as not to go 'wide of the mark'[374] (a phrase which has retained its familiarity whilst losing its ideological force).

Perhaps the best illustration of the ideological significance of cultural practices comes from horse-riding — not least because it generated extensive contemporary discussion. In his *Observations, Divine and Morall, for the furthering of knowledge and virtue* (1625), J. Robinson depicted the vicious, brutish (sic) man, 'swayed and led by the affections as a foolish wagoner by his horses'.[375] Owen Feltham echoed the sentiment: 'man's will without discretion . . . is like a blind horse without a bridle'.[376] The taming of the passions was represented as analogous to the art of riding. That this, again, was not mere simile becomes clear when we examine treatises such as Nicholas Morgan's *The Perfection of Horsemanship, drawne from Nature, Arte and Practice* (1609). Since the fall, Morgan begins, the obedience of creatures to man could no longer be assumed; it had to be secured by art. Nature, however, desired restitution to her primary perfection, and all creatures desired a return to their original nature. The art that might restore it was reason — 'all Art worketh by true reason'.[377] Even after the fall, man's reason could be efficacious: 'our natural reason is obscured by the disobedience of our first parents, and yet nature may not be said to be unperfect or faultie, for it hath put into all things possibility and aptness, and also act and perfection.[378] It is significant that Ben Jonson had uttered the same belief.[379] Just as he believed poetry might assist in man's moral regeneration, so Morgan argued that the art of horse-riding might restore the original order of nature and man's nature. Taming a great beast was a taming of nature's wildness and so, like the Caroline masques and paintings in which disordered nature is calmed, represented an act of government. In a marginal comment to his translation of Machiavelli's *Prince*, Dacres, moralizing his text, observed that Plutarch maintained 'a Prince excels in learning to

ride the great horse, rather than in any other exercise: because his
horse being no flatterer, will show him he makes no difference
between him and another man, and unless he keep his feet well
will lay him on the ground'.[380] The prince who learnt to keep his
feet well, by corollary, learnt how to govern. The emperor on
horseback depicts the man fitted to rule because he has tamed his
own nature and learnt to order the wildness of nature herself. His
mastery of the great horse expressed his virtue. And this was true
not only of the prince. Dukes, marquises and knights, Morgan
noted, all took their titles from the names of horsemen.[381] The
aristocracy, the most virtuous men, were the most skilful riders;
when they rode they re-enacted the moral paradigms which under-
pinned hierarchy and government.

Whilst many other such particular practices require consideration in this way, we need re-emphasize generally here that *being*
a nobleman or gentleman was itself a cultural practice of ideological significance. The vogue for courtesy books and manuals for
gentlemen in early modern England reflects not only the fluidity of
social status, the development of the court and the civilization of
society; it speaks to a new awareness of the responsibility of the
gentry and nobility in society. Gentlemen were to serve the state,
not only in the narrow sense of counselling the prince, sitting in
parliament, or attending the Quarter Sessions. The JP's role 'to
mediate, attone and determine all such differences as arise between
party and party' was the gentleman's role.[382] Gentlemen were to
be patterns, Richard Braithwaite instructed them, of temperance
and moderation: 'a true and generous moderation of his affections
. . . hath begot in him an absolute command of himself'.[383] When
a man was ennobled, he had thoughts he never had before. 'A
gentleman *will do* like a gentleman'.[384] To be a gentleman was a
performance; to do like a gentleman was to enact a political ideal.
Like kings, noblemen had the power to mould society. 'Blame
none but yourselves', Nicholas Caussin admonished them, 'if you
create not a world, that you banish not vice from the earth and
make a golden age return again'.[385]

VI Analogues, practices and new sources

Acting and being, everyday behaviour and existence. The historian
of modern political ideas is not used to taking these as his
documents. *Political ideas* are ideas articulated by those involved
in the discourse or performance of politics. We have seen, however, that in a system of correspondences all related to all. Order
was observed and sought in all experienced, believed (and perhaps

imagined), and the constitution of order is of course the matter of politics. As we turn then to treatises on gardening, music, on marriage, the family, on the body, we shall not be surprised to find their language politicized at every turn.[386] And we shall gain a brief glimpse of how the discourse of these analogical practices and experiences offers a rich fund of texts for the history of political ideas.

In the case of works dealing with the natural world, the multivalence of the very word nature in seventeenth-century usage is enough to alert us. The term could describe a state of perfection, an Eden, God's creation, man's innocent condition, that which was normative; or anarchic wilderness, the condition of fallen man. The natural world therefore was a glass in which the tensions between order and disorder, the ideal and the actual, the spiritual and secular were reflected; a glass into which contemporaries looked to see the world. Animals, because they knew no artifice, might teach man lessons from a less corrupted nature. To a conservative Catholic like Matthew Kellison, nature itself demonstrated the argument for hierarchy over Calvin's 'anarchie': all creatures turned to monarchy; 'Nature and natural reason seem to plead for a monarchy'.[387] To other observers, nature presented a more complex text, but one no less readily politically read. The inspiration for such readings came no doubt in part from Virgil's *Eclogues*, but again the adoption and adaption addressed topical concerns.[388] The seventeenth-century writers who shared, for example, his fascination with the kingdom of bees, had their own reasons for taking an interest in the subject. For as the title of Charles Butler's detailed examination brings starkly home, the bees were subject to *The Feminine Monarchy*.[389] That potentially discomforting fact aside (perhaps the recent memory of Elizabeth I made it less disturbing of the traditional politics of gender), the bees seemed to offer a model of nature's virtue: 'In their labour and order at home and abroad they are so admirable that they may be a pattern unto men both of the one and of the other'.[390] The bees had the ideal commonwealth, 'since all that they do is in common without any private respect'.[391] Temperate and averse to idleness, they laboured together for the common good. Bees abhorred polyarchy and anarchy, loving a monarch 'of whom above all things they have a principal care and respect ...'[392] They protected their estate, trained to use of their 'poisoned spear' in defence of their perfect kingdom. They were so naturally inclined to piety that when a woman placed a sacramental wafer in their hive to make them produce honey, they constructed a little chapel around it![393] The keeping of bees therefore was a pastime that was a lesson in statecraft and also one in personal conduct. For

loathing impurity, being chaste and clean, bees were inclined to
sting vicious keepers. If you do not want to be stung, Butler
advised the prospective beekeeper, 'thou must be chaste, cleanly,
sweet, sober and familiar'.[394] What the author himself learnt from
his observation comes as a startling conclusion to his study: a
condemnation of all who withheld tithes from the church and a
diatribe against the 'new fangled Brownist' who separated.[395] The
1619 translator of Virgil's *Eclogues* pursued more secular observations — whilst noting that in the beehive some were designated to
toil 'by a covenant made' amongst themselves.[396] One can only
guess what other meanings those who read such tracts, more
importantly those who kept bees, derived from the observation of
their commonwealth.

The same is even more true of other everyday habits and
pastimes. Not least because few historians have as yet followed
Bouwsma's agenda, we know considerably less than we would like
about the politics of music and other such recreation.[397] The term
recreation itself suggests that quest to reorder fallen nature, which
we have seen to inform poetry and the visual arts. In the case of
music the analogic significance becomes clear as soon as we recall
that the celestial bodies were believed to move to music, according
to musical harmonies of divine composition. Music was a gift of
heaven, Peacham taught the complete gentlemen, bestowed on
men so that they might praise their creator.[398] Hymns were sung,
prayers were chanted or intoned, because music was a means of
coming closer to God — a belief, for all the different forms it took,
that held as good for the puritans as the high church party. The
author of *Mottects or Grave Chamber Music* (1630), dedicating his
work to the new Lord Brooke, reminded his patron that Brooke's
predecessor had loved harmony and music 'the being whereof is
beyond mortalitie and regulates the whole frame of nature in her
being and motions'.[399] Music's haters, Sir John Davies of Hereford
put it, 'have no forme nor soule'.[400] In the individual, the right
music might harmonize the humours and set the soul free, as Campion claimed, from the passions.[401] The musician knew how to
regulate himself. The brother composers Henry and William Lawes
were, the poet Aurelian Townshend praised them, 'lawes of themselves, needing no more direction'.[402] Music that led to self-
government assisted too with the government of others: indeed the
two were one in their dependence upon harmony. The Earl of
Strafford perhaps revealed one of his own recreations as well as
much else when he observed in his defence speech of 1641: 'as on
the lute if anything be too high or too low wound up you have lost
the harmony, so here the excess of a prerogative is oppression, of
a pretended liberty in the subject disorder and anarchy'.[403]

Thomas Ravenscroft in his *Brief Discourse of the True . . . Use of Charact'ring the Degrees . . . in Music* compared what he saw as the disordered state of music with that of a commonweal. Music lamented 'my laws violated, my precepts neglected . . .'.[404] Arts were 'much altered from their Pristine State/Humors and fancies so praedominate'.[405] But, as a prefatory verse put it, in frank acknowledgement of the tensions we earlier identified, such problems were not new:

> Concord and Discord still having been at ods,
> Since the first hour the heathens made them Gods

the flats and sharps contending along with them.[406] Ravenscroft, however, in ordering music into degrees contributed to a larger order:

> But heere is One, whose Dove — like Pen of Peace
> Strives to out flie such strife and make it cease;
> And Discord brings with Concord to agree
> That from their strife he raises Harmonie.[407]

Ravenscroft himself described the power of music in language that evokes the court masques: 'we see the sovereignty of Music in this Affection, by the cure and remedy it affords the dispassionate . . . thereby to assuage the turmoils and quell the tempests that were raised in them'.[408] We would like to know more about the score for masques, how the antimasque cacophony of knackers and bells gave way to harmony,[409] as we would like to know more about the choreographical transformation from antic to measured paces in the dance. For like the playhouse, music and dance in early Stuart England appear to have presented a cosmological, social and personal drama of reason and passion, order and disorder. The injunction that the family be like a well-strung instrument, 'every thing in his place keeping his note and height',[410] leads us on to how contemporaries saw that political play enacted also on the domestic stage.

The description of the king as the father of his people was a familiar idiom of political discourse from Aristotle's *Politics* to the Victorian age.[411] In those centuries when kingship was lordship and the king's household not different in kind from those of his noble retainers, the language was literally as well as metaphorically appropriate. The network of clientage relationships that bound the monarch to his nobility and through them to all his subjects was not unlike an extended kinship network. Monarchical government was personal, to some extent household government until at least the later seventeenth century. There were important changes that become apparent by the end of the sixteenth century: the monarch was perceived as not just an overlord but as the ruler of a nation; and the court developed spectacularly to become a centre of the realm, as well as the household of the king.[412] The system of personal relationships had to accommodate these subtle shifts of perception and a growing political nation. The royal 'family' became the realm — as indeed during the crises of the mid-Tudor years the safety and survival of the realm depended upon the royal family. The power of this political analogue is demonstrated in its persistence through the reigns of a boy, two women and a virgin queen. Indeed Elizabeth I, always so skilled in the personal appropriation of the ideologies that sustained monarchy, took advantage of her childless condition to emphasize her place in the politic family: 'Though after my death', she told her subjects in 1563, 'you may have many stepdames, yet shall you never have a more natural mother than I mean to be unto you all'.[413] The succession to the throne after Elizabeth of two fathers underlined the associations of the king's personal and politic families.[414] James I frequently played on the association in his speeches; Charles I in the paintings of his family. Both penned their political testaments as personal advice to their sons. The force of the representation was acknowledged by the king's enemies in the Civil War: those who drafted the Army Remonstrance of November 1648 pointed out to parliament that for all his (as they saw it) chicanery and evil, the king 'comes in the only true Father of his People, you being proved the cruel foster-fathers'.[415] Milton perhaps recognized the power of the paterfamilias icon as part of the force of the *Eikon Basilike* when he dismissed the politic father as a conceit best left to the Muses.[416] During the early modern period, however, it was not confined to poetic territory, but was an accredited analogue of all political discourse.

Though historians have frequently pointed to the analogue and studied the images of father and family in political speeches and treatises, they have paid little attention to the tracts on the family and household, and the political reflections which they venture or imply.[417] Yet as soon as we examine such works, we immediately discern an address to public as well as domestic issues. Pierre Ayrault's *A Discourse of Parents Honour*, translated into English in 1614, was written by a French civil lawyer in the 1580s, during the wars of religion.[418] The English dedication, to Tobie Matthew, prefaced it as a tract for an age inclined to disobedience. The nature of authority and obedience are its subjects from the opening pages. 'A commonwealth is nothing else but a body incorporate of so many private families and so founded and begun by parents'.[419] Good government in the commonwealth began with good order in the home. The father Ayrault interestingly compares to a rider with his bit, spur and switch; it was for his children, as his horse, to obey his direction.[420] Some, Ayrault notes, had raised the question whether obedience were owed to unjust fathers. 'The determination of such question' he saw as 'exceedingly dangerous' — because of their political repercussions. 'Whether the Bishop of Rome be above or under a General Council, whether the Emperor be above the people . . . whether in religion contrarietie of sects may be tolerated, at first sight [such questions] be set forth with a marvellous fair show, but if you mark them well there is poison served in . . . for upon these and such like other disputes, every day ensue schisms, seditions, civil wars & *this question now in handling* [of obedience to fathers] *is much after the same sort'.*[421] Ayrault concluded that the obligations of parents and children were mutual and that natural bonds could not be broken. 'To take away filial obedience, and duty to parents, is to grab up nature by the root'.[422] He who renounced that obedience 'having begun with his father is like enough to finish it with insurrection against his Prince'; 'farewell all government when parents cannot be obeyed'.[423] In particular, Ayrault denied that differences of religion could break the bonds between father and son. This was not a surprising concern in the France of Henri III, but there was relevance there for England too.

In his *Observations Divine and Morall*, Robinson repeated the denial — in the cases both of families and commonwealths. 'No difference or alteration in Religion how great soever, either dissolves any natural or civil bond of society . . . A king, husband, father . . . though a heathen, idolator, atheist or excommunicate, is as well and as much a king, husband or father . . .'[424] To break the bond with parents was an irreligious act that no sectarian preference could justify. As Ayrault put it, 'do but once prove disobedient to parents, and presently you fall down headlong into atheism . . .'[425] The threat of religious difference to the politic and domestic family is dispelled by a reassertion of the obedience due naturally to fathers.

As well as parent–child relations, the family is the microcosmic stage of that enduring drama: the relations of the sexes. Once we might have read the many assertions of male authority in early modern England as straightforward descriptions of their world. More recent work, however, has pointed to tensions and strains in gender relations which surfaced in a variety of cultural practices and community actions: skimmingtons, shaming rituals, accusations of witchcraft, carnival inversions.[426] In default of any study, one is tempted to wonder what impact the (acknowledged) success of Queen Elizabeth's reign had on the traditional taboo of female government. What we can say is that questions were being aired

and books being published about the position of women in the
family and society and that such discussions have significance for
the historian of political ideas. C. Newstead's *An Apology for
Women* (1620) offers an interesting example, largely because it is
far less apologetic than its title suggests. For Newstead argued the
natural superiority of women. Their beauty itself, he noted, was a
'prerogative of nature' and displayed their virtues.[427] The
temperature of their bodies made them wittier, we might say more
intelligent, than men; they were more prudent in the management
of household matters, and 'our politic prudence sprung first from
oecumenical'.[428] As no element predominated in their bodies so
no passions usurped their souls. In consequence they were more
faithful and chaster than men because less slave to their appetites.
'It is the greatest conquest, when the body is the chariot, that
carries the mind triumphing over its affections'.[429] Women ruled
the family nourishing and educating their offspring. Far from the
male standing independent and commanding, 'there is nothing
more repugnant to man's nature than solitude'; 'a man is never
perfect until he is married'.[430]

Few went so far in their claims for the natural superiority of
women. But even in the more conservative treatises we detect a
debate about gender relations which both drew from and in turn
contributed to political discourse. The author of *Counsel to the
Husband* (1608) declared the broadest political significance in
familial relationships: 'there belongeth more to a family than
governors, servants, household stuff, and provision: there must be
laws and discipline, order and instruction, a watchman and over-
seers'.[431] Families had been subverted by wives disobeying and
husbands ruling badly; disagreement between the husband and
wife resulted in confusion. The *Counsel* therefore endeavoured to
prescribe the model, natural relationship. Here the husband's predominance is taken for granted and he should not 'give over his
sovereignty unto his wife', any more than he would don her
apparel.[432] Her place was to take light from him ('as the moon is
said from the sun') and to labour for his wealth and credit, in
whom her own were subsumed.[433] The woman's subject status,
because natural, was no condition of debasement. 'If . . . in a
kingdom, or family, there must of necessity be those degrees and
that we see men so subject to princes, that they constantly delight
therein, and neither count it slavishness . . . should not the wife
look unto the hand of God, which made her the wife, and not the
husband . . . to govern otherwise, is not to rule but to usurp'.[434]
But while the husband was possessed of natural authority he was
expected 'to command yet with love'.[435] What then when the
reality fell short of this ideal harmony, when the woman withheld

obedience or the man ruled not lovingly but 'tyrannously'?[436] In the year after Bate's case when the question of love and obedience between the king and his people had exercised the judges, the *Counsel* expressed a 'wish that it might never grow to question of law between man and wife whose is the duty . . . but for them to strive who should be most careful of each other's good'.[437] If the conduct of family affairs continued to be mishandled, if prayers were not said, the wife might counsel and ask 'for the reformation of those amiss'. Her only course was to persuade 'by warmth and fair means'.[438] 'As there is no striving with a prince because of his power; so there is (*or should be*) no contending with the husband . . . because of that absolute sovereignty which is in his hand'.[439] The greatest reproach to a wife (as James I might have said to a parliament?) was to be 'Solomon's contentious woman'.[440] The virtuous obedient wife, however, 'is a crown to her husband'. Fulfilling her obligations, she obliged her husband to honour his: to 'not disdain to be counselled by his wife'; to love and understand her, 'so to govern that he give not occasion by foolishness to be despised nor by overmuch severity to be hated or feared'.[441] In its recognition of strains and exhortation to mutual love and duty, *Counsel to the Husband* at every point politicizes the relations between husband and wife. That it also so often seems to echo with the language, issues and tensions of Jacobean politics is not least because marriage and love were, like the role of the father, analogues of political life.

Love we like to think of as the most private and personal of matters — perhaps despite evidence to the contrary in our own age. In the seventeenth century love did not describe only personal but also cosmic, spiritual and political relationships.[442] God's act in creating the world was perceived as an act of love. In his *Heavenly Academie*, Francis Rous wrote that 'love itself is a likeness to him who is love'.[443] God, Robinson put it simply in his *Observations Divine and Morall*, 'is love'.[444] Love bound the whole cosmic chain in a network of relationships within and between the corresponding spheres. Lovers who could not join together were indeed 'star-crossed'. In his philosophical enquiry *De Veritate*, Lord Herbert of Cherbury wrote of love as that which mediated between the world of spirit and the material world.[445] It brought man closer to God; love, his poem 'The idea' shows, might lead to knowledge, liberty, unity and harmony.[446] Recently I have shown how in the Caroline court masques love was the force that led men to virtue, to a perfected nature, to self-government. Herbert's poem, significantly 'Made at Alnwick in his Expedition to Scotland with the Army 1639', was no less political. Love was the unifying element in the cosmos, in families and in

kingdoms. As a consequence of the fall, however, love also had
become corrupted by appetite and required regulation. Christianity
prescribed marriage as the institution through which man's sexual
appetite might, instead of casting him down into the bottomless pit
of sin, procreate virtue and assist in his regeneration.[447] The
marginalia to the Genevan Bible pointed up the Pauline analogy of
the married couple to Christ and the church; the book of Common
Prayer described marriage as a condition of paradise and remedy
against sin.[448] Marriage was a polity; it regulated lust by its laws.
Love and marriage were normative analogues and vocabularies in
early modern England and so came naturally in political discourse
to men for whom the ideal of government was the replication of
God's divine order founded on love. Love expressed harmony and
balance; in loving relationships authority and subjection were as
one, not in contention; love unified the community. In his
Resolves Owen Feltham praised the Church of England because it
'constitutes so firm a love among men'.[449] I. Doughty, a fellow of
Merton College Oxford, exhorted controversialists in the church in
1628 to 'love and unamity', as the notes of Christians.[450] In a
Christian commonwealth, the relation between the monarch and
his people had to be founded on love. James I in a speech of 1624,
in this as in other respects, saw it as his duty to model himself on
God:

> it is a very fit similitude for a king and his people to be like a husband
> and wife, for even as Christ, in whose throne I sit . . . is husband to the
> Church and the Church is his spouse, so I likewise desire to be your
> husband and ye should be my spouse; and therefore, as it is the
> husband's part to cherish his wife, to entreat her kindly, and reconcile
> himself towards her, and procure her love by all means, so it is my part
> to do the like to my people . . .'[451]

The king so wed to his people also believed that 'there was such
a marriage and union between the prerogative and the law as they
cannot possibly be severed'.[452] It is important to appreciate that
the political tensions and quarrels of the early Stuart decades did
not invalidate this discourse. Sir Thomas Wentworth and John Pym
once again spoke a shared language, referring to the 'mutual intelligence of love' between king and people and the 'lust' that
depraved the realm if the bonds of law were not upheld.[453]
Illustrations of this discourse could be multiplied. It is more important to flip the coin and see that as politicians naturally employed
the vocabulary of love and marriage, so the representations of love
and marriage offer documents of political ideas. Recently I attempted to explicate the politics of love from the poetry and drama of
three Caroline writers. The subject needs broader exploration: not

only in Elizabethan and Jacobean plays and poems, but in paintings, sonnets, courtly airs, dance, the etiquette of courtship,
wedding ceremonies, divorce cases and so on. Jacobean drama, we
know, illustrates political tensions and ideals in plays about love
and marriage. In the Lord Mayor's show in London, the mayor was
portrayed as the bridegroom of the city.[454] At the level of court,
civic and county elites as well as the village community a *political*
history of love and marriage would offer invaluable insight into the
history of political thought.[455]

The public condition, the politics of the family, of marriage and
of love leads us to what we might think of as the last sanctuary of
private space: the self, the body. The phrase 'body politic',
however, though now emasculated of its analogic force, remains to
inform us of an age when the body was not only politicized, but
stood as the most familiar of all analogues for the commonweal.
The analogue, like that of the family, goes back to pagan, classical
times, and to the time of the apostles.[456] But it is in the
Renaissance period that the natural, not merely the rhetorical or
idealized body, was explicitly analogized to the state, and in that
age that the analogy was developed and worked out in detail. As
has been well argued, Menenius's comparison of the state and body
in *Coriolanus* 'is more than a device of rhetoric; it is a statement
of truth . . .'[457] This analogue of the natural body may tell us
much about changing attitudes towards the self and the community: the image realized the multiple forces in man and contained
the disparateness of society. It also brought the individual and the
polity together. The image was a means of overcoming a metaphysical problem of distance between subject and object.[458] The
many treatises entitled 'An Anatomy of . . .' indicate the desire to
relate and reduce the universe to human experience. In the
political realm the image (like the whole world-view) not only
unified a fragile state; it elevated and incorporated the person of
the king into that larger body of the commonweal at a time when
the monarch as personal overlord was becoming a monarch as
ruler of the nation.

The general use of the image in political discourse in Renaissance
England, because it is familiar, need not detain us long.[459] John
Pym in 1640 took it for a truism that 'A king and his people make
one body: the inferior parts confer nourishment and strength, the
superior sense and motion'.[460] Significantly the most detailed
working out of the analogy is found in one of the few self-
pronouncedly political treatises of the early Stuart years. In his
Comparative Discourse of the Bodies Natural and Politique,
Edward Forset anatomized the king's councillors as the understanding; his favourites as the fantasies; disordered manners as

diseases; 'nimble headed pragmatics' as amateur doctors.[461] What it is more important to observe — and a subject still not investigated — is how the image of the body was subject to varying interpretations and adapted according to circumstances.[462] The emphasis on the king as the head and the people as the body was traditional and conservative. But as James Daly pointed out, it left the political counterpart of the soul in a 'dangerously ambiguous position'.[463] Archbishop Laud in a 1628 sermon spoke of the church as the soul which unified the bodies politic and natural and so potentially forged a division between the ecclesiastical and secular power which, had its implications been pursued, would have damaged the Elizabethan world picture.[464] Pym, as we have seen, more radically claimed that parliament was the soul of the commonwealth.[465]

The metaphor of the king as the head was by no means a justification of absolute authority. The king could no more change the laws of the body politic, George More pointed out in his *Principles for Young Princes*, than the head could alter the sinews on which it depended.[466] In order to rule the body too, the head itself needed to be free of corruption. Again Pym was to claim that it was for parliaments to ensure that 'the intellectual part . . . be kept from distemper', and he was not the first to draw such conclusions from the metaphor of head and body.[467] Buchanan had described the laws as a check on the passions of the king, reminding us that in the head itself reason and appetite contended for government.[468] Ponet and Parsons even foresaw that 'decapitation is a reasonable remedy for a diseased body politic'.[469] Few drew such conclusions in early seventeenth-century England, but the emphasis on the natural body of which the politic was seen to be the analogue, drew attention to the frailties as well as authority of the head/king. 'To prescribe a man', Nicholas Coeffeteau wrote, 'that is not moved with any passion were to deprive him of all humanity'.[470] The king was human and *ergo* subject to the passions of humanity, for all that as the head he represented the source of reason. Monarchs then needed to order their affections and appetites. More's *Principles for Young Princes* shows concern for the actual body of the ruler in injunctions to the prince to moderate his diet because 'the body being full of meat corrupteth the judgement as maketh a man neither fit to . . . govern in a commonwealth . . .'[471] The prince should learn to know himself 'and his imperfections'.[472] More did not explore the consequences if the ruler failed in either that self-knowledge or self-government which qualified him to rule. But the acknowledged 'passions', 'imperfections' and possible distempers in the person of the king sit uncomfortably with the dictum that the king could do no wrong and open the way for others to question the unreasonableness of royal command. Such tensions are a common subject of Elizabethan and early Stuart plays — *The Winter's Tale* and *Lear* are two obvious examples — in which royal passions rob monarchs of the basis of their authority while leaving them the externals of power.[473] Such plays still await the full political readings that they invite.

More generally, however, we need to see the political import of any discussions of the relation of passion and appetite to reason, and so the politics of attitudes to learning, madness, emotion and zeal.[474] Contemporary writers readily politicized their mental conditions. Owen Feltham described his own 'passions and affections' as 'the chief disturbers of my civil state: what peace can I expect within me while these rebels rest unovercome?'[475] Bishop Joseph Hall frankly applied the rules of civil policy to the mind because, he believed:

> Every man hath a kingdom within himself. Reason, as the princess dwells in the highest and inwardest room; the senses are the Guards and attendants on the court . . . The supreme faculties (as will, memory etc.) are the Peers; the outward parts, and inward affections, are the Commons. Violent passions are as rebels . . .[476]

The royal condition was also human; the human psychology also political. Once we see this, we may come to see the political significance of changing attitudes to human psychology. In the *Table of Human Passions*, translated into English in 1621, Nicholas Coeffeteau attempted an analysis of human psychology. Man he saw as motivated by pleasure and pain. Passions he defined as 'a motion of the sensitive appetite caused by the apprehension of good or evil, the which is followed with a change or alteration in the body . . .'. This he regarded as 'contrary to the laws of nature'.[477] Writing two decades later, however, when the laws of nature were less easily equatable with order and reason, Thomas Hobbes was to turn the theory of motion not only into a new mechanistic psychology but into a radically novel political philosophy.

VII Ideas, politics and the English Civil War

We have viewed the world picture of early modern England as one might study a court masque. We have examined the philosophy that informed it, the ideals it expressed, the perfect harmony and government it represented. We have, too, detected the antimasque figures and tempests that threatened its ideal images: Machiavels and sectaries, foreign furies and disordered passions at home. At times, it seemed, the tensions might not be contained. But they were. They were fused into and artistically subsumed by the final scenes of calm landscapes, civilised cities, measured dances and royal power in which the cosmic order was framed and represented at Whitehall.

Whitehall, I think, may be the key to intellectual as to political history. Historians rightly viewing the English Civil War as an intellectual revolution have — perhaps naturally — searched for its intellectual origins.[478] The search never produced results that quite convinced. They detect those of radical political views like Buchanan or even Fulke Greville; they find ardent Calvinists and presbyterians like Cartwright, providentialists like Raleigh. They point to the emergence of a common law tradition led by Sir Edward Coke, to the novel epistemology heralded by the new science of Francis Bacon. But they never satisfactorily explain how these men and movements for long accommodated — in many cases within the court itself — came in 1642 to turn the world upside down. For all the puritan unease, Sir Edward Coke's quarrel with James I, or Baconian empiricism, the languages and analogues of political debate remained the same: the languages of Scripture, of the law, of history and the classics; a discourse of politics in terms (often derived from Aristotle) of the family, of love and marriage, of the body. What we find from hindsight see as revolutionary intellectual discoveries did not produce a revolution. Thomas Hobbes evidently became acquainted with the new mechanism in Paris as early as 1630. There is no evidence that it then led him to a new politics.[479]

There is little sign then that in the early seventeenth century new theories or ideas affected the course of politics. The course of politics, however, subjected prevailing ideals and axioms to the greatest strain. Bate's case and the debates over impositions raised uncomfortable doubts about the harmonious relationship between monarchical authority and the law.[480] The demands of war in the 1620s, the courses pursued by king and Council in order to raise, equip, feed and transport troops, revealed and fostered tensions between, on the one hand, individuals and their private property and, on the other, the state and commonweal. The debates in parliament leading to the Petition of Right began to make it clear that the shared language of law and common good could express different meanings and perceptions in practice.[481] And, like the debates over religion, they also demonstrated that there were very different views on how to right what was amiss. A shared sense of what ought to be did not prevent conflict about how to restore an earlier (idealized) harmony and unity. The articulation of such differences, certainly of different emphases, undoubtedly damaged the model of order. What weakened it most was the erosion of the cement that held the world-view together: trust. By 1629 there were some, by 1640 many, who were no longer sure that Charles I could be trusted to rule for the common good. Moreover, events suggested that the traditional antidotes to such a distemper were no longer effective. The decisions in the Five Knights Case and the Ship Money Case led many to fear that the law was no longer a safeguard of balance and harmony. Charles's choice of advisers, personal prominence in government, and wilful rule left — as some saw it — the cry for good counsel unanswered. Doubtless in some gentry houses and vestries the question was pondered: what could be done when the king did not do as he ought?

Yet when all this is said, what remains noteworthy is that such realizations and disputes did not before 1642 rewrite the *language* of politics. The debates on the Petition of Right still confirm that heated words, different emphases and attitudes, did not develop into a contest of rival ideologies, of two opposed theories of the commonweal.[482] Speakers still talked of differences between the king and Commons as a marital tiff which could be made up through love, a temporary imbalance which the reason of the law (shared by all) would resettle.[483] They held on to the ideal of one truth, one commonweal; there could be no alternative ideology because there was no moral order, no political life outside it. The solutions to the problems remained traditional. Those who disagreed with the king sought not to remove him but to persuade him, because they could think of no government that was not his. The language and the ideals it expressed survived the confrontations of the 1620s. Even after the personal rule of the 1630s, there were no proponents in 1640 of an alternative parliamentary government. There were those who in practice were prepared to try to compel the king to heed good counsel, but it was good monarchical government, not any opposed model, that they sought. Their values and discourse were traditional. For all the gulf that separated them, it is, as we have seen, remarkable how close is the *language* spoken by Pym and Strafford at the latter's trial for treason in the winter of 1640. There was little sign even in a political crisis of Englishmen drawing on the radical pamphlets of the wars of religion.

Events, however, had brought those foreign experiences much closer to home. For in 1637 a British kingdom had rebelled against the divine order of monarchy. Still more the Scots had justified rising in defence of their religion and liberties and against the institution of episcopacy. Though protesting their loyalty to the king, they drew on Buchanan to justify, in the words of one

newswriter, 'what tenets they hold and what invasion they would
make upon the civil and temporal parts of the king's office'.[484]
This is not the place to consider in detail the difficult question of
the impact of the Scots' rising on English attitudes.[485] On the one
hand, Charles I and several of his courtiers described, at least
initially, the Scots trouble in conventional language: of 'factious
spirits', of 'disease', of 'a burning fever', in Wentworth's words, 'a
war of liberty for their own unbridled inordinate lusts and ambitions'.[486] Others, however, saw a greater ideological challenge in
the Scottish rebellion. The French ambassador viewed the pamphlets distributed in England as 'fort dangereux pour cette Monarchie'.[487] 'I should believe', an English newsletter concurred, 'the
question . . . a king or no king . . .'[488] The Scottish rebellion, in
other words, had shaken the very trunk of the tree of order and
some had begun to wonder whether it would stand. A letter
allegedly written from the camp at Berwick in the spring of 1639
reported: 'the contempt of religion brings discord and confusion,
treadeth virtue under foot, giveth Authority unto vice, and soweth
quarrels and dissentions amongst men . . . and *in the end open and
civil wars*'.[489] The language of the opening phrases is conventional, but the recognition, the fear in the last words, takes us into
a new world: a world in which the axe would be laid to the root
of the tree.

Drawing upon the radical Calvinist pamphlets of the sixteenth
century in order to justify their actions, the Scots were perhaps as
important to the intellectual as to the political upheavals of the
1640s. Yet in 1642, in England, King and Parliament drifted into
civil war, confused at events, not controlling them by the blueprint
of an ideological agenda. Each side claimed the authority of the
Scriptures and the law; each claimed to defend the unity and
harmony of the Christian commonweal against heretics, schismatics and factions. They did not go to war because they articulated fundamentally opposed political ideologies. They went to
war because they could not trust each other to maintain what they
still believed to be common values and ideals. On both sides the
Civil War was waged between men who believed passionately that
their enemies sought to undermine order and truth, and the law
and church that sustained them. Both sides waged a war for
defence of the commonweal against schismatics. One might say
they fought because they could not accommodate difference to
their world-view.[490] The shared languages and absolutes they
continued to express had for long held their world together; now
they obstructed a political settlement that might have saved it. For
a settlement in 1642 would have required the *recognition* of
difference and contest and a politics that could incorporate them.

And, in the words of Brian Tierney, 'none of the conceptual apparatus available — neither the language of mixed constitution, nor of corporation law (nor indeed of classical republicanism) provided a solution for the problem of conflict . . .'[491] Events outran ideas; new political crises could not be contained within the frame of order, but the old picture was still the only pattern men could make of the world. Even after the fact of war, they tried for some time to restore it, to touch it up here and there, but leave it intact.

The Civil War, however, fractured the Elizabethan world picture — and irreparably. In itself the war, especially when it proved to be more than a temporary outburst of passion, shattered the ideas of wholeness and harmony. The commonweal as one community was no more.[492] The Commonwealth that emerged in the 1640s bore no relation to the old ideal — beyond perhaps the desire to appropriate a value-laden term. It was a body now without a head, the government too of a (minority) party. After the Restoration, the term 'Commonwealthsman' described a hardline republican whig, and was often employed as a term of abuse.[493] The very word that had summed up a whole world and shared ideology had become the label of a faction and of, by 1660, discredited tenets.

With the demise of the commonweal, a world of interlocking values fell too. As armies marched through the countryside, billeted on homes, evicted MPs from the Commons and seized, then executed, the king, it was impossible to sustain an ideal of harmony and increasingly hard to think of government and obedience as reciprocally founded on duty and obligation. Naked power backed by the force of arms became visibly divorced from authority, from its divine, metaphysical and moral base. Men began to speak less of duties than of rights, less of the common good than the preservation and advancement of their own interest.[494] Laws were seen now to be at the mercy of the sword. Writers like Henry Parker saw the inadequacy of the common law language and traditions to deal with these circumstances. Hobbes claimed that the political situation led him to abandon other projects to write *De Cive*. When he sat down later to write *Leviathan*, Hobbes had to confront what was now a clear and novel problem: the need to reconcile power and interest, the need to find a means of overriding the conflicting interests of citizens who might not believe in God or any natural order or authority.[495]

Hobbes's state was a *Leviathan*, a monster, an 'artificial' creature. The Civil War robbed the state of its foundation in nature. As the chain that linked the heavens, the commonweal and the natural world was broken, the state, civil society, had to be justified; it could no longer be assumed. Hence arose the fundamental

questions concerning why men should subject themselves to
government, what rights they had and could or should surrender,
what limits there were to authority. Because he was forced to
answer questions that would have been, quite literally, unnatural to
his predecessors, Hobbes wrote the first work of political philosophy in England;[496] thereafter it was difficult to write about
political life in any other way. With the state now detached from its
natural original, politics had to find its own moral codes — or
accept that it had none.

The conflict not only shattered the unity of the commonweal, it
cast its shared languages into the arena of contest. The Bible, the
language of the Scriptures, was anarchically appropriated by every
sect or individual who claimed divine inspiration. The readers made
their own texts of Scripture now to overturn the authority it had
once supported — and not only the authority of the government and
church. Women priests, advocates of free love, fanatics, Quakers
and fifth monarchists overturned the order of gender, morality,
temporality and rationality as they had been known.[497] As for the
texts and languages of histories and the classics, the religious radicals
rejected them for revelation; the Levellers claimed history itself had
been a yoke, making bondsmen of men who had rights not by precedent but naturally by being men.[498] Intellectual radicals dethroned
Aristotle and planned new curricula for universities and colleges.[499]
The authorizing texts and languages of early modern England were
appropriated, deconstructed or simply destroyed.

With the destruction of the idea of cosmic order and the
languages through which it had been articulated, the whole nature
of discourse was revolutionized. The metaphysical conceit which
spoke across the correspondences gave way to the plain prose that
spoke to only one discursive territory.[500] The need to address a
broader audience in the 1640s and 1650s, the people, led the most
poetic of imaginations to prose, and the more prosaic to plain
simplicity. The visual symbols of a world view — in churches,
paintings, statues, masques — fell prey to iconoclastic fury.[501] The
king's art collection was dispersed, and the Commonwealth and
Protectorate regimes displayed some discomfort with any visual
mode of representation.[502]

The final destruction of the world view took place, of course, in
1649, on the scaffold at Whitehall. On 30 January 1649, it was not
only Charles Stuart who met his end: the father of the politic
family was executed; the keystone of the arch collapsed; the head
of the body was decapitated; the light of the Sun of the
commonweal was extinguished. At the sight of the severed head,
the watching crowd was said to have uttered a deep groan. Pregnant women, on hearing the news, miscarried.[503] Analogically

this was the end of the family, of civil society, of nature, of the cosmos itself. And yet, for all the confusion, for all the world turned upside down, the heavens did not fall, the beasts did not overcome man. By the 1650s there was even some order in the realm. England was governed without a king — and even humiliated her ancient rivals the Dutch. The pieces remained and even co-existed, even when everything which (as it had been believed) held them together had collapsed. If 1642 showed their coherence was not certain or natural, the 1650s suggested, radically, that it was not necessary.

After 1660, most of the old political and social order was brought back. At first sight we might be tempted to think that the old intellectual order came with it, that the old world picture was dusted off and restored. Some believed that, or at least acted as if, it was. Charles II referred to his crown as 'that right which *God* and *Nature* hath made our *due*' (my italics);[504] Clarendon referred to the restored House of Lords as the 'Great Council' of the realm.[505] The languages of law, custom, history and Scripture became again Pocock's accredited and institutionalized vocabularies. Yet though the idiom persisted, the contest for and partisan deployment of these normative languages had made inroads in to the community of belief from which they had drawn their authority. The changes were profound. Even in the Declaration of Breda, Charles II himself had offered religious toleration to presbyterians. There was to be no one religious truth. Those who denied them toleration did so not in the name of unity, but from the interests of a section — what would soon be called a party.[506] The Declaration even offered a pardon to rebels — as though their treason against a king could be separated from their sin which only God could forgive. The office of monarch was restored by a political (and military) act; the monarch was granted an annual revenue for peacetime government; by the 1670s some spoke of transferring the office to another not the successor to the throne; in 1688 they did so. The Army's 1648 claim that authority resided in the office 'and but ministerially in the person'[507] was aired in the rhetoric of Exclusion, and again in 1688. The pursuit of interest overshadowed the old bonds of obligation and loyalty; even the king and the court felt the need to build an interest through a direct exchange of pension and place for service and co-operation in the Commons. Though it was to be some time before the language of contract widely permeated the discourse of politics, relations had indeed become contractual (the abolition of feudal tenures is significant)[508] — even between ruler and ruled. Society and government recoalesced not around the normative foundations of an organic community and divine order, but around the coincident interests of individuals who elected to enter into relationships with each other, but who yet retained an identity outside of the community. John Locke offers us the best verbal exposition of these changes which had taken place, but they are evident too in a myriad of cultural practices and mores: the emergence of politics as a self-conscious pursuit, the rise of party, the separation of morality from sin, the developed idea of privacy, perhaps the acknowledgement, with all its profound consequences, of the autonomous self.[509]

These profound changes were not sudden, or obvious. The survival of old vocabularies makes them difficult to date.[510] Men were still loathe to credit parties with more dignity than the name of factions; the old terminology of 'court' and 'country' co-existed with the new party labels.[511] But at times now one senses an archaism, a strategic conservatism in their usage and deployment. The old languages and texts were no longer universally normative but appropriated to serve a particular cause. By the end of the century, Charles Schmitt observed, reference to the authority of Aristotle was *reactionary*: 'scholastic philosophy had an ideological rather than an intellectual role to play'.[512] Scriptural politics having been shown to open the door to all confusion, the language of the Bible less often informed political discourse. The classics lost their force as the texts of moral philosophy to be consciously imitated by the 'Augustans' who aped the style of a civilization which they saw to be quite different from their own.[513] Slowly the study of history induced a sense of anachronism and relativism, little developed in England since its faint beginnings in the philological enquiries of the Elizabethan antiquaries.[514] Along with the ideology of order, its authoritative texts and languages, the analogues and correspondences fade too.[515] There are fewer references to the king as father of his people; and in society the family becomes more private.[516] The world of nature was no longer an analogue for virtue and government: Bernard de Mandeville's *Fable of the Bees* posited a society built on natural vice, prosperity and self-interest.[517] As for the body politic, the phrase lived on as a metaphor shorn of its literalism as ideas of interest and contract invalidated it.[518] With the collapse of such analogues and correspondences, literary styles and reputations were overturned. Pope and the Augustans appear not to have greatly valued metaphysical poetry, perhaps because the metaphysical conceit, the encapsulating of a world, a cosmos, in a microcosm, had passed;[519] some have even suggested that what we delineate as reason and feeling had become separated.[520] In its place there was a new literary genre which arose from the gradual acknowledgement of the autonomous self, as well as from a world in which the aesthetic had found its own space — the novel.[521]

One cannot place a year-date on ideological and cultural changes such as these. It 'took a long time for the interconnections and cross-references to disappear from the corpus of human learning'.[522] But if we accept that, for all that, we are by the end of the seventeenth century in a new intellectual world, the best date to pick in order to understand that profound shift is 1649. And 1649 must lead us to conclude that whilst the new political history will be the poorer if ideas are left out, the intellectual history of early modern England must — still more than it has been — be also a political history.

II Studies

2. Crown, parliament and locality: government and communication in Early Stuart England*

The history of England in the early seventeenth century is being rewritten. On both sides of the Atlantic since the mid 1970s, historians working, at least initially, independently, have questioned important aspects of the traditional view of early Stuart politics and the origins of the English Civil War. These historians — their critics have labelled them 'revisionists' — no longer accept that the period 1603 to 1641 saw an inevitable constitutional conflict centred upon rival claims to power between an absolutist monarchy and a developing House of Commons. It has been demonstrated that the House of Commons in early Stuart England never successfully used, and seldom attempted to use, the 'weapon' of withholding supply in order to secure the redress of grievances; indeed that leading MPs such as Sir Dudley Digges, Sir John Eliot and John Pym appreciated that an adequate and independent source of royal revenue was necessary for monarchical government. Secondly, it has been shown that rather than 'winning the initiative' in legislation, the record of parliaments in passing statutes was poor. After the long sessions of 1621, for example, only one bill — and that the subsidy bill — became law. Third, and most important, these historians have argued powerfully that the court and the House of Commons were not united blocs, belligerently eyeing each other across the terrain of issues that divided them. Rather, they suggest, both court and House of Commons were divided within themselves. Moreover, allegiances and connections ran vertically as well as horizontally: factions at court had clients in the Commons, and members of the Commons looked to patrons in the Lords and at court.

These are, and were intended to be, essentially critical contributions. They have made it hard to live with the old portrait of early Stuart politics, but offer no new picture in its place. The 'revisionist' historians have not attempted, nor are they likely to agree upon, one new synthesis; they are united mainly by a recognition of the need to question assumptions and return to the evidence. But we have seen some preliminary suggestions and sketches. The revisionists have illuminated factional struggles and, at times, the failure of the court to contain them; tensions in the relations between centre and locality and the effects of those tensions on parliaments; and, perhaps most cogently presented, the strains on the structure of government caused by the demands of war from 1625.[1] To the revisionists' criticisms and suggestions some have already reacted with concern, and even dismay. Some such reactions have exhibited more emotion than evidence or substantial argument, and a greater tendency to misread than to consider carefully the revisionist contribution.[2] But Professor Hirst has rightly re-emphasized that there were issues of importance in early Stuart politics, that men clearly attached importance to parliaments and they they spoke at times the language of law and liberty, of property and principle.[3] Such issues, however, are normal to all political life, and in the early seventeenth century the disagreements and discussions to which they gave rise were articulated within the royal family, the court and the Council, as well as in parliament and the localities. They do not in themselves explain the outbreak of violent conflict in 1642, nor the choice of sides. Issues and disagreements are a chapter in the story of the erosion of trust, but the full story has yet to be written.[4] It is perhaps what the revisionists have not yet addressed themselves to that is of greater concern than reservations about what they have. For despite the disclaimers the revisionists have still concentrated too much on parliaments, and especially the House of Commons, too little on the king, the court and the Council. Historians recently have paid too little attention to questions (for questions they remain) of social change, the inflation of honours, the influence of the press, or the role of the populace. And English historians too have been slow to consider the implications for the early Stuart period of the recent studies of European history — studies of the intendants and gouverneurs of seventeenth-century France, for example, or of the Thirty Years War.[5] In other words, we still await a study of parliaments in a broader political perspective.

Recently, historians of Tudor England have turned from the study of institutions to investigate the network of informal relationships and patterns of clientage which dictated the course of politics. Penry Williams has argued that the principal art of government in sixteenth-century England was that of 'winning compliance' — through patronage and the delicate cultivation of personal connections.[6] And Professor Elton, departing from his earlier emphasis upon the machinery of government, has directed our attention to the 'points of contact' which, perhaps in any age before advanced communications and a professional civil service, were the essence of government.[7]. It is, I believe, only by placing the recent specialized contributions in this broader framework that a more satisfactory picture of the early seventeenth century may emerge. In this essay, I shall attempt to draft a sketch of this wide landscape. My concern will be neither with the issues of early Stuart politics nor with the institutions of government as such, but with the processes of communication which, of course, were important to them both. Most of what will be touched on requires extensive further study, and doubtless many of my suggestions will be shown to be oversimplified. But if it is agreed that all the subjects sketched belong on the same canvas, we have at least the prospect, albeit after years in various studios, of a complete new picture rather than a fragmented series of miniatures.

Concerning the focus of all government in early modern England there was apparently no theoretical contention. Professors Judson and Kenyon some years ago and Weston and Greenberg more recently showed that the early Stuart kings and their subjects differed little in their ideas about monarchy. Most Members of Parliament endorsed James I's view that government was the king's business and that he ruled by divine right. Similarly, James I and Charles I believed in their obligation to rule in accordance with the law.[8] Now those who speak the same language do not always concur in their meaning or interpretation: the debates over impositions in 1610 and over the Petition of Right in 1628, Bate's case and Hampden's case are evidence of that. But it is important to emphasize that what those debates and cases reveal too is a shared belief in the harmony between law and prerogative, an agreement that laws could not cover all circumstances and that some discretionary power was essential to government. As the business of government expanded and the realm became threatened by foreign invasion, the scope of that discretion had necessarily become broader. By the end of the sixteenth century, there was a greater stress upon the responsibilities and prerogatives of the monarch than on the mixed polity of Sir John Fortescue's analysis.[9] Such developments had not been at the expense of the law nor of parliaments. By the sixteenth century, parliament was undoubtedly regarded as the supreme legislator. But Members of Parliament did not regard the business of government other than legislation as their concern. They showed no desire to participate in government, nor to tell the king how to govern. They only expected that the monarch should govern responsibly, with justice and for the good of his subject — in the manner, as Aristotle put it, that defined a monarchy as opposed to its corruption, tyranny. The king, of course, could not govern alone. Monarchical government, it was perceived, required good advisers who could inform the king and honest and efficient officers who would execute his decisions. It was the responsibility of councillors and royal officers to ensure that the king's will, always well-intentioned, was framed from the fullest knowledge and carried out honestly and impartially. In other words, communication to the king and from the king was the binding thread of government.

Here the court played a central role. For it was the junction of those communications, the nerve centre of politics. The court was a stage for the display of virtues and talents where the king might select able men for title and office. And through the court, the leading men of the realm, those powerful in their localities, could have access to the monarch — to proffer advice, press a suit, or prosecute a grievance. Access to and influence at court was the first goal of all political ambition. In making their most important political calculations, the aspirants of early Stuart England placed great emphasis on what might seem to us trivial incidents at court. 'Lake's restoration is talked of', Thomas Locke informed Sir Dudley Carleton in 1621, 'for he has his train borne after him in court, like a Privy Councillor . . .'.[10] When the Duke of Buckingham lay ill in 1623, while James I went hunting, the newswriters forecast the downfall of the favourite.[11] It was an understandable (if in this case inaccurate) reaction. The personal whims of the king could make or break a minister or a faction, and the position of a favourite was always fragile. Close proximity to the king then was the most desirable position for both office-holders and place-seekers. Thanks to the work of David Starkey, we have begun to see that we should not focus our attention on the great office-holders of early modern England — the Treasurer, the Lord Keeper, or the Secretaries of State — to the neglect of those who held places of ceremony or household offices which, though of little administrative importance, brought their incumbents into regular and close contact with the monarch.[12] It is obviously of significance that Queen Elizabeth's two favourites, the earls of Leicester and Essex, both held the position of Master of the Horse, a place that ensured their close attendance upon a 'saddle queen'. The politics of the Stuart bedchamber and privy chamber still awaits a full study,[13] but for the Jacobean period it is clear that access could determine fortunes and factions. Robert Carr, future Earl of Somerset, began his career as a page in the bedchamber and rose to hold the major office in the royal household, that of Lord Chamberlain. George Villiers, whom James met out hunting, rose from the positions of page, cupbearer and gentleman of the bedchamber: his appointment as Lord Admiral, one of the senior positions on the Council, was the product not the basis of his political influence. And significantly, in 1621, Buckingham's mentor, John Williams, advised him to renounce the Admiralty to become Lord Steward of the King's Household, for, he argued, that office 'makes you in all changes and alterations of years near the king and gives unto you all the opportunities of accesses without the envy of a favourite'.[14] Similarly in 1626 when in order to placate his enemies, the duke planned to surrender some of his offices, he was advised 'to part with some of those Places you hold, which have least relation to the court'.[15] Access and proximity to the king were the doors to and supports of favour.

For those ambitious for place, then, absence from court, even on the king's business, gave rise to anxiety. This was in particular the ambassador's dilemma. The newsletters of John Chamberlain are the product and evidence of Sir Dudley Carleton's fear that he would always remain an envoy because he was never at home to play the courtier, or, in his own words, 'because he is a stranger to the king'.[16] Carleton's fears proved ill-founded, but similar anxieties were experienced by Sir Thomas Roe and the earls of Bristol and Leicester, in each case with justification. Some even counselled Sir Thomas Wentworth to think twice before accepting the Lord Deputyship of Ireland, 'for never was there as yet such an officer that lost not ground at Court through his absence and the envy of malign persons'.[17] Once again Wentworth's correspondence with Laud, whom he came to rely upon as an agent at court, is our best evidence that he shared that fear — and once again not without reason. Those most familiar with the ways of the court were quick to agree that distance from the king spelled danger. Not all who aspired to place, of course, could gain access to the monarch. Most men owed the success of their suits to the mediation of others. It was necessary therefore to cultivate someone close to the king, for without such support, one remained, in Burghley's graphic phrase, 'like a hop without a pole'.[18] Those who gathered around the men of influence and power — factions — did so for a variety of reasons. Sometimes they were little more than family groups out for office, 'sometimes the bond was a religious or political one . . . But more often than not personal ambitions, family interests, religious beliefs and political ideals were all mixed up in a kaleidoscopic pattern that was perpetually changing its shape'.[19] Most often the policies and personnel that made up the pattern were shaken by a change of the king's will. But — and this is too seldom emphasized — the reverse was also true: the king's decisions were themselves influenced and even determined by the prevailing power balance at court. Contemporaries expected that this should be so because the king was expected to listen, especially to his noblemen, his natural advisers. As Sir Thomas Roe told the Earl of Holland in 1630, 'the world will value you not by how the king looks upon you but by what power you have and use with him . . .'.[20] In truth, Holland's position, as with all courtiers, depended upon both. Royal favour would determine influence and fortunes. But human nature and political reality meant too that the king should be influenced by the views of those at court, especially of the powerful nobles and gentry. The history of faction bears this out. The Howards fell from favour in 1618 not least because their leading rivals joined forces to conspire against them. If the monarch was the determinate, he could also be the weathercock of faction. The balance of these roles altered with the personality of the monarch and with events. Henry VIII was evidently more open to the influence of faction than Elizabeth, and James I more than Charles. The consequence of these differences for the politics of each reign would repay closer investigation. For in a personal monarchy, the responsiveness of the monarch to influence determined the course of politics.

At certain points and in some cases, the fortunes of factions were clearly linked to policies and the success of those policies. Some sought office in order to influence policy: Sir Robert Naunton, for example, desired place above all to promulgate an anti-Spanish foreign policy.[21] Others at times adopted policies as a strategy for the securing of place, as did those who followed Buckingham and Prince Charles from the Spanish match to a declaration of war against Spain. Policy and place were necessarily though not simply related in the history of factional politics. It was the task of those who enjoyed office and the king's favour to assist him with the business of government. When they conspicuously mishandled a problem, ministers might be expected to lose their place. And a change of personnel often then brought a change from the policy which had led to their downfall. Robert Cecil, Earl of Salisbury, for example, never completely recovered from his failure to carry through the Great Contract; his rival, Henry Howard, Earl of Northampton, advised a different programme of projects to tackle royal insolvency.[22] After the failure of the negotiations for a Spanish match in 1615, Somerset was succeeded by the Winwood-Abbot faction, which was hostile to a pro-Spanish policy, and which, in part for that reason, had pursued the charges of Somerset's involvement in Overbury's murder so vigorously. Royal policies, then, like royal favour, were — and were expected to be — open to influence. As John Bastwick put it, as kings were gods in their wisdom, 'so are they likewise in respect of invocation, only to be sought to and called upon of their subjects'.[23] No one at court should then have felt unable to obtain a hearing, or incapable of enjoying the king's favour or of persuading him to a particular course. This desideratum presented enormous difficulties: on the king's part too much resolution could reduce advisers to mere sycophants and so invalidate their counsel, whilst too little determination led to unstable changes of policy and personnel. The problem was no less for the leaders of factions: for them, advice for the good government of the realm had always to be reconciled with the desire to stay in power. For the best government, the king had to be above faction, free of dependence on any one group; resolute, yet open to advice; able to inspire a sense of security in those in office, yet provide some hope of favour in those who as yet aspired to it. This was a fine borderline, but a crucial one. For the court formed the first vital link in a chain which connected the king to the localities. It was meant to bear, not break under, the contrary pressures and strains produced at times by the momentum of political life.

This the court of the early Stuarts clearly failed to do. We await a full institutional and political history of the royal court and household in early modern England,[24] but some of the problems are clear. In 1601 the Earl of Essex, unable to influence the queen in the determination of policy or to secure her favour in the distribution of place, was driven to rebellion. Whilst earlier in the reign the Elizabethan court appears to have remained open to various factions and policies, by the 1590s royal patronage had become all but the monopoly of the Cecils,[25] the succession of Robert to William underlining the family's control. The rebellion of the Earl of Essex was perhaps only the most obvious evidence of the political damage done by such a monopoly and the narrow base of the court.[26] And it may be the hopes placed in James VI by those excluded — Catholics and puritans, Essex men and Howards — that alleviated their discontent. Certainly the succession of James VI and I completely changed the situation. For all that he continued to enjoy royal favour and power, Cecil now had also always to consider others — especially the Scottish attendants in the new bedchamber who lived in familiar intimacy with the king.[27] The early restoration of families such as the Howards and Percies to title and court favour may also have been an astute move by James I to offset Cecil's monopoly of patronage and influence. As Cecil himself lamented, the court in the early years of James I was more open and more volatile than in the last decade of Elizabeth.[28] James took a Scottish favourite, Robert Carr, from among his bedchamber servants but, at least initially, showed no inclination to entrust him with power. The position was to change after a decade of Jacobean rule. With the deaths of Cecil in 1612 and of

Henry Howard, Earl of Northampton in 1614, court politics descended to the manoeuvrings of lesser figures on a stage vacated by the principal actors. From the confusion, George Villiers emerged as the new favourite, not because he displayed ability or judgement, but because he was endowed with a grace and beauty that attracted James.[29] There was little reason why his emergence need have caused concern. As King of Scotland and during the years of Cecil's hegemony James had enjoyed his favourites, and in 1616 Villiers, like them, seemed destined more to play the courtly gallant than the governor. But such Villiers was not to remain. Not content with the benefits of royal favour, Villiers, successively Marquis and Duke of Buckingham, determined to wield influence and ultimately to dictate policy. Accordingly, after pursuing initially alliances with the old nobility, with the earls of Southampton and Pembroke his first patrons, with the earls of Arundel and Northumberland, Buckingham turned to building a party at court entirely dependent upon himself.[30] 'He makes family alliances', the Venetian ambassador reported, 'as a support to form a great party'.[31] The duke sought compliant creatures rather than allies and so lost the reciprocal benefits of patronage — the support that clients provided as well as received.[32] Even his admirers and apologists were critical of Buckingham's patronage: as Sir Henry Wotton put it in his life of Villiers, 'He did not much strengthen his own substance at Court, but stood there on his own feet; for the truth is most of his allies rather leaned upon him than shored him up'.[33] Clarendon, who married into the duke's family, agreed: the duke's 'numerous family and dependents' had 'no other virtue or merit than ther allyance to him'.[34] As far as Ben Jonson was concerned, Buckingham's men were a mere band of gypsies raised to places they did not merit either by birth or virtue.[35] The duke's exploitation of his patronage undoubtedly 'offended the auncient nobility and the people of all conditions. . .'.[36]

More seriously, Buckingham resolved to block the advance of any who did not enjoy his patronage and, after 1623, of all who disagreed with his policies. Reflecting perhaps on the fall of Carr and his own rise to favour from within the bedchamber, Buckingham attempted to control the avenues of access to the king and to deny that access to his rivals and enemies. So, one of the punishments of Lionel Cranfield, Earl of Middlesex, whose impeachment had been managed by Buckingham on account of Cranfield's opposition to war, was banishment from court.[37] His brother-in-law, Arthur Brett, tipped as a rival for James's favour, was despatched to France.[38] The Earl of Bristol, who continued to support the Spanish match, was refused an audience at court on his return from Spain.[39] Many might have expected or hoped that the death of James would see the downfall of the duke. But Buckingham had manoeuvred brilliantly to entrench himself in the favour of the prince. As Sir John North informed the Earl of Leicester in 1625, 'our great man of Power the Duke . . . disposeth all more absolutely than ever'.[40] The Venetian ambassador, in concurring, also drew attention to the dissatisfaction to which it gave rise: many, he wrote, 'cannot endure that one born a simple gentleman . . . should be the sole access to the Court, the sole means of favour, in fact one might say the King himself'.[41] The hostility to Buckingham's position and control of patronage is not difficult to understand, for it had repercussions throughout the political nation which still await elucidation. Those deprived of favour at court risked loss of reputation in the country. Court patrons were in some respects like trades union leaders. At court, they represented others' as well as their own interests, and when they did not succeed in obtaining a hearing when, that is, they failed to resolve grievances or secure advancements, they were in danger of losing the respect of their followers, on which in turn their position at court was founded.[42] There was little that those outside Buckingham's circle could do for their followers: 'who he will advance', Arthur Ingram explained to Sir Thomas Wentworth, 'shall be advanced, and who he doth but frown upon must be thrown down'.[43] As Buckingham advanced court acolytes entirely dependent for their fortunes upon his favour, the great magnates and powerful gentlemen of the realm were deprived of the capacity to act as patrons at court for their clients. In a society based upon the networks of patron and client relations, that was bound to affect the entire course of politics.

The court was traditionally the resort of the aristocracy. The nobles were held to be the king's natural, principal and permanent advisers. And to those with vast estates, patronage and local influence, the king turned first for assistance with the execution of royal commands throughout the country. In 1549, William Sharington, giving evidence against Sir Thomas Seymour, had stated that Seymour

> would divers times look upon a chart of England . . . and declare . . .
> how strong he was and how far his lands and dominions did stretch . . .
> and what shires and places were for him. And when he came to Bristol
> he would say this is my Lord Protector's and of others that is my Lord
> of Warwick's.[44]

His evidence presents a picture of England as a conglomeration of noble principalities, the heads of which acknowledged personal allegiance to the monarch. It is an exaggerated picture: tenurial power was never sufficient for the family dominance of an entire region, but the Percies with 1,900 tenants in Northumberland and 3,000 or so in Cumberland were a formidable force.[45] Even a government agent, Richard Topcliffe, told the young Earl of Shrewsbury in 1590, that he was 'a Prince alone in effect, in two counties in the heart of England.'[46] In the sixteenth century, the co-operation of a leading magnate with central government was of vital importance and could go far towards securing the support of the region in which he possessed his estates and of the clients who followed him.[47]

It is important that by the end of the sixteenth century this was less clearly the case. The sixteenth century, it seems, saw the decline of the vast seigneurial household and with it, to some extent, the sway wielded by the great lords over the country.[48] This, however, is not necessarily evidence for the economic, social and political decline of the aristocracy.[49] Rather it illustrates that unique talent of the English ruling class: the adjustment to changed conditions and circumstances. The establishment of peace under the Tudors and the extension of crown authority and patronage altered the position of the nobility. Favour, place and influence did not go principally to those with powerful retainers in the country. Rivalries were often determined more by influence at court than by show of force in the country. As Wallace MacCaffrey has shown, even the mighty George, Earl of Shrewsbury felt that his long absence from the court (in part as the custodian of Mary Queen of Scots) had caused him to lose ground in Nottinghamshire to his gentry neighbours, the Stanhopes, who had cultivated relations with Lord Burghley.[50] Lord Buckhurst confirmed his judgement in writing to the Earl's successor, Gilbert: by royal favour, he told the seventh Earl, and their 'continual presence' at court, the Stanhopes 'will always prevail with so great advantage against you . . .'.[51] Peace and the enhanced importance of influence at court were to effect one of the greatest changes of aristocratic life: the civilization of the ruling classes. The change was gradual and in the early modern period never complete. But during the sixteenth century, humanist literature and courtesy books for the education of gentlemen and noblemen stressed as much the courtly as the martial accomplishments requisite for a nobleman; and emphasized too as much their service to their prince at court, in Council and in their counties, as their support for the ruler in war.[52] Honour, Dr Mervyn James has argued, became associated almost entirely with the king's conferment of honour.[53] By the end of the sixteenth century, clients looked to a great lord less for his capacity to protect them by arms, but more, as the Earl of Newcastle was to note, for his 'power to serve them both in court and in Westminster Hall to be their solicitor'.[54] The power of the nobleman to act at court depended, of course, upon his influence in the country. But more than ever, maintenance of local prestige depended too upon the influence a magnate exercised at court. As a consequence, the nobility appear to have spent more time in London, away from their estates. The fashion for London houses, the development of the Strand, the West End and Covent Garden, indeed the cultural flowering of the capital in the late sixteenth and early seventeenth centuries are the best evidence for these changes.[55] With the vast costs of maintaining a London residence and presence at court, it does not require any thesis of a declining income to explain the reduction by some noblemen of their seigneurial households in the country. Rather than any crisis of the aristocracy, it is the decline of the great provincial households and the more frequent absence of the magnates that had consequences for local society and government — consequences which still await investigation.[56]

Undoubtedly the Crown came to see the change as a problem. Where in the earlier sixteenth century efforts had often been made to draw the nobility to court, by the end of Elizabeth's reign there was greater concern that they should not too long remain there.[57] Regular Jacobean proclamations (following that of 2 November 1596) ordered those nobles and gentlemen not needed on the King's business to leave London and return to their seats in the country, for, 'the government of the countreys will be weakened, Hospitalitie and the reliefe of the poore . . . decayed . . .'.[58] The proclamations reflected a reality: without a paid bureaucracy and developed communications, local government depended upon the presence of powerful local men. Between 1580 and 1590 William Cecil, Lord Burghley, compiled and kept up an annotated map of England, with lists of names of the men in each county who were either JPs and deputy-lieutenants or influential figures in local society suitable for elevation to office.[59] Similarly, among the State Papers for 1598 we find a list of 'Principall Gentlemen that dwell in their contreis'.[60] The lists, however, may suggest a problem as well as the recognition of a problem: for they are lists of gentry rather than noblemen, and their very existence implies the Queen and Council's need for greater knowledge of and contact with the men who increasingly governed on their behalf. Elizabeth's parsimony with her patronage may well have added to the problem. As Professor Elton has suggested, the small numbers in the House of Lords and on the Council at the end of Elizabeth's reign reflected a dangerous narrowing of royal patronage and of the government's connections with the localities.[61]

It may be that James I himself discerned that the dearth of noble creations under Elizabeth had to be reversed. It is customary to accuse James of foolish indulgence in the granting of titles. But his early creations were all of families of large estates and local influence, worthy of elevation. It was later in his reign, Firth argued for the years after 1615, that the correlation between local influence and elevation to the peerage was abandoned.[62] It was during the period of Buckingham's ascendancy that large numbers of peerages, for the first time Irish and Scottish titles as well as English, were granted or sold, often to men of little standing and small estate — to his brother Christopher Villiers and brother-in-law Sir William Fielding, to Sir George Calvert or Sir George Chaworth.[63] Not all of the creations were indefensible nor without political value: Buckingham's connections with the Manners and the Montagues tied significant local families more closely to the government.[64] But that those elevated through Buckingham's patronage and influence were, as a group, significantly less wealthy and less well endowed with local estates cannot be denied.[65] By 1629, a new courtier nobility had been created with often little influence in the country, but predominance at court. The House of Lords, doubled in size between 1603 and 1628,[66] reflected less the counsel of those with the largest stake in the realm, more a division between traditional families and parvenues.[67] When representatives of the older families began to protest against the selling of honours, Buckingham seemed only more determined to add to the number of his clients.[68] In 1626, Buckingham held thirteen proxy votes in the Lords, more than any other two nobles put together — and this not least because six of his creatures had been elevated to the Lords that session, probably in order to protect the duke against impeachment.[69] Between 1625 and 1629, twenty-six new peers and nineteen viscounts were created.[70] It is hardly to be wondered at that the Earl of Manchester in the Lords and the Earl Marshal, the Earl of Arundel, in the Privy Council urged 'that titles should not be distributed broadcast . . . but only to persons of quality and of noble birth'.[71] Members of the House of Commons and others regarded the sale of honours with no less dismay: in 1626 and 1628 they discussed, along with plans for resumption of alienated crown lands, 'a resumption also of honours', as one newswriter put it, 'the number of our nobility being grown too great for the commonwealth and for the ancient and due esteem of that order'.[72] They recognized, that is, that counsel at court and good government in the locality depended, to a large extent, upon a peerage of land and influence. But, as I have suggested, by the 1620s many with the greatest influence at court enjoyed little prestige in the country, while some of those with substantial estates and influence in the locality were supplanted by the favourite's creatures at court. The chain of communication between the central government and the locality had lost important links — and lost them at a time when local politics had begun to develop its own momentum, independently of the drive of central instructions.

One of the most important advances in our understanding of early modern history has been the study of the local communities. It has been well demonstrated that in the early modern period a tendency to centralization ran parallel with a growing sense of local identity and loyalty, especially to the county. In 1642, as Dr Morrill has shown, it was to their 'country' or, as they meant by the term, their county that men gave their first allegiance.[73] The many neutrality pacts of the Civil War and the creation of local 'club men' bands to oust invading foreigners, whether royalists or parliamentarians, provide evidence of the importance of local circumstances and allegiances. Yet a sense of local identity did not preclude, rather was related to, a greater awareness of national affairs.[74] The demands of war and the more frequent sessions of parliaments in the 1620s involved the localities to a greater extent in the affairs of central government. Pamphlets and corantos, the first newspapers, disseminated foreign and domestic news to the counties as well as the capital. Professor Hirst has argued that a greater awareness of national issues is evident at the hustings. In place of the traditional picture of rustic ignorance and corrupt oligarchy, he has suggested the existence of a well-informed populace, a wider franchise and an increasing number of contested elections at which relatively lowly people might make their influence felt.[75] And he has shown that counties and towns instructed MPs they sent to Westminster, and expected account from them when they returned. Sir Thomas Wentworth's explanatory addresses to the Yorkshire Quarter Sessions were perhaps not entirely exceptional, but were rather the reflection of a changed political world, a world in which, in Francis Bacon's words, 'now-a-days . . . there is no vulgar but all statesmen'.[76] At a time when local loyalties were strong and political awareness was developing, it was important that communications be maintained between court, Council and locality. It would seem that the traditional methods of communication informally through the great magnates were undermined as the nobility in many counties detached themselves increasingly from the localities to base themselves in London or at court.[77] It was therefore essential that those of local influence, those who remained to govern in the localities, should be able to communicate their needs, grievances and problems to the king. If this were no longer possible along the chain of patronage to the court, it was all the more important that the other channels of communication remained open.

Here we must turn to the Privy Council, the most important and least-studied organ of early modern government.[78] For the Privy Council combined the advisory and executive roles crucial to the effectiveness of personal monarchy; it helped formulate and carry out the king's wishes and orders. The institution, of course, derives its name from the first of these functions: the giving of advice, in contemporary eyes perhaps its most vital responsibility. To Francis Bacon, a meeting of the Council saw 'the king in his chair or consistory . . . where his will and decrees which are in private more changeable are here settled and fixed'.[79] The Council met frequently, membership was usually for life and it could exert considerable influence upon the monarch. An offspring of the great councils of all the king's aristocracy, the Privy Council was expected to provide the best advice: the counsel of able, experienced men, influential in the country, capable of independent advice from their own knowledge and experience. Here again we may detect problems in the later years of Elizabeth's reign when the Council shrank in size to a small coterie of office-holders dominated by Cecil's faction. Evidently the Queen had found it difficult to replace the generation of the 1580s, men like the Earl of Leicester.[80] After the deaths of Cecil and Henry Howard at the end of his first decade of government, James I met the same problem. In 1613 the Spanish ambassador Gondomar reported 'that the Council is composed of men of little knowledge'.[81] The king began to take the advice as well as enjoy the company of his favourite. Buckingham's meteoric rise exacerbated (perhaps also reflected) the problem; and as he determined to monopolize patronage and determine policy, the Council as an advisory body was seriously weakened. When he could not get his way in Council the Duke ignored it or by-passed it. Divided and overawed, the Council failed to give a lead in parliament.[82] For it was no longer policies discussed and agreed by the Council which were promoted, but courses devised without its approval or knowledge. The chaotic and confused sessions of parliaments in the 1620s owed something to the weakness of the Council[83] that was itself a consequence of Buckingham's position.

MPs certainly saw this as one of the nation's problems: the dominance of counsel by favourites. The language of 'evil counsellors' is too often dismissed by historians as mere rhetoric, as a convenient explanation of their problems invented by men who looked for scapegoats or who were reluctant to criticize the king. In fact it was a rational and understandable analysis.[84] Responsible monarchical government did depend upon advice. And good advice was believed to come in general from the aristocracy (the most virtuous as well as most powerful men) and in particular from a Privy Council on which they sat. Members of Parliament therefore, like the Earl of Arundel, urged James and Charles to take the advice of a full Council and to ensure that men of experience and noble birth were appointed to it.[85] Since Professor Hexter has misleadingly stated otherwise,[86] it is important to emphasize that few MPs believed that parliament could — indeed few appear to have desired it should — be the prime source of regular counsel to the king. The Council was an institution with regular times of meetings; parliament, in Conrad Russell's now famous phrase, was still more of an event.[87] The demand for responsible government in early Stuart England, as Clayton Roberts demonstrated long ago, was a demand for government in conjunction with the Privy Council not parliament.[88] During the period of Buckingham's hegemony, it was a demand that remained unsatisfied.

The Council was also the principal executive body. It issued proclamations and letters and briefed lords-lieutenant and deputies, sheriffs, JPs and constables whose duty it was to execute them. In the absence of a professional civil service, the formidable burden of supervising local government was borne by the Privy Council. It was then essential for the Council to include those men of power and influence in their localities who in their individual capacities might act as agents of, and lend extra authority to, the Council board. In 1534 Thomas Cromwell had listed among his remembrances: 'To appoint the most assured and substantial gentlemen in every shire to be sworn of the King's Council, with orders to apprehend all who speak or preach in favour of the pope's authority'.[89] At a time of potential danger, he recognized the role of the Council in tying closely influential local men to central government. Even in more settled times, the membership of the Council could be as important in winning co-operation as in the conduct of administrative business.[90] Almost a century after Cromwell's remembrance, in 1626, Charles I sent his privy councillors down to their own localities in order to urge subscription to the forced loan.[91] Privy councillors, like the Council as a body, could be a valuable point of contact between the central government and the locality. Such a role was even more evident in the position of a lord-lieutenant, most of whom were members of the Privy Council. In 1614, Henry Howard, Earl of Northampton, even suggested that lords-lieutenant should go into their counties and summon the men of quality to discuss grievances and taxes.[92] When a lord-lieutenant, such as the Earl of Newcastle, maintained close links with the locality and good relations with his deputies, the position could become the major point of communication between the Council and the counties.[93] But as the business of the

Council became greater, many lords-lieutenant were increasingly detached from the areas of their charge, leaving their deputies to execute Council orders in local circumstances about which they knew less and less. The problems of the Sussex militia in the 1620s were occasioned not least by the local ignorance and inactivity of the Earls of Arundel and Dorset.[94] Such long-term problems were again exacerbated by Buckingham. Concentration of patronage in Buckingham's hands, as even his client Sir John Coke acknowledged, damaged the effectiveness of the Council.[95] When the independence of councillors proved an obstacle to the enactment of his wishes, Buckingham had them removed; alternatively he by-passed the Council altogether.[96] In 1621, the Earl of Southampton had remarked that he 'liked not to come to the Council Board because these were so many boys and base fellows'.[97] The removing or alienating of powerful men from the Council or ignoring it altogether had dangerous repercussions, as the duke was to discover to his disadvantage. Conrad Russell has recently drawn attention to the great difficulties faced by the government of early Stuart England in trying to fight a war.[98] Buckingham, however, had not only to contend with the chronic difficulties of a shortage of men and supply, but also to do so without the full co-operation of powerful privy councillors and leading figures in the counties.[99] The peculiarly spectacular fiasco of English military campaigns in the 1620s owed much to a breakdown of effective communication and patronage.

Let us draw together the argument so far. Government was the king's business. But in order for monarchical government to work — that is in order for the king to be well advised and his wishes effectively executed, the organs of advice and execution (the court, the Council and the aristocracy) needed to maintain open communications — to the king from the country, and from the king to the locality. This in the 1620s they failed to do. This was not the only problem of early Stuart government: shortage of money, the pressure of business, issues and disagreements, most of all war imposed formidable strains. But better communications might have ameliorated difficulties, might have facilitated the process of compromise and discussion through which problems and issues normal to political life are tackled. Significantly the analysis sketched here follows closely that of members of early Stuart parliaments. They complained that the court had become inaccessible, that the nobility had been tarnished by sale of titles to parvenues, that the advice of the Council had been eclipsed by an irresponsible favourite who had usurped royal patronage and employed it to advance his family rather than men of desert. They urged the responsible exercise of patronage; they 'condemned the authority of a single individual and said that matters should be done by Council';[100] they asked that the king heed the advice of 'the ablest men for parts and breeding'.[101] Their suggestions, however, were not adopted; their remedies not applied. And Members of Parliament found themselves faced with a responsibility which they were neither willing nor qualified to shoulder.

During the period from 1603 to 1629 there were few requests from MPs for more frequent parliaments.[102] Parliament was not an ordinary institution of government. Its two most important functions — passing laws and voting taxes — were themselves extraordinary.[103] Laws were needed only to remedy abuses: change for the sake of improvement, the modern attitude to legislation, meant little to a society which believed that the passage of time brought decay, not progress. Grants of taxation were made not for the ordinary expenses of the government, but for special circumstances or emergencies, such as a war. As for private petitions or local suits, these had been traditionally advanced through the patronage networks to be promoted by a patron at court or in the Council. Administration, executive action, justice, the routine of government were none of parliament's business.[104] Nor did Members of Parliament show any desire that they should be. But as the other organs of government and communication came under stress, MPs were forced to adopt a different attitude. The grievances and wishes of the localities, now more articulated and pressed, often could not get a hearing at court or in the Council. So many MPs, themselves often justices of the peace and deputy-lieutenants, faced with the problems of governing the localities, brought those grievances and difficulties to parliament. Significantly it appears that it was the first parliament of James I that saw a large rise in the number of private and local bills in parliament,[105] at a time when Elizabeth's parsimony had narrowed the court's connection with the localities. In order to maintain their positions, powerful local gentlemen had to prove they could exercise influence at the centre — if not at court, then in the Commons. During the 1620s, many excluded from access to the court by Buckingham's near monopoly of patronage, turned to parliament in order to serve their localities and represent their interests. As Dr. Peter Salt has shown in an important article, it was only after the demise of his own court patrons and Buckingham's support for his Yorkshire rival, Sir John Savile, that Sir Thomas Wentworth's contest with the Saviles at the hustings 'became implacable'.[106] As others like Wentworth despaired of obtaining a hearing at court, the House of Commons, more than ever before, became the seminar of the English localities.

It was not a seminar likely to reach a conclusion. Members and leaders of the Commons changed, procedure was drawn out and often cumbersome; 'tyme wasted needlessly', as one member put it, 'is very considerable'.[107] Proposals were often abandoned before they had advanced far and problems were referred to committees from which they sometimes failed to emerge. The flood of local petitions and bills made things worse. Parliament was now being called upon to perform everyday tasks whilst meeting only occasionally, and to resolve a myriad of particular local problems by laws. 'Anything that may concern the welfare of your Town', James Howell told the aldermen of Richmond who had returned him as its Member of Parliament, '. . . I take to be the true duty of a Parliamentary burgess, without roving at random to generals'.[108] With so many such particular concerns and preoccupations it is little wonder that there were few laws. Parliament appeared united only when grievances and problems were common to most localities, as in 1628 when nearly all MPs came to the House to complain against billeting of troops, martial law and arbitrary imprisonment. Even then there were limits to the action that parliament could take. The Petition of Right was an attempt to settle particular grievances by a general statement. It was no solution to the problems that had emerged during the war years of 1625 to 1628. Charles I and his parliaments agreed in general about the inviolable status of the common law and the necessity for some discretionary power in the prerogative.[109] What they disagreed about was when and how prerogative powers had been employed, about, as J.P. Cooper put it, 'the means . . . and circumstances proper to the king's emergency powers rather than the principles, about the interpretation of the law rather than the law itself.[110] And again MPs reiterated that the problem had arisen from the actions of intermediaries and from misunderstandings. As Sir Henry Marten observed on 3 May 1628, 'The greatest calamity of this kingdom . . . is the distance between the king and the people'.[111] That distance is demonstrated perhaps by the Council's consulting the antiquary Sir Robert Cotton to advise them concerning the feeling in the country and the best strategy in parliament.[112] If the Petition of Right brought such joy, if it defused for a time the political tension, it was not because parliament had won (or believed it had won) a 'victory' *over* the king, but because the royal assent was evidence of the harmony *between* king and Commons and the fruit of direct communication between Charles I and his subjects. After years of urging the king to listen to sound advice, parliament by-passed the obstruction of favourites in order to appeal directly to the king. And the king, fulfilling expectations about his good intentions, had taken it. But the Petition of Right was not, as was soon discovered, a permanent answer to the basic problem of advice or executive government. The king, for example, did not believe that he had surrendered a right to imprison without cause shown. As Professor Relf and Dr. Ball agreed, 'as a practical measure its efficacy was limited to the grievances complained of'.[113] Legislation could not define the modes of government. To the wider problem, apart from renewed attacks on evil counsellors, the Commons had no answer. The frustrations of the parliamentary session of 1629 are evidence of a recognition of parliament's limitations. Its stormy and violent conclusion, in which the Speaker was illegally held in his chair, was the desperate action of men who recognized that laws had not resolved — perhaps could not resolve — their grievances. Sir John Eliot attempted instead to tackle the problem of counsel by declaring any who advised extra-parliamentary taxation or religious innovations to be 'a capital enemy to this kingdom and commonwealth'.[114] Reflecting during his imprisonment in the Tower, Eliot saw the problem starkly. His thoughts on government, the *De Iure Majestatis*, reflect the experience of a man who had realized that parliament had only a limited place in the government of England and define monarchical authority in a manner 'which might have served to destroy the independence of parliament'.[115] An awareness of its limited capacities to resolve the problems of government at a time of difficulties was at the heart of 'the crisis of parliaments'.

The comparative political calm of the years after 1629 has always been difficult to accommodate within a story of escalating political crisis. But our analysis, I think, makes it less difficult to understand. The termination of hostilities with France and Spain greatly relieved the tensions in central-local relations. Just as important, the assassination of the Duke of Buckingham in August 1628 removed a major grievance and political problem.[116] There was considerable optimism in the country that more responsible government might follow and that a change of counsel might see a different style of government.[117] During the early 1630s at least, such hopes were not entirely disappointed. In the first place, there was a change of personnel. Though Charles remained attached to the duke's memory and family, some of Buckingham's old enemies, such as Sir Dudley Digges or Wentworth exiled from court patronage, were introduced or reintroduced to royal favour. Despite Lord Treasurer Weston's prominent position in Council, no minister emerged to enjoy a monopoly of either patronage or influence upon royal policy. A wide variety of men and factions vied for place; many different policies and attitudes to religion, to domestic and foreign affairs once again found expression at court.[118] Charles I also showed greater concern for the maintenance of aristocratic privilege. He sold no titles of nobility throughout the 1630s and was cautious, as Wentworth discovered for long to his discontent, in conferring the highest honours.[119] Court ceremonies, rituals and entertainments all reflected an obsession with rank and degree.[120] Second, Charles eschewed the advice of favourites and restored an active Privy Council to its traditional position as adviser to the king and the principal executive body.[121] After 1628 Charles had no one first minister. The new formality at court distanced the king and so excluded most courtiers from developing the close relationship with Charles that Buckingham had enjoyed. Weston, Laud and Wentworth, often wrongly thought of as successors to Buckingham's place, never secured a monopoly of favour or influence and often doubted their position in the king's estimation. Charles I, as Clarendon and Secretary Dorchester concurred, 'resolved to hold the reins in his own hands and to put no further trust in others than was necessary for the capacity they served in'.[122] But personal rule was not autocratic government. Charles attended the Privy Council more often; he carefully pondered advice. Evidently he attempted to strengthen the Council's authority and usefulness by adding to its numbers those who might bring their own knowledge and influence to the board. He increased the number of lay peers and added to the Council by virtue of their office the Lords President of the Marches and the North, and Sir William Alexander, principal Secretary of State for Scotland, in order perhaps to promote better communications. The procedure of the Council was regularized and tightened; registers were more efficiently kept. Most important, Charles resolved the dilemma of the political need for a large body of councillors and the administrative desirability of a smaller working group by the further development of standing committees of Council with special responsibilities (for Ireland or the ordnance, for example) which reported to the full board. During the 1630s the Council was active again as the principal advisory and administrative body.[123] Third, it would appear that Charles attempted to tackle some of the problems of communication between centre and locality that we have been discussing. He took personal care — by ordering elaborate censuses — to enforce proclamations commanding nobles and gentlemen to leave London and provide hospitality and government in their countries. He added to the number of lords-lieutenant so that each county for the first time had its own lord-lieutenant and many more than one. For the collection of ship money the sheriff was chosen, not least because he was the sole agent with whom the Council needed to maintain contact and from whom it could expect account. Most important, when he reissued the Elizabethan orders for the relief of famine, poverty and plague, Charles I instructed JPs to send monthly reports on their enforcement to the justices of assize; and he established a large committee of the Council to examine them.[124] Such measures, typical of the vigorous tone of Caroline government, suggest that Charles appreciated that he could no longer depend for the maintenance of local welfare and order upon the patronage and power of the great lords. The innovations, rather the renovations of the personal rule, were designed to make local and central government more effective. For seven years they enjoyed at least relative success. The Book of Orders was reasonably effective at least in allaying the immediate crisis,[125] and more obviously ship money was collected with an efficiency which has caused some historians surprise and discomfort.[126] We do not need to follow complicated paths to explain, or explain away, that success. The Council was more effective and when it applied itself to the enforcement of a policy, it achieved considerable results.

But the problems of communication were not solved. For the course of politics to run smoothly, communications needed to run in *two* directions: from the locality to the centre, as well as from the centre to the locality. Good government depended upon a reasonable knowledge of local circumstances, and this was all the more important in the 1630s when there were no parliaments to air local views or express local grievances. It was such communication that was not re-established. Privy Councillors with more and more business knew less of their own localities and became more dependent upon what they were told. Often ignorant of local circumstances they were, in Professor Barnes's words, 'too ready to listen to those who professed the "king's interest" and too willing to forget the personal motives that actuated them'.[127] In the localities, many of those who worked locally as deputy lieutenants and justices began to despair of a government that seemed oblivious to the problems to which its orders gave rise, unaware of the greatly increased burdens of office and slow to reward diligent service.[128] If Charles enjoyed some success in enforcing the orders of the Council in the counties, the grievances and problems of the country were not sufficiently appreciated at court. Neither did the king see any need to explain or justify his orders; he regarded obedience as his due. In the absence of knowledge and explanation, myths — the children of ignorance — were born and grew. Archbishop Laud, who sought above all to unite the church, was feared as a popish innovator not least because he failed 'to make his designes and purposes appear as candid as they were'.[129] For his part, Charles was so ignorant of the mood of the localities that he believed that the Scots war would be popular. Having little independent knowledge of the localities, the Privy Council, burdened by central business and especially the collection of ship money, could do little but refer local business back to local men. 'Non-residence', Professor Barnes concluded of Somerset, 'robbed the lord lieutenant of the part he might have played as an informant to the Council', and the same was true in several counties.[130] Where the lords-lieutenant were resident, like the Earl of Newcastle in Nottinghamshire, we find the best response to the demands.[131] In other counties, with memories of the billeting of 1628 (in most places not remunerated), the lords-lieutenant were seen less as a point of contact, more as the hated agents of central interference. Those deputy-lieutenants and justices left to govern in the localities were then often left to stand alone between their local allegiances and difficulties and the demands of a central government that seemed all too ignorant of them. The most diligent service, the Earl of Newcastle complained to Wentworth, went unacknowledged, and 'if your Lop and I loose our Counties and have little thanks above neither, wee have taken a great deal of paynes in vayne'.[132] The demands of the Scots war from 1638 placed many local gentlemen in a near impossible position. For the most part, they attempted loyally to carry out the Council's instructions for the raising of men and money. But grievances were now expressed loudly, especially by the lower orders who were, as always, most hit by the demands and miseries of war. Ship money sheriffs complained that they could no longer depend upon the co-operation of their constables; deputy-lieutenants faced reluctant, even riotous, recruits. They protested that central demands threatened the order and stability of local government and society.[133] The Council did not listen and probably did not understand. In the end the gentry governors of several counties joined their subordinates in protesting against the consequences of government demands. Some may have welcomed the occasion to articulate long-felt frustrations, but others had little choice, faced with the danger of local insurrection and no help from above.[134]

A parliament was welcomed in 1640 because it gave the gentry of the localities a necessary platform to explain the problems which faced them and to express the grievances which swamped them. Those who were elected to the Short Parliament were no heralds of imminent revolution, nor even protagonists of a constitutional battle. They continued to place their trust in a king well-intentioned and well-advised. Though many petitions of grievances were sent up from the counties to the Commons,[135] few MPs thought it parliament's place to provide government or even permanent counsel.[136] Sir Benjamin Rudyerd condemned the carriage of some members in former assemblies who had acted 'so hauty as though Parliaments would last alwayes'.[137] Few MPs seem to have shared Pym's diagnosis that 'the intermission of Parliaments hath beene a true cause of these evells'.[138] More subscribed to Harbottle Grimstone's argument that good examples were needed more than good laws.[139] Lord Digby expressed the prevailing traditional feeling: 'great counsells must provide for the future'.[140] Perhaps Charles I did too precipitately dissolve an assembly that Clarendon believed was loyal and with which a settlement could have been reached.[141] Rudyerd and others, after all, might have been willing to vote twelve subsidies for the abolition of ship money.[142] If the Commons failed to agree upon an immediate grant of supply needed for the war, it may well have been, as some MPs indicated, from fear of the reaction in their counties, which in some cases were in a state of unstable agitation. Grimstone clearly expressed a widely-felt concern that if they proceeded to a subsidy bill before the resolution of grievances, 'the country would not agree to it and they would give but a bad welcome to us'.[143] It is perhaps worthy of note that even after the dissolution of the Short Parliament Charles raised a loan of £300,000 from the Council and gentry about the city — 'an unanswerable evidence', Clarendon believed, 'that the hearts of his subjects were not then aliened'.[144]

During the summer and autumn of 1640, however, law and order began to break down, as soldiers returned unpaid and the costs of a fruitless campaign mounted.[145] The Scots invaded and occupied Newcastle. The Long Parliament which assembled in November 1640 met in very different circumstances. By the winter of 1640, some MPs had come to believe that parliament should take a regular part in government and, in the absence of satisfactory alternatives, should perform functions which for decades it had striven to avoid. Lord Digby's change of mind represented this shift of perspective: 'It is true . . . wicked ministers have been the proximate cause of our miseries, but the want of parliaments (is) the primary . . .'.[146] The evidence of disputed elections suggests that there was a feeling in the country that parliament had more to do than present grievances and depart.[147] The bill for annual parliaments and the Triennial Act establishing an independent machinery for the calling of a parliament every three years were the product of this radically changed atmosphere. The Triennial Act *was* a revolutionary step. Never before in early modern England had parliament attempted to determine its own life or frequency of assembly. It may have been for most a step taken reluctantly. For most MPs, it would seem, still did not wish to take upon themselves the business of government.[148] As Gardiner put it succinctly: 'All the habits of men led them to look to the king for guidance. Parliaments were but bodies meeting at rare intervals, doing important work and then vanishing away.'[149] During the winter of 1640–1 attempts to solve the problems of counsel and government still revolved around the Privy Council not parliament.[150] Negotiations went on for Charles to appoint to high office and the Council Board the earls of Bedford and Essex, Lord Saye and Sele, Pym and St John, who enjoyed the confidence of the Commons and who might manage the House for the king. The schemes for these bridging appointments, however, floundered and finally died with the death of Bedford himself in May 1641.[151] They failed not least because it was doubtful whether Bedford and the 'country peers' could any more sway the backbenchers or secure the co-operation of the localities than could Charles. For by the summer of 1641 the questions being debated at Westminster were remote from the grievances of the localities. The leaders of the Long Parliament were not just alienated from the court; they were distanced too from the country.[152]

With the collapse of the schemes to elevate Bedford and others to high office, MPs faced a clear choice: parliament now had either to leave the business of government to Charles and his chosen advisers, or to take greater responsibilities itself. Those who, as the summer of 1641 wore on, drifted back to their localities leaving the House unquorate, probably expressed their preference for the former, while Pym and others who staffed the committees that continued to sit and act during the recess (and the king's absence in Scotland) already began to turn parliament into an organ of government. Shortly after parliament reconvened on 20 October, the choice was presented even more starkly when news came of the outbreak of the Irish rebellion, and the need for an army to suppress it. Pym's response was clear: from October he attempted to secure the agreement of the House to a demand that the king appoint his councillors with the advice of parliament. He failed. Only after Charles's attempted arrest of the five members in January 1642 did the Commons vote that no privy councillor should be appointed without its consent and so effectively assert its own position as the supreme Council.[153] And only after that attempted coup did Pym secure the passing of a militia ordinance by which parliament raised an army by its own executive authority. In that ordinance, attitudes to the king, the Privy Council and parliament, for long held, were now abandoned.[154] In their defence of the militia ordinance the parliamentary propagandists claimed for the Lords and Commons executive authorities and advisory responsibilities which for half a century they had insisted belonged to the king and his Council. Parliament, they declared

is likewise a council, to provide for the necessities, prevent the imminent dangers, and preserve the public peace and safety of the kingdom, and to declare the king's pleasure in those things as are requisite thereunto; and what they do herein hath the stamp of the royal authority, although His Majesty, seduced by evil counsel, do in his own person oppose or interrupt the same; for the King's supreme and royal pleasure is exercised and declared in this High Court of law and council, after a more eminent and obligatory manner than it can be by personal act or resolution of his own.[155]

Many even of those who fought for parliament were unhappy with the claim. Some were moving that the demand even to approve the king's choice of ministers be dropped from the Nineteen Propositions when Pym announced to the House that Charles was preparing for war.[156] Only reluctantly did parliament come to govern.

For half a century or more, Members of Parliament analysed the problems of government in terms of bad advisers and bad officers. Both were symptoms of the breakdown of patronage and communications which, when effective, had helped to ensure that the king was advised by, and that he govern through, men with experience of and influence in the localities. With the collapse of this chain of communication, problems, grievances and issues normal to political life (and normally ironed out by informal contact and action) came to parliament. Anxious to establish and maintain their local standing, the county gentry acted as the spokesmen of local discontents: if not at court, then in parliament. That is not to say that they necessarily believed that parliament was the *best* place to deal with them. Parliament, as some members came to see, was capable of only negative protest.[157] The ability to change counsel and policy, as Wentworth and Noy in 1628 and Pym and Bedford in 1641 well realized, lay at Court not in parliament. By the autumn of 1641, it was that realization and the differing responses to that realization which divided the house. Some MPs now wished, or saw the need, for Members of Parliament to govern — if not through participation in royal councils then through direct parliamentary control. Other members who had come to the House no less incensed with the grievances of personal rule, still believed that permanent counsel and executive government were none of parliament's business. Of these latter some, like Edward Hyde himself, were to be protagonists of the royalist cause. But others were and remained primarily the representatives of the country, men for whom the high politics of Westminster no less than of Whitehall were remote from and secondary to the protection of local interests.[158] During the 1640s the parliamentarians no less than the royalists, parliamentary governments no less than royal government, met with local independence, local intransigence and local hostility. The real problems of government in seventeenth-century England faced the victors no less than the defeated of the English Civil War.

3. The personal rule of Charles I*

I

The period of government without parliaments from 1629 to 1640, variously described as the 'eleven years tyranny' and 'The Personal Rule of Charles I', has been little studied (at least as far as the central government is concerned) since Gardiner completed his commanding narrative nearly a century ago.[1] Yet the 1630s is not only a decade of unusual fascination, worthy of investigation in itself. Because we may learn from those years so much about King Charles, so much about the nature and problems of early Stuart government, a study of the Personal Rule is also essential for an understanding of the crises which led to civil war. To some, perhaps, the place of that decade in the story of civil war is clear: the period of government without parliament intensified the conflicts between crown and subjects which had been set in motion since the succession of James I; accelerated, that is, the fateful journey towards civil war past many a milestone of divisive controversy. As Professor Rabb has put it, 'the attempt to do without parliament in the 1630s was in the long run untenable . . . Resistance to Charles's policy was inevitable'.[2]

But was it? To those on the road during the 1630s the journey seemed far from a headlong rush towards conflict. Even looking backward from a knowledge of later events, Edward Hyde, no uncritical flatterer of Charles I, recalled, as we have seen, the Personal Rule as a decade of calm and felicity.[3] His analysis prompts a number of questions. How, after two decades of alleged constitutional conflict between king and Commons, was Charles able to rule without consulting his subjects in parliament? How, if parliament was central to the government of England, was it possible (and even easier) to continue the business of government without it? Why did the gentry families represented in parliament,

indeed in many cases former MPs themselves, assist with the collection of levies and the enforcement of policies which made rule
without parliament possible? Unlike the kings of France, Charles I
had no standing army and no agents of the central authority in the
localities: his government rested upon co-operation. Why and how
far was that co-operation secured after 1629?

In order to begin to answer these questions, we must investigate
the circumstances in which the decision to govern for a time without
parliaments was made. We must attempt to understand the aims and
ideals of the king and his counsellors for the government of Church
and state. We must see how those aims and ideals became policies
and how, through the organs of central and local government — the
Privy Council, the courts, the lieutenants, the bishops, the sheriffs,
the justices and the constables — policies were translated into
actions. We must pay no less close attention to the responses and to
the nature of the responses, within Whitehall and in the counties and
dioceses, to those policies and to the methods by which they were
executed. Finally we must attempt to suggest why and when the co-
operation upon which personal government depended began to
break down and why the Personal Rule collapsed. These are questions which can only be touched upon here, but they are questions
which need to be asked and more thoroughly investigated.

II

Why then did Charles I in 1629 dispense with parliament for a
decade? Hitherto his short reign had exhibited no hostility to those
assemblies. Before he became king, Charles had been, as Rudyerd
described him, a prince bred in parliaments.[4] During the first four
years of his reign parliaments were summoned more frequently
than at any time during the previous seventy years. And, at least in
the declaration of war against Spain, royal policy had been framed
in accordance with the wishes of the Commons. Indeed it was
these very factors — the experience of parliaments and the heeding
of their counsel — which, in the end, persuaded the king to
dispense with them. Looked at from Charles's point of view parliament had proved reluctant to finance a war which it had advocated. The failures, defeats and abortive campaigns of the 1620s,
humiliating to a ruler as obsessed with honour and shame as was
Charles, were the direct consequences of inadequate supply.
Months after those failures, in April 1629, the Council discussed
questions arising from the king having been engaged, at the
entreaty of parliament, in three wars for which it had voted insuffi-
cient revenue. These were understandable questions. Acceptance

of parliamentary advice and expectation of parliamentary supply went hand in hand.[5] Secondly, the House of Commons had instituted judicial proceedings against the Duke of Buckingham, who was not only a favourite fully in the king's confidence, but the architect of the foreign policy advocated by parliament and, at least in Charles's estimation, the general best qualified to conduct the war.[6] It is hardly surprising if Charles expected that in time of war domestic quarrels, especially those stemming (as he believed them to be) from jealous pique and personal interests, should be subordinated to unity in the face of the enemy. Then when after three years of warfare, MPs assembled in 1628, they came to parliament not to offer their support, but to present as grievances the very measures — forced loans, billeting, martial law — which their own counsel, their failure to supply, indeed the very facts of war had necessitated. Few today question the emergency powers assumed by government in the name of common safety at a time of crisis. Few in 1628 questioned the need for some emergency power or doubted that it rested in the king's prerogative. But those who came to Westminster in 1628 did argue that the modes and the men through which those necessary powers had been exercised had led to an abuse of their purpose, to a breach of the rights and privileges guaranteed by law. With those engaged in trying to fight a war, these distinctions carried little conviction. To tie the government in wartime to the normal processes of law was to end its capacity to fight. Or as Sir James Bagg expressed the point to Buckingham, 'Magna Charta . . . is now made a chain to bind the king from doing anything'.[7] The king's decision to dispense with parliament originated from the failure to fight the war and from a feeling that the deliberations of the Commons bedevilled any action. It was a vision shared by many at court and not a few throughout the country. Within the House of Commons, Sir Thomas Wentworth experienced the same sense of frustration with parliament's fondness for debate, not action. Members of parliament he regarded as 'a generation of men more apt to begin business than obstinately to pursue and perfect them; and the part they delight most in is to discourse rather than suffer'.[8]

If the renewed attack on the duke, during the last weeks of parliament, presaged ill, the close of the session at least brought five subsidies. Charles had promised to resummon the House and evidently embarked on preparations to ensure the success of the second session. In July Buckingham surrendered some of his offices and was reconciled to some of his enemies. Clarendon suggests that he also considered a complete change of policy; a suggestion confirmed by Dorchester's belief that the duke had found 'his own judgement to have been misled'. Though preparations for the relief of La Rochelle continued during the summer of 1628, there was much noise of 'trading for a peace'.[9] Whatever Buckingham's intentions, they were cut short by Felton's dagger on 23 August. Buckingham's death was one of those incidents that changed the flow of traffic. For all his loyalty to the man and his memory, Charles now came into his own as master of affairs. More importantly, many estranged and alienated from the court returned to positions of favour and influence. And with the removal of the minister named as the cause of all grievances, there was good expectation of a harmonious session of parliament. Sir Francis Nethersole expressed that optimism bluntly only a day after the duke's assassination: 'The stone of offence being now removed by the hand of God, it is to be hoped that the king and people will come to a perfect unity'.[10]

Not all thought the problem so simple. There was disagreement at court about whether to recall parliament, some maintaining that the duke's death would give members of the Commons an opportunity 'to make appear their formal distempers were rather personal than real', others suggesting a period of respite and reform, before a second session in the spring. By the end of September it was decided to resummon parliament in January. Dorchester thought it the wisest course, 'for the *aegritudo* in men's minds requires time to take it away and the medicine of a constant and settled government . . .'.[11]

Metaphors of illness and cures pervade the language of 1628 and 1629.[12] The diseases discovered had not only affected relations between king and parliament. The war years had revealed symptoms of more fundamental disabilities and sores which, to the king and Council at least, threatened to infect the whole body politic: the weakness of the militia, divisions within the church, the pursuit of private interests before the public good, the decline of respect for authority, even a rejection of the wholesome purgatives which might have cleansed and restored the commonweal. It was a sense of impending fatality, of a terminal cancer of disorder threatening the collapse of all authority which governed the behaviour of king and Council during the winter of 1629.[13] That same sense, those same fears were articulated in the language of necessity, that is the needs of the state. But if the word 'state' is used more frequently in the letters and reports of this period,[14] it should not be understood in its modern sense, as an abstract authority detached from society, but as a description of the commonweal, that is of the common good. At the end of Hilary term 1628, Charles urged the judges leaving on circuit to see above all 'that every man in his quality and calling should have care of the common good, the rather because not every particular man, but the whole commonwealth is interested in it'.[15] The strains and stresses of war had not only brought about the crisis of parliaments; the safety and survival of the commonweal had been called into question.

King and Council embarked, as we shall see, upon a course of treatment: reform and retrenchment at court, the end of the sale of honours, reinvigoration of conciliar and local government. But for all the difficulties and frustrations of recent experience, Charles had by no means given up with parliaments. Rather the feverish activity of the autumn and winter of 1628 was an expression of the realization, eloquently expressed by the Secretary of State, that 'it imports more than anything else that the next meeting should be without the late disorders'.[16] It is important to grasp that having commenced a programme of reform, Charles I met his last parliament for a decade in a mood of not unmerited optimism.

That optimism, as we know, was misplaced. The session of 1629 proved contentious, abortive, unproductive and chaotic. The Commons refused to pass an act legitimizing the collection of tonnage and poundage, remained querulous about the religious issue, despite the king's declaration, and departed from Westminster after an unruly and disordered scene followed the order for their adjournment. The ill humours of the state had not been purged. Charles resolved not to call another parliament for a time, until, as his proclamation declared, his people might see his good intentions more clearly. The *aegritudo* referred to by Dorchester required longer and more radical treatment. There was business, not debate, to be conducted. As Attorney General Heath told Carlisle in reporting the dissolution: 'Now is the time to put brave and noble resolutions into action'.[17]

There can be little doubt that thereafter, whatever road the course of politics took, the king was his own master. Though foreign ambassadors, familiar with a Richelieu or an Olivares, tried to predict the rise of another favourite, none emerged to assume Buckingham's former place of influence and power. The arrangements which had followed Buckingham's death settled as an established pattern: 'The King holds in his hands the total directory leaving the executory part to every man within the compass of his charge'.[18] Even the queen, to whom Charles became a devoted husband and with whom he secluded himself whenever possible, was allowed almost no part in public affairs and showed no desire to exercise influence.[19] The state papers and registers of the Privy Council certainly reveal breadth of counsel and full consultation within the Council and the committees of the Council. But they indicate too that the decisions made, the aims and priorities pursued were often those of Charles himself.[20]

III

What were those aims and priorities? What were the ideals and purposes, for ideals and purposes there were, which underlay the directives and proclamations issued and published by king and Council during the decade of Personal Rule? It is not always possible to detect from the official language of public documents the minds most at work in their formulation. Those which were of the king's own devising, and those which, formed by the genius of another, bore only his stamp cannot always be differentiated. But the language of the king's own letters and speeches, the articulation of ideals in the culture of the court, the alterations made by his hand to official papers, the comparison of documents passing through the Signet Office with the business reported in the Council register enable us to form a fairly clear picture of what mattered most to Charles.[21] Central to all his directives was an obsessive concern with order — in matters both large and small. Always an aspect of his personality, it was a characteristic developed by experience: by the profound impression made on the prince by the decorous gravity of Spain; by (in contrast) the dislocation and chaos of the wars; perhaps by the social unrest which bad harvests and unemployment threatened.[22]

It was an obsession most visible in the royal court and household. In the Memoirs of her husband, Lucy Hutchinson recalled vividly the change of style from King James to King Charles. 'The face of the Court was much changed in the king, for King Charles was temperate, chaste and serious, so that the fools and bawds, mimics and catamites of the former Court grew out of fashion'.[23] It was a change of style which is more clearly detectable after 1628. In March 1629, for example, Charles announced his resumption of the ancient forms at court. With the ordinances of Henry VIII as his model, he ordered greater care concerning the distinctions and degrees of rooms and persons; he issued directives governing the behaviour of attendants when the court went abroad. In January 1631 royal instructions of greater detail delineated by rank those with rights of access respectively to the Privy, Presence and Bed Chambers; they commanded due distance to be kept when the king and queen were in public. Charles literally withdrew himself from the easy familiarity which had characterized the reign of James and from which, perhaps, court favourites had sprung. The style of Charles's court reflected the image of the king: formal and reserved.[24] But it was not only in the sphere of morality and manners that the concern for order was revealed. Charles instigated a programme of reform and retrenchment at court, a programme which, if never very successful, at least curtailed the curve of rising extravagances. During the 1630s, the court and household were, as Professor Aylmer concluded, relatively parsimonious. The reforming Jupiter who in *Coelum Britannicum* renounces the sins of extravagance and licence was not purely a character of the dramatic imagination inhabiting only the idealized world of the masque.[25] As always with Charles I, the image and the reality informed each other.

The concern with order was not confined to the court. Indeed it is important to understand that for Charles I the court was not to be, as some historians have maintained, a retreat from the world of reality, but rather a model for the reformed government of Church and state. Fear of the collapse of all authority and the dislocation of society directed the king's attention to the reordering of society and government. Where there were no laws, the Council was to act to tackle the problems, where statutes had already prescribed measures, the Council was to ensure that they were enforced.[26] The Book of Orders, perhaps the best known statement of Caroline social policy, was undoubtedly a response to the immediate circumstances of hardship and the threat of riot which they imposed. But, as has recently been emphasized, it is remarkable too as an innovative attempt to deal not only with the immediate problem and consequences but also with the symptoms of dearth and poverty. The Book of Orders looked to longer-term solutions and their enforcement. In informing his brother of the new orders in November 1630, the Earl of Manchester described that wider purpose clearly: 'It is time for Councillors to care [for] those things that concern government in these loose and dear times, lest mischief follow of it. The diligence of some justices and the good fruit of their pains show that there want no laws to reform all things, but good executioners of laws. Notice must be taken of such as use diligent and they known that are negligent to which end we are in purpose to have a commission'.[27] Manchester went on to explain that the commission would oversee relief for the poor, the putting of youths to apprenticeship, the regulation of alehouses and the suppression of rogues and vagabonds. The Book of Orders, in other words, was the start of a programme for the reformation of society and the reinvigoration of local government.

That programme, because it depended upon men of substance and ability, brought an end to the sale of honours. Profligate grants of office and title had been a feature of Buckingham's supremacy no less under Charles than under James. Soon after the duke's death, however, Charles resolved to grant no more. When a widow petitioned for the nomination of a baronetcy promised to her by Buckingham, 'the king told her he would not grant any

more of that kind'.[28] Action was taken to rectify the consequences of undiscriminating patronage. In June 1629 Charles
ordered that no peers with Irish or Scottish titles should be of the
commission of the peace, unless they also held estates in England.
Sir Edward Moundeford reported the new policy: 'There is a
general reformation in hand for court and county . . . offices shall
be given by desert, Sheriff-wicks shall be given as rewards of
honour to the best-deserving of the counties'. The 1630s saw a
return to the careful maintenance of aristocratic privilege.[29] It was
one characteristic of the old society of degree and deference for
which Charles increasingly yearned.

The king attached great importance to the role of the nobility
and gentry in the governance of the localities. Proclamations
ordering gentry dwelling in London to return to their country
seats, published since the late years of Elizabeth's reign, were
reissued in stronger language and enforced with great vigilance.
The prosecution of town dwellers in Star Chamber was not just a
fiscal device to bring money into the Exchequer. Charles was 'very
jealous of the prosecution of his proclamation against town
dwellers' and endeavoured, by ordering a detailed census of
inhabitants, to ensure that it was enforced.[30] The re-establishment
of authority in the localities, in the hands of the most important
local families, was a central beam of his social reconstruction.

That reconstruction incorporated action to suppress taverns and
tobacco, to end depopulation and dearth, to foster fishing and the
drainage of the fens.[31] How far the king's intentions went may,
perhaps, best be seen in London, 'our royal chamber and the principal state of our residence'. As London embodied the ills of the
age so it was, when reformed, to be the proof of the cure. The
treatment ranged from the work of the commission for buildings
to the regulation of hackney coaches, even to schemes for the
levelling and draining of streets, and the improvement of London
Bridge.[32] All were part of Charles's design to reduce the sprawling
anarchy of the metropolis to order, calm and decency.

It is in the context of these concerns, of this looking back to an
(idealized) society of harmony and deference that we should
understand Charles's religious policy. If order was Charles I's
private religion, then it behoved all the more that the religion of
the realm be ordered. Gardiner, in a perceptive phrase, captured
the central tenet of royal policy: 'the incongruity of dirt and
disorder with sacred things'.[33]

It is not usual to refer to the religious reforms and enactments
of the 1630s as the policy of Charles I. The name of Archbishop
Laud stamped itself on the religious history of that decade at the
time and has borne his imprint ever since. And yet it was the king's

policy. It is important to recall that Laud did not become Archbishop of Canterbury until August 1633 and that, until then, such influence as he exercised beyond his see of London, formidable though that was, he owed entirely to royal favour and support. In 1633 Laud was elected to oversee a programme with which he was known to be in sympathy, but which the king (albeit with his advice) had already devised. In 1626 and again in 1628 it was Charles who had attempted, over-optimistically and unsuccessfully, to stifle the growth of controversy by a declaration prefatory to the new edition of the Thirty-Nine Articles, a declaration which forbade 'unnecessary disputations' and ordered that 'all further curious search be laid aside'. In December 1629 the king issued instructions to the bishops, enjoining their residence, diligent performance of their duties and careful maintenance of their sees. Afternoon sermons were replaced by catechizing and lecturers were ordered to read divine service (in full vestments) before delivering their sermon.[34] Even after his elevation to Canterbury, the tone of Laud's letters suggests that it was the king who led and the archbishop who followed. The decision in the St. Gregory's case, for example, was the king's not Laud's: Laud specifically explained to John Williams that it was Charles and not he who disapproved of communion in the body of the church, not the chancel.[35] Throughout the 1630s royal letters reflect the king's personal concern with the Church, with the proper maintenance of the clergy and episcopacy, and with due observance of the forms of worship established by the Book of Common Prayer.[36] Charles determined to end theological controversy, to reform and to re-establish respect for the hierarchy of the Church and to order its service with a view to uniting the realm in a liturgy common to every parish. It was an ideal close to that of Elizabeth in 1559. It was now an ideal which embraced not only England, but all three kingdoms, and even the plantations. Supervision of ministers going to the colonies, instructions to the Lord Deputy of Ireland, and most of all royal policy towards the Scots all bear witness to 'that good conformity and unity in the church which his Majesty is careful and desirous to establish throughout his dominions'.[37]

It had been necessary to reform the court because it was the temple of God's lieutenant on earth. It was essential to order the Church because it was the palace of an invisible king. An ordered Church was also the foundation of the perfect commonweal which was the king's grand design. When he decided to govern without parliaments, Charles I did not resign himself to a hand-to-mouth struggle for mere survival; he embarked upon an ambitious renovation of the fabric of the Church and state.

IV

Policies and ideals without the instruments of their enactment belong to the world of utopia, not to that of affairs. Some indeed have argued that during the 1630s Charles was but a dreamer, concocting fantasies of a monarchical Elysium, ignorant of the obstacles to its realization and unconcerned with the measures by which ideal is translated into practice. Nothing could be further from the truth. No decade of seventeenth-century history was more concerned with (to borrow a phrase from the 1650s with which the 1630s have so much in common) the instruments of government.

In the first place, the Personal Rule saw the reinvigoration of the Privy Council. During the years of Buckingham's hegemony, the Council was eclipsed by private counsel, compromised by division and weakened by the exclusions of magnates powerful in their localities. During the war years and especially after 1628, the Council was formed into an efficient advisory body and an effective organ of government. Former enemies of Buckingham returned to the Council board.[38] The Lords President of the Marches and the North, and the Secretaries for Ireland and Scotland were added, presumably to facilitate communications with the outlying provinces and kingdoms. In the absence of a favourite, king and Council resumed their partnership for the government of the realm. The Council met regularly, usually twice weekly. The king himself was more frequently in attendance, especially after 1635 with the death of Weston and, more significantly, the launching of the ship-money fleet.[39] If the formal registers of the Council (like the formal journals of the Commons) provide the best evidence of the bulk and range of business, it is the notes of a secretary to the Council such as George Weckherlin which offer a valuable glimpse inside the Council chamber.[40] They suggest full debate, vocal differences, extensive research and renewed discussion prior to action. They indicate an ordered and efficient institution.

Pressure of business necessitated procedural developments. Committees of the Council, formerly *ad hoc* conventions, became standing bodies with regular times of meeting and their own clerical bureaucracy. The Irish committee, for example, met every Wednesday morning, and the committee for war (significantly in session until 1634) on Thursday afternoons. Committees generated sub-committees such as that for St. Paul's cathedral, a sub-division of the committee for charitable uses.[41] Royal requests for regular surveys, censuses and reports vastly increased the paperwork coming to the Council and, by consequence, improved its own record-keeping. Council orders of April 1632 required that the title of each subject discussed be entered in the margin of the appropriate page and indexed at the back of the book. In October of the next year, the clerk began to compile an abstract of unfinished business of the month, so that matters left incomplete would not lapse but would instead be given priority. Precedents were drawn up to facilitate the resolution of problems by references to past practice.[42] When we read through the Council register, when we peruse the clerks' notes or the memoranda left by Windebank and others, we cannot but be struck by the efficiency of the Council — by the sophistication of the procedure, by the diligence and continuity of its personnel. The 1630s might well be known for the winning of the initiative by the English Privy Council.

The Council was but the first link in the chain which connected the motor of central policy with the wheel of local action. There were no permanent agents of the central government to enact its will in the localities. And Charles I showed no desire, even had it been possible, to change the traditional structure. But he did attempt to revitalize the existing machinery and especially to improve the means by which the orders of the Council were communicated to the counties. In the absence of a parliament, that seminar of the English localities, it was all the more important to secure the other 'points of contact' between Council and county.[43]

Perhaps the most useful were the justices of assize making their twice-yearly circuit. At the end of Hilary term 1628 the Lord Keeper addressed them before they went, ordering them in the king's name to 'certify his Majesty of the state of the several places of the kingdom and how they found the counties governed and that they should cherish such as they found diligent and careful in the execution of justice and certify the names of such as they found negligent and careless'. The Book of Orders of January 1631 further extended and formalized the role of the justices as roving reporters and superintendents of royal policy. In the summer of the same year Charles exhorted them especially to oversee the execution of his orders and to ensure that the gentry maintained their seats in the country. In 1635, the justices went out to explain and to justify the second writ of ship money. Not without cause were they described by the Lord Keeper as 'visitors of the kingdom'.[44]

But that of course was *exactly* what they were: occasional visitors to counties and provinces of which they otherwise had little knowledge. As such they were of limited value both as agents in and reporters from the localities. There were potentially more effective instruments. In May 1629, one Lionel Sharpe, lamenting the parliament's misunderstanding of the king's good intentions, advised Secretary Dorchester, that 'to make the king known, there are no fitter instruments than the lord lieutenants and the bishops. They might make known the excellent mind and nature of the king to his people'.[45] It may be that the king and Council endorsed this analysis. During the 1630s the number of lords-lieutenant was increased so that almost every county had its own lieutenant and most more than one. Sons of magnates were joined in the commission with their fathers, perhaps in order to familiarize them with their charge and to establish a degree of continuity in office. Those not required at court on the king's business were ordered to reside in their lieutenancies and to oversee personally the organization of the militia and the mustering of troops.[46] Similarly, the bishops were placed on the commission of the peace and permitted to leave their seats only by licence from the king. They could, if they were as diligent as Bishop Wren, be an invaluable source of information and a reliable source of royal policy.[47]

And yet for all this the English counties were not governed from the centre. At the vital end of the chain of command were the unpaid local officers — the gentry deputy lieutenants and justices of the peace, the parish constables and church-wardens from the lower social orders. In so far as he derived his authority from letters patent under the Great Seal, was responsible for his behaviour to the Council and was reluctant to lose the prestige attaching to the position, the justice of the peace was the king's man in the county. But in so far as he there held his estates, there enjoyed the society of friends and neighbours, there felt responsibility for his tenants and inferiors, there himself paid the rates which he helped to levy, the justice was the pinnacle and embodiment of local society — bound by interest and expectations to protect its customs and represent its needs. The absence of parliament, and the Book of Orders itself underlined the duality of the position. Local government depended upon local knowledge. This remained essentially the monopoly of local men. The lords-lieutenant who diligently attended the Council, or wantonly sported in the West End, knew all too little of the counties in their charge. Devoid of any other agents, the Council was forced to rely upon the propertied gentry who resided on their estates. The compositions for knighthood demonstrated their dependence. At first the Privy Councillors compounded with offenders. But, after a poor start, the commission was extended into the localities and leading gentry were appointed because they alone would know who, possessed of £40 annual rent, should have come forward.

We are well assured that by your industries and knowledge of the persons of men and their estates you may . . . better the same in many things, for whereas our commissioners . . . were led for the most part by subsidy rolls . . . they might easily mistake the true values of men which you by your better knowledge of them may be more truly informed of.[48]

With or without parliaments, the government of early Stuart England rested upon co-operation and consent.

V

To what extent then was co-operation secured? Did the members of parliament who returned to their localities in 1629 seek to obstruct the government by Council? Were the aims and ideals of Charles I anathema to the gentry rulers of the counties? Were the problems encountered by king and Council manufactured by constitutional conflict or inherent in the structure of the English polity?

Such questions are hard to answer qualitatively. Silence, or even letters of support from the localities, could conceal diligent activity, grudging compliance, at times even outright resistance. The certificates performed according to the requirements of the Book of Orders ranged from the brief 'all well' to the multipage report.[49] And whilst we should not equate detail of information with extent of activity, we may still deduce something from it. As Rowland St. John advised Edward Montagu: 'It is observed to be a rule of discreet policy in general businesses to make a general answer, lest by descending too far into particulars something should be fastened upon which may produce an unexpected prejudice'.[50] Vagueness, in other words, could cloak a multitude of sins. It is impossible to calculate how many avoided composition for knighthood by a false return of their income, but the excuses certainly arouse suspicion.[51] On the other hand, few doubted the need for measures to deal with grain shortage and unemployment. Few questioned the legality of knighthood fines. For all the evasions, the Book of Orders was successful and the compositions for knighthood brought £173,537 into the Exchequer.[52] If there was opposition, it did not in the end prevent payment. Beyond that all we can say is that the curve of response ranged from grudging to enthusiastic.

At two points it is possible to be more specific: the quest for an 'exact militia' and the levy of ship money. In so far as the one required soldiers and the other money the response to each can be measured. The effort to increase the numbers, sharpen the skill and modernize the equipment of the local militia was beleaguered by a multitude of problems. After 1604 and the repeal of 4 and 5 Philip and Mary caps 2 and 3, the authority of lieutenancy lost its foundation on statute and rested entirely on the prerogative — exposed to challenge from those with more enthusiasm for legal niceties than for military exercise. In February 1632, one Walters, an attorney, refused to contribute to the musters in Northamptonshire and stood 'upon the letter of the law'.[53] But there were more serious difficulties even at the centre. In the first place the lords lieutenant who first received instructions were often the very members of the Council who had issued them. Absent from their commissions and preoccupied with other business they were content to pass the burden of supervision to the deputies who 'best understand the state of the county and men's abilities therein'.[54] But no less than the justices, among whose number they ranked, the deputy lieutenants were first and foremost local men. With an authority that some questioned and with little support from absentee superiors, they were obliged to muster the reluctant pikemen and corsleteers (many perhaps their own tenants) and, in the case of the horse, the gentry of the county, their social equals and fellow justices. It is hardly surprising that it was always the number of horse which was most deficient.[55] The difficulties which faced the deputies were exacerbated by memory of the war years during which they had assisted with the loan, imposed martial law and billeted unruly troops on unwilling households, often without funds to reimburse them. That memory, as it fuelled their unpopularity, so it sapped their authority. The repeated injunctions of king and Council suggests that orders were not obeyed. In 1638 Charles admitted that former directories were 'not finding effects answerable to our expectations'.[56] The perfect militia proved an unrealizable goal.

But was the programme an unrelieved failure? The answer to that must be no. The very complaints about musters during the 1630s, and about deputy lieutenants in 1640, suggest that some effort was being made locally.[57] And study of the extensive militia records among the papers of Sir Thomas Jervoise, a deputy lieutenant of Hampshire, indicates clearly that, for all it fell short of the ideal, the militia of that county saw some improvement. Jervoise and his fellow deputies were diligent in their attention to business. Even where there was less enthusiasm for service, the Council was not completely helpless. Sir John Holland, deputy lieutenant for Norfolk, felt acutely the need for action after signs of Council disapproval: 'The Council's letters requiring diligence and expedition, the tax of our late remissness from our lords lieutenants are all spurs to quicken us in this service . . . The lords, I believe, will listen after our diligence and there will be them at leisure to give intelligence'.[58] The county militia never rose to the standards for which Wentworth would have laboured. Foot-dragging was common and hard to prevent. But if the achievement fell short of the expectation, the horse and foot of the county militia were driven to greater activity, more frequent exercise, perhaps greater expenditure on arms than had been, or was considered desirable.[59]

The great success story, however, was ship money. Ship money was a rate, not a tax, collected at first from the maritime counties, but after 1635 from the whole country. It owed its origins to royal diplomacy, and especially the king's negotiations with Spain.[60] It was never a source of ordinary revenue and was received not into the Exchequer, but into the Treasury of the Navy. It is important to bear in mind that ship money was not, and was never demanded (whatever was intended), as a regular or permanent levy. Each writ was a *separate* request for aid in time of national emergency; the preface to each writ explained and justified the need to equip a fleet for the year. It may be that the early responses of the country reflected a genuine recognition (after the debacle of 1628) of the need for a strong navy in a worn-torn Europe.[61] It is significant certainly that when the writ was extended from the maritime counties to the country at large, the point at which the legality might have been questioned, only 2½ per cent of the sum requested failed to come in, and the amount raised, £194,864, was never exceeded. The success story continued as we shall see, and it was not until 1639 and 1640 that the collection of ship money collapsed.[62] So much for the figures. What may we learn from the success and final failure of ship money about Charles I's government, and reactions to his government, during the years of Personal Rule?

The first response to the writ was bewilderment in the localities: doubts about *how* to proceed to rate the maritime towns and individual inhabitants. The first writ of 1634 left the assessment of the corporate towns to the mayors and civic authorities meeting together. This immediately posed problems, as the mayor of Dover explained to the Earl of Suffolk, Lord Warden of the Cinque Ports: 'Such is the distance of these towns and cities . . . that [we] are at an exigent and know not where to begin or what to do'.[63] The Council learnt by the experience. When the writ was extended the following year, they suggested the amount to be paid by the corporate towns within the counties. Beyond those suggestions, the assessment was to be made by the sheriff, who was exhorted to have 'more than ordinary care and regard' in the apportionment 'to prevent complaints of inequality in the assessment whereby we were much troubled last year'. In general he was advised to rate according to the houses and lands within the county, or to follow the other public payments 'most equal and agreeable' to the inhabitants.[64] But if this were an attempt to resolve all the earlier problems, it failed. Rating disputes remained the biggest headache.[65] Complaints about unequal assessment and favouritism came to both the sheriff and the Council. Often they contradicted each other. On the one hand the Council had ordered the sheriff to rate according to property: on the other it enjoined that poor cottagers should be spared and those of no estate but considerable personal wealth be assessed in their stead. Amid these conflicting dictates there was room for much confusion, protest and misunderstanding. The most diligent sheriffs perhaps met with the greatest difficulties. Sir George Sondys, sheriff of Kent for part of 1636 and 1637, was well respected in his county for his efforts to give all complaints a hearing and to settle all disputes fairly. Not surprisingly, as a result, 'there was in some places not less than six if not seven warrants or orders from him and his undersheriff in one and the same matter, each contradicting the other'.[66] At times the Council created the problem. Continuing to act as the final and impartial arbiter of disputes, it overruled and contradicted the assessment made by a sheriff according to its own directions.[67] Ship money exemplifies the problems of early modern government: problems of interest, division and localism, most of all the problem of dependence — the dependence of the Council upon the sheriff, of the sheriff on the constable, ultimately the dependence of all upon the preparedness of those assessed to pay.

And yet because ship money was collected, because the proportion returned of the sum expected was far higher than subsidies, better than any contemporary levy and certainly more impressive than modern taxation, it must also be regarded as evidence of what could be done when the Council and local officers devoted themselves to the task. By making the sheriff solely responsible for payment, the Council ensured a devoted servant of central policy in the county. Because his own interest was at stake, the sheriff laboured to overcome the difficulties and to raise the whole sum. Why then did ship money collapse?

Here we should return to an earlier point: ship money was not a regular tax, but a levy for a specific purpose. The Council itself seemed to act upon that assumption. The writ of 1638 demanded less than a third of the sum previously required, presumably because the Scots War focused attention upon a different emergency, one which would require troops rather than ships. The return, as we have seen, was low and the next year, when the Council (unwisely) raised the sum to earlier heights, the response was poorer. For ship money was now demanded along with other more pressing, more costly and certainly more disruptive requests for men to join the army at York and money to equip and transport them.[68] Sheriffs preoccupied with raising troops could not devote their undivided attention to the collection of ship money. In some counties they even acquiesced, under the pressure of time and circumstance, in using the money they had garnered to speed the troops north. The most diligent collectors met with resistance, especially from the lower orders, those most affected by the demands of the war. And when they lost the co-operation of the parish constables, when they could no longer distrain goods, nor sell confiscated property, the sheriffs were powerless.[69] When the sheriff could do nothing, the exhortations and threats of the Council lost their force. The collapse of ship money in 1639 takes us back to the problems of the later 1620s: problems that arose when England was called upon to fight a war. It points too to the weakness of the Council when there was too much business to supervise, too little co-operation in the counties. The success and the failure of ship money reflect the strengths and weaknesses of early modern government.

In discussing ship money we have confined ourselves to the practical problems of government. We have said nothing of the constitutional grounds. That is because before 1637 there is little to say. Before Hampden there are almost no recorded instances of objection to the levy on legal or constitutional grounds.[70] Complaints were confined to rating disputes; protests were limited to unfair assessments. Some have argued that these complaints cannot be distinguished from more principled objections. Rating disputes, they argue, were the respectable veils which covered more principled objections. Those principles plaintiffs not unnaturally silenced when appealing to the Council for more practical measures, such as redress of unfair assessments.[71] Such arguments must be taken seriously. When we reflect that Tintinhull hundred, Somerset, the home of that irrepressible parliamentarian, Sir Robert Phelips, produced more rating disputes than any other hundred in the kingdom, we are bound to suspect some opposition from principle.[72] Certainly we should not lightly assume constitutional acquiescence from silence. For at least one adviser sympathetic to ship money considered that 'in every place there are some malevolent spirits that labour to poison and censure the most honourable actions, blasting this for an imposition, an innovation against the liberty of the subject'. . .[73] But yet the absence of vocal protest remains remarkable. Sheriffs who might have drawn some advantage, certainly some sympathy from the Council, from attributing delays to nice constitutional scruples seldom refer to objections of principle. More often administrative difficulties are set in contrast to a general willingness to pay — a willingness which is more convincing when endorsed by the sheriff and translated into action and money. In Gloucester in November 1634, for example, though feeling was strong that the city was overrated, 'the chief inhabitants encouraged the payment rather than the service should be retarded'.[74] Purses were more in evidence than principles. Doubtless there was in letters to the Council an element of loyal rhetoric which at times concealed resentment and antagonism; doubtless ship money was paid, like any tax, with resignation rather than with enthusiasm. But before 1637 there is little *evidence* at least that its legality was widely questioned, and some suggestion that it was becoming more accepted.

It was John Hampden who raised the issue of principle and so took ship money to the law.[75] Hampden's case, the arguments of counsel, the eventual decision for the crown by the narrowest majority are well known. The news spread widely at the time.[76] During the year of decision, many delayed payment in anticipation of the judgement, perhaps in hope that the king might abandon the levy. But whatever his place in the portrait gallery of martyrs for English constitutionalism, Hampden should not loom too large on the canvas of Personal Rule. As the Earl of Leicester was informed by his secretary, ship money was in debate, 'but in the interim the money is in collecting'. The case may also have caused as much concern to the country as to the crown. Clarendon suggests that before Hampden's case many were pleased to pay a levy which they were not bound to. And even before the final judgement, one newswriter was 'of opinion it had been better for the people that this question had never been put to dispute, for if the judgement be on the king's side, . . . then it will be as a perpetual case and law and may for ever be continued'.[77] He may have been right. As we shall see, in the year of Hampden's case more than 90 per cent was collected. If the trial delayed payments and raised the question of legality, the final decision, unwelcome though it was, may have resolved more legal doubts than it aroused.

VI

And so we come to the fundamental question. Did the Bishops' War accelerate the journey along the high road to civil war, or force a detour into a conflict which had never been in sight? Could Charles have succeeded, could the Personal Rule have continued without the rebellion of the northern kingdom?

The question itself is inappropriate, for it assumes that Charles had decided permanently to govern without parliament. This was not the case. The declaration of 1629, that the king would call another parliament, 'when our people shall see more clearly into our interests and actions' should, I think, be taken literally. Wentworth seems so to have understood it. In 1635, triumphant after the success of parliament in Ireland, he reflected upon the situation at home:

> Happy it were if we might live to see the like in England; everything in his season; but in some cases it is necessary there be a time to forget, as in others to learn, and howbeit the peccant . . . Humour be not yet wholly purged forth, yet do I conceive it in the way, and that once rightly corrected and prepared, we may hope for a parliament of a sound constitution indeed . . .[78]

If Wentworth saw a high road stretching before him, its destination was a world of harmony in which king and parliament would work together. But what of others?

After the unruly scene of 1629, the early 1630s were marked by calm and quiet, at court and throughout the country. Clarendon recalled that 'there quickly followed so excellent a composure throughout the whole kingdom that the like peace and plenty and universal tranquillity for ten years was never enjoyed by any nation'.[79] Peace brought the expansion of trade and the benefits of neutrality in a Europe at war. The merchants soon abandoned their protest about customs duties. Some MPs imprisoned in 1629 made their apologies and were pardoned. Sir John Eliot himself faded from the public eye. His death in the Tower in 1632 attracted little attention: 'Sir John Eliot is dead in the Tower who is no otherwise considerable here but among the dead'.[80] The events of 1629 had caused concern to MPs themselves and to the many who heard the news of them in the country. In 1630 there may well have been support for government initiatives like the Book of Orders which tackled pressing problems neglected by legislation. When Charles I went on progress to Scotland in 1633, he was evidently a monarch popular with his people. The king, it was reported, 'enjoyed the love and dutiful demonstrations of his subjects in every place': he received 'the acclamations of his people everywhere and their expressions of joy and contentment'.[81]

The calm and peace continued. The ordinary budget was better balanced. Ship money was generally paid despite the difficulties. Undoubtedly there were tensions and grievances: Charles's religious policy, framed to unite the realm in a common liturgy, divided the Church and alienated some of the gentry. But those tensions and grievances neither stymied government nor threatened revolt.

Most, Clarendon tells us, thought that *'imperium et libertas* were as well reconciled as possible'.[82] In the many volumes of correspondence, public and private, we find few demands for a parliament. Nor should that surprise us. James I had called no parliament from 1614 to 1621. After 1624 war necessitated frequent sessions; with the peace those circumstances changed. In 1629 parliament was still an event; it was not an institution.[83]

On the eve of Hampden's case, in October 1637, John Burgh penned his weekly despatch to Viscount Scudamore, then ambassador in Paris. The political climate, as he described it, was far from threatening:

All things are at this instant here in that calmness that there is very little matter of novelty to write, for there appears no change or alteration either in court or affairs, for all business goes undisturbedly on in the strong current of the present time to which all men for the most part submit, and that effects this quietness. And though payments here are great (considering the people have not heretofore been accustomed unto them) yet they only privately breathe out a little discontented humour and lay down their purses, for I think that great tax of the ship money is so well digested (the honour of the business sinking now into apprehension and amongst most winning an affection to it) I suppose will become perpetual; for indeed if men would consider the great levies of monies in foreign parts for the service of the state, these impositions would appear but little burdens, but time can season and form minds to comply with public necessities.[84]

Time indeed might well have done. But even without the Scots would Charles have had that time? For all his vision down the long road to parliamentary government, Gardiner remained unsure: 'How long this state of things would have endured if no impulse had come from without it is impossible to say'.[85] There were undoubtedly difficulties and problems which *might* in the long run have made personal government unsustainable. The co-operation of those who bore the massive burdens of collecting knighthood fines or ship money could not for certain be secured indefinitely. Yet the diligence exhibited by many, even in 1639 and 1640, must not be underestimated. The relative youth of the royalists in 1642 suggests, perhaps, a maturing generation supportive of the king's personal rule. To contemplate what might have happened had the Scots not risen is no idle parlour game; it is an exercise of the historical imagination, central to an understanding of the past.

In the end we come back to the Bishops' Wars. At first the troubles in Scotland presaged no major crisis. In January 1638, Sir John Finet, Master of Ceremonies, devoted more correspondence to his problems of seating ambassadors at the masque than to the news of events in the north. Only by April did he begin to fear that the Scots question would not be settled 'without mischief'.[86] It is important to reflect that when he resolved to enforce obedience by arms Charles was evidently optimistic — not only of victory, but of the willingness of the localities to co-operate with the levy of men and money. If this was misplaced optimism, it was at least shared by others and not without sense. For all his opposition to English involvement in Europe, Wentworth supported the decision to fight the Scots. In November 1639, Colonel Gage could not perceive 'why it should not be feasible to raise and maintain a good army at the charge of the shires of England, as it hath been to compass the contribution of the ship money. I am confident that if in the country there were fit ministers and willing to second such a design, it would be effected with a great facility'.[87] Even that condition did not seem beyond hope of fulfilment. The Scots were old enemies and ballads sung in 1639 gave voice to English jingoism. Sheriffs and deputy lieutenants worked loyally to conduct the troops to York. But the war proved unpopular and changed the whole course of affairs. Why?

War revived the problems and grievances of 1628. The demand for coat and conduct money raised legal, administrative and fiscal problems. In many counties the cost of equipping soldiers equalled (and at times surpassed) that of ship money which was still demanded. The levy of troops from the trained bands gave rise to fears of invasion in a realm schooled by ship money writs to anticipate imminent danger. Hampshire, remote from Scotland, offered excuses instead of men, on the grounds that the coast was vulnerable. The loss of young adult males caused more than emotional disturbance to many a village or hundred. Parts of Cornwall protested that the removal of men led to a labour shortage which resulted in the flooding of the tin mines. Grievances were expressed most vocally by the lower orders, those most affected in any age by the demands and miseries of war. The most diligent sheriffs, deputies and justices faced recalcitrance and riot. The Council could offer little help. Central policy now threatened local order. It was impossible to preserve them both. The issues at stake were not constitutional. 'What had changed between 1634 and 1639 was not the gentry's opinion of Charles's constitutional arguments, but the breakdown of peace, quiet and order in the local communities.[88] In 1640, the gentry no less than the king met with resistance from below.

The decision to summon parliament, for all that it defused the electric atmosphere, exacerbated some of the problems. Even in 1640 ship money was paid well in Hampshire until the issue of writs for elections to parliament. Few thereafter would pay a levy which might be questioned or when subsidies would certainly be granted. Similarly the deputy lieutenants of Devonshire, mindful of 1628, feared being criticized in parliament.[89] With the war and the summoning of parliament all was again in flux. Personal Rule was at an end.

War undoubtedly provided the opportunity for the expression of discontents. But more significantly, because on a wider plain, it created problems and grievances not in evidence before. At court, the decision to fight the Scots meant the end of domestic reform, a crash from financial stability to indebtedness and the distraction of the Council from the business of normal government.[90] In the counties, that decision, like the wars of the 1620s, strained the fabric of local government and threatened the peace of local society. The problems which faced Charles I from 1638 to 1640, problems similar to those which faced the kings of France and Spain, caused no less difficulty to the republican regimes of the 1650s. They were problems rooted less in the constitution than in the structure of English government. Charles was too conservative ever to seek to change that structure. It was his achievement to have governed so ambitiously and so successfully within it. If local intransigence and a stand on local customs are milestones on a high road of English history, it is a road which leads past civil war, indeed beyond the Restoration. It is a road which leads not to the triumph of parliament, but to the erosion of provincialism: a road which ends with the railways?

4. Archbishop William Laud and the University of Oxford*

1. A reappraisal

William Laud was a controversial figure from his student days in Oxford in the 1590s to his death on the scaffold in 1645. Laud rose to prominence in a period during which it became clear that the Church of England meant different things to different men. These were decades which witnessed theological wrangles between the Calvinists (who asserted that men were predestined to either salvation or reprobation) and the Arminians who believed in God's universal grace and the free will of man. They were years too of sharper disagreements over the liturgy between those who rejected and those who emphasized the ceremonies prescribed in the canons of the Church and the Book of Common Prayer. Laud's career reflected as well as affected the course of those wrangles and disputes. Not surprisingly he has remained the subject of controversy ever since.

To some a martyr for the Church of England, to others a crypto-Catholic who corrupted it, judgements on the archbishop have too often reflected religious preferences more than careful consideration of the evidence. Those who brought Laud to trial in 1644 charged him with innovation, Arminianism and popery. Recently, after centuries of disagreement, historians have come close to endorsing those charges: William Laud, the historical verdict now has it, was the prelate who introduced novel doctrines and elaborate ceremony, the archbishop who wrecked the Elizabethan and Jacobean compromise — in the words of Patrick Collinson, 'the greatest calamity ever visited upon the Church of England'. Some would argue that Laud thereby fostered an even greater calamity: by exciting fears that an Arminian was but the spawn of a papist, he fuelled the paranoia about popery which kindled the civil war.

Both the disagreements of contemporaries and the recent

unanimity among historians would have puzzled Laud himself. For where he met with controversy, he eschewed it; in contrast to the charge of innovation he asserted his conservatism. How are we to explain this? Not least of the obstacles in the way of understanding is the nature of the evidence. Laud is too often depicted from the standpoint and propaganda of his enemies. His own letters and speeches, even more his sermons and treatises, remain inexplicably neglected. Yet Laud's own words cast a different light upon his intentions and better knowledge of his intentions in turn illuminates his actions.

It seems appropriate some three hundred and fifty years after his elevation to the see of Canterbury, to allow William Laud to speak for and explain himself. On the supposedly crucial questions of theology, however, he spoke and wrote little. Laud framed no new articles, nor crafted any new catechism for the Church. His silence is itself informative: Laud did not debate doctrine because it was not of great interest to him. Whilst, on royal orders, he entered reluctantly ('I am no controvertist') into theological debate with the Catholics, he never took up the theological cudgel against the puritans. Laud's personal doctrinal beliefs elude us — and probably never taxed him. At his trial, he denied that he was an Arminian and if there is any evidence to question the denial it escaped the searches of his indefatigable prosecutor, William Prynne. Even during the more comfortable days of his ascendancy, Laud never attempted to create an Arminian clergy — either as Chancellor of Oxford or as Archbishop of Canterbury. Once again his position is perhaps best explained by his own words, to the Master of Trinity College, Cambridge, who was composing a pro-Arminian treatise on predestination: 'I am yet where I was, that something about these controversies is unmasterable in this life'.

But because he campaigned for no doctrinal position, we should not assume that Laud was loyal to no church. Laud was devoted to the Church of England, that is to a church of apostolic antiquity, that part of the universal Catholic Church which had preserved the purity of the primitive church by casting off the corruptions and accretions of Roman superstition. While the Church of England insisted upon subscription to certain articles of faith, it did not, like the Roman Catholic Church, press what were only opinions or preferences by 'making them matters of necessary belief'. When disputed questions arose, they were to be settled by the Head of the Church and the bishops. Concerning things indifferent men might hold what opinions they would in private, showing only such public obedience as was necessary for the peace of the Church.

For first and foremost, Laud sought peace and unity, urging that

'in and about things not necessary, there ought not to be a contention to a separation'. It was a philosophy which he practised as
well as preached. Laud resolved 'in handling matters of religion to
leave all gall out of my ink'. His support for royal proclamations
forbidding disputes, his friendship and correspondence with
Catholics and puritans, his patronage of divines with whom he
probably disagreed are all evidence of the enactment of that resolution. In the one work of theology which he published that men
'may see and judge of my religion', Laud declared a faith in Christ
'as it was professed in the ancient Primitive Church and as it is
professed in the present Church of England'. His greatest wish, he
maintained, was that theological differences 'were not pursued
with such heat and animosity'.

Laud's one work of theology, his *Conference with Fisher the
Jesuit*, is not often read. It is ironic that one of the best defences
of the Church of England against Rome was penned by a prelate
charged with popery. When we read its pages, we are struck by its
moderation and oecumenism, not by denominational zeal or
fanaticism. This was the work which together with Hooker's *Laws
of Ecclesiastical Polity* and the works of Lancelot Andrewes,
Charles I was to give to his daughter as the corpus of Anglicanism.
In the preface to the second edition of 1639, Laud took up the
subject which was central to his career as bishop, archbishop and
Privy Councillor: a concern for order and decency. To Laud:

> No one thing hath made conscientious men more wavering in their own
> minds, or more apt and easy to be drawn aside from the sincerity of
> religion professed in the Church of England than the want of uniform
> and decent order in too many churches of the Kingdom.

External worship was the outward witness and bulwark of the
inner faith. And external worship was manifested in and through
ceremonies. Ceremonies were not the essence of religion: men
should not place 'the principal part of . . . piety in them'. But
ceremonies were necessary as 'the hedge that fence the substance
of religion from all the indignities . . .' While there was room
within the Church for differences of belief and doctrine, the hedge
of ceremony, in order to protect the Church, had to be uniform in
all its parts: 'unity cannot long continue in the church where
uniformity is shut out at the church door'. A belief in uniformity
of ceremony as the essential prop of inner spirituality was not
new: it had been the policy of Archbishops Parker, Whitgift and
Bancroft and of Queen Elizabeth herself. And in the 1630s it was
not the concern only of Archbishop Laud, but of Charles I himself.

To the King and his archbishop the external fabric and outward
worship of the church were subjects of urgent concern. Churches

with decaying roofs and broken windows, churchyards with wandering swine or open privies, no less services devoid of prescribed ceremonies and canonical vestments, invited the papist to scoff at and the sceptic to suspect a poverty of faith within. In the eyes of Charles I and Laud, those who had laid stress upon the preaching of God's word had exhibited too little care of his home. Laud did not wish to denigrate sermons: he believed them 'the most necessary expositions and application of Holy Scripture'; he preached them regularly. But the Church embraced tradition as well as Scripture, the sacrament as well as the word. And so in the detailed articles of enquiry issued for Laud's metropolitical visitation, we find a painstaking concern for the condition of the church, the churchyard and the church furniture and for the diligence of the bishops, the clergy and the parish officers. Like the Statutes which as Chancellor he drew up for Oxford University, Laud's visitation articles, as Archbishop of Canterbury, were intended above all to secure order and discipline.

Order and discipline required effective authority within the Church. Because he believed the Church 'overgrown, not only with weeds within it, but with trees and bushes about it', Laud stressed the authority of the bishops and clergy as the gardeners who might best prune them. If he was concerned to repel the encroachments made by the laity upon the terrain of clerical jurisdiction, it was because only the clergy and episcopacy could enforce the order and uniformity which hedged the Church. Lay patronage to livings or the common lawyers' challenge to the church courts weakened the authority of the Church and undermined the uniformity which was its support. Charles I agreed: 'I will have no Priest have any necessity of a lay dependency'. Behind the attempts to bolster the fiscal independence, quality, power and prestige of the clergy lay their central purpose: the concern for decency and order in matters sacred.

It was a goal pursued with more moderation than fanaticism. Laud preferred persuasion to suppression, believing that the attractions of the 'beauty of holiness' would soon become self-evident. In answer to the charges of his enemies, Laud boasted that he had deprived fewer clergy than his predecessor, the latitudinarian Archbishop Abbot. There is much evidence to support the claim. Laud proceeded 'tenderly' with a mad lecturer at Leicester who had been expelled by the Dean of the Arches; with the foreign congregations at Canterbury, even in 1638, he believed it 'fitting to keep a moderate hand'. In visitation articles, he enjoined upon the clergy 'mildness and temperance' in order to win over recusants. With regard to receiving the communion at the altar rails, he left it as a matter of conscience, maintaining that 'the people will best be won by the decency of the thing itself'. Laud made painstaking efforts to win over the refractory. Only those who could not be won, those who would not subscribe to the articles and ceremonies prescribed in the Prayer Book and canons, were forced from the Church and, in some cases, the country. Concerning such refractory nonconformists, Charles I himself issued the orders: 'let him go; we are well rid of him'.

Throughout his archiepiscopacy Laud remained very much the King's man. A monarch obsessed with order and uniformity, in Church as in state, Charles I had elevated Laud not for his theology (he was no theologian) nor even primarily for his counsel (Charles knew his own mind) but for his concern with ceremony and his pertinacity as an administrator. Laud was not always 'master of this work, but a servant to it'. The King by letters, instructions, audiences, by marginal comment on visitation reports, chivvied the archbishop who in turn harried the episcopacy and clergy. Often Charles proved more intransigent that Laud. It was Charles I who, after hearing the St. Gregory's case at the Council board, recommended the altar be set at the east end of the church; Laud enquired only whether it was placed in 'such convenient sort within the chancel or church as the minister may be best heard'. But on most matters the architect and his patron shared a common vision of the final edifice: a church built from the fabric of decency and ceremony — the place for worship in peace and uniformity.

It is an irony that it was Archbishop Laud (and King Charles) with whom the puritans went to war. For both in his policies and in his personality, Laud had much in common with them. Like the puritans he sought an upright and well-educated clergy; like them he was virulent against popery, hard against clerical failings and intolerant of lay profligacy. Like the puritans he urged harsh measures against drunkenness and incontinency — be it in the counties or colleges of England. Personally too, Laud, like his royal master, was an intense, ascetic and self-disciplined figure. His diary, a record of dreams, omens, and insecurities, of the application of scriptural text to everyday life, has been aptly described as a puritan document. His portrait, a dark brooding figure, suggests a sombre demeanour and stern determination which even the flamboyant romanticism of Van Dyck failed, or never attempted, to soften. It was their tragedy — and that of the Church — that Laud and the puritans shared a mutual fear, a common paranoia. To him, the nonconformists, in undermining the uniformity of external worship, threatened the fabric of Church and State. To them, after years of laxity, an insistence upon ceremony and an emphasis upon the position of the clergy smacked of popery. By examining Laud's words, we have seen that had they known more of his intentions, the fears of the puritans might well have been calmed. Those who knew Laud well neither feared nor suspected him. Philip Warwick, a gentleman of the bed-chamber, thought his 'grand design was no other that that of our first Reformation'. But it was that Reformation which others felt Laud might reverse. As Clarendon was astutely to reflect, he failed to make 'his designs and purposes appear as candid as they were'.

2. Archbishop Laud and the University of Oxford

In April 1630 William Laud was appointed Chancellor of the University of Oxford. He regarded it as his first duty to reform the University 'which was extremely sunk from all discipline'. From the outset he addressed himself vigorously to the task. He sent frequent letters and injunctions to the university designed to prevent the accumulation of degrees, to end disorders at disputations, to enforce the wearing of proper academic dress and in short to maintain in all aspects of university life, order, decency and formality 'which are in a sort the outward and visible face of the university'. The outstanding result of his effort to reform was the new code of statutes which Strickland Gibson, that eminent Oxford scholar and Keeper of University Archives, described as 'perhaps the greatest piece of university legislation ever successfully brought to completion.[1] Few would argue with that verdict. Even more than for his generous gifts of coins and manuscripts, more than for his establishment of lectureships in Arabic and Hebrew, Archbishop Laud, as Chancellor of Oxford, is most remembered for the code of statutes which bears his name.

The process of compiling the new statutes was long and laborious. Laud's involvement began before his appointment as Chancellor when he urged William, third Earl of Pembroke, then Chancellor of Oxford, to instigate a complete reformation of the university statutes.[2] It ended seven years later in June 1636 when Secretary Sir John Coke delivered to the university a book of statutes signed by Laud and sealed by Charles I as the official volume to be lodged in the university archives.[3] During the intervening years Laud participated energetically in the compilation of the new code.[4] The bulk of the labour of collating and correcting old statutes was borne initially by the delegates appointed by Pembroke — most notably by Brian Twyne the antiquarian scholar and Fellow of Corpus. But after August 1633 when Convocation, the governing body of the university, sent the draft of the new statutes for his consideration,[5] the directing hand was that of Laud himself.[6] It was he who now composed the final version and arranged for the new statute book to be printed in 1634. Nor did Laud confine himself, in reviewing the delegates' draft, to mere forms or trifles. When the new statutes, now printed, were presented to Convocation in July 1634 — almost a year since his draft had been submitted — Twyne complained that not only by the delegates who compiled them, but also by the heads of colleges who attended the weekly meetings at which the draft statutes were read, 'there were many alterations perceived and discovered in diverse passages and particulars both in phrase and substance'. Indeed 'there were many innovations discovered which we thought not of and many things hooked in and left out'.[7]

These innovations and alterations were again Laud's own. For though in revising the delegates' draft he continued to call upon the assistance of one of their number — Peter Turner of Merton — Laud tells us that he reserved to himself 'the last consideration of all'.[8] After 1633 there was no consultation. Laud's statute book was delivered to the university as a *fait accompli* — to be obeyed, not discussed, to be received by Convocation not voted on by it. He intended it to be received by the university as royal legislation.[9] Even when the statutes were printed, however, Laud's labour was not ended. He announced to Convocation that the new code was to hold authority for only a trial period ending in September 1635 after which he would himself finally settle the statutes 'reserving to myselfe power . . . to adde that which shall be fit and alter or take away from those statutes that which shall be found to be either unnecessary or incommodious'.[10] The final version, in which manuscript emendations and additions were entered in the printed book, was not ready until the summer of 1636.[11] On June 22 Secretary Sir John Coke addressed the Convocation which was held to receive the new constitution of the university, and a commission, appointed by the King, took acknowledgement from the heads of houses that they accepted the statutes as the laws by which they would govern and be governed.[12]

It was three years since Laud had taken personal charge of the task — years during which he had been not only elevated to the see of Canterbury, but also appointed to committees of the Council for Ireland and the Treasury, for foreign affairs and finance. Why in the midst of his public business had Laud devoted so much time to the government of Oxford? What did he set out to achieve by the new statutes? How readily were they obeyed, how effectively enforced? Finally, what may we learn from Laud's activities as Chancellor about his wider aims and ideals for the governance of church and state? Such questions lead us to consider the nature and reception of the new statutes which enshrined Laud's policy for the university and, perhaps, his hopes for the future of the commonwealth.

The amended statute book of 1636 saw a myriad of revisions — most of them intended to explain the statutes more precisely and to plug the loopholes through which miscreants had escaped during the probationary year. They are testimony to Laud's concern for detail and the care and attention which he had brought to the task. Tutors were now admonished to supervise the behaviour and appearance as well as the studies of their students; provisions were made to ensure that lectures took place, lasted the specified hour and made an original contribution to the subject; fines were imposed on those who failed to attend at disputations; residence qualifications for degrees were defined more strictly; and, in general, more checks and severer punishments were decreed in matters of discipline. The statute book was supplemented too by an epinomis — an addition or appendix after Plato — which declared that those who offended against the statutes were not guilty of that crime alone. Because the statutes enjoined the taking of oaths, breach of them was also perjury. The new code not only prescribed in detail what was expected and required. It also invested wide powers in the university officers responsible for discipline. In particular, the authority of the Chancellor and Vice-Chancellor was increased so that all lapses not covered by the letter of the law might yet be caught in the web of a discretionary power vested in the magistrate.

As defined by the statutes of 1636, the powers of the Chancellor were extensive. In matters of discipline, authority was given him 'to punish offenders against the statute of the university with corporal chastisement, money-fine, imprisonment, degradation, suspension from degrees, discommoning, proscription, banishment or expulsion from the university, censures ecclesiastical, or in any other reasonable manner . . .' In addition a discretionary power was given him to punish all offenders where no provision was made for it in the statutes. As opponents of the statutes complained, the authority of the Chancellor was universal and unbounded.[13]

Effective authority within the university lay not with the Chancellor but with the Vice-Chancellor — who was resident. The 1636 code endowed him with jurisdiction over 'all which conduces to the honour of the university and the safety and welfare of one and all'. No less emphasis was placed on his duties: to see that offenders were not only punished but detected; 'to make diligent search not only during the day, but also by night after such delinquents; and also to take care that heretics, schismatics and all other persons who think otherwise than aright of the Catholic faith, and the doctrine and discipline of the Church of England are exiled . . .' The Vice-Chancellor's principal weapon in the enforcement of order and discipline was the Chancellor's Court of the university. Title XXI of the Laudian code stipulated that the court was to hold session every Friday in the North Chapel of St. Mary's, with the Vice-Chancellor and two proctors presiding and an under-bedell of the law attending. Its procedure closely resembled that of church courts;[14] its jurisdiction ranged over all matters in which members of the university were a part. Much of the business of the court concerned actions for debt, but it dealt too with 'reformatio morum' and specifically with 'transgressi statuti'.[15] Under these heads the records of the court reveal the examination of offenders charged with night walking, prostitution, slander and assault.[16] Defendants who failed to attend were automatically banished from the university and, at least on paper, penalties and sanctions (imprisonment and excommunication) were severe. Appeals were heard on Wednesdays but were to be refused 'to certain persons sometimes out of hatred to the offences which have been committed and sometimes to rebuke the audacity of persons who in the midst of popular disturbances . . . screen themselves'.[17] The statutes expressly precluded appeals by those contumacious of the court.

Then as now the principal disciplinary officers of the university were the proctors. Among other tasks it was their prescribed duty to attend frequently at university exercises, sessions and disputations to ensure that all was done in accordance with the statutes. The proctors also patrolled the city by night with powers to fine instantly. By statute they received half the fine. The revisions of 1636 empowered each of them to appoint two assistants among whose duties it was 'to range the streets, lanes, eating houses and wine shops during sermon time'.

However, the central institutions in Laud's quest for order and discipline were the colleges and halls. This was both necessary and convenient. As Mr. Curtis has shown, the sixteenth and seventeenth centuries had seen the emergence of the colleges as the most important and autonomous academic communities: heads of colleges had the right to dispense their members from any of the new statutes which conflicted with their own.[18] It was within these smaller communities of residential colleges that Laud hoped discipline would be most effectively enforced. At the heart of the statutes were orders to ensure that students came up to colleges, were matriculated from colleges, resided only in colleges and returned to colleges each evening by nine o'clock sharp. Tutors in colleges were expected to supervise discipline as well as study and Laud looked to the heads of colleges to ensure the conformity of their members to the code. Attempts were made to bring the heads of colleges more under the Chancellor's scrutiny. The statutes of 1636 invested the Chancellor with authority to nominate the principals of halls;[19] it also established the Hebdomadal Council, ordered by Charles I at the instigation of Laud in 1631, as a permanent assembly.[20] Critics of this innovation accused Laud of expanding the powers of the assembly beyond those envisaged by Charles I in his letter of 1631. The Hebdomadal Council with the Chancellor and Vice-Chancellor sat as a court, passed censures on delinquents and issued decrees on matters of discipline. In short it was to be employed as another agency for enforcing the letter and spirit of the statutes.[21]

These then were the offices and institutions through which Laud hoped to reduce the university to 'piety and sobriety', to 'peace and unity'. On 22 June 1636, the day the statutes signed and sealed were delivered, Secretary Coke praised the improvements already witnessed during the years of probation: students were no longer to be found in taverns or brothels, 'nor seen loitering in the streets or other places of idleness or ill example but all contain themselves within the walls of their colleges . . . And if those temporary and imperfect orders produced so good effect what may now be expected from this body of laws and statutes so complete and so digested . . .'[22] The university, Coke told them, might now become the perfect model for the commonweal, an academy from which those nurtured through discipline to virtue might emerge as governors of a well-ordered nation.

Later in the summer, at the end of August, Charles I came to visit his seminary of virtue and learning. The royal visitation of August 1636 is an important chapter in the history of the university and of the personal rule of Charles I. By it the students and governors of Oxford University would behold the 'royal Justinian', the author of their new law, the symbol of all authority.[23] And there at Oxford Charles could see a utopia of order and sobriety, the promise of a perfect commonweal in the future. The royal visit was the enactment in image and ceremony of the spirit and body of the statutes. As the King approached from Woodstock, the governors and students, correctly attired and ranked according to their degrees, lined the royal path to Laud's own college, St. John's, and thence to Carfax.[24] The royal entertainments carefully devised by the university mirrored the royal hopes and expectations for the realm.

On 29 August, in Christ Church Hall, William Strode, the Public

Orator of the university, presented his play *The Floating Island*, which was written at Laud's instigation.[25] The Floating Island was a kingdom distracted by dissenting passions and on the verge of anarchy. The monarch, King Prudentius, and his minister, Intellectus Agens, in vain attempt to bridle their licence; and the passions, led by Audax, Irato, Desperato, Sir Amorous and Hilario, break out into rebellion and plot to murder the King. Prudentius, hearing of their conspiracy, retires to safety, leaving them to govern. The passions elect Fancie as their queen, but soon become dissatisfied with her fickle rule and, quarrelling among themselves, bring her reign to an end and the realm near to ruin. Prudentius returns to save the kingdom and the passions willingly submit to restraints which they now understand to be necessary. Reason rules over passion, order over chaos. In accordance with the conventions of the masques, with the topos of Caroline iconography, and perhaps with academic taste, the characters of the play are Platonic 'essences'. But the immediate relevance of the moral both for the kingdom and for Oxford in 1636 becomes clear in the epilogue:

> The isle is setled; Rage of Passions laid
> Phancy to Prudence bowes. Let all be staid
> In your Acceptance too, and then each breast
> Will cease its floating . . .

Strode's play, however, did not meet with unqualified acceptance. Though the King expressed his approval, many spectators tired of the play, as having too much of morality, too little of wit in it.[26] More successful, because more exotic and colourful in scene and costume, was the next day's production, also arranged by Laud, William Cartwright's *The Royal Slave*.[27] The play, set in Persia, centred on the Persian custom of elevating a captive slave to be King for three days before being offered as a sacrifice to the Gods. Cratander, the slave chosen, displays not the libertinism typically exhibited by those enjoying such short rule, but a truly regal disposition. By his beauty and countenance, by his wisdom and discretion, by his condemnation of unnecessary luxury, by his respect for law and self-restraint in the exercise of authority, by his probity and resistance to the temptations of sensual pleasures, he emerges in the eyes of all the court as the model of monarchy. For Cratander is acquainted with philosophy, the disciple of Socrates: his virtues are 'the fruits of learning'. His fellow slaves of baser parts, frustrated that their licence too is bridled by his virtue, complain 'we live not under a King, but a pedagogue'. They plot to kill him and to give vent to their lust upon the ladies of the court. But Cratander saves the Queen and her attendants and wins freedom for himself and good terms of peace for the slaves. A King by nature, he is appointed by the Emperor monarch of the conquered provinces. Cartwright's play was not only a panegyric to the virtues of Charles I. Though the epilogue to the university excused the production as the sport of courtiers not scholars, there was, no less than in Strode's play, a message for the university too. Like Strode's Prudentius (and his minister), Cartwright's Cratander exemplifies the man of learning as the man of virtue; only he who is master of his own passions can rule for the good of others unable to bridle their own. Learning and virtue are the qualities required for government.[28] Charles I had underlined the same message more directly in his letter to Convocation: universities he regarded as 'the seminaries of virtue and learning from whence the better part of our subjects by good education may bee disposed to religion, vertue and obedience of our lawes, and enabled to do service both in church and commonwealth'.[29] The next year, Cartwright was nominated by Laud 'Architypographus', or overseer of the new Oxford press. In 1642, then reader of metaphysic in the university, he lived at Oxford on terms of familiarity with Charles I. His play had been well received: 'His Majesty and all the nobles commended it for the best that ever was acted'; the Queen, acknowledging its wider appeal, requested that it be restaged at court.[30]

But for all its appeal to the court, the students, it seems, preferred more flashy spectacles of lesser substance. When, after the King's departure, such a performance was prepared for the courtiers and others remaining in town, 'Such was the unruliness of the yonge schollars to come in that uppon their breakinge in the strangers [and] others could not be placed doe what the Vice-Chancellor would; and so there was no play at all.'[31] The world of perfect order had departed with the King. Even before there had been bad omens. Only a month before the statutes had been delivered, Laud had thought it necessary, in preparing for the royal visit, to admonish heads of houses that their students be made to wear prescribed academic dress, 'not any long hayre, nor any bootes, nor double stockins rolled downe or hanging loose about their legges as the manner of some slovens is to doe'. Heads of colleges were authorized to name a Fellow with proctorial power for the duration of the visit.[32] Though reason was now embodied in statute, it had not yet mastered the passions of Oxford youth. Indeed, the revisions which were made to the statutes in 1636 were an implicit recognition that the printed book of 1634 had not solved — perhaps could not solve — the problem of discipline. In those revisions it was admitted that scholars often dodged sermons and disputations, paid scant respect to seniors, stayed out of college all night, drank, gambled and debauched themselves. Often it was acknowledged that the problems were beyond the power and diligence of the magistrate: innkeepers were specifically ordered to block all back walls and 'wandering walks', 'through the labyrinths of which the night rakes so often steal away from the magistrates'.[33] Rigorous efforts were made to ensure at least that students could not plead ignorance of the requirements of the statutes.[34] In April 1635 orders were sent to all colleges and posted at Carfax commanding students to attend sermons, present themselves for matriculation, conform in dress and manners and avoid loitering in streets and taverns. The same year the whole text of the statutes was epitomized on one printed sheet — perhaps in the hope that the less there was to read, the more likely it was to be read. In 1638 Thomas Crosfield devised an epitome of the new statutes with a timetable of all compulsory lectures and especially a table of detailed injunctions on discipline. While the statutes were being reduced for the convenience of students, more were added to the full code as new problems arose. In November 1636 Laud ordered that communion services and prayers be in Latin and in the body of St. Mary's rather than the chancel.[35] If the enactment of laws could itself have solved the problem of discipline, the university would have become the ordered commonweal of Laud's dream.

But the reality fell short of the dream. Laws could not crush the young blades of Oxford who flaunted the latest fashions and enjoyed the lifestyle of their class.[36] Ignorance, drunkenness and violence remained features of student life. In 1638 Laud urged the Vice-Chancellor to prevent students loitering in alehouses during the vacation; in 1640 he recommended to Vice-Chancellor Christopher Potter, the Provost of Queen's, 'a more strict watchfulnesse and observance against all haunting of tavernes', for drunkenness was 'the mother or the nurse of almost all other distempers'.[37]

So serious were the complaints about drunkenness that some sent their children to be educated abroad in more sober environments.[38] Charges of violent assaults by student on student occur frequently in the case-books of the Vice-Chancellor's court.[39] But despite the severe sentences listed in the statutes, those convicted were only obliged to acknowledge their guilt in public, and swear not to offend again.[40] Public shame could be effective, but only when reinforced by severer punishment.[41] Greatest success came from the new examination statutes which replaced the submission of theses and participation in demonstrations with formal examinations for degrees.[42] It was a reform considered by all to be a real achievement. But the examination statute, like all the rest, required constant vigilance and the diligent co-operation of the magistrate

— and it is significant that even Peter Turner admitted that the
new statute had often worked by 'conniving at some defects now
and then . . . .'.[43]

As Laud himself acknowledged, laws could not cover all contin-
gencies and 'when the laws are silent . . . power must be
applied'.[44] In short the success of the statutes was largely dependent on the officers and magistrates who should enforce them.
Alarmingly they were often partners in crime. In 1636 it was
admitted that proctors made 'idle efforts' to detect students in
taverns and failed to exact fines. Tutors were often found in the
same alehouses as their charges. The revisions of 1636 made
proctors liable to any fines they failed to levy, and the epinomis
rendered officers as well as students open to a charge of perjury
'if (which Heaven forbid) they suffer any statutes to grow out of
date from lack of use and desuetude'.[45] Unfortunately it was only
Heaven that could forbid it. The central problem for Laud, for the
statutes, indeed for the policy of 'Thorough' in church and state,
was a dependence on personalities — personalities less endowed
with a sense of duty than the author of the statutes. The only
officer on whom Laud could totally rely was himself. Vice-
Chancellor Frewen told him that while he had been present the
disputations had been conducted well, but his absence for just a
fortnight saw the examinations brought to a 'dead stand'. While
Frewen took great pains over the examination statutes, Laud
acknowledged 'that the great business would greatly fall to nothing
if the Vice-Chancellors for the future did not take that prudent and
vigilant care'.[46] Sadly not all of them did. Laud had occasion to
complain to Vice-Chancellor Baylie that, unlike his predecessor
Pincke, he failed to supervise discipline. And when the Vice-
Chancellor failed to be vigilant, the other officers were left to act
as it best suited them. In February 1637 Laud complained that he
had heard nothing of the success of the statutes all year; he urged
special care of the decree against 'noctinavigation', for 'I doubt not
the proctors will be negligent enough . . . .'.[47]

Indolence and indifference were not the only problems. Direct
opposition to Laud, and to the statutes, from the city, and more
seriously from within the university, was another. In the case of
the city, Laud's chancellorship served only to enflame the long-
standing rivalry between town and gown.[48] For as Chancellor,
Laud was a fervent champion of the university's rights and
privileges over the town, not least because powers of licensing
inns and right of search were important to the success of the
statutes. In response to a university petition for more authority in
matters concerning the reformation of the youth of the university,
Laud helped secure a new charter granting the university extended

powers to search in the town and suburbs for robbers, gangsters, prostitutes and students lodging outside college.[49] The city was ordered to assist the search. There was no use establishing a perfect commonweal in the university if its enemies could take refuge in the town. But even the charter did not solve the problems. In 1634 Charles I stipulated that there should be but three licensed alehouses in Oxford: by 1639 it was said that there were 300 unlicensed,[50] and Vice-Chancellor Frewen told Laud that at least 100 inns had been licensed by a JP who was himself a brewer on condition that the innkeepers buy their beer from him.[51] Here was a symptom of a larger and long-experienced problem: the town refused to comply with university laws about student discipline when the interests of the town were at stake. And drunken students, if poor scholars, made good customers.

Within the university, Laud's authority as Chancellor was compromised from the very day of his appointment. For Laud won the contest for the honour against Philip Herbert, third Earl of Montgomery and later fourth Earl of Pembroke, by only nine votes. Within a week of the election, fifteen members of the university appealed against it to the King, arguing that Frewen, as Vice-Chancellor, had Convocation unconstitutionally summoned. On the death of a chancellor, it was argued, the office of vice-chancellor became also automatically void and authority descended to the senior doctor.[52] Secondly, it was alleged, the Convocation was 'surreptitiously held, no competent warning being given . . . the same being begun before the Beadle had fitly warned it'.[53] The election was therefore void. The appeal remained unheard and the suspicion that Laud had not been duly elected was never allayed. It cannot have helped the Chancellor to command the respect and co-operation upon which he depended. In 1641 Laud himself reflected, 'I suffered much by the clamours of the Earl of Pembroke, who thought it long till he had that place, which he had long gaped for.'[54]

Nor were the statutes themselves heralded as a great triumph by all members of the university. That is not surprising for after August 1633 the business was taken out of their hands. Twyne, we recall, reported the dismay of the delegates and heads of houses that the statute book of 1634 was substantially different from that which they had approved; he showed anxiety about the arbitrary power of amendment which the Chancellor reserved to himself and noted that some critics boldly believed 'the said statutes are not to be obeyed, as being not expressly and openly read in Convocation'. Thomas Crosfield reflected in January 1635 on 'the university statutes and what exceptions could be made against them'. Others in 1641 complained that, like Laud's election, they were illegal because imposed upon the university and not voted by it.[55] Their purpose was no other than the removal of all restraints upon the office of Chancellor and an assault upon the liberties of Convocation and Congregation. Through the Hebdomadal Council the Chancellor sought to predetermine all important issues, 'so that when the business comes to be passed in the Convocation, most come pre-engaged'.[56] At his trial Laud was charged with illegal innovations intended to subvert the university's liberties through an absolute power invested in the Chancellor.[57]

These protests and charges are evidence that the effects of the statutes had been felt. But they are evidence too of a faction within the university opposed to the code before it was promulgated and devoted to its destruction after it had passed. To Anthony à Wood and later to Mallet, the explanation for such opposition is again simple: protests about Laud's election and the statutes were puritan complaints against a new Arminian regime.[58] According to this interpretation, Laud's friends in the colleges were those who, like Juxon at St. John's, Frewen at Magdalen and Jackson at Corpus, shared his religious views. His enemies — Prideaux at Exeter, Brent at Merton, Kettell at Trinity, Hood at Lincoln, Radcliffe at Brasenose — were those for whom those views were anathema. Undoubtedly this analysis contains some truth: in all the complaints against the statutes there are hints of religious grievances, and a university petition to Parliament in 1642 pressed specifically for a new code which would foster 'the true reformed Protestant religion'.[59] There is evidence too of opposition within the university to restrictions on preaching and to a new emphasis on reverence and ceremony.[60] But in general Mallet's picture is oversimplified. For what is striking about the statutes is the *absence* of detailed injunctions on religious matters — beyond a general insistence on subscription and conformity to the Church of England.[61] True it is that in the 1630s there were wildly differing views about that, but, at least as Chancellor of Oxford, Laud was unwilling to place stress on those differences.[62] He rigorously enforced the royal proclamation forbidding public discussion of doctrinal controversies, and barred a proponent of Arminian doctrines no less readily than he punished those who railed against them.[63] He also seemed anxious to avoid confrontation over questions of ceremony. When Proctor Corbet refused to bow at the altar in St. Mary's Laud would 'not give him any command, either to do or desist or to appoint any substitute, but leave him and let him do as it shall please God and himself'.[64] Secondly it is clear that Laud was able to gain the co-operation, at least at times, of those who disagreed with him on points of theology. It was Prideaux, listed by Mallet as an enemy, whom Laud asked to revise

Chillingworth's *The Religion of Protestants a Safe Way to Salvation*, and Prideaux who replied that 'no man shall be more ready to execute the Archbishop's commands'. Laud showed similar respect to others, advancing men like Dean Fell irrespective of their religion.[65] When he wrote in 1635 to the Bishop of Winchester with advice on the education of scholars at New College, Laud even agreed that 'Calvin's Instructions may profitably be read, and as one of their first books for divinity . . .'.[66] He wished only that students be grounded first in philosophy and logic — in accordance with the traditional curriculum. On the evidence of his chancellorship at Oxford it is hard not to substantiate Laud's own defence of his actions: 'I have nothing to do to defend Arminianism . . . and yet for the peace of Christendom, and the strengthening of the Reformed Religion, I do heartily wish these differences were not pursued with such heat and animosity . . .'.[67] Within the university, Laud pursued not doctrinal controversy, but a learned ministry.

Opposition on religious grounds was not the principal obstacle. It was but one factor in a myriad of personal relationships, which then, even more than today, formed the hub of the university. Laud entered his hope for discipline on the college and, within the college, the effectiveness of discipline depended on the head. Opposition to Laud and to the statutes from within the colleges took many forms: personal antagonisms and jealousies, reaction against change, internal college politics, localist revolt against central interference — and indolence and ineptitude. As Potter pessimistically told Laud in 1635: 'One main reason of their irregularities is because they have been left every head to his own humour'.[68] Those differing humours did not always owe their differences to religion, but they were responsible for different results. At Queen's, Potter, one brought up in a strong Calvinist tradition, strictly enforced the statutes and all Laud's injunctions.[69] The President of Corpus, Thomas Jackson, reduced all to order and sobriety, winning even the respect of the usually vitriolic Prynne who, though he shared not Jackson's religion, yet regarded him as 'a man otherwise of good abilities, and of plausible, affable, courteous deportment'.[70] In 1638, Laud had occasion to complain about the conduct of disputations at Brasenose: 'I would have you speak with the Principal [ironically the puritan Radcliffe] that he would command their cellar to be better looked to, that no strong and unruly argument be drawn from that topick-place.' By 1640 the Vice-Chancellor protested in his defence that after all his efforts, drunken students had only moved from the streets into the colleges where eyes were less watchful.

We cannot know how watchful they were in every college. But

we do have a wealth of evidence for one notorious case — that of
Merton College. For here, as well as the formal college registers
and reports, we have the private letters to Laud of Peter Turner,
a senior master of the college who had been closely involved in the
compilation and revision of the statutes, and who now stood high
in the Chancellor's esteem. The long saga of Laud's relations with
Merton is too detailed to be told in full here. It began in the
autumn of 1637 when a serious quarrel between two of the
Fellows was referred to Laud's attention.[71] It seems probable that
during the winter of the same year information, and complaints
about the disorders in the college, reached Laud through Turner,
who in March 1638 was advising him how to order a visitation so
that it might not appear who had entered the protests. Laud
appointed a commission to investigate.[72] On 29 March a detailed
questionnaire (consisting of thirty articles) was sent to the Warden
and Fellows in order to discover whether university and college
statutes were correctly observed. It was an extremely thorough
document, of inquisitorial detail.[73] At the beginning of April the
Visitors appointed to investigate the college (Richard Baylie, John
Lambe, Arthur Duck and Gilbert Sheldon) reported on the
irregularities complained of or detected: postmasters' places were
sold, meals were not attended in the common hall, lectures were
not read, nor college records maintained. College properties were
corruptly administered, Bible reading and Latin were abandoned,
and students often spent the night outside college in the company
of whores or lay within it, unable to speak English, let alone Latin,
in a befuddled stupor induced by the illegal double-strength beer
favoured by the Warden.[74] After this catalogue of sins it seems a
mere footnote to add that the statute book was not in the
library.[75] So serious were these charges that Sheldon thought
Brent would be best advised not to endure a full enquiry, 'but
should lay the key under the door and be gone'. In view of this it
was surely an excess of academic understatement which prompted
Brent's reply and his regret 'that you should conceive amiss of
us'.[76]

Laud ordered that the college obey the visitors' injunctions until
the formal hearing in October. Throughout the summer he wrote
constantly for further information and reports. Brent replied that
all was enacted according to his command.[77] And there the
historian would have to leave it — were it not for the secret
missives of Peter Turner. For Turner informed Laud of the evasions
and deceit practised by Brent: first the Visitors' orders were
ignored; secondly the three fellows appointed to prosecute the
complaints abut the college were dismissed and replaced by more
malleable representatives who, having no objections to the existing

administration, replied to all enquiries *'omnia bene'*.[78] But by August, perhaps because he realized that Laud was well informed of the real state of affairs, even Brent admitted that all was not well. Two or three Master-Fellows regularly joined students in the alehouse, 'and some young women have lately been begotten with child where two of our masters frequently resort and sometimes lodge'.[79] The final hearing in October served only to incriminate Brent and others further. The orders sent by Laud and read by Turner on 15 October catalogued the sins of the college and the rules by which it was to be governed in future. All too often they only repeated the very statutes of 1636: students were to live in college and return by nine o'clock each night; Fellows and students should wear academic dress; copies of the statutes were to be displayed in the library.[80] Ironically even these injunctions were enforced but spasmodically and grudgingly.[81] Brent became Laud's bitter opponent.[82]

Merton is a notorious case of a college where Masters, Fellows, and students flouted their own and the university statutes. But we should not assume that because it was notorious, it was exceptional. We should recall that we are informed of the ills of Merton not through the reports of any university or college officer, but from the private correspondence of Peter Turner. What went on within the walls of other colleges where Laud had no confidant (and where the historian accordingly has no evidence) perhaps best remains to us, as to him, a mystery. We may only note that in 1640, Brent admitted that junior masters usually failed to attend early morning prayers, but yet believed them to be 'frequented as well by us as any other college'.[83] He may have been right.

By 1636, Laud had succeeded by 'indefatigable industry' in devising a code of law by which the university of Oxford was to be reduced to order, discipline and sobriety. When one reviews Laud's labours as Chancellor, when one reads his painstaking correspondence with the university, it is indeed, as Hugh Trevor-Roper put it, 'hard to realise that it was but an item in his vast programme for the reconstruction of the whole basis of secular and ecclesiastical government'. And yet it was more than a mere item. For the university to Laud was like the court to Charles himself — a model for the government of church and state. Universities were in the realm as in the body 'the noble and vital parts, which being vigorous and sound send good blood and active spirits into the veins and arteries . . .'.[84] As Chancellor, Laud hoped to establish at Oxford his ideal commonweal, a seminary for a wider world — a world in which liberty never descended to licence, where order was imposed on anarchy, beauty upon dilapidation, learning upon ignorance, unity upon faction. Because Oxford was his 'seminary',[85] we may learn much from the history of Laud's chancellorship about his ideals for the future governance of the realm and something, too, of the reasons for his failure to enact them.

As Archbishop of Canterbury Laud has been depicted recently as the man who destroyed the Elizabethan compromise by a rigid insistence upon conformity, as the prelate who provoked the rise of revolutionary puritanism by a breach with traditional and orthodox predestinarianism.[86] At first this judgement seems convincing, not least because it is endorsed by many contemporaries. At his trial Laud, as Archbishop and as Chancellor of Oxford, was charged with innovating in matters of doctrine and ceremony, with leading the church via Arminianism to popery. And the all but universal hostility shown to the Laudian bishops in 1641 is evidence of the conviction those charges carried. Yet when we turn from the testimony of his accusers and critics to the evidence of his writings and actions, that judgement and those charges seem less persuasive. The Laudian statutes and Laud's correspondence with the university are notable for their *silence* on questions of theological controversy. As Chancellor he rigidly enforced Charles's proclamation forbidding debate — in the universities as well as the pulpit — on questions of salvation and free will.[87] Tooker of Oriel was silenced for his defence of Arminianism no less than were its critics.[88] Laud's correspondence, orders and works as Bishop of London and Archbishop of Canterbury are similarly silent. Commitment to a belief in predestination had never been an official doctrine of the Church of England,[89] and, whatever the fears of his contemporaries, from the evidence of his works and correspondence it is hard not to endorse the view that Laud 'for all his schoolman's outlook allowed that some parts of doctrine were genuinely "indifferent"'.[90] Laud's chaplain and biographer Peter Heylyn tells us that in a sermon preached at Oxford in 1615 he 'insisted on some points which might indifferently be imputed either to Popery or Arminianism . . .'.[91] But the Laud of the 1630s should not be judged by one episode in 1615. Certainly by 1630 Laud told Dr. Brooke, Master of Trinity, Cambridge, who was preparing a tract on predestination, '. . . I am yet where I was that something about these controversies is unmasterable in this life'.[92] If the central tenet of Arminianism was a belief in God's universal grace and the freewill of all men to obtain salvation then Laud's Arminianism, as Prynne discovered in preparing the charges against him, is hard to prove.[93]

What cannot be denied is that during Laud's archiepiscopate there was a greater emphasis on *iure divino* episcopacy, on sacraments and ceremony. This was not, however, novel, nor exclusively Arminian, nor perhaps primarily the work of Laud. Whitgift and Bancroft zealously persecuted puritan nonconformity; in this the laxity of Abbot's long primacy was the exception rather than the rule.[94] And the renewed insistence upon reverence owed as much to the accession of Charles I as to the succession of Laud.[95] It was Charles who ordered the communion table to be placed at the east end of the church.[96] Whatever his own preferences, in his visitation articles and orders to the clergy, Laud had insisted only that it be placed in 'convenient sort'.[97] Concerning such questions and rites the revised canons of 1640, as even the nonconformist Gardiner acknowledged, are evidence less of a rigidity which breeds division, more of 'a serious effort to find a broad ground'.[98]

Few of Laud's contemporaries saw him in this light; few understood his ideals. As Clarendon acutely observed, he failed to make 'his designs and purposes appear as candid as they were'.[99] As Chancellor of Oxford and as Archbishop of Canterbury, Laud pursued order and unity, not discord and division. The statutes for Oxford, like the articles of enquiry for his metropolitan visitations, show Laud's primary concern with externals — with the details of conduct and discipline. It is in these that his industry most contrasts with Abbot's indolence, his firmness with Abbot's indulgence.[100] To Carlyle, Laud was 'like a college tutor whose world is forms, college rules'; to Mallet such rules seemed 'disproportionately rigid and minute'.[101] But these writers failed to understand that for Laud uniformity and order in externals were the means towards sound learning in the university and spirituality within the church. The decay of discipline in the universities, he told Gerard Vossius, 'is the cause of all our ills in church and state', for the order in the university was 'a thing very necessary in this age both for church and commonwealth since so many young gentlemen and others of all ranks and conditions have their first breeding for the public in that seminary'.[102] In the church, too, nothing had more conduced to draw men from piety than 'the want of uniform and decent order'.[103]

Order in the academic world as in church and state required authority — and the recognition of authority. As during his archiepiscopate he stressed the independent authority of the church and the prerogatives of its courts, its bishops and its clergy, so during his chancellorship he emphasized the independent jurisdiction of the university and the powers of its officers — Chancellor, Vice-Chancellor and proctors.[104] An insistence upon order and discipline and an emphasis upon authority were not, however, threads which spun a straitjacket for the conscience.

Prideaux remained Professor of Divinity throughout Laud's chancellorship; Proctor Corbet was left undisturbed despite his nonconformity; even William Hodges of Exeter who had offended by his
scandalous sermon was restored after submission.[105] Few in the
university, and indeed few in the church, were deprived of their
positions as a result of differences concerning doctrine or ceremony.[106] Rather Laud (and many Laudian bishops) are remarkable
for their patience with the obstinate and their attempts to win over
the refractory.[107] And among those whom Laud advanced in the
university and the church, we find men like Samuel Fell, Richard
Sibbes, and Joseph Hall who differed from him in belief and even
practice.

Nor did order and discipline forge chains for the intellect. The
Oxford of William Laud was not the Salamanca of Philip II. Rather
at Oxford during the 1630s the new learning, and especially the
new science, flourished — thanks not least to Laud's donations of
manuscripts and mathematical books, and his endowment of a
lectureship in Arabic. And at the court of Charles I, as even the
critical Lucy Hutchinson acknowledged, 'men of learning and
ingenuity in all arts were in esteem and receiv'd encouragement
from the King'.[108]

If by a study of Laud's chancellorship we may understand more
clearly his ideals and objectives, we may similarly comprehend
more easily the obstacles to their fulfilment. We have argued that
Laud as jealously guarded the freedom, privileges and jurisdiction
of the university within the city, as those of the church within the
commonwealth. Maintenance of the privileges of the university (as
of the church) was inextricably linked with discipline and order
within. Only if it was above reproach could the university, like the
church, defend its privileges and jurisdiction. Only it if enjoyed
independent jurisdiction could an institution properly reform
itself. That is why Laud took pains to secure for the university a
new charter of privileges to accompany a new code of discipline,
why he pressed for equal representation for gown and town on the
commission of the peace. But privileges attracted resentment. The
city was as hostile to the favours shown the university as was the
laity to the pretensions of the church. Vice-Chancellor Frewen
made the identification clearly in a letter to Laud in October 1640.
For all the university's efforts towards reform, 'some of our back
friends in Parliament will give us but little thanks: some there,
perhaps many, rather desiring we should be guilty, that they might
with more colour use us as they did the monasteries.'[109]

There were enemies within as well as assaults from without. In
the university as in the church and state Laud discovered that
'private ends are such blocks in the public way'.[110] As we have

seen the officers of the university responsible for discipline were often negligent, no less remiss were the bishops in the Laudian church, or the justices and deputy lieutenants in the counties. Even the diligent officers met with unreliable subordinate officials. In the diocese and the locality, no less than in the case of Merton College, a return of '*omnia bene*' could cover a multitude of sins. Hebdomadal Council may have been instituted as a governing body of the university, but in so far as it consisted of heads of houses, it was also an assembly of representatives from the colleges. Like the gentry governors of the provinces they too often served their private interest first, the demands of the government second. Like those leaders of county society, the heads of colleges jealously guarded their local autonomy against encroachment from above. Some heads of houses objected to the statutes, some opposed any increase of chancellorial power. There was little that Laud, as Chancellor, could do. Potter admitted as much: on hearing of Laud's intent to carry out a visitation of the colleges, he told him that he was 'like to find great necessity of it'.[111] When he sought the power of Metropolitan visitation, Laud acknowledged his weakness as Chancellor, and though he won the right, he never exercised it in practice. The history of the university shows the limits to the effectiveness of authority: the impossibility of complete supervision.

1636, the year in which the statutes were finally completed and a new charter secured, in which as if by celebration he entertained the royal party at Oxford, was also the year when 'it might well appear to Laud that his policy had triumphed wherever it had been applied'.[112] It soon became clear that this was but an illusion. As the dissensions grew within the realm, Laud clung desperately to the university as the hope for an ordered commonwealth, free from faction and vice in the future. As he told the sons of the Elector Palatine at the degree ceremony in 1636, students in particular must conquer youthful passions. But that hope depended upon the maintenance of discipline, and when he had perhaps abandoned his most strenuous efforts elsewhere he continued to chivvy the officers of the university. 'There is,' he urged, 'a greater necessity to hold up good order in the brokenness of these times.'[113]

Even within Oxford, however, Laud's triumph was qualified. Few within the university (perhaps in the realm) opposed his ideals when they understood them. Many opposed the means (the scant respect for interests, the extension of authority) and the methods (the detailed enquiry, the persistent hectoring) by which they were translated into practice. What to Laud were efficient procedures were to others arbitrary courses. The unity and co-operation for which he had asked on his appointment as Chancellor were, from the beginning, no more than a dream. Like the realm, the university was *not* just one body ruled by one head, but a series of commonwealths, some governed by reason, some by passion, often contesting with each other, at times divided within themselves. 'Thorough' in Oxford, as in the country at large, depended upon personalities: depended that is on those who governed identifying their local and private interests with the public good. Too few made the identification; too many had a different view of the public good.

But the story of Laud's chancellorship was not one of complete failure. As the troubles of 1640–1 mounted, Laud delayed his resignation as Chancellor because, despite some difficulties, 'I have found so much love from the university that I could not make myselfe willing to leave it'.[114] The Vice-Chancellor reassured him in 1641 that though he vacated the office, his gifts, his endowments, most of all the discipline and reformed manners which were the legacy of his statutes, assured his fame 'howsoever long care is taken for the study of the arts and the honour of letters'.[115]

As his days neared an end Laud feared for the future of the university and the church. One night in November 1642, he records, 'I dreamed that the church was undone and that I went to St. John's in Oxford where I found the roof off some part of the college, and the walls ready to fall down'.[116] Laud's college is still standing, and the statutes which he devised governed the university until the nineteenth century. Nor was the church undone. For in the 1640s Oxford emerged as the stronghold of church and crown. When the Long Parliament divided between Cavaliers and Roundheads, most of those Oxford men who had matriculated during Laud's chancellorship supported the monarchy.[117] When the troubles had passed, it was the zeal of the gentry which secured the restoration of a hierarchical, episcopal church along with the crown. And among the nominees to the vacant bishoprics were many best known for their roles in the university of Laud's chancellorship.

5. The image of virtue: the court and household of Charles I, 1625 – 1642 *

The government of seventeenth-century England was personal monarchy. The king was the centre of patronage and power. A change in the person (and personality) of the king fundamentally affected the course of politics. The continuity of institutions and offices, even of personnel, should not lead us to underestimate the power of the king's person. In the seventeenth century the succession of a new monarch was still the fundamental change in the political climate — the event which decided who would grow in the sun of royal favour and who would wither in the cold of obscurity.

At first sight the succession of King Charles in 1625 brought no major change. It was a peaceful and undisputed succession — the first succession of an adult male who was direct heir to the throne since the succession of Henry VIII in 1509.[1] The new king too was already a familiar figure in the world of affairs. Since 1623 he had played a major role in domestic and foreign policy in alliance with his father's favourite, George Villiers, Duke of Buckingham.[2] Buckingham's own career adds to the impression of continuity. For Buckingham managed with great political agility the feat rarely performed by favourites: surviving the death of one sovereign to entrench himself more firmly in the affections (though not the embraces) of another. Charles I succeeded too to the throne of a kingdom at war since 1625 — a war which, spanning the two reigns, tempts some historians to underplay the importance of the succession.

To those at court, however, things quite rapidly looked different. Charles I was in many respects a complete contrast to his father: where James was informal to the point of familiarity, at times unkempt and (by English standards) undignified, a lover of debate and wit even descending to vulgarity and irreverence, Charles I was stiff, proud and prudish.[3] His manner and morals owed little to the bawdy camaraderie of the Scottish court in which James I had learned his kingcraft. It was the grave ceremonial of Spanish court etiquette which appealed to Charles I's disposition.[4] As with any other head of a household, Charles I's manners and morals were soon reflected in his domestic arrangements, that is to say in the organization of the court. But the king's domestic world was also the world of politics. At a time when access and proximity to the king's person were the goals of political ambition, and access was determined by the arrangement of the royal household, a change of personal style could rearrange the patterns of court politics.

The king's person was not the only force for change in 1625. Charles I came to the throne betrothed to a princess who was Catholic and French. Since the death of Queen Anne of Denmark in 1619, the politics of influence had been played in two courts: that of James I and (certainly from 1621) that of Prince Charles himself. From 1625 there were also two courts, but the game was to be very different. For now the second court was that of a youthful queen who was (by treaty) to be attended by French, by Catholics and, of course, by women. For those outside the area of the king's entourage and favour the politics of reversionary interest fostered by an ageing king and an adult, politically active prince gave way to the politics of influence upon a young and hence impressionable foreign queen.

Though the personality and domestic circumstances of Charles I brought immediate changes, the succession did not see a complete turnover of personnel. For a time this was in doubt. Almost on the day of James I's death, the Venetian ambassador reported debate among courtiers concerning 'whether the household of the dead king or that of the prince shall be the household of the present king'.[5] It was after all a real problem, one which had not arisen for over a century. Charles had his own servants to reward. But he had to satisfy the officers of his father's household (whose tenure terminated with James I's death) who now petitioned for confirmation of their places — among them many Scots.[6] It seems that the eventual settlement was a compromise: Charles settled his own household 'for the most part with his then own servants', but retained James I's officers, either in their posts or as supernumeraries, until their death. This compromise inevitably resulted, for a time, in superfluity of officials, additional expense and some odd arrangements like that by which two Master Cooks (the one to James, the other to Prince Charles) shared the post and the diet assigned to the place at court.[7] It meant too that only gradually, with death or retirement, did the officers of the royal household reflect Charles's personal choice.

Change in the style of the court was more immediately effected. The Venetian ambassador reported a new regime within days of Charles I's succession:

> The king observes a rule of great decorum. The nobles do not enter his apartments in confusion as heretofore, but each rank has its appointed place and he has declared that he desires the rules and maxims of the late Queen Elizabeth . . . The king has also drawn up rules for himself, dividing the day from his very early rising, for prayers, exercises, audiences, business, eating and sleeping. It is said that he will set apart a day for public audience and he does not wish anyone to be introduced to him unless sent for.[8]

These preferences and rules enacting them spread rapidly throughout the court. Sir John Finet, Master of Ceremonies, discovered that on escorting an ambassador from the Council Chamber to the king, he was halted at the door of the Privy Chamber by a Gentleman Usher, 'all further passages being begun then to be debarred to all but Privy Councillors and Bedchamber men'.[9] A servant of the Spanish envoy was ordered to leave the Privy Gallery.[10] When he set off on his first summer progress to meet his queen at Dover, Charles issued a proclamation for the better order of his household, forbidding 'unnecessary pestering' of the court, or the resort thither of those not listed as required for the king's service.[11] While the commissioners appointed for the regulation of the household discussed,[12] the tone of the new court was already set: a tone of order, formality and decorum. We must now turn to describe the organization of and orders for the Caroline household and court and then to the political consequences of the changes in domestic arrangements.

Orders and organization

The king's principal residence was the sprawling Tudor palace of Whitehall — a building of perhaps two thousand or more rooms, with additional closets, garrets and kitchens.[13] The palace was divided into two geographically separate as well as administratively distinct sections — the king's and the queen's sides — because, given the distance of the queen's palace at Greenwich, Whitehall served as the London home for both monarchs. On both sides were lodgings for the household servants of the king and queen. The number of rooms assigned to each office reflected the duties and status of the place held. We know, for example, that in Charles II's reign the Lord Chamberlain occupied forty rooms, the Controller nineteen and the Master of the Horse twenty.[14] Since these last were described as 'once the duke's' and since the duke of Buckingham had been Master of the Horse, we may assume that the distribution of suites had not changed very much.[15]

Certainly little had changed in the structure of the building since the reign of Henry VIII. Even the furnishings and fabrics of the state rooms dated back to the early Tudors. As soon as he succeeded to the throne, Charles formulated plans to rebuild the palace with expedition. As early as February 1626, the month of the king's coronation, John Burgh, writing from court, expected that Whitehall would be rebuilt 'with much beauty and state and that suddenly'.[16] Through lack of money Whitehall was not rebuilt. Few physical changes were effected. As late as 1639, Abraham Van der Dort, the keeper of the king's pictures, referred (somewhat derogatorily) to the 'old fashioned and rusty iron tongs' and old furniture of the royal Chair Room.[17] Charles I then came to Whitehall like a vigorous new manager to an unwieldy, chaotic and decaying hotel. Perfect order and beauty demanded reconstruction along more rational, classical ordered lines (such as those proposed by Inigo Jones).[18] But if reconstruction remained a dream, then the best possible order must be established within the limitations of the old fabric. The palace of Whitehall, like our unwieldy hotel, contained large state rooms and intimate corners (below p. 161), grand halls and stairways and little known back passages and entrances. It housed a permanent staff of many hundreds, all vying for promotion and favour, for legitimate perquisite and illicit backhander. It also lodged a fluctuating horde of visitors, on public and private business, with *their* households and servants. It was this anarchy of rooms and persons which Charles early determined to organize, and which he fashioned gradually into what Sir Philip Warwick boasted was 'the most regular and splendid court in Christendom'.[19] The means by which he did so were orders for regulation and reform and measures of retrenchment.

Before we describe the various orders for the government of the several branches of the household, we shall need to pause to consider the evidence from which our picture will be drawn. Few of the books of orders which were issued have survived and none of those that I have used is authentically dated precisely. British Library Stowe MS 561, a collection of orders for the king's, queen's and royal family's households is listed as 'temp. Charles I' with no further information.[20] The fullest account is provided by a parchment book of household regulations in the Lord Chamberlain's department at the Public Record Office (LC5/180). This is signed, in the king's hand, 'Charles I' but the date inscribed at the top, '1630' is in a later hand.[21] There are, however, reasons for believing that it is correct. For in March 1629 a memorial concerning attendance on the king and queen, found among the papers of Secretary Sir John Coke, established principles which underlay the orders in LC5/180.[22] Moreover excerpts from the orders relating to behaviour in the Privy Chamber and royal Chapel, dated 1631, are among the manuscripts of the Earl of Bridgewater and in the State Papers Domestic.[23] These all, then, suggest a date between 1629 and 1631, as do other references to the settling of the king's household in the sixth year of his reign.[24] The parchment book may be used with confidence.

No book of orders has survived for the Caroline Bedchamber. We do, however, have a book of orders issued in 1689 for the Bedchamber of William III which announces that the orders are 'in the same form as they were established in the reigns of our royal uncle and grandfather of ever blessed memory'.[25] There is no reason to doubt the statement: William III's orders may well have been a direct repetition of Caroline ordinances.[26] But as disputes during Charles II's reign clearly illustrate, such orders were open to controversy and interpretation in practice.[27] Most obviously the distribution of authority and relationships between the Lord Chamberlain and the Groom of the Stool (Chief Gentleman of the Bedchamber) depended upon the personalities and status of those who held the posts. And for all his theoretically independent sphere of jurisdiction, Sir James Fullerton, Groom of the Stool to Charles I, could not have claimed equality with William, Earl of Pembroke, who as Lord Chamberlain and a courtier of massive political weight probably effectively governed the Bedchamber for all that it lay beyond his technical jurisdiction.[28] Our evidence then may be used, but it must be used with caution. And, as we sketch the orders for the government of the royal household, the Hall, the Presence, the Privy Chamber and the Bedchamber, we should never forget that there may have been other such interpretations and adjustments in practice.

The parchment book of orders signed by the king himself, like the Eltham Ordinances on which it is modelled, contains regulations concerning the government of the court from the outer precincts to the Privy Chamber.[29] The Knight Marshal and Porters at the Gate were ordered to scrutinize carefully those entering the precincts of the court and none was to enter but those enrolled upon a list kept at the Gate. The porters were to have 'special regard that no ragged boys nor unseemly persons be suffered to make a stay in any of the courts'. Royal servants were reminded, in language that was to become typical of Charles I's style, that their own domestics should be 'comely and seemly persons, well apparelled' and mannered. If any was 'noised to be a profane person or outrageous rioter or ribald, a notorious drunkard,

swearer, railer or quarreller', he was to be ousted from his place
and banished the court. A renewed emphasis upon decorum and
order was the hallmark of the Caroline ordinances. On Sundays
and offering days, it was decreed, the Lord Chamberlain was to
dine in the Great Chamber and all with tables at court were to
attend. The Gentlemen Ushers who waited at meals were ordered
to remain after dinner 'for some reasonable time that so strangers
and men of quality that shall have occasion to resort to our court
may not find it empty'. When the king dined in the Presence, only
peers, bishops and privy councillors were permitted to tread on
the carpet surrounding his table. The Gentlemen Ushers were
ordered to see that none pressed too close to the king in his
presence, or to the cloth of state in his absence. And they were
themselves reminded to keep the reverence and distance which it
was the duty of their office to safeguard.

At the time of the Eltham Ordinances of Henry VIII's reign, the
Presence Chamber had marked the formal divide between the
king's public rooms and the Privy Lodgings. Throughout the
sixteenth century it had been a door which had separated two
distinct worlds — in reality as well as in name. But by 1625, the
Privy Chamber had declined in importance and altered in function
with the creation of the Bedchamber by James I.[30] Charles I's
orders for the regulation of the household themselves acknowledge
the change and the somewhat redundant nature of the Privy
Chamber now that its staff no longer performed body service for
the king: 'for our Privy Chamber though we find it much changed
from the ancient institution both in the number of gentlemen and
their service, nevertheless we are pleased to continue a fit
number'.[31] Charles seems to have wished to reassert the
geographical (and psychological and political) significance of the
Privy Chamber as the first step inside the Privy Lodgings. The
Privy Chamber was closed to all but noblemen, councillors and
those sworn of it. None was to enter booted or spurred.[32] Most
interestingly, in houses where there was only one chamber which
served as a Presence Chamber and Privy Chamber, the king insisted
upon the maintenance of a distinction: 'the said chamber shall be
avoided and become the Privy Chamber after warning given to
cover the table there for our meals and also at other times when
our pleasure shall be to have the same private'.[33] And for all that
the Gentlemen of the Privy Chamber no longer lived in intimacy
with the king by reason of their duties, Charles I, the Venetian
envoy reported, 'every morning shows himself in the Privy
Chamber in the presence of all the lords and officials of that apartment. He detains them in conversation and salutes the others and
leaves them all happy and devoted'.[34] Other evidence suggests

that whilst they had declined from their earlier importance, Gentlemen of the Privy Chamber enjoyed access to the king and the favours which stemmed from it (below, pp. 164ff.).

The Privy Chamber, however, was no longer the innermost sanctum. Gentlemen of the Privy Chamber were barred admission to the Privy Lodgings beyond, and even peers and bishops who were permitted to enter the outer Withdrawing Room (next to the Privy Chamber) were denied further passage.[35] Here too the parchment book of orders for the regulation of the household concludes — with injunctions that they be read twice yearly and distributed to the various offices at court.[36] Significantly the book prescribes no rules for the government of the Bedchamber. In this, the nature of the archive reflects the new situation. The orders we have examined are concerned with household departments within the jurisdiction of the Lord Chamberlain. The Privy Chamber, once a separate commonwealth ruled by an independent head, has now fallen beneath his sway. Outside the Lord Chamberlain's authority, however, lies the Bedchamber, now performing the personal body service once the duty of the Privy Chamber; and here now we find an independent governor of familiar name — the Groom of the Stool.

It is during James I's reign that the Groom of the Stool emerges as First Gentleman of the (new) Bedchamber, with sole responsibility for admitting and supervising the officers of that chamber — 'excepting only at public ceremonies' when they observed the dictates of the Lord Chamberlain 'as the other noblemen usually do'.[37] Through all the changes consequent upon minor and female rule, the Groom of the Stool re-emerges in his former place of intimacy. In the reign of Charles I the orders suggest that he helps to dress the king in the mornings; he rides (along with the Master of the Horse) in the king's coach; he attends as cupbearer when the king dines in the Bedchamber or privately with the queen, and he performs, in general, 'all other offices and services of honour about our person'.[38] These evidently included the functions from which the officer derived his name, for it was specifically ordered that 'none of our Bedchamber whatsoever are to follow us into our secret or privy room when we go to ease ourself, but only our Groom of the Stool'.[39] As the symbol of his office, he wore 'a gold key in a blue ribbon'. This was a treble key to the Bedchamber which also opened 'every door of all our gardens, galleries and privy lodgings', and all the rooms in the various royal palaces.[40] Under his surveillance, Gentlemen of the Bedchamber waited on the king and slept by turns, either in the same room or in the Withdrawing Room, on a pallet (or put-you-up bed). Six grooms of the Bedchamber, waiting by rota, saw that linen and other necessaries were provided; pages, waiting beyond the doors, were brought in to make fires and beds. Leave to enter the Bedchamber could be granted only by the Groom of the Stool. His physical proximity to the king's person was not only implicit in his duties; it was recognized in his perquisites. For by virtue of his service, the Groom of the Stool enjoyed the rights of the leftovers after the king's repast — doubtless substantial 'scraps' from a diet of twenty-eight dishes.[41] He had also the right to the spoils of the king's goods, furniture and utensils on the death of the monarch.[42] It is clear that in moving from the now more ceremonial Privy Chamber into the Bedchamber, the Groom of the Stool had retained his personal services and proximity to the king.

When we step back and survey the ordinances, it would appear that the household of Charles I differed little from that of his immediate predecessors. There was nothing very novel about the orders promulgated. The parchment book of orders dated 1630 at most points echoes the Eltham Ordinances and the practices of Henry VIII. Throughout the 1630s, the various commissions appointed to investigate the household grounded their recommendations on Tudor precedents.[43] As the Reverend Garrard informed Wentworth in 1638, 'They look back to Henry the Seventh, Henry the Eighth and Queen Elizabeth's time'.[44] But we should not assume that what was grounded in precedent effected no alteration. Indeed by their very harking back to the days of Henry VIII, by the conscious renovation of rules and customs lost during the intervening years of a minor, two women and a Scot, the orders indicated a shift in the style, behaviour and character of the court. After the bawdy decadence of James I's reign, Charles sought to establish a well-regulated court as a shrine of virtue and decorum. Perusing the orders, we are struck by the repeated emphases on the moral *gravitas* expected of courtiers and the solemnity and ceremonial of court life. Any servant found 'so vicious and unmannerly that he be unfit to live in virtuous and civil company' was to be banished; passage to the king was not to be permitted via backstairs or privy galleries: rather 'all accesses generally shall be made through the rooms of state that thereby the honour of our court may be upheld'.[45] Elaborate rules prescribed a hierarchy of status 'limiting persons to places suitable to their qualities':[46] seats in the royal Chapel, places in the royal barge were reserved for those listed as entitled to them. None, Clarendon tells us, presumed to be seen 'in a place where he had no pretence to be'.[47]

Renewed emphasis on rules and forms was not the only change. The succession of the new monarch was also marked by a campaign of reform and retrenchment. Charles, we must not forget, inherited a war and a near impossible financial problem.[48] In the first year of his reign the Exchequer virtually stopped the payment of wages to household officers. By 1628 they in their turn were threatening to suspend the performance of their duties.[49] To add to the burden, the newly formed household was very large: as we have seen Charles retained many of his father's servants (probably hundreds) as supernumeraries; he had also to provide for a queen, both in addition to the thousand or more who constituted the regular household.[50] As well as superfluous officers, there were the endemic diseases of corruption and waste.

Early attempts were made to check these cancers. The records were studied and the number of places in each department was specified; none was to be admitted into any vacancy until the household was reduced.[51] Courtiers reported in 1629 that the horde of attendants was to be pared to the parsimonious level of Elizabeth's reign.[52] Courtiers and royal officials were forbidden to retain an excessive number of servants — presumably because these, along with their masters, fed at the king's expense.[53] Economies were ordered in all departments, in matters large and small: the Groom of the Stool was advised to purchase at the cheapest price rather than to take provisions automatically from the Great Wardrobe,[54] the number of carts assigned to each department on progresses was regulated and listed,[55] utensils of pewter, iron and wood were to be repaired rather than discarded;[56] and, amusingly, dogs were banned from household servants' chambers because they consumed food which might otherwise have gone to the poor.[57] On 5 May 1627, the Lord Chamberlain revived the ancient order of eating meat on trenchers made of bread in order to eliminate waste and provide scraps for the poor.[58] After 1634, the household expenses of visiting ambassadors were no longer defrayed beyond their first audience.[59]

Corruption was perhaps the biggest problem, not least because those responsible for its eradication were often those most guilty of peculation. Here in his own household Charles I adopted the methods which he was to apply to the government of the realm: the elaboration of detailed rules, the demands for regular reports, and the repeated hectoring enquiry, all of which reduced the scope and perhaps blunted the nerve for fraud.[60] The Clerk Controller was held personally responsible for seeing that provisions ordered were both received and serviceable.[61] Meat delivered was to be weighed daily, the weights entered in the books of the Counting House and the figures tallied monthly.[62] All officers were made accountable for arrears arising in their own departments. On 9 February 1627, for example, arrears in the Buttery, Pantry and Cellar were charged at the end of each month to those waiting during that period.[63] In 1628 the wages of all those in arrears were detained and when the sum held was inadequate to meet the deficit the relevant officers were summoned and discharged of their places.[64]

The most effective weapon in the war against corruption was an insistence upon efficient accounts. Accounting systems were evidently slack enough to allow many to purloin provisions without any risk of detection other than the occasional scrutiny of the Porter at the Gate. Some action was taken: in November 1628 it was ordered that arrears should be reckoned within fourteen days of the end of the month.[65] But deficient accounting remained. Auditors investigating the Board of Greencloth, as part of the commission for reform of the household in 1638, discovered serious deficiencies in the accounting of receipts and expenditure.[66] Blanks in the records and vague statements which made it impossible to attribute responsibility had very likely covered a multitude of sins. But for all the defects discovered, the arrears appear to have been greatest for the first two years of the reign 'at which time the household was unsettled and many occasions of waste and losses'.[67]

The attempt at reform was never more than a heavily qualified success;[68] arrears and losses, pilfering and peculation continued. The records reveal many instances of royal household property missing or found in private hands.[69] But this in itself is evidence, perhaps, that crimes were investigated and detected, even if they were not always solved. Whatever the verdict of historians, contemporaries felt the sharp edge of reform. Indeed requests like that of the Treasury commissioners in 1635 for a certificate of all fees and annuities paid 'together with a medium of all the receipts and the payments in your said office, cast up for the five years last past' must have chilled dishonest hearts.[70]

The limitations to reform lay often within the very nature of the court itself. Henry Lawton, Keeper of the king's Closet and hence a man close to the king, evidently stole a pair of candlesticks. Not only was he pardoned, he was given the candlesticks as a New Year's gift![71] More generally, retrenchment was always compromised by the king's overriding concern with maintaining the honour and majesty of the court. The St. George's day feast, for instance, was to be provided with all that was necessary and honourable 'and not with niggardliness nor yet with prodigality and waste, but in such a mean way as it may be seen and known to be most to the king's honour'.[72] The mean is of course a matter of interpretation. But Sir Thomas Herbert scarcely veiled his criticism of flamboyant extravagance when he reported to Lord Scudamore that at Newmarket many men were less well shod and fed than the gallants' horses.[73]

For if the accession of Charles I brought a new morality, a new formality and an impetus to reform and order, the new reign was most marked by another concern — a renewed emphasis upon ceremony and ritual. Emphasis upon the ritual associated with the person of the king and the office of monarchy not only pervades the regulations for the government of the court; it often provides the subject of ambassadors' and courtiers' correspondence. If the English as a race, then as now, were naturally inclined to formality, it was the king himself who fostered and insisted upon it. Charles, unlike his father but like Elizabeth, maintained the board of state in the Presence Chamber.[74] When he dined there, elaborate ceremony was prescribed. The Cupbearers and Carvers were ordered

> Before they give their attendance upon the king's person to wash their hands; the while they are with the Gentlemen Ushers in washing, every man in the chamber is to be uncovered; after the Gentleman Usher is to call for a bowl of sack . . . and to drink to one of the gentlemen that have washed. After the Carver hath his towel upon his shoulder, he and the Gentleman Usher goeth together in the Presence Chamber where they make three *congés* at three several parts of the Chamber and so come to the board.[75]

The ceremony of the king's retreat in the evening was similarly marked by a ritual which underlined the physical move from public to private rooms and the personal transmogrification from public office to individual person. At the command of the king, the Gentleman Usher called for torches at eight or nine o'clock; a Groom bearing the torch lights the way for the Yeoman Usher of the night watch who leads the party to the Pantry for refreshments. Thence they proceed to the Great Chamber where they surrender governance of the household to the Squires of the Body, until eight o'clock the following morning.[76]

This concern with ceremony in the daily round of court life becomes an obsession on public occasions, such as the receipt of ambassadors or festive days. Finet, we recall, commented early upon the new formality in receiving ambassadors.[77] The Reverend Joseph Mede noted in 1629 that envoys were now novelly entertained by great officers, not at the king's table.[78] Though he evidently spoke the language well, Charles addressed the envoy from France, for form's sake, not in French, but in English through an interpreter.[79] The duties of the Gentlemen Ushers concerning the reception of visitors,[80] the assigning of rooms and the conducting of envoys to audience were carefully delineated.[81] All were attended with due state, not least because on important public occasions the nobility were warned to attend at court.[82] The Venetian ambassador was clearly somewhat surprised (as well as flattered) to find that in 1626 he was accorded the honour of attendance by a privy councillor and knight of the Garter;[83] in 1637 it was the Earl of Arundel and duke of Lennox, the premier peers of England and Scotland, who escorted an ambassador to his coach.[84] Especial care was taken over public processions. When the king went to chapel, the Lord Chamberlain informed the Gentlemen Ushers what ambassadors would resort to court 'and then the Gentlemen Ushers shall send warning to all the noblemen, wheresoever they be in town . . .'.[85] When the nobility attended 'the Lord Chamberlain is to appoint the greatest estate [i.e. rank] at the time being present to accompany . . . the said ambassador till they come to the Closet'.[86] Meanwhile those in procession to chapel were ordered to progress in orderly ranks 'and not break them with pretences of speaking one with another', 'that being one of the most eminent and frequent occasions whereby men's ranks in precedence are distinguished and discerned'.[87] The service in the chapel repeated the elaborate ceremony of the household and undoubtedly the king's personal inclination to ritual was one of the major influences for liturgical changes.[88]

At the time of offering, a Groom of the Chamber was sent for the king's donation — a noble (i.e. 6s. 8d.). This was delivered to a Gentleman Usher who in turn handed the coin to the most eminent nobleman present, 'who shall kiss it and deliver it to the king immediately before the offering when the king is set on his knees . . .' After the king had kissed the chalice, he received the noble from the nobleman kneeling on his right and offered it to the cleric officiating.[89] If ritual was the court's religion, the religion of the court was undoubtedly ritualized.

Religion and ritual combined in the most spectacular public occasion in Caroline England — the feast of St. George. The ceremony associated with the order had declined since the death of Henry VIII. Elias Ashmole, the historian of the Garter, recalled, however, that 'in the beginning of King Charles I's reign . . . the gallantry of attendants began to increase and augment'.[90] Those attending the knights companions were conspicuous in greater numbers and for the enhanced richness of their habit.[91] Behind the renewed interest lay Charles I's own passionate concern for the Order of the Garter, and the due proprieties of its regulations and ceremonies.[92] The Garter exemplified the courtly culture of chivalry and piety, manliness and chastity.[93] Charles, one of his Bedchamber men tells us, never failed to wear the George.[94] In 1629 he revived the custom, long lapsed, of the sovereign's proceeding in person to Windsor on the eve of St. George's day.[95] He commissioned for the walls of the Banqueting House a magnificent canvas depicting the procession — though only Van Dyck's sketch for the painting was completed.[96] It is, however, sufficient to convey something of the majesty of the day — which was a public occasion of the sort in which the early Stuarts rarely showed an interest. In 1635 the Earls of Danby and Moreton 'disposed themselves for their more commodious passage and the people's view'.[97] For the ceremony of the investiture of Prince Charles in 1638, the king designed a public cavalcade from Somerset House in the Strand to the gates of Windsor Castle.[98] The Garter procession was clearly the public vaunting of the order, dignity and spirituality of the new royal court.

These then, for all the superficial continuity, were the changes apparent at court: retrenchment and reform, a return to the original rules and their enforcement and a renewed emphasis upon ritual and ceremony. Together they led Lucy Hutchinson to observe that 'the face of the court was much changed in the king'.[99] What was the significance for the court of these changes?

Charles I's court undoubtedly placed greater emphasis on the awful majesty of the king's presence. Custom and ritual, most notably the touching for the king's evil, had traditionally endowed the king's body with semi-divine qualities.[100] The new orders for the court reinforced this. Throughout stress is laid on the preservation of distance from the king's person, and rooms and objects immediately associated with the king's person. Gentlemen Ushers were ordered 'to see that no man of whatsoever degree he be of be so hardy to come to the king's chair, nor stand under the cloth of state . . . nor to lean upon the king's bed, nor to approach the cupboard where the king's cushion is laid, nor to stand upon his carpet'.[101] By extension, however, the mystical power of the king's person was evidently believed to rub off on objects and persons in contact with it. We recall that the Groom of the Stool inherited the personal objects of a deceased monarch. More graphically, it was ordered that that part of the towel which had been in contact with the king when he washed, the Gentleman Usher should raise above his head as he walked.[102] It was an emblem of the reverence due to the king, and a badge too of the special place held by his servant. These ideas were influential. It is not only the ignorant and superstitious, flocking to be cured of the king's evil, who bear testimony to the power of the king's person. Within their more sophisticated world courtiers themselves believed that the cramp rings given by the monarch to his servants (on Good Friday) had the capacity 'as it hath been often proved' to cure fits.[103] For the king's servants, living with their sovereign as the apostles with Christ, the image of divine monarchy became reality. Bishop Wren captured their world nicely when he turned to the king at grace and prayed: 'Give us this day our daily bread'.[104]

If more emphasis were placed on the mystical person of the king, fewer than ever enjoyed access to his presence. Charles I was not, it must be said, as isolated in Whitehall as some historians have maintained. He did, at least until 1637, undertake annual progresses — to Oxford and Woodstock, to Newmarket and the New Forest, even to Huntingdonshire and Lincolnshire.[105] But apart from the journey to Scotland in 1633, in the course of which the king dined with the Earl of Newcastle at Bolsover, with the earl of Exeter at Worksop, with Lord Willoughby en route to Grantham and enjoyed other 'great entertainments',[106] the progresses were confined to the south of England, to a circuit bounded by royal parks and residences.[107] Nor were they public displays in the style of earlier progresses: Charles did not, like Elizabeth, end his summer progress by a ceremonial procession through the city to Whitehall.[108] When Sir Thomas Herbert on progress in the spring of 1632 reported that 'the season and company conspiring together make Newmarket the theatre of our world', he referred not to the world of the county populace, nor even that of the minor county gentry, but to the confined world of the court.[109]

Even within the court, the renewed emphasis on formality, distance and privacy limited access to the king to a select few. James I's easy familiarity was succeeded by Charles I's near obsession with privacy.[110] Charles literally retreated behind closed doors. In 1626, to check the 'too much liberty given for the making and dispensing of the keys of his Majesty's privy lodgings', Charles ordered new treble locks to replace the old double locks.[111] A decade later a royal proclamation was issued further to prevent 'the freedom of access that sundry persons do take unto themselves into his Majesty's houses, gardens and parks by undue procurement of keys'. Only those in places of especial trust were issued keys, and Mr Boreman, the royal locksmith, engraved on each key the name of the person for whom it was made. The keys were then delivered to the Gentlemen Ushers.[112]

Few passed beyond the locked doors. Whilst the regular household of the king numbered in excess of a thousand, very few of these had direct contact with the monarch. A list of the names of the servants in the Privy Chamber in 1629 reveals four Gentlemen Ushers, eight Grooms, five Cupbearers, five Carvers, four Sewers and six Esquires of the Body.[113] The staff of the Bedchamber was smaller still. And apart from domestic servants, few were permitted to enter the Privy Lodgings. None below the degree of baron was allowed within the Privy Chamber,[114] and tighter still were the rules governing the Bedchamber. Only the Gentlemen themselves and the Princes of the Blood could come and go freely. The royal physicians, apothecaries and barbers were allowed in at specific times to discharge their functions; while the head officers of the household, the Lord Steward and the Lord Chamberlain, the rest of the Privy Council, and a handful of others who appeared on the Groom of the Stool's *entrée* list could also enter the apartment after leave had been asked and granted.[115] All others of quality waited upon the king in the Withdrawing Room where the Secretaries of State and Masters of Requests also had their audiences.[116] Most household officers dined with the Lord Chamberlain in the Great Chamber. Only the Gentlemen of the Bedchamber 'and those whom it shall please the king to appoint' supped with the monarch and partook of his own diet in the intimacy of his privy quarters.[117]

Here, for all the formality beyond, a more familiar world unfolds. This reflects not only human nature — the king's needs for informal communication, even for confidants — but also the geography and architecture of the palace. The stately grandeur of the Great Chamber and Presence gave way to the more domestic proportions of the Privy Lodgings. These, for all their majesty, may have been more confined that historians have believed. In 1633, for example, a quarrel over precedence arose between Sir Maurice Drummond and the Earl of Carlisle because the two met 'in a narrow passage next to the Bedchamber where two can hardly pass one by the other'. It is revealing too that whilst he could make no claim by his rank, Drummond must have presumed that his post of Gentleman Usher entitled him to vie for the precedency.[118]

Certainly the glimpses which the evidence allows shows the king living on close terms with his servants within the Bedchamber. Philip Warwick's *Memoirs* contain the intimate insights of a Gentleman of the Bedchamber whose 'near attendance', as the preface explains, provided details of the king's manners and conversation, personal habits and private devotions.[119] During the last two years of his reign, under the strain of war and defeat, Charles confided principally in Sir Thomas Herbert who attended in his Bedchamber. Herbert literally knew the king as one might a flat-mate: he noted the king's regular habits, his donning the George and Garter first thing in the morning and winding of his watch before bed; more interestingly he records discussions with the king of his dreams.[120]

The new emphasis on orders, rules and ritual underlined the proximity and authority enjoyed by those who waited personally on the king. When they handed over their keys at the service of all-night, the Gentlemen Ushers daily waiters surrendered their powers and the care of the king's person to the Esquires of the Body whose jurisdiction was total, overriding all rank.[121] One recalled

In the time of war, upon all occasions that required, I went into the Bedchamber and awaked his Majesty and delivered all letters and messages to his Majesty and many times by his Majesty's command, I returned answers to the letters and delivered orders. And I remember that coming to the king's Bedchamber door, which was bolted on the inside, the late earl of Bristol then being in waiting and lying there, he unbolted the door upon my knocking and asked me what news? I told him I had a letter for the king. The earl then demanded the letter of me which I told him I could deliver to none but the king himself, upon which the king said, 'the Esquire is in the right; for he ought not to deliver any letter or message to any but myself, he being at this time the chief officer of my house'.[122]

Examples such as these then remind us graphically of the intimacy and authority with the king that men holding no major functional office could enjoy. They suggest too that the Eltham Ordinances described a reality when they enjoined that Gentlemen of the Privy Chamber should come to know their king so well that they could tell his wants or moods by his countenance.[123]

Intimacy with the king was not confined to the Bedchamber. David Starkey has argued for the proximity which ensued (indeed the institutions of intimacy which emanated) from Henry VIII's pleasure of jousting with his courtiers.[124] Certainly we should not forget Charles I's relaxations and pastimes or those with whom he participated in games and sports. Charles, like his father, had a passion for hunting;[125] he enjoyed tennis and bowls — it was he who added a bowling green to the Privy Gardens at Whitehall[126] — billiards and a game of chess.[127] Just as important, he loved to gamble on his skills.[128] These were relaxed moments when ceremony was dropped: sports and wagers are the encounters of equals who have suspended social rank for the trial of force, expertise or wits. Charles not only dined and played bowls with Richard Shute at Barking Hall, he evidently peppered his conversations with the indiscretions which only unguarded relaxation indulges. Samuel Pegge relates one episode which is at least indicative, if not (without substantiation) reliable. 'Ah Shute', the king allegedly said, 'how much happier than I art thou in this blessed retirement from the cares of a crown'.[129] On occasions such as these, the king went attended by only a few select gentlemen — perhaps those who shared his interests — or, when hunting, the equerries and stable attendants who served him. Probably it was on such an occasion that a mere footman sold Charles a ring.[130] What we know for certain is that in and out of Whitehall a few men, men not always of the highest rank or most elevated office, enjoyed by their place access to and the trust of their king. If Clarendon is to be believed, Charles recognized the importance of these relationships: he 'saw and observed men long before he received them'.[131] Those who attended upon his person owed their places to the king's personal choice.

The importance which Charles attached to access and proximity can be clearly seen in the case of the queen's court. Charles, after all, was a young adult male; the new queen an impressionable teenager away from her mother and country for the first time. The king devoted great attention to the appointments of those who were to serve his wife.[132] Orders issued by Charles for the government of the queen's household, like those promulgated for the regulation of his own, were concerned with the maintenance of distance and with the control of access to the queen's Privy and Bedchambers.[133] In part this reflects the king's personal taste and desire for privacy with his wife. But the ordering of the queen's household was also at the centre of domestic politics and international diplomacy. For the first two years of his reign relations with France were dominated by the question of the queen's servants. The purge of the French from the English court in 1626 lay behind the breach and the war. Even after the peace of 1629 the debates continued. Successive French ambassadors manoeuvred to exact the terms of the original marriage treaty, to place a French bishop, doctor and chief Woman of the Maids as confidants to the queen. Charles I persistently denied their requests.[134] There can be little better evidence that domestic proximity meant influence. Within days of the expulsion of the French, Charles appointed four Protestant ladies to the queen's Bedchamber; Buckingham, anxious to secure his position in the new political circumstances, obtained one post for his mother.[135] The French ambassador, meanwhile, jockeyed to bring the countess of Carlisle into disfavour with the queen, largely because her husband was believed to be powerful and pro-Spanish.[136] The politics of Bedchamber appointments was the politics of access and influence. When policies depended upon personalities, the politics of access was the determination of power.

Politics

It is at this point that we must examine more carefully the importance of the domestic arrangements for court politics. Several questions present themselves: what were the fruits of access? How influential were the king's (and queen's) domestic servants? What part did the Privy Chamber and Bedchamber play in the factional struggles to place men or dictate policies? And more generally what was the importance of the household and court in the history of the reign of Charles I?

For many men the *raison d'être* of attendance at court was the quest for place or favour. It was a hazardous world where none who might be a rival could be trusted as a friend. As William Murray put it, 'the court is like the earth, naturally cold, and reflects no more affection than the sunshine of their master's favour beats upon it'.[137] It was the king alone who could fulfil or frustrate ambition. In the receiving of suits, as in all else, Charles insisted on order and formality. Philip Warwick recalled that 'in suits or discourses of business he would give way to none abruptly to enter into them, but looked that the greatest persons in affairs of this nature address to him by his proper ministers'.[138] The Master of Requests himself was obliged to wait for audience in the Withdrawing Chamber.[139] In the race for favour, then, the Gentlemen of the Bedchamber and Privy Chamber, those who depended upon no intermediaries, were undoubtedly the front runners. When we peruse lists of their names, we see that most of them received some grant or pension and many enjoyed a multiplicity of favours. Thomas Carey of the Bedchamber was granted in 1628 the profits of royal manors in Wiltshire and Somerset;[140] the same year William Murray received £800 worth of timber from the Forest of Dean.[141] George Kirke, Groom of the Bedchamber, was pardoned his offence of building houses on the Spring Garden wall and even granted that part of the wall on which he had built them.[142] Later, with his fellow servant Sir Robert Killigrew, he entered the infamous and profitable undertaking to drain the Great Level in Lincolnshire.[143] Posts within the Bedchamber led often and rapidly to profitable office: George Kirke became Gentleman of the Robes and keeper of the register in Chancery,[144] Sir James Levingstone, one of the auditors of the court of Wards,[145] Sir William Balfour, lord lieutenant of the Tower.[146] The most spectacular success story, of course, was Endymion Porter. A confidant of Charles as prince of Wales, he held no major formal office but that of Gentleman of the Bedchamber. But Porter was showered with grants and favours: royal lands, the customs on French wines, the farm of the wines at Chester, the surveyorship of the Petty Customs of the Port of London, the profits of the manufacture of white writing paper, and more.[147] By 1628, Porter's gross income was estimated at £3,000 a year, a sum which surpassed the wealth of some in the House of Lords. In 1631, he established a landed seat by purchasing — evidently on favourable terms — Hartwell Park, Northamptonshire from the king.[148] If few scaled Porter's peaks, all Charles's Bedchamber servants ascended with ease a mountain of patronage on which most scrambled for a toehold.

The king's personal servants not only advanced themselves, they promoted suits for others. Orders for the government of the Bed-chamber suggest that the Groom of the Stool 'and in his absence some one of the Gentlemen or Grooms of our Bedchamber' were those 'to whom we are pleased to give leave to move us as they shall see cause . . .'.[149] In 1628, for example, Thomas Carey of the Bedchamber successfully procured a pardon for his kinsman, Ferdi-nand Carey;[150] William Murray obtained for his son a scholar's place at Winchester College.[151] Several suitors wrote to Endymion Porter to request that he use his influence with the king on their behalf.[152] More significantly, even members of Buckingham's family worked through Porter in advancing their suits to the king.[153] Examples abound of the influence exercised by the Bedchamber in securing favours and grants for themselves, their families and their friends.

Nor was this the limit of their influence or activities. Even when they held no other official position, Gentlemen of the Privy Chamber and Bedchamber were often engaged on missions of a sensitive nature as personal appointees of the crown. The Eltham Ordinances had specified Gentlemen of the Privy Chamber should possess the linguistic qualifications which would enable them to act as occasional ambassadors, and this remained one of their important, if occasional, duties.[154] The king's privy servants attended ambassadors, and conducted them to their audience: in 1638 they were sent to meet Mary de'Medici, the queen's mother, at Harwich.[155] Porter, of course, was sent on a variety of missions in which his skills of connoisseurship and diplomacy were both called upon. Charles I also revived the responsibilities of his domestic servants for the guard of his person. In 1628, in addition to the Gentlemen Pensioners and the Esquires of the Body, 'his Majesty doth expect that the Gentlemen of the Privy Chamber . . . restore the practice and exercise of horsemanship'.[156] In 1633, on the progress to Scotland, the king was accompanied by a special regiment of horse consisting of servants from the Presence and Privy Chambers.[157] The performance of these duties could be the first rung on the ladder to high office: Lord Hunsdon, Lord Chamberlain to Elizabeth, explained to James VI that the Gentlemen Pensioners were no mere ornament to the monarchy, but 'a nursery to breed up deputies of Ireland and ambassadors into foreign parts'.[158] Occasionally we may catch glimpses of the king's domestic servants in overtly political roles: Lord Newburgh told Secretary Coke that in the summer of 1638 it was Patrick Maule, a Bedchamber Scot, and the marquis of Hamilton with whom Charles most discussed Scottish affairs.[159] Ten years earlier in 1628, when many tried to persuade the earl of Carlisle to hurry back to court, it was Thomas Carey whom lord treasurer Weston

sent to invite the earl into a 'strict friendship'.[160] The very infor-
mality and sensitivity of such roles makes it unlikely that many
instances survive in the records. But the evidence we have is sufficient to suggest that they were played often.

Clearly contemporaries believed this to be the case — even those
who were the greatest figures on the Council and in the conduct of
business. All too often we write history around the personalities of
the men who held the great offices of state. Contemporaries saw
things otherwise. Philip Warwick judiciously phrased what he knew
from experience: 'everywhere, much more in court, the numerous
or lesser sort of attendants can obstruct, create jealousies, spread ill
reports and do harm'.[161] During the 1630s Sir Thomas Wentworth
suffered constant anxieties about his position and reputation
because his distance deprived him of access to the king: 'a man's
presence', he knew well, 'moves much'.[162] Even those ministers
seemingly well entrenched at home sought to place agents close to
the king within the intimate confines of the Bedchamber. Archbishop William Laud, despite all the manifestations of Charles's
favour, manoeuvred to have his friend, William Juxon, dean of
Worcester, sworn Clerk of the Closet 'that I might have one that I
could trust near his Majesty, if I grow weak or infirm'.[163] Laud's
biographer, Peter Heylyn, adds that Laud promoted Francis Windebank to clerk of the Signet for the same reason — that so he might
have 'the king's ear on one side and the Clerk of the Closet on the
other.'[164] We cannot know how many such alliances were forged
between the Privy Lodgings and the king's ministers. But when
access was not the preserve of high office and the personal whim
of the monarch could make or break a career, ministers had to look
to their subordinates as well as to their equals.

Despite all we have said, however, there are no strong reasons for
believing that the Bedchamber or Privy Chamber were hotbeds of
factional politics in the reign of Charles I. There is no evidence for
Charles's reign that politics was controlled by ministers creating a
following in the Bedchamber, as the earl of Salisbury had done; nor
did any figure rise from the king's intimate service to the highest
place of power and influence as had first Sir Robert Carr, earl of
Somerset and, second, George Villiers, duke of Buckingham.[165]
Here what dictated the change appears to have been the succession
of Charles I in 1625. For, somewhat surprisingly, the evidence
suggests that, for all that he remained firmly in the king's
confidence, Buckingham never gained control of the Bedchamber.
In 1625 the new monarch had others to satisfy and many candidates
for his favour, as well as the duke. We have seen that Charles swore
in former members of his household as prince and retained James I's
former domestics — some of them Buckingham's enemies. The

Venetian ambassador also reports that Charles was anxious to secure the goodwill of the Scots and 'has confirmed many in their charges almost in greater numbers than the English'.[166] The list of domestic servants bears both statements out: the recurring names suggest continuity of families and personnel and a high proportion of Scots. Buckingham's exact position in the new Bedchamber remains something of an enigma. The duke, we know, was by Charles's side when news came of James I's death. The new king ordered that apartments be provided for Villiers next to his own.[167] Conway reports that Buckingham was the first to be sworn Gentleman of the Bedchamber, but here the problem starts.[168] For on 18 April 1625, dispatching the same news, Pesaro, the Venetian envoy, added that the duke had been made First Gentleman of the Bedchamber (presumably Groom of the Stool), 'receiving the golden keys and the pass everywhere, whereby he can have access to the king at all hours, even though shut in by triple keys, a confidence he enjoyed with the deceased'.[169] A week later, however, Pesaro, correcting his earlier report, informed the Doge that fuller enquiry had not borne this out: 'the duke did not take the oath as First Gentleman of the Bedchamber as I wrote, but was only received by his Majesty therein and so were the little duke of Lennox and the marquis of Hamilton'.[170] It is not clear what happened, but it seems likely that Pesaro had picked up a current rumour which had not materialized as fact. In the end Buckingham was made Master of the Horse, while the post of Groom of the Stool and First Gentleman of the Bedchamber went to Sir James Fullerton, former Gentleman of the Bedchamber and Master of the Wards and Liveries to Charles as Prince of Wales.[171]

This may have been significant, and deliberate policy. Though Buckingham clearly continued and even added to his strength as first minister, it was his personal relationship with the king rather than any control of the Bedchamber on which his power and influence rested. Later events show that it was a special relationship which was not repeated. It may be that from the beginning Charles determined to allow no one dominance of the Bedchamber: indeed the early arrangements for his household suggest attempts to heal faction, and incorporate a wide range of men and opinions. It was to Buckingham's house that Charles took the earl of Pembroke whom he then appointed to the junta for foreign affairs;[172] it was the young duke of Lennox who was sworn of the Bedchamber with Buckingham. The king's Privy Lodgings were never the preserve of the Villiers clan, their progeny or their policies.

Certainly after Buckingham's death the Bedchamber did not emerge as the key to factional politics. But this negative conclusion is not insignificant. The privacy behind which the king enshrined himself, the new formalities governing access at court, distanced Charles from his ministers, and separated too those who governed from those who held places of intimacy near the king. On the one hand, none from the Bedchamber rose to high office; on the other, many who governed in his name were in only infrequent personal contact with the king. This may have been deliberate policy: the separation of favour and proximity from functional office and the business of government. But whether or not it was so intended, the consequences were equally important. For free from the jockeyings of faction, within the privy quarters in which he spent much of his time, Charles was more able to exercise independent judgement on matters of policy. This independence, a determination to hear all sides of a question, was noted by the Venetian ambassador at the beginning of the reign; it remained a feature of the king's character in his handling of conciliar business.[173] Privacy too enabled the king to work uninterrupted, and whilst he never rose to the standards of bureaucratic diligence set by Philip II of Spain, Charles, by recent English precedents, was a monarch who worked — studying advice, perusing and annotating papers.[174] We know that when he thought and wrote, he liked to be alone.[175] And when the king was alone it was his own mind which was most at work.

The separation of personal service from government business, and the privacy and independence of the king influenced the political course of the reign. Charles, for the most part, remained above faction. Especially after the death of Buckingham, a wide variety of views on domestic and foreign affairs was expressed at court. And whilst on certain matters the king listened on some occasions to particular men — Weston on questions of finance, or Laud on religion — the evidence suggests that men were chosen to reflect rather than to determine the personal views of the king. None emerged as the king's confidant on all aspects of business: Clarendon and Sir Philip Warwick agreed that Charles limited 'persons to places suitable to their qualities', retaining what Secretary Dorchester called the 'total directory' in his own hands.[176] Charles was never really close to those like Weston and Laud whose views he most respected;[177] by contrast he seldom agreed with Holland and Hamilton who were among the principal recipients of his favour.

This may in turn have contributed to a reign of greater stability. Under James I factional rivalries had risen to such a level that they had overflowed into parliament and the localities, thrown up and swept away ministers and flooded the Council Chamber and the House of Lords. Rivalries of course persisted into the new reign. But after the death of Buckingham, newswriters commented frequently on the peace prevailing at court: James Howell told Wentworth in the spring of 1635 that 'All things pass calmly at court and no factions fomented';[178] the countess of Devonshire described a 'great calm'.[179] For all the satirical contempt which he expressed for 'Lady Mora' in his correspondence with Wentworth, Laud was obliged to live in peace with Weston and Cottington, and was rebuked by Charles when he tried to make political capital out of a minor incident.[180] The very longevity of Charles I's ministers bears testimony to the muted tone of factional rivalries. Weston died as the longest serving lord treasurer since Salisbury — a remarkable feat during a period of retrenchment. No minister during the 1630s lost his place as the consequence of factional warfare. Indeed Charles was quick to discourage and suppress attempts to unseat his ministers and followed as his policy the rule which he delivered to Wentworth: 'the marks of my favour that stop malicious tongues are neither places nor titles, but the little welcome I give to accusers and the willing ear I give to my servants'.[181] Wentworth grasped the point. When, in 1638, he advised Newcastle concerning conduct at court he urged him not to trust to factions nor 'to seek to strengthen or value yourself with [the king] by any other means than those of his own continued grace'.[182]

A balance of factions and a king who, exercising his own judgement, remained above the strife of faction was not pleasing to all. Those for whom personal favour was subordinate to the exercise of power, those for whom the advancement of personnel was linked with the promotion of particular policies were often discontented. It is both interesting and illuminating that the best example of discontent, of the frustration of favour without power, comes from within the Bedchamber itself. Henry Rich, earl of Holland, undoubtedly enjoyed the king's (as well as the queen's) personal favour. Appointed, for a time, Master of the Horse, the recipient of several grants and gifts, Holland was reputed in 1629, a, perhaps *the*, court favourite. By 1636 he was chief justice of the Forests and Groom of the Stool. But for all the favours he enjoyed, on matters of religion and foreign affairs, Holland never got his way. He remained puritan and pro-French. For these reasons, in addition to normal rivalries, he was hostile to both Weston and Laud and twice tried to embarrass the lord treasurer, on the second occasion with some measure of success. Yet Holland failed to unseat his enemies and to advance his policies.[183] He is the paradigm of the court in which personal favour was not the same as political power.

In order to wield greater sway, Holland, along with others, pursued another avenue of influence: the court of Henrietta Maria.[184] For in the queen's court Holland wielded influence as well as enjoyed favour. In Henrietta Maria's household, affection for persons and support for policies were more closely intertwined.

That is not to say that the queen's court was a monolith committed
to one cause, or dominated by one faction. Among the queen's
domestics and followers were her court ladies, and her minions
(such as Wat Montague and Thomas Jermyn) many of whom were
Catholic, and a third group described by Professor Smuts as the
queen's 'puritan followers'. These last may not be as puritan as
Smuts (and the ambassadors upon whose evidence he relies)
believes, but they were clearly a group distinct from and even
antagonistic to the queen's Catholic entourage. What assembled
them as a group within the queen's household was their commitment to a French alliance — as the arm of military intervention for
the restoration of the Palatinate. Under Henrietta Maria's patronage
and protection they attempted two goals: to overthrow those sympathetic to Spain or committed to peace and to use the queen in
order to persuade the king to their policy.[185] It is indicative of the
nature of Caroline court politics that on both counts they failed.

Charles remained hostile to attempts to proselytize or to mount
palace coups which stemmed from the queen's household. Courtiers were banned from the queen's chapel and the king scarce
concealed his anger at conversions to Rome fostered by the
queen's confessors.[186] Similarly, Holland's attempt, backed by the
queen, to unseat Weston by an affray with his son resulted for a
time in the earl's disgrace and the queen's embarrassed retreat.
Throughout the 1630s, the Catholic *dévots* and the 'puritan
followers' manoeuvring from within the queen's court remained
an irritant to the king. But there is no evidence that by means of
such machinations they came near to achieving their aims.

Indeed Charles I's relationship with his wife exemplifies his
domestic arrangements. After Buckingham's death, Charles, as
Thomas Carey reported, 'wholly made over all his affections to his
wife'.[187] But it would seem that the queen exercised little
influence or power.[188] Whatever her natural inclinations, there
were many who by interest pressed her to do so. Charles,
however, remained determined and the influence wielded by the
queen and her followers was limited to intrigues played behind the
scenes. Until the years of crisis and war, when his trusted ministers
were off the stage, Charles maintained even in his relations with
his wife the separation of favour from influence which had
characterized the style of his court.

Court and kingdom

It is time for us now to reflect on a broader question still: what
may we learn from the institutional organization and politics of the

court about Charles I as king or about his aims and values for the government of the country? It was, of course, a contemporary truism that subjects followed the examples set by sovereigns. John Owen versed it nicely in one of his popular epigrams, published in 1628.

> All subjects in their manners follow kings
> What they do, bids; forbearing forbids things
> A king's behaviour sways his subjects lives
> As the first mover all the fixt stars drives.[189]

Charles I clearly attached great importance to the belief. As he set a personal example of order, comeliness and sobriety at court, so in turn, the court, reflecting his virtues, would become the model for the country. The orders of 1630 for the regulation of the household made the wider purpose clear: 'to establish government and order in our court which from thence may spread with more order through all parts of our kingdoms'.[190] Sir Edward Moundesford writing to Framlingham Gawdy recognized the broader significance of changes at court. 'There is', he opined, 'a general reformation in hand for court and country'.[191]

The point is reinforced by a study of the culture of the court. Paintings, plays and masques were not an empty show for the self-enhancement of the king's majesty. Charles I personified the belief, shared by advanced connoisseurs such as Inigo Jones and the earl of Arundel, that art and architecture performed an essentially moral function, that art might elevate men to what they might become. This is an important subject which awaits full investigation. It is perhaps significant that in the privy galleries we find a predominance of paintings on religious subjects, suitable objects perhaps for the private meditations of a king who, exercising his power by divine authority, owed account to God. In the state rooms at St. James's, by contrast, hung the famous Van Dyck of Charles I and his riding master, placed at the end of a series of portraits of the emperors of Rome.[192] Its effect, as Sir Oliver Millar argued, 'must have been most spectacular, as if Charles were riding out through the arch to join the Roman emperors of Titian and Guilio Romano'.[193]

The masque was the fullest expression of the belief that culture might inculcate values to be emulated — by courtiers and ultimately those beyond. To take the best example, the theme of Thomas Carew's *Coelum Britannicum* was reform at court and throughout the realm.[194] The masque opens with a panegyric on the monarch whose exemplary life has 'transfused a jealous heat of imitation through your virtuous court'. The power of example, we are told, has spread outside the court even to the gods and the stars whose claims to virtue are upheld now only in so far as they reflect the standards of the king's shining example, the quintessence of virtue. Over the king's chamber door, behind which (in contrast to former profligate days) he lived in perfect love and harmony with the queen, is inscribed 'Carlo Maria', an emblem of the essence of all pure love, the model for all. With immorality banished, with love and union exemplified by the king and queen at court, it could not be but that their example would be followed in the country: 'there is no doubt of a universal obedience where the law giver himself in his own person observes his decrees so punctually'. *Coelum Britannicum* is all the more interesting to us because its author Thomas Carew was a Sewer in ordinary to Charles I, a Gentleman of the Privy Chamber and in high favour with the king. Something of a profligate himself, he evidently framed his masque in accordance with the king's tastes and values — and possibly under royal direction.[195]

If the court were to be the model for the reform of the country, the attempts to order the household, establish hierarchy and deference, remove abuses, cut waste, preserve honour and establish authority in the proper hands takes on a broader significance. For much suggests that the qualities which he sought at court, the fundamental conservatism which underlay them, the new vigour and intricate rules which were the methods by which he hoped to establish them, were those which he urged in the government of the country. The country, as we know, fell long short of the 'universal obedience', which in Carew's masque followed the king's example. Even at court, the perfect world was never established. Peculation continued; rivalries were thinly veiled. The king's favourite poet probably died of syphilis; his court painter, Van Dyck, kept a mistress.[196] At court as in the country, for all the reforms, the evils lurked in corners or underground. As Robert Reade ironically told Windebank in 1640: 'We keep all our virginities at court still, *at least we lose them not avowedly*'.[197] In the Caroline court itself lay the achievements and the limitations of Caroline government.

Study of the court and household has led us to reflect on the king's intentions for the government of the country. For in a personal monarchy, the changes made by a monarch in his own household are intimate revelations of his person, and the king was the government. This was perhaps never so true again after the reign of Charles I. After 1660 Charles II received a public revenue for the duties of public office; feudal revenues were abolished; ministers needed to account to parliament as well as the king; the emergence of parties linked royal favour to the capacity to wield influence; boards and departments removed the business of government yet further from the royal household. In 1688 ideas concerning the separation of the king's person from his office (first aired in 1642) were translated into action. The court lived on as an important focus of politics. Under Charles I it had been *the* focus of politics, the centre of personal monarchy.

6. History, English law and the Renaissance*
(with Christopher Brooks)

In 1970 Professor D.R. Kelley published an excellent book on the study of law and history in sixteenth-century France. He argued that the French scholars, combining legal and historical studies, came to examine institutions and customs in historical terms. This enquiry was prompted by intellectual stimuli and by the immediate political and legal situation. The philological investigations of classical scholars and the early growth of 'the archive tradition' advanced French historical scholarship; the multiplicity of French customs, the rival jurisdictions and the upheaval of the French wars of religion directed French scholars to the history of their own customs and institutions. The debate initiated by polemic emphasized the need for learned enquiry.[1]

In a recent number of *Past and Present*,[2] Professor Kelley, following Maitland and Pocock, has emphasized the comparative insularity of the English lawyers and historians of the sixteenth and early seventeenth centuries. According to Kelley, the acceptance of common law procedures and the relative order of the English polity deprived them of the stimuli for this new approach. English lawyers did not accept that their law was the product of time and historical development. Instead, from the days of Fortescue to the hegemony of Coke, they preferred the myth that the common law had emerged full-grown and perfect from the mists of time out of mind. Convinced of the perfection of their legal system, English lawyers agreed with Coke's claim that the 'common laws are the most equal and most certain, of greatest antiquity and least delay and most easy to be observed' of any possible laws. In short, the English 'had too strong a faith in a permanent and unchanging tradition' — a faith epitomized in their persistent denial of the impact of the Norman Conquest on English society, institutions and law. Instilled with these attitudes, English scholars were blind to the new perspectives. If they read the French writers, it was for the polemic of Hotman's *Franco-Gallia*, not for the scholarship of the disciples of Cujas.[3]

Only one light gleams at the end of the otherwise gloomy tunnel of early modern English scholarship — the light of Sir Henry Spelman.[4] Spelman 'acquired a remarkably broad knowledge of European law', feudal as well as civil and canon; significantly, he worked in contact with foreign scholars.[5] Spelman 'discovered' feudalism and interpreted English law, customs and institutions in the light of that discovery. But he was neither wholly published nor appreciated, for by the 1620s Sir Edward Coke had established an inviolable orthodoxy.

In this short comment, we would like to suggest that in the late sixteenth and early seventeenth centuries English lawyers were less confident about their legal code, and more aware of the influence of continental and civil law upon the common law than Professor Kelley has allowed. English historians showed at least as much interest in the study of customs and institutions as their French colleagues, whom they read with interest and whose techniques they applied to their own studies. Coke does not epitomize an attitude prevalent since Fortescue; he represents an important change in attitudes to the law and history.

In the late sixteenth century, any claim for the perfection of English law would have been highly contentious, even among English lawyers. From *c.* 1580, there was an apparently unique increase in central court litigation, and many changes in substantive law and in court procedures came with it. An important consequence of these developments was a growing anxiety about the uncertainty of the law. This concern was expressed most frequently by unsympathetic laymen,[6] but there is some evidence that it was shared by the common lawyers. In the 1590s, Francis Bacon pointed out that uncertainty was 'the principal and most just challenge that is made to the laws of our nation at this time'.[7] Lord Keeper Egerton listed it as a primary concern 'to propound to the Iudges howe the Incertentye of Iudicature maye be reformed and reduced to more certainty'.[8] Even those lawyers who praised the common law were at pains to defend it from this criticism.[9] Until the first decade of the seventeenth century, attempts to remedy the problem of uncertainty ranged from Bacon's proposals for a digest of the laws to a general improvement in the quality of legal literature.[10]

It is true that ideas about law reform stopped short of consideration of the civil law as an alternative to the English legal system. One reason for this may have been that by the early seventeenth century the civil law was associated with arbitrary government. But the numerous proposals to codify and reform continental laws suggest that the common lawyers were justified in claiming that their law was no less certain or more subject to delay than rival European systems.[11] Nor were such claims always based on mere ignorance or prejudice. One of the harshest attacks on the civil law is contained in Sir John Davies, *A Discourse of Law and Lawyers* (1615), a work which displays considerable familiarity with continental jurists.[12]

Professor Kelley observed that proposals made by Bacon for a digest of the common law probably received little response from his fellow practitioners.[13] But one part of Bacon's programme for change — the reform of the statutes — found wide support in the legal profession. It was generally held that the statutes were too numerous and too confused. In 1592, Coke told parliament that there were so many laws that they could aptly be called '*Elephantinae leges*'.[14] In 1597, Egerton, speaking for the Queen, said that there were too many laws, that many were obsolete or out of use, many too severe or too slack, and 'many of them so full of difficulties to be understood that they cause many controversies and much trouble amongst the subjects'.[15] Other lawyers who supported Bacon's plan were among the most learned of the day: James Whitelocke, William Noy, Thomas Hedley, William Hakewill, Henry Hobart, and the two Finches.[16]

Thus, far from vaunting the perfection of their legal system, Elizabethan lawyers saw the need for reform. Inevitably, reform raised questions about the nature of change. During the late sixteenth century there is nothing to suggest that lawyers were reluctant to face change. The common law was viewed as the application to particular circumstances of a set of principles or maxims which had their standards of proof in divinity, natural law and philosophy. The judicial decisions of the past were not held to be authoritative; they were of interest only in so far as they contained reasoning which helped to resolve a case in hand.[17] When Coke elevated past decisions into rules which bound the present, he introduced a major new innovation, one which gave history, albeit mythical history, an importance it had not enjoyed in the sixteenth century. For Elizabethan lawyers, reason, not history, was the guide. Given this outlook, change could be accommodated easily. A sixteenth-century writer on manorial jurisdictions, William Barlee, accepted without concern that the queen could reform the law on the basis of the principle, *Cum in novo Casu novum remedium abhibendum*.[18] In the parliament of 1601, two lawyers, Thomas Harris and Thomas Wiseman, seconded the assertion that the 'times are not what they have been, and therefore, the necessity of the times requires a necessity of the Alteration of the laws'.[19]

Indeed, in some respects, change was an accepted feature of the common law. This is illustrated well by the rules which were being developed for the judicial interpretation of statutes. The author of the *Discourse upon the Exposition and Understanding of Statutes*, which was transcribed by the future Lord Keeper, Thomas Egerton, readily accepted it as ordinary practice that judges should interpret statutes for the benefit of the commonwealth or according to equity even if the interpretation was contrary to the 'wordes' of the statute. This work demonstrates a clear appreciation that statute law changed the common law, and that judicial decisions altered the way statutes were applied during different historical periods.[20]

The common lawyers of the late sixteenth century were also a good deal less insular than Professor Kelley leads us to believe. Sir William Sta[u]nford, a lawyer said by Fulbecke to have been well versed in foreign learning, told his readers that to discover the origins of benefit of clergy, they should consult the canonists since the privilege had its origins in their law.[21] In the discussion of equity in his popular and practical book, *Symboleographia*, the attorney, William West, referred to Budé, Oldendorp and Corasius. Kelley has shown that of these Budé had particular importance in the development of the French historical school.[22]

This acquaintance with continental jurists is not surprising. From about 1570, an increasing number of English lawyers preceded their legal training at the inns of court by stays at Oxford and Cambridge,[23] where the civil law curricula offered contact with continental scholarship. From 1587, the Regius Professor of Civil Law at Oxford was Alberico Gentili, an Italian scholar with a European reputation.[24] As B.P. Levack has shown, the English civilians were not antagonistic to the common law.[25] There is even evidence that some of the common lawyers took up the study of civil law. The judge, James Whitelocke, had been a student of Gentili. Justice of the King's Bench, Sir John Doddridge, was learned in the civil and ecclesiastical law.[26] Professor Kelley writes that the English were reluctant to admit that the civil law had ever had any influence on the common law.[27] But an unsigned early seventeenth-century tract openly acknowledges that in the reign of King Stephen,

> the code and other *partes* . . . [of the civil law] . . . were familiarly read by our English Lawyers and I thinke as well by the Com*m*on as Canon Lawyers and in Henry the thirds time we see by Bracton that it was *parte* of the studye of a Com*m*on Lawyere . . .[28]

Only when the political disagreements of the early seventeenth century aligned the civilians with the champions of an omnipotent prerogative did the common lawyers show antipathy towards them. Although some parts of Dr. John Cowell's *Interpreter* were rejected because of their political implications, a later purged edition was used as a basic guide for two centuries of common lawyers.[29]

Maitland once observed that the desire for reform of the law nearly always goes hand in hand with a desire to know its history.[30] This appears to have been as true of the sixteenth century as it was of the early nineteenth. Far from being the basis of insularity and historical short-sightedness, the attitudes of Elizabethan lawyers were accompanied by a keen interest in the kind of history Professor Kelley has found in France.

The late sixteenth-century interest in history reached its zenith in the foundation of the Society of Antiquaries in 1588. In the 1590s, William Camden introduced the members of the Society to the etymological and philological scholarship of the humanists of Europe, especially those of France with whom he had entered into correspondence. Camden spoke directly of 'a consonancy and a correspondency between the name of a thing and the thing named'.[31] In the light of Camden's example, most members of the Society employed etymological analysis in their discourses on the history of English institutions and offices. Though the papers were marked by nationalistic pride, the antiquaries were ready to accept that many customs were not of ancient foundation. Some went so far as to argue that most offices had been borrowed from the Normans.[32]

These views were shared by the lawyer members of the Society, a number of whom were involved in Bacon's plan to reform the statutes. Sir John Davies, the future Solicitor for Ireland, appreciated the impact made by the Conquest on offices and institutions; William Hakewill argued that the Normans had altered Saxon laws.[33] Though some of the manuscript debates of the Society's last meetings are lost, we know that they intended to discuss the origins of the civil and common law in England.[34] The question for debate suggests that the issue was not prejudged. There is some evidence that the members of the Society were taking an interest in the importance of feudal tenures and service. Notes on holding land 'in capite' and on summonses to parliament may be evidence of an appreciation of the connection between tenure and service.[35] Certainly by 1610 one of the founder members of the Society, Sir Robert Cotton, had arrived at a full understanding of the impact of the Conquest on tenures:

I tak Escuag to be a Relation to a Knights fee, and so to be of the sam antiquity, both beginning with the Conqueror that intended perpetually

to hold and keepe in obedience what before he had achieved by
violence. . ... In this tenure som do immediately hold of the King others
from the Lords from whom they hav bin infeoffed.[36]

The meetings of the Society of Antiquaries came to an end perhaps
as early as 1605, but the members did not forget their acquaintance
with etymological techniques and continental humanist scholarship. In his *Argument upon the Question of Impositions*, John
Davies included as part of the law of England 'the generall law of
Nations, and the law merchant, the Imperial or Civil law, the
Canon or Ecclesiastical law . . .'.[37] During the debate on impositions in 1610, another member of the Society, John Doddridge,
argued that

old statutes are obscure and the reason is, for that we are so far
removed from the times wherein they were made. And therefore, there
are two excellent expositions to be admitted of them, the histories of
the time and present practice pursuant, for *usus est optimus legum
interpres*.[38]

When John Selden entered into the intellectual circle of Cotton
and Camden, he entered an arena of cosmopolitan scholarship. In
his *Titles of Honor* (1614), he praised Budé, Alciat, Hotman, and
Cujas as the most learned civilians. Following their works, he
argued that the Normans had introduced the military fief into
England.[39] Two years later, in his commentary on Fortescue,
Selden maintained that Norman customs had brought changes to
English law as 'new nations . . . bring alwaies some alteration'.[40]
Selden was not alone. The anonymous editor of Bracton's *De
Legibus et Consuetudinibus Angliae* urged his readers to excuse
Bracton's support for papal authority as but an expression of his
time. He insisted that Bracton be read in his own historical context
and argued that even if heresy were then considered to be law
'now it has been changed by the sanctions of more recent statutes,
just as in other causes, the judges' decisions have departed from
ancient ruling . . .'.[41]

It is clear that before Sir Henry Spelman published, others had
arrived at an understanding of feudalism and of the importance of
feudal tenure for English law. The meetings of the Society of Antiquaries of which he was a founder member were the stimulus for
Spelman's work. His *Antiquity and Etymology of Terms and
Times for Administration of Justice* (1614) shows the beginning of
his own understanding of feudalism. It was probably a fuller
version of a paper intended to be delivered at an earlier meeting
of the Society. Certainly it was written before Spelman entered
into correspondence with the French antiquaries, on the occasion
of his son's visit to the continent in 1619.[42]

There is no reason why the synthesis of legal and historical studies in England should surprise us. No less than in France, the late sixteenth century in England saw great improvement in the condition of the archives. Many of the archivists, men like William Bowyer and Arthur Agarde, became members of the Society of Antiquaries and made the records available to the lawyers and anti-quaries. Together they tried to improve the archives still further. Cotton worked with Arthur Agarde on compiling lists of exchequer records; he helped Ferdinando Pulton to make a book of statutes and worked on William Bowyer's private calendar of papers in the Tower.[43] The friendships of antiquaries, heralds and lawyers who had members of the Society kept them in close contact throughout the reign of James I.

Yet if we are to argue for an appreciation among lawyers of the development and change in the common law, we must still con-front Sir Edward Coke. If it is true that late sixteenth- and early seventeenth-century lawyers and historians did not share his attitudes, how was it that from the 1620s his views gained all but universal acceptance? It is unfortunate that we know all too little of Coke's own earlier thought. But, clearly, by the 1620s attitudes to the common law could not be divorced from the political con-flicts of Jacobean England. Most of the issues of James I's reign — impositions, parliamentary judicature, and so forth — arose from genuine doubt. The law had always been expected to provide guidelines; in times of disagreement, it was looked to as an arbiter — a view encouraged by James when he referred the contentious impositions to the judges. The parliamentary debate on impositions in 1610 illustrates how certainty of law was sought as a remedy for political confusion. Nearly every lawyer who spoke on this issue stressed the importance of having certain law. But Elizabethan legal thinking had emphasized legal change. Thomas Hedley struggled as he tried to accommodate the Elizabethan view of law to the Jacob-ean need for certainty. He denied the 'aspersion of levity and change and consequently of uncertainty', and argued that 'change of opinion upon good grounds is not levity but rather constancy to goodness and reason'. The common law of England was as certain as any law 'for it is the work of time, which hath so adopted and accommodated this law to this kingdom . . .'.[44] Though sophisticated, Hedley's argument was beset by difficulties. William Hakewill avoided them by a radical departure from Eliza-bethan attitudes and his own earlier historical outlook. He main-tained that the law was certain because it was unchanging and unchanged, constant from Saxon and pre-Saxon times to the present day and thus a reliable arbiter.[45] It was an argument born of the need of the moment rather than from a tradition of thought.

As consensus dissolved, a view of law based on natural law and divinity was no longer satisfactory.

As the political conflict intensified, the stand on precedent and the 'old constitution' became established. Sir John Davies, Sir Robert Cotton, even at times John Selden, who had all seen English law in a European and feudal context, themselves propagated the common law myth of Coke. Political division had been a source of inspiration for legal and historical scholarship in France; in England it narrowed scholarship. The past was looked to now to solve the problems of the present. From the etymological scholarship of the French humanists, the English historians turned to the politic histories of classical Rome and renaissance Florence.

Sir Henry Spelman, more than any other, remained aloof from the conflict. During the 1620s he worked on his Glossary, the *Archaeologus*. Merely developing earlier antiquarian investigations, he outlined clearly a feudal interpretation of English society, law and government.[46] He criticized those historians of parliament who looked at the past through the eyes of the present.[47] Did he have his colleagues in mind? Spelman's works were not appreciated until after his death. In part, this was because they remained scattered and unpublished. More important, they could not be entertained until the political conflict and the justification of present courses by past precedents had ended. Spelman's scholarship developed from the attitudes to law and the historical studies of the last decades of the sixteenth century. It is important that these decades should not be lost in an over-hasty sweep from Fortescue to Sir Edward Coke.

7. The Earl of Arundel, his circle and the opposition to the Duke of Buckingham, 1618 – 1628 *

Historians concentrating on the House of Commons have all but ignored the early Stuart nobility both as individuals and as members of the House of Lords.[1] Yet as a reward for their loyal service to his mother, Queen Mary of Scots, James I restored to power and office the Howard family which, in the decades before Elizabeth's reign, had counselled kings and broken favourites. We await a full study of the patronage and influence wielded by that family at court and in the localities. This essay will investigate the activities of Thomas Howard, Earl of Arundel, head of the senior Norfolk branch of the family, and examine from the evidence of his career the alignments in the Privy Council and the House of Lords during the 1620s.[2] The first section provides a detailed narrative of Arundel's position at court, a narrative which will demonstrate that issues concerning the constitution, religion, and foreign policy cannot explain Arundel's position or the political co-operation of the diverse men who made up his circle. In the conclusion, I shall suggest that, nevertheless, these men shared attitudes and values which have yet to be recognized and studied by the historian of politics.

Though best known as a great patron of artists, as 'The father of vertu', Arundel was prominent in his own age as one of the greatest noblemen and as Earl Marshal of England. His first biographer, Sir Edward Walker, Garter King at Arms, praised Arundel's personal qualities as well as his patronage of scholars and artists.[3] The Earl of Clarendon, however, depicted him in his History with an uncharacteristically venomous pen, dismissing those qualities as a mask behind which lived a contemptible man. Clarendon's Arundel was a nobleman apparently majestic and imperious yet in reality weak and vulgar, who donned an air of scholarship to disguise a lack of understanding, who appeared hospitable, but was arrogant and aloof.[4] But Clarendon's distaste for the Earl owed much to an inherited quarrel. In the Short Parliament of 1640 when he led the attack on the jurisdiction of the Earl Marshal's court, Hyde perhaps recalled that in 1624 his uncle had suffered at the hands of Earl Marshal Arundel.[5] In his later years as Earl of Clarendon, when he wrote his History, 'he still remembered with feeling the days when as Mr. Edward Hyde he was at cross purposes with this Earl of ancient lineage.'[6] But, whatever his own view, even Clarendon recognized the reverence held by many for Arundel 'as the image and representative of the primitive nobility and native gravity of the nobles'. We must attempt to understand the political importance of the Earl Marshal and the origins of this image during the years before Hyde encountered him.

I

Shortly after the accession of James I, Thomas Howard was restored to the earldom of Arundel, though not to the hereditary dukedom of Norfolk. Only some of his family estates came to him, while his great uncle Henry Howard, Earl of Northampton, and Charles Howard, Earl of Nottingham, enjoyed the rest.[7] He only repurchased Arundel House from Nottingham in 1607 with the aid of his wife's fortune and for some years he suffered financial hardship.[8] But Arundel soon became an important figure at court. He was frequently active in the tilts. He became intimate with Prince Henry, and friends from the prince's circle such as John Holles, future Earl of Clare, were to be his political allies in later years.[9] He earned the favour of the king and the regard of the ambassadors. When Arundel was about to embark on his first trip to Italy in 1612, the Venetian ambassador wrote to the Doge to urge that the young nobleman be shown hospitality:

> . . . he is the premier Earl of this kingdom, in which there are no Dukes save the King's sons . . . nor Marquises save Winchester who does not come to Court. Arundel will be, through his wife, a daughter of the Earl of Shrewsbury, heir to sixty thousand crowns a year; he is nephew of Northampton who has no children and is very powerful in the government.[10]

While Arundel was absent on his second trip to Italy in 1614, Northampton died, and he returned to claim his substantial inheritance in money and land.[11] He returned, too, as the senior representative of a family which after the Earl of Salisbury's death virtually monopolized court office and royal patronage. In May 1616 the death of the Earl of Shrewsbury added (through Arundel's wife

Alethea, heir and daughter of the Earl of Shrewsbury) the substantial Talbot inheritance, to the Howard legacy.[12] In the same year, having publicly expressed formal conversion to the Anglican faith, Arundel was chosen as a privy councillor and so gave evidence of his intention to follow his uncle into power and office.[13]

In 1616, it seemed that he would not wait long. The favourite Robert Carr, Earl of Somerset, fell to the machinations of a cabal of the old nobility led by the Earls of Pembroke and Southampton. There is no evidence for the Venetian ambassador's belief that Arundel, Pembroke's brother-in-law, played a part in those intrigues;[14] rather he shared with Somerset an interest in art and architecture which may have bound them in friendship.[15] But despite his known attachment to some of Somerset's circle, Arundel was never tainted, as were other Howards, by suspicion of involvement in the Overbury murder. The fall of Carr suggested Arundel as the natural successor to his uncle's office and influence.

The opposition to Somerset, however, was in part an expression of discontent with the policy of a marriage alliance with Spain, a policy with which the Howards were identified and sympathetic — if only because it was the royal policy. This issue may have alienated Arundel from his brother-in-law Pembroke, while resentment at the Earl of Suffolk's manipulations of family lands, which Arundel regarded as his own, estranged him from his Howard kinsmen.[16] Arundel's isolation from his family prevented the re-establishment of Howard control of patronage. Southampton's faction took advantage of the situation to promote as a candidate for royal favour a puppet, as they thought, of their policies — George Villiers.

It has not been sufficiently noticed that the years which saw the rise of Villiers to a viscountcy and intimacy with James saw the simultaneous promotion of Thomas Howard, Earl of Arundel, to membership of the Privy Council in three kingdoms and to prominence at court.[17] His estrangement from his family perhaps saved Arundel from the discredit which fell upon the Howards in 1618 with the removal of Suffolk from his post of Lord Treasurer, and from the suspicion of Villiers, Marquis of Buckingham, who ousted the Earl of Nottingham in order to obtain his office of Lord High Admiral in January 1619. Desirous now of an office which would confirm his importance at court, Arundel attached himself to Buckingham and sued through his patronage for the posts of Lord Treasurer and Lord Keeper — places which went to Buckingham's nominees Henry Montagu and Bishop John Williams respectively. Commenting on the competition for office, John Chamberlain thought 'the best plea I hear for the Earl of Arundel is his perpetual plieing the Marquis Buckingham with all manner of

observance . . .'[18] Arundel's association with the favourite need
not be ascribed to ambition alone. Though of comparatively lowly
birth, in 1620 Buckingham's 'handsome presence, amiable and
courteous manners, familiarity and above all his liberality seemed
to promise from him something . . .'.[19] If he was believed to be
courteous, his valuable work on the commission to reform the
navy won him the regard of all who abhorred court corruption,
and doubtless of Arundel whose uncle had first instigated the
enquiry.[20] More particularly, Buckingham's support for a policy of
a Spanish marriage pointed to an alliance with Arundel who
strongly favoured it.[21] In 1620, common interest and policy
suggested co-operation and friendship, not rivalry and enmity.

The events of the first session of the 1621 Parliament may serve
to illustrate that alliance. When the Lower House began enquiries
into the abuses of patents and monopolies, Buckingham avoided
difficult questions about his own involvement by sacrificing his
clients to the reforming zeal of the Commons.[22] In the Lords,
Arundel played a major role on the committee for customs, orders,
and privileges and served on most of the important committees of
the session. During the early examinations of Mompesson's patent
of gold and silver thread, Arundel displayed a cautious, exact
concern for justice, urging that none be asked to accuse himself,
but to give evidence only.[23] But as the Commons' investigations
increasingly threatened Buckingham himself, Arundel emerged as a
staunch supporter of the favourite in the Lords where some of the
peers seemed anxious to pursue enquiries into Buckingham's
influence. On 19 April, Arundel was chosen to investigate charges
sent up from the Commons against the Lord Chancellor, Francis
Bacon, a client of Buckingham.[24] Like Mompesson, Bacon was
sacrificed, and Arundel spoke on his behalf (against the sentence of
degradation) only after Bacon had been found guilty and the
Commons' anger had been assuaged.[25]

The most dangerous moment for the favourite came with the
examination of Sir Henry Yelverton's patent for inns and alehouses. On 30 April, defending himself in the Lords, Yelverton
accused Buckingham of promoting the monopolies which he now
condemned and of having threatened dismissal of those officers
who would not comply.[26] Arundel immediately moved that
Yelverton's speech was a dishonourable accusation against the king
and Buckingham and for the next few days was adamant for his
condemnation and for clearing Buckingham's name.[27] On 8 May,
Lord Spencer moved that Yelverton be given a formal hearing; he
reminded Arundel, who opposed the motion, that two of his
Howard ancestors had suffered condemnation without the opportunity of defence. The proud Earl acknowledged that his ancestors

had suffered 'and it may be for doinge the kinge and country good service, and in such time as [when] perhapps the Lords auncestors that spake last kept sheepe.' Arundel's stinging retort, an affront to the dignity of the House, caused his commitment to the Tower.[28] He remained there but a few weeks and only because he refused to apologize to Spencer. While in confinement, he was 'very much visited and courted by the Lord of Buckingham and all the grandees of that side'.[29] Buckingham with Prince Charles attempted to effect a reconciliation between Arundel and Spencer, because he needed Arundel's valuable service in the Lords. The first session of parliament came to a premature end in early July: 'some thinck yt is to enlarge the earle of Arundell the sooner.'[30]

Arundel believed that the incident had done him no harm; rather it 'shewed the king's constancy and favor to his servants that love him truly and made me see I had some true friends'.[31] His assessment seems to have been correct. Early in June, Chamberlain reported the court gossip that Pembroke would be made Lord Treasurer and Arundel Lord Chamberlain.[32] Though the detail was inaccurate, the spirit of the rumour was sound. On 29 August, Arundel was created Earl Marshal of England, a post which had been held by members of his family for several centuries and in which he had himself shown interest for several years. A pension of £2,000 per annum accompanied the grant of the office.[33] Buckingham evidently encouraged the appointment as a reward for Arundel's service in parliament, and it is probable that he had promised it in the spring. The release of the Earls of Southampton and Northumberland during the summer confirms the suggestion that Buckingham was anxious to strengthen himself in the Lords. Ironically, the bestowal of the Earl Marshal's office on Arundel was to be a major contribution to the restoration of Howard power and to the emergence of a group opposed to the favourite.

The new Lord Keeper, John Williams, Buckingham's protégé and mentor, was reluctant to pass Arundel's patent. He thought that the generous pension was impolitic with a new session of parliament pending. More important, he raised vital questions about the authority of the Earl Marshal's office. Firstly, Williams showed that the patent nowhere determined whether the powers of the revived Marshal's office were to be those exercised recently by the Earls of Essex, Shrewsbury, and Somerset, or those wielded by earlier Earls Marshal whose 'powers in those unsettled and troublesome times are vague uncertain and impossible to be limited'. Secondly, he drew the important distinction between the Marshal of England and the Marshal of the King's House, the power of which latter was 'to be searcht out from chronicles' and was potentially far greater. Williams assumed that the king intended for Arundel only the first place, 'But this new patent comprehendeth them both. . ..'[34]

Williams was worried about this great power passing irrevocably from Buckingham's control, especially at what seemed to be a difficult time. During the summer of 1621 news came of the failure to secure a truce in the Palatinate, news which hastened the recall of parliament and questioned the policy of a Spanish match. Any disagreements about foreign policy threatened to divide the tenuous personal groupings held together by Buckingham; it was no time to give power to those who might no longer be relied upon as friends. It seems likely that Buckingham seriously considered Williams's advice. In August it was rumoured that Buckingham would be made Constable of the realm, a post which would have overshadowed the marshalship.[35] In September, the Venetian ambassador reported that Williams could only be delaying Arundel's patent with the encouragement of a higher authority — an obvious allusion to Buckingham.[36] But the patent passed, either because Buckingham could not prevent it, or because he did not wish to. When the second session of parliament assembled in November, Arundel ceremoniously introduced the new Lords in his capacity as Earl Marshal.[37]

The second session began on 20 November with the king absent at Newmarket. Cranfield, Williams, and the ambassador John Digby outlined the progress of negotiations and requested a supply for defence of the Palatinate. On 29 November, however, amidst the debates and acting on the instructions of Buckingham, Sir George Goring advocated not only action in Germany, but a war against Spain, if Spanish troops were not withdrawn from the Empire. The motion caused great surprise.[38] Thinking that this lead by a prominent courtier was a signal to discuss the larger question of the Spanish match, the Commons began a full debate. James sent orders to his startled councillors to put an end to the discussion, and so began an unlooked-for dispute about the privileges of the Lower House. Buckingham's real intentions in this episode remain an enigma.[39] For his part, Arundel seems to have supported Digby's motion and the royal policy of intervention in the Palatinate, without discussion of relations with Spain.[40] But leaving the questions of policy aside, Goring's motion wrecked the second session of parliament and suggested a rash departure from the norms of conciliar discussion of parliamentary business.

While parliament still sat, on 12 December, the king wrote to his Privy Council to defend Arundel's Earl Marshal's court against the challenge made to its authority by the recalcitrant herald, Ralph Brooke:

wee take our owne honor to bee engaged to defend the power and reputation of that court, which is of so high a nature, so auncient and so immediatlie derived from us who are the fowntaine of all honor, as also that our said cousine may receive such encouragement and favour as both his generall faith in our service and his modest course shewed by appealing unto us in this particular doth deserve.[41]

Arundel's correct and precise behaviour had already made an impression upon James and the Venetian ambassador noted his proximity to the king.[42] The royal letter of 12 December enabled him to take the course which Williams had feared and to claim the widest jurisdiction for the Earl Marshal's office. Arundel consulted his friend and client Sir Robert Cotton, the antiquary, who had earlier researched into the antiquity and authority of the offices of Earl Marshal and Constable. In the summer of 1622 Arundel claimed the right to hold the old court of the Earl Marshal and Constable when there was no Constable of the realm.[43] James accepted the authority of the precedents which Cotton had supplied to Arundel and on 1 August 1622 the Privy Council formally decided in favour of the claim. On 16 April following, Arundel received the Constable's staff as final confirmation of his new authority.[44]

The decision invested Arundel with considerable power. Though not formally Constable, he exercised the authority and enjoyed the status of that office. The Constable was senior privy councillor by virtue of his office, and it is evident that great political importance was attached to the hierarchy of offices. In 1601, the Earl of Essex had sought the post in order to supplant Cecil; in 1619, the Earl of Nottingham had requested the Constable's staff in order to retain his precedence over Buckingham for whom he renounced the Lord Admiral's place.[45] Secondly, in medieval times the Constable's court had wielded near regal power and during the last four decades of the fifteenth century it had been used to attack opponents of the monarch.[46] Buckingham's advisers, moreover, reminded him of the importance of such offices: Williams was to recommend that the favourite renounce the Admiralty to become Lord Steward, while Thomas Wilson, keeper of the records, hoped that Buckingham would have himself made Earl Marshal.[47] Both posts brought those who held them close to the royal closet.

Arundel's new status certainly brought him into closer contact with the king. James perhaps raised to an appropriate position a nobleman who was a stickler for forms and proprieties to offset the developing monopoly of patronage by Buckingham. Court gossip about a new favourite, Arthur Brett, brother-in-law of Cranfield, in the autumn of 1622 suggests that Buckingham's position was not unassailable.[48] In November of that year, Buckingham sued to be Lord High Constable, presumably to reinforce his position in Council and at court.[49] Perhaps the growing influence of those devoted to the royal policy of a Spanish match induced him to send Endymion Porter to investigate the possibility of a successful negotiation. It may then be that Porter's optimistic reports and his own desire to reassert his position by the decisive diplomatic coup of a negotiated marriage were the direct motives behind the journey to Spain in the spring of 1623.[50]

In March, the Earl of Kellie reported that Lady Arundel had considered a trip to Spain, 'but that she is discharged', while, 'some say that my Lord of Arundel is in great danger that his Ladye is forbidden to go to Spaine, and that he is not to be imployed himself at this tyme.'[51] The Earl Marshal by no means approved of Buckingham's enterprise: Simonds D'Ewes believed that Arundel wanted no part in the negotiations while the prince was in Spain and the advantage was with the Spaniard.[52] Privy Councillors expressed grave reservations about such 'a dangerous and unexampled experiment'. Though he had earlier been won over by the arguments of the prince and Buckingham, James was now advised of the real dangers involved and 'now upone efter thochts I cannot think but it trubills his Majestie when the hazards thaye run are laide before him'.[53] As the Earl of Kellie noted, the whole affair was 'a subject that discontented folkes maye worke upon'.[54]

In addition to his reservations about the journey, Arundel had a more personal discontent. In May it was rumoured that Arundel was to be made a duke, but that he refused all but the Norfolk title, the premier duchy of the realm.[55] The patent sent to Spain making Buckingham a duke and so senior English nobleman much offended the Earl Marshal. An informant told Buckingham, 'since your patent, the Earl Marshal is become a great strainger at the Court.'[56]

In Spain, Buckingham anxiously sought information about the English court. In March, Tobie Matthew, son of the Archbishop of York and one close to Arundel, wrote to tell Buckingham that great men were plotting against him and advised him to hurry back lest enemies take advantage of his absence.[57] While in Spain, Buckingham quarrelled with the official ambassador John Digby, now Earl of Bristol, and removed him from all negotiations there. Attempts by Buckingham to cast aspersions on Bristol's abilities met with incredulity at the English court, while Bristol's own despatches, critical of Buckingham's carriage of business, made supporters of the match fear that the journey would disrupt years of delicate diplomacy.[58] If, as a staunch supporter of the match, Arundel was plotting against the favourite, his own influence was curtailed by the illness and death of his son in Flanders which

necessitated Arundel's departure from England in July.[59] Though
he gave Arundel permission to travel, James I was said to be displeased by his absence.[60] It would seem that they had become
much closer, within the limits of Arundel's reserved and formal
manner, while Buckingham and the prince were in Spain. Arundel
returned within a month but failed to attend at court because, as
he explained to Sir Dudley Carleton, 'his extreme sorrow makes
him incapable of this world's affairs.'[61] Sir John Hippesley
reported Arundel's retirement from court to Buckingham for
whom it was probably good news.[62] For if the enemies of Buckingham and the discontented were gathering, they would look to
Arundel as a leader.

Buckingham returned in September 1623, however, and the
evidence suggests that the king's relief at the safe return of his son
saw the favourite secure, for the time, in his position. Buckingham
had returned bent on breaking the Spanish match, while Bristol
stayed in Spain, with the prince's proxy, to complete negotiations
for it. The winning of the prince to his policy secured a major ally
for Buckingham.[63] But James continued to meet with the Spanish
ambassadors in the autumn, and those close to the king thought
'that it wilbe contrarye to his will if the match shall not goe
on'.[64] In December it was reported that, with the Council
divided, the king's will would certainly prevail.[65] Bristol
continued to correspond from Madrid and was said to have in
England 'a great and more powerful party in Court than you can
imagine'.[66] Buckingham now turned to deal with those whom he
regarded as his enemies because they had influence with the king.
On 26 December a newswriter reported a rumour that Arundel
would be confined to the Tower, a rumour confirmed by the Venetian ambassador's belief that Arundel was in danger while James I
vacillated between fear of his own son and fear of the Spaniard.[67]
Over Christmas 1623–4, Buckingham turned threateningly on Lord
Keeper Williams, his client who was now earnestly supporting the
match, and dismissed that policy as 'both dangerous to your coun-
trie and prejudicial to the cause of religion'.[68] Throughout
January, Buckingham tried to cajole the Privy Council into breaking with Spain. At the end of the month, Chamberlain wrote that,
led by Arundel, Williams, Lord Treasurer Cranfield, Sir George
Calvert, and Sir Richard Weston remained in favour of the match.
Only Carlisle and Conway voted to end it. The Earl of Pembroke,
despite his earlier support of Buckingham's motion for a parliament, and despite his distaste for the Spaniard, took the view that
if the king had engaged himself and the Spanish did not violate the
agreement then he could not with honour retreat from it.[69]
Pembroke's concern with honour and engagement was typical of

the behaviour of the early Stuart nobility. Buckingham was still in the minority, but in December the junta had voted to call parliament.[70] Council faction and personal rivalries were now to be played out on the floor of both Houses.

In December, Arundel had opposed the summoning of parliament,[71] but when it was called he used his influence at the hustings. His secretary, Humphrey Haggett, obtained a place at Chichester, second to Lord Percy, son of Arundel's friend, the Earl of Northumberland. Sir John Borough, who collected antiquities for the Earl and who was made herald through his patronage, took the first place at Horsham.[72] But Buckingham not only exercised some official as well as private patronage, he also organized a clear programme to direct the Lower House. The Earl of Kellie observed in March, 'Monye of theis Parlament men that did disturb the last Parlament ar now als mutche for my Lord of Bukkinghame as thaye warr then against him.'[73] Against that organization Arundel could only promote delaying tactics: he suggested that precedents of former treaties be fully investigated before any decision was made; he sat on the committee to investigate allegations made against Buckingham by the Spanish ambassadors, who tried thereby to discredit the Duke.[74] Such tactics were not futile: Bristol was en route for home promising a full report of all the negotiations in Spain, and rumours were already rife of the scandalous behaviour of Buckingham there. However, on 12 March both Houses advised the king to terminate marriage negotiations, and proceeded to promise a supply.[75] In vain Arundel and Cranfield, Earl of Middlesex, argued that parliament's offer of support was too general to be a basis for a war: the prince snubbed them.[76]

But though he could do little in the Lords, Arundel planned, perhaps, to work through his clients in the Commons. In the Lower House, one voice stood out from the clamour against the match. On 19 March, amidst a debate on supply for the war, Sir George Chaworth argued that the treaties for the marriage and Palatinate were already at an end but that the old peace with Spain remained and prohibited any assistance to the Low Countries. Chaworth maintained that the kingdom was in no danger and hinted that war was in the interest of a faction and not of the realm: 'yf a war ensue upon our petition wch you now wage were I to chuse, I had rather be in ye office of Admirall of Engd than K of Engd.' The country was too poor to finance a major campaign and was in greater need of good laws and reform of grievances.[77] The speech evidently caused a stir, and Pym observed that 'if there had beene bad humours enough in the Howse it might have done some hurt.'[78] But Thomas Wentworth, Recorder of Oxford, quickly rose to dismiss the speech as a 'diversion' and Chaworth

found no support.[79] By the end of the month he was dismissed
from the House after they had 'pricked a hole in his election'.[80]
Chaworth's speech may have owed something to his indignation at
not obtaining the viscountcy which was promised to him by Buckingham after his employment as an ambassador to Brussels in 1621.
Chaworth attributed Buckingham's hostility towards him to his
continued support for the Spanish marriage after the Duke had
abandoned it.[81] In 1624 he sat for Arundel borough in Sussex. It
is clear that the election had been irregular, the mayor having
returned Chaworth over one Richard Milles by reopening the poll
late in the afternoon when many electors had gone home. The
mayor would not have risked this course without connivance from
above — from the Lord Lieutenant of Sussex, the Earl of Arundel.
Not only was Arundel Chaworth's patron for the place, it appears
that Chaworth's cousin travelled to Italy with Lady Arundel, so
there may have been closer connections between them.[82] But
despite the irregularities of the election, the case against Chaworth
was not clear cut. Even at the first count four voters (all supporters
of Milles) had arrived after voices had been heard but before a
formal poll was taken.[83] Chaworth himself maintained that the
polling continued with the consent of all and complained that he
never received a formal hearing.[84] The situation might have
suggested a completely new election, but Buckingham was sus-
picious enough to see that no new writs were issued and Milles
took his seat.[85]

During the Easter recess, Buckingham attacked Chaworth, who
laid his defence, and a copy of his speech, before the king. He
claimed that James thanked him for it and swore 'that had [he]
beene in ye House of Parlament he wold have spoken just my
words'. When Buckingham upbraided him for his speech, James
broke out in impatience against the Duke, 'By ye wounds, you are
in ye wrong! for he spake my soule . . .'[86] There seems no reason
to doubt Chaworth's account in that his speech was a precise statement of royal policy. If the Duke had triumphed in parliament, he
had not as yet won the royal closet. His position was no stronger
than it had been in the spring of 1623.

After Easter, Buckingham returned to parliament determined
now to use it in order to break his opponents. His client Sir Robert
Pye brought into the Commons charges against Lord Treasurer
Middlesex who had continued a supporter of the match. When the
case came to the Lords, of the principal officers of the household,
only the Earl Marshal was not included on the committee to
investigate the charges.[87] Yet encouraged, perhaps, by James I's
half-hearted defence of Middlesex on 7 April, Arundel and Williams
asked the House to excuse the Treasurer's passionate accusations

against unnamed enemies and prompted him to name his perse-cutors.[88] John Holles, Lord Haughton, joined them in an effort to save Middlesex, but he was inevitably found guilty and sen-tenced.[89] Buckingham's next attacks struck Arundel directly. At the end of April and early May, Pye and Sir Robert Phelips raised questions about the heralds and the jurisdiction of the Earl Marshal's court. Sir Edward Coke's report that there could be no commission for the Constable's office threatened the very existence of Arundel's court.[90] If he failed to cajole the Privy Council, Buckingham showed that he had gained a monopoly of influence in parliament.

But his methods were both dangerous and caused offence. On 5 April, Pembroke, no friend of the policy of a Spanish marriage, yet urged moderation and caution in order to avoid firing a religious war.[91] And he refused to support Buckingham's plan to have Bristol, who returned in May, committed to the Tower in order to silence him.[92] Buckingham rightly feared that James had not been won over to the war and that the return of Bristol to court would be a threat to his very position.[93] Certainly James warned the prince and Buckingham against using parliamentary impeachment to crush their rivals and endeavoured to reconcile them with Bristol.[94] Arundel, powerless to prevent what had happened to Middlesex, determined to prevent its repetition against Bristol and, perhaps, himself. On 28 May, he reported that the sub-committee for privileges had decided to allow counsel to the accused in parliamentary judicial proceedings.[95] Three years before, he had denied Yelverton even a hearing. But times had changed: he could no longer look upon the Duke as a friend, and even those who had voted to end the match reacted against the obvious persecution of Cranfield and Bristol. The decision to grant counsel to the accused had been taken hurriedly and Arundel admitted the need for more consideration. But the main point was clear: 'God defend that an Innocent should be condemned.' The following day, parliament was dissolved.

Clarendon's belief that James I was openly displeased with Buck-ingham is confirmed by the Earl of Kellie who reported that the king rebuked the prince and Duke for courting too much popular-ity.[96] It seems that as the representative of justice and propriety (probably too of royal policy) Arundel rose in the king's estimation during the summer of 1624. On 5 June, James stayed at Arundel House and went stag-hunting while Buckingham lay ill at New-hall.[97] A week later, James made a second visit and it was rumoured that the Spanish ambassadors and Bristol met the king there in secret.[98] Both the prince and Buckingham were worried that Bristol's friends would gain him an audience.[99] Certainly

Buckingham's position was insecure: in June, Bristol sent in answers to the questions posed about his embassy and was later to claim that James was satisfied by them.[100] In August, Sir Robert Phelips advised his patron Buckingham to win over Bristol, for the Spanish match was already broken and persecution of Bristol could only lead to trouble.[101] Lord Keeper Williams endorsed this advice and counselled him to behave more modestly to the king so as to avoid offence.[102] In October, Pembroke, who rejected advances made by Buckingham, was reported as one of a group opposing a war against Spain unless France could be secured as a reliable ally.[103] It was to separate Pembroke from his enemies, and to prevent the return of the Spanish faction to power that Buckingham hurried the negotiations for a French marriage. Arundel, Calvert, and Williams were dropped from the commission for negotiations in July and by December even Pembroke and Hamilton had been excluded, 'and as I am informed the great Lords of the Consell . . . are not weill pleased, whoe was the Lords Stewart, Marshall and Chamberlaine . . .'[104] In order to prevent Arundel and Pembroke becoming dukes, Buckingham resigned his Irish titles.[105] He had reason to fear the great lords.

Perhaps the death of James I in March 1625 saved Buckingham from the fate of Somerset. Rumours about the medicines he had administered to the king on his death-bed and the scandal of a possible poisoning of James can only have gained currency from a belief that Buckingham benefited by his death. Certainly Buckingham's survival as favourite into the next reign caused some surprise and added to the animosity towards him.[106] At first the situation was confused: Council factions jostled for the ear of the new king, and Buckingham postponed taking the proxies for the marriage to France for fear of losing his place. His fears were justified. At the meeting of the Privy Council Arundel requested 'that the king should let his Council share the things which he wishes to announce' — a request which was a condemnation of Buckingham's behaviour since 1624 or earlier. Arundel's other proposal, to limit the sale of honours, not only reflected his contempt for the low-born who were raised to noble status, it overtly aimed at Buckingham's patronage and potentially at his influence over the House of Lords. Buckingham replied cleverly that there could be no limit to a king's ability to reward deserving subjects, and Arundel met with little support in a Council from which Middlesex, Bristol, Calvert, and the Earl of Suffolk were excluded for the first time. 'No one said any more and the Earl [of Arundel] was somewhat dashed.'[107] Buckingham had now secured the control of an emasculated Privy Council and the norms of Stuart government were brushed aside. As a body for the full discussion of business and as adviser to the crown, the Privy Council ceased to function until after Buckingham's death.[108]

The new reign, however, dictated the assembling of another parliament. Buckingham cannot have been happy at the prospect, for he was now identified with the policy of a French marriage, which was only a little less odious than the Spanish match, and the war against Spain, intimated in 1624, had not materialized. There were bound to be questions raised, and there were enemies to take advantage of them. In 1624, Buckingham went to parliament because he could not get his way in Council. Now, having removed his enemies from the Council, he had to defend himself against them in parliament.

The parliament of 1625 sat for three weeks in a plague-infested Westminster before a final disastrous session in Oxford early in August 1625. The Commons' committee for foreign affairs began careful examination of the abortive Mansfeldt expedition and of the activities of the Council of War.[109] Dangerous precedents circulated in August concerning the punishment of corrupt ministers, and the session was abruptly dissolved. Buckingham was convinced that those who opposed him in the Commons — Sir Thomas Wentworth, Sir Dudley Digges, and his quondam client Sir Robert Phelips — were supported and encouraged by his enemies in the Lords. Three days after the dissolution, Kellie reported a rumour that Arundel, Williams, Pembroke, and Archbishop Abbot were to be questioned concerning their activities.[110] Sir Arthur Ingram confirmed it, warning his friend Wentworth that Buckingham suspected these lords and others of the Lower House 'that were depending upon them, among which you are not altogether free'. He assured Wentworth that Arundel was a 'good friend'.[111]

Buckingham's suspicions seem to have been well founded. Williams had advised the king not to reassemble the parliament at Oxford because some were out to attack the Duke.[112] The French ambassador reported that Arundel and Pembroke, 'personnes puissantes dans le Parlement', were aware that Buckingham would be called to account. Thomas Lorkin told his patron Buckingham that Arundel and Pembroke were conspiring against him.[113] There are close and interesting ties between those Buckingham suspected in the Lords and Commons. The precedents for punishment of corrupt ministers were collected by Sir Robert Cotton who had been closely connected with Arundel since 1616 and who, in 1625, sat for the Howards' seat at Thetford, Norfolk, where Arundel was Lord Lieutenant.[114] A copy of the speech containing those precedents has been found among Sir Robert Phelips's manuscripts at Taunton.[115] Though the speech was not delivered, the Commons echoed its spirit in condemning advice given by one man only and endorsed Arundel's plea to the king to consult with his full Privy Council.[116]

In the Lords, as well as his brother-in-law Pembroke, Arundel had a friend in Holles, now Earl of Clare, a client of Arundel's friend the Earl of Northumberland, and personal friend of Lord Keeper Williams.[117] In 1624 Clare had been conspicuous for his attempt to defend Middlesex. In 1625 he failed to attend the second session of parliament at Oxford because his house was under suspicion of the plague. But he assured Arundel of his intention to have attended him there and asked him to prevent a friend from being pricked sheriff and so incapacitated from standing for parliament.[118] In November Clare wrote to Wentworth expressing his hope that Phelips and Sir Edward Coke would not be pricked sheriff and his satisfaction that the 1625 session, though brief, might 'make great ones even more cautious in wrestling with that high court.'[119] For all their different reasons, the enemies of Buckingham were gathering.

The king's desperate need for supply meant that another parliament was imminent, and Buckingham set about protecting himself. Wentworth, Coke, and Phelips were pricked sheriff, and evidently Arundel, who as Earl Marshal helped to choose the sheriffs, was unwilling or unable to prevent it.[120] But if he had clipped the leadership of the Commons, Buckingham still had to reckon with the Lords — with Arundel and Pembroke. Before parliament met on 6 February, Buckingham was presented with an opportunity to discredit Arundel. After nearly a year's delay, Charles was to be crowned early in February. The coronation was an important public function for all the nobles of the realm, an occasion on which to display their prominence at court and to show the new king that they merited his favour. Arundel, as Earl Marshal and one of the greatest nobles of the realm, prepared a grand reception for Charles in the garden of Sir Robert Cotton whose house in Westminster, next to parliament, backed on to the Thames. On the coronation day, however, the royal barges floated past the crowd at Cotton House and the king disembarked with some discomfort downriver. D'Ewes, a friend of Arundel and Cotton, observed that Buckingham had manoeuvred to embarrass publicly both Arundel and Cotton on the eve of the new parliament.[121] He thus demonstrated the price of opposition and his inviolable influence upon the king. Significantly, Buckingham had had himself made Constable for the coronation day.[122]

But clever manoeuvres alone could not end his troubles with parliament. Indeed, they may have served to sharpen the distaste felt for him. The Lower House, now led by his former client Sir John Eliot, determined to call Buckingham to account. The Earl of

Bristol, under confinement since May 1624, had become exasperated by his failure to obtain a hearing and resolved to bring his case to the Lords. The man behind all was Pembroke who, as Sir James Bagg warned Buckingham, had won Eliot to his circle, and had attempted to assist Bristol in the spring of 1625.[123] In the Upper House former supporters of the Duke, such as the Earl of Suffolk, shifted allegiance from him, and many seemed anxious to check his monopoly of patronage and influence.[124] On 25 February, Lord Mandeville reported from the committee of privileges a motion that no peer should hold more than two proxies.[125] This was a direct threat to Buckingham who held thirteen proxies in this session, many from newly ennobled Lords, and who depended on control of the Upper House lest charges be presented against him in the Commons. Amongst those who supported the motion were Arundel, Clare, and Arundel's friend the Bishop of Norwich, Samuel Harsnett. But the new ruling concerning proxies could not operate until the next session; it may have been intended as a warning to Buckingham not to use the House of Lords as the playground for his private vendettas. In 1626, Buckingham's most dangerous opponents were Pembroke, who held probably five, but whom the Duke still hoped to win over, and Arundel, who also held five proxies, and whom he looked upon as an inveterate enemy.[126]

Suddenly Buckingham was presented with a chance to remove him. In February, Arundel's son, Lord Maltravers, secretly married without royal consent the Duke of Lennox's daughter whom Charles had intended to match with Argyle's son. Arundel was imprisoned supposedly for this affront to the king, but more truthfully, as was observed, in order to remove him from parliament and so deprive the opposition to Buckingham of six votes and a leader.[127] Arundel, trusting still in Charles I, could not believe that he would remain long under royal displeasure, for the marriage had been desired by Lennox and by 'good Kinge James himselfe'.[128] An anonymous correspondent tried to discover for the Earl the cause of the King's displeasure. He had courted Buckingham to no avail — 'I might as well concluded the busyness as I began it' — but thought yet that a judicious explanation would settle everything: 'Let the Parlamt free those that stand in need of their helpe,' he advised, 'for God's sake make not yor case so desperat but ride it out with patience.'[129]

But Arundel's patience must have been taxed as the weeks passed without his release. Whether he wished to make his case desperate or not, his imprisonment raised in the Lords fundamental questions of parliamentary privilege and of the violated rights of those who had given their proxies to the Earl Marshal. The Lords' committee for privileges, after searching the precedents, discovered that no peer had ever been committed without trial while parliament was sitting. It was an issue that transcended the personal quarrel.[130]

On 30 March, Clare argued that proxies given to an absent lord should return to the peers who had given them that they might be conferred anew.[131] The question was raised again on 3 April.[132] The growing anxiety in the House about this question cannot be divorced from the show-down impending between Buckingham and Bristol, who in response to charges of treason against him had sent to the Lords similar charges (drawn up with Williams's assistance) against the Duke.[133] In the last resort, the outcome of that show-down would depend upon votes in the Lords.[134] On 19 April Bristol's petition was read in the House and the Lords made their first formal demand for the release of Arundel.[135] The House of Commons watched the proceedings in the upper chamber closely. Philip Mainwaring, a friend of Sir Thomas Wentworth, assured Arundel that he would soon be free: Bristol had presented his case and 'our house hathe some things now on foote in Parliament wch at the least makes a noyse.'[136] Buckingham showed relatively little anxiety about the investigation in the Commons, but he was worried about the Lords and proposed the creation of twenty new peers to boost his following there.[137] Bristol launched his full attack on 2 May[138] and the case against Bristol and counter-case against Buckingham were now to proceed. The Lords continued to demand the release of Arundel and the king repeatedly gave evasive answers, hoping perhaps to force a vote on both cases while the Earl Marshal was absent and his proxies were neutralized.[139] The Earl of Clare, who led the committee to enquire into the charges against Bristol, awaited Arundel's return, while the House of Commons demanded the commitment of the Duke (and hence the loss of his votes) pending the investigations. Sir John Skeffington, MP for Newcastle under Lyme, told his patron, the Earl of Huntingdon, that the Lords 'want only the company of such a Lord whose example and courage would give animation and boldness to some such as dare not wel looke out of theyr cold neutralities'.[140] Lady Cornwallis regretted Arundel's absence, 'in regard of the want of so able a man at this tyme in the upper house', but feared he would not be suffered to return.[141] The Lords, however, proved adamant. On 2 June the House voted to conduct no business until Arundel returned.[142] Buckingham made enquiries about the proxies held by the Earl Marshal[143] but concluded that there was no alternative to Arundel's release. Arundel returned to his place on 8 June. Pembroke immediately moved 'That the Duke of Buckingham his answere now be receaved.'[144] Bristol petitioned that his case be hastened and on the 13th he delivered the names of his witnesses. Two days later parliament was dissolved.[145]

Albeit reluctantly, Arundel had become a martyr to the cause of parliamentary privilege and head of the opposition to Buckingham. When he was expelled from court after parliament, his 'followers in consequence of this persecution have their ranks now swollen by a great part of the people in general . . .'[146] It was an unnatural alliance. No nobleman more despised the political activities of the lower orders than the aristocratic, reserved Arundel who had recommended the closing of all unruly taverns near Westminster.[147] No one was less suited to be a champion of the diverse discontented — the ambitious courtiers, the frustrated place-seekers, and the war-hawks. It was not a common policy that bound them but a common dislike for Buckingham and his rash bearing.

For eighteen months, Arundel remained debarred the court, months during which no parliament was called and the tangles of foreign policy demanded the subordination of domestic disagreements. As Lord Lieutenant of Norfolk and Sussex, Arundel was called upon to raise the county musters, and as Earl Marshal he was responsible for the discipline of billeted troops. Just as members of the Commons returned from parliament after heated debates to carry out their offices in the localities, so Arundel, ostracized from court, enacted Council orders.[148] There were still signs of tension: Buckingham supported the petition of the herald Henry St. George against Arundel, who had evicted him from Derby House, and St. George requested that the Earl Marshal 'may not be allowed to prejudice him out of spleen to the Duke'.[149] But without co-operation government would have collapsed completely in 1627, and Arundel suppressed personal animosities for the sake of order and stability.

Indeed, an accommodation with the Duke could not be ruled out. In December 1626 it was rumoured that Buckingham sought a reconciliation with Bristol and Arundel as a means of re-ingratiating himself.[150] He had also arranged a pacification with Pembroke in August, and Calvert returned to court by the end of the year.[151] Clearly these moves were an insurance for the next parliament, and may help to explain its being called. Early in 1628, Arundel's client, Sir Robert Cotton, offered to the Privy Council a blueprint for a harmonious parliament. Having remedied the abuses of the forced loan and arbitrary arrests, Buckingham was to request a parliament in which he would champion the cause of reform and so avert distrust in his administration. In 1628 Cotton sat for Arundel's borough of Castle Rising in Norfolk, and it is most probable that he wrote *The Danger Wherein The Kingdom Now Standeth and the Remedy* in consultation with his patron.[152] Both wished for the restoration of traditional and effective conciliar government rather than the pursuit of private quarrels. The proposal met with favourable reception in Council and it seems that its outlines were followed. In early April it was thought that Arundel and Bristol would commence impeachment proceedings against Buckingham in the Lords, but by the 20th one John Hope reported an agreement whereby, in return for concessions to the liberty of the subject, Buckingham was not to be named as a cause of the nation's grievances. Buckingham had effected a reconciliation with Arundel, Bristol, and Williams, having led them 'to believe he is theyr friend and layed all the blame of theire discord on mistakeings and they are so foolish to believe it . . .'[153]

Arundel certainly had no reason to place an unqualified trust in an agreement with Buckingham. On 6 May 1628 he reported from the committee of privileges recommendations that the liberties of peers and their goods be guaranteed during the session of parliament[154] — a precautionary measure against Buckingham's possible treachery. Yet throughout the debates on the Petition of Right, Arundel, as Miss Relf has shown, attempted to promote a moderate course in order to restore harmony.[155] While Buckingham abhorred all concessions and while Lord Saye and the Earl of Warwick advocated total support for the Commons' petition, Arundel and Bristol led a centre group composed of Williams, Bishop Harsnett, the Earl of Clare, and most of the old aristocrats. They proposed acceptance of the substance of the Petition, but modification of the language, 'with due regard to leave entire that sovereign power wherewith your Majesty is trusted'.[156] It was a position typical of Arundel's behaviour over a decade. Only when impasse threatened the failure of the Petition did Arundel's group join those who accepted it unrevised and then insist upon Charles giving his answer in due legal form.

Throughout the 1628 session of parliament, Arundel worked in close contact with his friends in the Lords and Commons. His associates in the Lower House helped to assist the smooth and rapid passage of his private bill (probably drawn up by Selden) for the annexation of the hereditary lands to the title of Earl of Arundel.[157] After the adjournment in June, Selden, Arundel's legal adviser who had played an important part in the debate on the Petition of Right, joined Cotton at Arundel House. There they all studied the engraved stones and marbles which Arundel had shipped from the East.[158] Sir John Eliot, formerly a client of Buckingham and Pembroke, entered into correspondence and friendship with Selden and Cotton and rested his hope for future good government in the Earl Marshal. The co-operation of these and others in 1628 was founded on discontent with Buckingham's administration: it masked differences of attitude to religion, foreign affairs, and questions of government. The assassination of Buckingham in August 1628 therefore undermined the foundations of that alliance and opened the way to new connections and the re-establishing of old associations. In late July Arundel had been admitted to kiss the king's hand, but not until October was he readmitted to the Council table.[159] Lord Percy believed correctly that with Buckingham off the stage the Lord Treasurer Weston would hold the greatest power and that he would bring in Buckingham's old enemies, Arundel, Bristol, and Sir Francis Cottington.[160] Arundel returned to his Whitehall lodgings and to prominence at court.[161] Clare expected that with Weston and Arundel at the Council table all would change 'for both thear habilities be such as they need nether fear nor envy able men . . .'[162] Weston himself believed that, with the Duke off the stage, 'our Affairs may be settled in the Ancient way.'[163] He commented not on policies, but on modes of government.

The 1629 session of parliament ended in violence in the Commons after noisy debate over religion and grievances. But this time the Commons were alone. In the Lords, Arundel, echoing an old petition to Charles, moved the king in the Earl of Oxford's cause 'to preserve ancient Honor especially when it is accompanied with virtue'. He proposed the establishment of a learned academy to educate the young nobles, the natural advisers of the crown, for service in government.[164] It was again a plea for the old forms. Arundel emerged as a leading figure on the Privy Council, and in his friend the Earl Marshal, Bishop Harsnett rested his hope for the revival of that 'vital spirit' which preserved 'the gallant ancient composition of our glorious state [which] is much declined . . .'[165]

II

In 1621 Arundel had led Buckingham's supporters in the Lords; from 1624, he emerged as the leader of his critics in the Lords and in the Council, and was looked to as a leader by the Commons. Why did Arundel break from Buckingham? Why did the enemies of the Duke look to Arundel as a leader? We must examine Arundel's circle.

Those who associated in opposition to Buckingham were often bound by ties of kinship. Arundel was Pembroke's brother-in-law; his wife's brother-in-law, the Earl of Kent, supported him in the

Lords. John Selden was steward to the Earl of Kent as well as legal adviser to Arundel. Sir Robert Cotton's son married Arundel's niece, while Clare's daughter married Sir Thomas Wentworth, Arundel's 'good friend'. Such connections were important, but disagreements and political alliances could cut across the ties of blood. In 1614 Arundel had observed 'that suspicions of jealousies are nowe between parties grown to that heights to dissolve . . . bondes of kindred.'[166] He remained estranged from members of his own family for most of James I's reign.

More recent historiography would trace the disagreements between Buckingham and Arundel and the emergence of Arundel's circle from attitudes to foreign policy. But Buckingham had no consistent policy: he wavered between the Spanish match and a war, while Arundel, though he has been described as one committed to peace, supported a proposal to intervene in the Palatinate and might have entertained, as he was to do in the 1630s, a war against Spain with French assistance.[167] The argument from attitudes to foreign affairs makes it difficult to explain the behaviour of Pembroke, who failed to support Buckingham though he was hostile to Spain. Religious divisions prove no more helpful. Buckingham advanced both puritan and Arminian divines until the last years of James's reign. Despite his probable private Catholicism, Arundel had openly taken Anglican communion in 1616. In 1617, Sir Dudley Carleton thought him to be the protector of the anti-Arminian group at court, yet in 1624 he supported the Arminian bishop Montagu.[168] The herald Edward Walker aptly remarked that 'in religion he was no bigot'. If Arundel was committed to the Spanish party and the Catholic faith, it becomes impossible to understand how he attracted as his followers men like Selden, Williams, Cotton, and Wentworth.

What is clear from a study of Arundel's associates is that many shared intellectual interests: in history and antiquities, in art and architecture. Arundel projected a history of his own family and planned a study of Roman Britain.[169] His library contained the major antiquarian works of the century and the great Italian histories of Machiavelli and Guicciardini.[170] A love of the past doubtless facilitated his friendship with Cotton, Selden, with Henry Spelman, his Norfolk neighbour, with John Williams and Samuel Harsnett who collected historical works for their own libraries and leisure.[171]

We need not document the artistic interests of the nobleman who is famous for his collections and for his patronage of Inigo Jones, Rubens, and Mytens. But it is less well known that the Earl of Northumberland, Arundel's friend, built up a classic collection of works on architecture and that the Earl of Clare studied the subject from books borrowed from that collection.[172] Sir Robert Cotton sat with his patron on the commission for buildings in London. Arundel's friends Cotton and Selden shared his interest in collecting antiquities and Pembroke was a friendly rival for the best pieces.[173] It may be that Buckingham developed his own interests in art and antiquities during his years of close association with Pembroke and Arundel, but he developed 'nothing of the older man's refinement or antiquarian sense'.[174]

These intellectual pursuits should not be ignored by the historian of faction and politics. Cultural attainment was of the essence of nobility in the seventeenth century. Competition for works of art was sharpened by more than aesthetic zeal. It is interesting that after 1625, when their political alliance had broken, Arundel refused to co-operate with Buckingham in collecting rarities from the East: he worked alone, to Buckingham's disadvantage, through his agent William Petty.[175] In 1626, writing to Buckingham at the time of his greatest crisis, Edmund Bolton understood the importance of these noble pursuits:

> By your favour I would say there is scarcely any greater cause of your loss of favour with the gentry and better bred sort, who usually delight in books, than that of late your Lordship hath not seemed to value the generously and soberly well-learned famous for free studies and liberal cyclopaedie . . .[176]

In short, interests in aspects of history, of art and architecture, of learning in general, reflected, and perhaps even inculcated, attitudes and values. In a letter to Arundel from Constantinople, his agent Sir Thomas Roe reported that there the arts were thought to debilitate martial spirits. 'But they are absurdly mistaken,' he argued, confirming Arundel's own beliefs, 'for civility and knowledge do confirme and not effeminate good and true spirits.'[177] When Arundel's librarian Franciscus Junius wrote on the paintings and artists of the ancient world, he outlined more clearly the links between aesthetic pursuits and social and political values. The arts, he argued, inclined men to peace, consecrated the memory of the great, and showed virtue as the pattern of the glorious life. For artists to work, they needed 'that stable tranquillitie of an unshaken peace', enjoyed during the greatest days of classical empires and praised by the humanist students of antiquity.[178]

We cannot divorce the political values of Arundel's circle from their interests in the world of antiquity. Arundel's own library and collections were a monument to classical scholarship and to an Italian intellectual tradition of classical scholarship. Arundel sent his sons to Padua so that there they would imbibe a classical heritage. In Harsnett's house another son was guided through classical texts, for Harsnett's library was a fine repository of humanist learning.[179] The Earl of Clare read widely in classical texts and projected a commentary on Bacon's essay 'of Empire'. Sir Thomas Wentworth read and annotated Polybius in his rural leisure; Sir Robert Cotton's historical writing revealed increasingly the influence of classical and Italian models.[180] Perhaps they sought in the histories of classical Greece and Rome a remedy for the instabilities of the 1620s. And if Arundel (and Harsnett) avidly collected Holbein's portraits, it may be because they depicted a period of humanist learning in England, the great age of the aristocracy at the court of Henry VIII, when the Howard family was supreme.

Certainly Arundel came to symbolize for many the old values of order and sobriety in public life. The French ambassador was told that in negotiating with Arundel and Pembroke, 'il faut aller avec mesure . . .', while 'even such as were no parties in contention with my Lord of Buckingham blame him that he was very rash in managing business . . . keeping no Motion of order or Measure . . .'[181] By his ostentatious behaviour, his insults to the nobility, his homosexual involvement with King James and his vulgar familiarity with the prince, by his indecorous behaviour in Spain, Buckingham offended many who sympathized with his policies.[182] Arundel, by contrast, was a nobleman for whom the forms and methods were at least as important as the ends, a great master of order and ceremony, as his biographer depicted him. The elaborate ceremonial life of the Marshal's court was not for him mere display, but the correct expression of the dignity and authority of the office. When he went on embassy to Holland in 1632, Arundel drew up elaborate rules to ensure the correct behaviour of his attendants there.[183] Such a concern for order and sobriety helps to explain his friendship with Harsnett who wanted to return to the old stability in local government,[184] and with Wentworth, the exponent of 'Thorough' and 'antiquas vias' in the 1630s. Buckingham had offended against this ideal of order by his meteoric rise to supremacy and by his irresponsible actions. Sir Dudley Digges (who became Arundel's client) and the Earl of Clare compared him to a comet which unsettled the order of the heavens and eclipsed less flashy luminaries.[185]

In the terrestrial sphere, Buckingham had upset the social and political order by sale of honours and by blocking the king from his aristocratic councillors — 'the great usurper', Lord Percy called him.[186] Arundel came to personify the interests of the old aristocracy and the values of honour and nobility. He refused to accept any duchy other than that of Norfolk to which he had a hereditary claim[187] and was anxious to preserve the honour of all noble families. Arundel supported the claim of Robert de Vere to the earldom of Oxford against the pretence of Buckingham's candidate Willoughby, and then petitioned the king to grant de Vere the estates necessary to support so ancient and so honourable a title.[188] In the Lords, Arundel was the champion of the privileges due to peers, such as the right to answer on honour not oath; in his Earl Marshal's court he made rigorous enquiries into claims to titles.[189] This concern for maintaining the old nobility caused friction between Arundel and Buckingham in 1620 when they agreed on major questions of policy.[190] In 1623 Arundel ruled that no man was to be made a baronet who could not prove gentle descent. In 1625, as we have seen, he petitioned Charles to stop the sale of titles.[191] He was not alone: the Earl of Northumberland was offended by Buckingham's ostentatious coach with its six horses; even the Earl of Clare, who bought his title, condemned the sale of honours.[192]

The members of the House of Commons were no less concerned with the maintenance of the aristocracy. Sir Dudley Digges advised the king 'above all to look into the several abilities of his noblemen and be served by ablest men for parts and breeding'.[193] In 1628, in support of Arundel's bill for the annexation of hereditary lands to his title, 'Sir Edward Coke wished every nobleman would do so that there might be convenient maintenance for the supporting the earldoms . . .'[194] The charge of selling titles was included in judicial proceedings against Buckingham in 1626. Evidently the Commons preferred the decorum of the old aristocracy to the vulgar pretensions of the upstart. And in Arundel they believed that nobility of birth met truly noble behaviour and inclination. Ben Jonson, whose works during the 1620s show great interest in the theme of honour and nobility, thought Arundel the man 'to shew and to open clear vertue the way'.[195] Franciscus Junius called his patron, 'the very pattern of true Nobility'.[196] All writers who dedicated books to Arundel stressed his nobility, his real worth, and solid virtues in contrast to the superficialities of the age.[197]

A concern with order and propriety, with honour and nobility — *gravitas* the Romans called it — alienated Arundel from a court dominated by Buckingham. His plain attire, scorned by Clarendon, separated him from the tawdry gaudiness of the new nobility; his formal behaviour distanced him from two kings who lived with their favourites in intimate familiarity. These values made Arundel appear, like Clarendon's Pembroke, to be of the court but never corrupted by it. They earned him the respect of those essentially conservative parliamentary gentry who loved their king but were contemptuous of Buckingham. Such values, the currency of political exchange in the 1620s, bound to Arundel a group of men in the Lords and Commons.

Edward Hyde had no part in that world. He came to court in the 1630s when Arundel was at the height of his influence and when the Earl Marshal's court, which he hated, was most active. He came to a court dominated now by the former enemies of Buckingham, shortly after he had married into the Villiers family and had undertaken a tract to vindicate the memory of the favourite. He saw only Arundel's arrogance, his ambition, and his reserve, where others living in the world of Buckingham had venerated the Earl's decorum and nobility.

Historians have singled out the 1620s as the decade of issues and conflict. The political activities of Arundel and his circle during these years suggest rather the importance of personalities and personal connections — not connections based on constitutional principles or ideological commitments nor connections founded on the mere pursuit of office, but connections strengthened by traditional beliefs about correct behaviour and modes of action, about methods not policies. The Arundel circle is a case study in the values and politics of Renaissance England.

8. The foundation of the Chairs of History at Oxford and Cambridge: an episode in Jacobean politics*

The establishment of a history professorship at Oxford by the antiquary William Camden in 1622 was, as we know, one of a series of new chairs founded at Oxford within a few years. The new post followed the Sedleian Chair of natural philosophy (established in 1618), Thomas Savile's professorships of geometry and astronomy (1619) and Dr. White's chair of moral philosophy (1621). By contrast Fulke Greville's history lectureship, founded in 1627, was the only newly created post in early seventeenth-century Cambridge. Both foundations, however, broke with tradition. For even if, in the last years of James I's reign, the endowment of university posts in modern subjects at Oxford was something of a fashion, the study of history was not.[1] Despite evidence of interest among students and college tutors, the study of history as an independent discipline had no place in the curriculum of either university.[2]

The story of historical and antiquarian scholarship in late sixteenth- and early seventeenth-century England leads us not to Oxford and Cambridge, but to London and, more particularly, to the houses of the herald William Dethick and, later, Robert Cotton. In those houses from 1586 to 1607 the Society of Antiquaries held their seminars on the history of English institutions; in Cotton's house, after the society had been dissolved, they continued to meet informally throughout the reign of James.[3] None of those whose names are found among the lists of the Society's members were academics. Rather they were men of affairs: lawyers such as James Ley, heralds like Francis Thynne or William Dethick, or office-holders like Arthur Agarde, deputy Keeper of the Exchequer.[4] When, in 1602, the members of the Society presented to the Queen a petition for the establishment of an 'Academy for the study of Antiquity and History', they pressed the practical advantages of historical knowledge. And, fearful perhaps of criticism, they denied any competition with the universities in which the study of history had no place:

> This Society will not be hurtful to either of the universities, for it shall not meddle with the arts, philosophy or other final studies there professed, for this society tendeth to the preservation of history and antiquity of which the universities being busied in the arts take little regard.[5]

The 1602 petition failed. But the quest for an institute of historical and antiquarian studies outside the universities continued. The revival of a Society of Antiquaries was mooted in 1614 and Edmund Bolton, the author of *A Rule of Judgement for Writing or Reading our Histories*[6], tried unsuccessfully for more than a decade to promote an academy of heraldic and historical studies. Once again few academics are found among his lists of potential members.[7]

The centre of any academy for historical study would have been a library of manuscripts and books. In their petition of 1602 the members of the Society of Antiquaries offered to pool their libraries with the Queen's to form such a collection. The universities, however, were less well equipped in this respect than the private libraries of the London antiquaries. At Oxford, the catalogue of 1620 suggests that the Bodleian library could provide only the most basic chronicles such as William of Malmesbury and Henry of Huntingdon.[8] In 1600 St. John's College had very few historical works.[9] At Cambridge, Corpus Christi housed the important collection of Archbishop Matthew Parker, a former fellow. But, as with many college libraries, it was difficult to obtain access.[10] In the main the universities of Oxford and Cambridge missed out on — or rather there is no evidence that they pursued — the splendid opportunities for acquiring historical books and manuscripts which the early Stuart period presented. The vast collections of John Dee and Henry Savile of Banke came to private libraries. Not until the Duke of Buckingham presented Cambridge with his manuscripts in 1626 and Oxford acquired the Barocci collection from Venice in 1629 were the universities' historical libraries of any note.[11]

During the early seventeenth century the best historical materials were in the hands of individual collectors and an interest in historical research led scholars first to London, especially to the library and house of Sir Robert Cotton. The most famous historians and antiquaries of Jacobean England — John Selden, John Speed, Henry Spelman — lived in London and enjoyed access to that library and to the friendship of Cotton and William Camden.[12] The London circle was not divorced from university scholarship. Camden corresponded frequently with Thomas Allen of Trinity, and the Saviles (Henry and Thomas) of Merton College.[13] Cotton's librarian, Richard James, a fellow of Corpus, was the nephew of Bodley's librarian, Thomas James. More importantly Bishop James Usher's project of writing a full history of the church in Britain brought the ecclesiastical historians of Cambridge and Oxford into contact and correspondence with the London circle.[14] But these were informal contacts. They bridged what remained a gulf. When in 1622 he founded his chair at Oxford, Camden excluded divines and stipulated that it be a chair of 'civil history' in which the universities had hitherto not participated.[15]

Why then did Camden who for fifty years had pursued his antiquarian and historical researches in London, who had been named in 1610 a foundation fellow of the projected college at Chelsea, turn his attention to the university of Oxford? Why did Fulke Greville, Lord Brooke, an intimate of the Camden circle and a prospective member of Bolton's Academy, look to Cambridge in order to encourage historical studies?

No satisfactory explanation has been advanced for the foundation of the Camden lectureship. Camden's first biographer, the non-juring antiquary Thomas Smith, believed that Camden had expressed such an intention in a closing remark in the first edition of Britannia (1586). There Camden had mentioned 'some monument unto the almighty and most gracious god and to venerable antiquity which now right willingly and of duty I vow and God willing in convenient time I will perform and make good my vow'.[16] The passage, however, is vague enough to refer to anything — a future book, or even the foundation of the Society of Antiquaries a few months later. The claim of Camden's Lecturer, Degory Wheare, in 1623, that 'by this votive tablet I am here' was probably purely rhetorical.[17] Even if we accept that in 1586 Camden was referring to the foundation of his chair, we must still explain why it took him thirty-six years to execute his vow. There is no other evidence of his interest before 1622.

Christopher Hill maintains that the foundation of the Camden chair should be seen as another attempt to 'Greshamize' the universities and as an example of the puritan promotion of modern subjects. Camden's lecturer, Degory Wheare, Hill points out, was the friend of Francis Rous (later Speaker of Barebones) as well as tutor to John Pym.[18] Yet there is little evidence of Wheare's puritanism. Camden was certainly no puritan: in the Annales of Elizabeth's reign, he refers to 'that odious style of puritans' and, desirous of unity in church and state, criticizes the Brownists for 'presuming to judge of religion according to their own imagination'.[19] It is, as Hugh Trevor-Roper has argued, 'really impossible to press Camden into Hill's tradition of "Puritan" history . . .'.[20]

It has also been suggested that Camden was influenced by the example of his friend Sir Henry Savile, the Provost of Eton and Warden of Merton, who in 1619 had founded chairs of astronomy and geometry.[21] The two men were close friends and Camden admired Savile's learning. Yet Savile makes it clear that Camden did not consult him. Writing from Eton on 25 October 1621, he informed his friend: 'I have half a quarrel with you, that being lately so long together and in so good leisure you did not impart to me that which it seems you have declared at large to my good Lord Paget concerning your worthy purpose of founding an Humanity lecture in Oxford'. Camden also ignored Savile's entreaty that he accompany his foundation with the donation of his historical library.[22] The Savile connection casts little light on the foundation of the Camden chair.

To these unsatisfactory explanations, Professor Smith Fussner, author of *The Historical Revolution*, adds the unhelpful suggestion that William Camden 'sensed that the study of history belonged properly in the modern university'.[23] In order to understand Camden's purpose, we must look more closely at the chair established in 1622.

Camden's first lecturer, Degory Wheare, was unknown to him. It would seem that Camden decided upon the foundation in the early autumn of 1621. On 19 November of that year Thomas Allen of Gloucester Hall wrote to his friend the antiquary recommending for the new post his colleague Wheare as an M.A. of twenty years standing and as a man of experience, 'having sometimes travelled'.[24] Wheare in fact had resigned a fellowship at Exeter college in 1608 in order to travel with Lord Chandos, with whom he had lived for a short time on his return, before occupying lodgings at Gloucester Hall. He may have been seeking profitable office outside the university: in 1603 he contributed to the *Academiae Oxoniensis Pietas*, the university's celebration of the accession of James I, and later wrote panegyrical verses on the return of Prince Charles from Spain.[25] He was not the only candidate for the history chair. In January 1622 the Warden and fellows of New College recommended one of their members, Daniel Gardiner.[26] But by the spring support for Wheare came also from William Piers, dean of Peterborough and Vice-Chancellor of the university, and from the chancellor, William Herbert, Earl of Pembroke.[27] Camden evidently made choice of him on the strength of these testimonials.

In some respects Wheare's appointment is puzzling. He had little or no experience of the careful study of manuscripts and etymological investigations for which Camden's own writings were famous. Within months, it would seem, his tenure of the position was in jeopardy. On 17 May 1622 Convocation, the governing body of the university, settled Wheare's appointment as lecturer.[28] Less than a year later, on 21 March 1623, the Register of Convocation records the grant of the reversion of the place to Brian Twyne of Corpus Christi.[29] Twyne seemed, in many ways, the more suitable man for the post: an indefatigably diligent reformer of Corpus (and later of university) archives, the industrious transcriber of Tower, Guildhall and university records, his scholarly career mirrored Camden's own.[30] He seems to have been ambitious for the chair and the reversion can hardly have been a satisfying prospect when Wheare was a near contemporary. Evidently Twyne worked to obtain it for himself. On 24 March 1624 Camden wrote to Wheare (who had with wise caution maintained a complimentary correspondence with his patron[31]) to explain that Twyne 'procured Sr Richard Cox and others of the Green Cloth to move me for my consent if he could buy you out, never acquainting me that Mr. Twyne was in holy orders and a beneficed man wherein foul play was offered to me. I never meant to have him your successor and hope you do not wish it . . . I assure yourself I never purpose to change as long as you are willing to hold the place'.[32]

Camden's letter, however, poses problems. For despite his claim of deception, he had, according to the Convocation register, granted Twyne the reversion *notwithstanding* his position as incumbent of Rye in Sussex.[33] Moreover, Twyne resigned the benefice in 1623 and was confirmed in his reversion in January 1624.[34] In 1634 he still held out hopes of succeeding to the place.[35] The scraps of evidence obviously conceal much jockeying for position and intrigue. But we can safely conclude that in the end Camden clearly preferred for his lectureship Degory Wheare — the man less experienced in archival research: for writing 'to my approved Good Friend Mr Whear . . .', Camden assured him 'I know that you Tecum Habes Ingenium, that you know *uti foro & aetatem habes*'.[36] These, as we shall see, were the qualities that mattered.

Meanwhile Camden's chair was embroiled in another controversy. When, on 14 May 1622, the foundation was recorded no rules were laid down: 'I appoint no other orders for my historical lecture than shall be prescribed and set down cum approbatione of the university'.[37] University delegates were left to draw up rules for both his chair and Dr. White's chair of moral philosophy founded the preceding year.[38] As a result, a problem arose. The university urged Wheare to lecture on ecclesiastical history and provoked from Camden an uncharacteristically aggressive, and revealing, letter. In the presence of Thomas Clayton, Regius

Professor of Medicine, Camden declared:

> Where I understand there hath been some doubt and question made touching the subject of my lecture and what kind of history I intended my reader should insist on I do hereby signify that it ever was and is my intention and meaning that (according to the practice of such professors in all the universities beyond the seas) *he should read a Civil History and therein make such observations as might be most useful and profitable for the younger students* of the university, to direct and instruct them in the knowledge of History, antiquity and times past. Whose advancement in that way my desires especially aimed at, and I trust both my present Reader . . . will carefully labour to effect and such as shall hereafter succeed him also diligently endeavour the fulfilling of my desires, not intermedling with the History of the Church or Controversy therein farther than shall give light unto those times which he shall then unfold . . . and that very briefly.[39]

Since the days of *Britannia*, Camden had shown himself reluctant to meddle with ecclesiastical history,[40] so his instruction was not out of character. But when we consider the subject he proposed for his lecture, all continuity with his earlier antiquarian studies ends. For Camden required Wheare should lecture on Lucius Annaeus Florus, the author of an epitome of Roman history, based on Livy, and the historian in Bacon's mind when he referred to such epitomes as 'the corruptions and moths of history'.[41] The greatest Elizabethan antiquary and historian recommended then as the basic text for the young students of Oxford a work inaccurate and inconsistent in chronology and geography.[42]

Wheare did not immediately take up the text of Florus.[43] His inaugural lectures, commenced in 1622, were a series of discourses on the uses of history, on the methods by which history should be studied and its lessons turned to greatest use. In his addresses on 'The Method and Order of Reading Histories'[44] Wheare stressed the importance of a broad chronological picture. Epitomes, despised by Bacon, were recommended especially to the young ('for whose sake this task is undertaken'), 'if they render the way to an improvement plain and easy'.[45] Gerard Vossius, after all, had commenced a universal history.[46] Wheare then guided his audience through the principal historians of classical Greece, recommending Thucydides as a guide for politicians, Xenophon for his style and prudence and Polybius, preferred by many before all others. Histories, Wheare advised, were to be read in conjunction with the lives of famous men: thus Thucydides was to be read with Plutarch's lives of Themistocles and Aristides.[47] Histories provided political instruction; lives of great men furnished ethical models.

Students were especially exhorted to study the history of Rome:

seeing their commonwealth . . ., if ever any did, experienced all the diversities of times according to the common laws of Nature, it will here become our reader of Histories to look back awhile and contemplate the rise and infancy of the Roman state (which began under the first monarchy) and to descend to its growth and increase and afterwards to consider its declination towards its fall and ruin, observing a right order both in the times and Authors . . .[48]

Roman history, as Justus Lipsius observed, excelled in examples. Wheare recommended that the course of study begin with Florus who despite errors and inaccuracies was the most useful.[49] Then Livy was lauded for his restrained, concise style, Tacitus for his precepts.[50] Julius Caesar was condemned for lacking one requisite of a good historian — 'the Moral and Politic part'.[51] Appianus's *History of the Civil Wars* was interestingly prescribed as 'one of the most lively Representations that is to be found in any history of the disorders of commonwealths, and the miseries that attend great changes in governments, *and so of great use in this our unsettled age'*.[52]

Turning to more modern historians, Wheare recommended Jacques August de Thou, historian of his own time, as 'the prince of the historians of this age' and Guicciardini 'who everywhere sprinkles grave sentences like salt'.[53] England still awaited its historian, but Bacon's *History of Henry VII* equalled, if it did not excel, the best histories. Camden's own *Annales* of Elizabeth's reign were comparable to the best of the ancient annals.[54]

For Wheare, history was a register of particulars 'undertaken to the end that the memory of them may be preserved and so universals may be the more evidently confirmed by which we may be instructed how to live well and happily'.[55] It was important then for the student to learn how to become a 'competent reader'.[56] In the rest of his lectures Wheare discoursed on 'the manner of collecting the fruits of histories'. Philology and philosophy were both to be gathered from history. Words, customs, events, causes were all to be studied. Most importantly it was the reader's part to observe, extract and compare all the examples he found in histories and to gather them together into precepts. These precepts were then to be applied to the laws and rules of life. The best reader of histories (like the best writer) was one endowed (in Vossius' phrase) with 'practick philosophy', ready to collate and apply the precepts which he had gleaned, 'for the principal end of History is practice and not knowledge or contemplation. And therefore we must learn, not only that we may know, but that we may do well and live honestly'.[57] In short, for Wheare history was 'moral philosophy clothed in examples'.

Drawing as they did on a host of earlier authorities, Wheare's lectures were not novel; they were familiar stuff. To Professor Trevor-Roper they were a poor show — 'a list of literary sources for the study of history . . . punctuated by trite observations' which 'reflected the old threadbare truisms of Elizabethan "puritan" historiography — that history is "philosophy teaching by examples"'.[58] But the inaugural lectures did not disappoint Camden. Camden's confirmation of Wheare's appointment, inserted in the Convocation register, refers to Wheare as recommended by letters of scholarly men 'and afterwards by experience and dissertations on history now completely observed by myself'.[59] In a letter of January 1623 to the university concerning his lecture, Camden spoke of the 'laudable beginnings which I have seen and do hear are well approved'.[60] Writing to Wheare himself Camden described him, in 1624, as the man for his age.[61]

Certainly the lectures were popular. The first Latin edition of the lectures, published in 1623 as *De ratione et methodo legendi historias* was 'eagerly sought after by many' and soon sold out.[62] There were five more editions before the end of the century and the book became a standard teaching text. Far removed as they were from Camden's painstaking antiquarian studies, the lectures evidently represented the approach to history which he wished the young scholars of Oxford to pursue. The foundation of the Camden chair, the choice of first incumbent, the subject appointed, and the inaugural lectures all pose problems which we must attempt to resolve.

Let us follow Wheare's advice and turn from the history of the foundation to the life of the founder. The story of Camden's life itself poses many problems.[63] It is relatively easy to trace his early career from the patronage of Lord Burghley to the publication of the first edition of *Britannia* in 1586, through the meetings of the Society of Antiquaries. With the demise of the society, Camden retired to Chiselhurst in Kent. But he kept in close touch with his pupil, now Sir Robert Cotton, and evidently acted as an adviser to Cotton's patron Henry Howard, Earl of Northampton, now rising to eminence and influence at court. We know that in 1606 Camden helped Northampton with a prosecution speech which the Earl delivered at the trial of the Powder plotter, Henry Garnet.[64] We know too that it was with royal encouragement that, in 1608, Camden resumed work on a history of Queen Elizabeth's reign; that thereafter his labours and drafts were subject to official scrutiny. Camden did not write the *Annales* of Elizabeth's reign in detachment from the world of politics and public affairs.[65]

The *Annales* has been rightly praised as a complete picture of the 'aevum Elizabetheum', of the economy, society, constitution and government of Elizabethan England conceived as one organism.[66] In that world Camden's values had been formulated. By 1615 when the first part of his work was published,[67] Camden was over sixty years old. Looking back it was obvious to him that the achievement and qualities of his heroine Gloriana were lacking both in the personality and the society of her successor. Criticisms of James were implied in praise of the Queen — a queen who neither debased the coin of the realm, nor sold crown lands; a queen who built a powerful navy and patronized voyages of discovery and conquest.[68] Condemnation of a more superficial and effeminate age was suggested by praise for nobles who shunned empty ostentation and superfluous apparel for virtuous action: 'and the youth was fashioned for wars and men imboldened to fight'.[69] It was not only in his handling of Scottish affairs that Camden showed dangerous indifference to the wishes of James I. The *Annales* presented a subtle picture of *two* ages. Through the narrative of the great days of Elizabeth, Camden penned a criticism of the new reign of James.

But it was meant to be constructive criticism. Just as Elizabeth herself had learned her statecraft not least from her reading of Cicero and Livy,[70] so her own life, and the lives of her great subjects — of Sidney or Drake — might serve as a model for youth. For, as Camden told his reader, his intention had been 'insensibly to instruct the mind'. He had called his history *Annales* after Tacitus for annals' 'principal office it is to take care that vertue be not obscured and by the relation of evil words or deeds, to propose the fear of infamy with posterity'.[71]

Between the publication of the first volume of the *Annales* in 1615 and the foundation of the Oxford chair of history in 1622, the evidence for Camden's life story is full of gaps. He was evidently disillusioned with the fate of his first volume which, not surprisingly, had not pleased King James, but he continued to work on the second part, dealing with the reign of Elizabeth after 1588. During these years Camden was well-informed about court politics. John Chamberlain wrote to him in Kent reporting the latest court gossip and recorded that in 1618 Camden journeyed 'once a week the more' to St. Paul's to exchange news.[72] Camden too kept in touch with his pupil Sir Robert Cotton who from 1616 was acting as amanuensis to Thomas Howard, Earl of Arundel, and so at the centre of court politics.[73] The second part of the *Annales* was completed — probably late in 1617 — in retirement from formal participation, but not from interest, in political life.

Camden was pessimistic about the fate of his history. The second part contained in general more implied criticisms of James and he feared that in particular his praise of Walsingham, enemy to Mary Queen of Scots, would offend the King.[74] Camden submitted his manuscript to Sir Robert Cotton, 'for his Majesty's judicious censure whether it please him they should be suppressed or published for I am indifferent'.[75] It appears that he then projected a sequel, the annals of James I's reign, for which broad chronological outline notes survive.[76] The annals of James's reign were never completed, nor was the second part of the *Annales* of Elizabeth published in Camden's (or James I's) lifetime. It is not improbable that the king who had taken offence at Sir Walter Raleigh's portrayal of Nennius, saw the implied criticisms of the *Annales* clearly. In 1621, however, Camden entrusted the manuscript of the second part to his friend Pierre Dupuy with a view to publication after his death.[77] In 1625 the complete *Annales: The True and Royal History of Elizabeth, Queene of England* was published from a French version of Camden's Latin: a complete picture of the Elizabethan age, a reign famous for a prudent ruler, a virtuous aristocracy and harmony in church and state.

Reviewing the life and works of his patron in 1626, Wheare saw the *Annales* as the crowning achievement of Camden's career. For the *Annales* was not just a true and thorough account, it was also a pertinent comment for the times. Camden had intended: 'Quicquid in usum praesentis cedere posse videatur colligere, eo iuventutem instruere, munire, praeparare ad prudentiam, ad virtutem . . .'.[78] Wheare's lectures on Florus were delivered to the same purpose: to draw from the examples of the past what might be of greatest use and instruction to the youth of the present.[79]

Closer scrutiny reveals that Florus's epitome of Roman history was an excellent text for Wheare's and Camden's intention. The broad view of Roman history, the structure imposed on the narrative, the analysis of the virtues which fostered Rome's greatness and the vices which precipitated its decline were all presented with brevity and a style which itself inclined to precepts and axioms.[80]

In a small volume, Florus took as his subject seven hundred years of the history of Rome from the time of Romulus. This was because the history of the Roman empire from its greatness to its decline was a microcosm of universal history. Book I begins

> The Roman people during the seven hundred years from the time of King Romulus down to that of Caesar Augustus, achieved so much in peace and war that, if a man were to compare the greatness of their empire with its years, he would consider its size as out of all proportion to its age. So widely have they extended their arms throughout the world that those who read of their exploits are learning the history, *not of a single people, but of the human race.*[81]

It was the historian's task therefore to represent that subject, as those who describe the geography of the earth, in a small picture. An overview of a universal process was the *raison d'être* of Florus's epitome. His picture too, like Camden's, took in the whole society: economic life, social change, war, politics and institutions. The Roman state was an organism. The 'populus' could be compared to a single individual. When such a comparison was made it could be seen that the history of the body politic of Rome mirrored the chronological stages of the natural body: 'if anyone were to contemplate the Roman people as he would a single individual and review its whole life, how it begun, how it grew up, how it arrived at what may be called the maturity of its manhood, and how it subsequently as it were reached old age, he will find that it went through four stages'.[82]

The manhood of Rome, its great age, stretched for one hundred and fifty years from the beginnings of expansion outside Italy to the time of Augustus Caesar. During this period, the achievements of Rome were built upon the vigour and virtue of her leaders and people, on religious unity, and upon an aristocracy devoted to the public cause. This was 'a golden age free from vice and crime while the innocence of the old pastoral life was still untainted and uncorrupted'.[83] History revealed an endless battle between 'fortuna' and 'virtus'. During the period of their greatness, the moral worth and virtue of the Roman people led fortune to look upon them beneficently. But age brought evil and vice. Profitable peace degenerated into fruitless war in Carthage and Corinth; corruption set in at home. The hundred years following the destruction of Carthage and Corinth were 'as deplorable and shameful'[84] as the previous century had been great. Excess wealth undermined the virtues of the people, 'spoiled the morals of the age and ruined the state which was engulfed in its own vices as in a common sewer'.[85] Change in the government, corruption and office sale saw pursuit of the public good lost in the quest for private gain. Factional rivalry and power struggles rent the unity of the empire: the rivalry between Caesar and Pompey exemplified the decline. The story of Rome's decline was the story of moral regression among the leaders and throughout the body politic. How nearly it is echoed for a later age in Camden's *Annales* of Elizabeth!

Florus's analysis of the ills that beset a society in decline, indeed his analogy from the human process of ageing, posed the problem of what might remedy the ailing state. Florus responds with a view of history as a series of cycles and the possibility of the evolution of a new great age, through the virtuous activity of a governor or governing group. In Florus's *Epitome* we find those brief

biographical sketches of the leaders possessed of virtuous qualities
— Cornelius Scipio, Augustus Caesar — as in Camden's *Annales*,
Drake, Sidney and Walsingham emerge as men who imprint their
greatness on their age. During Rome's greatness, the qualities of
her leaders were turned to the needs of the time. Her first seven
kings 'possessed just such a variety of qualities as the circumstances and advantages of the state demanded'.[86] So Fabius 'Cunc-
tator' adapted his policy to the time and saved the state; so Trajan
by his own activity renewed the vigour of the Roman people.
Rejuvenation required a return to traditional government, to traditional values and virtues. It required an understanding of the
historical process in order that action might best be fitted to
circumstance. For rulers and ruled, public and private life, history
was 'magistra vitae'.

We can begin then to appreciate the value placed on Florus, by
Camden and Wheare. Pausing to draw out the applicability of his
text to their own times, Wheare expounded Florus's epitome, his
axioms and precepts, to the young gentlemen of Oxford by whose
action and virtue the process of decline might be halted in
England. The value of Florus's history for inculcating such lessons
was not Camden's discovery. The great philologians, friends and
correspondents of Camden, Justus Lipsius and Janus Gruter, had
recommended, edited and annotated the text. Since 1470 Florus's
Epitome had been through several editions; from 1600 to 1649
with over thirty editions, it was second only to Tacitus in popularity.[87] When the *Epitome* was translated into French by Nicholas
Coeffeteau, bishop of Marseille, in 1621, it was recommended by
the translator to the king for 'le fruict que vostre Majesté' peut
donc receuillir de la connaissance de cette histoire et de toutes les
autres, c'est que son courage vrayement Royal et genereux se
sentira doucement obligé d'imiter les examples de ceux dont elle
admire les vertues'.[88] At a time when direct criticism was
dangerous it was important that Florus's, and Camden's, message
could be conveyed (like the dramatic satires of Camden's pupil
Jonson) 'doucement'. Through the lectures on Florus at Oxford the
ills of the state and their remedies could be safely aired.

*   *   *   *   *

While Camden was at work on the *Annales*, perhaps some time
before he had thought of the history chair at Oxford, Sir Fulke
Greville had determined to establish a history lectureship at his old
university of Cambridge.[89] The two founders were acquainted:
Camden owed to Greville his appointment, in 1597, as Clarenceux
King at Arms. He acknowledged other 'extraordinary favours' from

him and left him by will a piece of plate.[90] But there is no evidence that the two collaborated concerning their respective foundations nor that the two posts were directly or immediately connected. Like Camden's chair at Oxford, however, Greville's post, his lecturer and subject, gave rise to controversy and pose problems.

From the 1590s Greville showed an interest in and support for literary men, and especially historians: Samuel Daniel acknowledged his support; to Francis Bacon he was a friend and patron for life. John Speed, the author of *The History of Great Britain (1611)*, thanked Greville, 'the procurer of my present estate', for 'setting this hand free from the daily employments of a manual trade'.[91] In 1615, the year of the publication of the first volume of Camden's *Annales*, Greville turned his attention to the University of Cambridge. In that year he provided funds for 'the building of a public library', and made his first moves to establish a history lecture.[92]

Greville consulted Sir John Coke for advice. His projected candidate was, as he told Coke, 'a northern Briton', that is a Scot, thirty-five years old, 'industrious' and with years of education spent in Germany — probably Gilbert Jack, the metaphysician. Coke, former rhetoric lecturer at Cambridge, approved the choice of lecturer for his birth, industry and his 'quickness and ripeness both of wit and judgement: significant words and variety of manner well digested in a perspicacious and contracted style . . .'. He applauded his long period of study in Germany but asked 'whether experience of the world hath broken his thoughts to more than speculation; as it importeth very much in *this most active profession* . . .'. Coke went on to outline to Greville the role of a historian as he now conceived of it:

> For . . . *these times neither live nor govern by honour, nor patterns of times past*: but the chief use of this profession is now the defence of one church, and therein of one state . . . Wherefore in my poor opinion it is now as necessary to have diligent historians as learned divines: and that your historian be also a divine able to join church & commonwealth together which to separate is to betray. So shall your erection be a most fruitful and famous work: whereas if you plant *but a critical antiquary instead of an historian*, nothing can be more unthrifty nor vain.[93]

Nothing came of the approach, either because the candidate was unwilling to take the post — in 1621 Gilbert Jack declined the White professorship of moral philosophy at Oxford — or because, in the light of Coke's advice, Greville found him unsuitable.[94] The next we hear of the project was the offer made in 1624, evidently at the instigation of Sir William Boswell, resident at the Hague, to Gerard Vossius.[95] Vossius, antiquary, philologist and historian, enjoyed one of the greatest reputations in the scholarly world. Since 1618 he had been professor of chronology at the University of Leyden.[96] A correspondent with Camden and most other English antiquaries, he had recently become known for his *Ars Historica*, a treatise on the nature of history which was an important influence on Wheare's own.[97] Vossius was tempted by the offer and the opportunity to live among great scholars in Cambridge, 'where the church reproduced more closely than in any other the shape of the early church'.[98] But he seems too to have been uncertain about it: Leyden's excellent opportunities and his wife's poor health inclined him to stay.[99] After two years of correspondence and prevarication, he advised Greville (since 1621 Lord Brooke) to appoint another.[100]

Before he did so, Brooke decided to formulate, and to some extent revise, his plans for the lectureship. The 'Ordinances Established for a Publique Lecture of Historie in ye Universitie of Cambridge', ascribable to 1627, echo Sir John Coke's recommendations of 1615.[101] The lecturer was to be an M.A. of at least five years standing, learned in Greek, Latin, cosmography, chronology and other sciences required by the profession. The best candidates were also to be men of the world:

> Such as have travelled beyond the seas and so have added to their learning, knowledge of the modern tounges, and experience in foreign parts, and like-wise such as have been brought up and *exercised in public affairs* shall be accounted most eligible, if they be equal in the rest.[102]

But the ordinances also suggest a change of tack. In 1615 Coke had recommended a divine; Gerard Vossius was an Arminian clergyman as well as a scholar. In 1627, however, none in holy orders was eligible; the realm had preferments enough for divines, 'few or none for professors of humane learning, the use and application whereof to the practice of life is the main end and scope of this foundation'.[103] Married men were also excluded — perhaps as a result of the tangled negotiations with Vossius — and, in general, the founder's control over the appointment was more clearly laid down.[104] In 1627 Greville chose Isaac Dorislaus, a young Dutch civilian from Leyden who had settled in Essex and who was employed in his household.[105] With his appointment, the project conceived twelve years before was enacted.

A series of questions arises from the story of Greville's lectureship. Why did he decide to establish the position in Cambridge in 1615? Why did he wait until 1624, after the initial candidate had proved unsuitable? Why did he decide, between

1624 and 1627, to exclude divines? The subject of the lecture is no less a problem. For though the ordinances left the choice of subject to the discretion of the reader, Greville asked Dorislaus to lecture on the *Annales* of Tacitus.[106] It was a choice soon to plunge the lecture into controversy.

It would appear an unexceptional choice. Tacitus's *Annales* was the most popular classical work of the early seventeenth century, the subject of many editions (notably that of Justus Lipsius) and commentaries.[107] Like Florus, Tacitus's respect for Seneca, his portrayal of virtues and vices, his striking brief portraits of characters, concise and epigrammatical style commended him for the purpose of a lecture to the young nobles. But Tacitus's political values, like his attitude to religion, were ambivalent. Tacitus thought monarchy a necessity for Rome; there was no alternative: Tacitus disdained the multitude. But because he depicted so powerfully the vices and excesses of the emperors, many did not read him as a monarchist.[108] To Francis Bacon, he was the enemy of tyranny; from Tacitus Sir John Eliot in 1626 had culled the comparison of the Duke of Buckingham with Sejanus.[109] But if Tacitus's *Annales* were open to various interpretations there can be little doubt about the emphasis placed by Dorislaus in his exposition of them.

The theme of Dorislaus's first lecture, delivered on 7 December 1627, was the different types of monarchical rule — the legal and the tyrannical.[110] The main argument pervading the commentary was that the ruler's authority was limited, that the people retained certain powers and that when these were encroached upon the ruler could be resisted. On 12 December he continued. The tyrannical Tarquin had ruled bloodily, taking counsel not, as traditionally, from the Senate, but from private advisers. By his will alone he carried all. Brutus, 'Liberator', deposed him. So later the Dutch people had resisted will unrestrained by law and tradition and contested the King of Spain's arbitrary government of the Netherlands. Royal authority was necessary and to be obeyed, but a tyrant was no king. Monarchs governed by the rule of law for 'legum praecipuum in civitate robur est'.

Some took alarm at the lectures. Mathew Wren, Master of Peterhouse, attended both lectures. On 16 December he wrote to William Laud, Bishop of Bath and Wells, enclosing notes on the lectures, and his own opinion of them:

His first lecture December 7th did pass unexcepted at by any that I could meet with. But yet I forbore not to show the Heads in private that it contented me not, because howsoever he highly preferred a monarchy before all other forms and ours above all, yet he seemed to acknowledge no right of Kingdoms but whereof the people's voluntary submission had been the *principium constitutionem*. The second lecture December 12th was stored with such dangerous passages (as they might be taken) *and so applicable to the expectation of these villainous times*, that I could not abstain before the Heads there present to take much offence that such a subject should be handled here and such lessons published, and at these times . . .[111]

Wren persuaded the Vice-Chancellor, Thomas Bainbrigg, who had not attended, to investigate. He consulted two senior doctors who had been placed better than Wren to hear and they 'did somewhat blanch it, because he had used some distinctions towards the end which might well satisfy all'. Wren remained unsatisfied and secured copies of the lectures from which he extracted 'the principal passages'. Though Dorislaus privately satisfied him as to having intended no ill, Wren blocked the congregation that was the next day to have incorporated him a Doctor, and forwarded the papers to Laud.

Dorislaus's lecture thence became the pawn of factional rivalries within Cambridge. For Wren, a protegé of Laud, was one of the leading figures in what was known as the Arminian party, a group opposed in theology to the rigours of Calvinist predestinarianism and committed in matters of liturgy to more elaborate ceremony.[112] When he wrote sending the lecture notes, Wren urged Laud 'to have that regard of me as not to let my name be heard at all, but where my service will be rightly accepted, without the least hint thereby to the adverse faction (whose disfavour I have already incurred deeply by stopping the incorporation of him and bringing him into question) . . .'[113] The two doctors consulted by Bainbrigg, we recall, had found nothing of serious objection in Dorislaus. Samuel Ward, the Saxonist, Lady Margaret Professor and one of the leaders of the Calvinists in Cambridge, exonerated him unequivocally from any crime. Concerning Dorislaus, Ward wrote to Ussher, bishop of Armagh, in 1628:

> He read some two or three lectures beginning with Cornelius Tacitus, where his author mentioning the conversion of the state of Rome from government by Kings to government by consuls, by the suggestion of Junius Brutus; he took occasion to discourse of the power of the people under the Kings, descended to the vindicating of the Netherlanders for retaining their liberties against the violences of Spain. In conclusion he was conceived of by some to speak too much for the defence of the liberties of the people, though he spake with great moderation, and with an exception of such monarchies as ours, where the people had surrendered their right to the King, as that in truth there could be no just exception taken against him.[114]

Much of what happened thereafter took place behind the scenes. The Vice-Chancellor, fearful that the lecture might be lost, having heard Dorislaus's explanation, sent him to the Council to make a similar submission, and to his patron with a letter of recommendation from the university. Both were to no avail. Order came to the university in the King's name through Bishop Neile, prohibiting Dorislaus to read.[115]

Whether Greville had seen the lecture before delivery we cannot say. His attitude to the controversy surrounding it is unclear — not surprisingly given the factional tangles in which the fortunes of the lecturer were embroiled. He continued to pay Dorislaus his £100 stipend, but made no provision for financing the lecture in his will. In a death bed codicil, however, he not only provided for the permanent maintenance of the chair, he named Dorislaus as first incumbent.[116] There can be few clearer indications of Greville's approval of Dorislaus's performance and probably, as we shall suggest, of the views which he had expressed. It is time for us to leave the lecture and to turn to the founder.

Greville, after leaving Cambridge, obtained entrée to the court through his school companion at Shrewsbury, Philip Sidney, and through the Earl of Leicester, a friend of Greville's father, and Sidney's uncle. Through them, he made the acquaintance of Sir Francis Walsingham, Sidney's father-in-law, with whom he travelled on diplomatic missions during the 1570s. The deaths, between 1586 and 1590, of Sidney, Leicester and Walsingham robbed Greville of his friends and patrons, and removed from the political stage the leading protagonists of a more active foreign policy (and alliance with the Netherlands) to which Greville had himself become committed. During the 1590s, Greville attached himself, along with others of the Sidney–Leicester circle, to the Earl of Essex, becoming, in 1598, Treasurer to the Navy. With the triumph of Cecil and the death of Elizabeth, Greville's fortunes were checked. But after the death of Salisbury, he was appointed Chancellor of the Exchequer, through his connection with Lady Suffolk. Greville survived the fall of Suffolk in 1618; in 1621 a patent conferred on him the title of Baron Brooke.[117]

At each point in his life and career, Greville's poems and dramatic works express his reactions to prevailing political circumstances.[118] Though none is dated it is possible to ascribe most of them to a particular period of a few years, if not to a particular year.[119] *Mustapha*, for instance, a dramatic study of the problem of the Turkish succession at the time of Suleiman, was evidently penned in the 1590s (like so much of the literature of that decade) as a comment on the problem of Elizabeth's successor. But related as they are to time and circumstances, Greville's works are notable for the consistent attitudes and values which permeate them: values which were formulated in his youth and adhered to throughout his life. What were those values? They were the values of a man of learning engaged in court and political life, of a committed Protestant anxious for a more active policy to stem the tide of Catholicism and Habsburg imperialism. They were the values of a man for whom the stoic discipline was a model for human conduct, for whom the policies of Leicester and Walsingham were a blueprint for government, for whom Sir Philip Sidney was the exemplar of all noble virtues. They were, like Camden's, the values of an Elizabethan.

Greville greatly admired Elizabeth. To him the early years of her successor saw only decline: the deterioration of leadership and the decay of society. Early in the new reign, he redrafted his *Mustapha* incorporating revisions which were a thinly veiled criticism of James I and his favourites. Now, even more in retrospect, the reign of Elizabeth seemed an ideal to be reattained. About 1610 Greville projected a life of Elizabeth. In his *Life of Sidney*, probably first drafted about that time, he endlessly digresses to praise the qualities of the Queen and, by implication, to contrast them with the failings of the King. The portrait of Sidney, the model of all the public virtues of his age, the author of noble 'counsels and projects', pointed critically to the mere titled upstarts of lesser worth and substance who thronged the Jacobean court. Greville wrote the *Life of Sidney* so that 'our nation may see a sea-mark raised upon their native coast . . . and so by a right meridian line of their own learn to sail through the straits of true virtue into a calm and spacious ocean of humane honour'.[120] It was written, that is, in the spirit of Sidney's own conviction that 'the representing of virtues, vices, humours, counsels and actions of men . . . is an inabling of free-born spirits to the greatest affairs of state'.[121]

That same belief in the instructive qualities of examples of virtue and vice underlay Greville's *Treatise of Monarchy*. Arising in part from his tragedies, *Mustapha* and *Alaham, A Treatise of Monarchy* shows signs of composition and revision over more than two decades. Greville's theme is the declination of monarchy with the vicissitude of nature and the passage of time — 'Time that begeteth and blasteth everything'.[122] In an earlier ideal state princes and subjects had lived together in order and harmony. But with the fall of man from grace, kings, subject like all men to human vices, ambitiously sought more power. Monarchy decayed to tyranny and tyranny eroded the ethical basis of society which government was instituted to uphold:

'As where noe lymitts be to Powre or will
Nor true distinction between good and ill'.[123]

Monarchy, however, was still the best, indeed the only possible form of government. Aristocracy and democracy could lead only to anarchy. Kings alone guaranteed against chaos in the body politic as, in the body natural, reason checked the sway of passion. It was essential for the health of the commonwealth that monarchs be good and effectual. Monarchs must promote trade and wealth, preserve peace, uphold established religion and provide justice. This required able leadership by moderate princes who, by the help of uncorrupt counsel, could best act for the public good. Only the maintenance of a balance between the power of the ruler and the rights of the ruled could uphold the interests of each and the stability of the commonwealth. Consultation was part of that balance and of that stability. Parliaments could best expose the ills of the body politic and laws best provide a remedy,

'lawes being mappes and councellors the doe
show forth diseases and redresse them too'.[124]

Law, like ideal monarchy, embodied reason, the light of government.

Good government was guided by a 'second light' — the light of example. Examples from the past might offer instruction, especially lessons 'drawne from those monarchies which overran, in little tyme all this knowne worlde of man'.[125] The Greeks had shown the importance of representative assemblies; the experience of Rome taught the need for conservation of traditional customs and institutions. The Roman state was 'for all free states a glass'.[126] But rulers might take guidance from more recent examples. Under Elizabeth, England had returned to many of the glories of the best governments. In the art of war, for instance, the possibilities of great exploits

'by undertakings of a mayden Queene,
May, as in modells to the worlde be seen'.[127]

Whilst it is impossible to date *A Treatise of Monarchy* accurately, several allusions in the text indicate the period during which it was revised. Reference is made to the Venetian Interdict crisis of 1606; mention is made of 'late fourth Henrie' of France who was assassinated in 1610.[128] I would like to suggest that the text of *A Treatise* contains revisions of a much later date. In general the comments on the tensions between royal authority and custom and law (a central theme of the poem) might seem to reflect the political debates of the 1620s. In the parliament of 1621 Greville worked hard to establish an effective partnership between James and the House of Commons.[129] More particularly, *A Treatise of Monarchy* urges resistance to the growing threat of popery and the Habsburgs. Kings should not be adverse to war 'out of the harts effeminatish ground'.[130] Armed readiness and alliances with neighbouring states were advocated. If war broke out, the people would be willing to pay — people

> 'who when peace is turned to war
> finde subsedyes no taxes but revenues are'.[131]

Such passages seem to point to a period after the outbreak of the Thirty Years War, perhaps to the years 1621–4 when some at court advocated intervention on behalf of Frederick the Elector Palatine against the Habsburgs. We cannot be sure. But we know that Greville had always favoured a Dutch alliance against Spain, that from 1621 to 1623 while James listened to pro-Spanish advisers, he all but retired from court. In 1623, when Buckingham returned from Spain bent on war and so began a struggle with the king for control of foreign policy, Greville (like so many making calculations about the future in those tangled months) wavered. In his public life, that is, he wavered between support for the marriage treaty and advocacy of war in order to restore the Palatine.[132] To the privacy of his verse, however, he committed his real view of the inefficacy of diplomacy:

> '. . . when friends or foe draw swords
> They ever loose, that rest or trust to words'.[133]

Both the domestic and foreign issues of the 1620s are reflected in *A Treatise of Monarchy*. Both, I would suggest, prompted Greville's next political comment — the appointment of Isaac Dorislaus to lecture on Tacitus at Cambridge in 1627. It is perhaps significant that, against his own earlier inclinations and Sir John Coke's advice, the candidates in 1624, Vossius, and in 1627, Dorislaus, were Dutch.[134] In his lectures Dorislaus, we recall, praised the Netherlanders for their legitimate resistance to the tyrannical aggrandizement of Spain.[135] More generally, he stressed, as we have seen, the need for a balance in the constitution,[136] for imperial power to be limited and the rights of subjects regarded. In 1631, in a letter to Hugo Grotius, he was to speak more specifically of the need for royal authority 'moderationibus consiliis temperetur'.[137] Greville had always believed in the value of history; for more than a decade he had planned the lectureship at Cambridge. But in its final form, in the choice of lecturer and subject, the lecture was a comment on the immediate political circumstances.

*   *   *   *   *

The Camden and Greville lectureships were both a statement of their respective founder's attitudes to the immediate circumstances of the 1620s. There are differences between the two foundations, as there are between the men who established them. But when we review the history of the two posts, it is the similarities that strike us. Both chose as lecturers men who were not historians of experience, to deliver discourses on classical histories in order to show the fruits of historical examples as a guide for the conduct of private and public life. There were, of course, personal connections and common influences. Greville and Sidney went to the same school, Camden and Sidney shared the same tutor at Oxford. Both the lectureships reflect Sidney's own distinction between the mere chronologer who presented nothing but a narrative and the historian who 'is most commonly a moral philosopher either in the ethic part when he sets forth virtues or vices and the natures of passions, or in the politick when he doth meddle sententiously with matters of state'.[138]

There were other common influences: both Greville and Camden had read and derived much from the works of Buchanan and Bodin.[139] It has also been suggested that Greville wrote his treatise of *Humane learning* as a comment on Francis Bacon's *Advancement of Learning*.'[140] Wheare too saw in intellectual affinity between his patron and the younger Bacon when he coupled Bacon's *Henry VII* with Camden's *Annales* as the best of modern English history. Such influences, not least because they were part of the intellectual world in which Camden and Greville formed their values, cannot be discounted. But because they were part of the common intellectual coin they cannot alone explain the foundations at Oxford and Cambridge.

The major influence on both Camden and Greville was the practical circumstances of Jacobean politics. Sometime around the close of the first decade of early Stuart rule Camden and Greville, along with other historians and antiquaries, became aware of the harmful cycles of time.[141] To both men the reign of James witnessed a decline, throughout society and government, from the days of glorious Elizabeth. It is surely significant that Greville planned both a panegyrical life of Elizabeth and the foundation of a history lectureship and library in 1615, the year in which the first volume of Camden's *Annales* published to the world the achievements of Elizabeth and a new style of history. About that time the Essex divorce and Overbury affair revealed the moral turpitude of the Jacobean court; factional strife bedevilled good counsel as James retreated with his favourite; the parliament of 1614, dissolved in weeks, signalled the collapse of representative institutions and negotiations for a Spanish match overturned Elizabethan policy.

For Camden and Greville the years which followed brought

further disillusionment. While popery triumphed in Europe, England remained pusillanimous. At home rivalries at court and quarrels in parliament bedevilled action. Both men witnessed the final destruction of the Elizabethan age. Both were drawn to histories of past crises of empires. Both analysed the ills of their own age as Florus had described those of Rome in decline: the ills of unbalanced wealth, the decline of public virtue, a shift from traditional models of government and the failure of leadership. For Camden and Greville monarchy was the only acceptable form of government, but James I was not an adequate monarch. In the *Annales* of Elizabeth's reign and Greville's *Treatise of Monarchy* we detect the tensions between the ideal of kingship and the reality of Jacobean experience. History revealed that the great empires had been those where the interests of sovereign and subject, where prerogative and liberty were harmoniously reconciled. Such harmony and unity had marked the reign of Elizabeth, a queen who framed her own life to virtue through study. Camden praised her, in the preface to the *Annales*, for her study of Ascham, Cicero and Livy; Greville attributed her maintenance of a balance between power and freedom to 'the moderating education of King's children in those times'.[142] Education and experience helped rulers govern well.

Faced with a decline of leadership and public virtues, Camden and Greville, towards the end of their lives, turned to the young gentlemen, the future counsellors of kings, as the hope for England's rejuvenation. The traditional university curriculum, as humanist critics had for long complained, provided no adequate training for public service. Rather students nurtured on Aristotelian logic and rhetoric learned, in Bacon's phrase, 'to hunt more after words than matter'.[143] Camden had little time for mere rhetoricians; Greville described them as

'. . . busie idle fools
That serve no other market than the Schooles'.[144]

He came to doubt the value of academic education. What was needed was a practical training, as Greville advocated in his treatise of *Humane Learning*:

'Again the active necessarie arts
Ought to be briefe in bookes, in practise long,
Short precepts may extend to many parts
The practise must be large or not be strong'.[145]

Pure knowledge profited nothing if learning were not applied:

'The world should therefore her instructions draw
Back into life, and actions, whence they came'.[146]

The study of history, well directed, led the young 'back unto life and actions'. The collection of examples from the past led to the formulation of precepts as a guide to life. As Wheare had told the young students of Oxford, 'the principal end of History is *practice and not knowledge or contemplation*. And therefore we must learn not only that we know, but that we may do well and live honestly'.[147] Dorislaus told Grotius, in 1631, that he was returning to Cambridge to resume his lecture, that he might recall the young nobles to virtue, purer philosophy and the study of public affairs by historical examples.[148] The study of history might lead to a reinvigorated and virtuous society in the future.

It was that hope which underlay the foundations at Oxford and Cambridge. The purpose of the lectureships was not to provide an academic training in the study of history but to impart values and models culled from past examples. It is that purpose which helps us to understand why neither lecturer was noted for historical scholarship — Dorislaus, we recall, was a civil lawyer; why travel and experience were the qualities sought; why Florus and Tacitus were the texts chosen. It was that purpose which explains why, in the 1620s, history for the first time, became part of the curriculum of the English universities. It was the hope of Camden and Greville that the universities might play a vital role in the reform of society and government.

9. Cavalier critic? The ethics and politics of Thomas Carew's poetry*

Historians have argued that in the early seventeenth century there was a developing cultural rift as well as mounting political polarization. The contemporary labels 'court' and 'country', we are told, delineated distinct and antagonistic cultures and styles that presaged the division into Royalists and Roundheads in the English civil war.[1] In *The Causes of the English Revolution* Lawrence Stone proclaimed, 'By the early seventeenth century England was experiencing all the tensions created by the development within a single society of two distinct cultures, cultures that were reflected in ideals, religion, art, literature, and theatre, dress, deportment and way of life.[2] In *The English Civil War* Robert Ashton concurred, identifying the emergence of a distinct court culture that was 'exclusive, aristocratic and authoritarian.'[3]

Literary scholars have tended to agree. In his essay, 'Two Cultures? Court and Country under Charles I', Peter Thomas wrote of 'two warring cultures' emerging in the 1630s as an Elizabethan national culture fragmented into parts. One was a Caroline court, which 'seemed to speak for narrow snobbery and effete indulgence.'[4] Most recently, Graham Parry has attributed to the cultural interests of Charles I the most sinister political intents. When criticism of or obstacles to royal policies presented themselves, Parry argued, Charles I regarded it as the function of culture to dispel them: to present an ideal image that might mould a more tractable reality or that might at least divert men from consideration of that reality. So in the cult of Neo-Platonism, Parry maintained, Charles 'saw an admirable means of projecting a royal image in a way that distracted attention from the political aspects of his kingship.' In culture, as in politics, it was the 'grateful, uncritical mind' that was favoured by the court of Charles I.[5] Accordingly, the man of free spirit, independent judgement, and truly creative genius could find no home there. Milton was to become the literary antagonist of the Caroline regime.[6]

Such an interpretation of the cultural and political history of early Stuart England is enshrined in the idea of 'Cavalier' literature. When we think of Caroline dramatists or 'Cavalier poets', we think of a group of courtiers, flamboyant and gay, engaged only with the concerns of the courtly *précieux*, with love and the chase, irresponsibly insensitive to the moral questions and political problems of their age; or worse, uncritical servants and sycophants of an autocratic king who maintained them principally for their flattery.[7] Cavalier drama as characterized by Alfred Harbage was a fawning spectacle devoted only to the foolishly sentimental and romantic concerns of an exclusive coterie.[8] And, in the words of George Parfitt, 'Cavalier poetry shows a narrowing of range of reference and interest, becoming courtly in a sense which suggests a decisive split between "court" and "country" and a consequent concentration upon few areas of emotional experience.'[9] Where Jonson and Donne aired problems and criticisms within a world still united by common values, the Cavalier playwrights and poets of the 1630s, it is said, sang the swansong of an exclusive and authoritarian caste doomed to be defeated.[10]

Thomas Carew may stand as a test of any such characterization of Cavalier poetry and Caroline court culture.[11] For Carew was in the most exact sense a courtier: a gentleman extraordinary of the Privy Chamber and sewer in ordinary to the king, he attended personally upon the monarch in the royal privy lodgings.[12] Carew's place, diet, and livery freed him from the necessity of earning a living and might have qualified him to be one of those courtly gentlemen who, in Pope's phrase, 'wrote with ease.' He epitomized the amateur court poet. Moreover, Carew was evidently close to Charles I. In the words of Clarendon, 'He was very much esteemed by the most eminent Persons in the Court, and well looked upon by the King himself.'[13] Charles singled him out for office and advanced him over a rival Scottish candidate.[14] To damn him still further, Carew was also the author of a masque, allegedly that most courtly and sycophantic of modes, indeed, of what may claim to be the most brilliant court masque of the early Stuart period — a masque in which (at least at one level) the apotheosis of the monarch was taken to its greatest height.[15] Carew may be taken, then, to represent the court: during the 1640s he was regarded by the puritans as the emblem of its frivolity, immorality, and illegitimacy.[16]

Carew's biography, however, does not read like that of a model Caroline courtier. For Charles I's court reflected the new monarch's personal style, which was in marked contrast to the bawdy revelry of the Jacobean court: Charles I issued orders that

prescribed decorum, morality, and chastity. As a young man Carew
had led a profligate life and contracted syphilis.[17] Throughout his
life he was best known to his contemporaries for his erotic verse,
especially 'A Rapture', and as a libertine — a reputation to which
he himself alluded in his masque.[18] To describe Carew as a courtier, then, is accurately to define his official position at the
Caroline court, but it is not to illuminate his personal style; and it
should not substitute for an examination of his values and beliefs.
Carew is usually studied as one of the 'Cavalier Poets'. But to call
him a Cavalier is to be guilty of anachronism, for Carew died in
1640, two years before civil war divided the realm into these rival
camps.

It is my purpose in this essay to repatriate Carew in the decades
of early Stuart England *before* the civil war. This is the England of
Renaissance humanism: a commonweal of values in which virtue
and politics, morality and poetry were believed to be inseparable.
The leading citizen of that commonweal was Ben Jonson, whose
own art — be it verse epistle, epitaph, comedy of humours, or
masque — emerged from deeply held ethical premises and was
written for both private instruction and public counsel. Carew, I
wish to argue, was a 'son of Ben', not only as a legatee of Jonson's
style but, more important, as the heir of Jonsonian morality.

I

Since the 1640s many have depicted Carew as an exponent of unrestrained eroticism. Others have described him as a spokesman for
the graceful elegance of Caroline England. That both positions
have been powerfully argued may lead us to conclude that there
were contradictions and tensions in Carew's verse and life —
between explicit language and artful poise, between hedonism and
self-control. It is these tensions that I wish to examine further. For
through these ambiguities we may see Carew as a poet exploring
both personal dilemmas and some of the most important social and
political issues of his age, not disengaging from them. More
generally, by such a study of Carew, by an emphasis upon the
moral weight behind the lightness of touch, I hope to suggest that
in order to understand 'Cavalier poetry', we need to appreciate the
bequest of Jonson's ethical beliefs and concerns: the governance of
human nature; the relationship of virtue and politics; the role of
the artist in the commonweal. For once we relocate Carew and
other Caroline poets and playwrights in pre-civil war England, we
may begin to see serious consideration of such questions rather
than retreat from them, a preoccupation with common rather than

exclusive or partisan concerns, doubts and questions rather than self-congratulation, criticism of courtiers and king as well as compliment. We may begin to see a serious political vision and personal morality.[19]

In the sphere of personal morality, it might be thought that Thomas Carew had little to tell anyone. Known as a libertine in his own age, he has been chiefly remembered since then for 'A Rapture', one of the most erotically explicit poems in the language. Such an observation alone should cause us to reconsider any accusation of flattery, for Carew's eroticism seems out of place in a court devoted to the cult of Platonic love — a cult to which his poetry appears at times to be an irritated reaction: 'Let fooles thy mystique formes adore,/I'le know thee in thy mortall state.'[20] But to know Carew's poems only in their mortal state would be to misunderstand them — or to hear only one of the voices through which the poet spoke on love and morality.[21] For there is an ambiguity about love and passion both between various poems and within them. The first thirty or forty lines of 'To A.L. Perswasions to Love', for example, read as the conventional rhetoric of seduc-tion: as an incitement to a young girl to indulge in the pleasures of the flesh before time robs her of her beauty. All the seducer's persuasive tricks and tropes are there: the pleasure that the maiden will herself enjoy; the responsibility to use Nature's stock of beauty with liberality; the point that lesser lights shine when the greater are hid under a bushel.[22] These tropes are standard, but we note that it is precisely such persuasive eloquence that forms the subject of Carew's 'Good Counsel to a young Maid', in which, conscious of the seductive powers of (his own?) verse, he warns his pupil,

> Netts, of passions finest thred,
> Snaring Poems, will be spred,
> All, to catch thy maiden-head.[23]

The young woman is warned to be on her guard, for the rhetoric of seduction is not to be confused with the reality of love. She must resist the powerful anguished overtures of the seducer's eloquence lest consent bring her shame.[24] Chastity, the maid is told in this poem, is central to her honour, and only honourable love should be allowed to conquer it. And this, for all the seduc-tive opening lines, is also the point of 'To A.L. Perswasions to Love'. For, as we read on, it becomes clear that there the poet-lover offers not merely the sexual gratification of the moment but love for life. And like the young maid, A.L. is advised to select only such a suitor:

> Cull out amongst the multitude
> Of lovers, that seeke to intrude
> Into your favour, one that may
> Love for an age, not for a day;
> One that will quench your youthfull fires,
> And feed in age your hot desires.[25]

The conjunction that opens the last line lends its force to the whole verse. The poem becomes not simply an act of seduction but advice to use the gift of youthful beauty in order purchase that life-long love which might legitimize the indulgence of sexual passion without loss of honour.

Love involves physical passion, but mere lust is not the same as love. In another poem Carew tells his mistress of 'The difference/ Twixt heat of soule and sence'.[26] And he debates the difference between them in one of four songs that he wrote for a court entertainment:

> Quest. By what power was Love confinde
>   To one object? who can binde,
>   Or fixe a limit to the free-borne minde?[27]

The question evokes the arguments of fashionable Platonic lovers as expressed, for example, by Queen Atossa in Cartwright's *The Royal Slave*.[28] The answer, however, dismisses the implication of the question; before a court audience Carew denies the veiled polygamy in Platonic love:[29]

> An. Nature; for as bodyes may
>   Move at once but in one way,
>   So nor can mindes to more than one love stray.[30]

Unlike mere lust, Carew asserts, love is faithful. Unlike mere lust, it is also timeless. It is 'Eternitie of love protested' in Carew's song, as in 'To A.L. . . . .'.

> True love can never change his seat,
> Nor did he ever love, that could retreat.[31]

Honourable, faithful, and eternal love, love both physical *and* spiritual — such an interpretation of Carew's position seems to be at odds with our traditional reading of his most famous erotic ode. For in 'A Rapture' these qualities are scorned. Honour is 'but a Masquer': the 'nobler' lovers refute it and act oblivious of reputation.[32] The poem is usually read as an incitement to sexual licence, and it is easy to see why. At one level the poem reads as a playful but sophisticated act of seduction, in which the poet seeks to answer all his mistress's and society's objections to the free vent of sexual passion. To read the poem as *only* frank hedonism or as a mere *jeu d'esprit*, however, is to oversimplify it. For the context of Carew's sexual freedom is not society but an Elysium where 'All things are lawfull'.[33] Sexual licence here is not at odds with social order. Carew writes of a world apart from society, a paradise, a land of innocence free of sin where men do not know the names 'of husband, wife, lust, modest, chaste, or shame.'[34] In this Elysium men live virtuously by acting according to their natural instincts. Here what society has labelled sinful bears no such taint. In this Elysian ground Carew playfully sees Aretine's works, handbooks of sensuality, become 'divine' lectures of love and Daphne surrender to Apollo.[35] Here where 'Beautie and Nature, banish all offence', the social labels of moral and immoral, honourable and dishonourable, have no place.[36] This is Carew's own rapture: an Elysium in which the tensions between man's natural instinct and social order and morality are resolved. 'A Rapture' is, we might say, a laboratory in which Carew creates an ideal condition so that he may better explore an actual problem.[37]

In Elysium 'All things are lawfull — that may delight / Nature, or unrestrained Appetite.'[38] From this location honour is seen to be only a social attribute — one at times at odds with religion and values natural to man. Where honour dictates that men kill 'religion bids from blood-shed flye'; in Elysium he enjoys 'steadfast peace'.[39] Society, necessarily perhaps, erects codes that restrain men's natural instincts and so creates tensions between natural and social behaviour. Carew envisions a paradise in which man's innocence removes the need for restraint and dispels such contradictions. 'A Rapture' is located in and hankers for that world of natural innocence, a world, as 'The Second Rapture' describes it, 'of lust and lovers' — for in innocence they are one.[40] Carew's quest for a reconciliation of sexual passion and virtue may be behind 'The Second Rapture' as well. For all the frank eroticism of the imagined sexual union with a young girl, the imagery is religious and the maiden remains chaste. Lynn Sadler has observed that the poem plays on the biblical story of the virgin presented to David 'that my lord the King may get heat'.[41] The maiden may 'renew the age' by a reunion, a reconciliation of 'lust' and 'blisse' that man enjoyed before the fall tainted him with sin.[42] From this perfect state man had fallen. Though he knew all too well that man was a creature of appetite, Carew seems to have believed in man's potential for virtue. It may be, then, that Carew's hope for himself and mankind lay not in mere obedience to the social dictates of honour and reputation but in striving to live by the natural innocence of man's perfect state.

In society, it would seem, Carew at times suggests that the best reconciliation of love and passion, appetite and order, was found in marriage. The subject of his poem 'On the Marriage of T.K. and C.C. the morning stormie' is the resolution of tensions. Carew depicts marriage as a calm in a world of tempests. Marriage puts an end to the unruly winds and waters, the sighs and tears of unrequited love; it brings peace to the soul. And marriage unites lovers in a physical union now that they are joined by holy sacrament to each other. When the priest unites the bride and groom,

> From the misterious holy touch such charmes
> Will flow, as shall unlock her wreathed armes,
> And open a free passage to that fruit
> Which thou hast toy'ld for with a long pursuit.[43]

In society, outside matrimony, it had been forbidden fruit; within marriage it is the fruit of the garden of innocence to which, by partaking of it, the couple return. Marriage, that is, returns them to innocence. It removes them, like the Elysium of 'A Rapture', from the values and language of a fallen society. So the bride's exclamations of sexual pleasure become 'pleasing shreekes'; the 'fight of love' is become peace; ''Tis mercy not to pitty' the virgin for her blood spilt.[44] Their natural love expressed in marriage reconciles contradictions, rendering chaste what was impure, honourable what was shameful, moral what was immoral. Marriage, because it orders man's passions, enables him to partake of sensual pleasure without being debased by it.[45] It unites in harmony and orders the potentially contradictory and unruly aspects of his own nature. If, as Sadler points out, Carew writes with the most frank and free eroticism about married love, it is because in marriage pleasure is reconciled to virtue.[46]

Such an interpretation of Carew's verse and the morality of his poetry might seem to detach the poetry from the poet — a man who, we recall, was brought close to death by a life of licence and by syphilis. On the contrary, I suggest that a strong personal sense of the ungoverned anarchy of his own appetite and passion, some internal quest for order and regulation, dominated Carew's life as well as his poetry. Evidently he contemplated marriage: there were rumours in 1624-5 that he might wed the rich widow of Sir George Smith.[47] At a time when his fortunes were at a low ebb, economic motives might well have been to the fore. But Carew's correspondence with Sir John Suckling concerning his marriage plans supports the suggestion of the poet's search for regulation in his life as well as his art.[48] Suckling attempted to dissuade his friend from matrimony. With more than a hint of irony — induced, no doubt, by the prospect of the pox-ridden Carew taking the marriage vows — Suckling ribaldly urged him to consider that fruit trees multiplied only when transplanted. 'Do but make love

to another', he counselled, and the 'homely meal' of marriage
would soon pale before the varied dainty dishes available to the
lover's palate.[49] Carew, significantly, remained adamant in his
reply. Love, he agreed with Suckling, was natural, but 'if *love* be
natural', he added, 'to *marry* is the best *Recipe* for living
honest.'[50] For marriage he defined as the expression of love that
was fixed and immutable; and, as we have seen, Carew maintained
that there was no other love. '*Love* changed often doth nothing;
nay 'tis nothing: for *love* and *change* are incompatible.'[51] In
marriage alone love seeded, bore fruit, and multiplied. Carew
responded to Suckling in his friend's own coin: the tone of his
answer is jocular, bawdy, and coarse. To us, perhaps, Carew's
argument for sexual fidelity is couched in less than appropriate
language: 'one steed shall serve your turn as well as twenty
more.'[52] But, as often was the case with Carew, the language and
tone should not be simply equated with the meaning. As he told
Suckling, ''Tis not the want of love . . . if every day afford not
new-language, and new waies of expressing affection.'[53] Carew's
coarse language, like his erotic verse, also makes a point: it is itself
a frank acknowledgement of those physical, animal urges that
marriage accommodates and to which marriage may give vent. The
sensual and the physical are as significant in Carew's reply as in
Suckling's letter. Carew's final conclusion, however, is not the
same: 'I know what marriage is and know you know it not.' For
Carew believed that in condemning marriage, Suckling denied
what was natural, in the sense of that which might restore man to
his higher nature, the original innocence of his uncorrupted
nature. In the words of the *Book of Common Prayer* marriage was
'instituted of God in paradise in the time of man's innocency' and
'ordained for a remedy against sin.'[54]

Marriage for Carew was the literal as well as metaphorical
expression of the poet's 'attempt to impose a civilized order upon
the desperate chaos of man's inner realities.'[55] It accommodated
the physical and spiritual in man, natural instinct and social order.
Once we see that there is more to Carew than the libertinism of
'A Rapture', we may also begin to appreciate that there was more
to his love lyrics than the celebration of court love games played
by the *précieux*. We may come to see that while he worked within
the conventions of Petrarchan love poetry, Carew re-employed,
adapted, and even subverted them as he brought to them the
concerns and problems of his age. Through a poetry of beauty,
love, and nature, we may see, Carew did not retreat from contemporary issues and problems; rather, he examined not only amorous
but also social and political relationships.

II

The celebration of beauty is a *raison d'être* of the love poem. The equation of a lover's physical attributes with the features of the natural or celestial spheres was conventional in the poetry of the Renaissance. Carew's delightful song 'Aske me no more' places him firmly within the convention. Even in this poem, however, apparently sung simply in the key of celebration, the refrain transcends the mere flattery of a mistress. The lady's beauty is not compared to roses; it becomes the very essence or idea of roses and so captures the essence of nature itself.[56] In 'The Comparison' Carew makes his departure from the conventions of the love poem clear:

> Dearest thy tresses are not threads of gold,
> Thy eyes of Diamonds, nor doe I hold
> Thy lips for Rubies. . . .[57]

For Carew beauty does not reside in his mistress's fair hair (though 'threads of lawne'), her coral lips, her 'teeth of pearle', or even in her wit (though 'pure and quicke').[58] The poet loves her 'for all', and it is 'the complement' of each part to the other rather than the compliment of a suitor that gives the poem its title.[59] Beauty expresses the harmony of nature in the universe, not merely its earthly manifestations in a mistress. And so 'The Comparison' is that of the maiden with the purest essence of nature: her lips are 'Nector', her breath frankincense; her cleavage is a 'Paradise'. Celia is a 'faire Goddesse' to be worshipped: the goddess Nature herself.[60]

As Nature's legate, Beauty influences men with all the might of nature's sway. The beauty of nature leads men necessarily to love: 'Love flow from Beautie as th' effect.'[61] It has a magic that enchants men so that the greatest beauty most attracts. Such a power needs to be exercised with responsibility. Those endowed with nature's gifts must acknowledge it — 'Confesse thy beauty' — and attune their behaviour to their outward appearance: 'tis fit thou thine owne valew know.'[62] The beautiful, those endowed with the quintessence of nature, must lead the life of the beautiful — that is, the virtuous life. For beauty's authority is legitimate only when founded upon virtue. In his 'Epitaph on the Lady S.', Carew offers an encomium on the union of beauty and virtue to her:

> Whose native colours, and purest lustre, lent
> Her eye, cheek, lip, a dazling ornament:
> Whose rare and hidden vertues, did expresse
> Her inward beauties, and minds fairer dresse.[63]

Such a fusion of outer beauty and inner virtue represented and restored the divine image in which men were moulded before the fall of nature. Like the first man and woman, however, not all endowed with such beauty lived according to their divine image. The mistress of Carew's 'The Comparison', for instance, is a 'faire Goddesse' only in outward appearance. 'The Comparison', it becomes clear, is not only or primarily between the woman's beauty and the hues and features of nature; it is a comparison — or, rather, an unfavourable but forceful contrast — between a divine appearance and a personality that failed to live up to it. The mistress is not praised but chided:

> Faire Goddesse, since thy feature makes thee one,
> Yet be not such for these respects alone;
> But as you are divine in outward view
> So be within as faire, as good, as true.[64]

The powerful commandment of the last line emphasizes the didacticism of Carew's love poetry. Here, as elsewhere, Carew adopts the conventions of the poetry of compliment but, as Jonson, employs them with an independent and radical force. He instructs rather than flatters. And while appearing to describe the charms of a mistress he posits a view of beauty that implies a morality.

Beauty is depicted as vulnerable to the ravages of time, and Carew's treatment of this theme has encouraged us to read his verse in conventional *carpe diem* terms, hedonistically urging men and women to seize the pleasures of the hour. Does not 'A Rapture' open with a line redolent with the hot impatience of sexual passion: 'I will enjoy thee now my Celia, come'? Does not 'Perswasions to Enjoy' warn Carew's Celia of the pressing need to 'reape our joyes /E're time such goodly fruit destroyes'?[65] We must recollect, however, that 'To A.L. . . .' concludes not in advice to seize the moment but rather an exhortation to secure the long term, to lay the foundation of eternal love rather than to indulge immediate sexual urges. And this may offer us insight into Carew's more serious preoccupation. In the battle against time, the eternal enemy of mankind and the special preoccupation of the Renaissance consciousness, Carew's weapon is love. Love is shown to transcend the externals of beauty and so to be free of that decay natural to physical substance. Carew's Cleon reassures his fearful mistress: 'Though beautie fade, my faith lasts ever.'[66] For Cleon dotes not on Celia's 'snow white skin' but on her 'purer mind', and that is incorruptible.[67] When the two exchange their tokens of a love so founded they know that they have won the victory over time: 'Thus we are both redeemed from time.'[68] And the poet, by celebrating their love — any true love — may redeem others. The publicization of love by the poet may lead others to transcend time, as Celia acknowledges:

> . . . CE. And I
> Shall live in thy immortall rime,
> Untill the Muses dye.[69]

Cleon and Celia, like the shepherd and the nymph in another poem of the same title, are speakers in 'A Pastorall Dialogue'.[70] It is not only a dialogue between them but a conversation among Time, Love, and, as the title suggests, Nature. Nature, though it expresses the passage of time in the seasons, is yet eternity itself. Men conquer time then when they accord and act with nature. By returning to a virtuous life lived in accordance with innocent nature, Carew is arguing, man may triumph over his enemy, Time.[71]

Man, Carew suggests, returns to nature through love. In Carew's poetry metaphors drawn from nature (a commonplace of Renaissance love poetry) are employed with unusual freshness and vigour to articulate a real and philosophical rather than an allegorical or metaphorical relationship between nature and love. Love's language and tactics, in Carew's verse, are the voices and movements of nature. The mistress whose heart lies in 'The Torrid, or the frozen Zone' is unwarmed by the beams of love.[72] The bold lover, however, is a sun whose powerful rays cannot be resisted by the most unyielding of nature's flowers.

> Marke how the bashfull morne, in vaine
> Courts the amorous Marigold
> With sighing blasts, and weeping raine;
> Yet she refuses to unfold.
> But when the Planet of the day,
> Approacheth with his powerfull ray,
> Then she spreads, then she receives
> His warmer beams into her virgin leaves.
> So shalt thou thrive in love, fond Boy.[73]

That 'So' transcends simile. Nature *is* a lover and love is natural. In the Elysium of 'A Rapture' nature provides the lovers' bed and pillows from her stock of flowers and down.[74] The woman's body is itself a garden through which the lover wanders partaking of the 'warme firme Apple, tipt with corall berry' and 'the vale of Lillies'.[75] 'A Rapture' expresses an ideal state in which nature and love are one, pure and innocent. In society, nature no less than love has become corrupted and disordered. Passion and lust manifest the chaos of a wild, unruly nature. Carew has told us, however, that perfect, faithful, timeless love may restore men to innocence. So, we may see, that as perfect nature instructs lovers, the right love may reciprocally rule and reorder the chaos of fallen nature. The beauty of Carew's mistress, singing, 'Stills the loude wind; and makes the wilde / Incensed Bore, and Panther milde.'[76] Or, as the ode 'To the Queen' makes clear, the 'great Commandress', who orders love and tames lust, also disciplines nature. Her example of love

> . . . shews us the path
> Of Modestie, and constant faith,
> Which makes the rude Male satisfied
> With one faire Female by his side.[77]

The power of love's example subdues even the 'wilde Satyr'. Ultimately love's law will rule the flood and 'free' man through the 'deepe divinitie' of love from the fall.[78]

The love that may regulate nature must be the model of order, drawn from nature's first perfection. Love expresses the peace, order, and eternity of nature. Mutability and infidelity are not the attributes of love but of its opposite, lust, which is (the word is often used) 'wilde', the behaviour of man cast into the wilderness because he fell slave to appetite.[79] Legitimate love, by contrast, manifests 'calme desires' and displays 'milde aspects'.[80] It distils the harmony of nature, uniting body and soul, the physical and spiritual, appetite and order. Such a love, we have seen, Carew believed to be best found in marriage. Marriage may now be understood not only to calm the tempests of man's personal turmoil; as we shall argue, it might also restore the harmony and order of nature and so effect the redemption and reformation of society and the commonweal.

It is this universal ethical vision — the restoration of the state of perfect nature and reformation of society — that is the subject of two of Carew's poems usually described as 'country house poems':[81] 'To Saxham' and 'To my friend G.N. from Wrest'. At one level these poems, like 'To Penshurst', are undoubtedly charming celebrations of the pleasures Carew enjoyed at the country seat of two friends and patrons, Sir John Crofts and Henry de Grey, Earl of Kent.[82] Like 'To Penshurst', however, there is more to them than that. Like Jonson's, Carew's poems transcend their particular circumstances; they are representations of an idealized nature that was central to Carew's ethics and social attitudes.

'To . . . G.N. from Wrest' opens with a contrast between the 'temperate ayre' of Wrest and the 'raging stormes' of the 'cold nights out by the bankes of Tweed'.[83] Carew has just returned from the king's campaign against the Scots and the discomforts of the royal camp near Berwick-upon-Tweed.[84] He has also returned to a garden of peace from a wilderness that threatened disorder.[85] Wrest is described as a haven of nature, of an idealized, perfected nature: the garden is pregnant with Nature's seed and fertile with her fruits. It is a world free of social artifice; there are no compounds or 'forraigne gums' but 'pure and uncompounded beauties' expressing all the gifts of a fecund, ordered, and uncorrupted nature.[86] Where by the Tweed there were 'bleake Mountains', 'fierce tempests', 'everlasting winter', Wrest caresses its guest with 'balmie dew', 'odours sweete' and 'with the warme Suns quickning heate'.[87] Wrest symbolizes the harmony of perfect nature. And so in Carew's hands it becomes, like nature itself, a model of behaviour. Everything at Wrest follows nature's dictates and is good. The virtues of natural activity are found within the house as well as its fruits outside. Wrest offers the warm hospitality of 'cheerfull flames' to all strangers; its ornaments are 'living men'.[88] Hierarchy is respected here because it, too, is natural: 'Some . . . spun of a finer thred' are fed with daintier fare, but there is plenty for all, and all live together there in harmony.[89] A natural hierarchy does not preclude the natural community of men. At Wrest nature is not merely represented in images, in statues or marbles of gods. And Carew wishes us to appreciate that the natural imagery of his poem is more than poetic conceit or 'gay Embellishment'.[90] Wrest *is* a portrait of perfected nature. Ceres and Bacchus do not stand as stone figures in niches there, nor are they useless decorations for Carew's poem:

> We offer not in Emblemes to the eyes,
> But to the taste those usefull Deities.
> Wee presse the juycie God, and quaffe his blood,
> And grinde the Yeallow Goddesse into food.[91]

Those who 'presse the juycie God' are not only making wine; they are extracting nature's essence. And it is this that Carew wishes to distil through his poem. His readers are being urged not to live with the images of nature (or with a poetry concerned with them) but to return to nature itself.

Grey's house, of course, was built by man's art, but in it we find the gifts and attributes of nature. Outside in the garden, in the world of nature, 'we decline not, all the worke of Art.' In the garden the lake and winding stream represent man's capacity to order Nature's wilderness and to perfect her, as in the house Nature perfects man's art and society. Wrest 'directs' the 'course' of nature and so enjoys 'fertile waters', fecundity, and fruit.[92] Religious imagery pervades the poem, suggesting a garden paradise. Nature, we are told, doth 'blesse / this Mansion'. Here all men 'feely sit / At the Lords Table'.[93] In this garden of innocence, as in 'A Rapture', erotic love, once again innocent, has full rein: '*Vertumnus* sits, and courts / His ruddie-cheek'd *Pomona*' on the bank.[94] To this 'blest Place' Carew has come, perhaps from his own personal wilderness as well as the raging storms of the Scottish border. 'Thus' he announces to his friend G.N., 'I enjoy myselfe.'[95] The simple half-line has an unusually quiet force. Carew does enjoy *himself*; that is, he finds himself in this perfect state of nature and so finds calm. By contrast, his friend, hunting, strives against nature and so toils (the word is Carew's own) in the wilderness.[96] Wrest beckons all men who strive in the wilderness to return to the garden of innocence.

Saxham too is an idealization of nature. Where outside the house the inclement season bore little fruit, 'thou hadst daintyes, as the skie / Had only been thy Volarie.' Once again the language is religious: Natures' sweets 'blesse' Saxham; animals come thither 'as to the Arke.'[97] At Saxham there is no striving in the wilderness, for here animals freely offer themselves as sacrifice on this altar of Nature:

> The willing Oxe, of himselfe came
> Home to the slaughter, with the Lambe,
> And every beast did thither bring
> Himselfe, to be an offering.[98]

Even the elements paid 'tribute to thy fire.' Here is a paradise again, eternal, outside time. At Saxham it is 'endlesse day.' The shrine of Nature welcomes every 'weary Pilgrim' come to worship. Its 'chearfulle beames send forth their light', beckoning all who travel in darkness.[99] He who saw the light might, like the lamb, 'bring Himselfe' and so find, by worshipping at Nature's shrine, that 'inward happinesse' he seeks.

'To my friend G.N. from Wrest' and 'To Saxham' are usually studied as country house poems. In this context one critic has dwelt upon Carew's 'mutations' of the Jonsonian mode, pointing to the relative isolation of Saxham compared with Jonson's 'Penshurst' and to a sense of the Crofts' house as a retreat. So far I would not dissent. To M. McGuire, however, Saxham thus becomes a 'cavalier justification of the country house as a private stronghold, within which aristocratic comforts and powers can be preserved against the rising tide of opposition.'[100] Such an interpretation reveals extraordinary ignorance of the historical circumstances and, I would suggest, a misunderstanding of Carew's poetry and values. It is not clear who in the 1620s or 1630s was 'rising' in opposition to aristocratic comforts and powers: ideological challenge to aristocratic privilege was virtually non-existent. Although Saxham and Wrest are undoubtedly portrayed as retreats, they are not socially exclusive. Both households, it is stressed, open their doors and offer unlimited hospitality to the poor and strangers as well as those of 'finer thred':

> Thou has no Porter at the doore
> T'examine, or keep back the poore;
> Nor locks, nor bolts; thy gates have bin
> Made onely to let strangers in.[101]

Nature does not, as McGuire would argue, support only aristocratic society. It offers its fruits to all societies that live in accordance with its dictates. Saxham and Wrest are models of how men in society might return to nature: they are in some ways poetic parables. They offer the pattern of a peaceful, ordered, hier-archical, yet communal life that might bring men closer to the perfection of that first ideal commonweal: the kingdom of nature and love.[102]

III

In Saxham and Wrest we may begin to see, then, that nature and love are the bases of Carew's attitudes toward politics as well as ethics. This should not surprise us. For all Carew's poetry was public poetry, even (perhaps especially) that love poetry that we delineate as the most private.[103] The interrelation of love and politics pervades Carew's language and metaphors. Carew's lover may be now subject, now monarch but his relationship with his mistress is most often expressed in political terms. The lover acknowledges his duty to a mistress who commands him to return her letters: 'so powerful is your sway / As if you bid me die I must obey.'[104] Her letters have been merely her ambassadors, which now return to their 'Soveraigne', leaving the lover's 'vassall heart', 'ever hon'ring her', as a 'true Servant and subject to her Selfe.'[105] In 'A deposition from Love', by contrast, the lover is a conquering prince rather than a servant, waging a war against 'your rebell sex' in order to take the citadel of his mistress's heart. The victory, however, is short-lived and Carew's abandoned lover

> . . . he that is cast downe
> From enjoy'd beautie, feels a woe,
> Onely deposed Kings can know.[106]

This is the language of politics employed not merely as metaphor but as the discourse of a common world of lovers and kings, a world that does not rigidly distinguish what we would call the private and public domain. As Carew himself put it, 'Service in prose, is oft call'd love in verse.'[107] The relationships of men and women are described in political language because they are public and political relationships. No less, by corollary, political relationships may be examined through the language of love. Charles I and Henrietta Maria expressed their political ideals and values through the language of Platonic love, representing through their marriage the regulation of passion by higher understanding, the rule of the soul over the senses.[108] In his love poetry, then, Carew employed and articulated a discourse that was intrinsically political in Renaissance England and a language through which, in the 1630s, the monarch directly expressed his political values. The poetry of love and nature, therefore, should not be read as mere amorous banter or as Carew's retreat from political problems and realities, but as the discourse through which he examined political relationships and, in the guise of a lover, offered counsel and complaint to king, court, and commonwealth.

Carew is usually depicted as one of the court lackeys whose poetry celebrates uncritically the virtues and values of the Caroline court.[109] Once we have approached his attitudes towards nature and ethics, however, we may come to see that Carew's verse was independent and critical of the court. Let us consider the poem 'To the King at his entrance into Saxham', written by Carew to be delivered to James I by John Crofts.[110] Saxham, as we have seen, enshrines the virtues and gifts of nature. And here, as the king enters the house, his host welcomes him to country hospitality: the fruits and beasts of the local countryside rather than the 'rarities' or 'dainties' (compare the 'foraigne gums' of Wrest) 'that come from farre' but that are found, of course, at court.[111] At Saxham along with simple fare the king is offered plain entertainment, a country dance, and with it the plain language of loyalty, love, and 'pure hearts'. Here Crofts and his family are devoted to their country and to nature as well as to their monarch; they pay their 'pious rites' to 'our household Gods' as well as to their king.[112] Their tone is loyal and loving but not flattering or sycophantic. For the king himself is also expected to adjust to their world — to bring the mercy, 'not the greatnesse', of his majesty and to appreciate their endeavours.[113] In Saxham, as at Wrest, the king may find the greatness of the state of nature, which may enhance and direct even his rule. Both implicitly and explicitly the richness and honesty of their world is contrasted with the superficiality and deception of the court. Wrest, for instance, boasts no outward finery but offers sincere hospitality:

No Dorique, nor Corinthian Pillars grace
With Imagery this structures naked face,
The Lord and Lady of this place delight
Rather to be in act, then seeme in sight.[114]

At Wrest, we recall, Bacchus and Ceres are not merely represented in statuary; at Saxham there is no porter to exclude the poor. Pillars, porters, and statues, 'Emblemes to the eye', 'outward gay Embelishment'; the images evoke the Caroline court, its paintings and marbles, and perhaps the images that they in turn portrayed.[115] They also suggest a society that would seem what it is not, an unnatural society beside Saxham and Wrest where 'we presse the juycie God'.

Criticism of the insincerities of the court is made more explicit in other poems. Carew's 'Obsequies to the lady ANNE HAY' opens with the powerful shock of a death that has changed the normal course of all behaviour: 'I saw the sleeke / And polisht Courtier, channell his fresh cheeke / With reall teares.'[116] Sincerity beneath the polish is evidently exceptional at court, where everything is unreal, a veneer that covers a less attractive fabric. From such a world the most honest men were inclined to withdraw. The Earl of Anglesey (Carew reminded his widowed countess), a man of exemplary virtues, rather than compromise his credit 'chose not in the active streame to swim' but 'retir'd from the tumultuous noyse / Of Court, and suitors presse.'[117] Living apart from the court, and only by so doing, Anglesey enjoyed 'Freedome, and mirth, himselfe, his time, and friends'; 'all his actions had the noble end / T'advance desert.'[118] At court, by contrast, there was only dependence and hollow laughter, rivals rather than friends. At court a man must deny himself and his nature for falsehood and deception. And at court, Carew indicates, noble ends and desert find little place.

In early Stuart England the court was still expected to prescribe models for behaviour and values to be emulated.[119] But Carew contrasts the values of the court with those of the virtuous life. The court is supposedly concerned with honour and reputation. Honour to Carew, however, is 'but a Masquer' that deludes 'baser subjects' but is disdained by 'the nobler train.'[120] This appears to be paradoxical, but Carew's point is that honour as traditionally understood is a mere appearance — a concern with reputation in society rather than with true virtue, irrespective of public estimation. And society and reputation, he makes clear, may often be at odds with the truth:

> . . . malice can on vestals throw
> Disgrace, and fame fixe high repute
> On the close shamelesse Prostitute.[121]

When morality is so overturned, all order is subverted. True virtue lies not in potentially false reputation but in personal integrity, in a return to that innocence of man's first (and presocial) existence:

Vaine Honour! thou art but disguise,
A cheating voyce, a jugling art,
No judge of vertue, whose pure eyes
Court her own Image in the heart.

Carew's lines come from a chorus he wrote to the court performance of a play.[122] And that powerful 'Court' of the last line may
be intended to reinforce the point: virtue courts her own image in
the heart, but the image of the court, honour, is but a disguise for
the 'jugling art' practised there. The court continues to boast and
advocate a virtuous code of conduct, but in reality courtly values
have become detached from virtue and so the court has lost its
claim to prescribe morality.

During the 1630s, as we know, the courtly code of honour and
the ethical and political values of the court were expressed through
the idea of Platonic love. As the court gossip James Howell
described it, Platonic love was 'a love abstracted from . . . sensual
Appetite'; it consisted 'in contemplation and ideas of the Mind, not
in any carnal fruition.'[123] Some critics have dismissed its importance for Caroline poetry,[124] but there can be little doubt that
Carew recognized the importance of Platonic love for courtly
values and addressed some of his verse directly to the subject.
Some poems appear to be a critical response to it. Carew himself,
as we have seen, writes of a spiritual love that transcends the
merely physical, and his language at times suggests the influence of
Neo-Platonism. In 'A Pastoral Dialogue' Cleon dotes not on Celia's
pure white skin 'but on they purer mind.'[125] But Carew showed
little sympathy for the courtly cult of Platonic love or for its
ethical and political implications. In his poetry the spiritual relationship never supplants or negates the physical. Nor can the one
be divorced from the other. In the famous 'Disdaine Returned' ('He
that loves a Rosie cheeke . . .') Carew loves not with the spirit or
body alone: he seeks in his mistress both 'a smooth and steadfast
mind' *and* 'lovely cheekes, or lips, or eyes.'[126] The union of body
and spirit is the ultimate expression of love and of human nature,
beside which all else is second best. So Carew's lines to his mistress
'in absence' describing their closeness while apart emerge in the
end as a device to pass the time before they may come together
again in flesh as well as in spirit:

Wee'le cheat the lag, and lingring houres,
Making our bitter absence sweet,
Till soules, and bodyes both, may meet.[127]

That 'both' unites them all — soul to soul, body to body, and,
perhaps most significantly, body to soul. Here and there are
suggestions that in accordance with Neo-Platonic ideas, Carew

believed in a progress of perception from the world of sense and material to the sphere of spirit and knowledge.[128] Whether or not this is the case, physical love in the poetry does elevate men and women to a spiritual union. Spirit and sense feed each other, and love is the union of body and soul both within the lover and between the lover and his mistress. Carew's position, then, may be described as Neo-Platonic, but his emphasis is quite different from the Platonic love of the court and court masques in which the world of spirit and idea *transcends* the physical universe as masque dispels antimasque.

It is noteworthy that Carew's 'Separation of Lovers' was one of four songs, all on the subject of love and honour, that he wrote for 'an entertainment of the King and Queen' evidently in 1633.[129] It may be that the songs were intended as a commentary upon, and to some extent a criticism of, the cult of Platonic love that had just taken the court by storm in the production of Walter Montagu's *The Shepherds' Paradise*.[130] It is almost inconceivable that Carew would not have seen the play, and Rhodes Dunlap has drawn attention to the close echoes in lines 9–12 of 'To My Mistresse in Absence' of the speech by Melidoro, Montagu's Platonic lover.[131] Beyond that we cannot be sure, but what is clear is Carew's awareness of Platonic love and his reaction to the cult:

Let fooles they mystique formes adore,
I'le know thee in thy mortall state.[132]

It would appear that for Carew courtly Platonism was an abstraction that denied the senses and thereby negated what Carew lamented the absence of in 'A Divine Mistris' — the 'humanitie' of man, his nature.[133] If so, we may understand how he might have regarded it as an affront to his beliefs. The criticism, however, goes further, because Platonic love was the metaphor through which the court articulated a political philosophy as well as an ethical code.[134] Carew may well have been more optimistic than Charles I about the capacities of men, the king's subjects, to regulate themselves and so may have been less attracted to an ethical and political system that enshrined the king as the soul of the commonwealth, ruling over creatures of appetite. Carew's rejection of courtly Platonism amounted, as we shall see, to a challenge to the political ideology of the court, to a critique of the court's vision of the commonweal, of the monarchy, and of the relationship between the king and his people.

The description of the commonweal as the 'body politic', with the king the head and his subjects the members, is a commonplace Renaissance image. In Carew's poetry, however, the idea of the 'body' takes on literal as well as metaphoric reality. The king and people Carew presents with freshness as literally conjoined so that sensations in one part of the body rapidly affect the other. When sickness befalls the monarch,

> Entring his royall limbes that is our head,
> Through us his mystique limbs the paine is spread,
> That man that doth not feele his part, hath none
> In any part of his dominion.[135]

The language of feeling and pain imparts a physicality that transcends metaphor. The king and his people are one body physically as well as theoretically united, just as Carew's lovers are joined in body as well as soul. And it is just such a love, physical as well as spiritual, of the people for the king, that afflicts them with his pain:

> This griefe is felt at Court, where it doth move
> Through every joynt, like the true soule of love.[136]

Such a grief 'shewes a good King is sicke, and good men mourne.'[137] The repetition of the epithet underlines the fact that Carew as often is prescribing an ideal relationship while describing an actual one. The best relationship between a *good* ruler and *good* subjects is like the perfect union of true lovers: it is a physical togetherness as well as spiritual; it unites ruler and ruled, virtue and government. And so sickness, which threatens the good monarch, is a 'Tyrant' ruling by arbitrary will that king who has governed in conjunction and love with his people.[138] It is 'the minister of death', the most arbitrary of all rulers who knows no regimen but merciless conquest.[139] The union of king and subjects, and mutual love between them, Carew is saying, is essential to the health — indeed, the very life — of the body politic. And the good king of this ideal polity is not only God's lieutenant on earth but is possessed too, as was Carew's ideal mistress, of 'humanitie'; he is the 'Darling of the Gods and men.'[140]

To Carew, kings are not gods who may decree what is virtuous and what is vicious. They too live in and are of a society that has fallen from virtue and so may themselves be susceptible to the corruptions of fallen nature. Absolute authority is beyond them. Carew tells his mistress who commands the return of her letters that, although a monarch, she too must account for her actions and heed his wishes:

> If she refuse, warne her to come before
> The God of love, whom thus I will implore.[141]

Monarchs, Carew informs a lady resembling his mistress, may establish by their own authority values in their own kingdom, but

there remains an absolute morality, a universal virtue to which
they too are subject. The poet explores the idea, with unconventional implications, through the disarmingly familiar metaphor of
the coin that bears the king's stamp:

> To Lead, or Brasse, of some such bad
> Metall, a Princes stamp may adde
> That valew, which it never had.
>
> But to the pure refined Ore,
> The stamp of Kings imparts no more
> Worth, then the mettall held before.
>
> Only the Image gives the rate
> To Subjects; in a forraine State
> 'Tis priz'd as much for its owne waight.[142]

A debased coinage was regarded in early Stuart England as the
currency of an ailing kingdom. Here, of course, it is a kingdom fall-
ing from virtue and, incidentally, one in which outward values
have become detached from intrinsic (metallic) value. Thus, Carew
argues, a good king is he who comes closest to intrinsic worth, to
nature, and stamps its values with his image, so that society takes
by his authority nature itself as its currency. The good ruler's
responsibility is to return society to those inherent, natural values
of its first pure refined condition — that of man before society
(and its sham concern with reputation) in the garden of innocence.
A vision of nature, we may see, is central to Carew's political as
well as ethical system. The function of government he still
perceives as the rule of virtue: politics and morality are not
divorced; government and love are not distinct. Rulers, like lovers,
ought to renounce the empty considerations of honour and reputation by which princes, like all men, were evaluated in a fallen
world. They were to take their standards of government from
uncorrupted nature, to exemplify nature's first innocence in their
persons, and to codify nature's dictates as the maxims of their rule.

We have suggested in discussing Carew's ethics that men and
women rediscover their nature through a pure and eternal love, a
love sealed in society by the physical and spiritual union of
marriage. I would like to suggest that for Carew it is through the
marriage of ruler and ruled, of the king and his people, perhaps in
Parliament, that the commonweal too comes nearest to the
kingdom of virtue. Carew's lovers, as we have seen, are political
beings — sometimes monarch, sometimes subject. The lover is
unfulfilled, however, in either role if, in the one case, his
sovereign mistress spurns his 'vassall heart' or when, as a conquering prince, his power does not secure him her love.[143] Whether

ruler or subject, man as lover is complete and fulfilled only when love is spiritual and physical, mutual and reciprocated. So a king who conquers but rules without love is no king at all: He is, as 'A deposition From Love' makes clear, 'deposed.'[144] And so in the commonweal as in the polity of love (for the two are really one) true kingship depends upon reciprocal love. Monarchy is the marriage of ruler and ruled that conjoins authority and love and so leads society, as it does man, to the virtue of nature.

The place of love and marriage in Carew's political thought may be understood most clearly from his poem 'Upon my Lord Chiefe Justice his election of my lady A.W. for his Mistresse'.[145] Law and love are here betrothed. In consequence the 'government Tyrannicall' (compare the 'tyrant Mistresse' of 'An Elegie on the La: Pen') of 'Vsurping Beauties' is to be brought under the rule of law.[146] Law controls the passions by governing them. Law and government in their turn, however, are to lie 'In Love's soft lap' exchanging rigour and coercion for love and union:

Harke how the sterne Law breathes
Forth amorous sighs, and now prepares
No fetters, but of silken wreathes,
. . . Love hath fi'lde
His native roughness, Justice is growne milde.[147]

Their marriage improves both potentially arbitrary love and overrigorous law. In their union 'The golden Age returnes' — that is, an age in which outward appearances and inner virtues become one ('the fayre shall all be kind'); in which love is reciprocal ('who loves shall be belov'd'); in which men find their true and perfect nature (only the 'froward mind' is 'To a deformed shape . . . confin'd').[148] This is Carew's state of nature and perfect commonweal; it is the ideal vision of his politics of love: heavenly justice has now come to earth, as Astraea returns to rule.[149]

Carew's poem, however, is addressed to a specific person and has too a more particular application. The chief justice of the verse is Sir John Finch, who became Lord Chief Justice of the Court of Common Pleas on 16 October 1634. Finch was close to the court and a vigorous upholder of the royal prerogative; in 1637, he was the leading spokesman for the crown in the Ship Money case.[150] Finch, then, stands not only for justice in the abstract or in general but for royal justice and the exercise of royal justice during the years of the personal rule of Charles I. Finch's mistress, 'my Lady A.W.', is Anne Wentworth, niece to Sir John Crofts, whose country home, Saxham, Carew regarded as a haven of nature and virtue. In Saxham there is no crime because men cannot steal what is given freely: 'And as for thieves, thy bountie's such / They cannot

steale, thou giv'st too much.'[151] The rigour of justice has no place
in this perfect society, as there is no sin in 'A Rapture'. Even in
society, Carew tells us, men are not mere wild beasts to be tamed
by 'dreadfull Rods' of 'sterne law' but have the potential for virtue
in their nature.[152] And so in society and in the polity men should
be ordered by love as well as authority so that they might
rediscover their own higher nature and achieve that self-regulation
that is the best government of all. If marriage regulates the sexual
passions without denying man's sensual appetite, so in government
the marriage of love and justice may order society without denying
the humanity and inherent good of man. There is more than a hint
of criticism in the poem — that justice needs to be softened and
government should woo with 'silken wreathes', not 'fetters'.[153]
The reference to Astraea 'new enthron'd' could not but have
evoked memories of a Queen Elizabeth under whose rule love had
softened the harshness of government.[154] Carew's 'Upon my Lord
Chiefe Justice . . .' argues for in general what it celebrates in
particular: a union of love and justice as the best form of government.

Charles I, as we have seen, communicated his vision of the best
government through his marriage represented as a Platonic union
of souls. Significantly the royal marriage is the central subject of
the poetry that Carew addressed to both the king and queen, but
Carew's depiction of that marriage is very different from the
king's. Love and government are intertwined in a verse that wishes
for the monarch as 'A New-Yeares gift' the physical joys and fertile
fruits of marriage:

> Season his cares by day with nights
> Crown'd with all conjugall delights,
> May the choyce beauties that enflame
> His Royall brest be still the same,
> And he still thinke them such, since more
> Thou canst not give from Natures store.
> Then as a Father let him be
> With numerous issue blest, and see
> The faire and God-like off-spring growne
> From budding starres to Suns full blowne.

In this important extract many of the strands in Carew's ethical
and political thought are interwoven. Love ameliorates the cares of
government. The king retains his right to the title through a love
that is pure and constant, yet physical as well as spiritual. Such a
love, such a marriage is indeed 'from Nature's store'. In this
physical and spiritual union the king not only lives and rules
virtuously, he seeds and sires virtue as his offspring, giving birth
to 'God-like' children — that is, children made like the first man

in God's image, 'Suns' who, as nature's light, may rescue a fallen world from darkness. The perfect ruler is become the true lover. And in fashioning his government by his marriage the king may secure 'loyall hearts' and 'conjugal delights' with his subjects. *This* marriage — between the king and his people — would see 'One great continued festivall' of joy, that golden age of love and justice united.[155] It is the prescription of this perfect polity that is Carew's 'New-Yeares gift. To the King'.

It is, as it were, the other side of the government–love equation that Carew addresses to the queen. If the good ruler is, in Charles's case, the right lover, then here the true lover may have the best claim to rule. The queen, who exemplifies love, is a 'great Commandresse' who has ordered the unbridled excesses of 'wilde lust'. Her government flows directly from her love by example rather than coercion. She teaches men that love is constant and fruitful, and as a result of her influence disordered nature itself submits to her government willingly. The 'rude male' becomes satisfied with one partner; the very Satyr is 'reconciled' to order.[156] The queen in Carew's poem, however, is not the Platonic lover of the masques. Like the 'numerous issue' of 'God-like off-spring' wished for the king, the queen's example and love is fertile: a 'pregnant fire', which will engender virtue and order throughout the natural world. In both poems Carew's message is the same: true love is the government of nature, and the only true government is that which is founded on a love both physical and spiritual.

Carew's position on love and the politics of love, then, is very different from the tone and stance of the courtly Platonic love cult. The subject and images of Carew's love poetry are more physical; his language is more explicitly erotic than the abstractions of courtly Platonism. But we should not conclude from this that his poetry is less serious or less political. Language and tone reinforce Carew's argument. For Carew believes strongly in the potential for virtue in man's nature and so advocates not the transcendence or *denial* of the potentially wild manifestations of nature but that *marriage* of the senses and the spirit, or the reason, in which alone man may fulfil his nature. Accordingly, Carew sees right government not as the suppression of man's anarchic natural appetite by abstract authority ruling by coercion. Rather, he prescribes as the purpose of government that reordering of men's nature so as to restore them to the purer condition of their original state of nature in which no government was necessary. Such a regimen must be founded upon love. And in the commonweal as well as in the world of ethics (the distinction would have meant much less to him than to us) Carew advocates marriage — here the union

of the ruler and the ruled in love and virtue — as the mean
between the anarchy of unordered appetites and the sterility of an
authority that, in suppressing the sensuality of man, denied his
nature and nature itself.[157]

Marriage, we recall, Carew described as a condition of peace in
a polity of love beset by the tempests of tears and sighs of wild or
unsatisfied passion.[158] Love — illicit, unrequited, or lust — is
often depicted in Carew's poetry in Petrarchan martial imagery as
a struggle or battle. In returning his letters to the mistress who
now spurned him, Carew recalled in defeat his 'former fights,
'gainst fiercer foes, then shee / Did at our first encounter seeme to
bee'.[159] 'A deposition from Love' compares the conquest of a
mistress to a siege; it is 'Truce in Love entreated' by he who has
in his heart 'No voyd place for another Dart'.[160] Constant and
mutual love, by contrast, secures, as Carew describes it in 'A
Rapture', 'steadfast peace' where 'no rude sound shake us with
sudden starts', that 'Halcion calmnesse' of the Elysium in which
the poem is located.[161] It may be then, that it is *this* peace and
calmness — that of a paradise located outside time and history —
that Carew wished for society and the commonweal as well as for
individual men in prescribing a politics of marriage as the best
mode of government.

In this context we may begin to understand Carew's most difficult and most obviously political poem, 'In answer of an Elegiacall
Letter upon the death of the King of Sweden from Aurelian Townshend. . . .'[162] During his personal rule Charles I, it is often said,
was dedicated to a policy of peace in order to avoid resummoning
Parliament. Cavalier poetry celebrating the 'halcyon' days of the
1630s is accordingly read as uncritical idealization of the king's
ignoble and enforced withdrawal from European affairs — as, once
again, the sycophantic celebration of a royal policy that was not
for the good of the realm. Carew's poem is usually regarded as the
classic example of this flattery of Caroline foreign policy, and it is
not difficult to see why.[163] At one level Carew's poem exemplifies
that retreat from European engagement that characterized Charles
I's foreign policy and alienated some of his subjects. In reply to
Townshend's exhortations 'inviting me to write' on the death of
Gustavus Adolphus, Carew counsels his friend:

But let us that in myrtle bowers sit
Under secure shades, use the benefit
Of peace and plenty, which the blessed hand
Of our good King gives this obdurate Land.[164]

The poet's place, Carew argues, is to celebrate this peace rather
than to dwell upon the ravages of a European war from which

England is fortunately free. Townshend's own court masque, *Tempe Restored*, is held up as a more fitting subject for his muse.[165] And yet for all his disclaimer, the subject does concern Carew — for one of his longest poems of 104 lines! There is a suggestion of irony too — or at least of some divorce between words and meaning — in the poem. The forcefulness of 'Bellow for freedome' is a noise that must awake the reader, as Townshend's 'shrill accents' sounded an alarm to Carew's 'drowsie eyes.'[166] Gustavus Adolphus forces himself upon the stage of Carew's poem as a figure 'mightie', 'victorious', 'majesticke'.[167] Carew's obvious praise for the King of Sweden appears inexplicably at odds with his advice to Townshend about the appropriate subjects of his art. There is a tension within the poem that may reflect Carew's own ambivalent attitude toward royal foreign policy. The discrepancy may also be understood otherwise, for Gustavus is presented as a figure beyond poetry:

> His actions were too mighty to be rais'd
> Higher by verse, let him in prose be prays'd,
> In modest faithfull story, which his deedes
> Shall turne to Poems: . . .[168]

He is, for Carew, a figure *outside* poetry. Gustavus represents the flux and change, victories and defeat, of action in the world — a world of noise, of time and events, of death, of fate, of history. It is this world rather than Gustavus Adolphus that Carew rejects as a subject for his muse:

> Let us to supreame providence commit
> The fate of Monarchs, which first thought it fit
> To rend the Empire from the *Austrian* graspe,
> And next from *Swedens* . . .[169]

Carew does not reject Gustavus Adolphus specifically. He wishes to distance his verse from chronicle, from the relation of events, the rise and fall of states.[170] He does so because poetry, as Sidney had claimed, may express higher truths than history. Carew's poetry 'of Love and Beautie' has a more sublime purpose and engagement than with the flux of European power politics: it is concerned with reformation, the restoration of a golden age of innocence beside the calm of which the battles of Germany seem but a noise in time. So halfway through his 'answer' Carew commends to his friend Townshend's own poetry of love and nature as a more fitting subject for his muse. For Townshend's 'past'rall pipe' and 'Angel-shapes' in his masque for the queen 'brought us from above / A patterne of their owne celestiall love.'[171] Townshend's masque had risen above the world of events: its 'ravishing sounds' did 'dispense / Knowledge and pleasure, to the soule, and sense.'[172] Townshend had instructed in that pure love that might lift men and monarchs beyond the noise of time and events to the calm of an earlier condition of innocence. All man's strivings in the world could secure no more. The 'Halcyon days' Carew celebrates is that 'Halcyon calmnesse' of the lovers in the Elysium of 'A Rapture'.[173] It is far from clear whether Carew believed that those days had come to England during the 1630s: he acknowledges that England is not the land of perfect peace and harmony but an 'obdurate' country, resistant to reformation. But we may be sure that for Carew the securing of such a condition was the purpose of poetry. If Carew believed that the restoration of uncorrupted nature might be attained by the poetry of love, then we may more clearly understand his disclaimer that the noise of strife and battle (the antithesis of love) 'concernes not us.'[174]

If we are to argue that Carew's poetry expounded ethical and political beliefs, if we are to suggest that Carew believed in the power of poetry to effect important change, then we must withdraw Carew from Pope's company of gentlemen who wrote with ease. It is right that we do so, for too many since Pope have been led to assume that because Carew was a courtier, because his lines often read with effortless simplicity, he did not take his poetry seriously or have anything serious to say. His contemporaries, however, did not make the same mistake. Suckling, for example, rejected (probably with tongue in cheek) Carew's claim to the crown of the wits because

His Muse was hard bound, and th'issue of's brain
Was seldom brought forth but with trouble and pain.[175]

Carew himself acknowledged his painstaking industry in a less scatological metaphor, spurning what he called the 'unkneaded dowebak't prose' or ballad rhymes of his contemporaries. Carew worked at his poetry and admired others who laboured to refine their verse.[176] 'Thy labour'd workes', he assured Ben Jonson, 'shall live, when Time devoures / Th'abortive off-spring of their hastie houres.'[177] Such labour did not always guarantee appreciation. Poets, Carew reminded his mentor, wrote not for their reputation in a 'dull age' but for 'after dayes', 'immortall Bayes' that placed them, as it did their poetry, beyond reputation and time. Jonson, unlike the rhymesters, struck 'soules' into his verse and so wrote not for an age but for all time.[178]

Carew took his own poetry seriously because he appreciated and made claims for the importance — indeed, the power — of poetry. The claim to poetic power is conventional, but Carew asserts it with particular force to remind the lover of his authority. And given the political freighting of love poetry, this was also to argue, in the 1630s, for the power of poetry in the commonweal. When the poet speaks — often through the lover — in Carew's lines, he asserts the power of his art. Though she spurns him, Celia is forcefully reminded of the poet's power in the aptly titled 'Ingratefull beauty threatned':

> Know Celia, (since thou art so proud,)
> 'Twas I that gave thee thy renowne:
> Thou hadst, in the forgotten crowd
> Of common beauties, liv'd unknowne,
> Had not my verse exhal'd thy name,
> And with it, ympt the wings of fame.[179]

Celia's 'killing power' is the gift of the poet — and the poet may as easily take it away. The power to create and to 'uncreate' remains in the poet's hands.

Herein lay the power of poetry: the power of creation and immortality. The poet's power to create and to immortalize derived from a treasury of which he was the sole beneficiary — the treasure of nature. Carew offers to a mistress in return for her favours 'Rich Nature's store, (which is the Poet's Treasure).'[180] The only true poetry was that which distributed nature's wealth in order to give life. So Jonson's poems were 'births', as Donne 'kindled first by thy Promethean breath.'[181] Poetry alone offered images of virtue that could effect reformation. To Carew nature's perfection could not be represented in pictorial images. 'Canst thou', he challenges in 'To the Painter', '. . . tell how / To paint a vertue?' The answer is already clear: 'your Artifice hath mist.' But nature can be faithfully represented through love:

> Yet your Art cannot equalize
> This *Picture* in her lovers eyes,
> His eyes the pencills are which limbe
> Her truly, as her's coppy him,
> His heart the Tablet which alone,
> Is for that porctraite the tru'st stone.
> If you would a truer see,
> Marke it in their posteritie.[182]

Love is perfect nature's expression. And so the poet who writes of love does what the painter cannot: he distributes nature's treasure — virtue — in order to renew his age.

The inculcation of virtue through a poetry of love and nature was Carew's contribution to his age. But the inculcation of virtue in this age was also the business of government. We have seen how Carew's lover is depicted in political language. No less the poet, nature's lover, is presented as a monarch. Jonson, for example, is advised to dispel any concern about criticism of his verse, because his less good is judged by the standards of the best: 'the quarrel lyes / Within thine own virge.'[183] The virge is the boundary of the royal domain: poetry is Jonson's court and he, its monarch. The parallel is succinctly made in Carew's famous epitaph on Donne:

> Here lies a King, that rul'd as hee thought fit
> The universall Monarchy of wit.[184]

Carew defines wit in 'A Fancy' as the didactic content of art.[185] The monarch of wit, then, was a king indeed, leading men to knowledge and establishing rules of behaviour. For Carew the purpose of government was to make each man his own ruler by restoring him to the innocence of his first nature. Poets shared with kings this responsibility and power. Carew's purpose then could not have been loftier or his claim for the power of poetry greater. Studying Carew's poetry, we have come a long way from the stance of frivolity and flattery that allegedly characterized the Cavaliers:

> . . . cause you underneath may find
> A sence that can enforme the mind;
> Divine, or moral rules impart
> Or Raptures of Poetick Art.[186]

III Appraisals

10. The politics of literature in Renaissance England*

The subject of this essay may seem unusual; the books under consideration[1] most historians may regard as peripheral. If this is the case, it is only a measure of how reluctant historians have been — no, *are* — to take literature seriously. It would be comforting to think that such a charge is ill-founded, or at least overstated. Unfortunately it is neither. For though historians have often raided the great literary texts of their period for passages and quotations which nicely illustrate an interpretation of the age, they have refused persistently to accord literary works the status of primary historical evidence. In almost all historical writing, literary sources provide only the decorative gloss to arguments founded upon other allegedly more 'reliable' evidence — acts and proclamations, letters and charters. Behind such a historical view of evidence lies a series of unarticulated assumptions or, worse, unpondered questions. Chief among the unarticulated assumptions is a sharp distinction between, or a belief in a clear differentiation between, the realm of fiction and imagination on the one hand, and the factual 'real' world on the other. And among the questions too seldom considered is that of the precise status of any text — be it Privy Council order or play — as a document of authorial intention or of any recipient's interpretation. It is precisely such questions and assumptions that in recent years literary critics, notably the deconstructionists and reception theorists, have examined and exposed. If we may at times have been alienated by their most theoretical flights or the unnecessarily obfuscating jargon of their discussions, historians cannot afford to ignore the problems they have identified. Nor should the historian deny himself (out of a fear that they are forbidden?) the fruits of recent literary enquiry: that is, a more sophisticated awareness of the interaction of text and context, of literature and history, which has characterized a critical movement now described as 'the new historicism'.

It should not be surprising that some of the richest fruits are to be gleaned from recent work in the Renaissance.[2] For consideration of the relationship of the imagination to the actual, of what we delineate as literature to other branches of letters, takes us to the heart of Renaissance humanism. In sixteenth- and seventeenth-century England, what we generically distinguish as history, rhetoric, courtesy book or romance were delineated in common as *literae humaniores*. And the common purpose of humane letters was didactic: the role of art was the representation of virtue for the improvement of man and the common weal. In the age of humanism all branches of letters inhabited the public realm. Literature was, in the broadest sense, intrinsically political.[3] As such, literary texts not only reflected the social and political values of the age, they also helped to fashion them. In the study of political discourse in Renaissance England, literature is a rich and largely unexploited body of evidence.

The most popular, topical and ephemeral of literary genres is that which until recently has been most neglected by critics as well as historians: the prose fiction of the late sixteenth and seventeenth centuries which some would designate as the novel. The second half of the sixteenth century in England saw three times as many novels and novellas published as the previous half century and, for all the difficulties in identifying precisely the reading public, it seems clear that many of the works appealed to orders of society below the gentry, those classes which (as David Cressy and others have argued) most benefited from the great increase in literacy of the Tudor years.[4] Paul Salzman's *English Prose Fiction* sets out to map the ground of this unfamiliar territory by listing and describing the authors and modes of fiction popular with gentry and more humble readers from 1558 to 1700.[5] The most enduring mode was the romance, exemplified in its highest form by Sir Philip Sidney's *Arcadia* in which characters explored the nature of love in Arden. After Sidney, the subject of courtly chivalric love and the pastoral (which he had fused) became the fashionable motif and setting for the prose fiction of more than a century. The term 'romance' evokes for us that which is most detached from the reality of human affairs — we think of it as 'escapist', even frivolous.[6] But, as Salzman argues, the Renaissance romance was not an escape from the moral and political questions of the age, but a means of engaging those issues free from the restraints of the everyday.[7] Fiction was not the abnegation of truth, but an imaginative examination of the true. Nor did the mode of romance necessitate an uncritical celebration of courtly love conventions and the social and political ideology they enshrined. Indeed the romance form could be employed as the most effective device in challenging them. The pastoral of Greene's *Pandosto*, for example, is not the ideal setting for love and reconciliation, but the scene of suicide and loss;[8] similarly in Thomas Lodge's *Rosalynde* (1590), Arden is the home of outlaws living like Robin Hood. The court's idealization of Arden, Lodge and others imply, was not only distant from the reality, it masked an unpalatable reality. Far from being restricted by any supposed monotone or rigidity of the romance mode, Salzman argues, Lodge was 'able to utilize . . . romance conventions to create a fascinating exploration of the Machiavellian manipulations of appearance when characters rely on outward rather than inward eyes'. The form of romance fiction, that is, could be manipulated and inverted to articulate criticism as well as celebration of courtly values.

The longevity of romance lay in this flexibility and in its engagement with contemporary issues, not in rigidity or escapism. Indeed Salzman shows that in the late sixteenth, and especially in the seventeenth centuries, romance had 'a much closer relationship with the social and political turmoil of the period' than modern criticism has appreciated. The *roman à clef*, exemplified in John Barclay's *Argenis* (1621) became, as James I and the newswriter John Chamberlain were quick to appreciate, a vehicle for social comment. Lady Mary Wroth's *The Countesse of Montgomerie's Urania* (1621), a clear allusion to Sidney, immediately attracted controversy on account of its fairly direct drawing upon contemporary characters from the Jacobean court. The denunciation of 'uncertaine tyrant love' and the emphasis upon marriage in the work may also reflect not only the feminist critique of the chivalric love cult, but also the political circumstances and problems of Jacobean England. For in a society in which lovers addressed each other as subjects and sovereigns, and in which queens and kings spoke of being 'wedded' to their people, the language of love was part of the vocabulary of political discourse. Right love and right rule were not distinct because morality and politics, private and public virtue, were not separable.[9] Barclay's *Argenis* was a romance but, as Salzman rightly observes, it was too a disquisition on morality and politics — 'an interpretation of the use and abuse of power'. The Royalists' turning to romance during the decades of civil war has often been regarded as an escape from defeat. But Salzman convincingly interprets works such as Sir Percy Herbert's *The Princess Chloria* more as an exploration of the experiences and dilemmas than a retreat from them, and as a didactic political handbook rather than a withdrawal from politics. And so in *The Princess Chloria* the prince learns what in the 1650s Charles II also needed to learn: 'dissimulation is as necessary in Prince's actions as the sword of justice'.

The romance survived the civil war. But it was no longer the mode that could best debate the social and political questions of the age.[10] In the later seventeenth century, the picaresque and the rogue novel, co-existent with the romance in the decades before the war, came more into their own. The change mirrored a shift in perception brought about by civil war, for all the apparent similarity of the Restoration world. As Salzman writes with brilliant economy, 'In the romance, harmony is achieved through balance; the purity of ideal forms is conveyed through refined love, and the stability of marriage and monarchical rule. The picaresque on the other hand turns to Hobbes's crushing dictum: "I put for a general inclination of all mankind a perpetuall and restlesse desire of power after power that ceaseth only in death".' The rogue tradition and the anti-romance were the mode of a new society of commerce, interest and experimental science and philosophy. They demonstrate, like romance, that the prose fiction of the sixteenth and seventeenth centuries offers not only documents of the most important political and social changes of the age, but the most sophisticated contemporary discussions of moral and political questions.

The implications of Salzman's book then could scarcely be more important. His own purpose, however, as he defines it, is narrower and more modest: 'a little-known area needs the services of a cartographer before critics'. The disclaimer is fortunately not always adhered to. Salzman analyses well the complexities and possibilities within romance, demonstrates clearly its political engagement and introduces us to its range of political voices. He offers rich suggestions regarding the connections between literary genres and social changes, and the relationship between the romance and the anti-romance, or the ideal and the actual.[11] But in so far as the author does impose limits on his analysis, it is to be regretted. Few texts, Lyly's *Euphues* for example, receive the discussion that is required; the chapter on Sidney does not rise above a historiographical review of the subject. Many of the important suggestions concerning the conscious playing with literary forms and conventions remain undeveloped. Most frustratingly for the historian, the principal changes over the period are never satisfactorily explained. So, for example, we learn that 'by 1651 the direct imitation of Sidney's style was a difficult task', but we do not know why.[12] The unanswered questions and undeveloped suggestions are all the more frustrating because at all points one senses a great intelligence behind this book, even when the self-imposed limitations have not brought it fully onto the page. We should hope that Professor Salzman, having served as our cartographer, returns to this territory with a subsequent guide book.

Aspects of the interrelationship of novel and society in Elizabethan and Stuart England are also the subject of two recent, more specialized and more analytical studies, both written from the conviction that fiction not only reflected but also helped to shape consciousness in early modern England. David Margolies's *Novel and Society in Elizabethan England* grapples with the crucial questions of the positions of the author and the text vis-à-vis the prevailing social and political ideology and in relation to changes in social and political attitudes. The book has some important things to say. Margolies is, I believe, right to press the point that fiction in Elizabethan England did not, as it often does today, create a private world, a realm of the imagination as distinct, or so we appear to believe, from public life; the Elizabethan author's world (and reader's world) 'is the public world'.[13] Fiction, once again we note, is public discourse. Margolies also observes interestingly that the model for the author's role derived from the traditions of a pre-printed culture, from that direct relationship with the reader which resulted from personally reading aloud and from the intimate, personal world of manuscript circulation. Only during the late sixteenth century did authors adjust to a more distant relationship, an anonymous relationship which separated the author as an authority from the text and so freed the reader to perform his own readings without the author as a present interpreter. What Margolies calls 'the objectification of the novel' clearly suggests a way of thinking abut the impact of print culture not yet adequately explored. Such 'objectification' and the emergence of a reading public outside the essentially genteel circle of manuscript distribution produced important changes in the relationship of fiction to social ideology. In the case of Robert Greene and Thomas Deloney, Margolies argues, the novel not only reflects the 'bourgeois' values of the commercial classes and the tensions between them and the chivalric codes of the gentry, it asserts and shapes the ideology of the merchants, craftsmen and artisans, not least through a critical examination of the gentry's codes and mores. Greene was the first writer to make a livelihood by his pen, to depend upon the public. In moving from the elegant literature for gentlemen to, in *The Defense of Conny Catching* (1592), a more popular mode, Greene's 'enduring contribution was to provide an embodiment in the novel of a new world view, a coherent alternative model by which readers could interpret the world'. In Greene and Deloney, we encounter authors who responded to the market, and who also forged through print a 'class experience': a representation of reality evaluated according to a scheme of values different from that of the ruling classes.

The broad outlines of the argument seem enticing, if not convincing — for an alternative bourgeois ideology was clearly not established in Tudor England. But the exposition of the argument is worrying and is marred by naiveté, incautious generalization, poor history, anachronistic language and overzealous (and uncritical) Marxism. The Tudor historian will place little confidence in assertions that 'the new aristocracy's position was being eroded' in the 1590s, or that Thomas Nashe was caught between a disintegrating feudal world view and emerging 'bourgeois social relations', especially when Mr Margolies never stops to define his terms. The argument that there were changes in the relationships between author, text and reader and that those changes reflected and effected attitudes and values is well made, but that there ever was in Elizabethan England a 'bourgeois ideology' must remain more doubtful. Margolies acknowledges the problem himself in his admission that 'for all his bourgeois spirit, Deloney still retains a prejudice toward gentility'. And though Margolies may be right that metaphor fulfilled what was only later conceptualized, what was diffused through prose fiction in Elizabethan England may have been less a 'class experience' than a critical examination of the relationship of social ideals to realities that was of concern to all classes.

It is because she avoids such crude class categorization that Laura Stevenson's study is more subtle and persuasive. Like Margolies's book, *Praise and Paradox: merchants and craftsmen in Elizabethan popular literature* is written from the premise that 'a work of fiction is not just a distorted reflection of reality, but a structure that permits reflection upon it'. The novel therefore permits the historian clearly to see contemporaries' attempts to make sense of their experience. Laura Stevenson's purpose is to examine the representation of merchants in Elizabethan fiction as a barometer of changing attitudes to trade. The sample consists of nearly 300 works published over 44 years. Stevenson begins by reminding us that, though trade and crafts formed the subjects of much of the literature of the late sixteenth century, most popular authors of the Elizabethan period — many of them divines — 'were not middle-class men who wrote for the middle class'.[14] Moreover, though authors like Thomas Deloney (who was a craftsman) examined, in *Jack of Newbury*, the tensions between wealth and status, this was not the celebration of a new bourgeois ideology struggling to assert itself against the social norms, but rather an attempt to accommodate new social circumstances — the facts of money lending, the breakdown of the guilds and the pursuit of profit — within the still shared traditions of paternalism and the just price. In contradiction to Margolies, therefore, Stevenson more intelligently discerns that 'the inspiration behind the popular literature on merchants, clothiers and craftsmen . . . was not economic growth that generated a large middle class, but economic changes that called older social assumptions into question'. Far from combating the social ideology of gentry society, Stevenson shows, the authors of popular fiction attempted to find a place for merchants (significantly the wealthy merchants) of the metropolis within it. They found their solution not in the praise of mercantile pursuits but in representing the merchant as a servant of the common-wealth, as a principal citizen of honour and prowess possessed of civic virtues rather than business acumen.[15] In other words, despite the occasional gesture towards it in Dekker's *The Shoemakers' Holiday*, or in Deloney's works, the authors of Elizabethan novels did not advance the intrinsic merits of the world of commerce as later celebrated by Defoe and Steele, and so stopped short of formulating a new social ideology.

To historians such as Christopher Hill, the emphasis upon diligence and thrift in Elizabethan sermons or pamphlets is evidence of the development of a new bourgeois ideology. In a splendid dismantling of such incautious (and wishful) thinking,[16] Stevenson points out that such virtues, far from distinguishing the values of capitalist merchants from feudal courtiers, were the common bequest of a classical culture which praised such habits in the quite uncapitalistic context of magnanimous and charitable expenditure — 'it is in using money well not in making it industri-ously that the playwrights' heroes prove themselves virtuous'. Magnanimity and charity were aristocratic virtues against which no alternative code of behaviour was posited by the mercantile class. In Elizabethan England, 'whatever the facts of capitalism, the spirit of capitalism . . . was not even articulated, let alone familiar'. Like the chivalric merchant, the artisan could only find a place in a society of aristocratic values as a '*gentle* craftsman'. When he appeared as a hero in the literature of pastoral romance, it was as a nobleman in disguise. The popular literature of Elizabethan England, Stevenson concludes, could employ pastoral and romance to analyse universal problems, but it could not closely embrace the realities of social rivalry, nor could it present to the mercantile world an alternative self-defining ideology.

As a study in the value of literary evidence for historical ques-tions, *Praise and Paradox* itself deserves unqualified praise for its incisive common sense and jargon-free lucidity, most of all for its demonstration that literary evidence when read rather than plundered can deliver the most effective challenge to long-held assumptions. No other material, perhaps, could capture as well the tensions within contemporary awareness of the traditional and new, or the attempts of an intrinsically conservative culture to resolve them. My only reservation is related to Stevenson's overall sense of the *failure* of popular literature to promulgate an alternative social ideology, and to her assumption that the authors were unsuccessfully struggling to do so for, as many of her own case studies suggest, it was political and moral as much as economic problems that the authors of popular fiction were engaging. Jack of Newbury indeed 'has instructed his monarch in the duties of government' and declines a knighthood, preferring to remain prince of his own commonwealth. But this may represent not so much a means of celebrating merchants in the traditional language of civic virtue, as a device for criticizing the failure of the court and court aristocracy to uphold those codes in reality. We are familiar with sixteenth-century pastoral as a location for the critical examination of courtly values. The novel of urban life and mercantile magnanimity could also function in the same way — not merely by claiming for merchants a place in the world of aristocratic values, but by appropriating these codes for the mercantile world and so removing their authorizing power from the court and nobility which no longer displayed them as they ought. The appropriation of social ideology by a class formally outside it may not have been a failure but a significant redefinition of the relationship of virtue to class. Certainly the sense of decline in courtly standards deserves a greater place in the tensions Stevenson examines,[17] for like the 'country' or the Arden of pastoral romance, the 'city' of popular fiction was not a concept separate from the court or politics; it was another 'moral and aesthetic laboratory' in which ideas about society and the commonwealth could be analysed. The gentle craftsman or chivalric merchant may not have established the intrinsic merits of trade. But they could be, and were, effective contributors to the changing political discourse and political criticism of Elizabethan England.

It may not be difficult to persuade historians that the prose fiction that was, like the popular paperback, purchased cheaply, changed hands, and was regarded as ephemeral offers evidence of changing attitudes to and perceptions of society.[18] With poetry, however, the case is different. Is not poetry defined as the expression of 'beautiful and elevated thoughts in choice or elevated words . . . differing from those of ordinary speech'?[19] Is poetry not the loftiest mode of the literary arts, that which gives expression to those universals that are raised above the temporal and transient in human affairs — and so of little value to historians occupied most often with lowlier concerns? Such assumptions and reservations come from our tendency to think that art occupies the sphere of the sublime and that the least 'prosaic' (the most common usage of the term makes the point) of the literary forms are those most distant from everyday engagements. Such beliefs, as has been recently argued, have led us to deny or play down the topicality of references in the greatest of poets — Shakespeare.[20] Such belief, however, would have meant little to the artists of the Renaissance. Poetry in the age of humanism was not (nor was seen to be) distantly raised above ordinary experience, nor were universal and particular concerns held to be in irreconcilable confrontation. Rather, Renaissance poetry examined contemporary and particular experience within the context of inherited, principally classical, forms, and so within the context of the traditions and values bequeathed by those forms. Renaissance poetry, by integrating classical traditions and topical questions, not only passed the values of the ancients to the early modern age, but also endowed contemporary verse, written according to classical form, with an authority lent by tradition. The very imitation of form, in other words, was itself a political act.[21] The title of David Norbrook's study, then, *Poetry and Politics in the English Renaissance* signals a new approach and announces a book to be enthusiastically welcomed. Our enthusiasm does not end there. For Norbrook's reinterpretation of a century of English verse emerges from his challenging the premises of a tradition of criticism, a tradition that depicted Renaissance England as a unified and ordered polity and its poets as the defenders of that order. As a consequence of this tradition, Norbrook argues, the tensions and contradictions in Renaissance poetry have been 'flattened out into a mandarin formalism' which has silenced the more questioning and critical voices of the texts. The ambivalences which Norbrook seeks to identify are not only to be discerned in the subjects of the poetry. Norbrook draws upon the work of those post-structuralists who have contributed an awareness that poetic form is itself political and subject to manipulation as a political strategy. 'The radicalism of texts is now located not in their overt political content but in their subversion of the conventional processes of signification.' The suppressed radicalism of Renaissance poetry — a radicalism of form as well as language — is Norbrook's principal concern.

Poetry and Politics identifies the radical voice of English Renaissance poetry essentially with the Protestant reformers of the mid-sixteenth century, with their emphasis upon an inner spiritual authority and their implicit challenge to the authorizing power of the established public images and liturgies — of church and state. Whilst acknowledging that after the mid-century, especially the rebellions of 1549, there was a conservative reaction and a renewed interest in courtly forms, Norbrook argues for the concurrent and powerful survival, and for the political importance, of a literature of Protestant apocalypticism. The argument is not only made for lesser poets. Both Spenser and Sidney, most often studied as court poets, Norbrook reads as spokesmen of the prophetic tradition as much as priests of the new Neo-Platonic order. So Spenser's praise of the Protestant Virgin Queen he interprets as an oblique criticism of the French match which was opposed by the Leicester circle of which Spenser was part. Similarly, though Philip Sidney's *Old Arcadia* takes as its subject the courtly preoccupation with an aristocratic society of love and harmony, he *also*, according to Norbrook, 'subjects the Italian courtly ideals of retirement, contemplation and love to severe Protestant scrutiny'. Spenser and Sidney, then, are seen as exemplifying the tensions within the Elizabethan state, tensions between authority and conscience, order and liberty, conservatism and radicalism. In love poetry, in particular, those tensions could be expressed. The end of Elizabeth's reign, Norbrook argues, brought another shift to conservatism and further emphasis upon authority. Significantly, the principal poet of the Jacobean court, Ben Jonson, the villain of Norbrook's story, reacted against the Protestant prophetic tradition in poetry with its potential subversion of the authorities of church and state; the masque, the genre that Jonson made his own, was the liturgy of the divine Stuart kingship. But the prophetic poetry of Spenser and Sidney did not die; it found its heirs in Fulke Greville and George Wither, Samuel Daniel and Michael Drayton, and finally, and most triumphantly, in Milton. These were the poets — Norbrook calls them 'Spenserians' — who continued to propound 'an apocalyptic world view' and so found themselves in opposition now to a court that rejected it. In their political poetry, Norbrook concludes, Spenserians, notably Milton, politicized the aesthetic and so rejected and subverted the courtly forms of the Stuarts that aestheticized politics by representing (most obviously in masque) the commonwealth as an ideal order held together by the king's person. In the end, 'Charles's attempt to aestheticize politics floundered on the intensely politicized and rationalistic culture created by the Scottish reformation'. The prophetic traditions of Protestant poetry brought the Stuarts down.

Dr Norbrook offers the most challenging reinterpretation of English Renaissance poetry to have appeared for many years. No historian can afford to ignore it — not only because of his demonstration of the richness of poetry as evidence, but also because of the historical thesis he expounds. That said, the controversial argument is marred at times by its premises and by an excess of enthusiasm for, and for identifying, radical voices. Norbrook informs us that the main historical impulse to his study came from the writings of Christopher Hill which, as J.H. Hexter incontrovertibly demonstrated, is a shaky foundation on which to build a major interpretation.[22] Norbrook's is undoubtedly a more solid edifice, but he does draw too sharp a line between the Spenserians on the one hand and Jonson and the Sons of Ben on the other. Spenser, as Michael Leslie's close and detailed study shows, drew directly on the emblems and codes of chivalry suspected as popish by the strictest of Protestants, and manipulated emblematic allusions to express the highest compliment to the Queen.[23] 'Although occasionally critical of the reality, Spenser never wavers in his glorification of the Queen's ideal self.' If Norbrook overstates the case for the radicalism of Spenser, he undoubtedly too glibly writes off Jonson and the Caroline poets as uncritical of the court milieu in which they wrote. Norbrook himself has some difficulty explaining (or explaining away) Spenser's taking the post of secretary to Bishop Young who vigorously persecuted the Presbyterians; and he finds himself acknowledging that the too sycophantic Jonson who broke with the prophetic tradition 'can be found imitating some of the Spenserians' political rhetoric'. Such instances may more suggest that the tensions between conservative and radical impulses were to be found within most poets than divide them into ideological camps. Milton is no exception, for though *Comus* is different, in its emphasis upon spiritual struggle, from the Stuart court masque, the Milton of the 1630s had by no means abandoned hope in the courtly aristocracy, or a belief in the potential of humanity for reformation and poetry's power to achieve it. In this respect, in their commitment to poetry as an effective force of morality and improvement, Milton and the Spenserians are less rigidly divided from Jonson (and the Carolines) than Norbrook would suggest.[24] But in raising such doubts and criticisms, we must acknowledge that it is Norbrook who has stimulated them — and more. If *Poetry and Politics* does not command widespread agreement, it will help shape the discussion of the subject for years to come. There is no excuse in future for historians or critics to reduce these texts to that 'mandarin formalism' that Norbrook deconstructs. Nor, incidentally, was there any excuse for the discourtesy done to the author and readers by the publisher in producing one of the ugliest books to have appeared for some time — with unjustified margins, jumbled footnotes and no italics. Routledge should have known better;[25] an important book certainly deserves better.

In contrast to the prose fiction and even the poetry, the drama of early modern England has been exhaustively studied — or so it might seem. For, on further consideration, what has for the most part been studied is what the literary canon has selected from the vast array of theatrical performances and publications and, moreover, those aspects of that drama which most seemed to qualify for greatness. Many of the names that literally packed the Jacobean and Caroline theatres — Brome, Nabbes, Randolph, Rowley, Shirley, Davenant — remain unstudied and unedited. As we have seen, scholars still fear to 'reduce' the greatest of all playwrights by fuller exploration of his political engagement.[26] Any confidence we may have had that the most important drama has been studied must be dispelled by the realization that until Anne Barton's book, *Ben Jonson: dramatist*, there was no major study of the corpus of Jonson's dramatic works.

Professor Barton's book exemplifies critical scholarship of the most traditional kind. She sets out to understand Jonson through his plays — not only the Jonson of measured language and classical order, but also the other Jonson who always threatens to overturn it. And not only Norbrook's Jonson, the servant of the court, but also the playwright who sharply satirized courtly vices. From *The Case is Altered* to *The Sad Shepherd*, each play is carefully re-examined, with both Jonsons allowed on stage. The discussion of *Bartholomew Fair*, the text that perhaps most obviously exemplifies the tensions between chaos and discipline, is admirable. The historian will be particularly interested in Professor Barton's discussion of the theme of trust in human relationships which she sees as central both to this play and *The Devil is an Ass*. More generally, the chapter on names and naming, of the relation of names to reality in Jonson's plays, is an original essay on a central tenet of Renaissance culture, and illuminates interest in the philological studies which came from Italy and France to England towards the end of Elizabeth's reign. Here, as throughout the discussion of the plays, my only regret is that Professor Barton did not make greater use of Jonson's own theoretical pronouncements, especially *Timber or Discoveries*, to study the relationship within Jonson of the critic to the dramatist who often defied the critic's strictures. The most novel and most controversial contribution of Anne Barton's *Jonson* is her reassessment of the late plays — *The New Inn, The Magnetic Lady, A Tale of a Tub* and *The Sad Shepherd* — that marked Jonson's return to the theatre after a decade. These are treated often as the product of Jonson's dotage or, in the case of *A Tale of a Tub*, as early, immature work. Professor Barton is convinced, and convinces the reader, that the plays are all Caroline, but sees in them an affinity with Jonson's Elizabethan drama, especially *The Case is Altered*.[27] For unlike Jonson's Jacobean comedies, *The New Inn* is centred around love and marriage and abandons the metropolis for a country setting. Like *The New Inn*, *The Magnetic Lady* ends in marriage and in, as its subtitle *Humours Reconciled* announces, reconciliation and harmony. Indeed in the late 1620s, and 1630s, Barton suggests, Jonson became nostalgic for the world of Elizabethan England, or what he perceived of that world, and represented in his late plays a 'fresh, simple, essentially uncorrupted country world' in which men and women understand their mutual dependence as a community. Far from sinking into dotage, Jonson had a powerful dramatic statement to make.

It is not Professor Barton's first concern to explicate Jonson's political position, but it must be of major interest to the historian. Jonson's late plays appear to me to be not only criticisms of the court but criticisms of the court's culture, subtly articulated in the court's own language: the language of love. Charles I and Henrietta Maria liked to present themselves as Platonic lovers, who, having conquered their own base appetites and passions, were a model for the government of all baser natures. Love was government.[28] Jonson makes the equation too, but his perception of the relationship (both sexual and political) was quite different. During the 1630s, the king ruled over his people, governing, during a decade of no parliaments, by proclamations and personal decrees from Whitehall. This, to Jonson, was not love's polity. For love and marriage reconciled men and women, kings and subjects, in a union of mutual exchange and good.[29] Elizabeth had often spoken of being wedded to the people. But the Caroline court which spoke the language of love was no longer governed by the politics of love of Elizabethan England. Accordingly, it is in the country — in the New Inn or the rural community at Tottenhall of *A Tale of a Tub* — that Jonson finds the true understanding of love and his political model for communication and reconciliation. The late plays of romance and marriage were Jonson's powerful indictment of and counsel profferred to the court of Charles I.[30]

Criticism and Caroline drama we are not accustomed to thinking of together. During the 1630s, it is usually held, the stage was dominated by the court, and by what Alfred Harbage termed 'Cavalier drama' — a drama that pandered to the trivial concerns of courtly love and sycophantically reinforced the court's political values.[31] In one of the first direct challenges to Harbage's characterization, Martin Butler's *Theatre and Crisis* attempts both a re-evaluation of the drama and of the relationship between play and politics in the decade from 1632 to 1642. He has a clear historical thesis to argue as well as a powerful critical perspective to apply. Butler begins by exploding the myth of Cavalier drama — by demonstrating beyond doubt that, given an audience far larger than the exclusive circle of Whitehall, the playwrights were by no means dependent on the court.[32] Even within the court, he recognizes, the existence of different factions and disagreements made it possible for the dramatist to articulate criticism; the best court plays, he shows, took advantage of that freedom. But Butler's case for a reappraisal of Caroline drama does not focus on the court; the courtly tradition is 'both the least interesting and least significant aspect of the period'. Rather, in the private and public playhouses, away from the 'restricted medium' of the court, Butler identifies a more vital theatrical mode, exemplified by Thomas Nabbes and Richard Brome whose plays presented a searching and critical examination of political issues and courtly values. Such plays — Brome's *The Weeding of Covent Garden* or *The Lovesick Court* for example — Butler argues, constituted a culture of opposition during the 1630s when parliaments were removed from the stage of politics. The puritans, the core of the opposition to Charles, are too often held to have damned plays and playwrights.[33] Butler helpfully reminds us that the puritans were by no means universally hostile to the theatre, and argues (rather less convincingly) that the theatrical circles of the 1630s overlapped with the puritan leadership of the Long Parliament. According to this study, the 1630s stage provided, like the Providence Island Co., a focus for country criticism of the court, of its favourite preoccupations, love and spectacle, and of the social and political values they enshrined. It was not Harbage's 'Cavalier Drama' but these opposition plays, Butler concludes, that deserve re-evaluation as expressions of the 'most lively and challenging currents of opinion in the decade'.

There are serious flaws in Butler's argument and many soon become obvious. Among the opposition dramatists, for instance, he ranks the Earl of Newcastle, who became governor to the Prince of Wales; William Davenant, who wrote for the court, private and public stages, he does not know how to 'count'. The difficulty arises from Butler's rigid distinction between the court and the professional stage, 'between drama written principally for the court and drama intended for other wider audiences'. It is a false distinction, for most court plays transferred to the stage and during the decade of personal rule there were court performances of a broad spectrum of plays — including works of Rowley and Randolph and Butler's hero Brome — taken from the professional theatres.[34] In concentrating on the professional stage, *Theatre and Crisis* gives short shrift to court plays and so fails sufficiently to appreciate that in these too — in those of Davenant or Shirley for example — one may discern critical voices similar to those Butler praises in the work of Nabbes and Brome.[35] In the end, we have to conclude that, for all his efforts to integrate literary and historical perspectives, Butler's reading rests upon questionable historical assumptions. He takes it for granted that Charles I wished to establish an autocratic government, while the leaders of the Long Parliament pursued moderation and balance. Moreover, Butler's own politics may have been allowed to infect his history and his criticism. When he concludes that the country plays expressed 'the most central and passionate current of feeling', or that Brome wrote 'the most committed play of the decade', Butler tells us more of what is central to his own political passions and commitments than to those of the 1630s. But my belief that the thesis of *Theatre and Crisis* is simply false — or falsely simplified — does not detract from my sense of its importance, nor indeed from admiration for Butler's achievement. For this book has cracked, if it has not broken, a mould. No longer can the drama of the 1630s be dismissed as aesthetically or politically monotonous. Our ears henceforth will be more sensitive to multiple and discordant voices.

If poetry and drama found patrons and audiences outside the narrow confines of Whitehall, the festival and masque were a quintessentially courtly mode. Their *raison d'être* lay in the splendour and celebration of the royal court. Such festivals were once ignored, or dismissed as empty and frivolous shows, the occasions only of vast expenditure for the fleeting pleasure of the night. Thanks to the brilliant work of Stephen Orgel and Roy Strong they can no longer be so trivialized.[36] Behind the pageants and masques of the Renaissance court was the Neo-Platonic philosophy of forms and a belief in the power of symbols to effect reality. The masques were an expression of the loftiest aspirations of humane learning and monarchical ambitions. In *Art and Power*, Roy Strong returns to the subject that over ten years ago he helped to establish in his *Splendour at Court*.[37] Strong proceeds from a discussion of the nature of festival to trace its changes and development from republican Italy to the monarchical courts of Europe. The developments, he maintains, cannot be comprehended in isolation from the political changes of the period: 'the huge escalation of princely festivals went hand in hand with the identification of the mystical aura that surrounded crowned heads as the sixteenth century drew to its close'. The festival was not a diversion from royal responsibilities, but an instrument of government, a fundamental political gesture both reflecting and acting upon political perception and change. Accordingly, by a study of Renaissance festival we may gain a special understanding of the hold of the idea of empire, the desperate quest for universal order as Christendom was torn by religious schism; of Catherine de Medici's search for reconciliation and unity;[38] or of the ideals and aspirations of the Stuarts. As we follow Sir Roy around Europe, we cannot but be dazzled by the brilliant show he stages for us, as he presents a series of stimulating suggestions concerning, for example, the relationship between the geometric dance and the fragmentation of order.

It comes as a disappointment therefore that the least revised and least satisfactory section of *Art and Power* is the concluding case study of the English court masque in the reign of Charles I. For though Strong explains lucidly the 'textbook Renaissance' Neo-Platonism of Inigo Jones, he offers no critical re-reading of the Caroline masque texts, nor any comment on their authors. Discussion of the political circumstances of the masques is thin and undermined by obvious errors (the judges did not decide on ship money in 1633). And it is naive to read Thomas Carew's *Coelum Britannicum* as merely 'a court celebration of the triumphs of Stuart absolutist rule'.[39] Strong proclaims rightly that it is important to understand the politics if we are to study masque as part of the mainstream of the history of ideas. But no very sophisticated comprehension of the early Stuart court or the role of the artist in it is found here.

The court masque is the subject of more detailed literary analysis in a volume edited by David Lindley for the Revels Plays series. Given some first-rate recent work on the genre — one thinks of Leah Marcus and Jonathan Goldberg — we come to the book with a sense of excitement.[40] This, however, is an uneven collection which, though it makes a very useful contribution, promises much more than it delivers. The introduction is sound and sensible but too brief and has little novel to say. Helen Cooper's essay on location and meaning in masque takes up the interesting question of the relationship of performance to audience, only to decline into bland clichés about masque as escapism. Jennifer Chibnall castigates Stephen Orgel (curiously in my view) for paying too little attention to masque form, and then discusses the masque form in a manner that exhibits a naive reading of texts and ignorance of contexts. When she does stumble on an interesting (if only half-right) observation (*Coelum Britannicum* is 'the only masque which is both presented to, and presents, the king'), she fails to explore it. John Creaser writes well on *Comus*, but contrasts a subtle reading of Milton with a caricature of the court masque. The most original contributions or approaches are provided by John Peacock and Sara Pearl. Rather than the usual emphasis upon the Italian inspiration behind Jones's scenes, Peacock draws our attention to the French sources of many designs, from which he deduces an influence greater than has been appreciated of Henrietta Maria and the literary romances which had been 'very much a part of the Queen's cultural ambience', in the court of Henri IV. Sara Pearl examines Jonson's entertainments as a contribution to the debates on foreign affairs during the critical years 1620 to 1625. Historians will be dissatisfied that the analysis is not taken far enough, but the essay points to the sort of work that needs to be done. The Caroline masque in particular awaits a study both as text and occasion. For as we read the long antimasque debates that introduce Shirley's *The Triumph of Peace*, Carew's *Coelum Britannicum* or Davenant's *Britannia Triumphans*, we begin to see that masque was not only spectacle, and that within a supposedly rigid structure there was room for shift of balance and self-conscious play with form.[41] We then begin to appreciate the masque as drama, with some of the freedom of interpretation offered by dramatic gesture, tone and movement. And we begin to discern not uniformity, but also ambivalence, debate and irony. In offering little discussion of such questions — of the interplay of form and content, the particular and the universal, the ideal and the real, praise and criticism — Lindley's volume lost an opportunity to open new dimensions of its subject.

What is most significant in general about the corpus of works under review is the new approaches and new perspectives they offer — and offer to the historian as well as the critic. R.M. Adams's *The Land and Literature of England*, written 'to set forth the outline of history . . . as *background* for the study of English literature' now appears hopelessly naive in its conception,[42] as do the not-entirely-defunct chapters on 'literature' (or 'culture') in historical surveys. For the literature cannot be so separated from the history of the Renaissance, nor can the context be relegated to the background in the study of texts. A greater sensitivity to the interaction has enabled us to discuss, in literature once regarded as one-dimensional, complexity and ambivalence. This in turn must lead to fruitful new work on self-perceptions of early modern society, for which literature may prove one of the richest sources of evidence, as opposed to mere illustration. The books reviewed here point the way. But they also raise problems which are not in any of them adequately addressed. In any discussion of literature as an expression of values, we need to consider the freedoms and constraints of patronage and censorship (whether self or socially imposed); we need to investigate the licence of play as a phenomenon of early modern society with its traditional festivals of inversion and misrule. In general we need to engage the difficult problem of reception. Can we know *how* a work was read or whether a criticism was understood? And if we cannot find (and seldom in the history of ideas can we find) direct evidence of contemporary reception, can we reconstruct the readings that it was possible for any given society or group to perform? Such questions lead us to a subject, little debated in these volumes, that John

Pocock and Quentin Skinner have made their own: the study of languages and vocabularies and their capacities to reveal and conceal, legitimate and undermine, praise and criticize. Literature offers a special case study in the conscious (as well as unconscious) development and strategic manipulation of languages. Carefully studied, literary texts may help us to a fuller understanding of the sophistication of contemporary responses — a sophistication suggested by the plenitude of allusion and reference in drama for example. And they may lead us to a greater awareness of the relationship of genres and forms to cultural and political changes.[43] The investigation of literary languages and forms as the agent and barometer of social and political changes requires the skills of several disciplines. It is therefore noteworthy, and for an historian regrettable, that nearly all the recent works in this area — I think all but one of the books under review — have been published by literary scholars. It will be the historians' loss if they do not turn their attention to the exciting discoveries that are being made. It is time to see literature as a firm root of historical interpretation, not just the fairy on top of the tree.

11. Culture, politics, and the English Civil War*

The study of culture was, until quite recently, confined to the periphery of historical studies. And in surveys and textbooks a chapter on culture or the arts is still most often tacked on as an appendage to the more important business of institutions and politics, religion, economy, and society. If some historians — and they are still few — are at last beginning to redress this neglect, it is more thanks to developments in other disciplines than to the historical academy itself. In particular the work of Clifford Geertz has rendered indefensible the separation that left cultural history to critics and art historians, if it did not relegate it to oblivion.[1] For Geertz argued that the exercise of power is itself a cultural practice, integral to and dependent upon the mores and expectations, rituals and symbols of any social group; that power, especially in pre-modern societies which lacked armies, professional bureaucracies, and the technology necessary for the foundation of authority on force, depended upon *perception*. Once we see that ideas and images are intrinsic to power and authority, their mediating texts — literary, visual, oral, and enacted — necessarily become documents of political history. Cultural and political history, in short, cannot be divorced.

If Geertz's work has been largely responsible for a new school of cultural anthropology, it has also influenced greatly recent approaches to literary criticism, especially those critics who describe themselves as 'new historicists'.[2] The new historicists are reacting against the 'New Criticism' of the 1960s, which (like the cultural history of earlier historians) extracted the text from its society and elevated it above temporality as a sacred cultural artefact to be 'appreciated' by those with capacity. The new historicists both in studying texts as cultural practices and cultural practices (even when not written) as 'texts' argue for the symbiosis of artistic and religious or political behaviour in society and for a recognition of their tendency mutually to shape each other. The theatre, to take an obvious case, draws upon the everyday, the stage of life, regal, elite, and common, and yet behaviour and experience are themselves shaped by artistic performances as well (perhaps as much) as any other. Studied from this perspective Shakespeare can never be set apart from his or the critic's culture and society. Nor, more significantly, can plays and poems be neglected by the historian — of politics any more than of letters.

For early modern English history, the separation of culture and politics has never been other than discomforting, and never, to be fair, complete. The very labels of the parties that divided in civil war in 1642, 'Roundhead' and 'Cavalier', convey cultural associations as well as political allegiances. Between drinking songs and love poems, puritan sermons and diaries, or, at the village level, maypoles and godly assemblies, there are obvious cultural differences which are not easily divorced from politics. That there was a politics of style in early modern England is as apparent as that there was a style of politics. But the very obviousness of a connection led, I believe, to simplistic assumptions and, as far as a study of the interrelationship of politics and culture is concerned, to false starts. Given cultural difference and a political divide into civil war it was all too easy for historians to make the simple conclusion that the Civil War was a clash of cultures: of puritan godliness against popery, of sobriety and morality against drink and debauchery, of the simple, honest, 'country' virtues against court chicanery and corruption, of Milton against the Cavalier poets.[3] Political and literary historians even seized on such simplistic antitheses to *explain* the origins of civil war in two rival cultures — ignorant of, or unconcerned by, the shared values and assumptions, the many individuals who belie a thesis of polarity, most of all the fact that the 'court' and 'country' divided within themselves in 1642 rather than confronted each other.[4]

Naive and simplistic starts may have for some time deterred us from further exploring rich complexities of cultural and political practices and their interrelationship in Tudor and Stuart England. But, in part thanks to anthropologists and literary scholars, there are signs of a new and more fruitful endeavour and, most encouragingly, indications too that historians are interested in pursuing the subject seriously.

D.M. Bergeron's *Shakespeare's Romances and the Royal Family* (Lawrence, 1985) very obviously emerges from recent 'new historicist' readings and especially from Jonathan Goldberg's *James I and the Politics of Literature*.[5] Endeavouring to explain the novel preoccupations of Shakespeare's romances with family matters and parent–child relationships which were of little

consequence in his earlier comedies, Bergeron suggests the importance of the succession to the throne in 1603 of a monarch, James
VI and I, who was the first ruler since Henry VIII to be a father
(indeed also, though not here observed, a husband). Whilst observing that the fathers and offspring of the romances are often of
James I's and his children's age, Bergeron does not seek to press
a simple identification or to view the plays as specific address to
the monarch; rather he suggests that the royal family was itself a
'text' that Shakespeare drew on and incorporated into his own
artistic performance. In particular, the royal family, it is argued,
helped shape Shakespeare's representation of the politics of family
relationships and the drama of family conflict.

The royal family was certainly set, in one of James's favourite
metaphors, on the public stage. And the royal children — Henry,
Elizabeth, and Charles — certainly became the focus of an attention at times greater than that accorded to the king. In a society
in which perhaps all marriages and all families were more public,
or less private, than we are familiar with, the royal family — its
tragedies and joys, conflicts and celebrations — was the most
public of all. In 1606, Queen Anne lost two children, Mary and
Sophia, within weeks of childbirth. Bergeron sees it as a turning
point in the relationship between James and his wife, a relationship
already strained by religious differences and perhaps by James's
sexual preferences. Estrangement became conflict in 1612 over
James's choice of Frederick Elector of the Palatine as a husband for
his daughter Elizabeth. Prince Henry, the eldest son, often had to
mediate between his battling parents but his own relationship with
his father and mother were not without strains. The court he established at St. James's stood as a symbol of many values and aspirations not reflected in or satisfied by the king's own court; and
Queen Anne, at least according to Bishop Goodman, 'did ever love
Charles better than Henry' — possibly on account of her elder
son's ardent Protestantism.[6] In 1612 tension gave way to tragedy.
Henry died of a sudden illness aged nineteen, and with the departure of Elizabeth to her new home in Germany, the succession
rested solely on the young Charles who in 1613 had yet to make
his mark. From 1606–7 to 1612–13, the royal family experienced
dissension and death. Between these years Shakespeare's romances
were written.

Preoccupations with family matters was not, Bergeron observes,
confined to Shakespeare. Jealous husbands, shrewish wives,
libidinous widows, and the hungry pursuit of sex provide plots for
Middleton, Jonson, and others. But where here family relationships
(perhaps more accurately sexual and marital relationships) exhibit
fragmentation, dislocation, debasement, Shakespeare's plays —

plays about royal families — are romantic, pastoral idealizations of family life in which, for all that tension and conflict exist, they are reconciled; the separated are united. In creating such idealizations, Bergeron posits that Shakespeare had the royal family in mind. The argument offers some enticing suggestions and readings. *Cymbeline*, he suggests, may have been written in connection with the celebrations for the investiture of Henry as Prince of Wales. And more generally, in *Cymbeline* and *Pericles*, the conflict of political purpose and domestic desire may owe something to the playwright's observation of the royal family. The most persuasive case is that for *The Winter's Tale*. For here there are both particular and general resonances that are all but compelling. Perdita is sixteen at the end of the play, the same age as the princess Elizabeth, at the time of court performance.[7] Leontes is thirty when she is born, the same age as James at the birth of his daughter. More importantly, the conflict between Florizel and his father King Polixenes over the choice of a bride is, significantly, not to be found in Shakespeare's source, Greene's *Pandosto*. This, like the reconciliation and celebration that closes the play (and like the wedding of Ferdinand and Miranda in *The Tempest*) may owe much to the royal family and festivities for the Palatine marriage and signal or represent the hopes for the realm in the royal children, hopes for security and dynastic order.

Bergeron's study is extremely valuable as one of those recent works that rightly insist on the topicality of Shakespeare's plays.[8] In drawing attention to the royal family as a text that shaped art, the crucial role of the court as a model for what we think of as private as well as public behaviour is graphically underlined.[9] But there are too many errors, and in some matters too much ignorance to win most historians' confidence: James I did not introduce the metaphor of the king as father of his people; the theory of divine right was not 'to everyone's grief'; Queen Anne was not a negligible force in politics;[10] it is not true that James paid attention to state matters only when Cecil prompted him.[11] More disappointing than such slips though is the book's failure to pursue some of its own observations and the questions to which they give rise. It is intriguing and perhaps more revealing than is noted that, for all the public attention on the family, few pictures of James with his children were painted. That in this, as so much else, Jacobean culture was literary rather than pictorial may suggest much about the shaping force of the royal text on the culture of the age. Secondly, the differences between Middleton and Jonson on the one hand and Shakespeare on the other would repay further consideration. Bergeron observes that where Jonson's and Middleton's families are fragmented and set at odds, their relationships devoid of love and determined by wealth and interest, Shakespeare's are harmonious, affectionate and united. The first of course are city plays, their fragmented families and corrupted love a metaphor for the social dislocation exemplified in the metropolis; the second, plays about courts and pastorals, idealizations which not only represent rulers (in the end) as the harmonious resolution of strife but prescribe — through criticism of Leontes and Polixenes to take a case — that they should be so. Bergeron is wisely cautious about arguing for the plays as a conversation with James I. But through court performances they were of course addresses to the sovereign, and addresses which in their idealizations may not simply have drawn from but spoken to the royal father. *The Winter's Tale*, as we have it, with its final harmony and unity may reflect less the reality of royal family politics (with the king and queen divided) than the desirability of their union. For if the royal father was the father of the realm, familial discord might easily be associated with broader political faction and conflict. And in this conjunction we come to a subject little developed here: the rhetoric and language common to the politics of the family and the politics of the realm. Like Elizabeth who spoke of being wedded to her people, James I himself said 'I am the Husband, and the whole Isle my lawfull wife. . . .'[12] The royal family in its largest definition *was* the commonweal, as the origin of the commonweal, Aristotle's *Politics* argues, was the family. Shakespeare's plays of family tension and family reconciliation, therefore, drew on political language with a broader domain: we might say they were political commentaries. Bergeron writes that 'What Shakespeare pursues through these plays is not the love of power, but the power of love.' The tensions between power and love find microcosmic focus in the family, but in the macrocosm of the commonweal too they were central.[13] When we remind ourselves that broken families threatened ruined kingdoms in politics as in plays, when we reflect that in *The Winter's Tale* the shepherd and the clown are incorporated within the royal family, when we see that the hope for regeneration in the future lies in community, we may want to think more about the plays presented toward the less-than-happy close of the first decade of Jacobean government.

There has been surprisingly little study of political attitudes and ideas in early Stuart England, or of the many documents that offer rich evidence of them. In *Politics and Ideology in England 1603–1640* (1986) Johan Sommerville rightly laments the inadequacy of a history of political theory which has focused on the most systematic texts of political philosophy (Hobbes and Locke) to the exclusion of pamphlets, sermons and letters, and which has too often studied ideas separate from the practice of politics and government. Sommerville's criticism of traditional histories of political thought promises more than it performs. For whilst shifting the focus from great political thinkers to pamphlets and treatises, he largely ignores letters, memoirs, diaries, histories, fables, poems, and plays — the last, curiously, because he believes they offer no guide to educated (as opposed to popular) opinion. Nevertheless, drawing on tracts, pamphlets, and sermons, Sommerville has some valuable information to offer and a definite case to argue.

Divided into sections on theory or principles and practice, the book opens with discussions of what are seen as conflicting ideologies of government: theories of divine right, of consent and the doctrine of the ancient constitution. The case for absolutism, it is argued, derived from a theory of natural law. Absolutists denied that power had ever rested in the community and derived monarchical power from God. Kings might owe their titles to conquest, election, or hereditary right, their authority like that of fathers and husbands was natural, divine. A belief in absolutism did not argue for no accountability. Divine right implied the duty and responsibility of power. The chaplain Isaac Bargrave put it graphically to Charles I (who never needed reminding of this) that 'though Kings be Gods before men, they are but men before God.'[14] Nor was divinely ordained power unlimited. Kings were bound to rule in the public interest and for the common good. But in absolutist theory, they owed accountability to no human laws or authorities. The clerics and pamphleteers preached on the duty of all subjects to obey; though they stressed the duties as well as rights of sovereigns, they had nothing to say about remedies against the abuse of royal power.

Other traditions of thought, Sommerville maintains, challenged these premises: civic humanism — which he indefensibly dismisses as 'buried if not dead in England before the Civil War' — and ideas of custom and law. Those who challenged absolutist theory differed in their history of the origins of authority: they denied that the authority of the father was regal and, following Suarez, questioned the natural origin of monarchy, maintaining that natural law prescribed no one form of government. Monarchical power therefore rested upon the transference of power from the community or upon consent; the coronation oath bound kings and subjects 'by reciprocal conditions'. Laws, Selden argued, were contracts between kings and their subjects. The reciprocal and contractual basis of authority implied the right to question and to limit monarchical power when the contract was breached. And Sommerville is anxious to argue that, in contradiction to the view that in 1642 parliament was unable to justify its actions, there was a tradition of resistance arguments — theoretical if not practical — to hand in early modern England: Buchanan's works were well known; during the 1620s Isaac Dorislaus alluded to rights of resistance in his history lectures at Cambridge;[15] John Pym was to quote Suarez. Though no specifically English writers are cited, continental books circulated and theories of contractual monarchy were widely known.

To such arguments for limited monarchy, England made its own powerful contribution: the tradition and force of custom, law, and parliament. Legal thought emphasized the property and personal rights of the individual. And lawyers came to claim that the common law was nearest to the natural law, that it, indeed, embodied reason. Monarchical authority was not therefore above the law; the law was itself supreme. If defects were found in the law, men such as Thomas Hedley argued that it lay with parliaments to amend them, for parliaments' powers derived from the law. 'The dominant legal opinion . . .,' Sommerville concludes, 'was that Parliament and not the judges had the supreme power to interpret the laws.' And as need to interpret the law became more obvious, ideas that the law required annual parliaments began to be articulated. Together with continental contract theory, theories of laws and parliaments in early modern England limited the powers of kings.

These then were 'those major political theories' that, according to *Politics and Ideology*, '*divided* Englishmen in the early seventeenth century.[16] The first — royal absolutism — received its most vociferous support from the clergy, while the third — Coke's doctrine of the ancient constitution — was usually expressed by common lawyers particularly in the House of Commons.' Before we turn with Sommerville from theory to practice, we must examine these arguments. For, as well as some valuable insights, these chapters proffer some extraordinary assertions and fallacious conclusions.

Sommerville's claim that the basic premises of Richard Hooker's *Laws of Ecclesiastical Polity* were close to those of the *Vindiciae Contra Tyrannos* will astound most who have read these works (as it would have, I suspect, their authors!). The claim that the concept of sovereignty was familiar in England before Bodin is nowhere *argued*. The distinction between the cleric's concern with morals and the layman's with means is false. The statement that the English application of contract theory was 'to neuter the King's authority while leaving his person inviolate' seems the opposite of what in fact was argued in 1642.[17] It is highly questionable that 'dominant legal opinion' gave Parliament supreme power to interpret the law. The claim that common lawyers 'in

emphasising the rational nature of English liberties . . . came close
to asserting that these liberties did, in fact, belong to all men by
nature' is untenable.[18] If such statements rock our confidence in
particulars, more generally the discussions of natural law and the
rational basis of the common law are thin and ambiguous.

These, however, are not the most significant problems. Perhaps
the greatest is Sommerville's anxiety to find divisive and conflicting ideologies. For though his chapters rigidly distinguish absolutist
theories from ideas of contract and law, much of his evidence
suggests that they need to be discussed together — as tensions and
ambivalences within a body of shared beliefs rather than as rival
value systems. Both proponents of divine right and advocates of
original popular sovereignty, he acknowledges, believed that the
object of government was the common good. James I thought that
popular consent may have originated kingship; by some civil
lawyers even the idea of popular sovereignty 'was given an
absolute twist'. Pym acknowledged that William I had gained
power by conquest. Disagreements about the nature and origin of
authority did not divide men into two distinct camps. It is only by
the artificial division of Sommerville's chapters, his failure to
contextualize remarks, and his reluctance to recall that the same
individual might utter 'absolutist' and 'constitutionalist' views that
political theories can be portrayed as polarized. In early
seventeenth-century England, the literature indeed 'reveals a
wealth of arguments in favour of limited monarchy on the one
hand and, on the other, . . . of the thesis that . . . the king's
powers were not limited by human law', but the differences did
not muster into ideological camps.[19] Sommerville's failure or
unwillingness to see this arises from his neglect of the shared
assumptions — indeed of the fundamental texts — of political
theory. Aristotle's treatment of the origin of political society, and
of the nature of legitimate authorities, most of all his insistence
that government must be virtuous, receives little discussion. Yet in
the legacy of this body of reflection on the polis lay many of the
ambivalences and different emphases that Sommerville discusses,
Aristotle being deployed to defend both the natural and original
authority of kings *and* the right of the people to govern
themselves.[20] Like Aristotle's *Politics* and *Ethics*, Roman political
commentators such as Tacitus and Cicero could be interpreted
differently — not only by different readers, but by the same
readers on different occasions.[21] The same was true of the law.
James I and Charles I shared their subjects' belief that they should
rule in accordance with the law, but what the law permitted, or
what it was perceived it permitted, was subject to interpretation —
not only by kings but by MPs and JPs too. It was the Scots who

in 1640 argued that 'where necessity commandeth, the lawes of Nature and Nations give their consent'; a decade before Charles had antagonized his subjects by the claim. In 1621, Sir Edward Coke saw no objection to the king's power of imprisonment without cause shown; by 1628 it was declared anathema to the fundamental law of the realm.[22] What had occurred in each case was not the triumph of one theory (or party) over another, but the emergence of new circumstances, circumstances that pointed up tensions and ambiguities and prompted revised interpretations.

When Sommerville tells us Sir Walter Raleigh and Bishop Morton opposed James I and Charles I while remaining committed to a theory of absolutism, we may be tempted to deduce that the key to English political thought was not theory but circumstance, practical politics rather than philosophy. It is unfortunate then that when he turns to 'Application' (the singular noun may be revealing) Sommerville's grasp of his subject becomes shaky indeed. There are good and original passages: the discussion of Cowell's case is one of the most valuable; the fallacy that the Laudians granted the clergy powers prejudicial to the crown is rightly exploded; the significance of the theology of Arminianism in the grievances of 1640 is challengingly disputed;[23] the secular priorities (lay control) of the religious debates is helpfully reemphasized. But there are innumerable contentions if not errors. Charles's religious policy did not flout the *law*, for all it displeased many; the discussion of the tonnage and poundage grant for a year in 1625 is distorted; the claims for annual parliaments are exaggerated; Conrad Russell's arguments are misunderstood; the discussion of the ship money case is thin. More generally, assertions that an 'ideological gulf' or 'conflict' is 'blindingly obvious' is repeated noisily as if noise and repetition may substitute for argument. And extraordinary claims — such as that the people were the arbiters of necessity — are made without substantiation. It is far from 'obvious' that the king's sense of the need to disregard the law to preserve common safety was 'diametrically opposed' to the views of the House of Commons. And Bristol's comment that the Petition of Right dealt with subjects' rights not the king's prerogative is revealing in a way that Sommerville does not see.[24] (If monarchs and subjects were conceived of as scale pans, the only position that could be understood was balance.)

In his perhaps regrettably revealing postscript, Sommerville shifts (without explaining the fit) from rival ideologies to conflict between king and parliament. How, one wonders, does he accommodate a man like Wentworth who led the debate on the Petition of Right and became the king's leading councillor? If courtiers such as Pembroke and Sir John Coke articulated opposition, how does one sustain a thesis of court/parliament polarity? If ideology, as he asserts, made parliaments reluctant to grant money, what are we to make of Phelips, Eliot, Pym, and others who wished to strengthen the finances of the crown? If James I and Charles I held similar views of royal power, why did one die in his bed and the other on the scaffold? Finally if the civil war marked no watershed in political theory, why did Hobbes find it necessary to start from first principles? And why did Scripture cease to pervade the language of politics in later Stuart England?[25] The questions prompt suggestions that lead us far away from Sommerville's claims: to the view that circumstances not theories led in 1642 to actions that men could not justify and to events that dismantled the common assumptions that had characterized political thinking.

Though Sommerville confines himself to written texts, the cover of *Ideology and Politics*, depicting the splendid apotheosis of James I painted by Peter Paul Rubens for the Whitehall ceiling, turns our attention to other cultural modes. Art historians and architectural historians have typically shown more interest in the development of technique and form than in paintings or buildings as documents of social and political values and aspirations. That the more broadly historical approach has not gone by default owes much to Roy Strong, whose many books have elucidated the representation of monarchy from Henry VIII to Charles I.[26] His latest study, *Henry Prince of Wales and England's Lost Renaissance*, (1986), investigates the culture and image of the circle and court of Henry, Prince of Wales. The court at St. James, the first of a royal prince since 1537, became a focus for both values and policies different to those of James I. Most obvious to visitors, perhaps, was the very different style. Where the king's court was casual and at times indecorous and bawdy, Henry 'in all things . . . affected regularity in his chapel, chamber and household.'[27] The Prince's Treasurer, Sir Charles Cornwallis, informs us that Henry decreed his feasts 'should pass with decency and decorum and without all rudeness, noise or disorder.'[28] Prince Henry intended that his court should announce his regality and his values. The ambassadors who 'approached him rather as a king than a prince' suggest that the image was not without power.

The prince gathered around him men who shared his values: an Italianate style, a love of martial sports, passionate Protestantism, and an anxious concern for the security of the reformed faith in England, which then depended so much on the pro-Protestant Henri IV of France. Sir Thomas Chalenor, the prince's governor since 1607, had travelled to Italy and served in the Low Countries in the 1580s; Adam Newton, his tutor, had travelled in France and collected pictures. Among his privy and bedchambermen, those who waited on the prince in his intimate quarters, we find Sir Robert Dallington who published travel books on Italy and France, and John Harington, an ardent Protestant whom Sir Henry Wotton introduced at Venice as 'the right eye of the Prince'. Among his older friends ranked Edward Cecil, Earl of Exeter, the Earl of Southampton, and Thomas Howard, Earl of Arundel. The circle was united by experience of travel, chivalric pursuits, and, with the exception of Arundel (and some others),[29] religion. Together with the prince's obsession with the navy and interest in colonization, these values made the court of St. James the focus of the hopes and aspirations of the old Elizabethan war party, bereft of a leader since the death of the earls of Leicester and Essex.[30] As Europe prepared for war over the Julich–Cleves succession, the zealots for the Protestant cause, many veterans of the Netherlands war, looked to Henry in the year, 1610, of his investiture. The prince did not disappoint them. He supported Henri IV and Maurice of Nassau and entered negotiations with the German Protestants to whom he was connected through his mother, Anne of Denmark. He helped manoeuvre a Protestant match for his sister. Strong sees Henry's policy as the antithesis of his father's: where Henry regarded marriages as the cement of a Protestant alliance, James saw them as the salve that might secure peace. There was, he argued, a 'clash of two ideologies'. There was a marked difference too in the modes through which those ideologies were expressed.

King James's court offered little prestige or patronage to continental artists. Henry by contrast recruited them: Constantine de Servi, De Caus, Inigo Jones, de Critz, Peake. Through their buildings, gardens and pictures, Henry's architects and artists gave 'visible form to the idea of the ruler'. The prince took care over his image, favouring — unusually for England — portraits à l'antique and on horseback, to depict a 'Spenserian knight and Roman imperator rolled into one'. If such depicted the general image of the prince, it was the festivals he staged which 'were designed explicitly to present himself and his policy to both court and public'. In Prince Henry's *Barriers* performed on Twelfth Night 1610, Strong convincingly reads a tension between the King's desire for peace and the prince's martial ambition at the time of the Julich–Cleves succession crisis. The politics of values pervades, Strong concludes, all the prince's pursuits — his collections of Roman medals and bronzes as well as pictures and festivals. In the text of the *Barriers* Ben Jonson himself refers to

The niches filled with statues to invite
Young valours forth by their old forms to fight.[31]

Unlike his younger brother Charles whose aesthetic pursuits, it is said, dangerously exacerbated suspicions of popery and broadened the gulf between court and country, Henry harnessed the arts to his advocacy of the Protestant battle in Europe and to his own image of the chivalric Protestant knight. His death in 1612 shattered an icon as well as the hopes of a faction.

Strong never fails to stimulate and *Henry Prince of Wales* is no exception. Minor mistakes are legion. James Fullerton was not Prince Henry's Privy Purse, but a member of Charles's household; Oliver painted no large-scale portrait of Henry; Lord Lumley was not a member of the Society of Antiquaries; there is little evidence that Sir Arthur Gorges was a member of Henry's circle; Augustine Nicholl was not Henry's Receiver General; *two* William Cecils are not distinguished.[32] Important materials concerning the prince's household and revenues have not been consulted.[33] Some of the broader historical comments on Jacobean court politics are suspect or wrong. Sir Robert Carr, future Earl of Somerset, was not of significance as early as 1610 when Strong sees him damaging relations between James and Henry; the investiture of Henry and the Great Contract were not connected as is here stated; grooms of the bedchamber *were* often cognizant with the inner workings of politics, etc.[34] Of more importance to the thesis, there were many more Catholics within Henry's milieu than the claim that Arundel was the exception would suggest: the Earl of Nottingham, another Howard, the Earl of Worcester, Lord Lumley, Charles Cornwallis, and possibly Michael Drayton, one of the prince's poets.[35] Whatever the Protestant policies of Henry, his circle did not comprise only militant Protestants: Arundel was a staunch advocate of a policy of peace and alliance with Spain. The role of Queen Anne also is worthy of reflection. Bishop Goodman, as we have seen, commented on the queen's great affection for her younger son. Not only does she emerge here as an important influence on the prince's collection and aesthetic sense — an influence which, despite her Catholicism, suggests a closeness between them — her religion evidently did not prohibit her staging at her son's investiture an entertainment that also alluded to the old Elizabethan mythology that became part of Henry's image. The argument for two clashing ideologies also raises complications not addressed. As Strong observes with more innocence than perception, 'It was James himself who created a circle around the Prince.' Did then James naively allow an opposition to his policies to emerge from his son's court? Or was the recruitment of old Essexians and warmongers, as the integration of Scots and English in 1603, part of a shrewd and subtle policy, like the dual marriage alliances he pursued for his children, to manoeuvre a balance in domestic and foreign politics — a balance that gave him greater movement and control? The second court — of a prince or a wife — provided an opportunity, not enjoyed since the 1530s, to connect (or as Elton put it 'earth') to the centre of politics interest groups powerful in the country.[36] James, who had total control of appointments at least until Henry's investiture, might well have made full use of it.

Such cavils by no means invalidate Strong's thesis or achievement. In his breadth of vision, his integration of politics, foreign policy, art, architecture, and festival, he has demonstrated the complex ingredients of the prince's image and his conscious formation and manipulation of its representation. The aesthetic was intrinsically political in early modern Europe. That it became all the more so in early Stuart England owed much to Henry's innovations as a connoisseur and sharp sense of the power of image. It was not only his successor, Prince Charles, who inherited that sense. In 1626, a client was even to advise the Duke of Buckingham that not to favour learning and the arts lost a noble reputation.[37] Sophistication and style had become an essential characteristic of noble authority.

No figure more exemplified that belief, perhaps none did more to promote it than the 'exceptional' figure of Henry's entourage, Thomas Howard, 2nd Earl of Arundel. As the first nobleman conspicuously to collect pictures and drawings, marbles and antiquities, as a patron of Van Dyck, Rubens, and Inigo Jones, as well as historians, mathematicians, and men of letters, Arundel earned Horace Walpole's praise as 'the father of vertue' in England. His early interest in paintings and books he probably owed to John, Lord Lumley, who had married a daughter of Henry Fitzalan, 1st Earl of Arundel. In *Lord Arundel and His Circle* (1985), Howarth demonstrates, however, that the most significant influence in its development came, not from England, but in 1612 when Arundel (at the unusually late age of twenty-seven) sought a licence to travel to Italy. The journey was brief, but began a love affair with Italy; Arundel returned the next year with Inigo Jones in his train. On his journeys he met Rubens and Van Balen in the Low Countries, the famous collector Guistiniani and sculptor Moretti in Rome; he purchased books on architecture; he returned with statues and other treasures. Perhaps most of all Arundel brought back a desire to convey the riches of Italian art and architecture to the court of Jacobean England. He commissioned new fireplaces and windows in the classical style for Arundel House in the Strand; he sat with Jones on the commission for buildings in London, authorizing a classical amphitheatre for the capital; he introduced busts and statues as garden ornaments in his retreat at Highgate. He continued through his agents, especially the Rev. William Petty, avidly to acquire paintings and marbles, later drawings and prints. The mark of his influence was the increasingly sharp competition for the best pieces as other noblemen joined the race to establish impressive galleries.

Arundel's 'curiosity' was not confined to paintings and marbles. An interest in antiquity and history led him to associate with members of the Society of Antiquaries, and especially with William Camden, the author of *Britannia*, and Sir Robert Cotton, owner of the largest library of manuscripts in early modern England. Whilst he formed his gallery, Arundel continued to build a splendid library, purchasing the Pirkheimer collection in 1636 when he was at Nuremberg en route to Vienna. And increasingly over the 1620s and 1630s, Arundel House became a centre of learning and source of patronage for many men of letters as well as painters. For not only did Rubens, Van Dyck, and Jones work for the Earl, and Cotton, Camden, and other historians enjoy his favour, the Dutch philological scholar Franciscus Junius was appointed his librarian and wrote there the famous *De Pictura Veterum*; Henry Peacham, author of *The Compleat Gentleman*, became a protége; Wenceslaus Hollar the engraver, William Oughtred the mathematician, and William Harvey the physician were brought from abroad to join the community that gathered in the Strand or at Albury, Arundel's country estate in Surrey.

Arundel's aesthetic and intellectual pursuits have traditionally been investigated (or more accurately appreciated) for themselves. David Howarth begins to argue that they cannot be seen apart from wider dynastic, political, and ideological contexts.[38] For Arundel's family had a tradition of interest in Italy and the arts which the Earl was anxious to publicize as well as continue.[39] His obsession with obtaining Holbeins in particular — what he later himself described as 'a foolish curiosity' — may have owed less to aesthetic considerations than to the fact that Holbein painted the Duke of Norfolk and other worthies of the Howard family at the height of its political power in the reign of Henry VIII.[40] It may be, then, that in Rubens and Van Dyck, Arundel sought his own Holbein, artists who might project the sophistication but also (as Rubens's portrait of the Earl in armour, or Van Dyck's portrait of the family suggest) the martial prowess of the dynasty.[41] His strong sense of his ancestry and responsibility to his lineage clearly shaped Arundel's historical interests: he projected a history of his family and corresponded with Cotton about it. But the connections between aesthetics and personal values were broader than the consideration of family. The arts for Arundel and his circle performed an aesthetic function; he believed passionately in 'the moral purpose of culture'. Peacham's *Compleat Gentleman* and Junius's *De Pictura Veterum*, written under Arundel's patronage, give the most systematic statement of his values: statues, antiquities, and manuscripts, they believed, inspired virtue; in the words of one of Arundel's agents, Sir Thomas Roe, they strengthened 'good and true spirits', through images to be emulated.[42] The point may be graphically made in a fascinating sketch to which Howarth draws attention: a sketch of a head of the Empress Faustina, wife of Marcus Aurelius with, beneath, another of the Countess of Arundel. Other evidence points to Arundel's inclination to Stoicism (Aurelius was believed to be the author of the stoic *Meditations*) and the sketch indicates a desire to associate both his family and pursuits with the philosophy. Arundel's plain, black Spanish garb and Italianate manners publicized the values of the circle in other ways. Their political significance, as even Clarendon's grudging portrait acknowledges, was not lost on contemporaries.[43] For Arundel was a public figure, a man of affairs, for all his aloofness. As Earl Marshal of England, his interests in history, antiquities, family, and drawing all shaped his sense of his office, as his various offices and appointments — as envoy to the Emperor in 1636 or Lord General of the army against the Scots in 1639 — shaped his collections and commissions. Though he never obtained the dukedom of Norfolk nor perhaps the place at court he thought his due, Arundel was a political figure of weight and not least on account of his unrivalled reputation as a connoisseur and patron of learning.

The historian of culture then must be grateful for Howarth's essay in integrating into political and cultural history the formation of the Arundel collection. There are presented here some splendid 'texts' which few historians will have read: the tomb of Henry Howard, the sketch of Faustina discussed, Van der Gucht's and Hollar's drawings of Albury House (almost in themselves a denunciation of a court — country polarity);[44] Van Dyck's *The Continence of Scipio*, the magnificent apotheosis of Arundel, his heart juxtaposed to Holbein's Duke of Norfolk. It must be hoped then that readers will not be deterred by the many historical howlers, some of the most elementary kind. Howarth for example describes the twelve years truce of 1609 between Spain and the Dutch as the Seven Years Truce of 1607; he has Sir Edward Coke as Secretary of State, presumably a confusion of the Chief Justice with Sir John Coke; he erroneously dates to 1573 the foundation of the Society of Antiquaries (here wrongly called the Society of Antiquarians) despite several recent works which have established it correctly;[45] he elevates Thomas Sutton to a knighthood. Errors like this point not only to carelessness. Together with other

Thomas Howard, Earl of Arundel (1629–1630) by Rubens (by kind permission of the Isabella Stewart Gardner Museum, Boston)

Lord Arundel Walking in the Grounds at Albury by Hollar (by permission of the Syndics of the Fitzwilliam Museum, Cambridge)

The Grotto at Albury by Hollar (by permission of the Master and Fellows, Magdalene College, Cambridge)

extraordinary phrases and descriptions they indicate rather too slight an acquaintance with the historical context and historiography of early Stuart England. Wider reading would have prevented Howarth describing *The Shepherd's Paradise* as a masque, Sir Robert Cotton as a 'radical' politician, or depicting Arundel as reviving the Society of Antiquaries in 1613–14, as anxious to go on the embassy to Vienna in 1636, or as reluctant to return despite Charles's alleged impatient prompting (on both the last the reverse

is true).[46] Other passages suggest that the intellectual and political
contexts are not really comprehended. The idea that the Society of
Antiquaries pursued a systematic approach to history that 'was to
bring the discipline into a dialogue with social and political
thought' may surprise any who have read its proceedings;[47] the
statement that theology was a 'common diversion' for seventeenth-
century gentlemen is even more puzzling.

More significantly, further research and wider reading were, I
believe, needed to develop and strengthen the case — especially
for the interconnections of intellectual and political history. For
some asides and observations made point to important lines of
enquiry not pursued. One example is afforded by the newswriter
Chamberlain's letter about the Countess of Arundel who made

> a great feast at Highgate to the Lord Keeper, the two Lords Chief
> Justices, the Master of the Rolls, and I know not who else. It was after
> the Italian manner with four courses and four table cloths one under
> another and when the first course and table cloth were taken away, the
> Master of the Rolls thinking all had been done, said grace as his manner
> is when no Divines are present and was afterwards well laughed at for
> his labours.[48]

A social gaffe led to humiliation; style and sophistication
bequeathed authority. The significance and chronology of this
increasingly important association and Arundel's role in its
development calls for further discussion. So do other enticing snap
evaluations of the connections between aesthetic taste and political
styles. The Duke of Buckingham, Howarth writes, 'had the same
temperament in collecting as in politics. Just as he was to sweep
Prince Charles off to Spain, so he abandoned himself to the
sensuous delights of the Venetian School.' Comments like this, or
the observation that Van Dyck lacked the 'moral integrity' of a
Velasquez, promise invaluable insights into the history of political
values and relationships — but to fulfil that promise they need
fuller explication than they receive. The same is true of Arundel's
own political career, to which Howarth pays disquietingly little
attention. The observations of Sir Edward Walker, Arundel's first
biographer, concerning the Earl's behaviour in the Privy Council
and at court, and his ambivalent attitude to religion, receive no
comment;[49] nor do Clarendon's sneers about Arundel's self-
aggrandizement and *lack* of learning.[50] Most regrettably Howarth
has little to say about Arundel's relations with the leading courtiers
or with King James and Charles. In the case of the last, aesthetic
and political history clearly come together: the Earl of Hamilton's
rivalry for the acquisition of pictures stemmed in part from his
desire to present them to a king who clearly regarded such gifts as

one of the currencies that purchased favour. Why then were King Charles and the greatest connoisseur of his court estranged for much of his reign, and why did Arundel never enjoy the honours that might have come his way? That Howarth does not pose these questions may caution us that they cannot be easily answered. Interesting, however, is Arundel's deployment of images in fashioning his own reputation: evidently he commissioned a 25-foot mosaic of himself, and was not averse to ordering paintings that flattered himself, his family, his house, and his own collection.[51] But he may have had less grasp of the need so to cultivate others, and especially the king. Arundel appears not to have been generous with his gifts to his sovereign, with whom he could, in aesthetic matters, have well claimed equality if not superiority. The relationship between them, though much improved after Buckingham's death, seems never to have been other than formal and respectful. Buckingham and Hamilton, by contrast, enjoyed Charles's affection. Whatever there may be in the suggestion that Arundel employed less than effectively one of the currencies of power and authority, the interplay of paintings and politics, the role of art in self-fashioning, in the representation of authority, requires further explanation. In the England of Charles I there was no simple correlation between common cultural pursuits and political loyalties.

If the study of 'elite culture' and its relationship to politics is a recent historical development, the investigation of popular culture and popular politics has only just begun. Interest in the behaviour and attitudes of the orders below the gentry has been fuelled not only by the democratization and socialization of historical studies, but also by a growing sense that, in the absence of an effective police force, the authority wielded by magistrates and squires itself depended upon a large measure of acceptance of that authority — upon, again, customs, traditions, and perceptions which were part of the culture of the manor and village, hundred and county. Popular culture and politics of course are subjects fraught with even more difficulties than the study of elites. The attitudes of the illiterate and inarticulate have often to be deduced from the claims (or criticisms) of their superiors, or from actions which, contrary to popular proverb, do not always speak louder than words. It is not therefore surprising that here too there have been false starts which threatened to discredit the enterprise, in one case leading an inexperienced young historian into rash assumptions about and explanations for popular allegiance in the English Civil War.[52] Yet even unsatisfactory books remind us of important questions and problems. And in the exhaustively-researched history of the outbreak of civil war, the behaviour and sympathies of the people have received surprisingly little attention. It is from such basic questions that David Underdown's enticingly titled book, *Revel, Riot and Rebellion: Popular Politics and Culture in England 1603–1660* (Oxford, 1985) originates. Did the people, he asks, do their best to stay out of the war or did they wilfully take sides? Were they free to follow their own preferences or did they mass deferentially behind the banners of their manorial lords and local gentry? If they were free to choose, what factors influenced popular allegiance: national or local considerations? wealth and status? religious or constitutional sensibilities? or regional culture and mores? To the sceptic who might doubt whether the evidence permits an answer to such questions, Underdown replies that 'some general impressions of group behaviour in the civil war and of the complex social and cultural forces that helped to shape it' can be obtained. Focusing his study on three counties, Dorset, Somerset, and Wiltshire, he posits a complex argument for the interrelationship of regional economy and culture with political values and allegiance.

The main thrust of the argument is stated from the beginning. Rejecting the view that the populace followed their landlords or county elites, he advances the hypothesis that 'contrasts in popular allegiance had a regional basis, and were related to local differences in social structure, economic development and culture.' Agricultural historians have drawn attention to the different economic structures of the arable and woodland areas of early modern England.[53] Underdown wishes to stress the other differences to which that gave rise. In the closer-knit villages of arable land where the community centred on manor and parish church, order and stability were maintained by informal processes and mediation, which could not be effective in less coherent, more dislocated pasture and woodland. Immigration of landless poor exacerbated the inherent instability of these latter areas, distancing them even further from the ideal orderly, vertically-integrated society on which theories of authority and obedience were founded. In the pasture lands governing elites could place little dependence upon the self-regulation of the community. Quite contrary modes of village government stemmed from this difference. In the arable lands, village customs and games, cyclical festivals and rituals, maypoles and church ales were regarded — as they were too by Charles I and Laud — as reinforcing the bonds of community and the hierarchy. In the pasture and woodland, however, village elites endeavoured to suppress feasts and Morris dancers, maypoles and wandering players as occasions of potential unruliness and insubordination. They emphasized individual sobriety, hard work, and piety, not the rituals of community co-operation. As a consequence of their different social structures and of these alternate attitudes of the elites, two contrasting cultures emerged in the arable and pasture villages which were reflected in all aspects of life. The typical sport of the South Wiltshire down-lands, football, reflected the collective character of the commun-ities; stoolball with, it is argued, its emphasis on the individual confrontation of bowler and batsman was the favoured game of the North Wiltshire cheese country. In the pasturelands too, we are told, traditional ideas of family life and gender relations were subject to more strain, as evidenced by the charivari or shaming rituals against scolding wives who defied the authority of husbands and the expectations of female fidelity.

Religion exacerbated all these cultural differences. For the gover-ning elites of the pasture and woodlands, hostile to parish games and anxious to establish order, were attracted to puritanism with its stress on godliness and sobriety, and its abhorrence of church ales and sports. By contrast the cultural traditionalism of the arable villages 'was naturally often accompanied by Laudianism'. At a time when religious preferences and political positions were inseparable — Charles I ordered the clergy to read *The Book of Sports* — religio-cultural differences could not but lead to political polarization too. That popular political perceptions looked beyond the parish pump, Underdown is anxious to stress. As characteristic of 'the intense legalism of popular politics', he points to the bell-ringing that celebrated the Petition of Right, the rating disputes that expressed popular discontent with innovations like ship money which affronted popular ideas of law, the mounting viru-lence of anti-popery and the suspicion of Laud's ecclesiastical policies that 'simmered through the country'. The political con-sciousness of the people could not be ignored by their betters: in the elections to the Short Parliament, there are signs that candidates began to appeal to it. But popular politics were as divided as their communities: in some (arable) villages the godly were derided. When civil war broke out in 1642 there were suffi-cient determinants of popular allegiance to obviate any thesis of ignorant deference to the lead of gentry superiors. So, in drawing his map of the Civil War, Underdown shows the cloth and dairy lands of North Wiltshire and North Somerset, the pasture of West Dorset and the Somerset Levels in Parliament's colours, the down-lands, South and West Somerset and Blackmore Vale as Royalist. The fit of political allegiance with ecological type is, he argues, not exact but sufficient to sustain the hypothesis. Muster rolls, lists of pensioners, and notes of those catalogued as suspects by the Protectorate in 1655 support, it is said, in general a regional pattern of allegiance that closely traces socio-economic and cultural lines. Moreover, the divisions persisted. The Protectorate regime never succeeded in suppressing traditional popular pastimes and celebrations (including Christmas); indeed its attack on 'familiar and often colourful monuments' alienated popular support. And the Restoration, for all the seemingly universal rejoicing, did not heal the divisions. The Civil War was 'a conflict about the moral basis of English society.' That conflict was not resolved in 1660.

A brief summary cannot do justice to the complexity of Underdown's arguments, still less can a review indicate the riches of the book. Not least, that so much can be discovered about villages and popular behaviour has convinced one former sceptic that such enterprises are worthwhile. The emphasis too upon the social and religious divisions created by puritans — 'so frequent in James I's reign as to cast much doubt on the view . . . that this was a tranquil interlude of peaceful co-existence within the English church' — invaluably corrects some recent historical fallacies.[54] The popular appeal of Anglican rituals, even of some aspects of Laud's and Charles I's religious policy, soon to be exhaustively documented by Christopher Haigh, is here valuably argued.[55] And the demonstration of popular royalism as well as popular parliamentarianism disposes of what was left of the argument that denied it.[56] As well as many illuminating incidents related — disputes over seats in church for one — general observations, such as the commonwealth's 'reliance on verbal means of establishing its legitimacy', open exciting new lines of thought.

Yet for all the riches, for all that many of the separate ingredients are inviting, the overall argument cannot be consumed. Why? The first explanation must be that many of the important claims and connections are assumed rather than argued. The reader therefore is left to wonder why the moderate Protestantism of the 1559 settlement suited arable more than pasture communities; why puritanism (especially as a code of discipline) appealed to the middling sort as opposed to governing elites of whatever class. Better definitions — of middling and puritan for instance — seem necessary. And fuller discussion certainly is necessary before we can concur that gender relations, which seem to be strained in all historical periods and geographical regions, were especially so in early seventeenth-century pasture and woodland, or that rituals of community had less meaning there than in arable villages. No more can we accept the simple connection made between puritan/pasture regions and the ideology of the 'country' when the latter comprised many persons of quite secular, even anti-puritan sympathies as well as men from all geographical areas. The arguments for popular political consciousness too are not without problems. Buchanan Sharp's argument that forest riots were not directed against the court is denied without the case being argued.[57] When we note that quite customary local charges — for highways and bridge repair for instance — frequently generated rating disputes, we may wonder whether those prompted by ship money reflected a simple reluctance to open purses rather than constitutional principles.[58] The second reason for scepticism is the many contradictions in the argument. For at times Professor Underdown seems to want to have things both ways. So we are told the Laudian support for church ales and maypoles was popular in places, but that suspicion of his 'entire programme' ran throughout '*the country*'.[59] Similarly skimmingtons and charivari are characterized both as the practices of the more dispersed pasture and woodland and also described as quite elaborately organized rituals 'deeply rooted in folk memory'. Most problematic of all is the discussion of village games. The contrast between community football and individualistic stoolball (its individualism curiously compared to cricket)[60] is implausible enough, still more so when stoolball is later used to demonstrate a sense of community!

Thirdly, it is not always clear whether Underdown's characterization of village cultures describes popular preferences, those of the elite, or both. The survival of games and ales in puritan pasturelands at Ditcheat and Cameley suggests, we are told, that the lowest classes remained 'hostile and resistant to Puritan reformation.' If so, are we viewing contrasting popular cultures or contrasting elite attitudes to what remained a *common* popular culture? Statements that there were no clear rungs between the 'lower middling' sort and the poor compound the confusion, as does uncertainty about the social status of soldiers in the 1640s. It may be that the contrasts presented reflect more status than regional differences. The fourth and most damaging objection is the many exceptions to the case. Pasture and cloth districts are presented as those with the greatest extremes of wealth, yet in Blackmore Vale and the Somerset Levels more equal distribution 'was still the norm'. Skittles and beer, festivals and maypoles are found in the clothing regions; in Blackmore Vale puritanism had made few inroads. Even stoolball was played outside of its 'heartland' — in Worcestershire for example. That Professor Underdown himself catalogues such exceptions when lesser historians would have (indeed have) silenced them is another mark of his scholarship. But it does not, I think, explain them away. Rather the reminder that parishes like Mere, Warminster, and Westbury straddled chalk and cheese, the acknowledgement that adjacent parishes could differ markedly, weakens the whole geographical and ecological thesis.

It is undermined by the least satisfactory and most important chapter of all: the analysis of Civil War allegiance. Arable downland Dorset was only 'mildly' royalist; Blackmore Vale, however, was firmly so. Few parliamentarian pensioners turn up in the cheese and cloth districts; but the small market towns of the Wiltshire cheese country were royalist. The Dorset pasturelands produced more royalists than the downlands, and there were even large numbers of royalist pensioners in Gillingham, where there had been forest riots directed, according to Underdown, against the court. Even in North Somerset, Shepton Mallet proved a stronghold of royalism. Areas of quite different economies, social structures and settlement patterns were royalist. Underdown struggles to accommodate these problems, but they will not go away. Observations such as that 'Royalists, no less than the Parliamentarians, had their following among the middling and industrious sorts' question some of the earlier premises; the explanation for exceptions — the recognition of the importance of gentry control in some regions or of 'striking contrasts of allegiance within quite small areas' — seems to invalidate the broader map. Curiously the final chapters appear to abandon it. The discussion of 1646–60 is more a study of the nation than of regional difference — of the failure to establish Puritanism, or to overcome popular conservatism throughout the realm. Festive rituals return even in puritan areas. Other than 'a general mood of alienation from Parliament', to most the issues and parties were 'shadowy entities far away in Westminster'.[61] Underdown explains the change: 'before 1640 the Puritans stood for local liberties against the external forces threatening their communities. . . . By the 1650s . . . they themselves were tarred with the brush of centralization.' There is little of regional or cultural difference in that explanation; rather we are back with the theory of localism as an explanation for the behaviour that Underdown rejects at the outset. What is obvious is that circumstances had changed. Vast sums had been levied, troops had been billeted, the Prayer Book had been outlawed, an anointed monarch had been executed, bishops had been abolished, landlords had been killed, families had been divided, village (as well as national) authorities and elites had been challenged and replaced. All such circumstances helped determine the attitudes of the 1650s as these and others did the allegiances of the 1640s. Immediate circumstances perhaps determine behaviour as much as do structures of economy and society; that is why popular allegiance can be fickle while structures remain. And while economic arrangements are important aspects of culture, they may be less important than family and upbringing, than the influence of manorial lord, vicar, or schoolmaster, than personal relations and even individuality in determining attitudes. A model that fore-grounds the ecological to the exclusion of these cannot be accepted.

Yet if the argument for the ecological determination of political behaviour remains unconvincing, Underdown has demonstrated that village culture — traditions, customs, rituals, and expectations — was an important component of what might be called the ideology of order. And it is this perspective that has begun to reorient research on local government and its stability in early modern England. Where earlier histories concentrated upon institutions and officials — on Quarter Sessions, jails and the whip, on judges and JPs — important recent work suggests that the prosecution and punishment of crime depended more upon the co-operative processes of the local community, on understanding between governors and governed, and a preparedness to compromise. It has been estimated that in seventeenth-century England, eighty per cent of offences remained unprosecuted.[62] These new directions and findings have clearly influenced the editors of and contributors to *Order and Disorder in Early Modern England*, edited by A. Fletcher and J. Stevenson (Cambridge 1985).

The introduction points to many of the obstacles to law and order in early modern England: the absence of an army and bureaucracy, increasing extremes of wealth and poverty, dearth, plague, the weakening of the church as an agency of order after the Reformation, and, perhaps by the end of the seventeenth century, a widening gap between the people and their gentry governors. How then was order, in a century remarkably free of popular riot, maintained? Fletcher and Stevenson see the strength of the state in an idealization of the law which was shared by common folk and gentlemen — an idealization that left the idea of law inviolate even while specific abuses and criticisms defied or assaulted it in practice. The ideology could not be taken for granted; it had to be nurtured. But given that condition, a society of potentially anarchic instability remained 'surprisingly stable'. The suggestion, if not entirely novel, is important. But its exposition is spoiled by a rather hurried and careless prose (a feature alas of several of the contributions) and its force marred by some vague phrases of little meaning without further substantiation. Sentences such as 'hegemony could be sustained by the constant exercise of *theatre* and concession' clearly require elucidation; the statement that the idea of the rule of law made the ideology effective is approaching tautology. There is a tendency too to idealize. If the populace committed crimes but never challenged the rule of law, that may owe less to their ideological perspective than to their lack of one: we should not expect principled opposition from the illiterate and unsophisticated. The idea that popular riot when it did arise, in a sense 'confirmed the social order' seems perverse: that most criminals are not anarchists does not argue their defence of law and order. Emphasis on persuasion and propaganda (though not a discussion of them) may well be timely but we should not discount fear in explanations of social control. The populace *en masse* may have been able easily to rise against gentlemen and justices, but the prospective individual felon knew all too well who had the whip hand.

The other contributions explore ideas and ideologies that sustained order, threatened stability, or prompted riot. The microcosm of order was the family and household. Susan Amussen explores the interactions of domestic and public order in an essay on gender relations and the family and argues (as here Underdown does again) for mounting strains in the ideal of the husband's and father's authority that had, of course, implications for the commonweal.[63] 'The puritan belief in the spiritual equality of the elect,' Amussen maintains, 'existed in tension with assumptions about hierarchy' — within the family as well as the church. And increasingly too women were less willing to accept their assigned role as subordinate, modest, and even chaste.[64] Yet for all the breaches in practice, the ideal of the family as the focus of order was not challenged, even by civil war radicals. What changed it was the increasing privacy of the family in the years after the Restoration and hence its decreasing relevance to public life. The essay opens an important aspect of family history — and indeed of political theory — which has been too little explored. But there are slips: the husband/wife analogy in political discourse long predates the 1640s; there is some curious use of evidence; and the prose reads still very much like that of a Ph.D. thesis. The reasons for privatization of family life in the later seventeenth century require explanation, as its implications need further exploration. But in phrases like 'as political theory assumed the family, household manuals assumed politics' there are whole subjects opening. Amussen touches upon the concern with reputation among women in the village community; and the importance of reputation for the office-holding, governing class is the subject of Anthony Fletcher's essay. Honour, he reminds us, was still central to early modern England and the more public role a man played the more his honour, for which he often sought office, was on the stage. It was a fragile commodity for, in rivalries for power, factions could prove ready to besmirch each other's honour. Gentlemen were therefore careful not to abuse their place nor to lose the respect of their communities. Over the militia especially they were 'even more touchy than usual about how their good name might suffer as a result of public duties.' Honour and reputation were the basis of authority, but they were also the perimeter within which it was exercised. This I found an important but unsatisfying essay that, untypically for Fletcher, harried a subject rather than tackled it. It would have been clarified by a fuller definition of how honour and reputation were perceived both by JPs and deputy lieutenants and their subordinates. But in a discussion of honour the absence of the king or court is curious to say the least.[65] The very grant of place that bestowed so much honour in the local community depended upon the crown; and it was the local sense of an officer's reputation at court that often decided the respect he enjoyed in the locality. As Chaworth wrote to the king in 1635, concerning his appointment as sheriff, 'I . . . have the worst inlet into the service that is possible, a prepossession of the whole county that I am in your Majesty's disfavour.'[66] True, the king's favour did not license arbitrary or harsh local government, but magistrates so guilty lost reputation not least because they were believed to abuse the *king's* honour. The reputation and honour granted by the crown and earned in the locality are in a more complex symbiosis than is described here.

It has become fashionable in some recent historiography to study puritanism as a code of discipline and order, attractive to the parish elites of potentially unstable communities. Convincing for particular cases, such as Terling, the thesis becomes much more doubtful when incautiously applied to the realm.[67] In one of the finest essays of the collection, Margaret Spufford performs a polite surgical demolition of the case. She challenges assumptions that have been in danger of becoming facts: we do not know enough to associate puritanism with the yeomanry. She shows the same willingness to present neighbours for sexual offences in the late thirteenth and fourteenth centuries as the seventeenth century; and in pointing to similar economic, demographic, and social strains in both periods, she suggests the irrelevance of puritanism to social order. There have been few better demonstrations of the devastations that careful scholarship and logic can inflict on incautiously constructed models.

Other essays shift the focus from the rulers to the ruled. In an important contribution, C.S.L. Davies demonstrates the popular element in the Pilgrimage of Grace. For all the connivance of gentlemen, the origins and strength of the movement are shown to derive from popular rumours and fears of the spoliation of the church and assault on the faith — rumours that would easily carry conviction against the background of the dissolutions, the Ten Articles, the abolition of all but three sacraments and of purgatory, the end of saints' days. Defence of true religion, he argues, legitimized rebellion, as indeed its icons — the Pilgrim's banner displayed the five wounds of Christ — were images of an order they were anxious to preserve. Davies's emphasis upon the church as the centre of community, upon its splendours as 'some alleviation of the austerity . . . of everyday life' ought to make historians of puritanism think again. Studying the Fens, the scene of some of the rare riots of the next century, Clive Holmes, in contradiction to Keith Lindley, finds evidence of a popular political consciousness imbued with a strong constitutional sense of law. Yet though he subjects evidence used by others to effective criticism, his own argument fails finally to convince. If localities after 1660 most readily accepted schemes that had statutory sanction, this may reflect less the constitutionalism of the people than the greater likelihood of efficiency, completion, and secure finance. Legislation may often have sealed local agreements rather than facilitated them. And the absence of riot in some areas may owe more to the local agricultural circumstances and personal arrangements (e.g. over grazing and common) than to the leadership (or not) of a yeomen, middling sort with an inclination to go to law.[68] Circumstances as well as ideology determined whether men acquiesced or rebelled. And such is the conclusion of one of the best pieces in which John Morrill and John Walter attempt to explain why the Civil War did not see the much-feared popular revolution. They have done us a service in reminding us it did not — given the disproportionately large numbers of pages given elsewhere to minor sects and crackpots. Land and liberty never became the slogan of the English Revolution; radical millenarianism never infected the poor; the radical groups, especially the most important, never appealed to the rural poor. There was little connection, they show, between the riots that marked the early and the later 1640s; in 1649 too there was not only an army but better harvests. The burdens of war — billeted troops and new levies — threatened insurrection; and fears for religious change then, as a century earlier, could inflame popular passions. But the reluctance of the Protectorate to use force, the willingness to work through local elites kept the popular political temperature low. Morrill and Walter see the fear of the mob as out of all proportion to the actual threat it posed. The importance of that fear — in imposing limitations on governors, central and local — might now fruitfully be further considered. We might question the authors' rather lofty conclusion that 'ideologies of acquiescence and order had penetrated the people' and note that they were not hungry, but in either case their conservatism (be it conscious or indifferent) speaks volumes about the nature of England's revolution and the early modern English state.[69]

The general order and stability of early modern England, reaffirmed here, present a paradox. For England was of European countries one among those least governed from the centre: seventeenth-century monarchs sent no intendants from Whitehall into the shires; the experiment of the Major Generals was short-lived. Some of the best scholarship of the last twenty years has demonstrated in fact that government in early modern England was *local* government, and in the entrusting of local gentry with the responsibility for order, lay the strengths as well as the weaknesses of the English polity. Local officials did not always reliably enact central orders, but they governed with a strong knowledge of the circumstances and needs of the locality and so acted as safety valves which prevented any explosive tensions between the demands of the centre and the capacities of the counties and hundreds. Anthony Fletcher's *Reform in the Provinces* (1986) subsumes and synthesizes the product of a vast amount of research on the county government of England. He studies the commission of the peace — the numbers, personnel, quality, and regulation of JPs; the conduct of business — in Quarter Sessions, petty sessions, and by individual justices in their divisions. He analyses the enforcement of policies concerned with the relief of the poor, vagrants, and apprentices, with the regulation of alehouses and sexual behaviour. He describes the continued efforts of the Stuarts to form an 'exact militia' against a background at times of local indifference or hostility. Briefly he sketches the role of sheriffs and constables responsible for almost all government at the level of the hundred and village.[70] Ranging over counties north and south, coastal and inland, Fletcher controls and synthesizes information from hundreds of articles and monographs, in a manner that makes the book invaluable for students. His pursuit of his theme across the traditional divide of 1660 enables him to consider the question of localism after the Restoration and to demonstrate that, brought together as it is here, the research on later Stuart England may tell us more than we might have realized. The chronology across the century is also important to Fletcher's case. And *Reform in the Provinces*, though primarily descriptive, has a definite case — indeed cases — to argue. One is the large measure of continuity in the nature of magisterial rule. For all the particular changes, the commission of the peace remained fundamentally unaltered as the backbone of county government: many counties continued regular Quarter Sessions during the 1640s — Sir John Poole being active as a JP in Devon at the very time that he was being fined as a delinquent; from 1654 representatives of families which had for long staffed the commission began to return as county governors. Secondly, the book argues for an overall and increasing efficiency in dealing with local problems and in the procedures and conduct of government: in establishing rates for poor relief; in the gradual evolution of a system of licensing alehouses; in training and equipping a local militia; in developing petty sessions, more efficient archives and administration (printed forms for recognizances for example); and, at the end of the century, in building Sessions Houses which further strengthened as well as reflected the awe shown to magistrates. And thirdly Fletcher maintains that the efficiency and improvements were almost entirely local achievements. Of the 'stacks' of statues they were required to enforce and of the myriad responsibilities with which they were charged, the magistrates selected those of most concern (or interest) to themselves and their localities. They prosecuted such offences as they and the communities of village and hundred decided to bring to law; they enforced the observation of the sabbath and moral codes as they saw fit; they supervised musters with varying commitment and enthusiasm; they interpreted, followed, and ignored conciliar and royal directives as local circumstances and sensibilities suggested. 'County government was always a matter of selecting priorities' and it was the JPs and deputy lieutenants, not the Privy Council, who selected them. Such a decentralized system of government was not an inefficient one. Indeed the triumph of the gentry (here seen as a triumph of the whole century not, as traditionally, one secured in 1660) was a twofold triumph: the securing of their independence of central control and their success in coping with the local difficulties they encountered. Fletcher concludes:

> In tackling the new tasks that the gathering crisis of the early Stuart period erected, gentry who held local office were dependent upon neither the monarch nor the Council for direction or prompting. Their priorities at any particular moment might or might not be the Council's priorities; their judgement about the best way to proceed might or might not coincide with how they were told to act. But that they were willing and able to govern, that they could secure order, and that they not the Council held the whip hand . . . seems not to be in doubt.[71]

It is the force of this conclusion that raises some concern. As a reaction to an earlier historiography that saw in every central pronouncement a consequent local action to implement it, such a statement cannot be questioned. But the local history industry has taken us so far from that historiography, that the balance is now in danger, as some of the most recent work has appreciated, of tilting too far the other way.[72] That Fletcher overemphasizes the autonomy of local governors and underestimates the place of central authorities is suggested even by some of his own material.

His discussion of the Book of Orders is a case in point. Fairly contemptuous of the success of the book in affecting local government, Fletcher reminds us that only one-tenth of the certificates
due from the counties were returned, and that in 1633 only eighteen counties made a return. The reports that were filed became
increasingly brief and standardized; after 1632 the Council did not
bother to read them and ceased to supervise the enactment of the
orders. As for the petty sessions that the Book of Orders commanded, Fletcher argues that, except where they had already
become the norm, adoption by counties was spasmodic and in
some cases temporary. The impact of the Book of Orders was
minimal. The negative conclusion, however, is surely tempered by
Fletcher's acknowledgement that 'standards of reporting and standards of government' were not synonymous, and by the recognition that 'the pace of government was quickening during the
1630s.' In Cheshire an embryonic system of petty sessions was
brought into life; Devon began to adopt the practice for the first
time; in other counties they were held more regularly. The statement that 'Nothing changed . . . except that the petty sessions
were held more frequently' seems a curious contradiction, for it
was in quickening some and prompting others to follow that the
intentions of the Council lay. Nor is it entirely true that after 1632,
little attention was paid to the programme: in 1636 the Privy
Council issued detailed directions for the regulation of maltsters
and two years later the assize judges were charged to shake up
local enforcement of the orders.[73] Though the Council was preoccupied with other business — especially after 1634 with ship
money — the provision of food supplies and poor relief, the concern with employment and vagrants were not entirely neglected.
Fletcher doubts whether the Council, even when it intervened,
was very effective. Apart from the assize judges, the Council had
no source of information other than JPs and deputy lieutenants,
and the assize judges themselves had little capacity and showed
little inclination to act as intendants. There is certainly some truth
in this, as some of the rating disputes over ship money reveal; but,
as they also suggest, only half-truth. For when the Privy Council
issued unequivocal orders, they were not breached or ignored
lightly.[74] The city of York for example kept a file of all proclamations issued so that it could promptly act on them;[75] Sir John
Poulet and others were fearful of disobeying the proclamation
forbidding gentlemen to come to London: some even sought
licences from the Lord Chamberlain to come to the capital to
consult a doctor.[76] The Council (and the Star Chamber — little
discussed here) could punish recalcitrants; usually a summons to
the Board was punishment and instilled fear enough.[77] More

importantly where the gentry were concerned, rebuke from the Council could be damaging to a man's standing in the county and expose him to his enemies: the Earl of Manchester believed that muster defaulters were disgraced in their counties when they were summoned to appear at the Board.[78] It may, moreover, not always have been apparent to contemporaries that the Council was less than well informed. In 1634, Sir Edward Montagu was advised against pursuing any enclosures against Council orders: 'The state,' he was told, 'hath a severe eye upon all these new enclosures', and of some an example was made in Star Chamber.[79] Sir John Holland warned Sir Thomas Hobart that, concerning the militia, 'The Lords I believe will listen after our diligence and there will be them at leisure to give intelligence.'[80] Such observations indicate too that, even when occasionally resident in their localities, Privy Councillors could remind their neighbours that the Council board was not only a distant authority at Whitehall.[81] Those who dwelt close to the Councils of the North or the Marches would never have needed reminding. As for the assize judges, it is clear that their capacity to act as agents of the centre was limited by their occasional and brief visits and, as Fletcher points out, by the many changes of pairing that prevented any two judges becoming well acquainted with the same areas.[82] Yet if much of the JPs' authority lay, as it is suggested, in the theatre of magistracy, in the awe generated by Quarter Sessions, we should not underestimate the power of the Assizes, the meeting with the 'lions under the throne', as an occasion for reminding JPs of the importance of their charge, their responsibility and accountability to king and council. It is somewhat curious that Fletcher emphasizes the power of legislation in prompting local action, but is sceptical of the impact of the speeches delivered by the judges. There seems no evidence to doubt that they faithfully reported the concerns delivered to them in the Lord Keeper's charge before they went on circuit; and the king evidently attributed considerable importance to it, James I on occasions giving the charge himself. The Long Parliament's desire to control who went on circuit suggests that importance was not misplaced.

These observations should qualify, not overturn, Fletcher's thesis. As he says, the provinces of England were certainly *not* governed from Whitehall.[83] But it is as important to appreciate that no monarch seems to have desired that they should be. The Book of Orders dropped what Montagu has regarded as the sinister programme for deputies from the Council to the counties;[84] no new officers were created; even ship money revived the powers of a medieval official. The crown and Council were desirous to invigorate traditional and essentially local processes and officers and moreover to assist as well as cajole them to perform their duties. Charles I regarded the assizes as a two-way process: they were 'auditories, being assemblies of the principal persons of each county'.[85] And no less true, the local magistracy looked to the judges and Council as support as well as interference. The city of Dorchester, for example, petitioned the Council for the authority to set the poor to work; it was Justice Heath's decision that enabled assessments on wealth as well as land for the poor rate.[86] Local governors could not ignore the centre, nor did they wish to. Whilst it would be foolish to imagine each Council order met with enthusiasm and speedy execution, it is unduly pessimistic to dismiss the Council's letters as directives to be treated as one saw fit. In government as in politics, locality and centre, authority and consent were interdependent.

For all the tensions between the centre and the localities in early seventeenth-century England, for all the cultural differences, the troubles that led to civil war did not, perhaps, begin there. Rather the first violent resistance to the crown came from Scotland, which (as David Stevenson once put it wryly) was 'virtually all country and no court'. In *The Road to Revolution, Scotland under Charles I*, 1625–37 (Urbana 1985) Maurice Lee, the historian of James VI and I's Scottish rule, brings out the full meaning of that phrase.[87] After James VI's succession to the English throne, there was no court in Scotland, nor any viceroy in the king's stead. James ruled his northern kingdom (which he visited only once after 1603) by pen from London. His capacity to do so stemmed from his knowledge and experience of his Scots subjects, and from the carefully cultivated personal relationships that enabled him to entrust good advisers with responsibility. Both experiences and counsel led him to proceed cautiously with changes he desired for kirk and kingdom.[88] When James I died, that experience and personal contact died with him — not least because the Duke of Hamilton preceded him, by a few weeks, to the grave. Charles I therefore succeeded to his Scottish kingdom without able advisers or any knowledge of a land he had left at three years of age, but brought to his Scottish rule, as his English, a vigour and determination for reform, order, and uniformity. His early years were disastrous: talk of large-scale revocation of lands prompted concern for the security of property; the separation of the Council and court of session posed a challenge to the aristocracy; perhaps, most of all, the (typical) failure to explain fuelled more fears than were justified. The history of Charles's Scottish rule, however, was not thenceforth the story of inevitable drift to conflict. Lee argues that when the Scots sent a delegation to protest the changes in 1626, Charles listened and in particular came to place his trust in their spokesman, the Earl of Menteith. With Menteith's counsel, Charles returned to a more cautious Jacobean style: he was persuaded to drop an unpopular scheme to revive justice eyres; he did not press the enforcement of the Articles of Perth; some fears concerning the revocations were calmed; tensions were defused. There were problems and grievances: the heavy peacetime taxation disgruntled the Scots; the squabbles over the project for a Fishing Association of Great Britain revealed how ingrained was the distrust of the Scots for the English. But during Menteith's years, the Scots had the ear of the king and Charles had an accurate source of information. In 1633, however, Menteith fell from favour — brought down by his enemies and by rivals' accusations that he was ambitious to succeed to the Scottish throne. With his fall, the only link between Charles and the Scottish aristocracy was broken.

The royal visit of 1633 served ironically to demonstrate the distance between and alienation of the king and his subjects. For Charles who had exhibited in boyhood distaste for his father's familiar, casual style appeared aloof, alien, and *English*.[89] Here *was* a clash of cultures, and one clearly apparent in the matter of liturgical preferences: Charles's insistence on Anglican rituals aroused suspicion; and for his part the visit seems to have stimulated a wish to bring the Scottish kirk more in line with England. After 1633 Charles elevated to episcopacies and the Privy Council clerics sympathetic to his wishes; he sought to endow bishoprics from monastic properties; he ordered a new prayer book for the kirk. The Earl of Traquair (who succeeded Menteith as Charles's adviser) was no friend of the bishops, but, the king's man with no powerful following of his own, he was not inclined to oppose the royal will delivered through Laud. Charles I proceeded, ignorant of the opposition to his policy. The riot of July 1637 was, in large part, the consequence of that ignorance — of a breakdown of the communications which in Menteith's years had cooled temperatures before they overheated.

Lee offers us the clearest, most persuasive account yet of the origins of the rebellion. He places the religious problem in the more important and broader context of rumours and fears: fears of the nobility for their position, resentment at enhanced clerical authority, a sense of alienation, a concern that the Prayer Book was just one step towards replacing Scottish by English customs and government. If some of the blame for not communicating those fears lay with Traquair, the responsibility, Lee concludes, must in the end rest with Charles. In Scottish more than in English history the change of monarch in 1625 was crucial. This seems undeniable, but it is not entirely clear whether the ill consequences of that change lay entirely in Charles's personality. For there was no substitute for James's many years of experience and knowledge of Scottish government; and, as time passed, there were fewer Scots in England familiar enough with their homeland to offer counsel.[90] James's passionate desire for a union of the kingdoms reflected perhaps his own sense that the union in his person was fragile. After the failure of that project, nothing brought the two nations closer together. Few Scots regularly journeyed south; English nobles and privy councillors knew nothing of the other kingdom. The Marquis of Hamilton in whom Charles placed so much affection was much more a purely *English* courtier than his father.[91] Undoubtedly, as Lee argues, in placing trust in Traquair, Charles, not for the first time, proved an inadequate judge of a good minister. But it may be that the trust he placed in the Scottish clergy proved the bigger mistake. In preparing a draft of the new Prayer Book — during which time Bishop Maxwell travelled frequently between Edinburgh and London — the bishops made little mention of obstacles or difficulties and perhaps showed more concern for their own ends than sensitivity to the situation.[92] Interestingly, Laud (whom Lee shows has been wrongly blamed for the crisis) appeared to have thought so, when he wrote in 1639 to Bishop Bramhall of Ireland: 'to live in the midst of Scotland and not to discover the grounds of these tumults, argues either extreme obstinacy or too imperious a disposition to involve the state.' Though he supported their cause, Laud had advised the Scots bishops 'to be very careful what they did . . . that they should be very moderate . . . and temper themselves from all offence. But I doubt this counsel of mine was not followed as well as it ought to have been.'[93] The bishops' eagerness to enhance their own power may have brought down the king as well as the episcopacy.

And so we come back to the central problem of the Civil War and to the central questions which it poses: was the mid-century crisis caused by religious issues, by tensions between centre and locality, by constitutional disagreement, by ideological difference, or by cultural conflict and a growing distance between the king and his confidants on the one hand and the subjects of his kingdoms on the other? There has been more work done on, more different sources consulted for, and more disagreement about such questions in the last decade than for many years. Explanations with which we were familiar and to which some were, indeed are, emotionally attached have been challenged beyond rehabilitation, but new ones have not as yet been agreed. The pages and passions expended make the task of synthesizing in textbooks or books for general readers, though increasingly necessary, increasingly difficult and hazardous. Two new books have bravely taken on the challenge. Gerald Aylmer's *Rebellion or Revolution? England*

1640–60 (Oxford, 1986), in the Opus series, is written for the general reader as well as the scholar. It is a book that characteristically makes modest — and characteristically unduly modest — claims. For not only are we offered one of the clearest narratives yet of the complex events of the 1640s and 50s (the accounts of Ireland and Scotland exhibit enviable lucidity), *Rebellion or Revolution?* quietly assimilates the new scholarship into that narrative. The word quietly is important. Whilst many of these subjects have generated heat and noise, Aylmer adopts new findings whilst remaining politely critical of extravagant claims old or new. The book is a reassuring testament to the possibility for a continuing and constructive dialogue (and we needed reminding of that). At times, it must be said, Aylmer's judiciousness is a limitation as well as a strength: we miss on some pages the heat and passion of these decades and on others we regret the author's reluctance to press his own view. But that is because Aylmer's own insights and emphases have much to contribute. That, as we are told, no one was executed for a crime of state in the 1630s might lead those who persist with the word tyranny to reflect again; that Charles might successfully have charged leaders of the Long Parliament in 1640 with treasonous dealings with the Scots, but did not, reopens the question of royal strategy and intentions; that Oxford is portrayed as a more secure base than parliamentary London raises questions about the importance of London throughout the war; the suggestion that a regency in 1649 (rather than the execution of the king) might have won more to the regime offers a fresh perspective; the observation that by the late 1650s none of Cromwell's councillors was a regicide helps to explain the collapse of the Good Old Cause. Some of these emphases and suggestions will be questioned (I found the comparison of the major generals with the assize judges curious), but, as it title suggests, *Rebellion or Revolution?* whilst pursuing a narrative never fails to ask and repose questions — both of the history of these troubled times and of those historians who would proffer too simplistic answers.

Derek Hirst's *Authority and Conflict: England, 1603–1658,* (1986) covers a wider chronological period and makes greater claims: to be a work of much original scholarship, greater detail, and more balance than any other recent study. We cannot be surprised if not all these promises are fulfilled. Yet as the first textbook written after the revisionist scholarship of the 1970s, this is a work of considerable importance and value. Hirst has read a formidable volume of material, covers economic, social, and religious history as much as politics; his narrative, if in places rather flat, is clear and his prose unconvoluted. Where he synthesizes, he often still has his points to make: the character sketch of Charles I and his values and beliefs gets closer to the king than any of the biographies;[94] the discussion of religion, the recognition of an 'Anglican commitment' as hostile to Geneva as Rome, the acknowledgement that Laud's suspicions of the puritans 'were not without foundation' valuably overturn current orthodoxies;[95] the account of 1641–3 helpfully stresses Pym's vulnerability and desperation; the discussion of the split between Presbyterians and Independents cuts effectively through an obfuscating maze of scholarship; the loonies of the 1640s and 1650s are firmly put in their place: 'The world was not turned upside down.' The account of the 1650s is less original than claimed, but the case for Cromwell trying till the end to reconcile moderation and reform (rather than 'sudden swings . . . between reform and reaction') is well argued, and the similarities between the 1650s and 1630s as identified here are illuminating.

Why then must there be some reservations about adopting *Authority and Conflict* as the standard textbook? In small part because of the slips: it is not true the 1621 parliament passed no statutes; Winwood's Christian name was Ralph not Henry; Laud did not before 1634–5 serve on all the key Privy Council committees. In part too because there are some puzzling judgements and descriptions: of Kent as an 'isolated area'; that there were no Protestant leaders at court after the death of Pembroke (what of Holland and Henrietta Maria's 'puritan followers'?).[96] The publisher's stricture on footnotes is a real problem because it does not enable Hirst to document some of his more novel or contentious points and so prevents the reader exploring them. But of most significance are the recurrent ambiguities and unresolved contradictions. To some extent these emerge from Hirst's admirable attempt to reconcile revisionist and anti-revisionist scholarship, to see the strengths in both. But there is a difference between irenicism or a middle way and trying simultaneously to have things both ways and in too many instances the latter is more evident than the former. So, for example, we are told that the Calvinist consensus was not popular but academic and yet that it was 'unravelling in the universities'; that 'after 1625 we can talk of an ideological divide', but also that 'polarization had not yet come.' Most importantly, given recent debates, Hirst wants to argue both that the old crown and parliament 'adversaries' school of historians were not wide of the mark *and* that the growth of parliament 'owed more to political crisis than to the aspirations of most members' — indeed that there was little sign even in the spring of 1640 of a parliamentary 'onslaught on the king's government.' It may be that such contradictions can be resolved, but they are not explained here; accordingly, the reader is left somewhat confused and Hirst's own position, as opposed to the views of others, remains unclear. Since his own contributions to these debates have been important and challenging, this self-denying ordinance can only be regretted.[97]

But what must be enthusiastically applauded, in *Authority and Conflict* and in *Rebellion or Revolution?*, is the attention given in general surveys to subjects which would once have found little space: to ideas, values, customs, and cultural activities as intrinsic to politics. Hirst writes of the 'informal controls' and processes that were 'the key to the maintenance of order'; he explains Charles I's beliefs in terms of his 'intense commitment to Renaissance principles of . . . symmetry'; he points to classical as well as scriptual influences upon the puritan elite; he sees in Cromwell's commission of his portrait, 'warts and all', a style which represented the ambivalence of his Protectorate. Aylmer's chapter on the quality of life during the 1640s and 1650s opens with a discussion of culture and the arts. Like Hirst, Aylmer rejects the simplistic idea of a cultural divide. Milton, he reminds us, belies any identification of puritans and parliamentarians with a plain style that rejected courtly elaborateness; there was no reversion after 1640 to architectural styles that had been fashionable before the influence of Inigo Jones. William Lely the portraitist and Samuel Cooper the miniaturist served Cromwell and Charles II. But if he shows that simplistic identifications have failed, Aylmer also points to important questions that need to be asked: how would poetry have differed without the Civil War? Would the wig, that symbol of a conspicuous expenditure absent during the 1650s, have 'come into fashion when it did without the restoration of the monarchy?' It is the pursuit of such questions that might lead to a fuller investigation of the politics of values and styles in seventeenth-century England and hence to a better understanding of the interrelationship of culture, politics, and the English Civil War.

Notes

List of abbreviations

Note: Place of publication is London, unless otherwise stated.

Add. MS	Additional Manuscript
AHR	*American Historical Review*
AO	Archives Office
APC	*Acts of the Privy Council of England*
BIHR	*Bulletin of the Institute of Historical Research*
BL	British Library
Bodl.	Bodleian Library
BJPS	*British Journal of Political Science*
Bull. John Rylands Lib.	*Bulletin of the John Rylands Library*
Cal. Stat. Pap. Dom.	*Calendar of State Papers, Domestic*
Cal. Stat. Pap. Venet.	*Calendar of State Papers, Venetian*
Camden Misc.	*Camden Miscellany*
Camden Soc.	Camden Society
Chanc. Court MS	Chancellor's Court MS
CJ	*Journals of The House of Commons*
Colleg. Mert. Reg.	Collegii Mertonensi Registrum 1567–1731
Convoc. Reg.	Convocation Register
CUL	Cambridge University Library
DNB	*Dictionary of National Biography*
ECHR	*Economic History Review*
EHR	*English Historical Review*
ELH	*English Literary History*
ELR	*English Literary Renaissance*
Hist. Polit. Thought	*History of Political Thought*
HJ	*Historical Journal*
HMC	*Historical Manuscripts Commission Report*
Huntington Lib.	Huntington Library
Hunt. Lib. Quart.	*Huntington Library Quarterly*
Int. Rev. Soc. Hist.	*International Review of Social History*

JBS	*Journal of British Studies*
JHI	*Journal of the History of Ideas*
JIH	*Journal of Interdisciplinary History*
JMH	*Journal of Modern History*
Journ. Warburg &	*Journal of the Warburg & Courtauld Institutes*
Courtauld Inst.	
Law Quart. Rev.	*Law Quarterly Review*
LC	Lord Chamberlain's Department
LJ	*Journals of The House of Lords*
Midland Hist.	*Midland History*
OED	*Oxford English Dictionary*
Oxford Hist. Soc.	*Oxford Historical Society*
PC	*Privy Council*
Polit. Science Quart.	*Political Science Quarterly*
Polit. Theory	*Political Theory*
PRO	Public Record Office
Proc. Am. Philos. Soc.	*Proceedings of the American Philosophical Society*
Proc. Brit. Acad.	*Proceedings of the British Academy*
RO	Record Office (County)
Scottish Hist. Rev.	*Scottish Historical Review*
SO	Signet Office
SP	State Papers
STC	A.W. Pollard and G. Redgrave *A Short Title Catalogue* (1926)
Studies in Eng. Lit.	*Studies in English Literature*
Surtees Soc.	Surtees Society
Thoroton Soc.	Thoroton Society
TLS	*Times Literary Supplement*
Trans. Am. Philos.	*Transactions of the American Philosophical*
Soc.	*Society*
TRHS	*Transactions of the Royal Historical Society*
UL	University Library

Chapter 1

1. The old integration of intellectual and political history was unsatisfactory in its emphasis on a canon of texts and its consequently decontextualized history of ideas. But the point remains.
2. J.G.A. Pocock, *Virtue, Commerce and History* (Cambridge, 1985), 34.
3. L. Stone, 'The Revival of Narrative: Reflections on a New Old History', *P&P*, 85 (1979), 3-24; quotation, 20.
4. For evidence of the whiggery cf. L. Stone, *The Causes of the English Revolution* (1971), especially 57, 117.
5. Cf. J.C.D. Clark's comment on the early Hanoverian revisionists in *Revolution and Rebellion* (Cambridge, 1986), 65.
6. Revealingly those who have castigated revisionists for taking the meaning and ideology out of history have also charged them with writing Jacobite or Tory history (see L. Stone, 'The Century of Revolution',

New York Review of Books, 26 February 1987. The present writer was once introduced as a 'Tory historian'). See also D. Cannadine, 'British History: Past, Present — and Future?', *P&P*, 116 (1987), 169-91.

7. For a selection of methodological essays, see Skinner, 'Meaning and Understanding in the History of Ideas', *History and Theory*, VIII (1969), 3-53; 'On Performing and Explaining Linguistic Actions', *Philosophical Quarterly*, XXI (1971), 1-21; 'Some Problems in the Analysis of Political Thought and Action', *Polit. Theory*, XXIII (1974), 277-303; Pocock: 'The History of Political Thought: A Methodological Inquiry' in P. Laslett (ed.), *Philosophy, Politics and Society* (Oxford, 1956), 183-202; *Politics, Language and Time* (1972); 'Verbalizing a Political Act: Towards a Politics of Language' *Polit. Theory*, I (1973), 27-45; 'Texts as Events', in K. Sharpe and S. Zwicker (eds), *Politics of Discourse* (Berkeley, Los Angeles and London, 1987), 21-34; 'Political Ideas as Historical Events', in M. Richter (ed.), *Political Philosophy and Political Education* (Princeton, 1980), 139-58. See also M. Foucault, *The Order of Things* (1970).

8. I refer here to Skinner's methodological injunctions. In *The Foundation of Modern Political Thought* (2 vols, Cambridge, 1978) Skinner falls back on a study of great texts. Pocock, *Virtue, Commerce and History*, 13.

9. Pocock, *Virtue, Commerce and History*, 8.

10. Pocock, *The Machiavellian Moment: Florentine Political Thought and the Atlantic Republican Tradition* (Princeton, 1975).

11. Here the stimulus has come from literary critics: see especially H. Bloom, *The Anxiety of Influence* (1973); idem, *A Map of Misreading* (New York, 1975); S. Fish, *Self-consuming Artifacts* (Berkeley, 1972).

12. Pocock, *Virtue, Commerce and History*,3; idem, 'The Commons Debates of 1628', *JHI*, 39 (1978), 329-34.

13. I. Hampsher-Monk, 'Political Languages in Time: The Work of J.G.A. Pocock', *BJPS*, 14 (1984), 89-116, esp. 107; Pocock, *Virtue, Commerce and History*, 4.

14. Pocock, *Virtue, Commerce and History*, 4.

15. W. Camden, 'The Antiquity and Office of the Earl Marshal of England', in T. Hearne (ed.), *A Collection of Curious Discourses* (2 vols, 1771), II, 90; K. Sharpe, *Sir Robert Cotton: History and Politics in Early Modern England* (Oxford, 1979), 21-4; B. Jonson 'Timber or Discoveries', in C.H. Herford and P. Simpson (eds), *Ben Jonson Works* (11 vols, Oxford, 1925-52), VIII, 621; A. Barton, *Ben Jonson Dramatist* (Cambridge, 1984), ch.8.

16. A. Lake, *Sermons with Some Religious and Divine Meditations* (1629), 'A Short View of the life and virtues of the Author'. Cf. Puttenham's idea of language arising from consent, and Milton's description of language as an 'instrument', *OED* 'Language'.

17. I. Hampsher-Monk, 'Political Language, in Time', 89-116, esp. 109.

18. J.H. Tully, 'The Pen is a Mighty Sword: Quentin Skinner's Analysis of Politics', *BJPS*, 13 (1983), 489-510, esp. 505.

19. Q. Skinner, *The Foundations of Modern Political Thought*. Cf. the methodological articles cited above, n.6, and see Tully, art. cit.
20. Pocock's and Skinner's approach appears to be premised on the belief that experience and language are concurrent.
21. J.E. Toews, 'Intellectual History After The Linguistic Turn: The Autonomy of Meaning and the Irreducibility of Experience', *AHR*, 92 (1987), 879–907, esp. 898.
22. Tully, art. cit., 491.
23. Pocock, *Virtue, Commerce and History*, introduction. Pocock does not explain the place of aesthetic or cultural practices in his approach to the history of political thought. This is not to say that Pocock's methodology cannot accommodate these non-verbal texts; only to observe that hitherto it has not extended to them.
24. The inspiration here has come principally from C. Geertz; see esp. *The Interpretation of Cultures* (1975).
25. W.J. Bouwsma, 'Intellectual History in the 1980s', *JIH*, XII (1981), 279–91, quotation, 288.
26. A.O. Lovejoy, *The Great Chain of Being* (Cambridge, Mass., 1936); E.M.W. Tillyard, *The Elizabethan World Picture* (1943); W.H. Greenleaf, *Order, Empiricism and Politics* (1964); R. Eccleshall, *Order and Reason in Politics* (Oxford, 1978).
27. S.L. Bethell, *The Cultural Revolution of the Seventeenth Century* (1952), 45.
28. J.P. Kenyon (ed.), *The Stuart Constitution* (Cambridge, 1986), 193–5.
29. D.G. Hale, *The Body Politic: A Political Metaphor in Renaissance English Literature* (The Hague, 1971), 119.
30. See below, 51–2.
31. The relationship of attitudes to animals and social and political ideas has recently been explored in K. Thomas, *Man and the Natural World, Changing Attitudes in England, 1500–1800* (1983) and H. Ritvo, *The Animal Estate: The English and other Creatures in the Victorian Age* (Cambridge, Mass., 1987).
32. Below, 35–9.
33. H. Valentine, *God Save The King* (1639), 18.
34. See *CJ*, I, 139 and the excerpt in Kenyon, *Stuart Constitution*, 10.
35. Trial speeches offer another rich source for the specific assertion of norms; in so far as the approach suggested here is concerned, they have been neglected.
36. Hampsher-Monk, art. cit, 105; J.H. Salmon, *The French Religious Wars in English Political Thought* (Oxford, 1959), preface.
37. The phrase 'timeless trope' often used to designate the importance of an idea is as unhelpful as it is problematic. Cf. below, 35. For a fine example of the historian's capacity to historicize the timeless trope see J. Fliegelman, *Prodigals and Pilgrims: American Revolution Against Patriarchal Authority* (Cambridge, 1982).
38. B. Sk., *Counsel to the Husband* (1608), 53. Cf. below, 58–9.
39. K. Sharpe, 'Cavalier Critic?: The Ethics and Politics of Thomas Carew's Poetry' in K. Sharpe and S. Zwicker (eds), *Politics of Discourse*, 117–46; below, Ch. 9.

40. B. Jonson, *Hymenaei*, 1. 17, *Works VII*, 209, and see S. Pearl, 'Sounding to Present Occasions: Jonson's Masques of 1620–25' in D. Lindley (ed.), *The Court Masque* (Manchester, 1984), 60–77.

41. K. Sharpe, *Criticism and Compliment: The Politics of Literature in the England of Charles I* (Cambridge, 1987), 95–6.

42. C. Hill, *Intellectual Origins of the English Revolution* (Oxford, 1965), passim; idem, 'Censorship and English Literature', *Collected Essays* (Brighton, 1985), I, 32–71.

43. See e.g., Sharpe, *Criticism and Compliment*, 36–9, 290–7; S. Lambert, 'The Printers and the Government, 1604–37' in R. Myers and M. Harris (eds), *Aspects of Printing from 1600* (Oxford, 1987), 1–29 (I am grateful to Shelia Lambert for a copy of this important essay); B. Worden, 'Literature and Political Censorship in Early Modern England' in A.C. Duke and C.A. Tamse (eds), *Too Mighty To Be Free* (Zutphen, 1988), 45–62. I am grateful to Blair Worden for allowing me to read this important essay in advance of publication. Annabel Patterson in *Censorship and Interpretation* (Madison, Wisconsin, 1984) writes, I now think, too much from an assumption that censorship was widely practised, but demonstrates how it was circumvented.

44. B. Tierney, *Religion, Law and the Growth of Constitutional Thought 1150–1650* (Cambridge, 1982).

45. D. Norbrook, '*Macbeth* and the Politics of Historiography', *Politics of Discourse*, 78–116. Cf. J.H. Burns, 'The Political Ideas of George Buchanan', *Scottish Hist. Rev*, 30 (1951), 60–8; H.R. Trevor-Roper, *George Buchanan and the Ancient Scottish Constitution* (*EHR*, Supplement 3, 1966).

46. J.P. Sommerville, *Politics and Ideology in England 1603–1640* (1986), see below, 283–8.

47. Cf. J. Daly, 'Early Stuart England was not a congenial place for the production of the kind of mature theory which the latter part of the century has taught scholars to look for', 'Cosmic Harmony and Political Thinking in Early Stuart England', *Trans. Am. Philos. Soc.*, 69 (1979), 3.

48. T. Hobbes, *Leviathan* ed. M. Oakeshott (Oxford, n.d.), 5.

49. T. Taylor, *The Mappe of Moses, or A Guide for Governors* (1629), esp. 7–12.

50. Daly, 'Cosmic Harmony', 26.

51. J. Robinson, *Observations, Divine and Morall, for the furthering of knowledg and vertue* (1625), 65.

52. A. Fisher, *A Defence of the Liturgie of the Church of England or Booke of Common Prayer* (1630), 116. Sir Robert Filmer preserved the manuscript of the treatise for publication (epistle dedicatory).

53. H. King, *An Exposition Upon The Lords Prayer* (1628), 18.

54. G. Fleming, *Magnificence Exemplified and the Repair of St Paul's Exhorted Unto* (1634), 21. Fleming defined 'gentem nostram, that is church and commonwealth' and urged that both be preferred above individual considerations.

55. F. Levy, *Tudor Historical Thought* (San Marino, 1967); J. Bruce and

T.T. Perowne (eds), *Correspondence of Matthew Parker* (Parker Soc, 1853).

56. W. Struther, *A Looking Glasse for Princes and People* (1632), 84-6.
57. Below, 28-31.
58. R. Bolton, *The Saints Sure and Perpetual Guide* (1634), 126-9.
59. Sharpe, *Criticism and Compliment*, 71.
60. R.D. Bedford, *The Defence of Truth: Herbert of Cherbury and the Seventeenth Century* (Manchester, 1979), 101. This is an important work which deserves to be better known.
61. Ibid., 104-5.
62. Below, 20-31.
63. The phrase is from J. Davenport, *A Royal Edict for Military Exercises* (1629), 2. See also 6-7.
64. A.B. Ferguson, *The Articulate Citizen and the English Renaissance* (Durham, NC, 1965) 349. Ferguson documents the awareness among some writers of economic and private interest and yet the tenacity of traditional concepts and values.
65. Kenyon, *Stuart Constitution*, 15.
66. E.g. L.S. Marcus, *The Politics of Mirth* (Chicago, 1986), esp. 33. Cf. J. Montagu, *The Works of the Most High and Mighty Prince James* (1616), 212. James I saw the preference for private interest as a rejection of the 'mother, the Commonwealth'.
67. N. Faret, *The Honest Man or The Art to Please in Court* (translated into English 1632), 125-6; George Wither went so far as to argue that injustice to an individual might be defensible in the name of the common good, *Britain's Remembrancer* (1628), 236.
68. See OED 'Private', 'privacy' and J. Goldbert, *James I and the Politics of Literature* (Baltimore, 1983), passim.
69. Ferguson, *Articulate Citizen*, passim.
70. Below, 61-3.
71. Kenyon, *Stuart Constitution*, 240.
72. J. de Santa Maria, *Christian Policie or the Christian Commonwealth* (1632), 105-9. Daly, 'Cosmic Harmony', 13.
73. A. Fawkner, *Eiphnotonia or the Pedegree of Peace* (1630), epistle dedicatory.
74. The OED's first entry for 'constitution' in the political sense is 1610.
75. M.A. Judson, *The Crisis of the Constitution* (New York, 1971 edn), 84. Cf. P.G. Burgess, 'Custom, Reason and the Common Law: English Jurisprudence 1600-1650' (Ph.D. thesis, Cambridge University, 1988), 192-7.
76. Cf. the point of R.M. Smuts in *Court Culture and the Origins of a Royalist Tradition in Early Stuart England* (Pennsylvania, 1987), 260.
77. E. Forset, *A Comparative Discourse of the Bodies Natural and Politique* (1606), 10.
78. Aristotle, *Ethics*, Bk II, ch.6, ed. J.A.K. Thomson (Harmondsworth, 1955), 65.
79. R. Knevet, *TPAT TIKON or A Discourse of Militarie Discipline* (1628), f.F2.

80. R. Braithwaite, *The English Gentleman* (1630), 306.
81. See below, 46.
82. C.H. McIlwain, (ed.), *The Political Works of James I* (Cambridge, Mass., 1918), 291.
83. Sharpe, *Criticism and Compliment*, ch.6.
84. See R. Tuck, 'Power and Authority in Seventeenth Century England' *HJ*, XVII (1974), 43-61.
85. Daly, 'Cosmic Harmony', 10.
86. J. Donne, *Essays in Divinity*, ed. E.M. Simpson (Oxford, 1951), 80-1; and F. Oakley, 'Jacobean Political Theology: The Absolute and Ordinary Powers of the King', *Journ. Hist. Ideas*, XIX (1968), 323-46, esp. 337-40.
87. *Cal. Stat. Pap. Dom. 1640-1*, 542.
88. F. Greville, *Poems of Monarchy*, in A.B. Grosart (ed.), *The Works of Fulke Greville* (4 vols, 1870), I, 92; cf. James I to his son, 'You are rather born to onus than honos', Basilikon Doron, *Works of James I* (1616), 138.
89. F. Bacon, *The Advancement of Learning*, Book 2, ch.XXI, sections 7-10, ed. G.W. Kitchen (1965), 163-6.
90. O. Feltham, *Resolves, divine, morall, politicall* (1623), 30. It is worth emphasizing the accountability in divine-right theories of monarchy.
91. P. Scott, *A Table-Book for Princes* (1621), 10-11, 65.
92. Ibid., 6.
93. W. Struther, *A Looking Glasse for Princes and People* (1632), 14. Struther, a preacher of Edinburgh, dedicated his thanksgiving sermon for the birth of Prince Charles to the King.
94. R.C. Johnson et al. (eds) *Commons Debates 1628*, II (New Haven, 1977), 3.
95. P. Bethune, *The Counsellor of Estate* (1634), 77.
96. P. Massinger, *The Emperour of the East* (1632), sig. E1, P. Edwards (ed.), *The Plays and Poems of Philip Massinger* (5 vols, Oxford, 1976), III, 432.
97. Scot, *Table-Book*, 12.
98. Forset, *Comparative Discourse*, 4; cf. Scot, *Table-Book*, 4: 'scepters are not given unto kings (tyrant-like) to abuse their authority, but to be strict observers of the laws they impose upon others'.
99. J. Bodin, *The Six Bookes of a Commonweale*, translated by R. Knolles, 1606, ed. K.D. Macrae (Cambridge, Mass., 1962); G.L. Mosse, 'The Influence of Bodin's Republique in English Political Thought, *Medievala & Humanistica*, 5 (1948), 73-83. Cf. Burgess, 'Custom, Reason and The Common Law', 194-7.
100. T. Hobbes, *Eight Bookes of the Pelopennesian Warre written by Thucydides*, preface to the reader; I owe this reference to G. Oestreich, *Neostoicism and the Early Modern State* (Cambridge, 1982), 114.
101. J. de Santa Maria, *Christian Policie*, 164.
102. Bastwick, below, 80, n.23.
103. Cf. K. Sharpe, *Faction and Parliament* (Oxford, 1978; 2nd edn,

London, 1985), 37-42.

104. See, for example, *The Works of Joseph Hall* (1628), 231: 'As where no sovereignty so where no counsel is, the people fail; and contrarily where many counsellors are, there is health . . .'.

105. Santa Maria, *Christian Policie*, 7; cf. 60-1, 76, 164, 273.

106. Ibid., 7; G. More, *Principles for Young Princes* (1611), e.g. 7, 29-30, 55-7, 59-61.

107. The *Vindiciae* and the *De Iure* were available in Latin from 1579. The *De Iure* went to three editions by 1580. Thomas Wentworth collected in his youth aphorisms from works which included Duplessis Mornay, J.W. Stoye, *English Travellers Abroad 1604-1667* (1952), 64. See also J.H. Salmon, *French Religious Wars*; and E.H. Kossman and A.F. Mellink (eds), *Texts Concerning the Revolt of the Netherlands* (Cambridge, 1974).

108. See J.E. Phillips, 'George Buchanan and the Sidney Circle', *Hunt. Lib. Quart.*, XII (1948), 23-56; W.D. Briggs, 'Political Ideas in Sidney's Arcadia', *Studies in Philology*, XXVIII (1931), 137-61; D. Norbrook, *Poetry and Politics in the English Renaissance* (1984), 15, 96ff.

109. Salmon, *French Religious Wars*, 12; D.G. Hale, *The Body Politic* (The Hague, 1971), 80.

110. See M. Judson, *The Crisis of the Constitution* (New York, 1971 edn), 83-4; E.O. Smith, 'Crown and Commonwealth: A Study in the official Elizabethan Doctrine of the Prince', *Proc. Am. Philos. Soc.*, 66, 8 (1976), 30-3.

111. J. Stoye, *English Travellers Abroad 1604-1667* rightly illustrates the easier contacts between England and the Huguenots in the reign of James I, but the point here is that political circumstances in England, as in France itself, were less conducive to *radical* political thought.

112. See C.H. McIlwain, *The Political Works of James I*, introduction.

113. D. Norbrook, 'Macbeth and the Politics of Historiography', 82; K. Sharpe, *Sir Robert Cotton*, 89-90.

114. P. Holmes, *Resistance and Compromise: The Political Thought of the Elizabethan Catholics* (Cambridge, 1982); I owe this reference to Keith Thomas.

115. P. Bethune, *The Counsellor of Estate* (1634), quotation, 2.

116. There was, for example, little discussion of sovereignty in early Stuart England; and see Knolles, *Six Bookes* and Mosse 'Influence of Bodin'.

117. J.F. Le Petit, *The Low Country Commonwealth*, translated by E. Grimestone (1609), 303.

118. J.H. Salmon, *French Religious Wars*, 12.

119. See P. Donald, 'The King and the Scottish Troubles, 1637-1641', (Ph.D. thesis, Cambridge University, 1988).

120. Kenyon, *Stuart Constitution*, 264.

121. See ch.8 below.

122. For an interesting discussion of the emergence of this relativism see B. Shapiro, *Probability and Certainty in Seventeenth Century England* (Princeton, 1983).

123. A. Pagden, *The Fall of Natural Man: The American Indian and the Origins of Comparative Ethnology* (Cambridge, 1982).

124. Sir Thomas Herbert, *A Relation of Some Yeares Travaile Begun Anno 1626 into Afrique and the Greater Asia* (1634). Herbert unfavourably contrasted the behaviour of Madagascan women who revealed their pudenda for food with the modesty of the English (p.15)!

125. H. Lord, *A Display of Two Foreign Sects in the East Indies* (1630), 93.

126. Ibid., 95.

127. P. Heylyn, *Microcosmos: A Little Description of the Great World* (Oxford, 1629). See, for example, the nationalism on pages 460–90.

128. *A Relation of the Successefull Beginnings of the Lord Baltemore's Plantation in Maryland* (1634), 7, 8.

129. Heylyn, *Microcosmos*, 771.

130. M. de Montaigne, *The Essayes or morall, politike and millitarie discourses* (1603).

131. R.D. Bedford, *The Defence of Truth*, 43.

132. J. Florio, *Essayes written in French by Michael Lord of Montaigne* (1613 edn), prefatory poem by Daniel, sig. A3.

133. Bedford, *Defence of Truth*, 50.

134. Shapiro, *Probability and Certainty*, 17.

135. Like other 'revisionists', I have been charged with idealizing the early Stuart age. From the whig perspective of inevitable conflict, however, any depiction of the seventeenth century in its own terms is open to the charge of idealizing.

136. J. Donne, 'An Anatomy of the world: the first Anniversary'.

137. T. Scot, *Philomythie or Philomythologie wherein Outlandish Birds, Beasts and Fishes are taught to speake true English* . . . (1616), sig. A2. The reference to Ignatius's brood is to the Jesuits who justified resistance to heretics and excommunicated monarchs. Cf. *Ignatius His Conclave, or his inthronizacon in a late eleccon in Hell* entered in the Stationers company register in 1611 (III, 208).

138. Cited in D.P. Norford, 'Microcosm and Macrocosm in Seventeenth Century literature', *JHI* XXXVIII (1977), 409–28, 416. Cf. the battle of Romans and Carthaginians that raged at night around Ben Jonson's great toe, Barton, *Jonson*, x.

139. E.T. *The Lawes Resolution of Women's Rights* (1632), 377.

140. See M. Walzer, 'On the Role of Symbolism in Political Thought', *Polit. Science Quart.*, 82 (1967), 191–204, especially 202; S. Greenblatt, 'Invisible Bullets: Renaissance Authority and its Subversion', *Glyph*, 8 (1981), 20–61.

141. F. Heal, 'The Idea of Hospitality in Early Modern England', *P&P*, 102 (1984), 86–93; L.S. Marcus, *Politics of Mirth*, 143 and passim.

142. *Works of James I*, 211.

143. G. Wither, *Britain's Remembrancer* (1628), 221–4, 229. Though he recognizes these problems, Wither throughout sees their solution in the reassertion of traditional ideals. This is an important work which deserves a full discussion.

144. See, for example, N. Carpenter, *Achitophel, or the Picture of a wicked Politician* (1629), 10: 'He that goes about to persuade a multitude they are not so well governed as they ought to be shall sooner want argument than attention'; M.R., *Micrologia, Characters or Essays* (1629), 11: on the popularity of songs 'interlarded with anything against the state'.

145. See below, 59-61.

146. Wentworth's speech as Lord President of the North, December 1628, Kenyon, *Stuart Constitution*, 16. Ironically this was one of the principal charges against Wentworth at his own trial for treason, article VII, F. Hargrave, *A Complete Collection of State Trials* (11 vols, 1776-81), I, 723.

147. J. de Santa Maria, *Christian Policie*, 21.

148. Walzer, 'Symbolism', 202; Greenblatt, 'Invisible Bullets', passim.

149. C. Geertz, 'Centers, Kings and Charisma: Reflections or the Symbolics of Power', in J. Ben-David and T.N. Clark (eds), *Culture and Its Creators* (1977), 168.

150. Hale, *Body Politic*, 83; John Carey has related these tensions to Hooker's style, 'Sixteenth and Seventeenth Century Prose', in C. Ricks (ed.), *English Poetry and Prose 1540-1674* (1970), 379-90, esp. 384-7.

151. See Barton, *Ben Jonson*, ch.9; on the significance of the broken circle see the forthcoming biography of Jonson by David Riggs. I am grateful to Professor Riggs for showing me this important study in advance of publication and for stimulating discussions of Jonson at Stanford University. See also L.A. Beaurline, *Jonson and Elizabethan Comedy* (San Marino, 1978).

152. I do not wish here to separate representation from reality, but rather to stress their interaction.

153. Smuts, *Court Culture*, 193.

154. de Santa Maria, *Christian Policie*, 21.

155. Norford, 'Microcosm and Macrocosm', 427.

156. Hale, *Body Politic*, 110.

157. M.C. Bradbrook, *The School of Night: A Study in the Literary Relationships of Sir Walter Ralegh* (Cambridge, 1936), 19.

158. On Herbert, see Bedford, *Defence of Truth*; on Jones, J. Lees-Milne, *The Age of Inigo Jones* (1953), 52; on Arundel, below, 201-6; on Suckling and Davenant, Sharpe, *Criticism and Compliment*, 71-2 and J. Suckling, *An Account of Religion by Reason* (1646); on Falkland, H.R. Trevor-Roper, 'The Great Tew Circle', in *Catholics, Anglicans and Puritans* (1987), 166-230.

159. Scot, *Philomythie*, sig. E3; cf. J. Earle, *Microcosmographie* (1630), 53.

160. W. Pemble, *A Plea for Grace* (1629), 133.

161. *Philomythie*, sig. E3.

162. R. Braithwaite, *The English Gentleman* (1630), 97.

163. A. Stafford, *The Guide of Honour* (1634), 16.

164. See Smuts, *Court Culture*, 222-34.

165. Thomas Wentworth to George Butler, November 1636, in W.

Knowler (ed.), *The Earl of Strafford's Letters and Despatches* (2 vols, 1739), II, 39; D. Howarth, *Lord Arundel and His Circle* (1985), 85–6; cf. below, 293.

166. Smuts, *Court Culture*, 233.

167. It is worthy of note that in N.O., *An Apology of English Arminianisme* (1634), Arminius speaks with more control and reason than 'Enthusiastus'.

168. Cited by Bedford, *Defence of Truth*, 199.

169. M. Casaubon, *Marcus Aurelius Antoninus His Meditations* (1634); the epistle dedicatory told Laud that in reading them he would read himself.

170. R. Harris, *The Way to True Happinesse* (1632), 4–5.

171. Knowler, *Strafford Letters*, II, 170; Bishop Hall wrote against the tendency to stoicism: 'Not Athens must teach . . . but Jerusalem', *The Works of Joseph Hall* (1628), 73.

172. Smuts, *Court Culture*, 233.

173. C. Dow, *Innovations Unjustly Charged upon the Present Church and State* (1637), 10. Cf. Wither's concern in *Britain's Remembrancer* to prove that the plague did not, as others were claiming, arise from natural causes.

174. A. Grosse, *Two Sermons* (1632); R. James, *A Sermon Delivered in Oxford* (1630), sig. F2.

175. Sharpe, *Criticism and Compliment*, 262, 300; Smuts, *Court Culture*, passim.

176. Bedford, *Defence of Truth*, 40.

177. E. D[acres], *Nicholas Machiavel's Prince* (1640), but even then 'with some animadversions noting and taxing his errors'; *Machiavels Discourses upon the first decade of T. Livius* (1636).

178. See F. Raab, *The English Face of Machiavelli* (1964).

179. Machiavelli was widely read at Oxford; see M. Curtis, *Oxford and Cambridge in Transition 1558–1642* (Oxford, 1959), 119, 137.

180. See for this last point, Q. Skinner, *Machiavelli* (Oxford, 1981), 46.

181. Cf. Sharpe and Zwicker, *Politics of Discourse*, 19–20.

182. J.H. Hexter, *The Vision of Politics on the Eve of the Reformation* (New York, 1973), 210–11 and chs 3 and 4, passim.

183. Raab, *English Face of Machiavelli*, 70–6; N. Orsini, *Bacono e Machiavelli* (Genova, 1936); J.G.A. Pocock, *The Machiavellian Moment*, 355–7, 386, 388.

184. Sharpe, *Sir Robert Cotton*, 233–4; F.J. Levy, *Tudor Historical Thought* (San Marino, 1967), 196–9.

185. *Machiavells Dogge* (1617). The classic denunciation of Machiavelli was Innocent Gentillet, *A Discourse Upon the Meanes of Wel Governing against N. Machiavell* (1602). These extracted maxims, with Gentillet's rebuttals, were the only form in which Machiavelli was translated into English prior to 1640. I owe this point to David Riggs.

186. G. More, *Principles for Young Princes* (1611), 69.

187. Scot, *Philomythie*, sig. A4. Mattaeus Tortus was Cardinal Bellarmine's almoner, under whose name Bellarmine had published his

Response to James I's *Apology for the Oath of Allegiance*. At James's command, Bishop Andrewes replied to this work in his *Tortura Torti sive ad Matthei Torti Librum Responsio* (1609). Scot casts him as a Machiavellian figure, as Jesuits were often so branded by Protestant polemicists.

188. See jacket for this frontispiece.
189. *The Uncasing of Machivils Instructions to His Son* (1613), 16.
190. Ibid., 29ff.
191. Ibid., sig. G4 (the work is curiously paginated).
192. *Nicholas Machiavel's Prince*, epistle to the reader.
193. Ibid., 121, my italics.
194. NB. O. Feltham, *Resolves, Divine, Moral, Politicall* (1628 edn), 9–10: 'I find many that are called Puritans; yet few or none that will own the name. Whereof the reason sure is this; that 'tis for the most part held a name of infamy, and is so new that it hath scarcely yet obtained a definition; nor is it an apellation derived from one man's name, whose tenets we may find digested into a volume: whereby we do much err in the application. It imports a kind of excellency above another . . . As he is more generally in these times taken, I suppose we may call him a church rebel, or one that would exclude order that this brain might rule.'
195. M. Walzer, *The Revolution of the Saints* (1966).
196. Notably N.R.N. Tyacke, 'Puritanism, Arminianism and Counter-Revolution' in C.R.S. Russell (ed.), *The Origins of the English Civil War* (1973), 119–43; idem, *Anti-Calvinists* (Oxford, 1987). For an effective challenge see P. White, 'The Rise of Arminianism Reconsidered', *P&P*, 101 (1983), 34–54; S. Lambert, 'Richard Montagu, Arminianism and Censorship', a vitally important paper which awaits publication. I am grateful to Shelia Lambert for an early view of this paper.
197. Bedford, *Defence of Truth*, 143.
198. P. Sidney, *Apology for Poetry*, ed. G. Shepherd (Manchester, 1973).
199. H. Burton, *The Christian's Bulwarke Against Satan's Battery* (1632), 2; W. Prynne, *The Church of England's Old Antithesis To New Arminianism* (1629), sig. C2.
200. H.R. Trevor-Roper, 'Milton in Politics', in *Catholics, Anglicans and Puritans*, ch.5; J.E.C. Hill, *The World Turned Upside Down* (1972).
201. Cf. M. Judson, *Crisis of the Constitution*, ch.8, esp. 321–7.
202. James I's speech to parliament, 21 March 1610, Kenyon, *Stuart Constitution*, 12.
203. For an earlier study, see D. Little, *Religion, Order and Law: A Study in Pre-Revolutionary England* (Oxford, 1970).
204. L. Damrosch, 'Hobbes as Reformation Theologian: Implications of the free-will Controversy', *JHI*, XL (1979), 339–52, esp. 350.
205. P. Collinson, *The Religion of Protestants* (Oxford, 1983), ch.5.
206. McIlwain, *Works of James I*, 274; Sharpe, *Criticism and Compliment*, 70, 245–7. In the Basilikon Doron, James wrote of the puritans: 'before that any of their grounds be impugned, let King, people, law and all be trod under foot', *Works of James I* (1616), 143.

207. Cf. Marcus, *Politics of Mirth*.
208. A point made by Sir Philip Warwick, *Memoires of the Reign of King Charles I* (1701), 74. I shall be developing this argument in *The Personal Rule of Charles I*.
209. P. Studley, *The Looking-Glasse of Schisme* (1634).
210. Feltham, *Resolves* (1628), 10-11.
211. Robert Saunderson, *Twelve Sermons Preached* (1632), I, 26; cf. his reference to Arminius's corrupt doctrine, ibid., 35.
212. E.g. W. Lamont, *Richard Baxter and the Millenium* (1979).
213. A.F. Scott Pearson, *Church and State: Political Aspects of Sixteenth Century Puritanism* (Cambridge, 1928), 37.
214. J.P., *Christ's Confession and Complaint Concerning His Kingdom and Servants* (1629), 29-30.
215. Ibid., 70; for a refutation of this argument see below, 57.
216. *The Fall of Babylon* (Amsterdam, 1634), preface to the reader.
217. Cf. Hale, *Body Politic*, 8.
218. Sommerville, *Politics and Ideology*, 12.
219. R. Tuck, *Natural Rights Theories* (Cambridge, 1979), 144.
220. S. Fish, *Is There a Text in This Class? The Authority of Interpretive Communities* (Cambridge, Mass., 1980).
221. Pocock, *Virtue, Commerce and History*, 21-2.
222. Ibid., 22.
223. Above, 23; James I tore out the Protestation at a Council meeting to which MPs were summoned with the journal, *Cal. Stat. Pap. Dom. 1619-23*, 326.
224. Sharpe, *Sir Robert Cotton*, 80-2, 144-6; for Coke, *Cal. Stat. Pap. Dom. 1629-31*, 490; *HMC Cowper* II, 266. Cf. *Cal. Stat. Pap. Dom. 1631-3*, 567; PRO PC 2/42/419. I am pursuing this official concern with manuscripts further in *The Personal Rule of Charles I*.
225. Sharpe and Zwicker, *Politics of Discourse*, 12-13. Eccleshall has shown that after the Restoration, because Hooker's *Laws of Ecclesiastical Polity* had been used to justify opposition to Charles I, attempts were made to deny its authenticity. R. Eccleshall, 'Richard Hooker and the Peculiarities of the English: the Reception of the Ecclesiastical Polity in the Seventeenth and Eighteenth Centuries', *Hist. Polit. Thought*, 2 (1981), 63-117, 75.
226. Tuck, *Natural Rights*, 63.
227. C.B. Schmitt, *Aristotle and the Renaissance* (Cambridge, Mass., 1983), idem; *John Case and Aristotelianism in Renaissance England* (Kingston, Ontario, 1983). I am grateful to the late Charles Schmitt for stimulating discussions on the reception of Aristotle in England.
228. Schmitt, *Aristotle*, 61.
229. Ibid., 36, 89.
230. Bedford, *Defence of Truth*, 20.
231. Schmitt, *Aristotle*, 113.
232. Cited by Bedford, *Defence of Truth*, 148.
233. L.B. Campbell, 'The Use of Historical Patterns in the Reign of Elizabeth', in L.B. Wright (ed.), *Collected Papers of Lily B. Campbell*

(New York, 1928), 355; idem, *Shakespeare's Histories: Mirrors of Elizabethan Policy* (San Marino, 1947).

234. E. Edwards, *Libraries and Founders of Libraries* (1864), 164-5; another example is James I's interpretation of Revelations, *A Paraphrase upon the Revelation* (in *Works of James I* (1616), 7-80).

235. H.R. Trevor-Roper, *Queen Elizabeth's First Historian: William Camden and the Beginnings of English 'Civil History'* (1971).

236. See C. Geertz, 'Centers, Kings and Charisma', 150-71.

237. Marcus, *Politics of Mirth*, 11.

238. D.M. Bergeron, *Shakespeare's Romances and the Royal Family* (Lawrence, Kansas, 1985); see below, 280-3.

239. See, for example, Basilikon Doron, *Political Works of James I*, 18; K. Sharpe, 'The Image of Virtue, the Court and Household of Charles I', in D. Starkey (ed.), *The English Court* (1987), 226-60, esp. 258; below, Ch. 5.

240. P. Scot, *A Table-Booke for Princes* (1621), 9.

241. R. Powell, *The Life of Alfred* (1634), 'To the Reader'; cf. Machiavelli's dedicatory epistle to Lorenzo Medici in *The Prince*.

242. Powell's Life of Alfred is '*together with a Parallel of our Soveraign Lord K. Charles*'.

243. See A. Barton, 'Harking Back to Elizabeth: Ben Jonson and Caroline Nostalgia', *ELH*, 48 (1981), 701-31; see, for example, D. Primrose, *A Chaine of Pearle: or a Memoriall of the peerles Graces and Heroick Vertues of Queene Elizabeth* (1630).

244. T. Heywood, *England's Elizabeth, Her Life and Troubles* (1632).

245. Christopher Hill recently described the ideas of Thomas Carew as 'banal', evidently because they were conventional, *TLS*, 1 January 1988, 17.

246. See K.A. McEuen, *Classical Influence Upon the Tribe of Ben* (New York, 1968); T.M. Greene, *The Light in Troy: Imitation and Discovery in Renaissance Poetry* (New Haven, 1982); R.W. Peterson, *Imitation and Praise in the Poems of Ben Jonson* (New Haven, 1981).

247. Oestreich, *Neo-Stoicism*, 40.

248. I am grateful to John Morrill for stimulating my thinking about this question.

249. M.S. Rostvig, *The Happy Man: Studies in the Metamorphosis of a Classical Ideal* (New York, 1962 edn), 101.

250. Smuts, *Court Culture*, 113.

251. N. Faret, *The Honest Man* (1632), 404-5.

252. C. Edmondes, *Observations upon Caesar's Commentaries* (1609), prefatory verse; in his own dedication to the prince, Edmondes reminded Henry that his father James I had recommended Caesar in his *Basilikon Doron*.

253. Edmondes, *Observations*, prefatory verses.

254. Ibid., sig. A5.

255. Ibid., 40.

256. P. Heylyn, *Augustus* (1632), 45, 50; NB. also 126, 150, 186, 223-4.

257. See Peterson, *Imitation and Praise*. Structuralist and post-

structuralist criticism has made us more sensitive to the politics of generic adaption and manipulation. See D. Norbrook, *Poetry and Politics in the English Renaissance* (1984); below, 269–71.

258. S. Birkbeck, *The Protestants Evidence* (1634), 64–5.

259. G. Chaucer, *The Ploughman's Tale Shewing by the doctrine and lives of the Romish Clergie that the Pope is antichrist* (1606).

260. Primrose, *A Chain of Pearle* (1630); above, 35.

261. A. Patterson, 'Fables of Power' in Sharpe and Zwicker (eds), *Politics of Discourse*, 271–96.

262. Ibid., 295–6.

263. T. Scot, *Philomythie*, C2ᵛ–C3.

264. Ibid.

265. Smuts, *Court Culture*, ch.3.

266. Ibid., 189.

267. J.H. Salmon, *French Religious Wars*, 17. This was an English edition of the fourth part.

268. B. Worden, 'Marvell, Cromwell, and the Horatian Ode', *Politics of Discourse*, 162–7.

269. Sharpe, *Sir Robert Cotton*, 246. It is surprising how little use is made of the chronological cards of the STC for this purpose.

270. Tuck, *Natural Rights*, 125.

271. I. Box, 'Bacon's *Essays*: from Political Science to Political Prudence', *Hist. Polit. Thought* 3 (1982), 31–50, esp. 37.

272. E.W. Talbert, *The Problem of Order* (Chapel Hill, 1962), 7.

273. Smuts, *Court Culture*, 26.

274. G. More, *Principles for Young Princes* (1611). See R. Strong, *Henry Prince of Wales and England's Lost Renaissance* (1986); below, 288–91.

275. P. Pelletier, *A Lamentable Discourse* (1610). The interplay of general axioms and the specific moment characterizes this work.

276. P. Matthieu, *The Powerfull Favorite or the Life of Aelius Sejanus* (Paris, 1628); Sir Francis Hubert, *The Deplorable Life and Death of Edward II* (1628).

277. Cambridge Univ. Lib. MS Dd 12, 21 f.99; F. Thompson, *Magna Carta, its Role in the Making of the English Constitution 1300–1629* (Minneapolis, 1948), 324.

278. The *Deplorable Life* was first written in Elizabeth's reign, but was refused a licence. An incorrect edition appeared in 1628 and prompted Hubert to issue the correct text (see STC 13901). The circumstance of Buckingham clearly prompted the publication, *DNB*, Hubert.

279. *Deplorable Life*, 17–18, 23.

280. M. Butler, *Theatre and Crisis, 1632–1642* (Cambridge, 1984), 33.

281. For one example, see *Cal. Stat. Pap. Dom. 1639*, 140–1.

282. P. Massinger, *The Roman Actor* (1629), sig. C2ᵛ. This is a frequent and frequently unconvincing disclaimer.

283. Scot, *Philomythie*, sig. B2.

284. Ibid., sigs D2–D3; B. White, *A Cast of Ravens: The Strange Case of Thomas Overbury* (1965).

285. *The Second Part of Philomythie*, sig. C2.
286. Kenyon, *Stuart Constitution*, 184.
287. R. Gray, 'Hobbes's System and His Early Philosophical Views', *JHI* 39 (1978), 199–215.
288. We have not concentrated enough on the role of languages in communicating such sentiments and emotions.
289. On the different views of the common law that could be held by those who spoke the same language, see Burgess, 'Custom, Reason and the Common Law'.
290. C.A.J. Skeel, 'The Influence of the Writings of Sir John Fortescue', *TRHS*, 3rd series, 10 (1916), 77–114, 97.
291. Cf. below, 64–5.
292. Pocock, 'The Commons Debates of 1628'.
293. W.J. Jones, *Politics and the Bench: the Judges and the Origins of the English Civil War* (1971).
294. James I's speech to parliament 1610, Kenyon, *Stuart Constitution*, 82–3.
295. S.E. Prall, *The Agitation for Law Reform During the Puritan Revolution 1640–1660* (1966); G.B. Nourse, 'Law Reform under the Commonwealth and Protectorate', *Law Quart. Rev.*, 75 (1959), 512--29; D. Veall, *The Popular Movement for Law Reform* (Oxford, 1970).
296. The present writer plans a study of perceptions of the past and politics from Foxe to Burnet.
297. Sharpe, *Sir Robert Cotton*, passim; J. Levine, *Humanism and History: Origins of Modern English Historiography* (Ithaca, 1987).
298. P. Bethune, *The Counsellor of Estate*, 260.
299. T. Hobbes, *Eight Bookes of the Pelopennesian Warre*, sigs A1–A2.
300. Below, Ch. 8, p. 213.
301. J. Stoye, *English Travellers Abroad*, 64–7.
302. C. Hill, *Some Intellectual Consequences of the English Revolution* (1980), 59.
303. C. Hill, 'The Norman Yoke' in idem, *Puritanism and Revolution* (1958), 50–122; B. Worden, 'Classical Republicanism and the English Revolution' in Worden et al. (eds), *History and Imagination* (1981), 182.
304. J. Levine, *Humanism and History: Origins of Modern English Historiography*.
305. W. Notestein, *The English People on the Eve of Colonization* (1954), 53, 120.
306. T. Godwin, *Romanae Historiae Anthologia Recognita et Aucta: An English exposition of the Roman Antiquities* (1628); for examples of 'senate' and 'senators', see W. Prynne, *A Briefe Survey and Censure of Mr Cozens his Couzening Devotions* (1628), dedication to parliament; A. Leighton, *An Appeal to the Parliament* (1628), 1. Gustavus Adolphus was referred to as 'that Caesar and Alexander of our times' in *The Swedish Intelligencer* (1632), preface to the reader.
307. P. Matthieu, *Unhappy Prosperitie, expressed in the histories of Aelius Sejanus and Philippa* (1632), 148.

308. Peterson, *Imitation and Praise*; K.E. Maus, *Ben Jonson and the Roman frame of Mind* (Princeton, 1984); P.J. Ayres, 'The Nature of Jonson's Roman History', *ELR*, 16 (1986), 166-82.
309. H. Crosse, *The Schoole of Policie* (1605), passim.
310. Stafford, *The Guide of Honour*, 61, cf. 72-3, 129.
311. H.F. Kearney, *Scholars and Gentlemen: Universities and Society in Pre-Industrial Britain 1500-1700* (1970), 43.
312. See J. Morgan, *Godly learning: Puritan Attitudes Towards Reason, Learning and Education 1500-1640* (Cambridge, 1986).
313. J.O. Halliwell (ed.), *The Autobiography and Correspondence of Sir Simonds D'Ewes* (2 vols, 1845), I, 49; above, n.298.
314. Rostvig, *Happy Man*, 122.
315. Above, 24-25.
316. Z. Fink, *The Classical Republicans* (Evanston, Illinois, 1945) and B. Worden, 'Classical Republicanism and the English Revolution'.
317. T.M. Greene, *The Light in Troy*, 293.
318. Smuts, *Court Culture*, ch.6.
319. Sharpe, *Criticism and Compliment*, 207-9.
320. D.J. Gordon, 'Poet and Architect: the intellectual setting of the quarrel between Ben Jonson and Inigo Jones', *Journ. Warburg & Courtauld Inst.*, 12 (1949), 152-78.
321. Kenyon, *Stuart Constitution*, 16. My comment here is a convenient shorthand. The metaphors current in any age are among the most valuable documents of deep cultural values and deserve fuller explication as such.
322. Ibid., 193.
323. Quoted by J.W. Gough, *Fundamental Law in English Constitutional History* (Oxford, 1955), 41.
324. J. Daly, *Cosmic Harmony*, 12.
325. C. Newstead, *An Apology for Women* (1620), 37.
326. Ibid., 36.
327. Feltham, *Resolves* (1623 edn), 251.
328. N. Morgan, *The Perfection of Horsemanship* (1609), sig. A2^v.
329. Sharpe, *Criticism and Compliment*, 123-4.
330. *Timber or Discoveries*, in Herford and Simpson, *Ben Jonson* VIII, 581, 593; cf. ibid., IV, 33: 'To the Special Fountaine of Manners: The Court', dedication of *Cynthia's Revels*.
331. Feltham, *Resolves* (1623 edn), 252.
332. G. Fleming, *Magnificence Exemplified* (1634), 42; cf. 40.
333. Despite the famous quarrel between Jonson and Jones, the literary and the visual were usually regarded as complementary. In *Mythomystes . . . of the Nature and Value of True Poesy* [1632], H. Reynolds spoke of painting as 'a silent poesy' and poetry as 'a speaking painting' (dedication to Lord Maltravers); cf. Nicholas Faret, who described painting as 'a silent poem', *The Honest Man* (1632), 100. Peacham relates that Rubens had history or poetry read to him while he painted, *The Compleat Gentleman* (1634 edn), 110. See L. Gent, *Picture and Poetry, 1560-1620: Relations Between Literature and The Visual Arts in the English Renaissance* (Leamington Spa, 1981).

I owe this reference to Keith Thomas.

334. L. Anderton, *The Triple Cord* (1634), epistle dedicatory.

335. W. Cartwright, *The Royal Slave*, Act I, scene iv, in G. Blakemore Evans (ed.), *The Plays and Poems of William Cartwright* (Madison, Wisconsin, 1951), 208; see below, 133–4.

336. W. Struther, *A Looking Glasse for Princes and People* (1632), 12.

337. It is worth noting here that it is the *sight* of the monarch that orders the wilderness of nature in the masques, for the king did not speak.

338. *The Works of Joseph Hall* (1628), II, 233.

339. H. King, *An Exposition Upon the Lords Prayer* (1628), 105.

340. The interest was avidly shared by subjects. Increasingly histories of kings were illustrated by pictures of the monarchs. See, for example, Henry Holland, *BraziliWlogia, a booke of Kings* (1618), a series of pictures of monarchs from William I. It was reissued in 1628 and in 1630 with copper engravings.

341. Smuts, *Court Culture*, 143 and plate 6. R. Strong, *The Cult of Elizabeth* (1977); F. Yates, *Astraea* (1977).

342. Smuts, *Court Culture*, 204.

343. Below, 51–2.

344. Massinger, *Emperor of the East* (1632), sig. E1^v.

345. M. Walzer, 'On the Role of Symbolism in Political Thought', *Polit. Science Quart.*, (1967), 191–204, esp. 196.

346. I am grateful to Professor Steve Mailloux of Syracuse University for discussions we had of this subject at the Stanford Humanities Center in 1986.

347. The present writer will soon be working on representations of royal authority in early modern England.

348. See J. Montagu (ed.), *The Workes of the Most High and Mighty Prince James* (1616), 'The Preface to the Reader'.

349. Kenyon, *Stuart Constitution*, 81; *Workes of James I*, 382.

350. Charles I to Louis XIII (n.d.), Huntington Library MS HM 20365.

351. Sharpe, 'Image of Virtue'; J.F. Larkin (ed.), *Stuart Royal Proclamations Vol II: Royal Proclamations of King Charles I, 1625–46* (Oxford, 1983), 80.

352. Kenyon, *Stuart Constitution*, 71.

353. E.O. Smith Jnr, 'Crown and Commonwealth', 8.

354. R. Strong, 'Queen Elizabeth and the Order of the Garter', *Archaeological Journ.*, 119 (1962), 245–70; E. Ashmole, *The History of the Most Noble Order of the Garter* (1715).

355. *Christian Policie*, 24.

356. E.g. T. Heywood, *England's Elizabeth*, 181–2.

357. *The Order of My Lord Mayor, the Alderman and the Sheriffes* . . . (1629).

358. For a good example, see Bulstrode Whitelocke's account of the procession before the masque *The Triumph of Peace*, in S. Orgel and R. Strong (eds), *Inigo Jones: the Theatre of the Stuart Court* (2 vols, Berkeley, 1973), II, 541–3.

359. See P. Burke, *Popular Culture in Early Modern Europe* (1978). For a detailed study of a more modern festival, see D. Cannadine, 'Civic

Ritual and the Colchester Oyster Feast', *P&P*, 94 (1982), 107-30.

360. C. Geertz, 'Ritual and Social Change', *Interpretation of Cultures*, 142-70; Marcus, *Politics of Mirth*, 149.

361. D. Underdown, *Revel, Riot and Rebellion: Popular Politics and Culture in England 1603-1660* (Oxford, 1985); below, 298-303.

362. R. Bolton, *The Saints Sure and Perpetual Guide* (1634), 212.

363. *An Alarm to Awake Church Sleepers* (1640), 122ff, 141.

364. O. Feltham, *Resolves or Excogitations with Resolves, Divine, Moral, Politicall* (1628 edn), 64-5, my italics; *An Alarm* also pointed out that, though men slept through sermons, they stayed awake for plays (p.96).

365. C. Dow, *Innovations Unjustly Charged Upon the Present Church and State* (1637), 206. John Gerhard called the sacraments the visible word, *The Marrow of Divinitie* (1632), 239; Bishop Griffith Williams pointed out that 'we do often times adore and worship without any words . . .', *The True Church* (1629), 163.

366. S. Hinde, *A Free Will Offering* (1634), 83.

367. Sharpe, *Criticism and Compliment*, 92.

368. D. Cressy, *Coming Over: Migration and Communication between England and New England in the Seventeenth Century* (Cambridge, 1987), ch.6.

369. Interestingly, Joseph Hall pursued generic classification so far as to say that on the world stage the good acted out a comedy and the wicked a tragedy, *Works*, II, 27.

370. A.S., *The Famous Game of Chesse Play* (1614). Searle points out that it originated from martial discipline.

371. 'And coming at the last in place,
Where knights and lords did dwell,
Their king shall give to them like grace,
Because they served him well.' (ibid., 'To the Reader').

372. Feltham, *Resolves* (1623 edn), 31.

373. As is evident from the masques, *Criticism and Compliment*, ch.6; cf. R. Strong, *The Renaissance Garden in England* (1979).

374. G. Markham, *The Art of Archerie* (1634), 6.

375. J. Robinson, *Observations, Divine and Morall, for the furthering of Knowledge and Vertue* (1625), 274.

376. Feltham, *Resolves* (1623 edn), 108.

377. N. Morgan, *The Perfection of Horsemanship, drawne from Nature, Arte and Practise* (1609), 6.

378. Ibid., 58.

379. Herford and Simpson, *Jonson*, VIII, 567, 607, 619.

380. E.D., *Nicholas Machiavel's Prince* (1640), 197.

381. Morgan, *Horsemanship*, 10.

382. R. Braithwaite, *The English Gentleman*, 147.

383. Ibid., 457.

384. Ibid., 266. Cf. the simultaneous acknowledgement and satire of this perception in *The Winter's Tale*, Act V, scene ii, lines 124ff.

385. N. Caussin, *The Holy Court*, 41.

386. As I first read through the STC I was struck by the politicization of

language over a broad range of works. And even when this is not obviously the case the prefaces appear to invite a politicization of the treatise which follows.

387. M. Kellison, *A Treatise of the Hierarchie* (Douai, 1629), 49.
388. See the fine study of P. Alpers, *The Singer of the Eclogues: A Study of Virgilian Pastoral* (Berkeley, 1979).
389. C. Butler, *The Feminine Monarchy: or a Treatise Concerning Bees and the Due Ordering of Them* (1609).
390. Ibid., sig. A1.
391. Ibid., sig. A1–A1^v.
392. Ibid., sigs A2–A3.
393. Ibid., sig. B3.
394. Ibid., sig. A5^v.
395. Ibid., 'The conclusion to the Reader'.
396. J. Brinsley, *Virgil's Eclogue* (1619), 121. The language is significant; Brinsley was a puritan divine of note, see *DNB*.
397. Bouwsma, 'Intellectual History in the 1980s', 288–91.
398. Peacham, *Complete Gentleman*, 96.
399. M. Peerson, *Mottects or Grave Chamber Musique* (1630), dedication to Lord Brooke.
400. Prefatory verse to T. Ravenscroft, *A Brief Discourse of the True..Use of Charact'ring the Degrees..in Music* (1614).
401. Ibid., prefatory address by Campion.
402. C. Brown (ed.), *The Poems and Masques of Aurelian Townshend* (Reading, 1983), 122.
403. J.P. Kenyon, *Stuart Constitution*, 193.
404. Ravenscroft, *Brief Discourse*, 'Apologie'; cf. Thomas Carew's identification of problems on the stage and in the state, R. Dunlap (ed.), *The Poems of Thomas Carew* (Oxford, 1949), 96.
405. Prefatory verse of M. Pierson to Ravenscroft's *Discourse*.
406. Prefatory verse of William Austin.
407. Ibid., cf. Shakespeare *Henry V*, Act I, scene ii, lines 178–83.
408. Ravenscroft, *Brief Discourse*, sig. A3. See S.K. Heninger, *Touches of Sweet Harmony* (San Marino, 1974); J. Hollander, *The Untuning of the Sky: Ideas of Music in English Poets 1500–1700* (Princeton, 1961).
409. See M. Chan, *Music in the Theatre of Ben Jonson* (Oxford, 1980); M. Lefkowitz, *William Lawes* (1960); M. McGowan, *L'Art du Ballet de cour en France 1581–1643* (Paris, 1963); B. Pattison, *Music and Poetry of the English Renaissance* (1970).
410. B., Sk., *Counsel to the Husband* (1608), 38.
411. Significantly one of the powerful Victorian images here came from the seventeenth century. See R. Strong, *And when Did You last See Your Father? The Victorian Painter and British History* (1978).
412. Cf. D. Starkey, 'Court History in Perspective', in idem (ed.), *The English Court* (1987), 1–24.
413. J. Neale, *Elizabeth I and Her Parliaments* (2 vols, 1953), I, 109.
414. D. Bergeron, *Shakespeare's Romances*; below, 282.
415. Kenyon, *Stuart Constitution*, 286.

416. Walzer, 'On the role of Symbolism', 195. Milton grudgingly recognized its power for an 'image doting rabble', cited by Trevor-Roper, *Catholics, Anglicans and Puritans*, 268.

417. Susan Amussen announces her intention of pursuing them in 'Gender, Family and the Social Order' in A. Fletcher and J. Stevenson (eds), *Order and Disorder in Early Modern England* (Cambridge, 1985), 196–217.

418. P. Ayrault, *A Discourse of Parents Honour* (1614), dedication to Tobie Matthew.

419. Ibid., 39.

420. Ibid., 18.

421. Ibid., 43, 45; above, 30.

422. Ibid., 156.

423. Ibid., 45, 157.

424. Robinson, *Observations, Divine and Morall*, 48.

425. Ayrault, *Discourse of Parents Honour*, 157.

426. Amussen, art. cit. and D. Underdown, 'The Taming of the Scold: the Enforcement of Patriarchal Authority in Early Modern England', in *Order and Disorder*, 116–36.

427. C. Newstead, *An Apology for Women* (1620), 36.

428. Ibid., 33.

429. Ibid., 17.

430. Ibid., 42, 47. I detect no obvious irony in this treatise.

431. *Counsel to the Husband*, 11.

432. Ibid., 42. Given the frequency and at times ritual accreditation of cross-dressing in early modern England, the fragility of the assertion is clear.

433. Ibid., 49.

434. Ibid., 50.

435. Ibid., 49.

436. Ibid., 55.

437. Ibid., 53.

438. Ibid., 62, 69. The language echoes that of a parliamentary petition.

439. Ibid., 63. My italics: the parenthetic aside of the original both speaks to a recognition of tensions and a desire to pretend that they do not exist.

440. Ibid., 76.

441. Ibid., 77, 85, 88.

442. See A.J. Smith, *The Metaphysics of Love* (Cambridge, 1985); Sharpe, *Criticism and Compliment*, ch.6. See below ch.9 and 262–4.

443. F. Rous, *The Heavenly Academie* (1638), 115.

444. Robinson, *Observations, Divine and Morall*, 204.

445. Bedford, *Defence of Truth*, 121.

446. Ibid., 6.

447. Cf. Herbert, '. . . the feeling which relates to the perpetuation of the species, so long as it is not infected with unlawful lust or concupiscence, is humane and may spring from the faculty which seeks the general good', Bedford, 121.

448. R. Greaves, *Society and Religion in Elizabethan England*

(Minneapolis, 1981), 118; J.E. Booty (ed.), *The Book of Common Prayer 1559* (Washington, DC, 1976), 290–1.

449. O. Feltham, *Resolves* (1628 edn), 49.
450. I. Doughty, *A Discourse Concerning the Abstruseness of Divine Mysteries* (1628), 20.
451. Kenyon, *Stuart Constitution*, 43. Professor Kenyon did not draw attention to the frequency and importance of this language.
452. Speech of the Earl of Salisbury reporting James I, 8 March 1610, ibid., 11.
453. Ibid., 16, 196.
454. J. Daly, 'Cosmic Harmony', 14.
455. In Burton's *Anatomy of Melancholy*, love is the unifier of families and kingdoms. Significantly Scot (*Philomythie*, sig. C2ᵛ) saw, 'The bond of marriage betwixt man and woman; the bond of loyal obedience between subjects and sovereigns' as the knots which the pope sought to cut asunder.
456. See 1 Corinthians 12, verses 8–31.
457. D.G. Hale, *The Body Politic*, 12.
458. Cf. Norford, 'Microcosm and Macrocosm'.
459. Two full studies are Hale, *Body Politic* and L. Barkan *Nature's Work of Art: The Human Body As Image of the World* (New Haven, 1975).
460. Kenyon, *Stuart Constitution*, 192.
461. E. Forset, *A Comparative Discourse of the Bodies Natural and Politique* (1606) 85; Hale, *Body Politic*, 91.
462. Barkan shows how the analogue was attractive to those who watched the disintegrating polis of the 5th century, *Nature's Work of Art*, 65.
463. Daly, 'Cosmic Harmony', 16. Forset identified the soul with the sovereign, *Comparative Discourse*, 3.
464. W. Scott and J. Bliss (eds), *The Works of . . . William Laud* (7 vols in 5, Oxford, 1847–60) I, 151–82, esp. 162–3.
465. Above, 39–40.
466. G. More, *Principles for Young Princes*, 1.
467. Kenyon, *Stuart Constitution*, 184.
468. J.H. Burns, 'Political Ideas of George Buchanan', 63.
469. Hale, *Body Politic*, 81.
470. N. Coeffeteau, *A Table of Humane Passions* (1621), 67.
471. More, *Principles for Young Princes*, 44–5.
472. Ibid., 42; cf. Marcus on Ben Jonson and James I, *Politics of Mirth*, 11, 102, 122–3.
473. See also *Criticism and Compliment*, 39–44; ch.2.
474. Michael McDonald argues that the wife's desire to leave her husband was seen as a psychological disturbance, *Mystical Bedlam: Madness, Anxiety and Healing in Seventeenth Century England* (Cambridge, 1981), 101 and 98–105.
475. O. Feltham, *Resolves* (1623 edn), 48.
476. J. Hall, *Works* (1628), I, 14.
477. N. Coeffeteau, *Table of Human Passions*, 5, 31; hope and despair

are differentiated 'by reason of the divers motions they excite', 49.

478. Most notably, C. Hill, *Intellectual Origins of the English Revolution.*

479. Above, 40 and cf. 10.

480. See the speeches of Nicholas Fuller, Thomas Hedley, James Whitelocke and William Hakewill, in E.R. Foster (ed.), *Proceedings in Parliament 1610* (2 vols, New Haven, 1966), II 152–65; I 70–97; 221–4; S.R. Gardiner (ed.), *Parliamentary Debates in 1610* (Camden Soc., 1st series 81, 1861), 79–83; *State Trials*, II, 407.

481. See C. Russell, *Parliaments and English Politics* (Oxford, 1979), ch.6; J. Guy, 'The Origin of the Petition of Right Reconsidered', *HJ*, XXV (1982), 289–312; R. Cust, 'The Forced Loan and English Politics' (Ph.D. thesis, London University, 1984).

482. Pocock, 'Commons Debates of 1628'; Judson, *Crisis of the Constitution*, passim. J. Sommerville has recently argued otherwise (*Politics and Ideology in England, 1603-40*, 1986). See my comments below, 283–8.

483. C. Russell, 'The Nature of a Parliament in Early Stuart England', in H. Tomlinson (ed.), *Before the English Civil War* (1983), 123–50, 132.

484. John Castle to the Earl of Bridgewater, Huntington Library, Ellesmere MS 7824.

485. The subject is thoroughly treated in Peter Donald's Cambridge thesis, above n.119.

486. Huntington Lib., Hastings MS 1349; Ellesmere MS 7828, *HMC Cowper II*, 227.

487. PRO 31/3.71, f.23, despatch of 3 March 1639.

488. Bodl. MS Tanner 67, f.53.

489. Bodl. MS Rawlinson B210, f.16.

490. Malcolm Smuts makes the point that the perception of politics as a world of contending passions waging a struggle against public interest 'led individuals on both sides of any serious issue to place the worst possible construction on the motives and designs of their opponents', *Court Culture*, 275.

491. B. Tierney, *Religion, Law and the Growth of Constitutional Thought*, 98.

492. D.W. Hanson, *From Kingdom to Commonwealth: the Development of Civic Consciousness in English Political Thought* (Cambridge, Mass., 1970), ch.10.

493. See Sharpe and Zwicker, *Politics of Discourse*, 5.

494. Tuck, 'Power and Authority'; Hanson, op. cit.; J.W.A. Gunn, *Politics and the Public Interest in the Seventeenth Century* (1969).

495. D. Wotton, (ed.), *Divine Right and Democracy* (Harmondsworth, 1986), 61.

496. Hampsher-Monk writes of Pocock's belief that 'Political theorizing emerges from ordinary political discourse in times of crisis' ('Political languages in Time', 105). But it is not clear from his discussion *how* this occurs, and it seems more likely that Hobbes was driven by experience to depart from rather than develop the paradigms of ordinary political discourse. Cf. D. Johnston, *The*

Rhetoric of Leviathan: Thomas Hobbes and the Politics of Cultural Transformation (Princeton, 1986).

497. C. Hill, *The World Turned Upside Down* (1972).
498. Hill, 'Norman Yoke'; cf. Overton's claim: 'whatever our forefathers were or whatever they did or suffered, . . . we are the men of the present age and ought to be absolutely free from all kinds of exorbitancies, molestations or arbitrary powers'. *A Remonstrance of Many Thousand Citizens*, in W. Haller (ed.), *Tracts on Liberty in the Puritan Revolution* (3 vols, New York, 1934), III, 354–5.
499. See H.R. Trevor-Roper, 'Three Foreigners: the Philosophers of the Puritan Revolution', in idem, *Religion, the Reformation and Social Change* (1967), 237–93.
500. See. J. Carey, 'Sixteenth and Seventeenth Century Prose'. In his preface to *Troilus* Dryden said of Shakespeare that many of his 'words, and more of his phrases are scarce intelligible . . . and his whole style is so pestered with figurative expressions, that it is as affected as it is obscure' (cited in W. Griswold, *Renaissance Revivals* (Chicago, 1986), 116). The comment aptly summarizes the revolution in style.
501. See A.L. Rowse, *Reflections on the Puritan Revolution* (1986).
502. An important observation here is made by Professor Underdown, 'The republic's reliance on verbal means of establishing its legitimacy . . . reflects the characteristic puritan preference for rational discourse over pictorial modes of communication.' *Revel, Riot and Rebellion* (Oxford, 1985), 257. This is a subject that awaits a full discussion.
503. C. Hill, *Intellectual Origins*, 5.
504. Kenyon, *Stuart Constitution*, 331.
505. Ibid., 421.
506. Bedford points out that where nonconformists had before been prosecuted in the name of truth, by Locke's day the concern was with good order, *Defence of Truth*, 231. For remarks on the intellectual importance of the accommodation of party see Sharpe and Zwicker, *Politics of Discourse*, 7.
507. Kenyon, *Stuart Constitution*, 264.
508. This has been underestimated. The end of feudal tenures marks a crucial shift from personal monarchy to the king as a public figure, governing a nation.
509. See M. McKeon, 'Politics of Discourses and the Rise of the Aesthetic in Seventeenth Century England', *Politics of Discourse*, 35–51; idem, *The Origins of the English Novel, 1600–1740* (1987) and J. Bender, *Imagining the Penitentiary: Fiction and the Architecture of Mind in Eighteenth Century England* (Chicago, 1987). I am grateful to John Bender for stimulating discussions at Stanford in 1986.
510. S.L. Bethel argued that 1660 is still 'the best date to choose as a dividing line' (*The Cultural Revolution of the Seventeenth Century* (1952), 12). I would suggest that 1649 marks the crucial divide.
511. D. Hayton, The 'Country Interest and the Party System 1689–c.1720' in C. Jones (ed.), *Party and Management in Parliament*

1660-1784 (Leicester, 1984), 37-79.

512. C.B. Schmitt, *Aristotle and the Renaissance*, 107.
513. Cf. the remark of T. Greene, above, 44.
514. Just as it took the Reformation for the medieval church to be seen in historical perspective, so the Civil War induced a sense of anachronism and change in secular as well as religious affairs.
515. Cf. Walzer, 'Once those images and analogues had been called into question, it was not impossible, but it was increasingly difficult to think the old thoughts', 'On the Role of Symbolism', 193-4.
516. Amussen, 'Gender, Family and the Social Order'.
517. B. Mandeville, *The Fable of the Bees* (1714).
518. Hale, *Body Politic*, 8.
519. I am grateful to A.J. Smith for discussions on this subject; cf. above, n.492 and below 264.
520. Bethel, *Cultural Revolution*, 115. Cf. T.S. Eliot, 'The Metaphysical Poets' in *Selected Essays* (1969), 281-301. This argument now appears too simplistic, but the suggestion pays careful consideration. See also below 263-4.
521. See the works by Michael McKeon cited in n.501.
522. Bethel, *Cultural Revolution*, 12.

Chapter 2

* Originally published in *English Historical Review*, No. CCCXCIX, April 1986, 321-50. An early version of this chapter was given at Glasgow in 1979 where Simon Adams and Jenny Wormald made valuable suggestions. It was revised for a meeting of the Shelby Cullom Davis seminar at Princeton and I am grateful to Lawrence Stone for the opportunity and his criticisms. Many colleagues have read or discussed parts of this with me, but I am particularly grateful to George Bernard, C. S. L. Davies, Gerald Aylmer, John Morrill, Conrad Russell, Penry Williams and Anthony Fletcher for their constructive criticism.

1. See C. Russell, 'Parliamentary History in Perspective 1604-29', *History*, lxi (1976), 1-27; idem, 'The Nature of a Parliament in Early Stuart England', in H. Tomlinson (ed.), *Before the English Civil War* (1983), 123-50; idem, *Parliaments and English Politics 1621-1629* (Oxford, 1979); P. Christianson, 'The Peers, the People and Parliamentary Management in the First Six Months of the Long Parliament', *JMH*, xlix (1977), 575-99; M. Kishlansky, 'The Emergence of Adversary Politics in the Long Parliament', *JMH*, 49 (1977) 617-40; K. Sharpe (ed.), *Faction and Parliament* (Oxford, 1978, revised edn, 1985); idem, *Sir Robert Cotton: History and Politics in Early Modern England* (Oxford, 1979).
2. J.H. Hexter, 'Power Struggle, Parliament and Liberty in Early Stuart England', *JMH*, 1 (1978), 1-50; D. Hirst, 'Unanimity in the Commons, Aristocratic Intrigues and the Origins of the English Civil War', *JMH*, 1, 51-71; T.K. Rabb, 'The Role of the Commons', *P&P*,

xcii (1982), 181–215; J.H. Hexter, 'The Early Stuarts and Parliament: Old Hat and the *Nouvelle Vague*', *Parliamentary History*, i (1982), 181–215. For a reply see K. Sharpe, '"Revisionism" Revisited', in *Faction and Parliament* (1985).

3. D. Hirst, 'The Place of Principle', *P&P*, xcii (1982), 79–99.

4. Much of it has already been written for the years 1640 to 1642 by A. Fletcher, *The Outbreak of the English Civil War* (1981).

5. E.g. R. Bonney, *Political Change in France under Richelieu and Mazarin 1624–1661* (Oxford, 1978); R.R. Harding, *Anatomy of a Power Elite: the Provincial Governors of Early Modern France* (New Haven, 1978).

6. Williams, *The Tudor Regime* (Oxford, 1979), 351.

7. G.R. Elton, 'Tudor Government. The Points of Contact. i Parliament, ii The Council; iii The Court', *TRHS*, 5th series, xxiv (1974), 183–200; xxv (1975), 195–212; xxvi (1976), 211–28.

8. M. Judson, *The Crisis of the Constitution* (New Brunswick, 1949); J.P. Kenyon (ed.), *The Stuart Constitution* (Cambridge, 1966); C.C. Weston and J.R. Greenberg, *Subjects and Sovereigns* (Cambridge, 1981).

9. R. Eccleshall, *Order and Reason in Politics* (1978).

10. Tho. Locke to D. Carleton, 5 Feb. 1621, *Cal. Stat. Pap. Dom. 1619–23*, 220.

11. R.F. Williams (ed.), *The Court and Times of James I* (2 vols, 1849), ii, 443, 457.

12. D.R. Starkey, 'The King's Privy Chamber, 1485–1547' (PhD thesis, Cambridge University, 1974).

13. See the chapters by N. Cuddy and K. Sharpe in D. Starkey (ed.), *The English Court from the Wars of the Roses to the Civil War* (1987), chs 6, 7.

14. *Cabala sive scrinia sacra* (1654), 101.

15. J. Howell to Buckingham, 13 Feb. 1626, in J. Jacobs (ed.), *Epistolae Ho-Elianae* (1892), 233.

16. N.E. McClure (ed.), *The Letters of John Chamberlain* (2 vols, Philadelphia, 1939); *Cal. Stat. Pap. Dom. 1611–18*, 495.

17. E. Nicholas to Ld. Fielding, 13 Dec. 1631, *HMC Denbigh*, v, 8.

18. Quoted in P. Zagorin, *The Court and the Country* (1969), 45.

19. R. Lockyer, *Buckingham: The Life and Political Career of George Villiers, First Duke of Buckingham, 1592–1628* (1981), 13.

20. *Cal. Stat. Pap. Dom. 1625–49*, 415.

21. R. Schreiber, *The Political Career of Sir Robert Naunton, 1589–1635* (1981), 44, 109.

22. Sharpe, *Sir Robert Cotton*, 120–4.

23. J. Bastwick, *The Answer . . . To the Exceptions Made Against His Letany* (1637), cited by P. Christianson, 'The Causes of the English Revolution: A Reappraisal', *JBS*, xv (1976), 53.

24. For a valuable introduction to the sort of further research needed, see D. Starkey (ed.), *The English Court*.

25. See S. Adams, 'Eliza Enthroned? The Court and its Politics', in C. Haigh (ed.), *The Reign of Elizabeth I* (1985), 55–78. I am grateful to Simon Adams for his kindness in sending me earlier drafts of this very

important essay.

26. Penry Williams plays down the significance of the rebellion (*The Tudor Regime*, 350); Adams suggests, I think rightly, that it reflected serious broader problems that await investigation.
27. See the chapter by Neil Cuddy in D. Starkey (ed.), *The English Court*.
28. 'I wish I waited now in her Presence Chamber, with ease at my foode and reste in my bedde. I am pushed from the shore of comforte, and know not where the wyndes and waves of a court will bear me', Sir Robert Cecil to Sir John Harrington, 29 May 1603; *Nugae Antiquae*, i, 345. I owe this reference to Neil Cuddy.
29. R. Lockyer, *Buckingham*, 19-25.
30. In 1621, Buckingham dealt to secure Southampton's and Northumberland's release from confinement, R.F. Williams (ed.), *The Court and Times of James I* (2 vols, 1849), ii, 268. R. Lockyer, *Buckingham*, 215; K. Sharpe, 'The Earl of Arundel, His Circle and the Opposition to the Duke of Buckingham', *Faction and Parliament*, 212-5; below, 184-7.
31. Relation of Girolamo Lando, 21 Sept. 1622, *Cal. Stat. Pap. Venet. 1621-3*, 439.
32. P. Christianson, 'The Causes of the English Revolution', 68.
33. H. Wotton, *A Short View of The Life and Death of George Villiers, Duke of Buckingham* (1642), 27.
34. E. Hyde, Earl of Clarendon, *The History of the Rebellion and Civil Wars in England*, ed. W.D. Macray (6 vols, Oxford, 1888), i, 12.
35. B. Jonson, *The Gypsies Metamorphosed*, in C.H. Herford and P. and E. Simpson (eds), *Ben Jonson* (11 vols, Oxford, 1925-53), vii, 565-615; D. Randall, *Jonson's Gypsies Unmasked* (Durham, NC, 1975).
36. Clarendon, *History of The Rebellion*, i, 12.
37. *Cal. Stat. Pap. Dom. 1623-5*, 245.
38. On his return, he was ordered not to come within forty miles of the court; ibid., 310.
39. S.R. Gardiner (ed.), *The Earl of Bristol's Defence of his Negotiations in Spain* (Camden, Misc., VI, 1871), v-vi; cf. the conditions of Somerset's pardon, *Cal. Stat. Pap. Dom. 1623-5*, 333, 352.
40. 28 Sept. 1625, in A. Collins (ed.), *Letters and Memorials of State . . . from the originals at Penshurst* (2 vols, 1746), ii, 360.
41. *Cal. Stat. Pap. Venet. 1621-3*, 439. Cf. The comment of Sir Simonds D'Ewes, that Buckingham was 'but a younger son of an ordinary familie of gentry of which the coat armoure was so meane . . .', quoted in K. Thomson, *Life and Times of George Villiers, Duke of Buckingham* (3 vols, 1860), i, 9.
42. J.P. Cooper (ed.), *Wentworth Papers 1597-1628* (Camden Soc., 1973), 5; D. Hirst, 'Courts Country and Politics before 1629', in *Faction and Parliament*, 105-38; S.P. Salt, 'Sir Thomas Wentworth and the Parliamentary Representation of Yorkshire, 1614-1628', *Northern History*, xvi (1980), 130-68. See P.R. Seddon (ed.), *Letters of John Holles 1587-1637* (Thoroton Soc., xxxi, 1975).
43. 7 Nov. 1625, W. Knowler (ed.), *The Earl of Strafford's Letters and Despatches* (2 vols, 1739), i, 27.

44. Cited by J.P. Cooper in G.E. Aylmer and J.S. Morrill (eds), *Land, Men and Beliefs* (1984), 87.

45. P. Williams, *The Tudor Regime*, 3.

46. Quoted by J. Dias in 'Politics and Administration in Nottinghamshire and Derbyshire 1590–1640' (D.Phil. thesis, Oxford University, 1973), 211, an important thesis that deserves to be read widely.

47. Cf. B. Coward, *The Stanleys, Lords Stanley and Earls of Derby 1385–1672* (Manchester, 1982); G.W. Bernard, *The Power of the Early Tudor Nobility* (Hassocks, 1985).

48. L. Stone, *The Crisis of the Aristocracy* (Oxford, 1965), passim; M. Girouard, *Life In The English Country House* (Harmondsworth, 1980), ch.iv.

49. As was shown conclusively by J.P. Cooper in 'The Counting of Manors' *ECHR*, 2nd series, viii (1956), 377–89 (*Land, Men and Beliefs*, 1–16); and in 'The Social Distribution of Land and Men in England, 1436–1700', *ECHR*, 2nd series, xx (1967), 419–40 (*Land, Men and Beliefs*, 17–42).

50. W.T. MacCaffrey, 'Talbot and Stanhope: An Episode in Elizabethan Politics', *BIHR*, xxxiii (1960), 73–85.

51. Ibid., 79.

52. M.E. James, *English Politics and The Concept of Honour* (*P&P* Supplement, 3, 1978). I am grateful to C.S.L. Davies for discussions of this subject.

53. M.E. Jones, op. cit., 18.

54. J. Dias, 'Politics and Administration', 173.

55. N.G. Brett-James, *The Growth of Stuart London* (1935); L. Stone, 'The Residential Development of the West End of London in the Seventeenth Century', in B. Malament (ed.), *After The Reformation* (Manchester, 1980), 167–212.

56. Preachers and moralists drew attention to this and lamented the decay of hospitality in consequence. Note, for example, Charles Fitz-Geoffrey's praise of Sir Antony Rous: 'He was none of those lay-Non-residents, who build fair houses, and immediately flie from them into some cabbine in Towne. . .'; *Elisha His Lamentation* (1622), 46. I owe this reference to Conrad Russell.

57. G.R. Elton, 'Tudor Government: the Points of Contact. III. The Court', *TRHS*, 5th series, xxvi (1976), 217

58. P.L. Hughes and J.F. Larkin (eds), *Tudor Royal Proclamations* (3 vols, New Haven and London 1964–1969), iii, 169; J.F. Larkin and P.L. Hughes (eds), *Stuart Royal Proclamations* (Oxford, 1973), i, 44, 323, 365, 369, 561 (quotation, 323–4). Charles I continued to issue the proclamations (J.F. Larkin (ed.), *Stuart Royal Proclamations* (Oxford, 1983), ii, 112, 170, 350, 648) and attempted to enforce them by ordering a survey of those nobles and gentlemen living in London in defiance of the proclamations: Bodl. Bankes MSS, bundle 14, 62. Cf. the difficulties caused by the absence of governors in seventeenth century France; R.R. Harding, 'Aristocrats and lawyers in French Provincial Government, 1559–1648: from Governors to Commissars', in B. Malament (ed.), *After the Reformation*, 102–3.

59. BL MS. Royal 18 DIII.
60. PRO SP 12/269/46. I owe this reference to J.R. Dias. See P. Williams, 'Court and Polity Under Elizabeth I', *Bull. John Rylands Lib.*, lxv (1983), 259–86.
61. G.R. Elton, 'Tudor Government: The Points of Contact. II The Council', 208–11.
62. C.H. Firth, *The House of Lords During the Civil War* (1910), ch.I.
63. Ibid., 11–19; Stone, *Crisis of The Aristocracy*, 97–119; D.J. Dawson, 'The Political Activity and Influence of the House of Lords 1603–29' (B.Litt. thesis, Oxford University, 1953); R. Lockyer, *Buckingham*, 54; Sir Edward Walker, *Observations Upon the Inconveniences that have attended the Frequent Promotions to the Titles of Honour and Dignity since King James came to the crown of England* (1653), in Walker, *Historical Discourses*, (ed.) H. Clopton (1705), ch.VI. Between 1615 and 1628 the number of peers rose from 81 to 126, most of them with Irish and Scottish titles.
64. Lockyer, *Buckingham*, 41–2. Significantly, Buckingham was advised to defend his creations on the ground that they established representatives in the localities; *Cabala*, 228.
65. Stone, *Crisis of The Aristocracy*, appendix xi; cf. J.H. Hexter's comments on 'the narrow territorial base of the creations of the Buckingham ascendancy', in *On Historians* (1979), 195 ff. Hexter points out the need to draw a line between the earlier creations and the visibly 'land short peers' of the Buckingham era (197). A colleague has pointed out that my argument here is in close agreement with Hexter. This must be worthy of record.
66. From 55 at Elizabeth's death to 126 in 1628.
67. Lockyer doubts the existence of a division between the old and new families (*Buckingham*, 96). But cf. K. Sharpe, 'The Earl of Arundel, His Circle, and the Opposition to the Duke of Buckingham, 1618–1628', *Faction and Parliament*, 241–2; below, 204–5.
68. The peers petitioned against the sale of Irish and Scottish titles in 1621, and in 1626. See J.O. Halliwell (ed.), *The Autobiography and Correspondence of Sir Simonds D'Ewes* (2 vols, 1845), i, 80–81, 388; N.E. McClure (ed.), *The Letters of John Chamberlain*, ii, 286, 346–8; *HMC Lonsdale 13th Report* Part VII, 2; *HMC Buccleuch-Whitehall*, iii, 335–6; Dawson, op. cit., 10, 126.
69. *Lords Journals*, iii, 491; Lockyer, *Buckingham*, 324.
70. Dawson, op. cit., 10.
71. *HMC Buccleuch-Whitehall*, iii, 335–6; Pesaro to Doge and Senate, 18 Apr. 1625, *Cal. Stat. Pap. Venet. 1625–6*, 12–13. Sir Edward Walker believed that Buckingham's sale of honours was 'one of the beginnings of general Discontents, especially among Persons of great extraction'; *Historical Discourses*, 300.
72. J. Mead to M. Stuteville, 29 March 1628, in T. Birch (ed.), *The Court and Times of Charles I*, i, 335; *Faction and Parliament*, 20.
73. J.S. Morrill, *The Revolt of The Provinces* (1976).
74. Professor Clive Holmes has helpfully re-emphasized this relationship in *Seventeenth Century Lincolnshire* (Lincoln, 1980), and in 'The

County Community in Stuart Historiography', *JBS*, xix (1980), 54–73.
I do not think, however, that those he criticizes were ever in
disagreement. Cf. A. Fletcher, 'National and Local Awareness in the
County Communities', in H. Tomlinson (ed.), *Before The English
Civil War*, 151–74. I am grateful to Anthony Fletcher for stimulating
discussions of this subject.

75. D. Hirst, *The Representative of The People?* (Cambridge, 1975). In a
revision of some of Professor Hirst's figures and conclusions,
however, Mark Kishlansky informs us that only 7 per cent of elections were contested in the period up to 1640. See M. Kishlansky,
*Parliamentary Selection: Social and Political Choice in Early
Modern England* (Cambridge, 1986). Recently Clive Holmes, J.R. Dias
and D. Underdown ('Community and Class: Theories of Local Politics
in the English Revolution', *After The Reformation*, 147–66) have
drawn attention to the relatively lowly men who held local office and
hence became involved in national affairs. This requires further
investigation.

76. J.P. Cooper (ed.), *Wentworth Papers*, 152–7; J.P. Kenyon (ed.), *The
Stuart Constitution*, 18–19; J. Spedding (ed.), *The Works of Francis
Bacon* (14 vols, 1857–74), xiv, 129. And cf. the proclamations issued
to explain the dissolutions of parliaments.

77. Shortly after the Civil War, the Earl of Newcastle reflected concerning an earlier age when 'whattsoever business his Majestie had in any
Countie in Englande, or in all Englande, itt was but speakinge to
Shrewsburye or Darbye & such greate men & itt was done with ease
and fasiletye.' (Quoted Stone, *Crisis of The Aristocracy*, 256.) He may
have exaggerated but his perception of such a change is important.

78. E.R. Turner, *The Privy Council of England from 1603 to 1784* (2
vols, Baltimore, 1927–8) dwells little on the political role of the
Council.

79. *Faction and Parliament*, 38.

80. G.R. Elton, 'Tudor Government: The Points of Contact. II. The Council', 207–11; cf. P. Williams, *Tudor Regime*, 428.

81. Turner, op. cit., i, 82; cf. *Cal. Stat. Pap. Dom. 1611–18*, 199.

82. 'The Council was so split it was an impediment to action rather than
a promoter of it'; Lockyer, *Buckingham*, 225. In 1625, the Privy
Councillors in parliament failed to back Buckingham's motion for a
subsidy because they had not been consulted concerning it, ibid.,
247.

83. A situation that was repeated, as Conrad Russell has reminded me, in
1641.

84. *Faction and Parliament*, 17–18, 37–42.

85. Pesaro to Doge and Senate, 25 Apr. 1625, *Cal. Stat. Pap. Venet.
1625–6*, 21; Sir John Borough's notes of the Commons in 1625, BL
MS Harl. 6445, fos 1–38; Sir William Walter's Propositions, 20 Mar.
1626, Bodl. MS Rawlinson, 674, fos. 9–9^v; *Cal. Stat. Pap. Venet.
1625–6*, 146.

86. J.H. Hexter, 'Power Struggle, Parliament and Liberty in Early Stuart
England', *JMH*, 1 (1978), 1–50, esp. 27–50.

87. C. Russell, 'The Nature of A Parliament in Early Stuart England', *Before The English Civil War*, 124-5.

88. C. Roberts, *The Growth of Responsible Government in Stuart England*, chs 2, 3.

89. *Letters and Papers of Henry VIII*, vii, 177, no. 420; I owe this reference to Elton, 'The Council', 201.

90. P. Williams, *Tudor Regime*, 81.

91. 18 Dec. 1626, *Cal. Stat. Pap. Venet. 1626-8*, 62: 'some of the members of the Council have gone into the country to urge subscription to the subsidies'; Birch, *Court and Times of Charles I*, i, 170. Cf. D. Hirst, 'The Privy Council and Problems of Enforcement in the 1620s', *JBS*, xviii (1978), 46-66, esp. 59-60.

92. Northampton's memorandum on the parliament of 1614, BL MS. Cotton, Titus F. IV, fos, 325-8. Dawson, 'House of Lords', 351.

93. J. Dias, 'Politics and Administration', chs vii, viii.

94. A. Fletcher, *A County Community in Peace and War: Sussex 1600-1660* (1976), 183-8.

95. Hirst, 'Privy Council', 55.

96. Turner, op. cit., i, 104; Dawson, 'House of Lords', 128. Between 1625 and 1626, the Earls of Bristol, Arundel and Suffolk were removed from the Council at Buckingham's bidding.

97. Lockyer, *Buckingham*, 101.

98. *Parliaments and English Politics 1621-29*, passim.

99. This was not true everywhere, but the co-operation of men like Sir John Drake at Plymouth, secured through patronage, appears to have been all too rare.

100. *Cal. Stat. Pap. Venet. 1625-6*, 146.

101. Letter of Sir Dudley Digges (Jan. 1626), PRO SP 16/19/107.

102. Few not none. See E.R. Foster (ed.), *Proceedings in Parliament 1610* (2 vols, New Haven, 1966), ii, 230; W. Notestein, F.H. Relf and H. Simpson (eds), *Commons Debates in 1621* (7 vols, New Haven, 1935), vi, 309.

103. Cf. Russell, 'The Nature of a Parliament'.

104. Even in Charles II's reign, Sir William Coventry was to remark: 'We do not take ourselves to be part of the government . . . We are only part of the legislature'; J. Miller, 'Charles II and his parliaments', *TRHS*, 5th series, xxxii (1982), 4. I owe this reference to Conrad Russell.

105. I owe this observation to an unpublished paper by Professor Elton, 'The Problems of Tudor Parliaments'. We need to know more about the chronology of numbers of private bills.

106. S.P. Salt, 'Sir Thomas Wentworth and The Parliamentary Representation of Yorkshire 1614-1628', *Northern History*, xvi (1980), 130-68, 136.

107. Bodl. MS Ashmole 1149, 172. Cf. Sharpe, *Faction and Parliament*, 25-8: S. Lambert, 'Procedure in the House of Commons in the Early Stuart Period', *EHR*, XCV (1980), 735-81.

108. J. Jacobs (ed.), *Epistolae Ho-Elianae or Familiar Letters*, 250.

109. Salt observes that 'A conflict between "Court" and "opposition"

can scarcely be discerned in the election of 1628, art. cit., 146.

110. *Land, Men and Beliefs*, 102.

111. R.C. Johnson et al. (eds), *Commons Debates 1628*, vol. iii (1977), 247; cf. the speech of Coryton, ibid., iii, 94.

112. R. Cotton, *The Danger wherein The Kingdom now Standeth and the Remedy* (128), in J. Howell (ed.), *Cottoni Posthuma*, 309-20; K. Sharpe, *Sir Robert Cotton*, 142-3, 182-3.

113. F.H. Relf, *The Petition of Right* (Minneapolis, 1917), 57; J.N. Ball, 'The Parliamentary Career of Sir John Eliot, 1624-9 (Ph.D. thesis, Cambridge University, 1953), 274-9; idem, 'The Petition of Right In The English Parliament of 1628', *Anciens Pays Et Assemblées D'Etats* (1964), 45-64.

114. C. Thompson, 'The Divided Leadership of The House of Commons in 1629', in *Faction and Parliament*, 245-84; Russell, *Parliaments and English Politics*, ch.vii.

115. J. Eliot, *De Iure Majestatis*, ed. A.B. Grosart (1882); Cooper, *Land, Men and Beliefs*, 100.

116. See the letter of Sir Francis Nethersole, 24 Aug. 1628, *Cal. Stat. Pap. Dom. 1628-9*, 268.

117. *HMC Various*, viii, 30, Miles White to Sir Arthur Ingram, 16 Dec. 1628; Mead to Stuteville, 20 Sept. 1628, Birch, *Court and Times of Charles I*, i, 396.

118. K. Sharpe, 'The Court and Household of Charles I', in D. Starkey (ed.), *The English Court*, 226-60, below, ch.5; idem, 'Faction at the Early Stuart Court', *History Today*, xxxiii (Oct. 1983), 39-46.

119. Stone, *Crisis of the Aristocracy*, 750-2; Sir Edward Walker, *Historical Discourses*, 309. Cf. Charles I's responses to petitions against the inflation of honours, *HMC Cowper*, i, 373; *Acts of The Privy Council 1629-1630*, 69.

120. PRO LC5/180, 16; Sharpe, 'Court and Household of Charles I'. Note the comment made by John Pory on 3 Jan. 1633 concerning the attendance at masques: 'No great lady shall be kept out though she have but mean apparell .. and no inferior lady .. shall be let in ..'; *Court and Times of Charles I*, ii, 214.

121. 'From 1629 to 1640 Charles returned to the Tudor ideal of government by a Privy Council'; Roberts, *Growth of Responsible Government*, 75.

122. *History of the Rebellion*, i, 62.

123. Sharpe, 'Personal Rule of Charles I', in Tomlinson, *Before The English Civil War*, 64-5, below, 110-11. Stone, *Crisis of The Aristocracy*, 751.

124. Sharpe, 'Personal Rule of Charles I', Tomlinson, 61, 65; below, 108, 111.

125. Professor T.G. Barnes believed the book of orders to be effective for most of the decade; *Somerset 1625-40: A County's Government During The 'Personal Rule'* (Cambridge, Mass., 1961), 177-202; cf. B. Sharp, *In Contempt of All Authority* (1980), 78-81; less optimistic about its success are P. Slack, 'Books of Orders: the Making of English Social Policy, 1577-1631', *TRHS*, 5th series, xxx

(1980), 18–22, and B. Quintrell, 'The Making of Charles I's Book of Orders', *EHR*, xcv (1980), 562–72.

126. See, for example, P. Haskell, 'Ship Money in Hampshire', in J. Webb, N. Yates and S. Peacock (eds), *Hampshire Studies* (Portsmouth, 1981), 73–113; and J.S. Morrill, *The Revolt of The Provinces*, 24–9.

127. Barnes, *Somerset*, 90.

128. See the Earl of Newcastle's observation, Stone, *Crisis of The Aristocracy*, 488; cf. Dias, 'Politics and Administration', 371.

129. Clarendon, *History of The Rebellion*, i, 125.

130. Barnes, *Somerset*, 101. For an overview, see A. Fletcher, 'National and Local Awareness in the County Communities'.

131. Dias, 'Politics and Administration', 393.

132. Quoted in ibid., 355.

133. Morrill, *Revolt of the Provinces*, 28–31.

134. It is not always easy to determine which was the case. Recently Anthony Fletcher has questioned T. Barnes's evaluation that in Somerset Sir Robert Phelips was the creature not the creator of opposition (*Somerset*, 295; Fletcher, art. cit., 157–9, 161). Cf. Dias, 'Politics and Administration', 392–400, 436–45.

135. E.S. Cope and W.H. Coates (eds), *Proceedings of The Short Parliament of 1640* (Camden Soc. 4th series, xix, 1977), 275–89.

136. See the comment of Sir John Byron on the parliament; Dias, 'Politics and Administration', 396.

137. *Short Parliament*, 139–40.

138. Ibid., 155.

139. Ibid., 137.

140. Ibid., 191; cf. Lord Keeper's speech (115–18) and Speaker Glanville's (127).

141. *History of The Rebellion*, i, 173–83.

142. This is my reading of the speech of 4 May, *Short Parliament*, 194; cf. *History of The Rebellion*, 180–2.

143. *Short Parliament*, 171; cf. Sir Francis Seymour's speech, ibid., 170.

144. *History of The Rebellion*, i, 184. Cf. the parallel of 1626 when Charles succeeded in raising a loan, having met resistance to a benevolence.

145. Morrill, *Revolt of The Provinces*, 28–30.

146. *The Speeches of Lord Digby* (1641), 16.

147. Hirst, *Representative of The People?*, 147–53.

148. The large numbers drifting away towards the summer suggests that many neither expected nor desired a Long Parliament.

149. S.R. Gardiner, *History of England from the Accession of James I to the Outbreak of the Civil War* (10 vols, 1883–4) ix, 352.

150. Clayton Roberts, *Growth of Responsible Government*, ch. 3.

151. Ibid; idem, 'The Earl of Bedford and the Coming of the English Revolution', *JMH*, xlix (1977), 600–16.

152. My own judgement concurs with Morrill, *Revolt of The Provinces*, 30. For a greater emphasis upon the interactions of the Long Parliament and the localities, see A. Fletcher, *The Outbreak of The English Civil War* (1981), but note 79–81.

153. For an account of the issue of counsel during the first weeks of the second session, see Clayton Roberts, *Growth of Responsible Government*, 105–10; B.H.G. Wormald, *Clarendon: politics, history and religion, 1640–60* (Cambridge, 1951), 4–46.
154. S.R. Gardiner (ed.), *The Constitutional Documents of the Puritan Revolution* (Oxford, 1899), 245–7; cf. the king's proclamation condemning the ordinance, ibid., 248–9. See C.C. Weston and J.R. Greenberg, *Subjects and Sovereigns* (Cambridge, 1981), ch.2.
155. Declaration of the Houses in defence of the militia ordinance; Gardiner, *Constitutional Documents*, 256–7.
156. Clayton Roberts, *Growth of Responsible Government*, 113–14.
157. Cf. D. Hirst, 'Court, Country and Politics before 1629', *Faction and Parliament*, 116.
158. One recalls that the MPs returned for Northamptonshire to the Long Parliament were instructed to promote a bill for the better navigation of the River Nene; Hirst, *Representative of The People?*, 182.

Chapter 3

A draft of this chapter was read at the Institute for Advanced Study, Princeton. I am grateful to John Elliott and the participants of the seminar for their helpful comments. I would also like to thank Gerald Aylmer, John Morrill, Conrad Russell and Lawrence Stone for their valuable advice and criticism.

I am grateful to the Duke of Buccleuch KT for permission to see the Montagu MSS cited in note 39 and to Lord Downshire for permission to see the Trumbull MSS cited in note 40.

* Originally published in H. Tomlinson (ed.) *Before the English Civil War* (Macmillan, 1983) 53–78.

1. S.R. Gardiner, *History of England from the Accession of James I* (10 vols, 1883–4). His account is not always read with the same balance and subtlety with which it was written.
2. See, for example, L. Stone, *The Causes of the English Revolution* (1972), 117–35; T.K. Rabb, 'The Role of the Commons', *P&P*, 92 (1981), 65.
3. E. Hyde, Earl of Clarendon, *The History of the Rebellion* (ed.), W.D. Macray (6 vols, Oxford, 1888) I, 93.
4. C. Russell, *Parliaments and English Politics 1621–29* (Oxford, 1979), 212.
5. *Cal. Stat. Pap. Dom. 1621–9*, 531; cf. ibid., 482; G.L. Harriss, 'Medieval Doctrines in the debates on supply 1610–1629' in K. Sharpe (ed.), *Faction and Parliament* (Oxford, 1978), 73–104.
6. For a favourable view of Buckingham's military leadership which bears out Charles's confidence, see R. Lockyer, *Buckingham: The Life and Political Career of George Villiers, First Duke of Buckingham, 1592–1628* (1981).
7. Russell, *Parliaments and English Politics*, ch.6; *Cal. Stat. Pap. Dom. 1627–8*, 473, Sir James Bagg to Buckingham, 20 December 1628.

8. Compare the views of Sir John Coke and George Wither: *Cal. Stat. Pap. Dom. 1625–49*, 244; G. Wither, *Britain's Remembrancer* (1628); W. Knowler (ed.), *The Earl of Strafford's Letters and Despatches* (2 vols, 1739), II, 53; cf. Gardiner, VII, 26–7.
9. Sir Rob. Aiton to Carlisle, 18 July 1628, *Cal. Stat. Pap. Dom. 1628–9*, 218; E. Hyde, Earl of Clarendon, *The History of the Rebellion*, ed. W.D. Macray (6 vols, Oxford, 1888), I, 51; Gardiner, VI, 346; Dorchester to Queen of Bohemia, 27 August 1628, *Cal. Stat. Pap. Dom. 1628–9*, 270; *Cal. Stat. Pap. Dom. 1628–9*, 117, 178–9, 218, 239, 247.
10. *History of the Rebellion*, I, 56; *Cal. Stat. Pap. Dom. 1625–49*, 291–3; K. Sharpe, 'The Earl of Arundel, His Circle and the Opposition to the Duke of Buckingham, 1618–28', *Faction and Parliament*, 237; below, 201; *Cal. Stat. Pap. Dom. 1628–9*, 268, Nethersole to [Carlisle], 24 August 1628.
11. *Cal. Stat. Pap. Dom. 1628–9*, 339, Dorchester to Carlisle, 30 September 1628: ibid., 340.
12. *Britain's Remembrancer*; cf. *Cal. Stat. Pap. Dom. 1628–9*, 258, 268, 340, 388.
13. PRO SO 1/1/173^v, Charles I to Conway, 21 September 1628; PRO SO 1/2/108, Charles I to Pembroke; J.P. Kenyon (ed.), *The Stuart Constitution* (Cambridge, 1966), 18.
14. E.g. PRO SO 1/1/173^v; SO 1/2/108.
15. BL Lansdowne MS 620, f.74; cf. PRO SO 1/2/128 and *Cal. Stat. Pap. Dom. 1629–31*, 40.
16. *Cal. Stat. Pap. Dom. 1628–9*, 339.
17. C. Thompson, 'The Divided Leadership of the House of Commons in 1629', in *Faction and Parliament*, 245–84; T. Rymer (ed.), *Foedera* (20 vols, 1727–35), XIX, 62; Heath to Carlisle, 7 March, 1629: PRO SP 16/138/45; cf. Coke, *Cal. Stat. Pap. Dom. 1628–9*, 516.
18. B. Donogan, 'A Courtier's Progress: Greed and Consistency in the Life of the Earl of Holland', *HJ*, 19 (1976), 317–53; G.E. Aylmer, *The King's Servants, The Civil Service of Charles I* (1961) 62; *Cal. Stat. Pap. Dom. 1628–9*, 339, Dorchester to Carlisle, 30 September 1628; *History of the Rebellion*, I, 61.
19. Chateauneuf reported to Richelieu that with respect to the queen Charles 'vit en grande amitié, familiarité et privauté, mais il ne lui donne ni lui laisse prendre aucune part dans les affaires'. PRO (Baschet Transcripts) 31/3/66, f.121. He also described the queen as 'timide et craintifre', ibid., f.213.
20. P. Warwick, *Memoires of the Reigne of Charles I* (1701), 70; *Cal. Stat. Pap. Dom. 1631–3* , 427. Note the way in which the decision concerning ship money was made, *Cal. Stat. Pap. Dom. 1634–5*, 161–3.
21. 'The King's personal commands and his private letters were sealed with the signet only', G.E. Aylmer, 'Studies in the Institutions and Personnel of English Central Administration 1625–1642' (D.Phil. thesis, Oxford University, 1954), 370. Signet Office letters from 1628 are in PRO SO 1/1–3. They are somewhat misleadingly catalogued as

'Irish Letter Books'.

22. R. Ollard, *The Image of the King* (1979), 30; P. Gregg, *King Charles I* (1981).

23. L. Hutchinson, *Memoirs of the Life of Colonel Hutchinson*, ed. C.H. Firth (2 vols, New York, 1885), vol. I, 119; P. Warwick, *Memoires*, 64–5, 113.

24. *HMC Cowper*, I, 382; *Cal. Stat. Pap. Dom. 1629–31*, 478; T. Birch (ed.), *The Court and Times of Charles I* (2 vols, 1848), vol. II, 91; (Pory to Puckering, 13 January 1631); Warwick, *Memoires*, 66.

25. G.E. Aylmer, 'Attempts at Administrative Reform, 1625–1640', *EHR*, 72 (1957), 229–59; *Court and Times of Charles I*, vol. II, 36, 40; *HMC De Lisle and Dudley*, VI, 88, 139; Aylmer, D.Phil. thesis (see n.21 above), 286; *The Poems of Thomas Carew* (1870), 197–235, especially 204–6.

26. The work of the commission of buildings is an example.

27. B. Sharp, *In Contempt of All Authority: Rural Artisans and Riot in the West of England 1586–1640* (Berkeley, 1980), 78–80: *HMC Buccleuch-Whitehall*, I, 270–1.

28. Stone, *The Crisis of the Aristocracy* (Oxford, 1985), ch.III. Conrad Russell has pointed out to me that the sale of titles, revived in 1642, may have been a feature of war finance; Stone, *Causes of the English Revolution*. 125; *Cal. Stat. Pap. Dom. 1628–9*, 379.

29. *HMC Cowp.*, I, 373; *HMC Gawdy*, 136; Stone, *Causes of the English Revolution*, 125–6, idem *The Crisis of the Aristocracy*, 94–6, 117, 351.

30. Rymer XIX, 374; PRO PC 2/42/242; 2/42/290; 2/43/65; 2/44/161; PRO C115 M36 8439; M36 8437. Bundles of returns of those living in London are in Bodl. Lib. Bankes MSS 14, 62.

31. Bodl. Lib. Bankes MSS 49/8; 50/48, 49; PRO PC 2/42/263; 2/43/157; PRO SO 1/2/4^v; *Cal. Stat. Pap. Dom. 1631–3*, 185; D. Coke, *The Last Elizabethan: Sir John Coke 1563–1644* (1937), 211–12.

32. PRO SO 1/2/187; cf. BL MS Add 11, 674; PRO PC 2/43/81; 2/43/311; 2/44/99, 336; 2/45/320; 2/48/59; SO 1/2/187-7^v.

33. Gardiner, VII, 125.

34. J. Rushworth, *Historical Collections* (8 vols, 1680–1701), II, 7; *Cal. Stat. Pap. Dom. 1628–9*, 547; *Cal. Stat. Pap. Dom. 1629–31*, 118. *Articles Agreed Upon by the Archbishops and Bishops of Both Provinces and the Whole Clergie, reprinted by His Majesties Commandment with his Royal Declaration prefixed thereunto. Bibliotheca Regia or The Royal Library* (1659), 224; P. Heylyn, *Cyprianus Anglicus* (1671), 188–90.

35. *Cal. Stat. Pap. Dom. 1633–4*, 212; *Cal. Stat. Pap. Dom. 1634–5*, 88. PRO PC 2/43/304; W. Scott and J. Bliss (eds), *The Works of William Laud* (7 vols, Oxford, 1847–60), VI, 350, 479.

36. E.g. PRO SO 1/2/55^v, 73, 112^v, 134^v, 141, 152, 177^v.

37. PRO PC 2/49/293.

38. See Sharpe, *Faction*, 37–42; ibid., 236–7.

39. When Charles went on progress to Scotland, the Council met twice weekly and also reported to the queen on Sundays, PRO C115/M.31/

8152; Manchester reported to Montagu in December 1635, 'The King every Sunday afternoon sits to see what returns each sheriff makes . . .', Northants Record Office Montague MSS 33, box B2, f.21.

40. Berks. RO, Trumbull MSS, Trumbull Add. MSS 54, 55, 56.
41. PRO PC 2/41; PRO PC 2/41/354; 2/42/142.
42. PRO PC 2/41/514; *Cal. Stat. Pap. Dom. 1633-4*, 266; PRO PC 2/44, at end.
43. G.R. Elton, 'Tudor Government: The Points of Contact: I, Parliament; II, The Council; III, The Court', *TRHS*, 24-6 (1974-6).
44. BL MS. Harleian 6988 f.74. PRO C115/M32/8348. *Cal. Stat. Pap. Dom. 1635*, 128. *Cal. Stat. Pap. Dom. 1633-4*, 352.
45. *Cal. Stat. Pap. Dom. 1628-9*, 542.
46. J.C. Sainty, *Lieutenants of Counties, 1585-1642, BIHR* Supplement 8 (1970); PRO PC 2/50/208.
47. Bodl. Lib. MS Tanner 148, f.67; See, for example, Bodl. Lib. MS Tanner 68, visitation of the diocese of Norwich, 1635-8.
48. Gardiner, VII, 167. PRO SO 1/2/26, Charles I to commissioners.
49. PRO SP 12/206/25.
50. Montagu MS I, f.60.
51. Kent AO, Dering MSS, U.1311 02 compositions for knighthood.
52. H. Leonard, 'Distraint of Knighthood: the last phase. 1625-41, *History*, 63 (1978), 23-37.
53. *Cal. Stat. Pap. Dom. 1631-3*, 278.
54. See Wentworth's remarks on the problems caused by this, *Strafford Letters*, II, 411; PRO SO 1/3/109.
55. *Cal. Stat. Pap. Dom. 1625-49*, 493; Hants RO, Herriard Collection, Jervoise MSS, boxes 012, 013 militia Papers. I am grateful to Mr J.L. Jervoise for permission to see and cite papers in his collection.
56. *Cal. Stat. Pap. Dom. 1629-31*, 15, 20; PRO SO 1/3/109.
57. Bodl. Lib. Bankes MS 42/55, Northamptonshire election 1640.
58. Bodl. Lib. Tanner MS 177, f.19ᵛ.
59. L. Boynton, *The Elizabethan Militia* (1967), ch.8.
60. *State Papers Collected by Edward, Earl of Clarendon* (3 vols, Oxford, 1767), vol. I, 80, Hopton to Windebank, 7 Apr. 1634.
61. PRO C115/M31/8215.
62. See chapter 5; J. Morrill, *The Revolt of the Provinces* (1976), 24.
63. Rushworth, II, 258-9; *Cal. Stat. Pap. Dom. 1634-5*, 295-6.
64. Rushworth, II, 259-61.
65. They dominate the Council registers and state papers for 1635.
66. Kent AO, Twysden MSS, U47/47/Z1, 234.
67. For a classic example, see C. Holmes, *Seventeenth Century Lincolnshire* (Lincoln, 1980), 132.
68. Bristol was assessed at £250 for ship money in 1638, £640 in 1639. Coat and conduct money cost the town £700: *Cal. Stat. Pap. Dom. 1640*, 121.
69. CUL Buxton MSS, box 96. I am grateful to Clive Holmes for drawing my attention to this collection. Morrill, *Revolt of the Provinces*, 28: ibid., 29; PRO SP 16/459/21.
70. Garrard told Cottington that he would rather pay 'ten subsidies in

parliament than ten shillings this new old way of dead Noye's'. But significantly he did not question the legality, *Strafford Letters*, I, 357. Cf. Saye and Sele's objections in 1635. Gardiner, VIII, 93.

71. P. Lake, 'The Collection of Ship Money in Cheshire during the 1630s: A Case Study in the Relation between Central and Local Government', *Northern History*, 17 (1981), 44-71. I am grateful to Peter Lake for his kindness in sending me a typescript of this article.

72. I am grateful to Conrad Russell for this observation.

73. BL Harleian MS 3796, f.70. I owe this reference to Dr Patricia Haskell.

74. *Cal. Stat. Pap. Dom. 1635*, 470.

75. The king himself had first submitted ship money to the opinion of the judges, Gardiner, VII, 206-10.

76. There was a full discussion of the question at Maidstone: Kent AO, Twysden MS U47/47 Z1, 2, 102-10.

77. CUL Buxton MSS, box 96; *Court and Times of Charles I*, vol II, 275; *HMC De Lisle and Dudley*, VI, 138, 21 December 1637; *History of the Rebellion*, I, 87; PRO C115/N4/8619. John Burgh to Viscount Scudamore, December 1637.

78. See the comments of the French ambassador, PRO 31/3/66, 131-8; Rymer, *Foedera*, XIX, 62; *Strafford Letters*, I, 419.

79. *History of the Rebellion*, I, 84.

80. PRO C115/N3/8152.

81. *History of the Rebellion*, I, 84: T.G. Barnes, *Somerset 1625-40: A County's Government during the 'Personal Rule'* (Cambridge, Mass., 1961), ch.VIII; *Cal. Stat. Pap. Dom. 1633-4*, 61, 94.

82. *History of the Rebellion*, I, 96.

83. I owe this phrase to Conrad Russell.

84. PRO C115/N4/8617. The hundreds of letters in the Scudamore collection have never been used systematically. I am preparing a short report on these papers.

85. Gardiner, VIII, 302.

86. PRO C115/N8/8814, 8815.

87. *Strafford Letters*, II, 189: Bodl. Lib. MS Clarendon 14, no. 1321.

88. Hants, RO, Jervoise MSS.; *Cal. Stat. Pap. Dom. 1640*, 314, 315; Morrill, *Revolt of the Provinces*, 29.

89. *Cal. Stat. Pap. Dom. 1639-40*, 420; *Cal. Stat. Pap. Dom. 1640*, 123, 152. I am grateful to Caroline Bartlett for these references; *Cal. Stat. Pap. Dom. 1639-40*, 588-9; *Cal. Stat. Pap. Dom. 1639-40*, 564; *Cal. Stat. Pap. Dom. 1640-1*, 148-9.

90. Aylmer, D.Phil. thesis (see n.21 above), 324.

Chapter 4

* Originally published in (1) *History Today* 33 (August 1983) 26–30 and (2) H. Lloyd-Jones, V. Pearl and B. Worden (eds), *History and Imagination: Essays in Honour of H.R. Trevor-Roper* (Duckworth, 1981) 146–64.

1. W. Scott and J. Bliss (eds), *The Works of the Most Reverend Father in God William Laud* (7 vols, Oxford, 1847–60), v, 13, 16, 26–8, 82; Oxford University Archives. Convoc. Reg., R 24, f.44^v; S. Gibson, 'Brian Twyne', *Oxoniensia*, v, 106.
2. Convoc. Reg. R 24, f.12; *Works of Laud*, v, 14; S. Gibson, *Statuta Antiqua Universitatis Oxoniensis* (Oxford, 1931), xlviii.
3. *Works of Laud*, v, 126–32; *HMC, Cowper*, II, 121; Convoc. Reg. R 24, fos 125–9.
4. Laud helped devise the statutes which enacted the new collegiate cycle for electing proctors and those which governed appeals: Bodleian Library, Twyne MS. XVII, 65; *Cal. Stat. Pap. Dom. 1628–9*, 341, 361, 398, 408, 414, and 1631–3, 134; Convoc. Reg. R 24, f.37^v; *Works of Laud*, v, 56, 59. For other matters referred to him see Twyne MS, XVII, 65.
5. Convoc. Reg. R 24, f.67; Twyne MS. XVII, 66. Laud endorsed the university's letter 'The submission of Oxford statutes to me and my ordering of them': *Cal. Stat. Pap. Dom. 1633–4*, 189.
6. For a general history of the delegates' work see Gibson, 'Brian Twyne'; C.E. Mallet, *A History of the University of Oxford*, II: *The Sixteenth and Seventeenth Centuries* (1924), ch.17; Gibson, *Statuta Antiqua*, x–lxix; J. Griffiths (ed.), *Statutes of the University of Oxford* (Oxford, 1888), preface; G.R.M. Ward (ed.), *Oxford University Statutes*, I: *The Caroline Code* (Oxford, 1845), preface. All the above underestimate Laud's role which emerges clearly in Twyne MS. XVII. I shall be developing this argument more fully in the seventeenth-century volume of the History of Oxford University.
7. Convoc. Reg. R 24, f.91; *Works of Laud*, V, 101; Twyne MS, XVII, 72. Twyne was not given time to make a copy of his draft: ibid., 67.
8. Gibson, 'Twyne', 103, and *Statuta Antiqua*, lxiii; *Works of Laud*, V, 99.
9. 'A Remonstrance', in Bodleian Library, Bodleian MS. 594, f.140, complained that the book was imposed on the university. Twyne refers to widespread opinions that the statutes were invalid because 'not expressly and openly read in Convocation': Twyne MS. XVII, 79. See H.R. Trevor-Roper, *Archbishop Laud* (1962 edn), 279.
10. Convoc. Reg. R 24, f.91.
11. No modern edition of the statutes distinguishes the 1634 code from the revised version of 1636. The emendations and additions can be clearly read in the original books in the Bodleian, NI Jur. Seld., Arch. Bodl. B 120 E. See S. Gibson, 'The collation of the Corpus Statutorum Univ. Oxon', *Bodleian Quarterly Record* (1925), 271–4.
12. Convoc. Reg. R 24, fos 123^v, 125; *HMC Cowper*, II, 121.
13. Bodl. MS. 594, f.140: 'all other statutes which gave any limitation to

the Chancellour's power are in the said late book of statutes quite removed and taken away, as impediments to his absolute government.'

14. For procedure in the sixteenth century see 'Praxis iudicaria in Curis Cancelarii Oxoniensis', Lambeth Palace MS 2085; cf. 'Praxis Curia Academicae' (c. 1770), Oxford University Archives, CC/131/1/3. See also M. Underwood, 'The structure and operation of the Oxford Chancellor's Court from the sixteenth to the early eighteenth century', *Journal of the Society of Archivists*, VI (1978), 18-27.

15. Oxford University Archives, Chancellor's Court MS, 27/6; Underwood, op. cit., 25.

16. E.g. Chanc. Court MSS 18/15, 18/19, 18/89.

17. Griffiths, *Statutes*, 221, 226-7; Underwood, op. cit., 24-5; Bodl. MS. 597, f.141.

18. M. Curtis, *Oxford and Cambridge in Transition 1558-1642* (Oxford, 1959); Mallet, *History of the University*, II, 331; Griffiths, *Statutes*, 138.

19. The complaint (in Bodl. MS. 594, f.141) that this was an unfounded innovation is substantiated by a report sent to Laud in ?1633 that there was 'No evidence for it in any record of the university': *Cal. Stat. Pap. Dom. 1633-4*, 386.

20. *Cal. Stat. Pap. Dom. 1631-3*, 135-6.

21. Bodl. MS. 594, fos 143-4ᵛ. Laud thought it crucial: *Works of Laud*, V, 82.

22. *Works of Laud*, V, 12, 130.

23. Ibid., V, 129.

24. Convoc. Reg. R 24, fos 132-4; Twyne MS. XVII, 187, 191-5; *Works of Laud*, V, 148-55; J. Taylor, 'The royal visit to Oxford in 1636: a contemporary narrative', *Oxoniensia* (1936), 151-9.

25. B. Dobell (ed.), *The Poetical Works of William Strode* (1907), 137-240. Strode, Public Orator of the university since 1629, told his audience that he wrote the play 'at the instance of those who might command him' (ibid., 139). Laud paid the expenses and it seems likely that it was penned at his request (ibid., xxvii).

26. *Works of Laud*, V, 148; *Poetical Works of Strode*, xx. Strode was made a Canon of Christ Church in 1638.

27. Twyne MS. XVII, f.191; G. Blakemore Evans (ed.), *The Plays and Poems of William Cartwright* (Madison, 1951).

28. The plots to kill Prudentius and Cratander as 'heavy philosophical spoil sports who place restrictions upon all the natural passions of man' are strikingly similar: ibid., 599.

29. Convoc. Reg. R 24, f.125ᵛ.

30. Blakemore Evans, *Cartwright*, 13-21.

31. Twyne MS. XVII, f.194ᵛ.

32. Convoc. Reg. R 24, fos 134, 136; *Cal. Stat. Pap. Dom. 1635-6*, 92; Twyne MS. XVII, f.191.

33. Griffiths, *Statutes*, 160; Convoc. Reg. R 24, f.108.

34. See Laud's letter of 5 May 1637 to the Vice-Chancellor requiring him to ensure that every college had a correct copy of the statutes: *Works*

of Laud, V, 168.

35. Twyne MS, XVII, f.130 & ᵛ; Bodleian Library, Wood MS, 423, 15; *Statuta Selecta e Corpore Statutorum Universitatis Oxon.* (1638); F.S. Boas (ed.), *The Diary of Thomas Crosfield* (1935), xv; *Works of Laud*, V, 156-7.

36. Cf. *Works of Laud*, V, 258.

37. Ibid., V, 201; Convoc. Reg. R 24, f.180.

38. *Works of Laud*, V, 258.

39. Vice-Chanc. Court MSS 18/15, 18/89.

40. See for example the acknowledgement of John King of his fault in assaulting one Fisher: Magdalen College Oxford. MS 281, 'Frewen's book 1628-40', f.10 (I would like to thank Mr. Gerald Harriss for permission to cite this MS).

41. Laud recommended public whippings: *Works of Laud*, V, 196-7.

42. Convoc. Reg. R 24, f.167 (Laud); *Works of Laud*, V, 212 (Turner), 235 (Frewen), 256-7 (Baylie).

43. Ibid., V, 212.

44. Griffiths, *Statutes*, 227.

45. Ibid., 188; Ward, *Statutes of the University of Oxford*, I, 345.

46. *Works of Laud*, V, 267-8; cf. *Cal. Stat. Pap. Dom. 1637-8*, 438.

47. *Works of Laud*, V, 163-4, 260. Laud required weekly reports.

48. See e.g. *Works of Laud*, V, 276-8; Queen's College Oxford MS, 378, fos 2ff.

49. S. Gibson, *The Great Charter of Charles I to the University of Oxford* (1933), 33. For this clause see Public Record Office (hereafter PRO), SP 16/315/27; for privileges confirmed and extended, see 'Confirmatio generalis omnium veterum chartarum et privilegiorum Almae universitatis Oxon . . .', Bodleian Library, Gough Oxford MS, VI, and Bankes MS, 12/7.

50. *Cal. Stat. Pap. Dom. 1633-4*, 386; *Works of Laud*, V, 238. In August 1637 Dean Fell reported 94 unlicensed taverns: ibid., V, 179.

51. *Cal. Stat. Pap. Dom. 1639*, 372-4.

52. Mallet, *History*, II, 303-4; *Works of Laud*, V, 4; cf. *Diary of Crosfield*, 42.

53. Bodl. MS, 594, f.139&ᵛ.

54. *The History of the Troubles and Tryal of William Laud* (1695), 181.

55. Above, p.129; *Diary of Crosfield*, 77; *HMC Leybourne-Popham*, 4-5; cf. Bodl. Ms, 594, fos 139-40.

56. Bodl. MS, 594, f.144ᵛ.

57. *History of Troubles and Tryal*, 435; *Works of Laud*, IV, 187-9.

58. Mallet, *History*, II, 304.

59. E.g. the complaints against oaths, and especially the oath *ex officio* ('whereby men are enjoyned to . . . accuse others, to detect and accuse themselves') and subscriptions in Bodl. MS. 594, fos 141, 145; *HMC Leybourne-Popham*, 4-5.

60. Bodl. MS. 594, f.144, complains that Hebdomadal Council issued orders to restrain preaching. See *CJ*, II, 191 (petition of 22 June 1642).

61. Griffiths, *Statutes*, 182. The text of orthodoxy was subscription to

the 1562 articles and 1603 canons.

62. Cf. below, 142.

63. W.C. Costin, *William Laud, President of St. John's College and Chancellor of the University of Oxford* (1945), 16.

64. *Works of Laud*, V, 205–6; cf. ibid., IV, 220–1, and *Cal. Stat. Pap. Dom. 1638–9*, 46, 68.

65. *Cal. Stat. Pap. Dom. 1635–6*, 486; *History of Troubles and Tryal*, 369.

66. *Works of Laud*, V, 118. However, he thought it dangerous to read the works of Calvin too early.

67. *History of Troubles and Tryal*, 353.

68. *Cal. Stat. Pap. Dom. 1635*, 142.

69. *Diary of Crosfield*, xix–xxiv. Potter ordered the wearing of round caps on Sundays in accordance with 'the command given by the Chancellor' and the abstention from flesh in Lent 'commanded by the Chancellour'. Whilst remaining a Calvinist, he encouraged bowing and an emphasis on ceremony. (Ibid., 44, 50, 74.)

70. T. Fowler, *The History of Corpus Christi College* (1898), 189–90; *Brasenose Quarter-Centenary Monographs*, II: *The Sixteenth and Seventeenth Centuries* (Oxford Hist. Soc., 1909), 29; *Works of Laud*, V, 261.

71. *Cal. Stat. Pap. Dom. 1637*, 393.

72. *Cal. Stat. Pap. Dom. 1637–8*, 316; Merton College, 'Collegii Mertonensi Registrum 1567–1731', 328–9. I am grateful to Mr Roger Highfield for his permission to see and cite this register.

73. PRO SP 16/376/68; G.C. Brodrick, *Memorials of Merton College* (Oxford Hist. Soc. 1885), 78.

74. Broderick (op. cit., 81–4) summarizes the ordinances issued by the commissioners to deal with the grievances pending a full enquiry. See *Cal. Stat. Pap. Dom. 1637–8*, 341–2; cf. 'Colleg. Mert. Reg.', 330, and *Cal. Stat. Pap. Dom. 1637–8*, 453.

75. College. Mert. Reg., 331.

76. *Cal. Stat. Pap. Dom. 1637–8*, 348, 573.

77. 'College. Mert. Reg.', 330–1; *Cal. Stat. Pap. Dom. 1637–8*, 561, 607; *Works of Laud*, VII, 460–2, 478–9.

78. *Cal. Stat. Pap. Dom. 1637–8*, 562. Laud ordered Brent to reappoint the first three: *Works of Laud*, VII, 460–2; cf. Turner's letters of 20 and 26 August; *Cal. Stat. Pap. Dom. 1637–8*, 588.

79. Ibid., 588.

80. Ibid., 221; 'Colleg. Mert. Reg.', 333–6.

81. *Cal. Stat. Pap. Dom. 1638–9*, 174; cf. *Cal. Stat. Pap. Dom. 1639–40*, 508.

82. *History of Troubles and Tryal*, 308, 343; *Works of Laud*, IV, 193–4.

83. *Cal. Stat. Pap. Dom. 1639–40*, 508.

84. *Works of Laud*, V, 129; Trevor-Roper, *Archbishop Laud*, 273; *Works of Laud*, V, 130.

85. Below, 143.

86. N.R.N. Tyacke, 'Puritanism, Arminianism and counter-revolution', in C. Russell (ed.), *The Origins of the English Civil War* (1973), 119–43;

R. Ashton, *The English Civil War* (1978), ch.5.

87. S.R. Gardiner (ed.), *The Constitutional Documents of the Puritan Revolution 1625-60* (Oxford, 1906), 75.
88. *Works of Laud*, V, 15.
89. Russell modifies Tyacke in stating that predestination was 'the normal though not quite the official doctrine of the Church of England': *Parliaments and English Politics 1621-9* (Oxford, 1979), 29. Cf. the debates in Parliament in 1629 for the uncertainty concerning the articles of the Church of England: W. Notestein and F. Relf (eds), *Commons Debates for 1629* (Minnesota, 1921), 23-8, 33-5, 95ff., 119.
90. Trevor-Roper, *Archbishop Laud*, x; cf. Laud's own remark: 'in and about things not necessary there ought not to be a contention to a separation': *Works of Laud*, II, 218.
91. Cited by Nicholas Tyacke in 'Arminianism and English culture', in A.C. Duke and C.A. Tamse (eds), *Britain and the Netherlands*, VII, *Church and State since the Reformation* (The Hague, 1981). I am grateful to Mr Tyacke for allowing me to see a typescript of this essay.
92. *Works of Laud*, VI(i), 292.
93. W. Lamont, *Godly Rule* (1969), 65.
94. Ibid., ch.3.
95. I shall be developing this argument in a book on the personal rule of Charles I.
96. PRO PC, 2/43/304, 3 Nov. 1633; *Cal. Stat. Pap. Dom. 1633-4*, 273.
97. See Laud's visitation articles as Bishop of London in 1628 and as Archbishop of Canterbury in 1635 in *Works of Laud*, V(ii); cf. ibid., VI(ii), 312, 348-50.
98. J.P. Kenyon (ed.), *The Stuart Constitution* (Cambridge, 1966), 166-71; S.R. Gardiner, *History of England from . . . James I to the . . . Civil War* (10 vols, 1883-4), IX, 143.
99. Edward Hyde, Earl of Clarendon, *The History of the Rebellion* (ed. W.D. Macray, 6 vols, Oxford, 1888), I, 125.
100. Compare Laud's visitation articles with Abbot's less detailed proceedings: *Works of Laud*, V(ii).
101. W.H. Hutton, *William Laud* (1895), 239; Mallet, *History*, II, 333.
102. Trevor-Roper, *Archbishop Laud*, 117; *Works of Laud*, V, 101.
103. *Works of Laud*, II, xvi.
104. For Laud's defence of proctorial authority against the Dean of Christ Church, see *Works of Laud*, V, 223.
105. *Works of Laud*, V, 66.
106. Evidence of Laud's metropolitan reports; cf. Hutton's comment on the High Commission Act books (*William Laud*, 99).
107. E.g. *Works of Laud*, V(ii), 318, 335, 340-1, 356.
108. N. Tyacke, 'Science and religion at Oxford before the Civil War', in D. Pennington and K. Thomas (eds), *Puritans and Revolutionaries* (Oxford, 1978), 73-93, and 'Arminianism and English culture'.
109. *Works of Laud*, V, 42, 179, 283, 291.
110. Ibid., VI(i), 310.

111. *Cal. Stat. Pap. Dom. 1635*, 142.
112. Trevor-Roper, *Archbishop Laud*, 271.
113. *Works of Laud*, V, 149.
114. *The True Copie of a Letter sent from the Most Reverend William Lord Archbishop of Canterbury to the University of Oxford when He Resign'd his Office as Chancellor June 25, 1641*, 2; cf. *Cal. Stat. Pap. Dom. 1640–1*, 253.
115. *Works of Laud*, V, 302.
116. *History of Troubles and Tryal*, 197.
117. Of 30 graduates who matriculated between 1628 and 1639, 18–20 can be identified as royalist (biographical information from M.E. Keeler, *The Long Parliament 1640–1641* (Philadelphia, 1954). This contrasts with the 169 Oxford graduates of all ages in the Long Parliament who divided into 73 royalists and 91 parliamentarians (D. Brunton and D.H. Pennington, *Members of the Long Parliament* (1954), 7).

Chapter 5

* Originally published in D. Starkey (ed.), *The English Court From the Wars of the Roses to the Civil War* (Longman, 1987) 226–60.

1. For a suggestion concerning the importance of this, see K. Sharpe, 'Personal Monarchy' in Lesley Smith (ed.), *The Making of Britain: the Age of Expansion* (1986)
2. R. Ruigh, *The Parliament of 1624* (Cambridge, Mass., 1971).
3. J. Wormald, 'James VI and I: two kings or one?', *History*, 68 (1983), 187–209. There is no really satisfactory biography of Charles I. See R. Ollard, *The Image of the King* (1979); P. Gregg, *Charles I* (1981); C. Carlton, *Charles I: the personal monarch* (1983).
4. For an example that Charles experienced, see the account of the ceremony to mark the departure of the Prince of Wales from the Spanish Court, BL, Additional MS 30,629.
5. Pesaro to Doge and Senate, 25 April 1625, *Cal. Stat. Pap. Venet. 1625–26*, 21.
6. Petition of George Kirke, *Cal. Stat. Pap. Venet. 1625–26*, 16; 'His Majesty does not wish to exclude his father's old servants or abandon his own'. (*Cal. Stat. Pap. Venet. 1625–26*, 21) and cf. reports of the Venetian ambassador, 2 May: 'The king is trying to keep the Scots satisfied and has confirmed many in their charges, almost in greater numbers than the English' (ibid., 26–7).
7. Petition of Thomas Smith, 31 July 1633, *Cal. Stat. Pap. Dom. 1633–34*, 157. LS13/30 contains an order that 'Supernumerary officers and servants of Household to our late royal father King James are to be our servants and to have these allowances ensuing during their lives and then to cease'. Compare the list with LC2/6, a list of officers of the household of James I; Order for payment to some Grooms of the Bedchamber to James I, now supernumeraries, *Cal. Stat. Pap. Dom.*

1625, 564; T. Rymer ed. *Foedera* (20 vols, 1727–35) *Foedera* XVIII, 225.

8. *Cal. Stat. Pap. Venet. 1625–26*, 21.
9. LC5/1, f.94; *Finetti Philoxenis: Some Choice Observations of Sir John Finett Knight and Master of Ceremonies to the two last Kings* (1656), 145.
10. LC5/1, f.94v.
11. *Foedera* XVIII, 78–80.
12. Pesaro to Doge and Senate, 2 May 1625, *Cal. Stat. Pap. Venet. 1625–26*, 26–7.
13. I take my calculation from 'A Survey or Ground Plot of His Majesty's Palace of Whitehall' (BL Lansdowne MS 736). This manuscript is believed to be *temp.* Charles II, but references to lodgings held by courtiers of Charles I confirm the impression that little of the fabric had been changed in the interim.
14. BL Lansdowne MS 736, f.5v.
15. Ibid., f.5.
16. John Burgh to Viscount Scudamore, 24 February 1625/6, C115/N4/8606: Chancery Masters Exhibits, duchess of Norfolk deeds. Scholars have not appreciated the richness of this cache of newsletters for early seventeenth-century history. I am preparing a short report on the papers.
17. BL Additional MS 10,112, f.17: 'An Index or Catalogue of all such implements and other things in the . . . Chair Room'. 'This Catalogue was drawn up by Van der Dort himself' (ibid., f.1).
18. E. Shepphard, *The Old Royal Palace of Whitehall* (1902) prints an engraving of Charles I's projected palace. On the projected palace, see J. Harris, S. Orgel and R. Strong, *The King's Arcadia: Inigo Jones and the Stuart Court* (1973), 147. They suggest (p. 170) that we may discern an expression of Jones's vision of a new classical palace in the masque *Albion's Triumph*. See S. Orgel and R. Strong (eds), *Inigo Jones: The Theatre of the Stuart Court* (2 vols, Berkeley and London, 1973) II, 454–78.
19. Sir Philip Warwick, *Memoirs of the Reign of King Charles I* (1701), 113.
20. 'Orders for the king's family Temp. Car I', BL Stowe MS 561. F.18 is headed 'Orders signed by the King's and Queen's Majesty, Nov. 1631'.
21. 'Household Regulations 1630', LC5/180. The MS also contains marginal notes by Charles I (e.g. p. 18).
22. *HMC, Cowper MSS* I, 382.
23. Huntington Library, San Marino California, Hastings MS Miscellaneous Box I, 'Orders for correct Behaviour on entering the Royal Chapel and Privy Chamber'; *Cal. Stat. Pap. Dom. 1629–31*, 478: Orders dated 9 January 1631.
24. LS13/169, p. 299.
25. 'A book Containing His Majesty's Orders for the Government of the Bedchamber and the Private Lodgings . . .', BL Stowe MS 563, dated 1689. Quotation from f.2.

26. 'It appears they have ever been most exact and particular in their care . . .', ibid., f.2.

27. An account of 'Points in dispute between the Ld. Chamberlain and the Groom of the Stool May 1683', and 'The Lords' opinion in the difference . . . 15 June 1683', manuscript lately in the private possession of Hugh Murray Baillie. I am grateful to David Starkey for copies of this MS.

28. This was certainly the claim of the Lord Chamberlain in 1683. The suggestion that in Charles I's reign Pembroke governed the Bedchamber (which was technically beyond his jurisdiction) is supported by the Wilton Van Dyck of the earl which shows him, as was claimed in 1683, wearing the triple keys to the bedchamber (Christopher Brown, *Van Dyck* (Oxford, 1982), 201; below, 160, 167). I am grateful to David Starkey for advice on this problem and for the observation that the Pembroke portrait shows the keys on a blue ribbon knotted to his belt beneath the sash. Of course the authority of Groom of the Stool may well have revived when the Earl of Holland held the place.

29. LC5/180, passim.

30. See Neil Cuddy's account, in Starkey, *English Court*, 183ff.

31. LC5/180, p. 21. A copy of these orders in the hand of Sir John Coke is to be found in the State Papers, with the duties of the Privy Chamber clearly specified, see N. Carlisle, *An Enquiry into the Place and Quality of the Gentlemen of his Majesty's Most Honourable Privy Chamber* (1829), 109-16; *Cal. Stat. Pap. Dom. 1637-38*, 216.

32. LC5/180, pp. 22-3.

33. Ibid., 24.

34. *Cal. Stat. Pap. Venet. 1625-26*, 26-7.

35. LC5/180, p. 22.

36. Ibid., 29-30.

37. Cf. Cuddy, in Starkey, *English Court*, 186ff., 214; BL Stowe MS 563, fos 3-3^v.

38. Ibid., f.5^v.

39. Ibid., fos 14^v-15.

40. Ibid., fos 7^v-8; but cf. note 28 above.

41. Ibid., fos 6^v-7. 'A Declaration of the particular fare of the king's Majesty on a flesh day', LS13/30, shows the king's diet to be 28 dishes at dinner.

42. BL Stowe MS 563, f.18.

43. E.g. BL Stowe MS 561; BL Harley MS 7623, f.16, an order to Newcastle to enquire into the number of servants allowed in the prince's household, 'having regard therein to such ancient records as shall specify the same'. The Lords Commissioners for the Household in 1637 took the Eltham Ordinances as the yardstick by which to determine the diet of the Groom of the Stool (PC2/44, f.244, 15 March 1637).

44. Rev. Garrard to Sir Thomas Wentworth, 16 December 1637, W. Knowler (ed.), *The Earl of Strafford's Letters and Dispatches* (2 vols, 1739) II, 140.

45. LC5/180.
46. Sir Philip Warwick, *Memoirs*, 67.
47. E. Hyde, Earl of Clarendon, *The History of the Rebellion*, ed. W.D. Macray (6 vols. Oxford, 1888), IV, 490.
48. The preamble to the Eltham Ordinances makes it clear that war was the impetus behind them.
49. See, for example, *APC 1625-26*, 14, 221, 441; cf. ibid., 37-8; F.C. Dietz, *English Public Finance, 1554-1641* (1932), 223, 228; *APC 1627-28*, 501.
50. G. Huxley, *Endymion Porter: The Life of a Courtier* (1959), 126.
51. LS13/30, though the order adds 'except upon special occasion His Majesty shall think fit to increase the same'.
52. Sir George Gresley to Sir Thomas Puckering, 15 November 1629, T. Birch (ed.), *The Court and Times of Charles I* (2 vols, 1848) II, 36; in 1637 attempts were still being made to secure the same economy, *HMC, De Lisle and Dudley MSS* VI, 139.
53. SP16/386/97; cf. Knowler, *Strafford Letters* II, 140-1.
54. BL Stowe MS 563, f.16^v.
55. LS13/30; LS13/169, 196.
56. BL Harley MS 7623, f.17^v (prince's household).
57. Ibid., f.15^v.
58. Order of 27 May 1627, LS13/169. For the effects of these attempts to reduce the costs of diet, see G.E. Aylmer, 'Studies in the Institutions and Personnel of English Central Administration, 1625-1642' (D.Phil. thesis, Oxford University, 1954). I am grateful to Gerald Aylmer for permission to cite this thesis and for his generous advice.
59. Order of 22 August 1634, LS13/169, p. 243.
60. I shall be developing this argument in my study of the personal rule of Charles I.
61. BL Harley MS 7623, f.18.
62. Ibid., fos 18-18^v.
63. Order of 9 February 1627, LS13/169.
64. Order of 17 November 1628, LS13/169.
65. Ibid.
66. There is a full and detailed report on the deficiencies of accounting methods in LS13/169, pp. 313ff. The commissioners recommended major changes. See, for example, 342.
67. LS13/169, pp. 34-5.
68. G.E. Aylmer, 'Attempts at Administrative Reform, 1625-40', *EHR*, 72 (1957), 229-59.
69. See, for example, a list of losses of plate from the royal scullery between September 1634 and April 1640, LS13/169, PC 2/42, pp. 106, 235 and BL Harley MS 7623, f.15^v. One dish was reported 'lost between the kitchen and the waiters' chamber at Whitehall'!
70. LS13/169, p. 256.
71. 'New Years Gifts given by the King's Majesty . . .' BL Harley Roll T2. The candlesticks were 'pardoned by his Majesty to Henry Lawton'.
72. BL Sloane MS 1494, f.45.
73. Sir Thomas Herbert to Viscount Scudamore, 2 March 1632,

C115/N3/8548.

74. LS13/169, p. 221. Cf. *HMC, Denbigh MSS* V, 8.

75. BL Stowe MS 561, f.4ᵛ.

76. Ibid., fos 6–7; cf. 'The order of All-Night as described by Ferdinando Masham Esquire of the Body to K. Charles I and K. Charles II', in S. Pegge, *Curialia or an Historical Account of Some Branches of the Royal Household* (1782), 19–23.

77. Above, 149 and also Finet's observation that the ambassador of the United Provinces was no longer after 1628 admitted by the backstairs, *Finetti Philoxenis*, 200-1.

78. Mead to Sir Martin Stuteville, 25 July 1629, in Birch (ed.), *Court and Times of Charles I* II, 24.

79. Ibid., II, 25.

80. BL Stowe MS 561, fos 5ᵛ-6.

81. On Easter day, for example, BL Sloane MS 1494, f.34.

82. Ibid., fos 9, 21, 34.

83. Contarini to Doge and Senate, 4 September 1626, *Cal. Stat. Pap. Venet. 1625-26*, 524-5,

84. Sir J. Finet to Scudamore, 17 April 1637, C115/N8/8804.

85. BL Sloane MS 1494, f.9.

86. Ibid., f.9.

87. LC5/180, p. 16.

88. I shall be arguing in a study of the personal rule of Charles I that Charles rather than Laud was the prime initiator of the liturgical changes of the 1630s.

89. BL Sloane MS 1494, f.10.

90. Elias Ashmole, *The History of The Most Noble Order of the Garter* (1715), 438.

91. Ibid., 85, 317-8.

92. For Charles's proposals for 'the most complete and absolute Reformation' of the order, Ashmole, *History of the Garter*, 148-9.

93. The Van Dyck portraits of Caroline courtiers, like those of Charles himself, show the Garter prominently displayed. See R. Strong, *Charles I on Horseback* (1972).

94. Sir T. Herbert, *Memoirs of the Last Two Years of the Reign of King Charles I by Sir. Tho. Herbert, Groom of the Chamber to his Majesty* (1813), 146. Charles intended that his body should be laid in the Tomb House of the chapel at Windsor, Ashmole, *History of the Garter*, 85.

95. Ashmole, *History of the Garter*, 444.

96. C. Brown, *Van Dyck*, plate 190. Sir Robert Crane, the Chancellor of the Order of the Garter, had three drawings by Van Dyck, probably relating to this, BL Egerton MS 1636, f.89.

97. Ashmole, *History of the Garter*, 318. For a full description of an elaborate Caroline procession see BL Sloane MS 1494, fos 40-60.

98. Ashmole, *History of the Garter*, 319; LC5/193: 'Earls and Lords to attend the King's Majesty at St. George's Feast 1638 . . .'

99. L. Hutchinson, *Memoirs of the Life of Colonel Hutchinson*, ed. C.H. Firth (1906), 69.

100. See M. Bloch, *The Royal Touch: Sacred Monarchy and Scrofula in England and France* (1973).
101. BL Stowe MS 561, f.5.
102. BL Sloane MS 1494, fos 12-12^v.
103. Ibid., fos 30^v-31. I am grateful to David Starkey for a discussion of this subject.
104. BL Harley MS 4931, f.8.
105. I have followed the royal progresses through the *Calendar of State Papers Domestic* 1625 to 1640.
106. The Privy Council at Berwick to the Privy Council in London, 11 June 1633, *Cal. Stat. Pap. Dom. 1633-34*, 94.
107. D. Townshend, *The Life and Letters of Mr. Endymion Porter: Sometime Gentleman of the Bedchamber to King Charles the First* (1897), 116; G. Huxley, *Endymion Porter*, 226; L. Aikin, *Memoirs of the Court of King Charles I* (2 vols, 1833) I, 345-6.
108. Aikin, *Memoirs* I, 345.
109. T. Herbert to Viscount Scudamore, 2 March 1632, C115/N3/8548.
110. J. Wormald, 'King James VI and I'.
111. Warrant to Mr Boreman, LC3/31, p. 3.
112. Order of 26 March 1636, *Foedera* XX, 122; Order of Council, 1 January 1637, PC 2/47, p. 105. Significantly the warrants for the making and issue of the keys came from the Lord Chamberlain, cf. note 28 above.
113. SP16/154/76. We do not have complete lists for the reign of Charles I; cf. for 1625, SP16/2/118; for 1647, Bodl. Tanner MS 317.
114. LC5/180, p. 22.
115. BL Stowe MS 563, fos 14-14^v.
116. Ibid., f.15.
117. BL Sloane MS 1494, f.15; LC5/180.
118. See the Privy Council investigations of 25 March 1633, PC2/42, f.529.
119. P. Warwick, *Memoirs*, preface, and passim; cf. K. Digby, *Private Memoirs of Sir Kenelm Digby, Gentleman of the Bedchamber to King Charles I* (1827).
120. T. Herbert, *Memoirs of the Last Two Years*, 145, 146, 184.
121. BL Stowe MS 561, fos 6-7; Pegge, *Curialia*, 16.
122. Ibid., 22-3.
123. Eltham Ordinances, ch.64 (*A Collection of Ordinances and Regulations for the Government of the Royal Household* (1790), 156); Carlisle, *Gentlemen of the Privy Chamber*, 37.
124. D. Starkey, 'From Feud to Faction: English politics c. 1450-1550', *History Today* 32 (1982), 16-22.
125. The French ambassador frequently complained of difficulty in obtaining audience because Charles was hunting, e.g., PRO31/3/66, f.139, 'leurs chasses . . . qui est leur plus grand divertissement' and PRO31/3/68, f.120.
126. Warrant to pay Thomas Hooker, keeper of the tennis court at St. James's, money the king had lost to him at play, *Cal. Stat. Pap. Dom. 1625-26*, 577; Shepphard, *The Old Palace of Whitehall*, 84-5.

127. A payment for billiard staves for the king is listed in BL Additional MS 32,476, f.32; Herbert, *Memoirs of Last Two Years*, 17.

128. *Cal. Stat. Pap. Dom. 1625–26*, 577.

129. S. Pegge, *Curialia Miscellanea: or Anecdotes of Old Times* (1818), 317–18.

130. LC3/31, p. 27: warrant for payment.

131. N. Carlisle, *Gentlemen of the Privy Chamber*, 116.

132. The transcripts of French ambassadorial correspondence are dominated by this subject, e.g., PRO31/3/66–8. Cf. *Cal. Stat. Pap. Venet. 1624–26*, 198, 457, 495, 607.

133. BL Stowe MS 561, fos 12ff.

134. PRO31/3/66–72, passim.

135. Pesaro to Doge and Senate, 31 July 1625, *Cal. Stat. Pap. Venet. 1625–26*, 129.

136. Soranzo to Doge and Senate, 11 January 1630, *Cal. Stat. Pap. Venet. 1629–32*, 264.

137. William Murray to Sir Henry Vane, 18 December 1631, *Cal. Stat. Pap. Dom. 1631–33*, 205.

138. Warwick, *Memoirs*, 66.

139. LC5/180; BL Stowe MS 563, f.22.

140. *Cal. Stat. Pap. Dom. 1627–28*, 573; *Foedera* XVIII, 95.

141. *Cal. Stat. Pap. Dom. 1627–28*, 269.

142. Dockets of Letters Patent, 1634–40, BL Harley MS 1012, f.42.

143. Ibid., fos 49v, 63, 68v; *Cal. Stat. Pap. Dom. 1638–39*, 558.

144. *Foedera* XIX 37; *Cal. Stat. Pap. Dom. 1629–31*, 553.

145. BL Harley MS 1012, f.34v.

146. *Cal. Stat. Pap. Dom. 1629–31*, 362.

147. Huxley, *Endymion Porter*, 214–17, 219–20.

148. *Cal. Stat. Pap. Dom. 1629–31*, 265; ibid., *1633–34*, 331.

149. BL Stowe MS 563, f.13^v.

150. *Cal. Stat. Pap. Dom. 1627–28*, 224.

151. Ibid., 167.

152. To take one year, see ibid., 237, 521, 566, 567.

153. Huxley, *Endymion Porter*, 195.

154. Carlisle, *Gentlemen of the Privy Chamber*, 26.

155. Ibid., 107.

156. Order of Council, 18 January 1628, *APC 1627–28*, 240.

157. Carlisle, *Gentlemen of the Privy Chamber*, 117. A special guard of Privy Chambermen was mentioned in 1639, *Cal. Stat. Pap. Dom. 1638–39*, 378; C115/N3/8854.

158. Pegge, *Curialia* (1782), 57–8.

159. D. Coke, *The Last Elizabethan: Sir John Coke, 1563–1644* (1937), 254.

160. *Cal. Stat. Pap. Dom. 1628–29*, 412.

161. P. Warwick, *Memoirs*, 116. Cf. the competition for a place in the Bedchamber on the death of Thomas Carey, *Strafford Letters* I, 242. Pory reported that Newcastle paid £2,000 to be sworn of the Bedchamber, Birch, *Court and Times of Charles I*, II, 187.

162. *Strafford Letters*, II, 410.

163. The 'Diary' of William Laud, 10 July 1632, in W. Scott and J. Bliss (eds), *The Works of . . . William Laud* (7 vols in 9, Oxford, 1847-60) III, 216.

164. P. Heylyn, *Cyprianus Anglicus* (1668), 214.

165. Cuddy, in Starkey, *English Court*, 208ff.

166. *Cal. Stat. Pap. Venet. 1625-26*, 26-7.

167. Ibid., 3.

168. Conway to Dudley Carleton, 31 March 1625, Birch, *Court and Times of Charles I*, I, 4.

169. Pesaro to Doge and Senate, 18 April 1625, *Cal. Stat. Pap. Venet. 1625-26*, 11.

170. Ibid., 21.

171. G. Aylmer, *The King's Servants: the Civil Service of Charles I, 1625-42* (1961), 317. Fullerton had been Groom of the Stool to Charles as Prince of Wales. It may be that he was not Chief Gentleman of the Bedchamber and that in 1625, as in 1536, the two posts were separated — though there is no evidence for this. Buckingham clearly remained the king's intimate but with Fullerton as Groom, Pembroke, the Lord Chamberlain appears to have wielded influence even in the Bedchamber. Above, p. 151 and note 28.

172. R. Lockyer, *Buckingham: the Life and Political Career of George Villiers, first Duke of Buckingham, 1592-1628* (1981), 235.

173. *Cal. Stat. Pap. Venet. 1625-26*, 26-7; K. Sharpe, 'The Personal Rule of Charles I', H.C. Tomlinson (ed.), *Before the English Civil War* (1983), 53-78; above, ch.3.

174. This has been specifically denied by C. Carlton, *Charles I. The Personal Monarch* (1983). Both Warwick and Herbert, however, claim that Charles read his papers. The best evidence that he studied letters carefully comes from his emendations to Sir John Coke's drafts, Coke MSS, Melbourne Hall, Derbyshire. I am grateful to Lord Lothian and Derbyshire Record Office for permission to use this important collection.

175. Herbert, *Memoirs of the Last Two Years*, 62.

176. Warwick, *Memoirs*, 66; above, p. 154; Dorchester to earl of Carlisle, 30 September 1628, *Cal. Stat. Pap. Dom. 1628-29*, 339.

177. Weston failed to get a place for his son at court, *Strafford Letters* II, 389; Laud remained paranoid about his position with the king, above, 166.

178. Howell to Wentworth, 5 March 1635, *Strafford Letters* II, 377.

179. *HMC, Portland MSS* II, 126.

180. S. Gardiner, *History of England from the Accession of James I to the Outbreak of the Civil War, 1603-42* (10 vols, 1883-84) VIII, 87-8.

181. Charles I to Wentworth, 3 September 1636, *Strafford Letters* II, 32.

182. Wentworth to Newcastle, 1 June 1638, ibid., II, 174.

183. *Strafford Letters* II, 225; *HMC Buccleuch-Whitehall* III, 346; *DNB*; B. Donagan, 'A Courtier's Progress: Greed and Consistency in the Life of the Earl of Holland', *HJ*, 19 (1976), 317-53; Gardiner, *History of England* VII, 218.

184. R.M. Smuts, 'The Puritan Followers of Henrietta Maria in the 1630s',

EHR, 93 (1978), 26–45.
185. Ibid.
186. J. Flower to Scudamore, 13 March 1630, C11/M31/8124. Garrard to Wentworth, 15 March 1636, *Strafford Letters* II, 524.
187. *Cal. Stat. Pap. Dom. 1628–29*, 393; cf. ibid., 412.
188. The French ambassadors frequently complained of her powerlessness.
189. John Owen, *Certain Epigrams* (1628), 31.
190. LC5/180, p. 1.
191. 8 November 1631, *HMC, Gawdy*, 136.
192. BL Additional MS 10,112, Van der Dort's Catalogue.
193. M. Whinney and O. Millar, *English Art, 1625–1714* (1957), 72.
194. T. Carew, *Coelum Britannicum* (performed 18 February 1634), in Orgel and Strong (eds), *Theatre of the Stuart Court*, II, 567–80.
195. R. Dunlap, (ed.), *The Poems of Thomas Carew* (Oxford, 1949), introduction.
196. BL Egerton MS 1636, f.2.
197. Robert Reade to Tho. Windebank, 23 January 1640, *Cal. Stat. Pap. Dom. 1639–40*, 364.

Chapter 6

* The world copyright of this article rests with The Past and Present Society, 175 Banbury Road, Oxford. It is reprinted with the Society's permission from *Past and Present*, 72 (August 1976) pp. 133–142 and with the kind permission of Christopher Brooks. Professor Donald Kelley replied to the article in *Past and Present*, 72 (August 1976) pp. 143–146.

1. D.R. Kelley, *Foundations of Modern Historical Scholarship: Language, Law and History in the French Renaissance* (New York, 1970).
2. D.R. Kelley, 'History, English Law and the Renaissance', *P&P*, 65 (Nov. 1974), 24–51.
3. Ibid., 28.
4. Ibid., 47.
5. Ibid., loc. cit.
6. See, for example, BL Cotton MS., Titus B, V, fos 419–23: 'Gerard Malignes Discourse for Reducing the Laws to Order': Historical Manuscripts Commission, *Hatfield House*, xviii, 60: a note by Sir Ferdinando Gorges about his proposals 'to reform . . . abuses and errors of the law'.
7. F. Bacon, 'Maxims of the Law' (1596), in J. Spedding (ed.), *The Works of Francis Bacon* (7 vols, 1857–9), vii, 319.
8. T. Egerton, 'Memorialles for Iudicature. Pro Bono Publico'. We are very grateful to Dr. L.A. Knafla for his transcription of this manuscript which is in the Henry Huntington Library, San Marino, California, Ellesmere MS, 2623.
9. Sir John Davies, 'A Discourse of Law and Lawyers' (1615), in A.B.

NOTES TO PAGES 175-177

Grosart (ed.), *The Complete Works (including Hitherto Unpublished MSS) of Sir John Davies* . . ., (3 vols, 1869-76), iii, 255.

10. See below, 180. There are many examples. Bacon's desire to produce a work on the basic principles of the common law was to some extent realized in Henrie Finch, *Law or A Discourse Thereof in Foure Bookes* (first published in law French, 1613, English edn, 1627). For the sixteenth century, see the dedication in W. Sta[u]nford, *An Exposicion of the Kinges Prerogative Collected Out of the Great Abridgement of Justice Fitzherbert* . . . (1567). Sta[u]nford praised the common laws, but added that the knowledge of them was dark and 'farr off'. He recommended that lawyers publish more books like his own which aimed to help students. It is also worth noticing that Sta[u]nford may have been responsible for the first printed edition of 'Glanville'. For this, see Sir W. Sta[u]nford, *Les Plees del Coron*, ed. P.R. Glazebrook (1971), editor's introduction.

11. For some European proposals for law reform, see Jacques Vanderlinden, *Le concept de code en Europe occidentale du XIIIe au XIXe siècle* (Etudes d'histoire et d'ethnologie juridiques. Editions de l'Institut de Sociologie, Université Libre de Bruxelles, 1967), 'Annexe'. We owe this reference to Mr. J.P. Cooper.

12. Davies, op. cit., 262-8.

13. Kelley, 'History, English Law and the Renaissance', 40.

14. H. Townshend, *Historical Collections or An Exact Account of the Proceedings, of the Four Last Parliaments of Q. Elizabeth of Famous Memory* . . . (1680), 37.

15. Ibid., 79.

16. F. Bacon, 'A Proposition to His Majesty . . .', in *Law Tracts* [ed. anon.] (1737), 14.

17. For the use of precedents in Bate's case, see G.D.G. Hall, 'Impositions and the Courts', *Law Quart. Rev.*, lxix (1953), 200.

18. W. Barlee, *A Concordance of All Written Lawes Concerning Lords of Mannors, Theire Free Tenantes, and Copieholders* (Manorial Society Publications, vi, 1911), 45.

19. Townshend, op. cit., 190.

20. Anon., *A Discourse upon the Exposition and Understanding of Statutes*, ed. S.E. Thorne (San Marino, California, 1942). The tract was probably written between 1557 and 1567.

21. W. Fulbecke, *A Direction or Preparative to the Study of the Law* (1600; 2nd edn, 1620), 28. W. Sta[u]nford, *Les Plees des Coron* (1557, STC 23219; 1567 edn, STC 23221), f.123: 'Mes coment cest priulege commensast inquires del doctours del ley cannon du quel ley cest Priulige suer sa nessance . . .'.

22. W. West, *Symboleographia* (1590, STC 25267; 1611 edn, STC 25272), f.174^v. The work of Joannes Corasius to which West refers seems to be the *Miscellaneorum Iuris Civilis, Libri Septem* (Cologne, 1590). For Budé, see Kelley, *Foundations of Modern Historical Scholarship*, ch.iii.

23. L.A. Knafla, 'The Matriculation Revolution and Education at the Inns of Court in Renaissance England', in A. Slavin (ed.), *Tudor Men and*

Institutions (Baton Rouge, Louisiana, 1972), 241.

24. B.P. Levack, *The Civil Lawyers in England, 1603-1641* (Oxford, 1973), 232.

25. Ibid., 134-7.

26. For Doddridge and Whitelocke, see E. Foss, *A Biographical Dictionary of the Judges of England* (1870), 232, 721-2.

27. Kelley, 'History, English Law and the Renaissance', 29.

28. BL MS Stowe 423, f.37^v.

29. W.S. Holdsworth, *A History of English Law* (16 vols, 1922-66), v, 21.

30. F.W. Maitland, 'Materials for the History of English Law', in E. Freund et al. (eds), *Select Essays in Anglo-American Legal History* (3 vols, Boston, Mass., 1907-9), ii, 57.

31. W. Camden, 'The Antiquity and Office of the Earl Marshall of England', in T. Hearne, *A Collection of Curious Discourses*, ed. J. Ayloffe (2 vols, 1771), ii, 90-7. Camden corresponded with the Hotmans: T. Smith (ed.), *Guliemi Camdeni . . . Epistolae* (1691), 21; *Francisci et Joannis Hotmanorum Epistolae*, ed. J.G. Meelii (Amsterdam, 1700), 331, 49. Camden introduced the members of the Society to the etymological approaches which he had employed in his *Britannia* (1586).

32. Some of the contributions are in Hearne, op. cit. The others are in BL Cotton MS, Cleopatra E, I, and MS Stowe 1045. References to the 'French writers' are often found. For example, Hearne, op. cit., i, 54, ii, 38; i, 28; ii, 2, 8. On attitudes to the Norman Conquest, see Joseph Holland, 'Of the Antiquity of Terms for the Administration of Justice in England', in ibid., i, 32-3, and the debates on the herald's office, ibid., i, 50-64, and on the inns of court, ibid., i, 64-83. Cotton said of the Earl Marshal that 'the name and office now in use, we borrowed, as *all other fashions* by the imitation of our French neighbours': ibid., ii, 99. Our italics.

33. Sir John Davies, 'The Antiquity and Office of the Earl Marshal of England', in Hearne, op. cit., ii, 108-11. Davies cites Bodin, ibid., 108; W. Hakewill, 'The Antiquity of the Laws of This Island', in ibid., i, 1-7.

34. Hakewill's contribution was part of a larger series. See BL Cotton MS Cleopatra E, I, f.242: '1605 The Question against Easter Terme is the Antiquity and Authority of the Civill Lawe in England'.

35. See F. Tate, 'Of Knights made by Abbots', in Hearne, op. cit., i, 84-90. Tate refers to an earlier seminar on Knights' fees, ibid., i, 85. This was held in Nov. 1599. BL Cotton MS Faustina E, V, f.67; notes for another paper on the same subject are in BL Stowe MS 1045, f.60.

36. BL Cotton MS Titus F, IV, fos 60-2.

37. Sir John Davies, 'The Question Concerning Impositions', in *The Works of Sir John Davies*, iii, 8.

38. E.R. Foster, *Proceedings in Parliament, 1610* (2 vols, New Haven, 1966), ii, 207.

39. J. Selden, *Titles of Honor* (1614), preface and pt. ii, ch.viii.

40. Sir John Fortescue, *De Laudibus Legum Angliae*, [ed. J. Selden]

(1616), 7-9, 14-20.

41. Henrici de Bracton, *De Legibus et Consuetudinibus Angliae,* [ed. anon.] (1640; entered by Stationers Co., 5 Mar. 1620), 'Candido Lectori', sig. A3: *'Praeterem lector, si quid quod tum temporum pro lege habebatur, nunc recentiorum statutorum sanctionibus immutatum sit, vel aliis de causis Justitiariorum opiniones ab antiqua sententia recesserint . . .'.*

42. Sir Henry Spelman, 'Of the Antiquity and Etymology of Terms and Times for Administration of Justice in England', in Hearne, op. cit., ii, 331-75. Cf. *Reliquiae Spelmannianae,* in E. Gibson (ed.), *The English Works of Sir Henry Spelman, Kt.,* (1973), 68-104. Both Ayloffe and Gibson ascribe the paper to 1614, but an earlier paper by Joseph Holland (BL Cotton MS Faustina E, V, f.8) suggests that the subject had been discussed before. For Spelman's correspondence with the French, see BL Add. MS 25,384, fos 3, 12; ibid., Add. MS 34,359, f.59.

43. Ibid., Lansdowne MS 137, f.2; Historical Manuscripts Commission, *Salisbury,* XXX, 272. BL Cotton MS Julius C, III, f.310; W. Prynne, *An Exact Abridgement of the Records in the Tower of London* (1657). Cotton assisted Bowyer with the work on which this was based. See also M. Friedlander, 'Growth in the Resources for Studies in Earlier English History, 1534-1625' (Ph.D. thesis, Chicago University, 1938).

44. Thomas Hedley's speech, 28 June 1610, in Foster, op. cit., ii, 174-87.

45. T.B. Howell (ed.), *A Complete Collection of State Trials* (21 vols, 1809-14), ii, 414ff.

46. J.G.A. Pocock, *The Ancient Constitution and the Feudal Law: English Historical Thought in the Seventeenth Century* (Cambridge, 1957), ch.iv.

47. Sir Henry Spelman, 'Of Parliaments', in *Reliquiae Spelmannianae,* 57-65.

Chapter 7

* Originally published in K. Sharpe (ed.), *Faction and Parliament: Essays on Early Stuart History* (Oxford University Press, 1978) 209-44.

I would like to thank His Grace the Duke of Norfolk, P.M., C.D., C.B.E., M.C. for permission to cite letters from Arundel Castle.

1. Work has commenced on procedure in the House of Lords (see especially E.R. Foster, *The Painful Labour of Mr. Elsyng* (Philadelphia, 1972), also J. Flemion, 'Slow Process, Due Process and the High Court of Parliament', *HJ,* xvii (1974), 3-17). We still await a political study of the Lords. I would like to thank Christopher Brooks, John Cooper, Conrad Russell, and Hugh Trevor-Roper for their most valuable comments on an earlier draft of this essay.

2. M.F.S. Hervey's excellent biography, *Thomas Howard Earl of Arundel* (Cambridge, 1921), pays little attention to the detail of political alignment. I plan a political biography of the Earl.

3. BL MS Harl. 6272.

4. Edward Earl of Clarendon, *The History of the Rebellion and Civil*

Wars in England, ed. W.D. Macray (6 vols, Oxford, 1888), i, 69–70.

5. A. Wagner, *The Heralds of England* (1967), 235.
6. D.N. Smith, *Characters from the Histories and Memoirs of the Seventeenth Century* (Oxford, 1920), 265.
7. *Cal. Stat. Pap. Dom. 1603–10*, 117, 225; Hervey, op. cit., 20–3, 464.
8. *Cal. Stat. Pap. Dom. 1603–10*, 390; Hervey, op. cit., 124.
9. J. Nichols, *The Progresses, Processions and Magnificent Festivities of King James I* (4 vols, 1828), ii, 80, 270, 307, 361; Hervey, op. cit., 465.
10. *Cal. Stat. Pap. Venet. 1610–13*, 438–39.
11. Hervey, op. cit., 102.
12. M.A. Tierney, *The History and Antiquities of the Castle and Town of Arundel* (2 vols, 1834), ii, 553.
13. *APC 1615–16*, 674; Hervey, op. cit., 114–16.
14. *Cal. Stat. Pap. Venet. 1615–17*, 245.
15. T. Longueville, *Policy and Paint* (1913), 25.
16. Hervey, op. cit., 21.
17. Nichols, iii, 348.
18. N.M. McClure (ed.), *The Letters of John Chamberlain* (2 vols, Philadelphia, 1939), ii, 272, 368; cf. J. Hacket, *Scrinia Reserata* (2 parts, 1693), i, 51.
19. A remark made by Contarini in 1626, *Cal. Stat. Pap. Venet. 1625–6*, 599; in 1626 Sir Robert Pye observed that those who were Buckingham's enemies then had been his friends in 1621. *HMC 13th Rep.*, app. vii (Lonsdale MSS), 13.
20. *Cal. Stat. Pap. Dom. 1611–18*, 582, 586; Arundel was also appointed to it: *APC 1617–18*, 263.
21. They received ambassadors together: *Cal. Stat. Pap. Venet. 1617–19*, 569; *Cal. Stat. Pap. Venet. 1619–21*, 372.
22. For this parliament see R. Zaller, *The Parliament of 1621* (Berkeley, 1971).
23. *LJ*, iii, 62, 67.
24. *LJ*, iii, 47.
25. S.R. Gardiner (ed.), *Notes of Debates in the House of Lords 1621* (Camden Soc., 1870), 62; *Letters of Chamberlain*, ii, 356; *HMC Mar and Kellie Supplement*, 111–12.
26. *Debates in the Lords 1621*, 47–9.
27. Ibid., 49, 57–9. There was some sympathy for Yelverton. Ibid., 55; C.G.C. Tite, *Impeachment and Parliamentary Judicature in early Stuart England* (1974), 122.
28. *Debates in the Lords 1621*, 73–4; *Cal. Stat. Pap. Dom. 1619–21*, 254, 257; *Cal. Stat. Pap. Venet. 1621–3*, 53.
29. *Cal. Stat. Pap. Venet. 1621–3*, 55; *Letters of Chamberlain*, ii, 374–5.
30. *Cal. Stat. Pap. Dom. 1619–21*, 262; *Letters of Chamberlain*, ii, 378.
31. *HMC Portland*, ii, 120, 5 June, 1621.
32. On 9 June 1621, *Letters of Chamberlain*, ii, 381.
33. *Cal. Stat. Pap. Dom. 1619–23*, 283, 285, 426; Arundel had been Marshal for Prince Charles's creation as Prince of Wales (*Cal. Stat. Pap. Dom. 1611–18*, 401), having served as commissioner for the

office since October 1616. In 1617 an antiquary delivered him notes on the Marshal's office. Bodl. MS Ashmole 862, f.66.

34. *Cal. Stat. Pap. Dom. 1619–23*, 291; Williams to Buckingham, 1 Sept. 1621, *Cabala* (1654 edn), 62–5.
35. G. Roberts (ed.), *Diary of Walter Yonge 1604–1628* (Camden Soc., 1848), 42.
36. *Cal. Stat. Pap. Venet. 1621–3*, 137–8.
37. *Cal. Stat. Pap. Dom. 1619–23*, 293; A. Wagner, 'The Origin of the Introduction of Peers in the House of Lords', *Archaeologia*, 101 (1967), 119–50.
38. Zaller, op. cit., 151–2; Sir George Goring to Buckingham, 29 Nov. 1621, in W. Notestein, F.H. Relf, and H. Simpson (eds), *Commons Debates 1621* (7 vols, New Haven, 1935), vii, 620–1.
39. Zaller, op. cit., 152–3; S.L. Adams, 'Foreign policy and the Parliaments of 1621 and 1624' in K. Sharpe (ed.), *Faction and Parliament*, esp. 155, 163.
40. *Debates in the Lords 1621*, 122, and see below, 202. Arundel had close personal ties with the Queen of Bohemia. Arundel Castle Autograph Letters 1617–1632, fos 228, 292.
41. *APC 1621–3*, 99.
42. *Cal. Stat. Pap. Venet. 1619–21*, 120.
43. PRO SP 14/132/83; T. Hearne, *Curious Discourses*, ed. J. Ayloffe (2 vols, 1771), i, 97; ii, 65.
44. *Cal. Stat. Pap. Dom. 1619–23*, 436, 559.
45. R.F. Williams (ed.), *The Court and Times of James I* (2 vols, 1849), ii, 159; R.W. Kenny, *Elizabeth's Admiral: the Political Career of Charles Howard, Earl of Nottingham* (Baltimore, 1970), 330–1.
46. G.D. Squibb, *The High Court of Chivalry* (Oxford, 1959); A. Wagner, *The Heralds of England*, 229–35.
47. Williams to Buckingham, 2 Mar. 1625, *Cabala*, 101–3; *Cal. Stat. Pap. Dom. 1623–5*, 561.
48. *HMC Mar and Kellie Suppl.* 140–2, 145.
49. *Diary of Yonge*, 57.
50. S.L. Adams, 'The Protestant Cause: Religious alliance with the West European Calvinist Communities as a Political Issue in England, 1585–1630' (D.Phil. thesis, Oxford University, 1973), 333.
51. *HMC Mar and Kellie Suppl*, 156. Kellie added, 'I know him to be wyser than to take onye exceptions at this time.'
52. E. Boussier (ed.), *The Diary of Simonds D'Ewes 1622–4* (Paris, 1975), 146.
53. *Cal. Stat. Pap. Dom. 1619–23*, 495, 503; *HMC Mar and Kellie Suppl.* 152–3, 175.
54. *HMC Mar and Kellie Suppl.*, 157.
55. Chamberlain to Carleton, 17 May 1623, *Letters of Chamberlain*, ii, 497.
56. *Cabala*, 160; *Cal. Stat. Pap. Venet. 1623–5*, 28
57. BL MS Harl. 1581, f.60; cf. f.244.
58. R. Ruigh, *The Parliament of 1624: Politics and Foreign Policy* (Cambridge, Mass., 1971), 354 n.22.

59. *Cal. Stat. Pap. Dom. 1623–5*, 20.
60. Ibid., 33.
61. Ibid., 81.
62. *Cabala*, 316.
63. Bristol claimed that he remained in Charles's favour when the prince left Spain leaving him with the proxy for the marriage. By May, however, the prince was reported to be of Buckingham's party in his quarrel with Bristol. S.R. Gardiner (ed.), *The Earl of Bristol's Defence of his Negotiations in Spain* Camden Misc., vi (1871), v–vii.
64. *HMC Mar and Kellie Suppl.*, 183–4.
65. *Cal. Stat. Pap. Venet. 1623–5*, 169–70.
66. *Cabala*, 160.
67. Locke to Carleton, 26 Dec. 1623, *Cal. Stat. Pap. Dom. 1623–5*, 134; *Cal. Stat. Pap. Venet. 1623–5*, 178.
68. J. Packer to J. Williams, 21 Jan. 1623/4, *Cabala*, 86.
69. *Cal. Stat. Pap. Dom. 1623–5*, 156.
70. Salvetti Correspondence 5 Jan. 1624, BL MS Add. 27962, vol. III, f.88, cited in D.H. Wilson, 'Summoning and Dissolving Parliament 1603–25', *AHR.*, xlv, (1940), 299 n.66.
71. Wilson, art. cit., 299.
72. Ruigh, *Parliament of 1624*, 101–2.
73. *HMC Mar and Kellie Suppl.*, 193.
74. *LJ*, iii, 236, 238.
75. *LJ*, iii, 259.
76. *Cal. Stat. Pap. Dom. 1623–5*, 191.
77. *CJ*, i, 742: *Cal. Stat. Pap. Dom. 1623–5*, 197; A.J. Kempe (ed.), *The Loseley Manuscripts* (1836), 479–80; Northants RO, Finch Hatton MS 50 (Parliamentary diary of John Pym), f.34 (I am grateful to Conrad Russell for lending me a microfilm of this manuscript); Ruigh, op. cit., 224–5.
78. Northants RO, MS 50, f.34.
79. Ibid., fos 34–35; *CJ*, i, 742–3.
80. PRO SP. 14/161/30. I owe this reference to Ruigh, op. cit., 224 n.129.
81. *Loseley Manuscripts*, 470–6.
82. Ibid., 472.
83. For accounts of the election see Pym's diary, f.40; BL MS Add. 36856, fos 108ᵛ–109.
84. 'And though I had 16 witnesses to cleare and justefie my election, yet ye Committee entred to ye hearing ye cause, but just as sunne sett and being then darkeish (before Easter) they made it such a [i.e. dark] worke, and in one quarter of an houre, without so much as hearinge one witnes for me, or more than one witness against me, they sentenced my election voyde.' *Loseley Manuscripts*, 482.
85. See ibid., 482.
86. Ibid., 480–3.
87. *LJ*, iii, 301.
88. BL MS Add. 40088, f.25.
89. Hacket, *Scrinia Reserata*, i, 189–90.
90. *CJ*, i, 786, 701; Pym Diary, f.81ᵛ; P.H. Hardacre, 'The Earl Marshal,

the Heralds and the House of Commons 1604–41', *Int. Rev. Soc. Hist.*, 2 (1975), 106–25. On 8 May complaints were also delivered against Bishop Harsnett of Norwich, a close friend of the Earl of Arundel, concerning his Arminian practices and alleged sympathy towards Catholics. *LJ*, iii, 362; Pym, f.89ᵛ; Arundel Castle Letters 1617–1632, f.225; BL MS Add. 15970, f.15.

91. BL MS Add. 40088, f.13.
92. S.R. Gardiner, *Camden Misc.*, vi, p.v.
93. Ibid., v; speech of James I, 7 May reported in Pym, f.89.
94. Gardiner, op. cit., vii; Clarendon, *History of the Rebellion*, i, 28.
95. *LJ*, iii, 418.
96. *History of the Rebellion*, i, 29; *HMC Mar and Kellie Suppl.*, 201, 203.
97. *Cal. Stat. Pap. Dom. 1623–25*, 267, 5 June, 1624.
98. *Cal. Stat. Pap. Venet. 1623–25*, 343, 14 June 1624.
99. Ruigh, op. cit., 361.
100. S.R. Gardiner, op. cit., xi–xii.
101. *Cabala*, 264–6.
102. *Scrinia Reserata*, I, 150.
103. *Cal. Stat. Pap. Venet. 1623–25*, 453.
104. *HMC Mar and Kellie Suppl.*, 206, 216.
105. *Cal. Stat. Pap. Venet. 1623–25*, 511.
106. C.S.R. Russell (ed.), *The Origins of the English Civil War* (1973), 16.
107. 18 Apr. 1625, *Cal. Stat. Pap. Venet. 1625–26*, 12; 25 Apr., ibid., 21.
108. See my *Faction and Parliament*, introduction, 37–42.
109. BL MS Harl. 6645.
110. *HMC Mar and Kellie Suppl.*, 282, 15 Aug. 1625.
111. W. Knowler (ed.), *The Earl of Strafford's Letters and Despatches* (2 vols, 1739), i, 28. Wentworth had shown great concern about the treatment of Bristol, ibid., 21.
112. *Scrinia Reserata*, i, 14.
113. BL MS Add. 30651 (French transcripts), fos 12ᵛ–13; *Cabala*, 301.
114. James Howell (ed.), *Cottoni Posthuma* (1651), 273–81. K.M. Sharpe, 'The Intellectual and Political Activities of Sir Robert Cotton c. 1590–1631' (D.Phil. thesis, Oxford University, 1975), 216–19.
115. Somerset RO Phelips MSS DD/Ph 216/19. I owe this reference to Conrad Russell.
116. *Cal. Stat. Pap. Venet. 1625–6*, 146.
117. C. Holles (ed.), *Memorials of the Holles Family 1493–1656* (Camden Soc., 1937), ch.12.
118. Earl of Clare to Arundel, 23 Oct. 1625, Arundel Castle Letters 1617–1632, f.277.
119. Earl of Clare to Wentworth, *Strafford Letters*, i, 31.
120. BL MS Add. 6297, f.283.
121. J.O. Halliwell (ed.), *The Autobiography and Correspondence of Simonds D'Ewes* (2 vols, 1895), i, 291.
122. D'Ewes to Sir Martin Stuteville, 4 Feb. 1625/6, BL MS Harl. 383, f.24.
123. S.R. Gardiner, op. cit., xv–xxxi; *Cal. Stat. Pap. Dom. 1625–49*,

112, Sir James Bagg to Buckingham, Mar. 1626.

124. The Earl of Suffolk transferred his proxy from his elder to his younger son who was an enemy of the Duke. T. Birch (ed.), *The Court and Times of Charles I* (2 vols, 1848), i, 106.

125. S.R. Gardiner (ed.), *Notes of the Debates in the House of Lords 1624-1626* (Camden Soc., 1879), 113-14.

126. For proxies see *LJ*, iii, 491; Ruigh, op. cit., 377 n. 76.

127. *HMC Skrine MSS* 54; V.F. Snow, 'The Arundel Case', *Historian*, xxvi (1964), 323-50. It is interesting to note that Buckingham had copies of letters between Arundel and his son Lord Maltravers on this question. BL MS Harl. 1581, f.390.

128. Tierney, *History of Arundel*, ii, 454; cf. *Court and Times of Charles I*, i, 90-1.

129. Arundel Castle Letters 1617-1623, f.284.

130. H. Elsyng, *The Ancient Method and Manner of Holding Parliaments in England* (1660), 151-2.

131. *Lords Debates 1624 and 1626*, 135.

132. Ibid., 139.

133. For the charges, see *HMC 13th Report*, App. 7, p. 11; T. Ball, *Life of The Renowned Doctor Preston* (1885), 116-17.

134. Bristol drew up for his own instruction a list of proxies held in the Lords, Ruigh, op. cit., 377 n.77.

135. *Lords Debates 1624 and 1626*, 144; *LJ*, iii, 504.

136. Arundel Castle Letters 1617-1623, f.285; Arundel had recommended Mainwaring for a seat at Steyning in 1624. Ruigh, op. cit., 10.

137. *Cal. Stat. Pap. Venet. 1625-6*, 390.

138. *LJ*, iii, 576.

139. *LJ*, iii, 591, 646, 652; *HMC Skrine MSS* 63, 65, 66.

140. Bodl. MS. Carte 77, f.104.

141. Lord Braybootle (ed.), *The Private Correspondence of Jane Lady Cornwallis 1613-1644* (1842), 146.

142. *LJ*, iii, 653.

143. Edmund Bolton to Buckingham, 29 May, 1626, *Cal. Stat. Pap. Dom. 1625-49*, 129.

144. *Lords Debates 1624 and 1626*, 214.

145. Ibid., 224-6; I have benefited greatly from conversations with Norman Ball and Conrad Russell on the Parliament of 1626. The above account is basically endorsed by J. Flemion, 'The dissolution of Parliament in 1626: a revaluation', *EHR* 87 (1972), 784-90, but Flemion pays little attention to Bristol's case.

146. *Cal. Stat. Pap. Venet. 1625-6*, 512, 21 Aug. 1626.

147. BL MS Add. 40087, fos 89, 96^v.

148. *HMC Skrine MSS*. 76; *HMC Cowper* i, 320; *Cal. Stat. Pap. Dom. 1627-8*, 461; *APC 1627*, 250. Arundel was not listed as one of the recalcitrant peers who refused the loan, *Diary of Walter Yonge*, 98.

149. *Cal. Stat. Pap. Dom. 1627-8*, 230-1.

150. *Court and Times of Charles I*, i, 175.

151. C. Russell, 'Parliamentary History 1604-1629 in Perspective', *History*, 61 (1976), 18-19; S.L. Adams, 'Protestant Cause', 399-400.

152. R. Cotton, *The Danger Wherein the Kingdom Now Standeth and the Remedy* (1628) and in *Cottoni Posthuma*, 309-20. The copy in BL MS Lansdowne 254, fos 258-69 is dated 27 Jan. 1627/8..

153. *Cal. Stat. Pap. Dom. 1628-9*, 60: PRO SP 16/101/43; cf. *Court and Times of Charles I*, i, 309.

154. *LJ*, iii, 782.

155. F.H. Relf, *The Petition of Right* (Minneapolis, 1917).

156. *Court and Times of Charles I*, i, 346-7, 349; *LJ*, iii, 801; V.F. Snow, *Essex the Rebel: The Life of Robert Devereux, 3rd Earl of Essex 1591-1646* (Lincoln, Nebr., 1970), 170.

157. *HMC 13th Report*, App. vii (Lonsdale MSS), 42, 11 June 1628; *LJ*, iii, 837-8; *CJ*, i, 911, *HMC Cowper* i, 351; Tierney, *History of Arundel*, i, 132.

158. J. Selden, *Marmora Arundelliana* (1628); Hervey, op. cit., 279-83.

159. *Court and Times of Charles I*, i, 381; *HMC Skrine MSS.* 169. Salvetti commented in October: 'Now that he [Arundel] is replaced he will take a distinguished part in the government of the State.'

160. *Cal. Stat. Pap. Dom. 1625-49*, 291-3.

161. *Court and Times of Charles I*, i, 419. In December the king and queen paid the Earl the honour of a visit to Arundel House, ibid., 451.

162. J.P. Cooper (ed.), *The Wentworth Papers 1597-1628* (Camden Soc., 1973), 308, Clare to Wentworth, 15 Nov. 1628.

163. *Strafford Letters*, i, 47, Weston to Calvert, 8 Sept. 1628.

164. *LJ*, iv, 34, 39.

165. *Cal. Stat. Pap. Dom. 1629-31*, 167.

166. Arundel to Sir Thomas Edmondes, 23 Feb. 1614, BL MS Stowe 175, f.244.

167. Ruigh, op. cit., 33; *Cal. Stat. Pap. Dom. 1625-49*, 336. Arundel to Vane, 10 Aug. 1629; Hervey, op. cit., 396.

168. Carleton to Vere, Oct. 1617, Arundel Castle Letters 1586-1617, f.222; H. Bouchier to Ussher, C.R. Elrington and J.M. Todd (eds), *The Works of James Ussher* (17 vols, Dublin, 1847-64), xv, 194; G. Ornsby (ed.), *The Correspondence of John Cosin* (Surtees Soc., lii, 1869), 85, 91.

169. Hervey, op. cit., App. ii; BL MS Harl. 4840; G. Carracoli, *The Antiquities of Arundel* (1776), 213.

170. *Bibliotheca Norfolciana* (1681); BL MS Sloane 862 is a manuscript list of Arundel's library.

171. *Cabala*, 105; G. Goodwin, *A Catalogue of the Harsnett Library at Colchester* (1886).

172. *HMC Portland*, ix, 152; *Memorials of Holles*, 112.

173. Arundel Castle Letters 1617-32, f.251; *HMC Downshire*, iii, 189-90; *Cal. Stat. Pap. Dom. 1611-18*, 356; Tierney, *History of Arundel*, ii, 435.

174. M. Whinney and O. Millar, *English Art 1625-1714* (Oxford, 1957), 2.

175. *The Negotiations of Sir Thomas Roe* (1760), 386, 434, 444-6, 495.

176. 29 May 1626, *Cal. Stat. Pap. Dom. 1625-49*, 129.

177. W.N. Sainsbury, *Original Unpublished Papers Illustrative of the Life of Sir Peter Paul Rubens* (1859), 283.
178. F. Junius, *De Pictura Veterum* (Amsterdam, 1637).
179. *Cal. Stat. Pap. Venet. 1619-21*, 34, 81; Arundel Castle Letters 1617-1632, f.267; P.C. Molhuysen (ed.), *Briefwisseling Van Hugo Grotius*, Vol. ii, (The Hague, 1936), 240.
180. *DNB* Holles; Bodl. MS Firth B2, f.104^v; Sharpe, 'Sir Robert Cotton', passim.
181. BL MS Add. 30651, f.53^v; *Scrinia Reserata*, i, 183.
182. Lord Percy wrote in September 1628 that Buckingham's sordid death befitted a life 'which was granted by all men to be dishonourable and odious', *Cal. Stat. Pap. Dom. 1625-49*, 291-3.
183. Tierney, *History of Arundel*, 457.
184. Ibid., 437; Arundel Castle Letters 1617-32, f.225.
185. *Autobiography of Simonds D'Ewes*, ii, 183; *Memorials of Holles*, 103.
186. *Cal. Stat. Pap. Dom. 1625-49*, 291.
187. *HMC Hatfield*, xv, 190; *Letters of Chamberlain*, i, 412.
188. Bodl. MS Ashmole 857; *LJ*, iv, 31.
189. *LJ*, iii, 41.
190. *Letters of Chamberlain*, ii, 286.
191. *Cal. Stat. Pap. Dom. 1623-5*, 95; Bodl. MS Ashmole 846, f.37.
192. C.H. Firth, *The House of Lords During the Civil War* (1910), 14.
193. *Cal. Stat. Pap. Dom. 1625-6*, 243.
194. *HMC 13th Report*, App. vii (Lonsdale), 42.
195. Ben Jonson, *Works*, ed. C.H. Herford and P. and E.M. Simpson (11 vols, Oxford, 1925-52), vii, 585.
196. F. Junius, *The Painting of the Ancients* (English edn, 1678), Dedication to Countess of Arundel.
197. E.g. *The Mirrour of Majestie* (1618); G. Markham, *The Booke of Honour* (1625).

Chapter 8

* Originally published in *History of Universities*, Volume II, 1982, 127-52.

1. H.R. Trevor-Roper, review of Christopher Hill, *Intellectual Origins of the English Revolution*, in *History and Theory*, 5 (1966), 63. I would like to thank Hugh Trevor-Roper for his valuable comments on an earlier draft of this paper.
2. M. Curtis, *Oxford and Cambridge in Transition* (Oxford, 1959), 119, 136-40; W. Costello, *The Scholastic Curriculum at Early Seventeenth Century Cambridge* (Cambridge, Mass., 1958), 39; E.J.L. Scott (ed.), *Letter Book of Gabriel Harvey A.D. 1573-1580*, Camden Soc. new series, 33, (1984), 78-81; L.F. Dean, 'Bodin's *Methodus* in England before 1625', *Studies in Philology*, 39 (1942), 160-6.
3. L. Van Norden, 'Sir Henry Spelman on the chronology of the Elizabethan College of Antiquaries', *Hunt. Lib. Quart.*, 13 (1949-

50), 131-60; L. Van Norden, 'The Elizabethan College of Antiquaries' (Ph.D. thesis, University of California, Los Angeles, 1946), ch.II; Kevin Sharpe *Sir Robert Cotton* (Oxford, 1979), ch.I.

4. BL Harleian MS, 5177 f.48; Oxford Bodl. MS Ashmole 7631V; Sharpe, *Cotton*, ch.I.

5. BL Cottonian MS. Faustina E V, fos 89–90^v; E. Flugel, 'Die Alteste englische Akademie', *Anglia*, 32 (1909), 261–8.

6. E. Bolton, *Hypercritica: or a rule of judgement for writing or reading our history's* Oxford (1722).

7. E. Portal, 'The Academy Roial of James I', *Proc. Brit. Acad.*, 7 (1915–16), 189–208; J. Hunter, 'An Account of the Scheme for the Erection of a Royal Academy in England in the Reign of King James', *Archaeologia*, 32 (1847), 132–49; Bolton's first attempt was in March 1618. He tried in 1620 (BL MSS Harleian 6103, 6143, 7571; *Journals of the House of Lords* II, 36) in 1622 (*Cal. Stat. Pap. Dom. 1619-23*, 411–2); in 1624 (BL Add. MS 24488 fos 66–87) and in 1628 (Van Norden 'College of Antiquaries' 34). See R.L. Caudill, 'Some Literary Evidence of the Development of English Virtuoso Interests in the Seventeenth Century', (D.Phil. thesis, Oxford University, 1975), ch.8, appendices I, II.

8. *Catalogus Universalis Librorum in Bibliotecha Bodleiana* (Oxford, 1620).

9. J.F. Fuggles, 'A History of the Library of St. John's College Oxford from the Foundation of the College to 1660', (B.Litt. thesis, Oxford University, 1975).

10. E.C. Pearce, 'Mathew Parker', *The Library*, Series IV, 6 (1925), 209–28; J. Butt, 'The Facilities for Antiquarian Studies in the Seventeenth Century', *Essays and Studies* 24 (1934), 64–80.

11. Seymour de Ricci, *English Collectors of Books and Manuscripts* Cambridge (1930), 22–4; R. Parr, *The Life of James Ussher . . . with a Collection of 300 Letters* (1686), 342–3.

12. Sharpe, *Cotton*, ch.II.

13. T. Smith (ed.), *Gulielmi Camdeni Epistolae* (1691), passim; F.J. Levy, 'The Making of Camden's *Britannia*', *Bibliotheque d'humanisme et Renaissance*, 26 (1964), 84.

14. Sharpe, *Cotton*, 33–4, 107, 215.

15. Below, 212.

16. T. Smith, 'Vita Camdeni' prefaced to *Gulielmi Camdeni . . . Epistolae* (1691), lix; W. Camden, *Britain* (translated Philemon Holland, 1610), 233; H. Stuart Jones, 'The Foundation and History of the Camden Chair', *Oxoniensia*, 8–9 (1943-4), 169–92, esp. 172.

17. D. Wheare, *Parentatio historica sive commemoratio vitae et mortis V.C. Guliemi Camdeni Clarentii* (1623), 17 in *Prael. Hist. Camdeniani Pietas erga benefactores* (1628).

18. Hill, *Intellectual Origins*, 174–7.

19. W. Camden, *Annales, The True and Royal History of Elizabeth* (1625).

20. Trevor-Roper, *History and Theory*, 1966, 65.

21. Smith, 'Vita Camdeni', lix; Stuart Jones art. cit., 313–4.

22. T. Smith, *Guielmi Camdeni . . . Epistolae*, 313-4. Camden left his books to Cotton; PRO Prob. 11/142(2)/111.
23. F. Smith Fussner, *The Historical Revolution* (1962), 252.
24. Smith, *Camdeni Epistolae*, 315, 317.
25. *DNB*; W.H. Allison, 'The First Endowed Professorship of History and Its First Incumbent', *AHR*, 27 (1922), 733-7.
26. Smith, *Camdeni Epistolae*, 316.
27. Ibid., lix, 327.
28. Oxford University Archives, Convoc. Reg. N., f.144.
29. Ibid., f.172.
30. Stickland Gibson, 'Brian Twyne', *Oxoniensia*, 5 (1940), 94-112.
31. Bodl. MS Selden Supra 81 (Letter book of Degory Wheare) fos 63^v-4, 68^v-9, 70-70^v.
32. Bodl. MS Bodl. Add. 241 (Unfoliated), Camden to Wheare.
33. Convoc. Reg. N., f.172, 'beneficio ecclesiastico non obstante'; *DNB*.
34. *DNB*: Convoc. Reg. N., f.172, Jan 8. 1624; Twyne records an interview with Camden in February 1623 at which, on his departure, Camden 'pulled me by the cloak, and took me by the hand, saying: Well Mr Twyne fare you well, ply your studies and follow your good courses as I hear you do, for I have appointed you to be Mr Weare's successor in my Historical lecture . . .' Bodl. Twyne MS 22, fos 385-6.
35. See K. Sharpe, 'Archbishop Laud and the University of Oxford', in H. Lloyd-Jones, V. Pearl and A.B. Worden (eds), *History and Imagination: Essays in honour of Hugh Trevor-Roper* (1981), 146-64; above, ch. 4.
36. Bodl. MS Bodl. Add. 241 (Unfoliated) at back.
37. Convoc. Reg. N., f.144.
38. Ibid., f.144. It is not clear whether the delegates were to draw up the same, or different, rules for the two chairs. The text states 'Gulielmus Camdenus nulla adhuc condidit statuta, vel ordinationes, de lectura praedicta et penes Academiam haec esse voluit, ut nominentur Delegati qui statuta et ordinationes faciant, *et de lectura historiarum et de lectura moralis philosophiae* . . .' The juxtaposition is interesting.
39. MS Bodl. 241 (Unfoliated), Jan 6 1622/3, my italics.
40. E.g. Camden, *Britain* (1610), 365; *Annales*, 377.
41. J. Spedding (ed.), *The Works of Francis Bacon* (1857-9), III, 334; J. Spedding (ed.), *The Letters and The Life* (1861-74), II, 23.
42. Lucius Annaeus Florus, *Epitome of Roman History*, ed. E.S. Forster (1929), xi.
43. The evidence suggests that Camden urged Wheare to lecture on Florus, having heard the discourses on history.
44. D. Wheare, *De ratione et methodo legendi historias dissertatio* (1623); reprinted 1625, 1637, translated into English in 1685. All quotations are from the 1685 edition.
45. Wheare, op. cit., 14, 38.
46. Ibid., 42.
47. Ibid., 57.

48. Ibid., 75–8. This reads like a paraphrase of Florus, see below 216–8.
49. 'I will not deny there are many errors, but he digests his relations by heads and species, rather than times. Yet though there are more accurate accounts, we should pardon the few errors we meet in so useful a work as Florus'. Ibid., 79. This is scarcely an attitude in line with Camden's careful scholarship and criticism.
50. Ibid., 105; Wheare echoes Lipsius's comment on Tacitus, 'a garden and seminary of precepts'.
51. Ibid., 96. That, argues Wheare, is why Caesar entitled his works *Commentaries*, not histories.
52. Ibid., 102, my italics.
53. Ibid., 126, 127.
54. Ibid., 157; F. Bacon's, *The Historie of the raigne of King Henry the seventh* was published in 1622.
55. Wheare, op. cit., 14.
56. Ibid., part II, 'Concerning a Competent Reader'.
57. Ibid., 298–303.
58. Trevor-Roper, *History and Theory* 1966, 67.
59. Convoc. Reg. N., undated insert next to f.144.
60. MS Bodl. Add. 241. Unfoliated.
61. Above, 211.
62. Preface to 1637 edition.
63. No life of Camden has been written since Thomas Smith prefaced his edition of Camden's letters with a brief 'Vita Camdeni'. See F.J. Levy, 'The Making of Camden's Britannia', art. cit.; W. McCaffrey (ed.), *The History of the Most Renowned and Victorious Princess Elizabeth* (1970), introduction; H.R. Trevor-Roper, *Queen Elizabeth's First Historian: William Camden and the Beginnings of English 'Civil History'*, Neale Lecture (1971); Sharpe, *Cotton*, passim.
64. Sharpe, *Cotton*, 116.
65. I have not here told the tangled story of Camden's and Cotton's involvement with the rewriting of the story of Mary Queen of Scots which James I wanted to be included in De Thou's *Historia sui temporis*. See Trevor-Roper, *Queen Elizabeth's First Historian*, and Sharpe, *Cotton*, ch.III.
66. Trevor-Roper, *Queen Elizabeth's First Historian*, 27.
67. W. Camden, *Annales rerum Anglicarum et Hibernicarum regnante Elizabetha* (1615).
68. Camden, *Annales* (1625 edn & translation), 65, 82.
69. Ibid., 80–1.
70. Ibid., 'Lectori', preface.
71. Ibid., 'Lectori', preface.
72. N.M. McClure (ed.), *The Letters of John Chamberlain* (2 vols, Philadelphia, 1939), II, 138; BL MS Cotton Julius C V, f.196.
73. Sharpe, *Cotton*, passim; ch.IV.
74. 'I fear I have offended in the eulogy of Sir Thomas Walsingham in the page 523', Camden to Cotton. BL MS Cotton Vespasian F IX, f.140.
75. Ibid., f.140.
76. Trinity College Cambridge, MS 715; 'Annales ab anno 1603 ad annum

1623', printed in Smith, *Camdeni Epistolae*.

77. Trevor-Roper, *Queen Elizabeth's First Historian*, 34.

78. *Dedicatio imaginis Camdenianae in schola historica 12 Nov 1626*, 46.

79. Some of the lectures are in Bodl. MS Auct f.5. nos. 5, 10, 11.

80. On Florus as a historian see V. Alba, *La concepcion historiografica de Lucio Anneo Floro* (Madrid, 1953).

81. Florus, *Epitome*, ed. E.S. Forster, 5–6.

82. Ibid., 7.

83. Ibid., 213.

84. Ibid., 213.

85. Ibid., 215.

86. Ibid., 25.

87. Alba, op. cit., 156–63; P. Burke, 'A Survey of the Popularity of Ancient Historians, 1450–1700', *History and Theory*, 5 (1966), 135–52, esp. 137, table 2. Richard Holdsworth, fellow of Emmanuel College, recommended Florus, along with Camden and Speed, to his students (Curtis, *Oxford and Cambridge in Transition*, 132). Edmund Bolton translated the epitome as *The Roman Histories*, in 1619.

88. Alba, op. cit., 159.

89. Greville's lectureship has received more attention. I draw on N. Farmer, 'Fulke Greville and Sir John Coke; an Exchange of Letters on a History Lecture and Certain Latin Verses on Sir Philip Sidney', *Hunt. Lib. Quart.*, 33 (1969–70), 217–36; R. Rebholz, *The Life of Fulke Greville* (Oxford, 1971), 293–8. Neither account, however, deals satisfactorily with the period 1624 to 1627.

90. *DNB*; Camden.

91. Rebholz, op. cit., 143; J. Speed, *The History of Great Britain* (1614 edition), 53.

92. Farmer, art. cit.

93. Coke to Greville, 16 Sept. 1615, printed in Farmer, art. cit., 230–3, my italics.

94. *DNB*: Jack.

95. Vossius to Boswell, September 1624, Bodl. MS Rawlinson 84B, f.21, printed in *G.J. Vossii et clarorum virorum ad eum epistolae* (1690), 90.

96. M. Michaud (ed.), *Biographie Universelle* (Paris, 1843–1958), Vossius.

97. G.J. Vossius, *Ars historica, sive de historiae, et historices natura, historiaeque scribendae praeceptis, commentatio* (Leiden, 1623); D. Wheare, *De ratione* (Part II). Vossius had also written on the Greek and Roman historians, *Biographie Universelle*

98. Vossius to Boswell, June 1625, Bodl. MS Rawlinson 84 B, f.32; cf. ibid., f.19, Vossius to Greville Sept. 1624.

99. Vossius to Dudley Carleton, 28 April 1625, Bodl. MS Rawlinson 84 B, f.23; to Greville, June 1625 ibid., f.30; to Boswell, Sept. 1626, ibid., fos 38–9. See *Vossii . . . Epistolae*, 89–93.

100. Vossius to Boswell, Sept 1626, Bodl. MS Rawlinson 84 B, fos 38–9.

101. 'Ordinances Established for a Publique lecture of Historie in ye universitie of Cambridge founded by Folke Lord Brook', Bodl. MS Rawlinson D 1005. The manuscript is not dated, but the clause excluding divines places it after the collapse of negotiations with Vossius in 1626, and before the appointment of Dorislaus in 1627.
102. Bodl. MS Rawlinson D 1005, f.4ᵛ (my italics).
103. Ibid., f.4ᵛ; cf. Camden's comments on ecclesiastical history above, 212.
104. Ibid., f.4ᵛ. The *DNB* states that Dorislaus married 'in or about 1627'. This may well have been after his appointment.
105. Wren described Dorislaus as Brooke's 'domestic' PRO SP 16/86/87; see below 221-2.
106. Bodl. MS Rawlinson D 1005, f.5, states that the lecturer was free to choose his subject 'provided it be either of secular or ecclesiastical history . . .'. Wren told Laud that the *Annals* of Tacitus 'were by his Lord (the founder of the lecture) appointed him for his theme', PRO SP 16/86/87.
107. P. Burke, 'A Survey of the Popularity of Ancient Historians'; J.J. Lipsius (ed.), *C. Cor. Taciti Opera* (Leiden, 1619); also *J. Lipsii ad annales C. Taciti liber commentarius sive notae* (Leiden, 1585).
108. Tacitus, *The Annals and the Histories*, ed. Hugh Lloyd-Jones, (New York, 1964), introduction; F.R.D. Goodyear (ed.), *The Annals of Tacitus* (Cambridge, 1972); H. Furneaux (ed.), *The Annals of Tacitus* (Oxford, 1896).
109. Lloyd Jones (ed.), *Annals*, xxiii; S.R. Gardiner, *History of England from the Accession of James I to the Outbreak of the Civil War* (10 vols, 1904 edn), VI, 105.
110. Our knowledge of the contents of the lectures is dependent on notes of them sent to Laud by Wren, PRO SP 16/86/88 'Notes out of his two first lectures De regia potestate mutuata a populo'.
111. Wren to Laud, PRO SP 16/86/88 (my italics).
112. Dorislaus was the son of a Dutch Calvinist minister.
113. PRO SP 16/86/88.
114. Ward to Ussher, Parr, *Life of Ussher*, 393.
115. Rebholz, *Greville*, 298-9.
116. Ibid., 300: Sr John Coke to Vice Chancellor of Cambridge enclosing a codicil to Greville's will dated 10 December 1628, Bodl. MS Rawlinson D 1005, fos 1ᵛ-2. The codicil transferred an annuity of £100 from the value of lands in Lincoln to the lectureship 'not provided for in my will'.
117. Rebholz, *Greville*, passim.
118. A.B. Grosart (ed.), *The Works of Fulke Greville* (4 vols, 1870); G. Bullough (ed.), *Poems and Dramas of Fulke Greville* (2 vols, 1939); F.A. Wilkes (ed.), *Fulke Greville, The Remains* (Oxford, 1965).
119. For some guidance on dating see Rebholz, *Greville*, Appendix I.
120. Nowell Smith (ed.), *The Life of Sir Philip Sidney* (Oxford, 1907), 31. Cf. Camden's description of Sidney 'whom as Providence seems to have sent into the world to give the present Age a specimen of the Ancients', cited by G.B. Johnstone, 'Poems by William Camden',

Studies in Philology, 72 (1975), 1-143.

121. Greville, *Remains*, ed. Wilkes, 3.
122. Greville, *Remains*, ed. Wilkes, 55, verse 81.
123. Ibid., 45, verse 41.
124. Ibid., 96, verse 246. The emphasis placed on law in Jacobean England was closely related to fear of time. See C. Brooks and K. Sharpe, 'History, English Law and the Renaissance', *P&P*, 72 (1976), 133-42; above, ch. 6.
125. *Remains*, 160, verse 500.
126. Ibid., 111, verse 304.
127. Ibid., 180, verse 578.
128. Ibid., introduction, 7.
129. Rebholz, *Greville*, 260-71.
130. Ibid., 167, verse 527.
131. Ibid., 178, verse 571.
132. Rebholz, *Greville*, Chapter XVI, esp. 276-80.
133. Greville, *Remains*, 170, verse 538.
134. Farmer, art. cit., 220.
135. Camden also praised the independence of the Netherlands: 'Those Nations have not only kept by their care and diligence the liberty which they hold by their ancestors wholly to themselves against Spain, against the French and English . . . yea against the Prince of Orange himself', *Annales*, 227.
136. Rome sustained her government and laws by balance. Greville, *Remains*, 111, verse 306.
137. Dorislaus to Grotius, 10 Feb. 1631, *Briefwisseling van Hugo Grotius* IV ed. B.L. Meulenbroek, (The Hague, 1964), 325.
138. Quoted in Farmer, art. cit., 221.
139. For Greville see H.N. Maclean, 'Fulke Greville: Kingship and Sovereignty', *Hunt. Lib. Quart.*, 16 (1953), 237-72. Sir John Davies appended Buchanan's *De iure regni* to his manuscript of Greville's *Mustapha*. Camden respected Buchanan as the 'Prince of Poets' (*Annales* 1625, III, 25). See too J.E. Phillips, 'George Buchanan and the Sidney Circle', *Hunt. Lib. Quart.*, 12 (1948), 23-56. It has also been suggested that Greville's political thinking was much influenced by Machiavelli, N. Orsini, *Fulke Greville tra il mondo e dio* (Milan, 1941).
140. Bullough (ed.), *Poems and Dramas of Fulke Greville*, I, 54-5.
141. Sharpe, *Cotton*, ch.VII.
142. *Annales* 'Lectori'; Maclean, art. cit., 265.
143. Curtis, *Oxford and Cambridge in Transition*, 115; Bacon *Works*, VI, 119, 122.
144. Greville, 'A treatie of Humane Learning' in *Poems and Dramas*, I, 170, verse 64.
145. Ibid., 171 verse 68. The Earl of Essex had told Greville that learning should be related to the practical world and had particularly recommended the study of history, Curtis, *Oxford and Cambridge*, 127.
146. *Poems and Dramas*, 171, verse 71.
147. Above, 226.

148. *Briefwisseling van Hugo Grotius* IV, 325.

Chapter 9

* Originally published in K. Sharpe and S. Zwicker (eds), *Politics of Discourse* (University of California Press, 1987) 117-146.

1. P. Zagorin, 'The Court and the Country: A Note on Political Terminology in the Earlier 17th Century', *EHR*, 77 (1962), 306-11; idem, *The Court and the Country* (1969).
2. L. Stone, *The Causes of the English Revolution* (1972), 106.
3. R. Ashton, *The English Civil War, 1603-1649* (1978), 22, 29, 30.
4. P. Thomas, 'Two Cultures? Court and Country under Charles I', in C.S.R. Russell (ed.), *The Origins of the Civil War* (1973), 168-96; cf. P. Thomas, 'Charles I: The Tragedy of Absolutism', in A.G. Dickens (ed.), *The Courts of Europe* (1977), 191-212.
5. G. Parry, *The Golden Age Restor'd: The Culture of the Stuart Court 1603-1642* (New York, 1981), 189, 191, and passim. Parry offers only superficial readings of Caroline literature.
6. Thomas, 'Two Cultures', 185-91; Parry, *Golden Age Restor'd*, 265.
7. See Parry, *Golden Age Restor'd*, passim.
8. A. Harbage, *Cavalier Drama* 1st edn, (1936); 2nd edn, (New York, 1964).
9. G. Parfitt, 'The Poetry of Thomas Carew', *Renaissance and Mod. Studies*, XII (1968), 56-68.
10. See, for example, Parry, *Golden Age Restor'd*, ch.9; Thomas, 'Two Cultures'.
11. There are two book-length studies of Carew: E.I. Selig, *The Flourishing Wreath: A Study of Thomas Carew's Poetry* (Hamden, Conn., 1970), was the first to argue for a recognition of the irony and ambivalence in his verse; L. Sadler, *Thomas Carew* (Boston, 1979) is marred by preconceptions about 'Cavalier culture'. The best short life is to be found in the introduction to R. Dunlap (ed.), *The Poems of Thomas Carew* (Oxford, 1949). See also BL Add. MS 24489 (Hunter's Lives).
12. Dunlap, *Carew*, xxxv. For the importance of this post at the court of Charles I, see my 'The Court and Household of Charles I', in D. Starkey (ed.), *The English Court*; above, ch. 5.
13. E. Hyde, Earl of Clarendon, *The Life of Edward, Earl of Clarendon* (Oxford, 1761), 36.
14. Ibid., 36.
15. T. Carew, *Coelum Britannicum* (1634). See the remarks of S. Orgel and R. Strong, *Inigo Jones: The Theatre of the Stuart Court* (2 vols, Berkeley, Los Angeles, London, 1973), I, 66-70. I show the ambivalent, ironic dimension to this masque in *Criticism and Compliment: The Politics of Literature in the England of Charles I* (Cambridge, 1987), 232-43.
16. See *The Great Assizes Holden at Parnassus by Apollo and his*

assessours (1645); J.E. Ruoff, 'Thomas Carew's Early Reputation', *Notes and Queries*, 202 (1957), 61-2; Dunlap, *Carew*, xlvi–lii.

17. K. Sharpe, 'The Court and Household of Charles I'; Dunlap, *Carew*, xxi–xxvii.
18. Ruoff, 'Carew's Early Reputation', 62; *Coelum Britannicum* lines 62–5 in Dunlap, *Carew*, 157.
19. E. Miner, *The Cavalier Mode from Jonson to Cotton* (Princeton, 1971), offered fruitful suggestions toward a re-evaluation of the morality and politics of Cavalier poetry. Since this essay was drafted, Lauro Martines has published a manual for the historical reading of poetry, *Society and History in English Renaissance Verse* (Oxford, 1985).
20. 'Ingratefull beauty threatned', lines 15-16; Dunlap, *Carew*, 18. See below, 248.
21. I. Selig, in *The Flourishing Wreath*, distinguishes the singing and speaking voices in Carew's poetry: 'the singing voice of the poet in Carew's songs derives a certain vitality from its being forced at all times to contend with the speaking voice, with the recalcitrant world of statement' (p. 59).
22. Dunlap, *Carew*, 4.
23. 'Good Counsel to a young Maid', lines 10-13; ibid., p. 13.
24. See another poem of the same title, 'Good Counsell to a Young Maid', ibid., p. 25.
25. 'To A.L. . . .', lines 55–60; ibid., 5.
26. 'To her againe, she burning in a feaver', lines 11–12, ibid., p. 35.
27. 'Incommunicabilitie of Love', lines 1-3, ibid., p. 62. See note, p. 244.
28. *The Royal Slave*, lines 1003-1014, 1029-1045 in G. Blakemore Evans (ed.), *The Plays and Poems of William Cartwright* (Madison, 1951), 231-2.
29. Several playwrights of the Caroline period satirize Platonic love as a mask for promiscuity. See, for example, W. Davenant, *The Platonic Lovers,* in *The Dramatic Works of Sir William D'Avenant* (5 vols, 1872-74), vol. II.
30. 'Incommunicabilitie of Love', lines 4-6, Dunlap, *Carew*, 62.
31. 'Eternitie of love protested', lines 7-8, ibid., p. 23.
32. 'A Rapture', lines 4, 6. For a recent discussion of this little-discussed poem, see P. Johnson, 'Carew's "A Rapture": The Dynamics of Fantasy' in *Studies in Eng. Lit.*, 16 (1976), 145-55.
33. 'A Rapture', lines 111-112, Dunlap, *Carew*, 52. Cf. Miner, '"A Rapture", depended precisely on everything happening in Elizium', *The Cavalier Mode*, 199.
34. 'A Rapture', lines 108-109.
35. 'A Rapture', lines 115-116, 131-135.
36. Ibid., line 26.
37. Cf. Miner, *The Cavalier Mode*, 80, 200.
38. 'A Rapture', lines 111-112.
39. Ibid., line 163. Dunlap, *Carew*, 53. See below, p. 254-5.
40. 'The Second Rapture', line 9, ibid., p. 103.
41. See 1 Kings 1:1-5; Sadler, *Carew*, 69.

42. 'Second Rapture', lines 17, 26. The rearousal of sexual passion is related to ideas of renewal.
43. 'On the Mariage of T.K. and CC. the morning stormie', lines 21-24, Dunlap, *Carew*, 80.
44. Ibid., lines 31, 32, 36.
45. Cf. the poem, 'A Married Woman', included in the 1642 edition of Carew's poetry; on marriage see lines 11-14:

> For in habituall vertues, sense is wrought
> To that calme temper, as the bodie's thought
> To have nor blood nor gall, if wild and rude
> Passions of lust and Anger, are subdu'd;

46. Sadler found it 'strange that in some of his amorous lyrics to women not his wife, Carew tries to Platonize the erotic while in most of his celebrations of marriage, he blatantly declares for sexual fulfilment' (p. 115). This is to fail to appreciate the central place of marriage in Carew's morality.
47. Dunlap, *Carew*, xxxii; Sadler, *Carew*, 15.
48. The correspondence is printed as an appendix in Dunlap, *Carew*, 211-12. T. Clayton suggests that the 'Answer' to Suckling is not by Carew but also by Suckling himself. T. Clayton (ed.), *The Works of Sir John Suckling: The Non Dramatic Works* (Oxford, 1971), lxxxvi, 332. There can be no final conclusion because manuscript copies are found subscribed 'T.C.' as well as 'J.S.' If Carew did not write the letter, evidently Suckling thought it a representation of views held by Carew, quite at odds with his own.
49. 'A Letter to a Friend', lines 35, 44, Dunlap, *Carew*, 211-12.
50. 'An Answer to the Letter', lines 21-23, Dunlap, *Carew*, 211.
51. 'An Answer', lines 13-16, Dunlap, *Carew*, 211; cf. 'Eternitie of Love Protested', 23.
52. 'An Answer', lines 31-32.
53. Ibid., lines 44-45.
54. Ibid., lines 24-25.
55. The phrase is B. King's, 'The Strategy of Carew's Wit', *Rev. Eng. Lit.*, 5 (1964), 42-51, esp. 51.
56. 'A Song' ('Aske me no more . . .'), lines 1-4; See Dunlap's commentary, 265. The poem employs the conceit of the phoenix dying in the woman's bosom in order to depict the mistress as the home of nature herself.
57. 'The Comparison', lines 1-3, Dunlap, *Carew*, 98; cf. Shakespeare's sonnet 130.
58. 'The Complement', lines 9, 20, 21, 55, Dunlap, *Carew*, 99-100.
59. Cf. 'Epitaph on the Lady S.', 55.
60. 'The Comparison', lines 13, 24, 25, Dunlap, *Carew*, 98-99. 'On a Damaske rose sticking upon a Ladies breast', line 6, Dunlap, *Carew*, 108.
61. 'To A.D. unreasonable distrustfull of her owne beauty', line 35, Dunlap, *Carew*, 85; cf. 'Incommunicabilitie of Love', lines 10-15, ibid., p. 62.

62. 'To A.D.', lines 54, 60.

63. 'Epitaph on the Lady S.', lines 7-10, Dunlap, *Carew*, 55.

64. 'The Comparison', lines 25-29, Dunlap, *Carew*, 99. A classic illustration of 'that wrenching final couplet for which Carew should be better known', Sadler, *Carew*, 52.

65. 'A Rapture', line 1, Dunlap, *Carew*, 49. See Johnson, 'A Rapture', 149; 'Song Persuasions to enjoy', lines 5-6, Dunlap, *Carew*, 16.

66. 'A Pastorall Dialogue', line 19, Dunlap, *Carew*, 43.

67. Ibid., lines 21-2.

68. Ibid., line 45, ibid., 44. Cf. '*Nym*. Then let us pinion *Time* and chase / The day for ever from this place.' 'A Pastorall Dialogue. *Shepherd Nymph Chorus*', lines 29-30, ibid., p. 46.

69. 'A Pastorall Dialogue', lines 46-48, Dunlap, *Carew*, 44.

70. The two poems share the same title.

71. Several of Carew's poems, including 'A Rapture', are concerned with appropriate time. See, for example, 'The Spring', Dunlap, *Carew*, 1; A. Long and H. Maclean, '"Deare Ben", "Great DONNE" and "my Celia": The Wit of Carew's Poetry', *Studies in Eng. Lit.*, 18 (1978), 75-94. Miner observes that in Cavalier poetry the remedy against time is not the enjoyment of the happy life as much as the virtue of the good life, *Cavalier Mode*, 154.

72. 'Mediocritie in Love rejected', lines 1-2, Dunlap, *Carew*, 12; cf. 'The Spring', ibid., p. 1; 'A Looking-Glasse', line 16, ibid., p. 19.

73. 'Boldnesse in love', Dunlap, *Carew*, 42; cf. 'A Prayer to the Wind', 11.

74. 'A Rapture', lines 35-40, ibid., p. 50.

75. Ibid., lines 66-69, ibid., p. 51.

76. 'Song. *Celia* singing', lines 3-4, ibid., p. 38.

77. 'To the Queene', lines 13-16, ibid., p. 90.

78. Ibid., lines 20, 22, 28, ibid., p. 91.

79. For example, 'Loves force', line 1, ibid., p. 116; 'Song. *Celia* singing', line 3, ibid., p. 38; 'Incommunicabilitie of Love', line 9, ibid., p. 62; 'To my friend G.N. from Wrest', line 7, ibid., p. 86.

80. 'Disdaine returned' ('Hee that loves a Rosie cheeke, . . .'), line 8, Dunlap, *Carew*, 18; 'To one that desired to know my Mistris', lines 3-6, ibid., 39.

81. See, for example, G.R. Hibbard, 'The Country House Poem of The Seventeenth Century', *Journ. Warburg & Courtauld Inst.*, 19 (1956), 159-74; W. McClung, *The Country House in English Renaissance Poetry* (Berkeley, Los Angeles, London, 1977), passim; M.A.C. McGuire, 'The Cavalier Country House Poem: Mutations on a Jonsonian tradition', *Studies in Eng. Lit.*, 19 (1979), 93-108.

82. Dunlap points out that the manor of Wrest Park, Bedfordshire 'with the title of the Earl of Kent, had passed in 1631 to Anthony de Grey who died in 1643.' This is erroneous. The title passed in 1624 to Henry de Grey, who died in 1639, succeeded by Anthony.

83. 'To my friend G.N. from Wrest', lines 1-3, Dunlap, *Carew*, 86. For an interesting discussion of this poem, see M.P. Parker, '"To my friend G.N. from Wrest": Carew's Secular Masque', in C.T. Summers

and T. Larry Pebworth (eds), *Classic and Cavalier: Essays on Jonson and the Sons of Ben* (Pittsburgh, 1982), 171–92.

84. Dunlap, *Carew*, xli.
85. Compare Carew's opening lines with the first scene of *Salmacida Spolia*, Davenant's masque, performed amid the Scots war on 21 January 1640. 'A curtain flying up, a horrid scene appeared of storm and tempest. No glimpse of the sun was seen, as if darkness, confusion and deformity had possessed the world . . .', lines 111–114 in Orgel and Strong, *Inigo Jones*, II 731; cf. fig. 401, p. 743: Cf. Sharpe, *Criticism and Compliment*, 251–6.
86. 'To . . . G.N. from Wrest', lines 15, 19; Dunlap, *Carew*, 86–7.
87. Ibid., lines 9, 11–12.
88. Ibid., lines 28, 34.
89. Ibid., lines 35–46.
90. Ibid., line 54.
91. Ibid., lines 65–68, ibid., p. 88.
92. Ibid., lines 69–80.
93. Ibid., lines 19–20, 42.
94. Ibid., lines 93–96. See A.B. Giametti, *The Earthly Paradise and The Renaissance Epic* (Princeton, 1966).
95. 'To . . . G.N. from Wrest', line 107.
96. The bucks and stags chased by Carew's friend are the 'embleme of warre' and may too signify that war on the borders from which Carew has just escaped to nature's haven. See lines 107–110. Cf. below, 253–5.
97. 'To Saxham', lines 18–19, 22, Dunlap, *Carew*, 28. Cf. 'To Penshurst', lines 30–34.
98. Ibid., lines 23–26.
99. Ibid., lines 35, 38.
100. McGuire, 'The Cavalier Country House Poem', 93–4.
101. 'To Saxham', lines 49–52, Dunlap, *Carew*, 28–9; compare the implied 'open house' at Wrest, 'To . . . G.N. from Wrest', lines 34–45, 60. Cf. 'To Penshurst', line 48.
102. See Giametti, who points out the connections between the Garden of Eden tradition and that of the secular garden of love, nicely combined in 'To . . . G.N. from Wrest', *Earthly Paradise*, chap. VII.
103. For incisive comment on the interdependency of the realms of love and government, see J. Goldberg, *James I and the Politics of Literature* (Baltimore, 1982), 55, 85, 107, and passim. I am extremely grateful to Jonathan Goldberg for several informative and stimulating discussions on this subject. Also see Martines, *Society and History*, 4, 12, 68–76.
104. 'My Mistris commanding me to returne her letters', lines 5–6, Dunlap, *Carew*, 9.
105. Ibid., lines 15, 24, 70, ibid., pp. 9–11.
106. 'A deposition from love', lines 27–30, ibid., pp. 16–17.
107. 'My Mistris commanding . . .', line 28, ibid., p. 9.
108. Orgel and Strong, *Inigo Jones*, I, ch.iv.

109. Parry, *Golden Age*, 211; Parfitt, 'Poetry of Carew', 56; Sadler, *Carew*, 85.
110. 'To the King at his entrance into Saxham, by Master Jo Crofts', Dunlap, *Carew*, 30-1; for suggested dates of the poem, see ibid., 226.
111. 'To the King', line 25; 'To . . . G.N. from Wrest', line 15.
112. 'To the King', lines 3, 4, 6.
113. Ibid., lines 37-39. There is almost a tone of reciprocity in the language and structure of the poem.
114. 'To . . . G.N. from Wrest', lines 29-32, Dunlap, *Carew*, 87.
115. See below, p. 257, for Carew's attitude to the plastic arts.
116. 'Obsequies to the Lady Anne Hay', lines 1-5, Dunlap, *Carew*, 67.
117. 'To the Countesse of Anglesie upon the immoderately-by-her lamented death of her husband', lines 57, 65. Like Jonson, Carew turns an epitaph to an individual into a critique of courtly society.
118. Ibid., lines 55-56, 66-67. Cf. 'himselfe' with 'my selfe' of 'To . . . G.N. from Wrest', line 107.
119. The very words 'courteous' and 'court' (meaning 'to woo') come from a society that believed that as the centre of virtue the court should prescribe manners to men in public and private life. Hence the best-selling courtesy book remains Castiglione's *The Courtier*. See my *Criticism and Compliment*, ch.1.
120. 'A Rapture', lines 4-6.
121. 'Feminine Honour', lines 16-18, Dunlap, *Carew*, 61.
122. Ibid., lines 19-22. Dunlap suggests the date was 1633.
123. J. Jacobs (ed.), *Epistolae Ho-Elianae* (1890), 317.
124. Miner, *The Cavalier Mode*, 220.
125. Above, 239.
126. 'Disdaine Returned', lines 7, 12 of a stanza carefully balanced to enfold them both.
127. 'To my Mistresse in absence', lines 32-35, Dunlap, *Carew*, 22. Once again, the final couplet forcefully turns the sense to an anticipated *physical* union.
128. See, for example, 'Separation of Lovers', lines 21-22, ibid., 62.
129. Ibid., 244.
130. Walter Montagu's *The Shepherd's Paradise* (1659) was acted on 10 January 1633 at Somerset House, Beaulieu to Puckering, 10 January 1633, T Birch (ed.), *The Court and Times of Charles I* (2 vols, 1848), II, 216. For the court reaction see J. Jacobs (ed.), *Epistolae Ho-Elianae*, 317.
131. Dunlap, *Carew*, 22.
132. 'Ingratefull beauty threatned', lines 15-16, ibid., p. 18.
133. 'A Divine Mistris', line 16. Once again note the almost subversive final line.
134. For a useful discussion, see Orgel and Strong, *Inigo Jones*, I, chap. IV.
135. 'Upon the Kings sicknesse', lines 19-22, Dunlap, *Carew*, 35. See notes on ibid., 229. The date must remain uncertain. I incline to 1633.

136. Ibid., lines 25-26. The parallel perfectly illustrates the unity of Carew's ethical and political attitudes.

137. Ibid., lines 41-42.

138. Ibid., line 17. Cf. The 'government tyranicall / In loves free state . . .' cited below, 251.

139. Ibid., line 1.

140. Ibid., line 37.

141. 'My Mistris commanding me to returne her letters', lines 31-32, Dunlap, *Carew*, 9. This is a nice reminder that divine right theory involved a responsibility to God, as well as power derived from Him.

142. 'To T.H., a Lady resembling my Mistresse', lines 16-24; ibid., p. 27.

143. See above, 244.

144. 'A deposition from Love', line 30, ibid., p. 17.

145. Ibid., pp. 83-4.

146. Ibid., lines 2-3; 'An Elegie on the La:Pen: . . .', line 1, ibid., p. 19.

147. 'Upon my Lord Chief Justice . . .', lines 8-14. We have seen how Carew uses the term 'milde' to describe the havens of nature and the condition of true love.

148. Ibid., lines 19-21. The 'deformed shape' of the froward evokes the antimasques of the 1630s, and especially those of the depraved lovers in *Tempe Restored*.

149. Ibid., lines 22-23.

150. See W.H. Terry, *The Life and Times of John, Lord Finch* (1936); *A Complete Collection of State Trials* (1771), VII: 506-719.

151. 'To Saxham', lines 57-58, Dunlap, *Carew*, 29.

152. 'Upon my Lord Chiefe Justice', line 12. It is this optimistic belief in the intrinsic and potential good of human nature that is central to Carew's ethics and politics. It differentiates him sharply, of course, from the Puritans.

153. 'Upon my Lord Chiefe Justice', line 10.

154. See F. Yates, *Astraea: The Imperial Theme in the Sixteenth Century* (1975).

155. 'A New-Yeares gift to the King', Dunlap, *Carew*, 89-90.

156. 'To the Queene', ibid., 90-1. Perhaps significantly the 1640 edition of Carew's poetry has this poem follow 'A New-Yeares gift to the King'.

157. The idea that virtue lay in the mean, the text of Aristotle's *Ethics*, was evidently of importance to Carew. Cf. his lines by way of an epilogue to a court play, included in the 1642 edition of his poems: 'The pleasure lyes, not in the end, but streams / That flowe betwixt two opposite Extreames' (Dunlap, *Carew*, 127).

158. See above, p. 236.

159. 'My Mistris commanding me to returne her letters', lines 37-38, Dunlap, *Carew*, 10.

160. 'A deposition from Love', ibid., 16-17; 'Truce in Love entreated', ibid., 41.

161. 'A Rapture', lines 97-99, 110.

162. Dunlap, *Carew*, 74-7; Townshend's 'Elegy on the death of the King of Sweden: sent to Thomas Carew', in C. Brown (ed.), *The Poems*

and Masques of Aurelian Townshend (Reading, 1983), 48-9.

163. See C.V. Wedgwood, *Poetry and Politics Under the Stuarts* (Cambridge, 1960), 44.

164. 'In answer of an Elegiacall Letter . . .', lines 45-48. The recognition of the obduracy of Charles I's subjects indicates a greater awareness of political reality in Carew than Wedgwood and others have allowed. See below, p. 256.

165. 'In answer . . .', lines 52-8. Carew refers to 'The beauties of the SHEPHERDS PARADISE'; but it is clear that the masque of Townshend he is describing is *Tempe Restored*.

166. Ibid., lines 2-3, 96-97. Cf. the 'drowsie eyes' with the 'slumbers' and 'amorous languishment' of 'A Rapture', lines 41, 52.

167. 'In answer . . .', lines 5, 9.

168. Ibid., lines 15-18.

169. Ibid., lines 35-38.

170. Cf. Carew's masque, *Coelum Britannicum*, lines 684-760, in which Fortune presents an antimasque, 'the representation of battle'. Orgel and Strong, *Inigo Jones*, II, 576.

171. 'In answer . . .', lines 52, 60, 63-64.

172. Ibid., lines 75-76.

173. Ibid., line 96; cf. 'A Rapture', line 92.

174. 'In answer . . .', line 97. For an interesting but different interpretation of this poem, see M.P. Parker, 'Carew's Politic Pastoral: Virgilian Pretexts in the "Answer to Aurelian Townshend"', *John Donne J.*, I (1982), 101-16.

175. '(The Wits) (A Sessions of the Poets)', lines 35-36, Clayton, *Works of Sir John Suckling*, 73.

176. 'An Elegie upon the death of the Deane of Pauls, Dr. John Donne', lines 4, 69, Dunlap, *Carew*, 71-3.

177. 'To Ben Johnson', lines 45-46, Dunlap, *Carew*, 65.

178. Ibid., lines 22, 23-25, 44.

179. 'Ingratefull beauty threatned', lines 1-6, ibid., p. 17.

180. 'To a Lady that desired I would love her', line 31, ibid., p. 82.

181. 'To Ben Johnson', line 12; 'An Elegie', line 23.

182. 'To the Painter', lines 12-14, 43-50, ibid., pp. 106-7.

183. 'To Ben Johnson', lines 47-48. The poem exemplifies the capacity for frank criticism within the context of praise.

184. 'An Elegie . . .', lines 95-96.

185. 'A Fancy', lines 16-18, ibid., p. 117. This poem was included in the 1642 edition.

186. Ibid., lines 15-18.

Chapter 10

* Originally published in *History*, vol 71 1986. pp 235-247.

1. P. Salzman, *English Prose Fiction 1558-1700: A Critical History* (Oxford University Press, 1985).

D. Margolies, *Novel and Society in Elizabethan England* (Croom Helm, 1985).

L.C. Stevenson, *Praise and Paradox: Merchants and Craftsmen in Elizabethan Popular Literature* (Cambridge University Press, 1984).

D. Norbrook, *Poetry and Politics in the English Renaissance* (Routledge and Kegan Paul, 1984).

M. Leslie, *Spenser's 'Fierce Warres and Faithfull Loves': Martial and Chivalric Symbolism in 'The Faerie Queen'* (Boydell and Brewer, 1984).

A. Barton, *Ben Jonson: Dramatist* (Cambridge University Press, 1984).

M. Butler, *Theatre and Crisis, 1632–1642* (Cambridge University Press, 1984).

R. Strong, *Art and Power: Renaissance Festivals 1450–1650* (Boydell and Brewer, 1984).

D. Lindley (ed.), *The Court Masque* (Manchester University Press, 1984).

R.M. Adams, *The Land and Literature of England: A Historical Account* (W.W. Norton, 1984).

2. See, for example, S. Greenblatt, *Renaissance Self-Fashioning from More to Shakespeare* (Chicago, 1980); idem (ed.), *The Power of Forms in the English Renaissance* (Norman, Oklahoma, 1982); J. Goldberg, *James I and the Politics of Literature* (Baltimore, 1983).

3. For a fuller exposition of this point see my *Criticism and Compliment: The Politics of Literature in the England of Charles I* (Cambridge, 1987), ch.I.

4. D. Cressy, *Literacy and the Social Order* (Cambridge, 1980), cf. Stevenson, *Praise and Paradox*, ch.3.

5. The bibliography lists 'all the known extant works of fiction published between 1588 and 1700, including translations'.

6. OED.

7. In Aristotle's *Poetics* imitative art is seen as passing beyond the bare reality of nature; it 'expresses a purified form of reality disengaged from accident', S.H. Butcher, *Aristotle's Theory of Poetry and Fine Art* (1895), 40.

8. In contrast to the role of pastoral in *The Winter's Tale*, though Shakespeare took *Pandosto* as his source.

9. *Criticism and Compliment*, passim.

10. See A.J. Smith, *The Metaphysics of Love* (Cambridge, 1985), 245–9.

11. See the interesting comments on *Don Quixote* in Salzman, 281, 286.

12. Salzman discusses *Sir Philip Sidney's Arcadia, Modernized by Mrs Stanley* (1725), but does not elucidate the metaphysical and social changes that have 'impoverished' the text.

13. Michael McKeon has recently suggested that the eighteenth-century novel signals the emergence of a distinct literary sensibility. See McKeon, 'Politics of Discourses and the Rise of the Aesthetic in Seventeenth-Century England' in K. Sharpe and S. Zwicker (eds), *Politics of Discourse* (Berkeley, Los Angeles and London, 1987).

14. Of 76 authors from families whose status is recorded, Stevenson found 36 from gentry, eight from clerical and 33 from non-gentle families (pp. 41–2).
15. Cf. Salzman, 98.
16. Stevenson, ch.vii; NB, p. 137, note 17.
17. The tension is explored in D. Javitch, *Poetry and Courtliness in Renaissance England* (Princeton, 1978).
18. See Stevenson, ch.3, for a discussion of the price, availability and ownership of books.
19. OED.
20. See D. Norbrook, 'Shakespeares', *London Review of Books*, 18 July 1985, and idem, '*Macbeth* and the Politics of Historiography', in *Politics of Discourse*, 78–116.
21. The sixteenth-century novel, of course, did not have such traditions to inherit. The politics of inherited (and created) genres and forms would repay further investigation.
22. J.H. Hexter, 'On the Historical Method of Christopher Hill' in *On Historians* (1979), 227–51 (first printed *Times Literary Supplement*, 24 October 1975). There has been no satisfactory response to Hexter's article; see Stevenson, 137 and note 17.
23. Leslie shows a close relationship between the fictional Arthurian world of Spenser's poem and the representations and festivals of Queen Elizabeth at court.
24. For a development of this argument, see Norbrook, 'The Reformation of the Masque' in D. Lindley (ed.), *The Court Masque*. I am more convinced by Smith, *The Metaphysics of Love* and especially by C. Brown, *John Milton's Aristocratic Entertainments* (Cambridge, 1986). I am grateful to Dr. Brown for permission to read this important book in proof.
25. In fairness, the same charge must be levelled at Croom Helm for Margolies, *Novel and Society*, but with Routledge it is a new and regrettable decline from standards.
26. Above note 20.
27. For an earlier articulation of this argument, see A. Barton, '*The New Inn* and the Problem of Jonson's Late Style', *ELR*, 9 (1979), 395–418; 'Harking Back to Elizabeth: Ben Jonson and Caroline Nostalgia', *ELH*, 48 (1981), 701–31.
28. See S. Orgel and R. Strong (eds), *Inigo Jones: The Theatre of the Stuart Court* (2 vols, Berkeley and London, 1973), I, iv. Salzman, Norbrook and Butler show how love expressed political positions in the literature of Renaissance England.
29. Cf. Norbrook on Fulke Greville: 'In the old constitutional order "love" meant a relationship between equals and based [sic] on a clear idea of mutual obligation, but "time and selfenesse" turn "love into compliment" . . .' (p. 165).
30. I develop this argument in *Criticism and Compliment*, ch.vi.
31. A. Harbage, *Cavalier Drama* (1936; 2nd edn, New York, 1964).
32. In his Appendix II, 'Shakespeare's unprivileged playgoers 1576–1642', Butler offers a completely convincing critique of J. Cook's *The*

Privileged Playgoers of Shakespeare's London (Princeton, 1981). Cf. Stevenson, ch.3 and the important essay by R.M. Smuts, 'The Political Failure of Stuart Cultural Patronage' in G.F. Lytle and S. Orgel (eds), *Patronage in the Renaissance* (Princeton, 1981), 165–90.

33. A view derived principally from Prynne's *Histrio-Mastix* (1633). Prynne was not typical.

34. See G.E.D. Bentley, *The Jacobean and Caroline Stage* (7 vols, Oxford, 1941–68), especially Vol VII.

35. Cf. *Criticism and Compliment*, ch.ii.

36. S. Orgel, *The Jonsonian Masque* (Cambridge, Mass., 1965); idem (ed.), *The Complete Masques* (New Haven, 1969); *The Illusion of Power* (Berkeley and London, 1975); *Inigo Jones*.

37. R. Strong, *Splendour at Court: Renaissance Spectacle and Illusion* (1973).

38. Interestingly, Strong argues that the festivals, with their theme of peace and reconciliation, 'decisively eliminate' any hypothesis that the massacre of St Bartholomew was premeditated by Catherine (p. 113).

39. See Annabel Patterson, *Censorship and Interpretation* (Madison, 1984), 107–11.

40. Goldberg, op. cit.; L. Marcus, 'Masquing Occasions and Masque Structure', *Research Opportunities in Renaissance Drama*, 24 (1981), 7–16.

41. *Criticism and Compliment*, ch.v.

42. Adams does nothing to show the interrelationships of literary texts and cultural contexts.

43. See *Politics of Discourse*, introduction.

Chapter 11

* Originally published in *Huntington Library Quarterly*, 57, 1988 95–136.

1. See C. Geertz, *The Interpretation of Cultures* (1975); also Geertz, *Negara: Theatre-State in Nineteenth-Century Bali* (Princeton, 1980); and Geertz, 'Centres, Kings and Charisma: Reflections on the Symbolics of Power', in J. Ben-David and T.N. Clarke (eds), *Culture and Its Creators* (Chicago, 1977), 150–71.

2. See. S. Greenblatt, *Renaissance Self-Fashioning* (Chicago, 1980); and Greenblatt (ed.), *The Forms of Power and the Power of Forms in the Renaissance* (Norman, Oklahoma, 1982); L.A. Montrose, 'A Poetics of Renaissance Culture', *Criticism*, 23 (1981), 349–59; J. Goldberg, *James I and the Politics of Literature* (Baltimore, 1983).

3. P. Zagorin, *The Court and The Country* (1969); L. Stone, *The Causes of The English Revolution* (1972), 105–7; P. Thomas, 'Two Cultures? Court and Country under Charles I' in C. Russell (ed.), *The Origins of The English Civil War* (1973), 168–96.

4. Cf. D. Hirst, 'The most telling comment on the relationship of court and country came in 1642, when both split down the middle',

Authority and Conflict, 31. For a critique of the thesis of cultural polarization see my *Criticism and Compliment: The Politics of Literature in the England of Charles I* (Cambridge, 1987), ch.1.

5. Bergeron previously studied the relationship of text to kingship in *English Civic Pageantry 1558–1642* (1971).

6. G. Goodman, *The Court of James I*, ed. J.S. Brewer (2 vols, 1839), 1, 251; Bergeron, 66.

7. E.K. Chambers, *The Elizabethan Stage* (4 vols, Oxford, 1923), iv, 135–7, dates the court performances 5 Nov. 1611 and Christmas 1612. Elizabeth was born in 1596.

8. For a fine example of this new emphasis see D. Norbrook, '*Macbeth* and the Politics of Historiography', in K. Sharpe and S. Zwicker (eds), *Politics of Discourse* (Berkeley Los Angeles and London, 1987), 78–116.

9. See my *Criticism and Compliment*, ch.1.

10. On Queen Anne's role see Neil Cuddy, 'The Revival of The Entourage: The Bedchamber of James I, 1603–1625' in D. Starkey (ed.), *The English Court* (1987), 173–225.

11. See the important article by J. Wormald, 'James VI and I: Two Kings or One', *History*, 68 (1983), 187–209, which Bergeron nowhere cites; and R.C. Munden, 'James I and "the growth of mutual distrust": King, Commons and Reform, 1603–4' in K. Sharpe (ed.), *Faction and Parliament* (Oxford, 1978; 2nd edn, London, 1985), 43–72.

12. C.H. McIlwain (ed.), *The Political Works of James I* (Cambridge, Mass., 1918), 272; Bergeron, 28; cf. Marc Antonio De Dominis, *De Republica Ecclesiastica pars secunda* (1620), 526–8.

13. Sharpe, *Criticism and Compliment*, ch.6.

14. Isaac Bargrave, *A Sermon Preached before King Charles March 27, 1627* (1627), 16; Sommerville, 33. The stress on duty in divine right theory needs emphasizing.

15. See K. Sharpe, 'The Foundation of the Chairs of History at Oxford and Cambridge: An Episode in Jacobean Politics', *History of Universities*, 2 (1982), 127–52; above, ch. 8.

16. Sommerville, 115, my italics.

17. See the Declaration of the Houses in Defence of the Militia Ordinance, in S.R. Gardiner (ed.), *The Constitutional Documents of the Puritan Revolution* (Oxford, 1899), 254–8.

18. It was this claim that was denied by Henry Ireton at Putney. See A.S.P. Woodhouse (ed.), *Puritanism and Liberty* (1938) esp. 53–5.

19. Lawrence Stone's phrase concerning the conflict 'within the mind' of allegiance to locality and centre applies well here to attitudes to kingship and law (*Causes of English Revolution*, 108).

20. Sommerville himself points out that Aristotle was deployed both to support a republic and favour kingship, *Politics and Ideology*, 58.

21. See, for example, H. Lloyd-Jones (ed.), *Tacitus, The Annals and The Histories* (New York, 1964), xxiii.

22. *Faction and Parliament* (1985 edn), xiii–xiv; Sommerville points out that Secretary Sir John Coke maintained that whatever law was made,

'If I discharge the place I bear I must commit men and not discover the cause . . .' (171).

23. The near silence of the Short Parliament on Arminianism is striking.
24. Sommerville fails to see J.G.A. Pocock's important point about the enduring belief in 1628 in a 'natural harmony between prerogative and law', 'The Commons Debates of 1628', *JHI*, 39 (1978), 329-34.
25. For some thoughts on this see *Politics of Discourse*, introduction.
26. See for example, Strong's *Splendour at Court* (1973); *Holbein and Henry VIII* (1967); *The Elizabethan Image* (1969); *The Cult of Elizabeth* (1977); *Art and Power* (Woodbridge, 1984).
27. Sir John Holles to Lord Gray, 27 February 1613, *HMC Portland*, IX, 9; Strong, *Henry Prince of Wales*, 7.
28. Charles Cornwallis, *A Discourse of The Most Illustrious Prince, Henry* . . . (1626) in *Harleian Miscellany IV*, 336; Strong, *Henry Prince of Wales*, 26.
29. See below page 290.
30. See S.L. Adams, 'The Protestant Cause: Religious Alliance with the West European Calvinist Communities as a Political Issue in England 1585-1630', (D.Phil. thesis, Oxford University, 1973).
31. S. Orgel and R. Strong (eds), *Inigo Jones: The Theatre of The Stuart Court* (2 vols, Berkeley and London, 1973) I, 160; II, 58-9; *Henry Prince of Wales*, 196.
32. I owe the identification of some of these errors to Mr. T.V. Wilks of Mansfield College, Oxford.
33. There are patent rolls of Prince Henry's household officers and servants, revenue accounts and orders for the government of the Prince's household at the Duchy of Cornwall Record Office. I would like to thank Professor Conrad Russell, Dr. Graham Haslam and Dr. Edward Chaney for drawing these manuscripts to my attention.
34. See N. Cuddy, 'The Revival of the Entourage'.
35. On Drayton's probable Catholic leanings, D. Norbrook, *Poetry and Politics in the English Renaissance* (1984), 197.
36. On the importance of the court as a means of earthing factions to the centre of government, see G.R. Elton, 'Tudor Government: The Points of Contact: III The Court', *TRHS*, 26 (1976), 211-28; D. Hirst, 'Court, Country and Politics before 1629' in *Faction and Parliament*, 105-34; and the essays by N. Cuddy and K. Sharpe in D. Starkey (ed.), *The English Court* (1987).
37. Edmund Bolton to Buckingham, 29 May 1626, *Cal. Stat. Pap. Dom. 1625-49*, 129; above, 203.
38. Professor T.K. Rabb (who is attracted to 'ologies' and 'isms') questioned my rejection of the word ideology to describe the values of the Arundel circle (*Faction and Parliament*, 244). The term can be usefully employed provided it does not lead us to think of too elaborate systems of ideas.
39. Howarth points out (2) that William Camden's inscription for the Sculpture Gallery at Arundel House referred to the earl's continuance of what his ancestors had begun.
40. It seems that when Arundel reluctantly gave up a Holbein in

exchange, he chose Holbein's portrait of Sir Richard Southwell, partly 'because he felt he would not mind the loss of the man who had brought his ancestor the poet Earl of Surrey to his knees'. He also had a copy of the portrait made. Both actions suggest a dynastic as well as an aesthetic interest in Holbein. Howarth, *Lord Arundel*, 71.

41. See illustration here and Howarth, plate 115.
42. The point was first made in my 'The Earl of Arundel, His Circle and the Opposition to the Duke of Buckingham, 1618–1628', *Faction and Parliament*, 209–44 (above, ch. 7), an essay not cited by Howarth. Junius and Peacham seem to be echoing for the visual arts the claims to moral force made for literature by Sidney in his *Apology for Poetry* (1595).
43. 'He wore and affected a habit very different from that of the time . . . all which drew the eyes of most and the reverence of many towards him, as the image and representative of the primitive nobility . . .', E. Hyde, Earl of Clarendon, *History of The Rebellion and Civil Wars in England*, ed. W.D. Macray (6 vols, Oxford, 1888), 1, 70.
44. See two illustrations reproduced here.
45. L. Van Norden, 'The Elizabethan College of Antiquaries' (Ph.D. thesis, University of California, 1946); Van Norden, 'Sir Henry Spelman on the Chronology of the Elizabethan College of Antiquaries', *Huntington Library Quarterly*, 13 (1949–50), 131–60; K. Sharpe, *Sir Robert Cotton: History and Politics in Early Modern England* (Oxford, 1979); see also J. Evans, *A History of The Society of Antiquaries* (1956).
46. For Arundel's desire to return, see Bodl. MS Clarendon 8 fos 802, 853; PRO SP German SP 80/10 passim especially 80/10/55, 80/10/27, 80/10/16; for a narration of the embassy by Sir John Borough, SP 80/10/55.
47. Several of the Society's papers are collected in T. Hearne, *A Collection of Curious Discourses*, ed. J. Ayloffe (2 vols, 1771).
48. Chamberlain to Carleton, 21 June 1617, in N.M. McClure (ed.), *The Letters of John Chamberlain* (2 vols, Philadelphia, 1939), II, 83; Howarth, 65.
49. Howarth, however, prints extracts in Appendix B. See Sir Edward Walker, 'A Short View of The Life of the Most Noble . . . Thomas Howard, Earl of Arundel and Surrey', BL MS. Harleian 6272; and printed in E. Walker, *Historical Discourses* (1705).
50. Macray (ed.), *History of The Rebellion*, 1, 69–70.
51. Howarth demonstrates fascinatingly that Arundel commissioned Mytens to make his Tudor Long Gallery *look like* a Roman palace interior (57–9).
52. See J. Malcolm, 'The King in Search of Soldiers: Charles I in 1642', *HJ*, 21 (1978), 257–68; and Malcolm, *Caesar's Due: Loyalty and King Charles I 1642–46* (1983); and for searching criticisms, M.D.G. Wanklyn and P. Young, 'A King in Search of Soldiers: A Rejoinder', *HJ*, 24 (1981), 147–54; and R. Ashton's review of Malcolm in *History*, 70 (1985), 130–1.
53. J. Thirsk (ed.), *The Agrarian History of England and Wales*, vol. IV

(Cambridge, 1967).

54. Such as that of N.R.N. Tyacke, 'Puritanism, Arminianism and Counter-Revolution', in C. Russell (ed.), *The Origins of The English Civil War* (1973), 119-43.

55. Christopher Haigh is preparing a study of the Church of England and its people 1558-1642. I am grateful to him for several stimulating discussions of what he has helpfully termed 'parish Anglicanism'.

56. See note 52 above.

57. Buchanan Sharp, *In Contempt of All Authority: Rural Artisans and Riot in the West of England, 1586-1660* (Berkeley, 1980).

58. For examples of rating disputes over poor relief, see Hants, RO Herriard MSS Box 13; Kent Archives Office Quarter Sessions Orders WI f.22ᵛ; over highway and bridge repair, Oxon. RO Dillon MSS XII g 1; Kent Archive Office Dering MSS U507/01; and over all local payments, Gorges to Coke, 18 Apr. 1637, Melbourne Hall Coke MS 56. I am grateful to Lord Lothian and the Derbyshire Record Office for permission to cite these important manuscripts.

59. Underdown, 130 (my italics).

60. Curiously, because modern cricket would appear to be every bit as much a team game as football.

61. This reference to 'shadowy entities far away in Westminster' appears to contradict the argument for popular political consciousness made earlier in the book.

62. See J.S. Cockburn (ed.), *Crime in England 1550-1800* (1970); C. Herrup, 'The Common Peace: Legal Structure and Legal Substance in East Sussex 1594-1640' (Ph.D. thesis, Northwestern University, 1982).

63. D. Underdown, 'The Taming of the Scold: The Enforcement of Patriarchal Authority in Early Modern England', *Order and Disorder*, 116-36. Cf. above, 57 to 59.

64. Cf. S.W. Hull, *Chaste, Silent, and Obedient: English Books for Women, 1475-1640* (San Marino, 1982).

65. Cf. M.E. James, *English Politics and The Concept of Honour* (Past and Present Supplements, 3, 1978).

66. George Chaworth to Charles I, 18 Dec. 1638, *HMC Cowper*, II, 205.

67. K. Wrightson and D. Levine, *Poverty and Piety in an English Village: Terling, 1525-1700* (New York, 1979). For an unsuccessful attempt to argue the case more broadly cf. W. Hunt, *The Puritan Moment: The Coming of Revolution in an English County* (Cambridge, Mass., 1983).

68. K. Lindley, *Fenland Riots and The English Revolution* (1982). For an example of an agreement that preceded statutory confirmation, see *Cal. Stat. Pap. Dom. 1631-3*, 513.

69. It is unfortunate that *Order and Disorder* does not have a better index to enable readers to pursue subjects across several essays.

70. See now J.R. Kent, *The English Village Constable 1580-1642: A Social and Administrative Study* (Oxford, 1986) which appeared after the publication of *Reform in the Provinces*.

71. *Reform in the Provinces*, 355.

72. See C. Holmes, 'The County Community in Stuart Historiography', *JBS*, 19 (1980), 53-73; A. Hughes, 'Warwickshire on the Eve of the Civil War', *Midland History*, 7 (1982), 42-72.
73. Huntington Lib., Ellesmere MS 6967; Bodl. MS Rawl. 243, Lord Keeper's speech to assize judges, 14 June 1638; cf. PC 2/49/272. And see also, 'A Proclamation commanding the due execution of the laws made for setting the poor to work', 20 May 1640, in J.F. Larkin (ed.), *Stuart Royal Proclamations* (Oxford, 1983) II, 712-14.
74. Note that the Privy Council believed that most officers were more diligent when commanded by 'express letters', Hirst, *Authority and Conflict*, 57.
75. City of York RO, House Books 35 f.162ᵛ.
76. Poulet to Coke, 8 March 1635, Melbourne Hall Coke MSS 50; Chaworth to Coke, 8 Dec. 1632, *HMC Cowper* 1, 485; cf. Nottingham UL Clifton MSS C1/C307.
77. Fletcher points out that in Hampshire the deputy lieutenants 'found that an authoritarian tone and a personal summons worked wonders' (310). We should not discount their effectiveness when employed by the Council.
78. *Cal. Stat. Pap. Dom. 1627-8*, 15, 12 Jan. 1627.
79. Northants RO, Montagu MS 15. f.46.
80. Bodl. Tanner MS 177 f.19ᵛ.
81. For the importance of a resident nobleman or Privy Councillor, see the speech of the Earl of Huntingdon to the Epiphany Sessions in Leicestershire 1638, Huntington Hastings MSS Box 26; and J.R. Dias, 'Politics and Administration in Nottinghamshire and Derbyshire, 1590-1640', (D.Phil. thesis, Oxford University, 1973).
82. We should note, however, that individual judges could spend several years on the same circuit, albeit not in the same pair; see J.S. Cockburn, *A History of English Assizes 1558-1715* (Cambridge, 1972), appendix 1.
83. I independently come to the same conclusion in *The Personal Rule of Charles 1* (in draft).
84. Montagu MS 10 f.47.
85. Bodl. MS Tanner 71 f.142.
86. *Cal. Stat. Pap. Dom. 1625-49*, 349; Kent Quarter Sessions Orders WI, f.65.
87. D. Stevenson, *The Scottish Revolution 1637-1644* (Newton Abbot, 1973), 324; Lee, 240.
88. See M. Lee, *Government by Pen: Scotland under James VI and I* (Urbana, 1980).
89. The distance between Charles I and his father has serious implications for Scottish history which have not been considered.
90. The same Scottish names continue to appear in the lists of Charles I's grooms and gentlemen of the bedchamber and privy chamber but by 1625 these were anglicized Scots or the sons of James's servants.
91. An anonymous correspondent advised Charles I of the need to send Hamilton and Lennox back to Scotland to serve him there, National Library Scotland, Dunlop MS 9303.

92. Some ministers early expressed their doubts. See, for example, Gilbert Durie to Coke, 31 Jan. 1634, Coke MSS 47.
93. Laud to Bramhall, 2 Sept. 1639, Huntington Lib. MS HA 15172.
94. There are no satisfactory biographies of Charles I. Some of the best insights are found in R. Strong, *Charles I On Horseback* (1972).
95. See above, note 54.
96. R.M. Smuts, 'The Puritan Followers of Henrietta Maria', *EHR*, 93 (1978), 26–45.
97. See D. Hirst, 'Revisionism Revised: The Place of Principle', *P&P*, 92 (1981), 79–99.

Index

theology 5, 11, 29, 60, 296
  see also religious practices
Thirty-Nine Articles 109
Thomas, P 230
Thomas Howard, Earl of Arundel
  (Rubens) 294
Thynne, F 207
Timber or Discoveries (Jonson) 272
Titles of Honor (Selden) 179
To the King at his entrance into Saxham
  (Carew) 245-6
To my friend GN from Wrest (Carew)
  241-3, 244
To My Mistresse in Absence (Carew) 248
To the Painter (Carew) 257
To Penshurst (Jonson) 241, 243
To Saxham (Carew) 241, 243-4
Townshend, A 254-6
  Tempe Restored 255-6
translations 18
  of the Bible 33
Traquair, John Stewart *1st Earl of* 312,
  313
travel 19
Treatise of Monarchy (Brooke) 224-6,
  228
Treatise of the New Covenant (Harris) 24
Trevor-Roper, H R 209, 214
Triennial Act (1641) 97-8
Turner, P 129, 136, 140-1
Twyne, B 128, 129, 137, 211

*Uncasing of Machiavelli's Instruction to
  His Son* 27
Underdown, D 49, 298-303
Upon my Lord Chiefe Justice . . . (Carew)
  251-2
Ussher, *Bishop* J 209

Van der Dort, A 150
Van Dyck, *Sir* A 46-7, 127, 158-9, 171,
  172, 291, 296
verbal discourse 5, 6-7, 40, 87
  see also textual sources
de Vere, R 205
De Veritate (Herbert of Cherbury) 59
Vindiciae Contra Tyrannos 37, 285-6
Virgil:
  Eclogues 53, 54
visual images 297
  of monarchy 46-7, 282, 289
Vossius, G 212, 213, 220
  Ars Historica 220

Walker, *Sir* E 182, 202, 296

Walpole, H 291
Walter, J 306
Ward, S 222
wars:
  and political change 6
Warwick, *Sir* P 128, 150, 164, 166, 168
  Memoirs 161
Weckherlin, G 110
Weeding of Covent Garden (Brome) 274
Wentworth, A 251-2
Wentworth, *Sir* T *see* Strafford, Thomas
  Wentworth *1st Earl of*
West, W:
  Symboleographia 177
Weston, Richard *1st Earl of Portland*
  168, 169, 170
Wheare, D 41-2, 209, 229
  and Camden 210-11, 212, 214,
  216-18
  De ratione de methodo 214
whig history 3, 4, 6
Whitehall, palace of, 149-50, 162
Whitelocke, *Sir* J 177
Williams, *Bishop* J 79, 184-5, 186-7,
  188, 190, 192-4
Williams, P 76
Wilson, T 188
Wimbledon, Edward Cecil, Viscount
  Wimbledon 289
Winter's Tale (Shakespeare) 282, 283
Wither, G 270
  Britaine's Remembrancer 21-2
women 304
  beauty 45, 238-9, 240-1
  marriage 60-1, 236-7, 251-4, 282
  position of 58-9, 304
  see also physical passion, spiritual
    passion
women's rights 21
Wotton, *Sir* H 82, 289
world picture 7-8, 9-20, 23, 28-9, 46
  and civil war 65-7, 68-9
  Elizabethan 35, 40, 43-4, 45
  Florus's 216-18
Wren, *Bishop* M 221-3
writers 265
  and the monarchy 34-5, 38-9
  and the public 265
  professional 265
  see also literature, textual sources
Wroth, *Lady* M:
  Countesse of Montgomerie's Urania
    263

Yelverton, *Sir* H 185-6

DATE DUE

DEC 31 '97			
JUN 2 8 2006			